# Windows Server 2008 R2 & SQL Server 2008 R2 High Availability Clustering

## (Project Series)

**Jonathan Ruffing**

**ScreamPublications.com**
**6467 Zinnia Ln. N., Maple Grove, MN, 55311 USA**

# Windows Server 2008 R2 & SQL Server 2008 R2 High Availability Clustering (Project Series)


www.screampublications.com



ISBN-13: 978-0615490342

ISBN-10: 0615490344

## Trademarks

Trademarked names may appear in this book. Rather than use a trademark symbol with every occurrence of a trademarked name, we use the names only in an editorial fashion and to the benefit of the trademark owner, with no intention of infringement of the trademark.
All terms mentioned in this book that are known to be trademarks or service marks have been appropriately capitalized. The publisher cannot attest to the accuracy of this information. Use of a term in this book should not be regarded as affecting the validity of any trademark or service mark.

## Warning and Disclaimer

Every effort has been made to make this book as complete and as accurate as possible, but no warranty or fitness is implied. The information provided is on an "as is" basis.

**COVER DESIGNER**
Eric Neumann

# Contents at a Glance


**CHAPTER 1:** Overview of the Completed Project ........ 1
**CHAPTER 2:** iSCSI Physical Network Topology ........ 9
**CHAPTER 3:** Configuration of the iSCSI Switches ........ 12
**CHAPTER 4:** Configuring iSCSI Connections on the SAN ........ 19
**CHAPTER 5:** Configuring iSCSI Connections on the Servers ........ 29
**CHAPTER 6:** SAN Performance- Planning Disk Layout & Creating Disk Groups ........ 51
**CHAPTER 7:** Configuring the Server Access to the Virtual Disks ........ 69
**CHAPTER 8:** Disk Performance- Configuring Shared Disks and Aligning Partitions ........ 73
**CHAPTER 9:** Creating a Windows Cluster with the Cluster Shared Volumes (CSV) Feature ........ 80
**CHAPTER 10:** Creating the Hyper-V Virtual Networks and Configuring Network Settings ........ 90
**CHAPTER 11:** Preparing the Virtual/Physical Servers for SQL Clustering ........ 100
**CHAPTER 12:** Creating the Windows Cluster that will Host the SQL Cluster's Resources ........ 118
**CHAPTER 13:** Installing SQL Server 2008/R2 on the Initial SQL Cluster Node ........ 124
**CHAPTER 14:** Installing SQL Server 2008/R2 on Additional Nodes to Make the Cluster Highly Available ........ 150
**CHAPTER 15:** Optimizing SQL Server's Performance by Adding Additional TempDB Files ........ 161
**CHAPTER 16:** Enabling the SQL Server 2008/R2 Program through the Windows Firewall ........ 167
**CHAPTER 17:** Applying Updates to an SQL Server 2008/R2 Cluster ........ 171
**CHAPTER 18:** Creating the CSV Virtual Machines to Host the Front-end Application Servers ........ 172
**CHAPTER 19:** Installing and Configuring the Microsoft Network Load Balancer (NLB) in an Active/Active Cluster ........ 187
**CHAPTER 20:** Installing and Configuring SQL Server 2008/R2 Reporting Services Scale-Out Deployment on Load Balanced Servers ........ 208
**CHAPTER 21:** Installing Microsoft Dynamics CRM 4.0 on the NLB Cluster ........ 251
**CHAPTER 22:** Configuring Microsoft Dynamics CRM 4.0 Security Settings ........ 277
**CHAPTER 23:** Applying Microsoft Dynamics CRM 4.0 Update Rollups ........ 292
**CHAPTER 24:** Importing a Previous Microsoft Dynamics CRM 4.0 Organization into the New CRM Cluster ........ 294
**CHAPTER 25:** Installation and Configuration of the CRM SRS Data Connector when Utilizing an NLB Cluster ........ 305
**CHAPTER 26:** Installation and Configuration of the CRM Internet Facing Deployment (IFD) Tool when Utilizing an NLB Cluster ........ 313
**CHAPTER 27:** Installing, Configuring, and Clustering the Microsoft Dynamics CRM E-mail Router ........ 321
**CHAPTER 28:** Configuring Microsoft Dynamics CRM for Outlook Clients to Connect to the New NLB Cluster ........ 367

# Table of Contents

**Introduction** ........ xx
**Terms and Conventions Used in this Book** ........ xxii

**Chapter 1: Overview of the Completed Project** ........ 1
Overview of the Completed Project ........ 2
Windows Physical Server and Network Load Balancer Clusters ........ 2
Windows Virtual Machine and SQL Clusters ........ 2
SAN Disk Layout ........ 3
Overview of the SAN iSCSI Network Topology ........ 4
Overview of the Clusters from within Windows Failover Cluster Manager ........ 5
Overview of the Cluster Shared Volume (CSV) Windows Failover Cluster ........ 5
Overview of the SQL Server's Windows Failover Cluster ........ 6
Overview of Our Network Load Balancer (NLB) Cluster ........ 8

**Chapter 2: iSCSI Physical Network Topology** ........ 9
iSCSI Network Topology for Multi-path Input/Output (MPIO) Redundancy ........ 9
SAN Physical Network Topology ........ 10

**Chapter 3: Configuration of the iSCSI Switches** ........ 12
Connecting to the Switch via the Console and the COM1 Port ........ 12
Erasing the Switch's Current Configuration ........ 13
Running the Switch's Setup Wizard to Create the Initial Configuration ........ 14
Configuring Jumbo Frames via the Console ........ 15
Finishing the Switch Configuration via the Web User Interface (UI) ........ 16
Applying the Jumbo Frames Configuration Changes ........ 16
Configuring the iSCSI Optimization Options ........ 17
Configuring the Individual iSCSI Ports ........ 18

**Chapter 4: Configuring iSCSI Connections on the SAN** ........ 19
Overview of the iSCSI Topology with Multi-path Input/Output (MPIO) Redundancy ........ 19
Storage Area Network (SAN) Topology Prerequisites ........ 20
Installing the Storage Area Network (SAN) Management Software ........ 21
Connecting the Modular Disk Storage Manager (MDSM) to the SAN ........ 24
Configuring the Initial Setup Tasks on the SAN ........ 25
Configuring the Ethernet Management Ports ........ 26
Configuring the iSCSI Host Ports ........ 27

**Chapter 5: Configuring iSCSI Connections on the Servers** ........ 29
Creating a Naming Convention for the Network Adapters ........ 29
Configuring the iSCSI Network Adapters- Enabling Jumbo Frames ........ 31
Configuring the iSCSI Network Adapters- Installing the Broadcom Advanced Control Suite 3 (BACS) ........ 32
Configuring the iSCSI Network Adapters- Setting the Sub-interface to use Jumbo Frames ........ 34
Configuring the IP Properties- First iSCSI Network Adapter ........ 36
Configuring the IP Properties- Second iSCSI Network Adapter ........ 37
Configuring the IP Properties- Heartbeat Network Adapter ........ 38
Review of the First Server's Network Connections ........ 39
Configuring the Initial Server's iSCSI Initiator ........ 40
Configuring the iSCSI Initiator- Dell Modular Disk Storage Manager Install ........ 40
Configuring Microsoft iSCSI Initiator- Discovery Portals ........ 41
Configuring Microsoft iSCSI Initiator- Multi-path Connections ........ 44
Configuring Microsoft iSCSI Initiator- First iSCSI Target ........ 44
Configuring Microsoft iSCSI Initiator- Second iSCSI Target ........ 45
Configuring Microsoft iSCSI Initiator- Third iSCSI Target ........ 47
Configuring Microsoft iSCSI Initiator- Fourth iSCSI Target ........ 48
Configuring Microsoft iSCSI Initiator- Verifying the of iSCSI Targets ........ 49
Review of iSCSI Multi-path Topology ........ 50

**Chapter 6: SAN Performance- Planning Disk Layout & Creating Disk Groups** ........ 51
Overview of the SAN Disk Layout ........ 52
Configuring the SAN RAID Arrays for the Best Performance ........ 52

RAID Level Selection ..... 52
Virtual Disk Configuration and LUN Id Selections ..... 54
Drive Selection and Number of Spindles ..... 54
Creating a Virtual Disk Ownership Balance Between RAID Controllers ..... 55
Creating Disk Groups and Virtual Disks that Allow Flexibility ..... 55
Disk Layout Considerations for Windows and SQL Cluster Quorum Disks ..... 56
Configuring the Dell PowerVault MD3000i Storage ..... 58
Creating Disk Groups with the Dell Modular Disk Storage Manager (MDSM) ..... 59
Creating Disk Groups with MDSM- First Disk Group ..... 59
Creating Virtual Disks with the Dell Modular Disk Storage Manager (MDSM) ..... 61
Creating Disk Groups with MDSM- Second Disk Group ..... 62
Creating Disk Groups with MDSM- Third Disk Group ..... 63
Creating Disk Groups with MDSM- Fourth Disk Group ..... 64
Viewing Logical Unit Number (LUN) Id's ..... 65
Modifying Logical Unit Number (LUN) Id's ..... 65
Assigning the Global Hot Spare Disk ..... 67

**Chapter 7: Configuring the Server Access to the Virtual Disks** ..... 69
Adding the First Physical Server's iSCSI Connection to the SAN ..... 69
Creating the Initial Host Group on the SAN ..... 71
Mapping the Virtual Disks to the Host Group ..... 72

**Chapter 8: Disk Performance- Configuring Shared Disks and Aligning Partitions** ..... 73
Overview of Shared Disk Behavior ..... 73
Configuration of the Shared Disks- Initialization ..... 74
Configuration of the Shared Disks- Formatting ..... 75
Viewing the Allocation Unit Size of a Previously Formatted Disk ..... 77
Configuration of the Shared Disks- Partition Alignment ..... 78
Calculating Partition Alignment ..... 79

**Chapter 9: Creating a Windows Cluster with the Cluster Shared Volumes (CSV) Feature** ..... 80
Installing the Prerequisites for Windows Clustering and Hyper-V Virtualization ..... 80
Creating the Windows Failover Cluster that will Host the CSV Virtual Machines ..... 81

Running the Validate a Cluster Wizard ... 82

Assigning the Cluster Name and IP Address ... 83

Adding Shared Disks to the Cluster ... 84

Renaming Cluster Disks ... 85

Enabling the Cluster Shared Volumes (CSV) ... 86

Adding Disks to the Cluster Shared Volumes (CSV) ... 87

Configuring a Quorum Disk for the Cluster ... 88

**Chapter 10: Creating the Hyper-V Virtual Networks and Configuring Network Settings** ... 90

Creating the Hyper-V Virtual Networks ... 90

Verifying the Virtual Network's Connection to their Network Adapter ... 93

Creating the Remaining Hyper-V Virtual Networks ... 94

Renaming the New Hyper-V Virtual Networks ... 95

Assigning Network Adapter Binding Orders and Metrics ... 95

Assigning Network Adapter Binding Orders on the Physical Servers ... 96

Assigning Network Adapter Metrics on the Physical Servers ... 98

Disabling the Network Adapters Power Management ... 99

**Chapter 11: Preparing the Virtual/Physical Servers for SQL Clustering** ... 100

Connecting to Multiple Servers with Hyper-V Manager ... 100

Creating the Virtual Machines for the SQL Nodes ... 101

Adding the Network Adapters ... 102

Configuring the Network Adapters- Assigning a Naming Convention ... 103

Removing Phantom/Ghost Network Adapters from Virtual Machines ... 104

Adding the SQL Virtual Machines to the Active Directory Domain ... 105

Configuring the Network Adapters- Assigning Static IP Addresses ... 106

Configuring the Network Adapters- DNS Properties ... 106

Configuring the Network Adapters- Binding Orders ... 107

Configuring the Network Adapters- Metrics ... 108

Configuring the iSCSI Network Adapters- Enabling Jumbo Frames ... 109

Configuring the iSCSI Network Adapters- Verifying Jumbo Frames are Enabled ... 110

Installing the Dell Modular Disk Storage Manager (MDSM) software ... 111

Configuring the Microsoft iSCSI Initiator Multi-path Connections to the SAN ... 112

Adding the SQL Virtual Machines to the SAN's Host Group for Disk Access ........ 113
Configuring the SQL Virtual Machine Shared Disks ........ 114
Adding Prerequisites for SQL Clustering- Windows Features ........ 115
Adding Prerequisites for SQL Clustering- Windows Roles ........ 116

**Chapter 12: Creating the Windows Cluster that will Host the SQL Cluster's Resources** ........ 118
Creating the Windows Cluster with the Initial SQL Node ........ 118
Running the Validate a Cluster Wizard ........ 118
Assigning the Cluster Name and IP Address ........ 119
Configuring the Newly Created Windows SQL Cluster ........ 120
Adding Shared Disks to the Windows Cluster ........ 120
Renaming Cluster Disks ........ 121
Configuring a Quorum Disk for the Windows Cluster ........ 122

**Chapter 13: Installing SQL Server 2008/R2 on the Initial SQL Cluster Node** ........ 124
Understanding SQL Cluster Install Options and Modes ........ 124
Prerequisites- Adding the Microsoft Distributed Transaction Coordinator (MSDTC) to the Windows Cluster as a Service ........ 125
Selecting the DTC Service ........ 126
Assigning the Client Access Point ........ 127
Selecting a Shared Disk ........ 128
Installing the SQL Server 2008/R2 on the Initial SQL Cluster Node ........ 128
Prerequisites- When Installing SQL Server 2008 on Windows Server 2008 R2 ........ 129
Launching the SQL Server 2008/R2 Installation ........ 130
Setup Support Rules Screen ........ 131
Resolving Common Warnings and Errors of the Setup Support Rules Screen ........ 132
Windows Firewall (Warning) ........ 133
Microsoft Cluster Service (MSCS) cluster verification errors (Failed) ........ 134
Microsoft Cluster Service (MSCS) cluster verification warnings (Warning) ........ 134
Network Bindings Order (Warning) ........ 134
Distributed Transaction Coordinator (Failed) ........ 135
SQL Feature Selection and How It Relates to a Reporting Services Scale-Out Deployment ........ 135
Selecting SQL Features for Installation ........ 136

Assigning the SQL Cluster and Instance Names ..... 137
Selecting the Shared Disks to be Included in the SQL Cluster ..... 139
Assigning the Client Active Directory Network as the Cluster's Network ..... 140
Assigning User Accounts to SQL Services ..... 141
Selecting the Authentication Mode ..... 142
Distributing SQL Directories Across the Shared Disks ..... 143
Assigning a User Account to the Analysis Services ..... 145
Distributing Analysis Services Directories Across the Shared Disks ..... 146
Re-Applying the SQL Server 2008 Service Pack when Installing on Windows Server 2008 R2 ..... 147
Verifying that the SQL Cluster is Online ..... 148
Connecting to the SQL Cluster with SQL Server Management Studio ..... 149

**Chapter 14: Installing SQL Server 2008/R2 on Additional Nodes to Make the Cluster Highly Available** ..... 150
Adding Additional Nodes to the Windows SQL Cluster ..... 150
Installing the SQL Server 2008/R2 on the Additional SQL Cluster Nodes ..... 150
Prerequisites- Temporally Disabling the Windows Firewall ..... 150
Prerequisites- When Installing SQL Server 2008 on Windows Server 2008 R2 ..... 151
Launching the SQL Server 2008/R2 Installation ..... 152
Selecting the SQL Instance for Additional SQL Cluster Nodes ..... 153
Selecting the SQL Service Accounts for Additional SQL Cluster Nodes ..... 154
Re-Applying the SQL Server 2008 Service Pack when Installing on Windows Server 2008 R2 ..... 155
Testing High Availability of the Newly Completed SQL Cluster ..... 156
Testing Failover- Moving the SQL Application to a Different Cluster Node ..... 156
Testing Failover- Moving the SQL DTC to a Different Cluster Node ..... 157
Testing Failover- Testing Connections to the New Active Cluster Node ..... 158
Testing Failover- Stopping the Cluster Service on the Passive Node ..... 159
How to Safely Shutdown the Passive SQL Cluster Node ..... 159

**Chapter 15: Optimizing SQL Server's Performance by Adding Additional TempDB Files** ..... 161
Overview of the Optimum Configuration for SQL Temporally Database Files ..... 161
Summary of Best Practices for TempDB Configurations ..... 161
Configuring the Initial TempDB's Properties ..... 162

Creating Additional TempDB Files with an SQL Script ........ 164
Modifying the Script to Create Multiple TempDB Files ........ 165
Verifying the Newly Created TempDB Files ........ 166

**Chapter 16: Enabling the SQL Server 2008/R2 Program through the Windows Firewall** ........ 167
Allowing Traffic Through the Firewall- SQL Server Management Studio ........ 167
Allowing Traffic Through the Firewall- SQL Instance ........ 168
Allowing Traffic Through the Firewall- Selecting Networks ........ 169
Enabling the Firewall and Testing Communications ........ 170

**Chapter 17: Applying Updates to an SQL Server 2008/R2 Cluster** ........ 171

**Chapter 18: Creating the CSV Virtual Machines to Host the Front-end Application Servers** ........ 172
Creating New Virtual Machines on the Cluster Shared Volume (CSV) Disk ........ 173
Copying Existing Virtual Machines into the Cluster Shared Volume (CSV) ........ 174
Importing Existing Virtual Machines into the Cluster Shared Volume (CSV) ........ 175
Verifying the CSV Virtual Machines in Hyper-V Manager ........ 176
Adding Virtual Machines to the Windows CSV Cluster with the High Availability Wizard ........ 177
High Availability Wizard- Selecting the Virtual Machine Application ........ 178
High Availability Wizard- Selecting the Virtual Machines ........ 179
Verifying the Virtual Machines were Added to the Windows CSV Cluster ........ 181
Managing the New CSV Virtual Machines ........ 182
Managing the New CSV Virtual Machines- Live Migration ........ 182
Managing the New CSV Virtual Machines- Shutting Down ........ 183
Managing the New CSV Virtual Machines- Setting Preferred Owners ........ 184
Managing the New CSV Virtual Machines- Virtual Machine Advanced Policies ........ 185
Managing the New CSV Virtual Machines- Virtual Machine Configuration Advanced Policies ........ 186

**Chapter 19: Installing and Configuring the Microsoft Network Load Balancer (NLB) in an Active/Active Cluster** ........ 187
Four Key Things to Know About Configuring the Microsoft Network Load Balancer (NLB) that Aren't Highly Publicized ........ 187
Configuring the Prerequisites for the Microsoft Network Load Balancer on the CSV Virtual Machines ........ 188

Adding and Configuring the Network Load Balancer (NLB) Network Adapter ... 189
Configuring the NLB Network Adapter's Properties ... 191
Disabling IPv6 on the NLB Network Adapters ... 191
Configuring the IPv4 Properties on the NLB Network Adapters ... 192
Configuring the Advanced IPv4 Properties on the NLB Network Adapters ... 193
Configuring the Network Adapters to Route Traffic Between Each Other on Windows Server 2008 or Later ... 194
Changing the Network Adapter Security Settings of Windows 2008 or Later for Multi-homed Servers ... 195
Creating the Network Load Balancer (NLB) Cluster ... 195
Creating the NLB Cluster- Adding the Initial Node ... 196
Creating the NLB Cluster- Configuring Host Parameters ... 197
Creating the NLB Cluster- Assigning the Cluster IP Address ... 198
Creating the NLB Cluster- Configuring Cluster Parameters ... 198
Creating the NLB Cluster- Configuring Port Rules ... 199
Creating the NLB Cluster- Reviewing the Port Rules ... 200
Adding Additional Nodes to Make the NLB Cluster Highly Available ... 201
Adding Additional Nodes- Second Node ... 202
Adding Additional Nodes- Configuring Host Parameters ... 203
Adding Additional Nodes- Configuring Port Rules ... 204
Verifying the Network Load Balancer's Final Configuration ... 205
Managing the NLB Cluster ... 206
Managing the NLB Cluster- Stopping Traffic to a Node ... 206
Managing the NLB Cluster- Setting the Default State ... 207

**Chapter 20: Installing and Configuring SQL Server 2008/R2 Reporting Services Scale-Out Deployment on Load Balanced Servers** ... 208
Installing SQL Reporting Services on the Initial NLB Cluster Node ... 208
Prerequisites- Creating the Active Directory Service Account ... 208
Prerequisites- Temporally Disabling the Windows Firewall ... 209
Prerequisites- When Installing SQL Server 2008 on Windows Server 2008 R2 ... 209
Installing SQL Reporting Services- Launching the Install ... 210
Prerequisites- When Installing SQL Server 2008/R2 on Windows Server 2008 ... 210

Installing SQL Reporting Services- Selecting Install Type ..... 212

Installing SQL Reporting Services- Feature Selection ..... 213

Installing SQL Reporting Services- Instance Configuration ..... 214

Installing SQL Reporting Services- Service User Account ..... 215

Configuring SQL Server Reporting Services (SSRS) on the Initial NLB Node ..... 216

Configuring SSRS on the Initial NLB Node- Connecting to the Instance ..... 217

Configuring SSRS on the Initial NLB Node- Creating the Report Server Database ..... 218

Configuring SSRS on the Initial NLB Node- Connecting to the SQL Cluster ..... 219

Configuring SSRS on the Initial NLB Node- Assigning Database Name ..... 220

Configuring SSRS on the Initial NLB Node- Assigning Database Credentials ..... 221

Configuring SSRS on the Initial NLB Node- Completing the Database Configuration ..... 222

Configuring SSRS on the Initial NLB Node- Creating the Web Service URL ..... 223

Configuring SSRS on the Initial NLB Node- Creating the Report Manager URL ..... 224

Configuring SQL Server Reporting Services (SSRS) on Additional NLB Nodes to Create a Scale-out Deployment ..... 225

Configuring SSRS on Additional NLB Nodes- Connecting to an Existing Database ..... 226

Configuring SSRS on Additional NLB Nodes- Connecting to the SQL Cluster ..... 227

Configuring SSRS on Additional NLB Nodes- Selecting the Existing ReportServer Database ..... 228

Configuring SSRS on Additional NLB Nodes- Assigning Database Credentials ..... 229

Configuring SSRS on Additional NLB Nodes- Completing the Database Configuration ..... 230

Configuring SSRS on Additional NLB Nodes- Creating the Web Service URL ..... 231

Configuring SSRS on Additional NLB Nodes- Creating the Report Manager URL ..... 232

Creating the SQL Reporting Services Scale-out Deployment ..... 233

SSRS Creating the Scale-out Deployment- Connecting to the Instance ..... 233

SSRS Creating the Scale-out Deployment- Joining the NLB Cluster Nodes ..... 234

Synchronizing Encryption Keys of the SSRS Scale-out Deployment Nodes ..... 235

SSRS Synchronizing Encryption Keys- Backing Up the Initial Node's Key ..... 236

SSRS Synchronizing Encryption Keys- Importing the Key on Member Nodes ..... 237

Modifying the SQL Reporting Services (SSRS) .Config File for the NLB Cluster Configuration ..... 239

Modifying the SSRS .Config File- Adding the NLB Cluster's Hostname ..... 239

Modifying the SSRS .Config File- Adding the NLB Cluster's URL Root ..... 240

Modifying the SSRS .Config File- Adding the NLB Cluster's Authentication Type ..... 241

Modifying the SSRS .Config File- Saving the Changes ..... 242
Configuring Internet Explorer Security on the NLB Cluster Nodes ..... 243
Configuring Internet Explorer Security- Disabling Protected Mode ..... 243
Configuring Internet Explorer Security- Adding Nodes to Local Intranet Zone ..... 243
Configuring Internet Explorer Security- Moving Sites to the Local Intranet ..... 244
Configuring Internet Explorer Security- Disabling Protected Mode Warnings ..... 245
Disabling the LoopbackCheck in the Registry of Each NLB Cluster Node ..... 246
Testing the SQL Reporting Services Scale-out Deployment on each NLB Cluster Node ..... 247
Testing the SSRS Scale-out Deployment- Web Service URL ..... 248
Testing the SSRS Scale-out Deployment- Report Manager URL ..... 249

**Chapter 21: Installing Microsoft Dynamics CRM 4.0 on the NLB Cluster ..... 251**
Prerequisites- Installing Windows Roles ..... 251
Prerequisites- Creating an Active Directory Organizational Unit (OU) for the CRM Security Accounts ..... 253
Installing Microsoft Dynamics CRM 4.0 Server Role on the Initial NLB Cluster Node ..... 253
Installing the CRM Server Role- Specifying Install Type ..... 255
Installing the CRM Server Role- Selecting the SQL Cluster to Host the Database ..... 256
Installing the CRM Server Role- How the Organization Name and CRM URL's Relate ..... 257
Installing the CRM Server Role- Specifying the CRM Organization Name ..... 258
Installing the CRM Server Role- Selecting the Website ..... 259
Installing the CRM Server Role- Specifying the Report Server URL ..... 260
Installing the CRM Server Role- Specifying the Security Account ..... 261
Installing the CRM Server Role- Understanding the CRM Email Router Role ..... 262
Requirements for Clustering the CRM Email Router Service ..... 262
Installing the CRM Server Role- Specifying the CRM Email Router Server ..... 263
Installing the CRM Server Role- Verifying System Requirements ..... 264
Installing Microsoft Dynamics CRM 4.0 Server Role on the Remaining NLB Cluster Nodes ..... 265
Prerequisites- Installing Windows Roles ..... 265
Installing the CRM Server Role- Launching the Install ..... 267
Installing the CRM Server Role- Specifying Install Type ..... 269
Installing the CRM Server Role- Connecting to an Existing Deployment ..... 270

Installing the CRM Server Role- Selecting the Website ..... 271
Installing the CRM Server Role- Specifying the Report Server URL ..... 272
Installing the CRM Server Role- Specifying the Security Account ..... 273
Installing the CRM Server Role- Specifying the CRM Email Router Server ..... 274
Installing the CRM Server Role- Verifying System Requirements ..... 275
Verifying the Install from within the CRM Deployment Manager ..... 276

**Chapter 22: Configuring Microsoft Dynamics CRM 4.0 Security Settings** ..... 277
Overview of the CRM 4.0 Active Directory Security Groups Created During the Installation ..... 277
Configuring Active Directory User and Computer Accounts for CRM 4.0 ..... 278
Moving the CRM Service User Account into the CRM Organizational Unit (OU) ..... 278
Assigning Group Membership to the CRM Service User Account ..... 279
Adding and Verifying Members of the Active Directory CRM Security Groups ..... 280
Adding and Verifying Members of the CRM NLB Cluster Node Local Groups ..... 281
Configuring CRM 4.0 Services- Understanding the Roles of each Service ..... 282
Configuring CRM 4.0 Services- User Accounts ..... 282
Overview of the IIS Application Pool Account Used for CRM's Web Components ..... 283
Configuring the CRM Application Pool Identity in Internet Information Services (IIS) 7.5 to use the CRM Service User Account ..... 284
Disabling Internet Information Services (IIS) 7.5 Enable Kernel-mode Authentication for Windows Server 2008 R2 ..... 285
Configuring Service Principle Names (SPN) Security for the Microsoft Network Load Balancer Cluster ..... 286
Using the ADSI Edit Tool to Edit the Service Principle Names (SPN) ..... 286
Adding the CRM NLB Cluster's Information to the Service Principle Names (SPN) of the CRM Service User Account ..... 287
How to Troubleshoot Service Principle Name (SPN) Conflicts ..... 289
Enabling Trust Delegation for the CRM Service User Account ..... 290

**Chapter 23: Applying Microsoft Dynamics CRM 4.0 Update Rollups** ..... 292
How and When to Apply Update Rollups to Each Different CRM Component ..... 292

**Chapter 24: Importing a Previous Microsoft Dynamics CRM 4.0 Organization into the New CRM Cluster** ..... 294

Backing Up the Previous CRM 4.0 Database(s) for Migration to the New CRM 4.0 Cluster ... 295

Restoring the Previous CRM 4.0 Database(s) into the New CRM 4.0 Cluster ... 296

Importing Previous CRM 4.0 Organizations- Deployment Manager ... 297

Importing CRM Organizations- Selecting the CRM Database ... 298

Importing CRM Organizations- Specifying the Organization Name ... 299

Importing CRM Organizations- Specifying the Report Server ... 300

Importing CRM Organizations- Selecting a Method for Mapping Users ... 301

Importing CRM Organizations- Edit User Mappings ... 302

Importing CRM Organizations- System Requirements ... 303

Verifying the CRM Organization was Imported Successfully ... 304

**Chapter 25: Installation and Configuration of the CRM SRS Data Connector when Utilizing an NLB Cluster** ... 305

Editing the Registry for CRM to Ignore Checks during the Installation of the CRM SRS Data Connector.. ... 305

Installing the CRM SRS Data Connector on each of the CRM NLB Cluster Nodes ... 308

Installing the CRM SRS Data Connector- Specifying the SQL Cluster as the Database Server ... 310

Installing the CRM SRS Data Connector- System Requirements Error ... 311

**Chapter 26: Installation and Configuration of the CRM Internet Facing Deployment (IFD) Tool when Utilizing an NLB Cluster** ... 313

Prerequisites- Setting Up Internet DNS Records ... 313

Prerequisites- Configuring the Internet Firewall ... 314

Downloading and Installing the Microsoft Dynamics CRM Internet Facing Deployment (IFD) Configuration Tool ... 314

Verifying that the CRM IFD Configuration was Successful ... 317

Verifying that the CRM IFD and SRS Data Connector are Working Together ... 318

Verifying that the CRM SRS Data Connector- Running a Test Report ... 319

**Chapter 27: Installing, Configuring, and Clustering the Microsoft Dynamics CRM E-mail Router** ... 321

Installing the CRM E-mail Router Cluster- Initial Node ... 322

Installing the CRM E-mail Router- Prerequisites ... 322

Installing the CRM E-mail Router- Launching the Install ... 323

Installing the CRM E-mail Router- Selecting Router Components ........ 324
Applying the Update Rollup to the CRM E-Mail Router ........ 324
Configuring the CRM E-mail Router Security- Assigning the CRM Service User Account Permissions ........ 325
Configuring the CRM E-mail Router Security- Adding PrivUserGroup Members ........ 326
Configuring the CRM E-mail Router Security- User Account and Startup Type ........ 327
Configuring the CRM E-mail Router Security- Adding the CRM Service Account to the CRM Organization(s) ........ 328
Granting the CRM Service User Account Access to Exchange Mailboxes ........ 331
Configuring the CRM E-Mail Router- Granting the Send As Permissions with the Exchange Management Console (EMC) ........ 331
Configuring the CRM E-Mail Router- Granting Full Access Permissions with the Exchange Management Console (EMC) ........ 333
Configuring the CRM E-Mail Router- Granting the Send As Permissions with the Exchange Management Shell (EMS) ........ 334
Configuring the CRM E-Mail Router- Granting Full Access Permissions with the Exchange Management Shell (EMS) ........ 335
Changing the CRM E-mail Access Configuration- Users ........ 336
Changing the CRM E-mail Access Configuration- Queues ........ 337
Creating a Deployment within the E-mail Router Configuration Manager ........ 338
E-mail Router Configuration Manager- Creating an Incoming Profile ........ 338
E-mail Router Configuration Manager- Creating an Outgoing Profile ........ 339
E-mail Router Configuration Manager- Creating a Deployment ........ 341
E-mail Router Configuration Manager- Loading Data ........ 342
E-mail Router Configuration Manager- Testing E-mail Router Access to Exchange Mailboxes ........ 343
Creating the CRM E-mail Router Service's Shared Disk on the SAN ........ 344
Creating the Virtual Disk- Selecting the Disk Group ........ 345
Creating the Virtual Disk- Specifying Capacity and Name ........ 346
Creating the Virtual Disk- Specifying the Host Group and LUN Id ........ 347
Configuring the Virtual Disk- Bringing the Shared Disk Online ........ 348
Configuring the Shared Disk to Host the CRM E-mail Router ........ 350
Configuring the Shared Disk- Creating the Directory Structure ........ 350
Configuring the Shared Disk- Assigning Permissions ........ 351

Configuring the Service for Clustering ........ 352
Configuring the Service for Clustering- Placing the Application Files on the Shared Disk ........ 352
Configuring the Service for Clustering- Modifying the Registry's Path ........ 353
Installing the CRM E-mail Router Cluster- On Secondary Nodes ........ 354
Creating a Clustered Generic Service for the CRM E-mail Router ........ 355
Creating the Clustered Generic Service- Adding the Shared Disk ........ 355
Creating the Clustered Generic Service- Renaming the Shared Disk ........ 356
Creating the Clustered Generic Service- Adding the Service ........ 357
Creating the Clustered Generic Service- Selecting the Type of Service ........ 358
Creating the Clustered Generic Service- Selecting the Microsoft CRM Email Router Service ........ 359
Creating the Clustered Generic Service- Creating the Client Access Point ........ 360
Creating the Clustered Generic Service- Selecting the Shared Disk ........ 361
Creating the Clustered Generic Service- Entering the Registry Settings ........ 362
Creating the Clustered Generic Service- Verifying the Settings ........ 363
Creating the Clustered Generic Service- Correcting the Parameters Path ........ 364
Testing Failover of the CRM E-mail Router Service ........ 366

**Chapter 28: Configuring Microsoft Dynamics CRM for Outlook Clients to Connect to the New NLB Cluster** ........ 367
Configuring the CRM Client for Outlook- Launching the Configuration Wizard ........ 367
Configuring the CRM Client for Outlook- Specifying Web Addresses ........ 368
Configuring the CRM Client for Outlook- Selecting the Organization ........ 369

**Index:** ........ 370

# About the Author

**Jonathan Ruffing** is a systems engineer who first became Microsoft certified in 1998. He has been designing and building server and network environments over the last thirteen years. He continuously works with the latest technologies by choosing to only work for information technology companies. He currently works for an internet media company that has pioneered the automation of video creation for the auto industry. He specializes in taking complex subjects and communicating them in a step by step way for anyone to learn.

# Dedication

I dedicate this book to my lovely and intelligent wife Yaneth, who is my love, my best friend and from the beautiful country of Panama. I also dedicate this book to my parents who have always showed me love, been supportive and who put up with a difficult teenager during my younger years.

# Give Us Your Feedback

The next book could include your ideas! Scream Publications is always looking for your opinions on our current books and ideas for future books. Tell us what you liked, didn't like or contribute ideas for future books. Scream Publications grew out of the need for real How To documentation that now so many technology companies neglect to create. With technology companies increasingly relying on end users to document their products for free on the internet Blogs and Forums there are bound to be areas that Scream Publications could help document with future books.

**Visit:** www.screampublications.com

**or**

**Email:** feedback@screampublications.com

# Introduction

The world of high availability and clustering is evolving faster than ever and is definitely a very exciting place to be. Windows Server 2008 R2 & SQL Server 2008 R2 have opened up the world of high availability, clustering, virtualization, live migration and failover technologies to the small and medium size companies by including it with the server license. Accompany this new software technology with multi-core processors and you have a very powerful and cost effective combination by being able to run many redundant virtual machines across a few physical servers.

This book guides the IT novice to professional through the process from start to finish of building a complex and highly available system for their real world enterprise applications. Microsoft's new technology is complex and needs to be put together in largely a chronological order where by each new part is depended and built upon its prerequisites.

We will start from scratch by outlining our clusters' physical topologies and then build up to a highly available clustering solution for our enterprise application. Our project will begin at the very root of iSCSI technology by first configuring our switches to be optimized for the best iSCSI performance possible. We will then build upon this foundation by setting up our physical servers' iSCSI network connections to maximize Microsoft and Dell's Multi-path Input/Output (MPIO) technology for performance and redundancy. Next, we will spend considerable time laying out our disk configurations on our iSCSI Storage Area Network (SAN) to give our Windows Server 2008/R2 clusters the best overall performance possible. After we have our SAN layout complete we will dive deep into setting up our Windows Server 2008 R2 Cluster Shared Volumes (CSV), SQL Server 2008 R2 and Microsoft Network Load Balancer (NLB) clusters. Once we have our clusters in place we will build upon their highly available foundation to make our SQL reporting redundant by creating an SQL Reporting Services Scale-out Deployment. The Scale-out Deployment will make our reporting available across all of our front-end servers that are members of our NLB cluster. In the final chapters, we will deploy Microsoft's Dynamics CRM 4.0 into our clustered environment as our real world enterprise application. This will give you real world knowledge of how to deploy CRM 4.0 and other enterprise level applications into your new clustered environment. During this process we will take CRM 4.0's E-mail Router service that is designed to only be installed on one server within a CRM organization and make it highly available. This will demonstrate how you can take an application or service that doesn't have built-in high availability and then build a custom failover cluster to overcome the service's limitation. Our finished highly available CRM application will be full featured with SQL 2008 R2 Reporting Services running our reports, CRM E-Mail Router routing our emails and with Microsoft's software Network Load Balancer (NLB) handling our intranet & internet traffic.

## Different Setup Options When Following this Book

- The iSCSI network settings are for the most part universal and not dependent upon particular hardware vendors for your switches and/or SAN. If you are using a different hardware vendor then our project's Dell equipment, then most likely your particular vendor's configuration steps will be slightly different. Since this book outlines exactly what needs to be configured you should be able to adjust your steps to end up with the book's same basic configuration.

- The SAN disk layout in this book for Microsoft's SQL Server is for the most part universal for best overall performance and is not dependent on particular hardware vendors. The information in this book will allow you to adjust your disk layout according to your particular applications and SAN hardware.

- The SQL Server configuration and installation steps are the same whether you are installing SQL on physical servers or into a virtual environment, such as we are using in our project.

- Whether you choose to install SQL Server 2008 SP1 or SQL Server 2008 R2 the steps are basically the same and we will cover the few differences that exist during the installation process.

## Goals

The goal of this book was to take many different technologies and show you how you can put them all together step by step into one highly available solution. With that being said, it is likely that you won't be using the same exact hardware or software as used in this book's project; however the high availability configuration will more or less be the same for your different hardware and software. A few quick hardware examples would be using Jumbo Frames for iSCSI network connections, aligning your disk partitions, or short-stroking your disks will all significantly increase your performance regardless of what brand of hardware you're using. A few quick software examples would be Microsoft's Network Load Balancer (NLB), Microsoft's SQL Reporting Services Scale-out Deployment, Windows Cluster Shared Volumes and SQL Clustering for application high availability. Regardless of what front-end applications your servers will host they will still be able to take advantage of some or all of these redundant technologies for high availability.

## Who is this Book for

This book is aimed at Network Engineers and System Administrators with an experience range from novice to the professional. The book is crafted to make learning the latest Microsoft and iSCSI technologies easy by guiding the reader step by step through the building process. The reader should have some prior experience with Windows Server 2008/R2 and SQL Server 2008/R2.

# Terms and Conventions Used in this Book

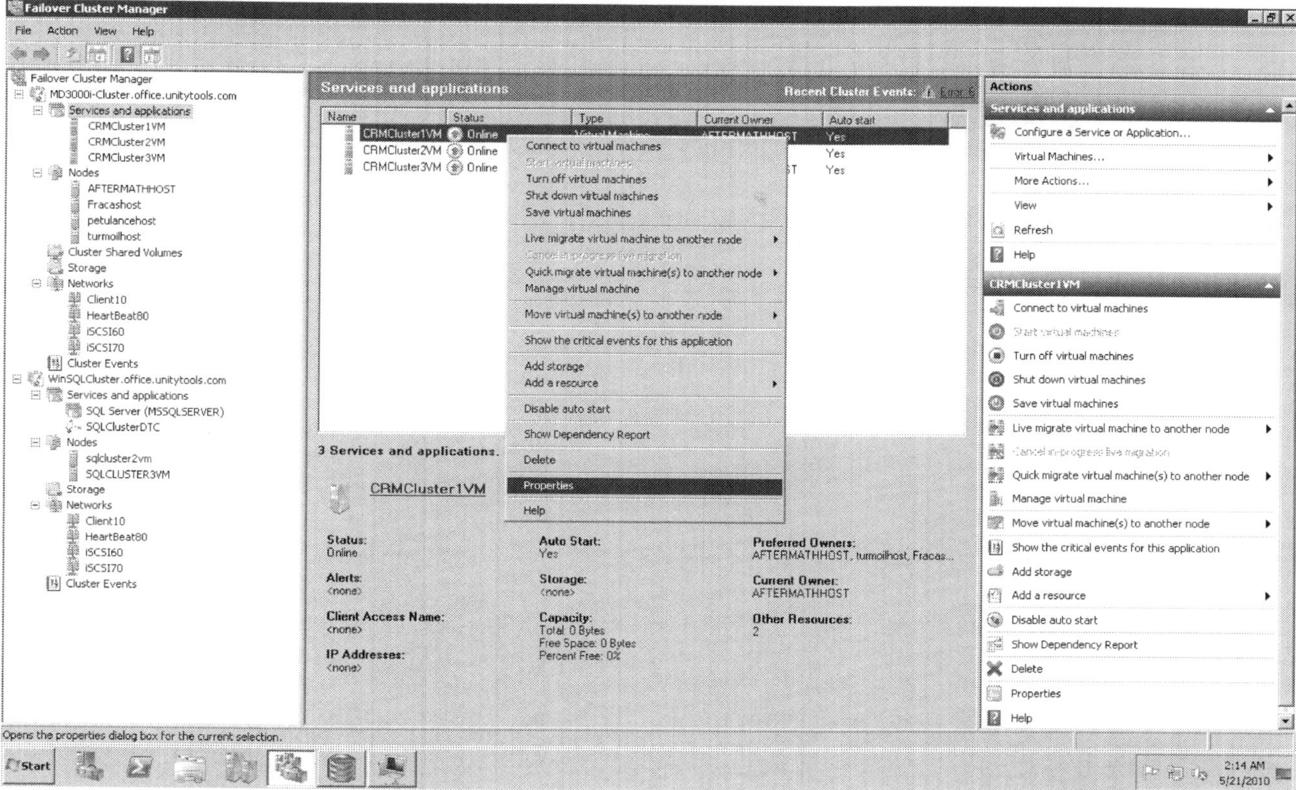


**Figure i.1**

- Paths to programs and settings have been condensed. For example in **Figure i.1**, we want to open the **Properties** of the cluster shared volume virtual machine named **CRMCluster1VM**. In this book the instructions and path may be written like this.
    - Browse to **Windows Failover Cluster Manager\MD3000i-Cluster\Services and Applications** and right click on the **CRMCluster1VM** virtual machine and then select **Properties**.
- The text displayed in **BOLD** is to highlight things such as **Names**, **Programs**, **Properties**, **Settings**, **Paths** and so on. The above condensed path is a good example of how text in bold is used to help guide you throughout this book.
- **Acronyms** for terms and programs are enclosed in ( ) parenthesis for at least the first few times that the term or program is introduced. After the term or program is introduced just the acronym may be used. For example, if we were talking about Microsoft's Network Load Balancer for the first the time it would be displayed as **Microsoft Network Load Balancer (NLB).** Then in subsequent text may just be referred to as the **NLB.**
- **Graphics** used in this book are labeled as **Figures** and have corresponding numbers based on which chapter as well as which number of figure it is within the chapter. The first number indicates the chapter, while the number after the decimal indicates which figure within the chapter it is. **Figure 2.3** for example

indicates that the graphic is located in the second chapter and that it is the third graphic within that chapter.

- **Synonyms** are used for the following words and terms interchangeably throughout this book due to different manufactures using their own terminologies. For example, when talking about a clustered server **Dell's Modular Disk Storage Manager** refers to a clustered server as **Host**, while **Microsoft's Failover Cluster Manager** refers to a clustered server as a **Node**. For this reason the following words and terms are synonymous:
    - Server, Node and Host
    - Virtual disk, partition, LUN
    - RAID array, disk group
- The areas labeled **NOTE**, **HOT TIP** and **BEST PRACTICES** you'll want to pay extra attention to as they note information of significance such as tricks of the trade, performance recommendations, manufactures misrepresentations and special absolute do's or do not's.

## Summary of Microsoft and Dell's Best Practices Followed in this Book

We will follow Microsoft and Dell's best practices whitepaper when building our PowerVault MD3000i Array with Windows Server 2008 R2 servers. The following is a summary of these best practices:

- It is recommended that you use virtual hard disks (vhd's) with your virtual machines. This will allow you to utilize Windows Server 2008 R2's Cluster Shared Volumes (CSV's) failover features such as the new live migration feature. For best performance it is recommended that you a use fixed vhd.
- Enabling Jumbo Frames on the SAN, switches and server network adapters will give you the best performance by reducing TCP/IP overhead.
- Use Dell's Multi-Path Input/Output (MPIO) driver on every system that you connect to the MD3000i.
- Utilize four network connections per server and dedicate the connections as follows:
    - Use two networks adapters for server-to-storage communications.
    - Use one network adapter for client-to-server communications.
    - Use one network adapter for cluster heartbeat communications.

Further Dell recommendations can be found in Dell's whitepaper titled "PowerVault MD3000 and MD3000i Array Tuning Whitepaper".

## Errata

Any corrections to errors will be posted on **www.screampublications.com**.

## Contacting the Author

The author can be contacted through his website **www.jonathanruffing.com**.

# Chapter 1: Overview of the Completed Project

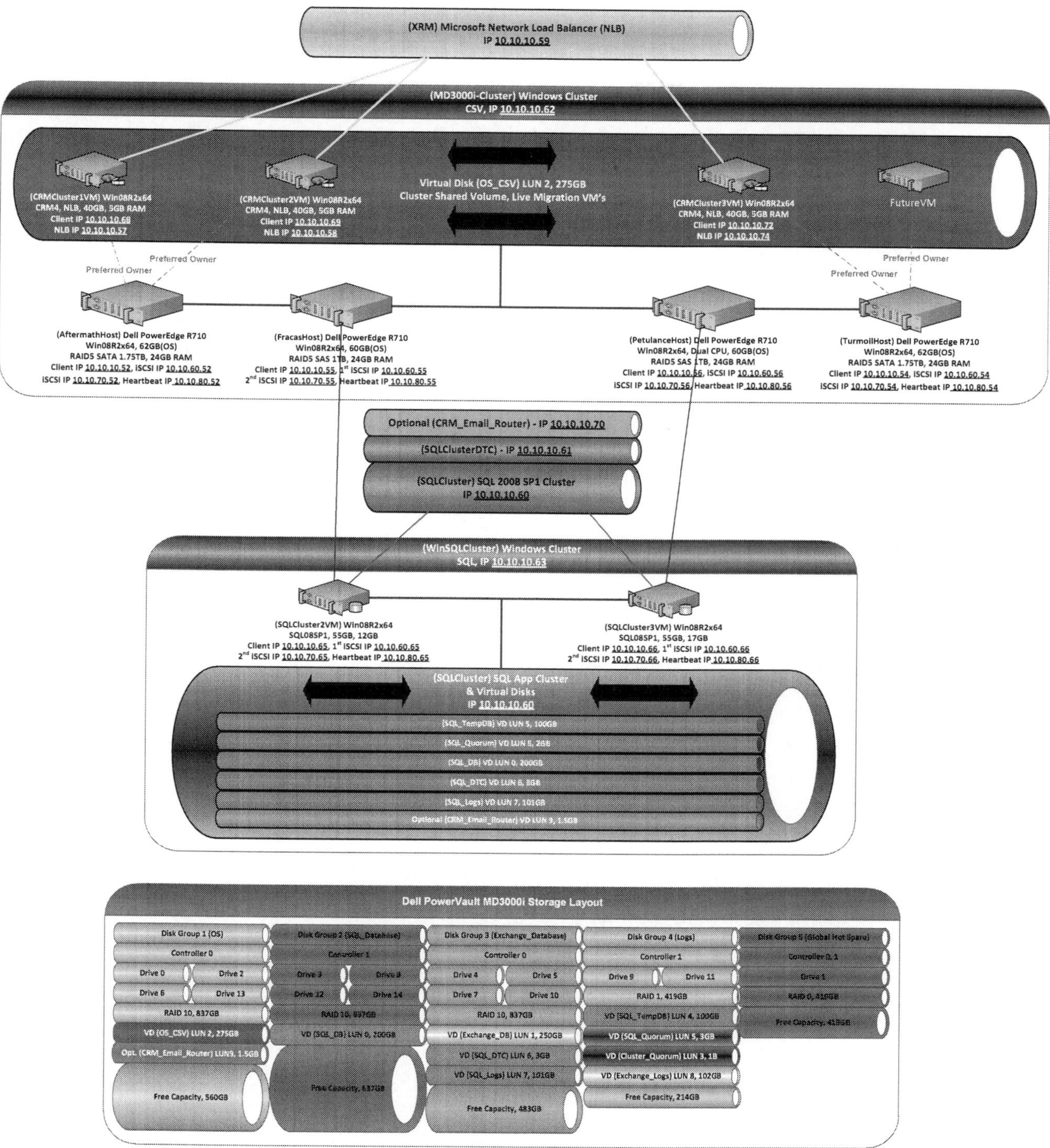


**Figure 1.1**

## Overview of the Completed Project

Let's begin by first taking a look at what the completed project will look like. The diagram in **Figure 1.1** shows what the finished project will look like. It may appear quite complex at first glance, but once we break it down into components it will help you understand what is involved. As you follow the steps going through each chapter you can always refer back to this diagram to see where we are at in the building process. Our project will include four clusters in total. Two of the clusters will be Windows Failover Clusters followed by an SQL cluster and a Microsoft Network Load Balancer (NLB) cluster. By the way don't be put off by the word failover in the term Windows Failover Cluster as this does not mean that the Windows cluster can only be Active/Passive. You will see that we have both Active/Active and Active/Passive clusters in our project.

## Windows Physical Server and Network Load Balancer Clusters

We first start with the Windows Failover Cluster that consists of our physical servers. In **Figure 1.1** this cluster is labeled MD3000i-Cluster and is color coded black. This cluster contains four physical servers that ultimately will host all four of our different types of clusters in conjunction with our SAN. These four physical servers host all of our virtual machine servers. If any one of these physical hosts goes offline then their virtual machines will be automatically migrated to one of the other physical hosts. Four of these virtual machines that are hosted by these physical servers are stored on the Cluster Shared Volume (CSV) disk which resides on the SAN. Virtual machines that are stored on the CSV disk can use Windows Server 2008 R2's new feature of Live Migration. These virtual machines can live migrate onto any of the physical servers that are part of the MD3000i-Cluster without disrupting the end users who are connected to them. Three of these virtual machines labeled CRMCluster1VM, CRMCluster2VM and CRMCluster3VM use Microsoft's Network Load Balancer (NLB) software to form another cluster labeled XRM and color coded yellow. The network load balancer allows these front-end CRM web servers to form an Active/Active cluster where each of them actively takes some of the workload that comes in to XRM's IP of 10.10.10.59. If one of the CRMClusterVM virtual machines goes offline then the remaining two online will automatically distribute the offline virtual machine's load between them. So as you can see these two clusters are truly highly available.

## Windows Virtual Machine and SQL Clusters

Next we have our second Windows Failover Cluster that consists of our two SQL virtual machines. In **Figure 1.1** this cluster is labeled WinSQLCluster and is color coded green. This cluster contains two SQL virtual machines labeled SQLCluster2VM and SQLCluster3VM. These two virtual machines form our fourth and final cluster labeled SQLCluster and color coded in red. Virtual machines are able to form a Windows Failover Clusters similar to the physical servers where they have their own independent resources. Therefore, these two virtual machines function completely independent of the first Windows Failover Cluster consisting of the physical servers. They connect directly to their own virtual disks on the SAN. As you can see in **Figure 1.1** the virtual disks labeled SQL_DB, SQL_Logs, SQL_TempDB, SQL_DTC and SQL_Quorum in orange are shared between the two virtual machines. The disks are shared between the two SQL virtual machines; however only one virtual machine at a time has ownership of the disks making our SQL cluster an Active/Passive cluster.

## iSCSI Storage Area Network (SAN) Disk Layout

The diagram labeled Dell PowerVault MD3000i Storage Layout at the bottom of **Figure 1.1** displays how we will distribute our four clusters' resources throughout the SAN's fifteen SAS drives. If you look closely you will notice that we have the SQL virtual disks distributed across three of the SAN's physical disk groups. This will provide the best possible performance by placing each of SQL's labor intense components DB, Logs and TempDB on their own RAID arrays. The disk groups are distributed across each of the MD3000i's Dual Controllers as well to provide the best possible performance by balancing the workload across both RAID controllers. We will setup our other virtual disks such as the CSV, Windows Quorum, Exchange DB and Exchange Logs to balance the workload as well.

**NOTE:** We don't cover clustering Exchange 2007 in this book, as you'll see there's plenty to cover already with our CRM front-end application servers and with our SQL back-end servers. However, I did want to include Exchange in our virtual disk layout, to give you an example of how you could distribute other labor intense applications among our SQL and CSV disks. In our example you are able to see how you could layout the SAN's disks to have a good balance of performance between our Exchange, SQL, and CSV workloads. If your company is planning on using Exchange Server 2010 then you can disregard allocating space for Exchange on the SAN as Exchange 2010 does not require a Windows Failover Cluster hosted by a SAN to be redundant.

## Overview of the SAN iSCSI Network Topology

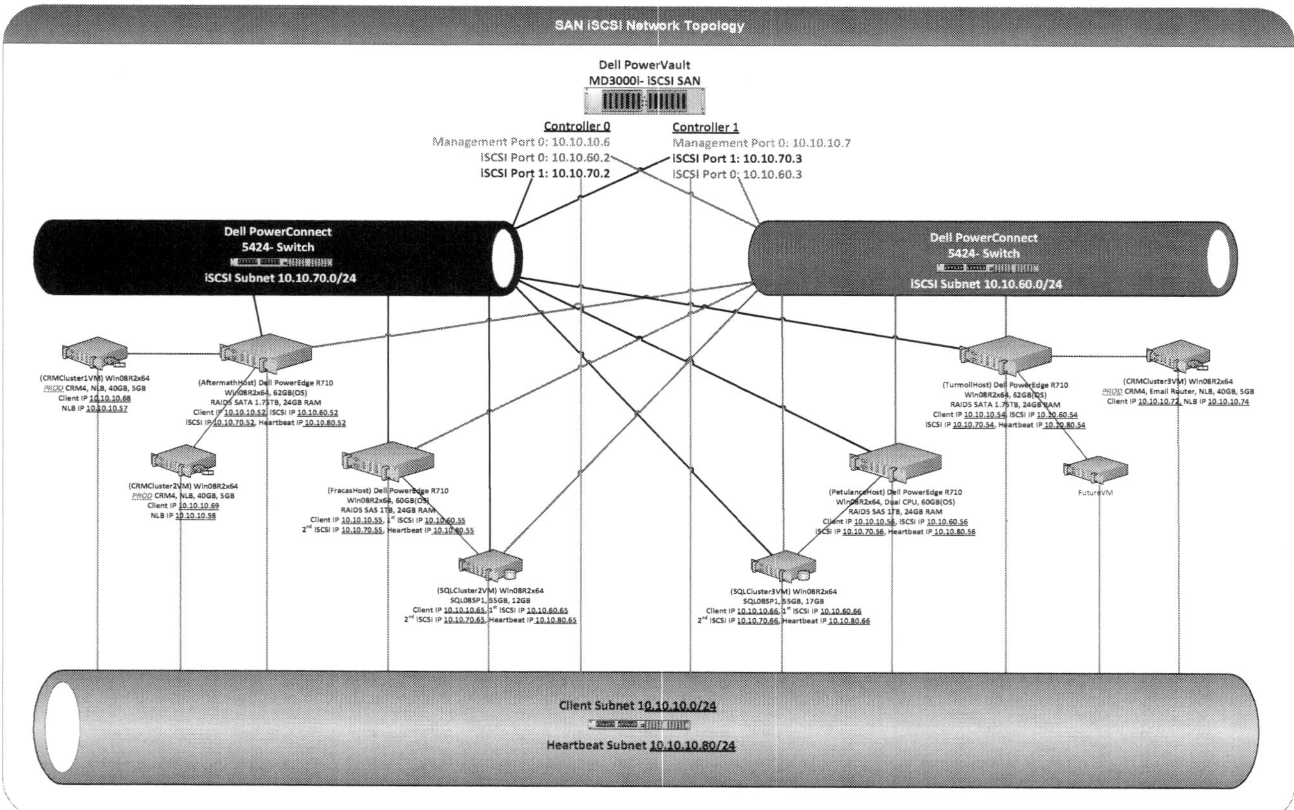


**Figure 1.2**

When our SAN iSCSI network is completed it will appear like **Figure 1.2**. The diagram of **Figure 1.2** shows how our subnets, switches, physical host servers, virtual machines and SAN components will interconnect to form our redundant iSCSI network topology. The redundant iSCSI subnets are represented by the two smaller tubes located towards the top of the diagram with the IP ranges of 10.10.60.0/24 and of 10.10.70.0/24. The client and heartbeat subnets are represented by the one large tube at the bottom of the diagram. The client and heartbeat connections are physically all on one set of switches, but are configured with different subnets to separate their traffic, while the iSCSI connections each use their own switch and subnet for redundancy. All of our physical servers are connected to each of the four subnets and have direct access to our SAN's resources. Our virtual machines are connected to different subnets depending on their role in the cluster. The clustered front-end web virtual machines only connect to the client subnet, while the clustered back-end SQL virtual machines are connected to each of the four subnets and have direct access to our SAN's resources as our physical servers do. Once we are finished building out our iSCSI network topology we will have a completely redundant network in place.

## Overview of the Clusters from within Windows Failover Cluster Manager

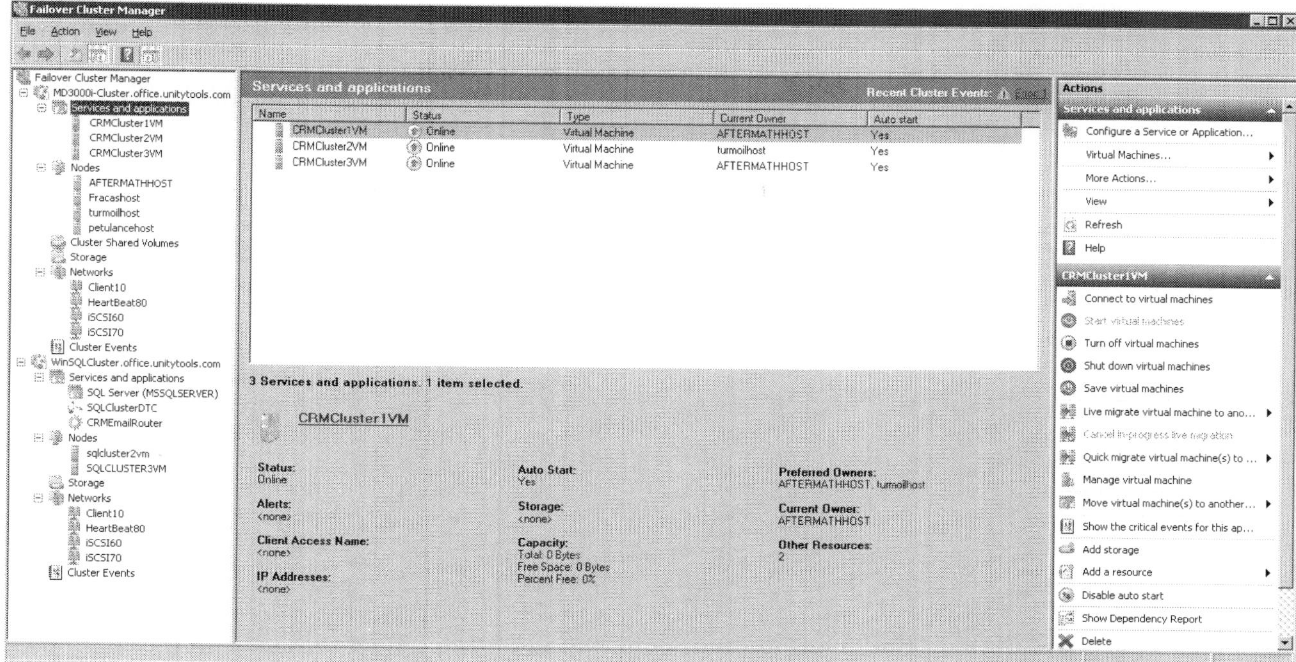


**Figure 1.3**

## Overview of the Cluster Shared Volumes (CSV) Windows Failover Cluster

We will take a quick look to see what the finish project will appear like from within Windows Failover Cluster Manager. In **Figure 1.3**, in the left pane we have both of our Windows clusters shown. Below each cluster name you can see the resources that belong to each cluster such as Nodes, Networks, Storage, Services and Applications. We have the MD3000i-Cluster's Services and Applications highlighted in the left pane and this shows us the virtual machines that are stored in the Cluster Shared Volume (CSV). These three CRMClusterVM's can live migrate between any of the servers listed under the Nodes section. We will cover the Failover Cluster Manager in depth in later chapters, so for now just get a visual of what our finished project will look like.

# Overview of the SQL Server's Windows Failover Cluster

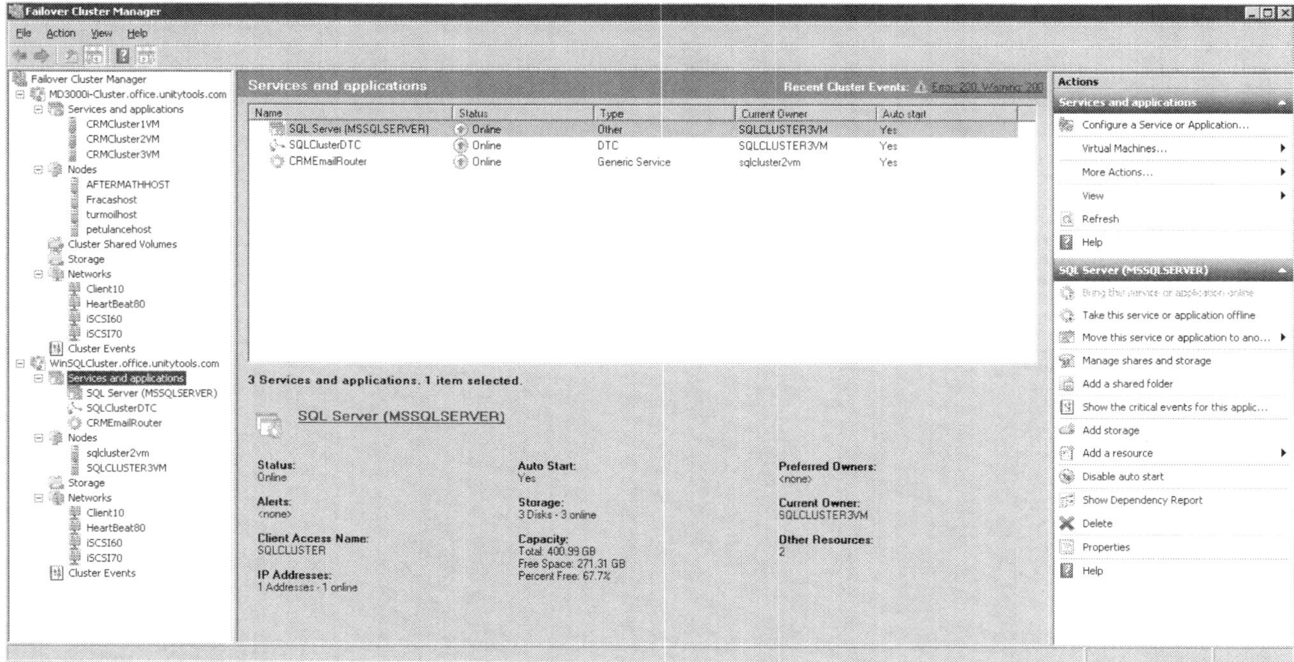


**Figure 1.4**

In **Figure 1.4**, we have the WinSQLCluster's Services and Applications highlighted in the left pane, which shows us our clustered SQL server components of the SQL Server application and the SQL Distributed Transaction Coordinator (DTC) service. In addition, if you are planning on installing Microsoft Dynamics CRM 4.0 as in our project, then you'd also have the clustered CRM E-Mail Router service hosted by this cluster. Each of these clustered services and applications can move independently of each other between any of the servers listed under the Nodes section of this cluster. This means that you can load balance your workload between the cluster's nodes by having the SQL Server application active on one node and the CRM E-Mail Router service active on the other node. The SQL Server application usually fails over within less than 15 seconds, while the SQLClusterDTC can failover in less than 10 seconds between nodes.

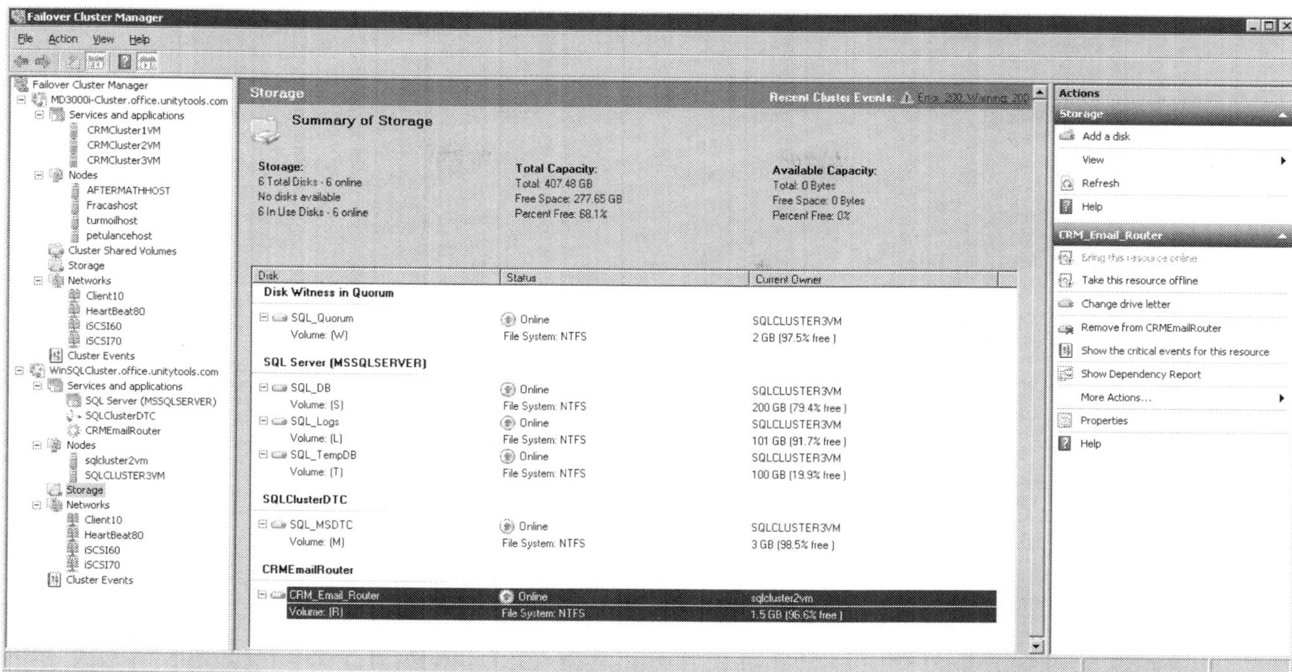


**Figure 1.5**

In **Figure 1.5**, you can see that when the Storage node of our WinSQLCluster is highlighted that all the SQL cluster's shared disks are visible in the center pane. The shared disks you see here are considered regular failover cluster disks and can only be accessed by one cluster node at a time. These shared disks can have applications, services and virtual machines stored on them as well as being able to failover between cluster nodes, however they do not have the ability to live migrate such as our CRMClusterVM's do that are stored on our CSV cluster disk. CSV cluster disks are able to be accessed simultaneously by all the nodes of the cluster which makes the new live migration feature of Windows Server 2008 R2 possible. However, the CSV virtual machines themselves that reside on CSV disks can only be hosted by one cluster node at a time. For most regular failover cluster disks, you can enable the CSV feature with the exception of failover cluster disks that will be hosting cluster aware applications, such as SQL Server and Exchange Server 2007.

## Overview of the Microsoft Network Load Balancer (NLB) Cluster

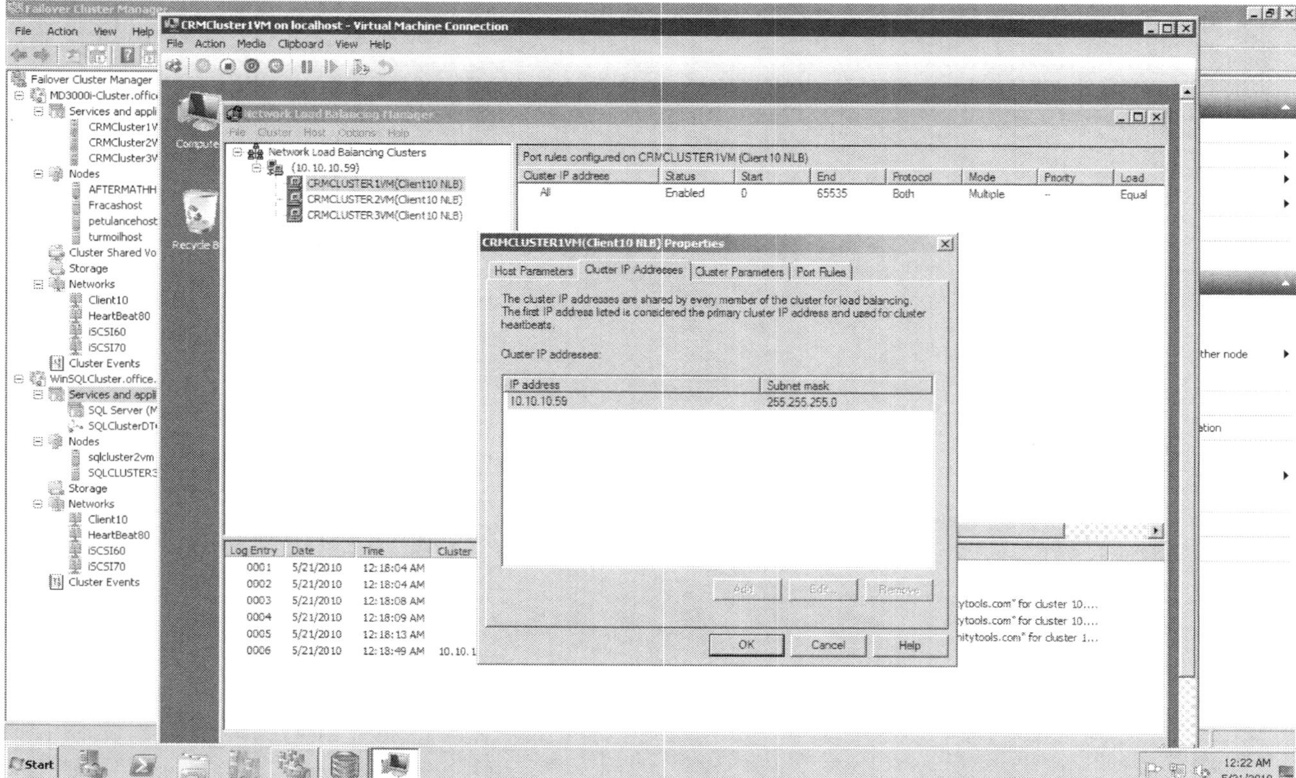


**Figure 1.6**

In **Figure 1.6**, we have our Microsoft Network Load Balancer (NLB) cluster which is made of up of our three front-end CRM application servers. This is an Active/Active cluster that balances the workload between the nodes based on the cluster's configuration. We can stop traffic to any of the nodes at any time and as long as at least one NLB cluster node remaining online then our end users will continue to have access the CRM application. The NLB cluster's name is determined by us creating an internal DNS record for the IP address that is assigned to our NLB cluster. In our project this cluster's DNS name is XRM, and all client access to our CRM application is sent to this XRM name.

# Chapter 2: iSCSI Physical Network Topology

In this chapter, we will begin covering the best practices to use when setting up our physical iSCSI network. We will take advantage of Multi-path Input/Output (MPIO) technology to give us the best overall performance and redundancy on the network. You will need to have your iSCSI physical network connections setup similarly to as outlined in the chapter before we can continue with our project's configuration.

## iSCSI Network Topology for Multi-path Input/Output (MPIO) Redundancy

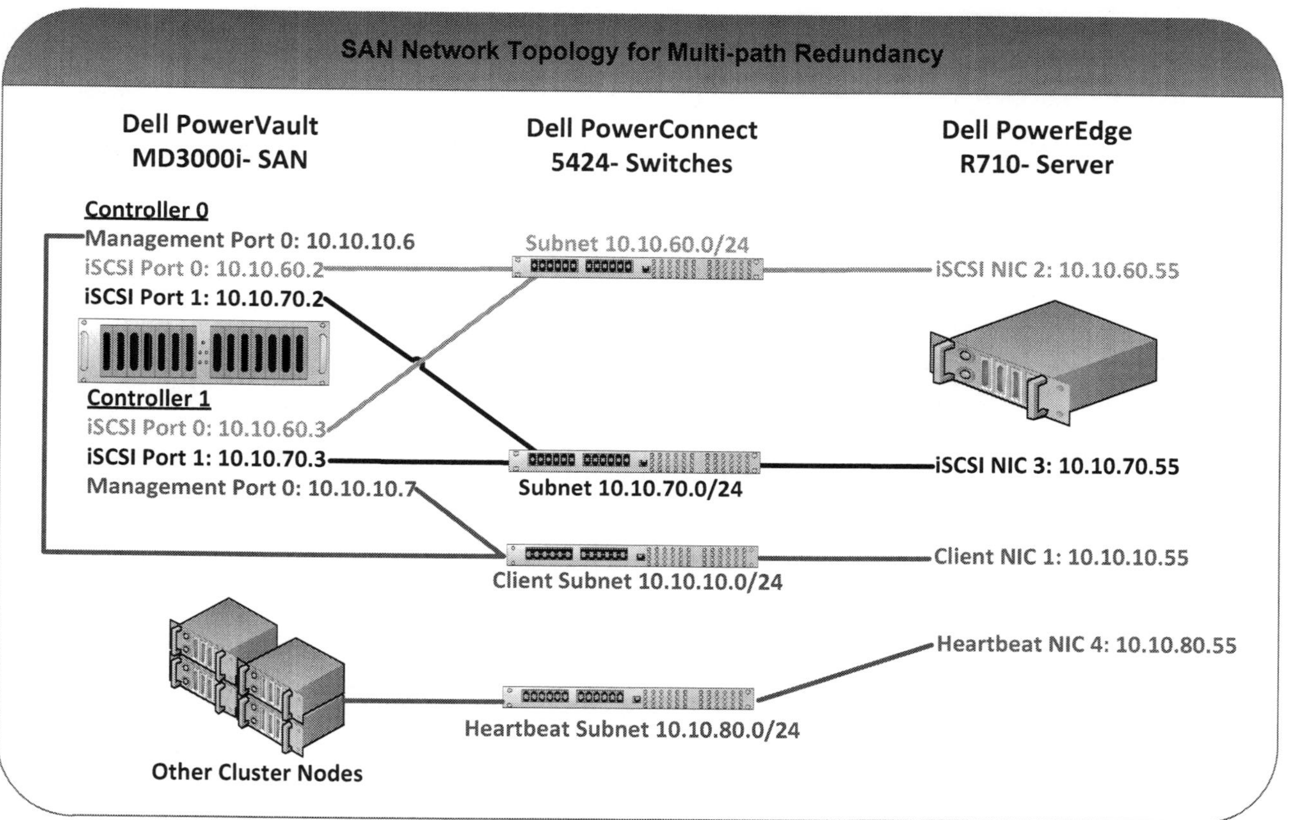


**Figure 2.1**

In **Figure 2.1** the diagram lays out how we want our SAN network topology configured to take advantage of Dell and Microsoft's Multi-Path Input/Output (MPIO) technology. You can use a single or dual controller SAN in your network topology. In our example, we have chosen to use a dual controller SAN for its superior performance and redundancy. This will also give us an opportunity to cover the more complex setup of the dual controller. The layout is as follows:

- On the left hand side of **Figure 2.1** we have our **Dell PowerVault MD3000i** Dual Controller iSCSI SAN which has a total of six network adapters with three per each controller. Each of the RAID controllers has two iSCSI network adapters and one management network adapter. We will connect each controller's iSCSI network adapter to a different iSCSI switch for redundancy to our servers. We will then connect each controller's management network adapter to the client subnet giving us two different IP's to access the SAN by.

- In the middle of **Figure 2.1** we have our two **Dell PowerConnect 5424** iSCSI switches along with one regular switch for our client network and one regular switch for our heartbeat network. Ideally you would have a separate switch for each of the four network connections, however if you do not have four separate switches available you could choose to combine the client and heartbeat subnets on to one switch.

- On the right hand side of **Figure 2.1** we have our **Dell PowerEdge R710** server which has four network adapters. We will use two of the network adapters for iSCSI connections, one for our client network and one for our heartbeat network.

## iSCSI SAN Physical Network Topology

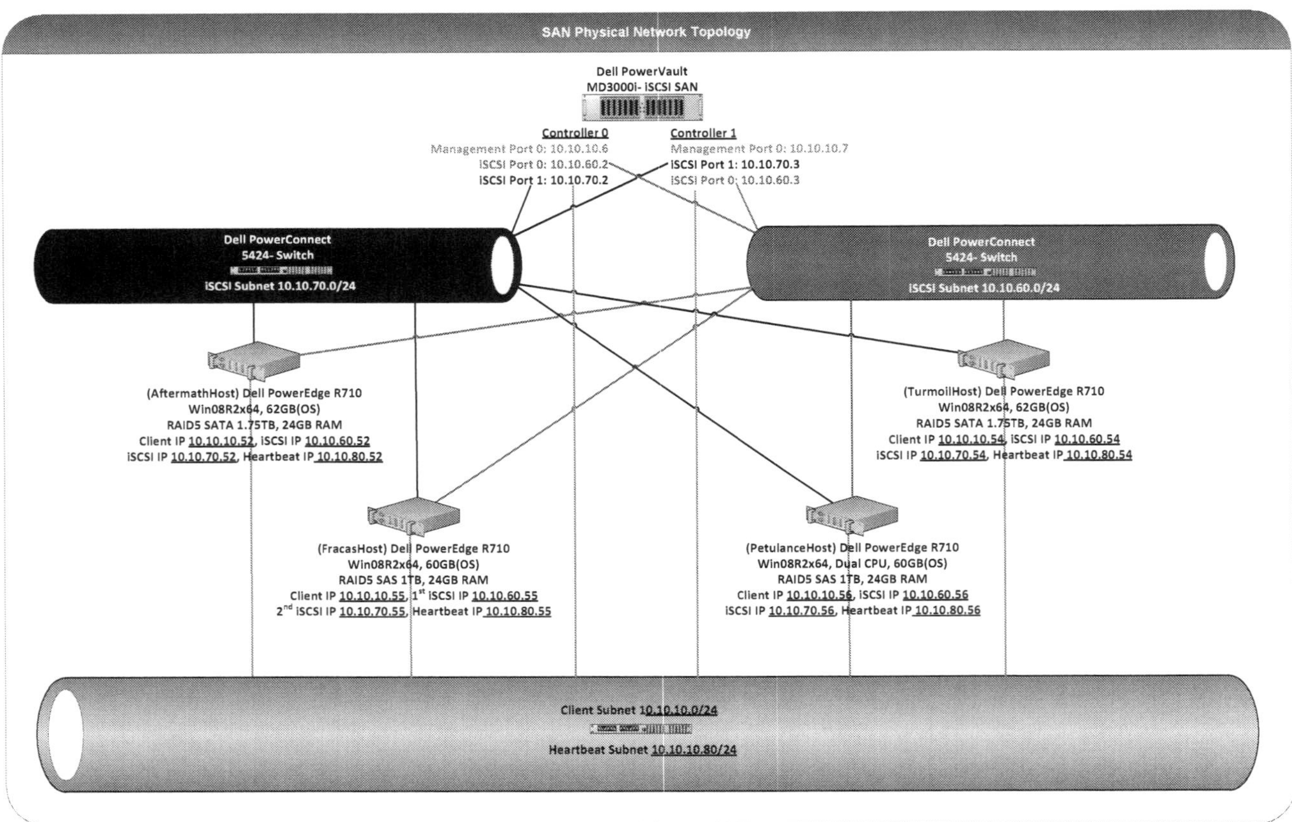


**Figure 2.2**

In **Figure 2.2** we have the physical topology of how all our cables, switches, servers and SAN components should be setup for our project. The iSCSI subnets are represented by the two smaller tubes located towards the top of the diagram with the IP ranges 10.10.60.0/24 and 10.10.70.0/24. The client and heartbeat subnets are represented by the one large tube at the bottom of the diagram. The client and heartbeat connections are physically all on one set of switches, but are configured with different subnets to separate their traffic, while the iSCSI connections each use their own switch and subnet for redundancy. You could choose to place your heartbeat subnet on one of the iSCSI switches if you don't have room on the client switches, or you could choose to use a completely separate fourth switch dedicated solely to the heartbeat network. Using a separate fourth switch for the heartbeat network would increase redundancy as well. Once you have all your physical connections setup then we'll be ready to begin configuring our switches for optimal iSCSI performance.

# Chapter 3: Configuration of the iSCSI Switches

Configuring the newly acquired hardware can be a challenge, especially if the devices were previously used and have unknown configurations or passwords. This process can be time consuming, so we'll cover how to erase unknown configurations first to get us started. In our project we have chosen to use two Dell PowerConnect 5424 iSCSI optimized switches for our iSCSI network. These two switches will be dedicated only to our redundant iSCSI networks. It is highly recommended that you use iSCSI optimized switches for your iSCSI networks when possible as they'll provide better overall performance, however it is not absolutely required. Don't worry if you're not using the exact same model or brand of switch as in our example, as the configuration settings for good iSCSI performance are fairly universal. You will want to read through this chapter to insure that your switches have the same settings for best overall iSCSI performance regardless of the model or brand of switch that you are using.

We will start out by connecting to our switches via the console to erase the current configuration and start fresh. We will then run through the initial setup process followed by configuring Jumbo Frames for the best possible throughput. Once our initial configuration is in place, we will cover how to use the OpenManage Switch Administrator web user interface to finish our remaining configurations. In the final steps we'll set our iSCSI settings at the port level following by enabling flow control. Once we have all our configurations set, we will be ready to take advantage of our switches optimized performance.

## Connecting to the Switch via the Console

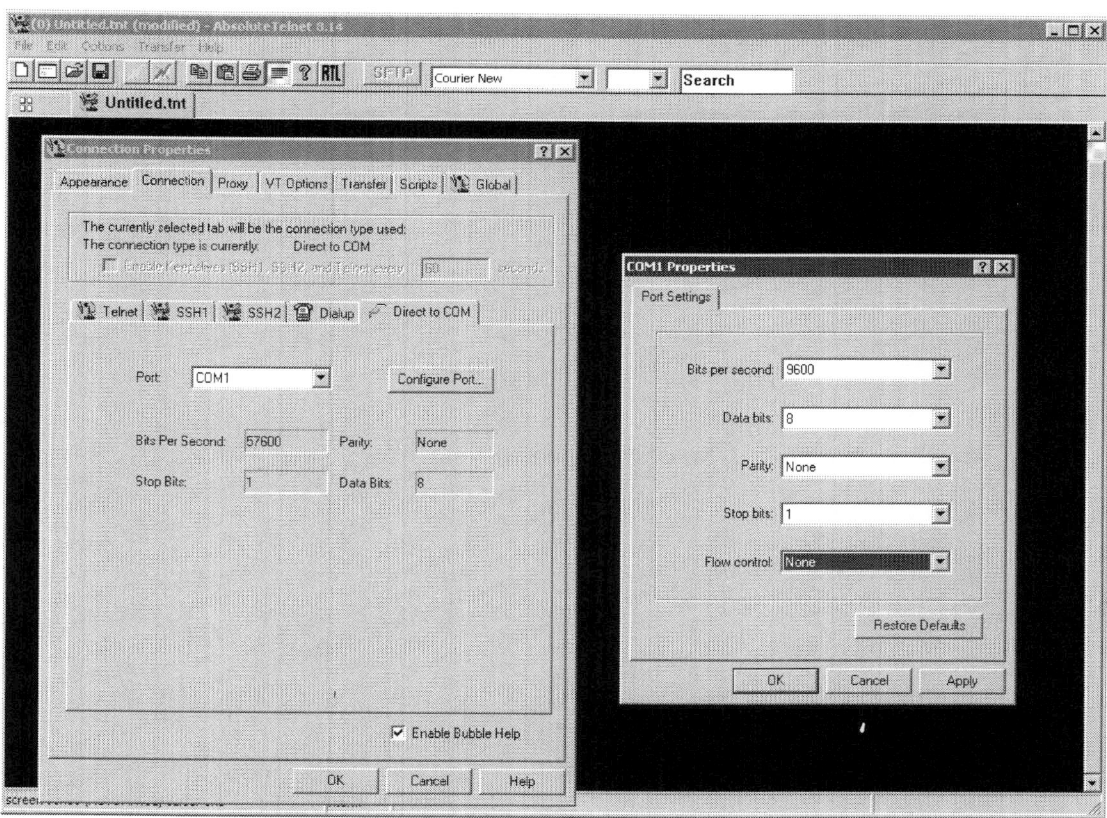


**Figure 3.1**

1. If you do not have access to the device via an IP connection, then you will have to begin by connecting a **Serial Cable** between your **Switch** and the **COM1** port of your server or laptop. If you already have access to your switches IP, Password and/or Web UI then you can skip to **Step 5**.

   a. Next, we need to use a **VT100** terminal emulation software such as **AbsoluteTelnet** or Microsoft's built-in **HyperTerminal** program on older Windows servers will work as well. The HyperTerminal program on **Windows Server 2003** is located under **Start\All Programs\Accessories\Communications**. For our project, we will use the free version of **AbsoluteTelnet** software to connect to our switches, as shown in **Figure 3.1**.

   b. Create a new connection for the **COM1 Port** with the following settings.

      i. **Bits per second/Baud rate = 9600**

      ii. **Data bits = 8**

      iii. **Parity = None**

      iv. **Stop bits = 1**

      v. **Flow control = None**

   c. Click on the **OK** button of the **COM1 Properties** screen to save your settings.

   d. Click on the **Apply** button, and then on the **OK** button of the **Connection Properties** screen to connect to your switch. You might have to hit the **Enter** key once or twice until a response from the switch shows up on the console screen.

## Erasing the Switch's Current Configuration

2. If you don't currently have access to the switches password or IP address, then we'll first want to erase the switch's configuration. Disconnect the power cord and hard power cycle the switch. While the switch is restarting the screen will look like the below text, and once the ***Autoboot*** message appears we want to hit the **Enter** key to enter the menu that will allow us to erase the current configuration.

```
**************************************************
***************** SYSTEM RESET *****************
**************************************************

UART Channel Loopback Test........................PASS
Testing the System SDRAM..........................PASS
Boot1 Checksum Test...............................PASS
Boot2 Checksum Test...............................PASS
Flash Image Validation Test.......................PASS
BOOT Software Version 1.0.0.20 Built 22-Jan-xxxx 15:09:28
Processor: FireFox 88E6218 ARM946E-S , 64 MByte SDRAM.
I-Cache 8 KB. D-Cache 8 KB. Cache Enabled.
Autoboot in 2 seconds - press RETURN or Esc. to abort and enter prom.
Preparing to decompress...
```

a. Once at the startup menu we want to select option number **[2]** and then hit the **Enter** key.

**[1] Download Software**
**[2] Erase Flash File**
**[3] Password Recovery Procedure**
**[4] Enter Diagnostic Mode**
**[5] Set Terminal Baud-Rate**
**[6] Back**
**Enter your choice or press 'ESC' to exit**

b. When you receive the **Warning! About to erase a Flash file** message, hit the **Y** key for yes.

c. When the next message asks for a config flash file type **config** as the name and hit the **Enter** key. The configuration is erased and the device reboots.

**Write Flash file name (Up to 8 characters, Enter for none.):config**
**File config (if present) will be erased after system initialization**
**======== Press Enter To Continue ========**

## Running the Switch's Setup Wizard to Create the Initial Configuration

3. Once the switch reboots we want to hit the **Y** key for yes to run the **Setup Wizard** once prompted. This will run us through the switch's initial setup where we can assign our IP address and password. For our project's redundant iSCSI switches, we will configure our first switch as **VLAN60** with a subnet of **10.10.60.0/24**, and then our second switch as **VLAN70** with a subnet of **10.10.70.0/24**.

## Configuring Jumbo Frames via the Console

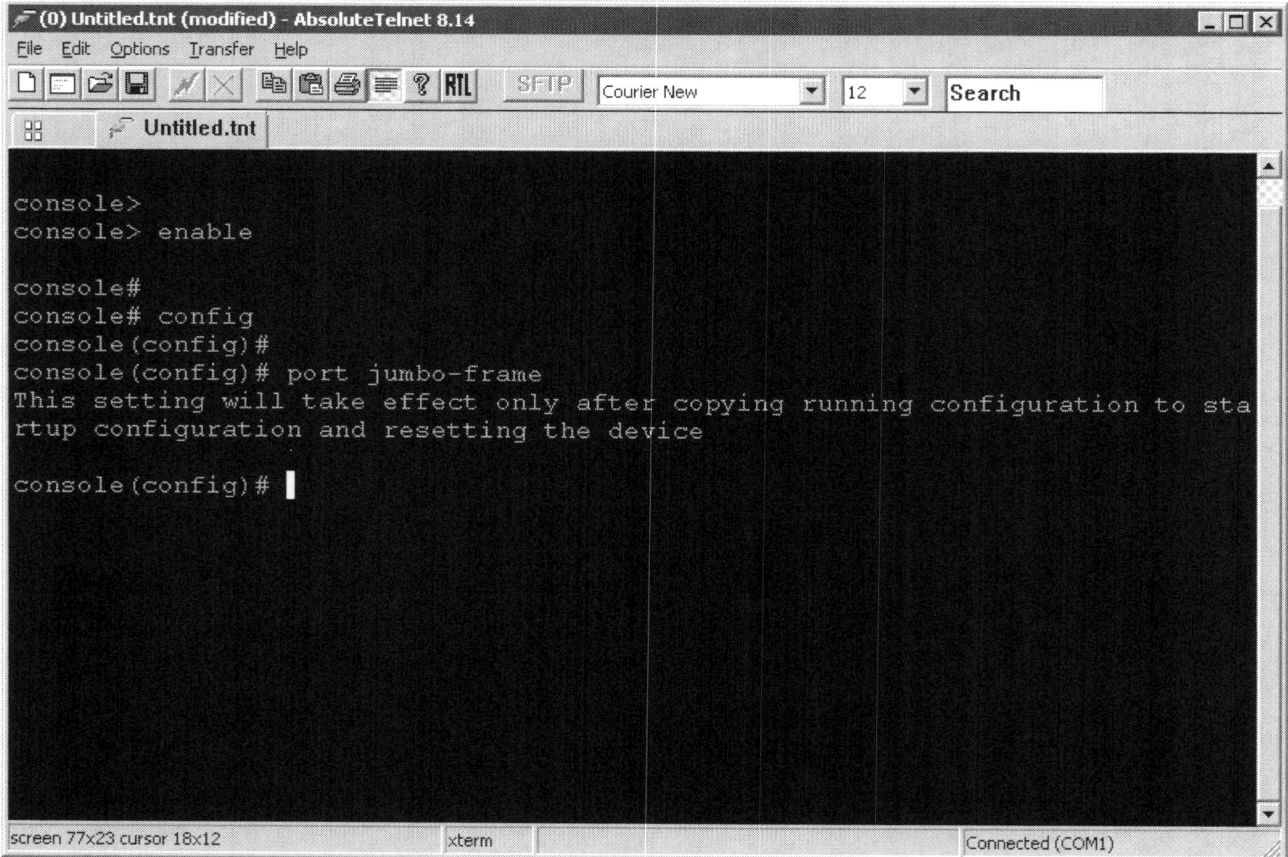


**Figure 3.2**

A Jumbo Frame refers to the Maximum Transfer Unit (MTU) that a network interface can use to send packets. A typical network usually uses a packet size of a 1500 MTU, while a Jumbo Frame network will typically use a packet size of a 9000 MTU. When utilizing Jumbo Frames on your iSCSI network it is important to make sure that all your network devices such as switches, routers, and network adapters are configured to handle Jumbo Frames or your network packets can become fragmented by devices that have their MTU size set smaller than the size of packets coming from devices configured to use Jumbo Frames. For this reason, we will insure that all our network devices have Jumbo Frames enabled with an MTU size of 9000. This will greatly increase our performance between our SAN and clustered servers.

4. Now that we have access to the switch, we can start configuring the iSCSI settings that will affect our performance. The first thing we want to do is to enable **Jumbo Frames** to allow a Maximum Transfer Unit (MTU) size of 9000. Type in the following commands as outlined below.

    a. At the **console>** prompt, type in the command **enable**, and then hit the **Enter** key, as shown in **Figure 3.2**.

       **NOTE:** That the enable command shown in **Figure 3.2** doesn't require a password as your switch might, this is due to our project's switches not yet having their password set.

b. At the **console#** prompt, type in the command **config**, and then hit the **Enter** key.

c. At the **console(config)#** prompt, type in the command **port jumbo-frame**, and then hit the **Enter** key. The console should return a message stating that **The setting will only take effect after copying running configuration to startup configuration and resetting the device.** The message indicates that we have only changed the configuration file and that for our changes to take effect we have to save our modified configuration file to the actual switch.

## Finishing the Switch Configuration via the Web User Interface (UI)

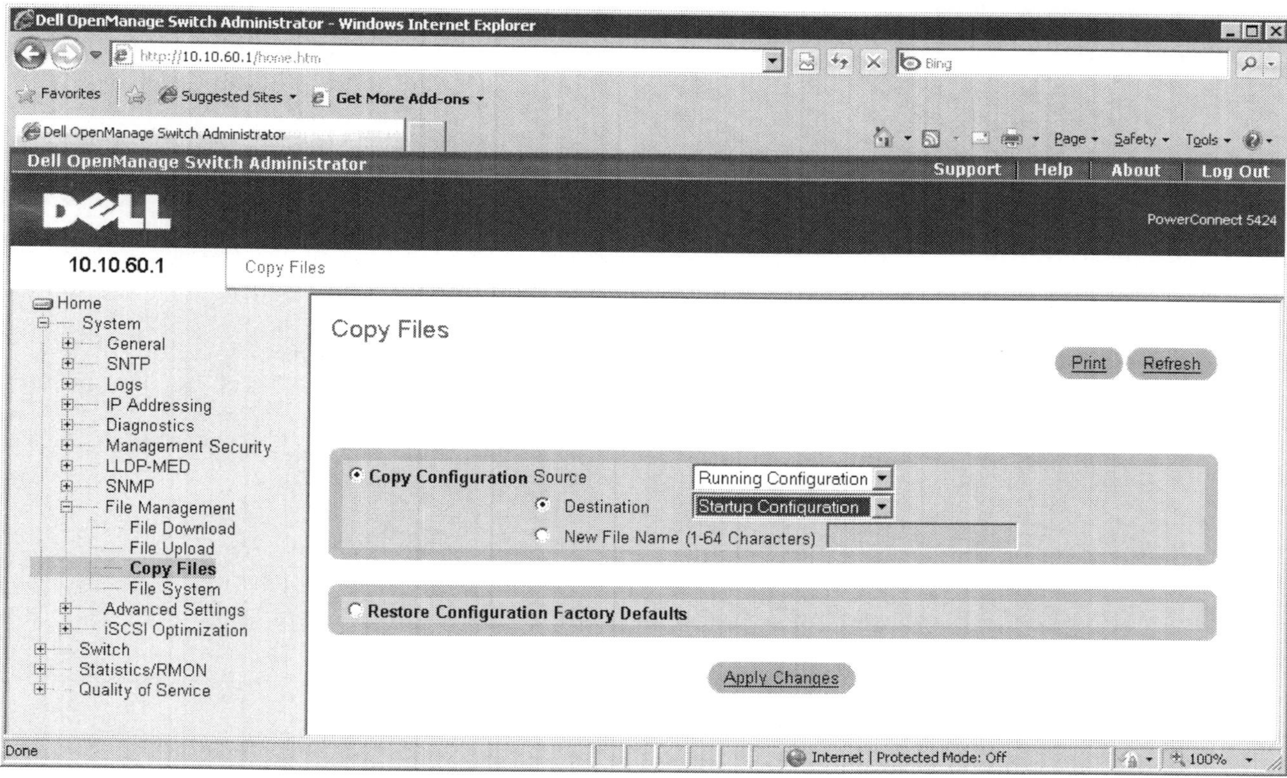


**Figure 3.3**

## Applying the Jumbo Frames Configuration Changes

5. Open **Internet Explorer**, and enter in your switch's IP address in the browser. This will launch the **Dell OpenManage Switch Administrator** user interface. For our project, we will enter the IP address of **10.10.60.1** to connect to our first switch's web UI.

   a. Login to the **Dell OpenManage Switch Administrator**, and then browse to **System\File Management\Copy Files** in the left pane.

      i. On the **Copy Files** screen, select the **Running Configuration** option for the **Source** field, as shown in **Figure 3.3**.

ii. For the **Destination** field, select the **Startup Configuration** option, and then click on the **Apply Changes** button in the bottom center of the screen.

b. We now have our new configuration set to take effect when the switch reboots. To reboot the switch browse to **System\General\Reset** in the left pane, and then click on **Reset** button in the right hand pane. Click on the **OK** buttons of the pop-up screens to end all sessions and reboot.

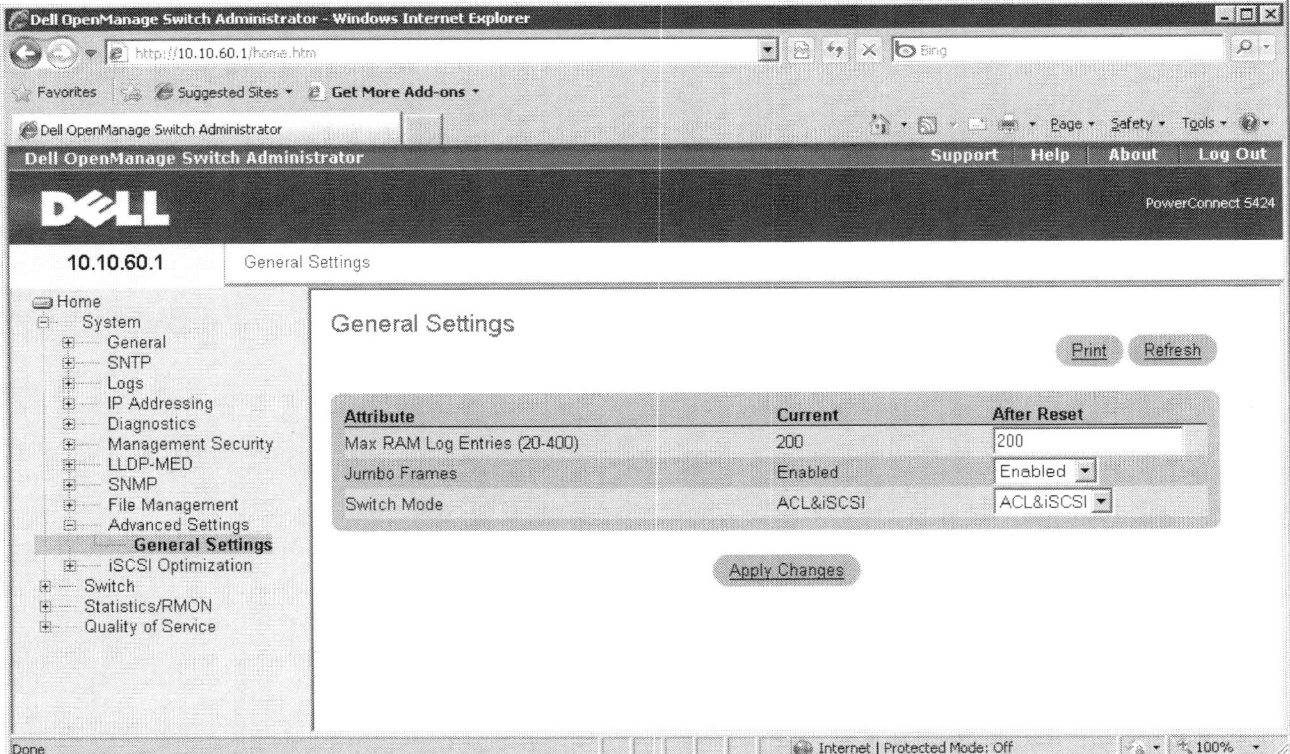


**Figure 3.4**

c. Once the switch has rebooted we want to login into the **Dell OpenManage Switch Administrator** web UI again, and verify that the Jumbo Frames are enabled.

d. Browse to **System\Advanced Settings\General Settings** in the left pane, and verify that the **Jumbo Frames** field is now set to **Enabled** in the right hand pane, as shown in **Figure 3.4**. You may have noticed that the Dell OpenManage Switch Administrator does have the option to configure Jumbo Frames, however this configuration change from within the web UI doesn't always work. For this reason we choose to enable the Jumbo Frames for our project from within the telnet console.

## Configuring the iSCSI Optimization Options

In this step, we want to manually disable one of the switch's iSCSI Optimization settings for better performance.

6. Browse to **System\iSCSI Optimization\Global Parameters\iSCSI Status** in the left pane, and select **Disable** option from the dropdown list, and then click the **Apply Changes** button in the bottom center of the screen.

## Configuring Individual iSCSI Ports

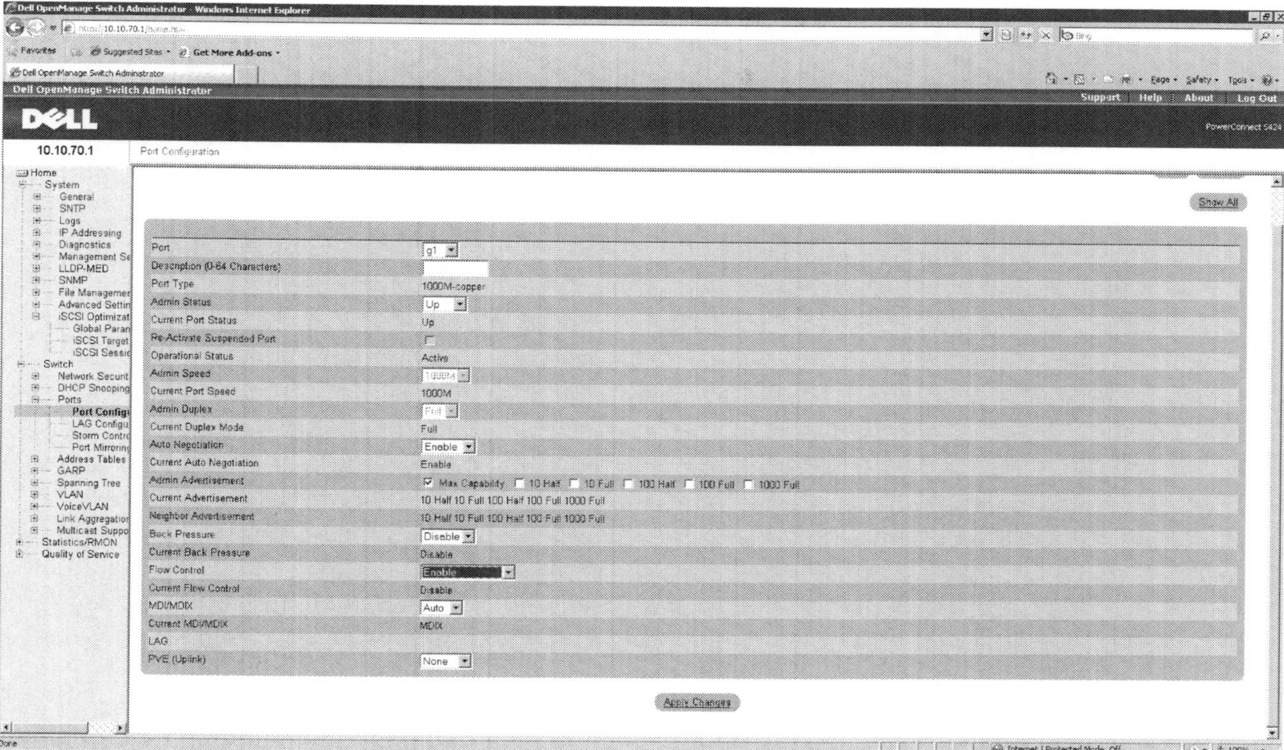

**Figure 3.5**

For each port connected to our iSCSI networks we want to enable the flow control option. The flow control option allows lower speed devices to communicate with our higher speed devices without them having a buffer overflow. The lower speed device requests that the higher speed device refrains from sending additional packets until it is caught up.

7. Browse to **Switch\Ports\Port Configuration**, and then select the first switch port being used for your iSCSI network from the **Port** dropdown field. For our project, we will select the **g1** port from the dropdown, as shown in **Figure 3.5**.

   a. For the **Flow Control** dropdown field, select the **Enable** option, and then click on the **Apply Changes** button in the bottom center of the screen.

   b. Repeat **Step 7** for each port that will be part of your iSCSI network.

8. Repeat the steps outlined in this chapter for your second iSCSI switch. For our project, we will repeat the setup process and assign our second iSCSI switch the IP address of **10.10.70.1** for our **VLAN70** network.

# Chapter 4: Configuring iSCSI Connections on the SAN

In this chapter, we will perform some initial setup tasks to manage our SAN. We will begin by making sure that all of our physical iSCSI network prerequisites are in place. Then we will proceed with installing the Dell Modular Disk Storage Manager (MDSM) software and making the initial connection to our project's Dell PowerVault MD3000i SAN. Once we have the MSDM software connected we will configure our management ports, enable jumbo frames, and configure our iSCSI ports to take advantage of Microsoft and Dell's latest Multi-Path Input/Output (MPIO) technologies. When we are finished with this chapter our iSCSI SAN connections will be in place and we will be ready to configure our server connections.

## Overview of the iSCSI Network Topology with Multi-path Input/Output (MPIO) Redundancy

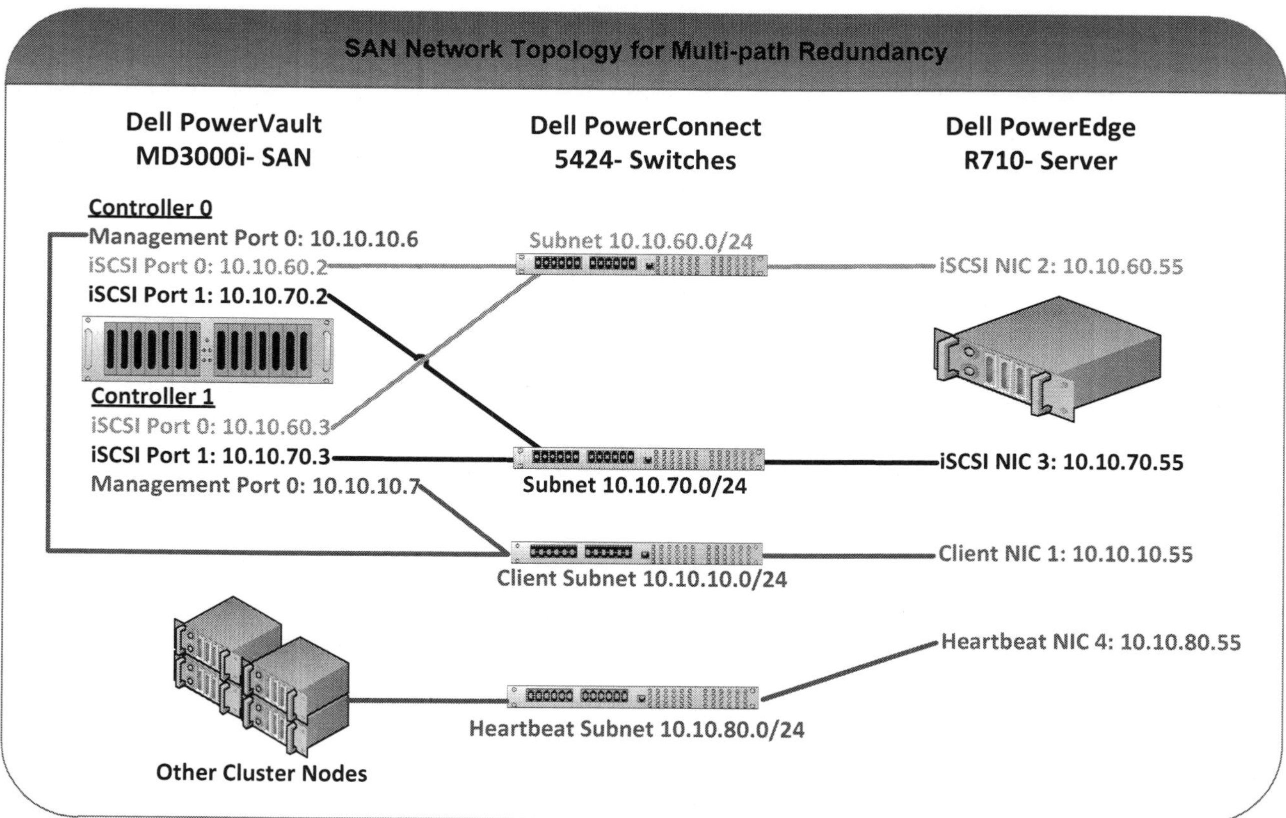


**Figure 4.1**

The diagram shown in **Figure 4.1** is an overview of how we want our SAN topology configured with our dual controller MD3000i SAN. We will utilize Dell and Microsoft's MPIO connections to give us full redundancy with the best overall performance. If you have a single iSCSI controller you can still take advantage of the redundancy and performance of using two switches, however you do have a potential single point of failure if the controller goes offline. The MD3000i's management ports will be connected to our Active Directory domain subnet, so that we can manage our SAN from our workstation. For our project, we will configure our iSCSI topology as outlined in the below bullet points.

- Each Dell PowerEdge R710 server will have two dedicated iSCSI network adapters communicating to our Dell PowerVault MD3000i through our redundant iSCSI switches.
- Our Dell PowerVault MD3000i has dual RAID controllers, each with two iSCSI network adapters and one management port.
- Each of our Dell PowerVault MD3000i's RAID controllers will have two dedicated iSCSI network adapters communicating to our servers through our redundant iSCSI switches.
- Each of the iSCSI network adapters for both the Dell PowerEdge R710 servers and the Dell PowerVault MD3000i SAN will be connected to their own dedicated subnet and iSCSI switch.
- Each of our Dell PowerVault MD3000i's RAID controllers will have their management network adapter connected to the client subnet where our Active Directory domain resides.

## iSCSI Storage Area Network (SAN) Topology Prerequisites

Before we continue on to the initial setup tasks of the SAN, we first need to make sure that the following prerequisites have been completed.

1. You should have the following tasks completed before continuing on to the next steps.
   a. All your devices that make up your iSCSI topology should be in place. Your switches, servers and SAN should all be physically connected, as shown **Figure 2.2** of **Chapter 2**.
   b. Each of your servers that will be connected to the SAN should have a static IP address and be connected to the client subnet where the Active Directory domain resides.
   c. Each of your physical servers should be a member of the Active Directory domain. The Windows Failover Cluster Manager requires that all clustered servers are part of the same Active Directory domain.

# Installing the Storage Area Network (SAN) Management Software

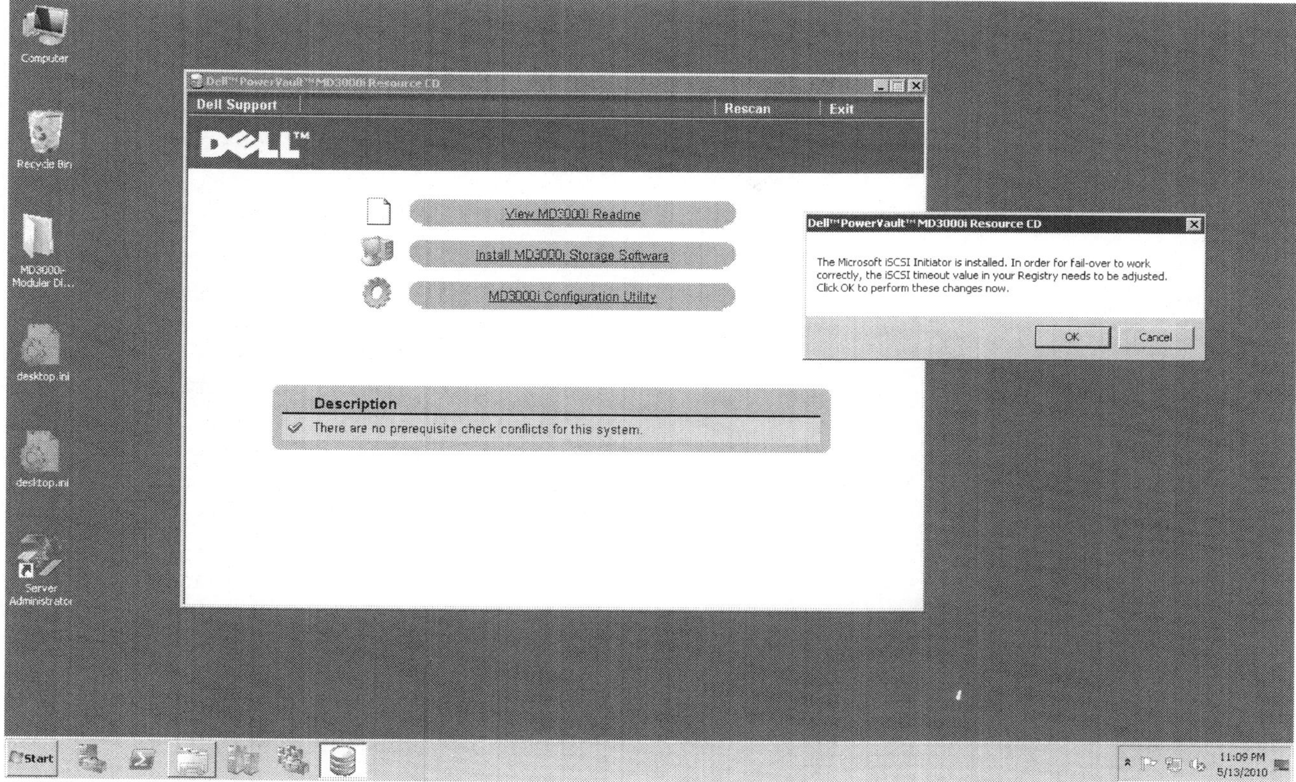


**Figure 4.2**

In this section, we will install the Dell Modular Disk Storage Manager (MDSM) management software for our project's Dell PowerVault MD3000i.

2. Download the **Dell PowerVault MD3000i Resource CD** software from Dell's website to one of the servers that will be part of the cluster.

    a. Launch the **Setup.exe** from the **Windows** folder of the installation media, and select the **Install MD3000i Storage Software** option, as shown in **Figure 4.2**. This will begin the installation of the **Dell Modular Disk Storage Manager (MDSM)** software that we will use to manage our MD3000i.

    b. Click on the **OK** button of the **Dell PowerVault MD3000i Resource CD** pop-up screen that states **The Microsoft iSCSI Initiator is installed**, as shown in **Figure 4.2**.

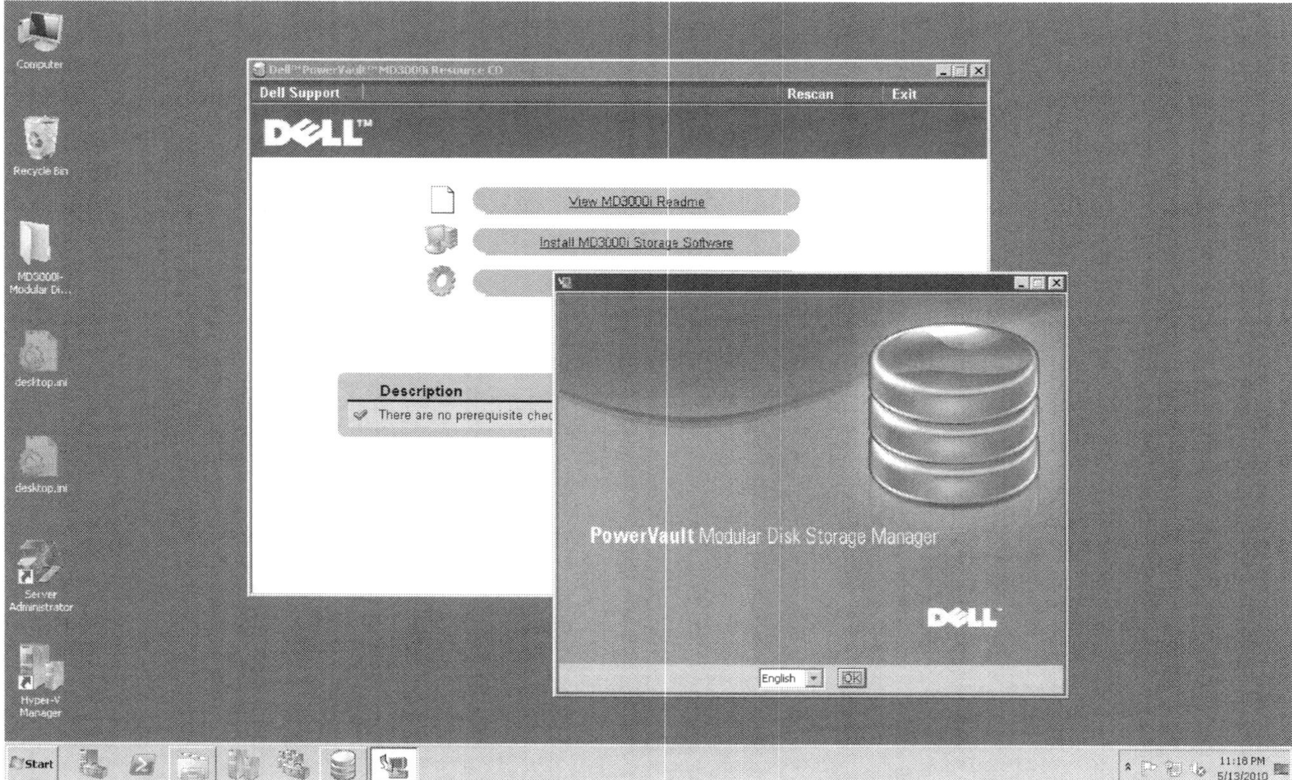


**Figure 4.3**

c. On the **PowerVault Modular Disk Storage Manager (MDSM)** screen, select your language, and then click on the **OK** button to continue.

d. Continue through the installation by clicking on the **Next** button for the **Introduction**, **License Agreement** and the **Choose Install Folder** screens.

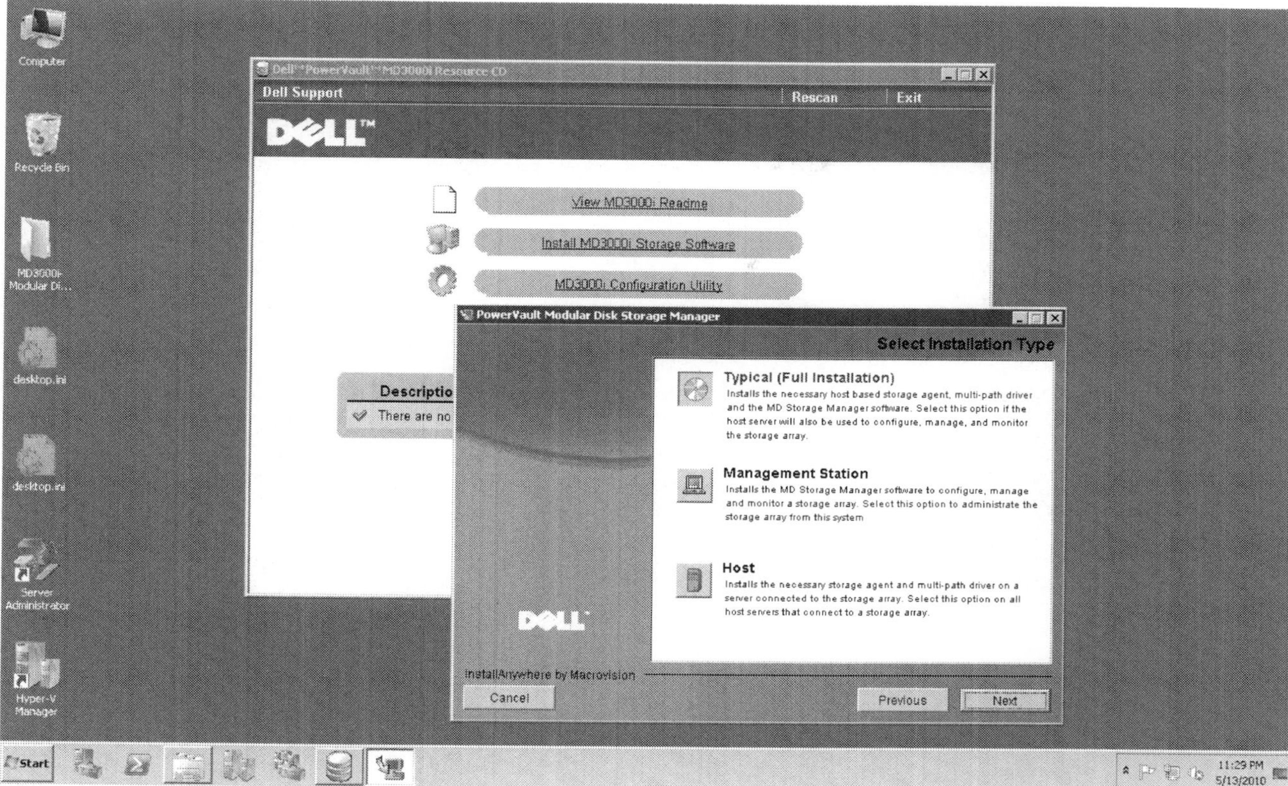


**Figure 4.4**

e. On the **Select Installation Type** screen, select the **Typical (Full Installation)** option, as shown in **Figure 4.4**. The Typical (Full Installation) option will install the following Dell components iSCSI Initiator, Multi-path Input/Output (MPIO) and the Dell Modular Disk Storage Manager (MDSM) software.

f. On the **Automatically Start Monitor** screen, select **Automatically Start Monitor (Recommended)** option, and then click on the **Next** button to continue.

g. On the **Pre-Installation Summary** screen, click on the **Install** button to continue.

h. On the **Install Complete** screen, select the **Yes, restart my system** option, and then click on the **Done** button to complete the installation.

# Connecting the Modular Disk Storage Manager (MDSM) to the SAN

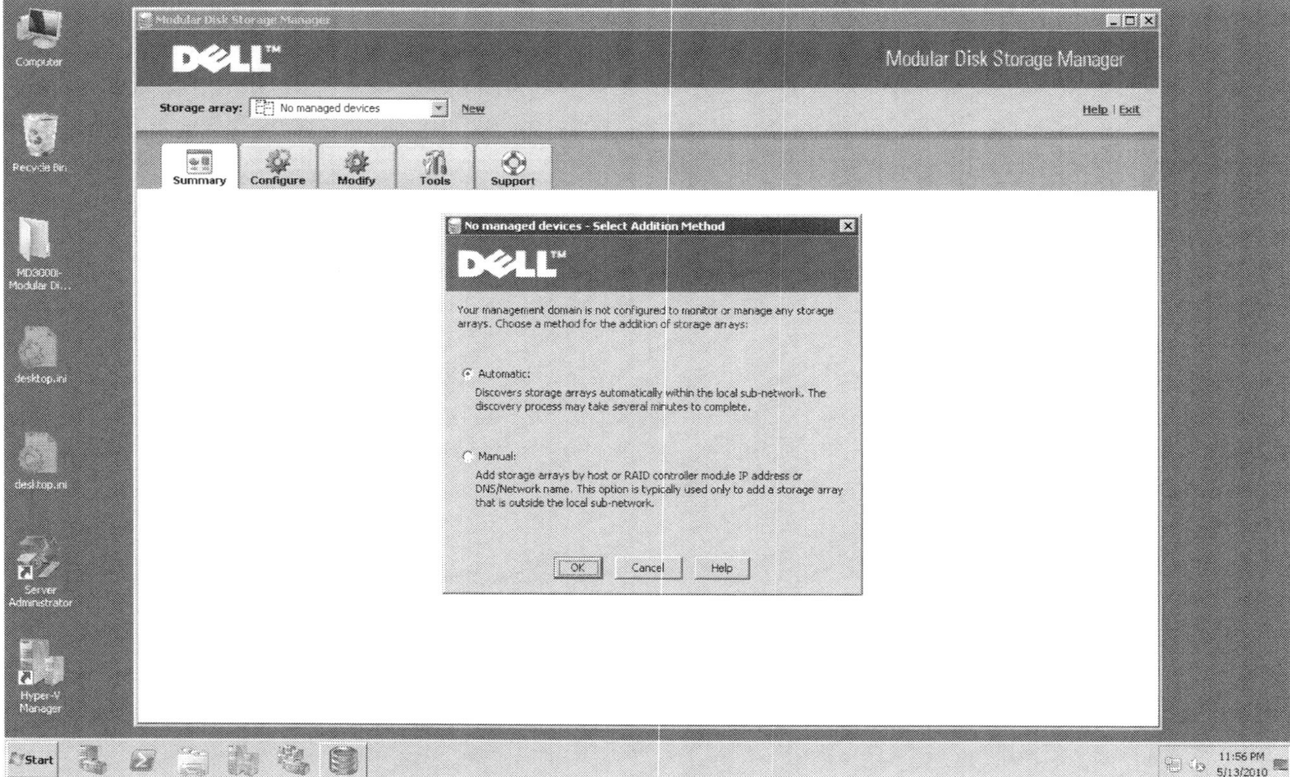


**Figure 4.5**

3. Once the server's reboot has completed, we want to launch the **Modular Disk Storage Manager Client** program from the **Start\All Programs\Dell\MD Storage Manager**.

    a. On the **No managed devices – Select Addition Method** screen, select the **Automatic** option, and then click on the **OK** button to continue. Your SAN's management ports and the computer that you are running the MDSM software from should both be connected to the subnet. If the SAN and client subnet both use DHCP, then the MDSM software should be able to connect to your SAN automatically.

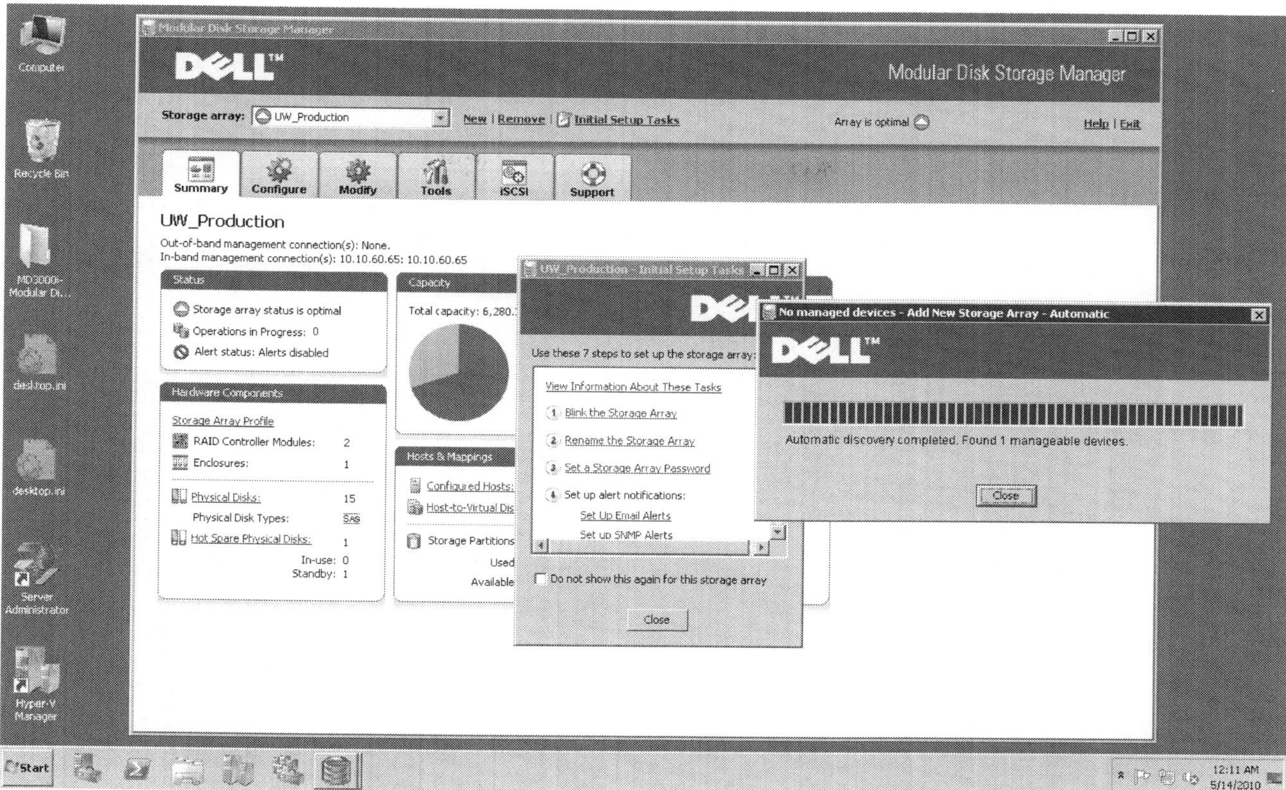


**Figure 4.6**

b. Once your SAN has been discovered, click on the **Close** button of the **No managed devices – Add New Storage Array** screen.

## Configuring the Initial Setup Tasks on the SAN

4. On the **Initial Setup Tasks** screen, complete **Steps 1-4**. In **Step 2** you have the option to rename the **Storage Array**. The **Storage Array** name is actually the name of your SAN, so you'll want to name it accordingly. For our project, we will give our SAN the name of **UW_Production**, however feel free to name your SAN accordingly.

# Configuring the Ethernet Management Ports

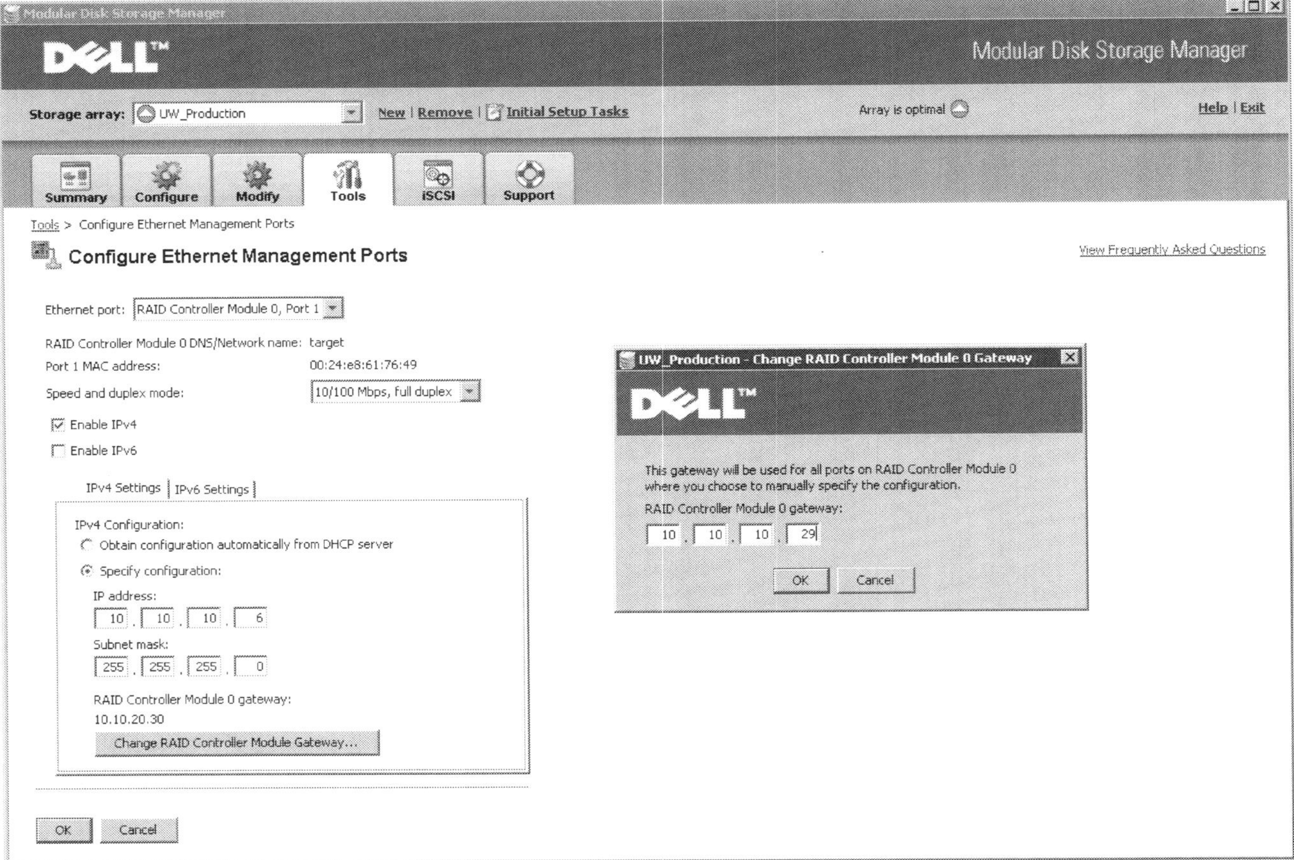


**Figure 4.7**

5. In the **MDSM** console, browse to the **Tools tab\Configure Ethernet Management Ports** option.

   a. On the **Configure Ethernet Management Ports** screen, select the **RAID Controller Module 0, Port1** option for the **Ethernet port** dropdown field, and then click the **IPv4 Settings** tab.

      i. In the **IPv4 Configuration** section, select the **Specify configuration** option, and then enter a static IP and subnet for your first management network adapter. If you prefer to leave your management network adapter set at its default of DHCP, then feel free to do so as these settings will not affect our other configurations. For our project, we will enter the IP address of **10.10.10.6** with the subnet of **255.255.255.0** for our first management port.

      ii. Click on the **Change RAID Controller Modular Gateway** button, and then enter your management network adapter's gateway IP address on the **Change RAID Controller Modular 0 Gateway** pop-up screen. Click on the **OK** button of the pop-up screen to save your changes.

   b. Repeat **Step A** to assign a static IP to your second management network adapter, by selecting the **RAID Controller Module 1, Port1** option from the **Ethernet port** dropdown field. If you have a single RAID controller SAN, then please disregard this step. For our project, we will enter the IP address of **10.10.10.7** with the subnet of **255.255.255.0** for our second management port.

c. Once complete, click on the **OK** button at the bottom of the **Configure Ethernet Management Ports** screen to save your changes.

**NOTE:** If you did decide to change the IP of the management ports you will most like have to reestablish your connection to your SAN with the Modular Disk Storage Manager (MDSM) software after the change.

## Configuring the iSCSI Host Ports

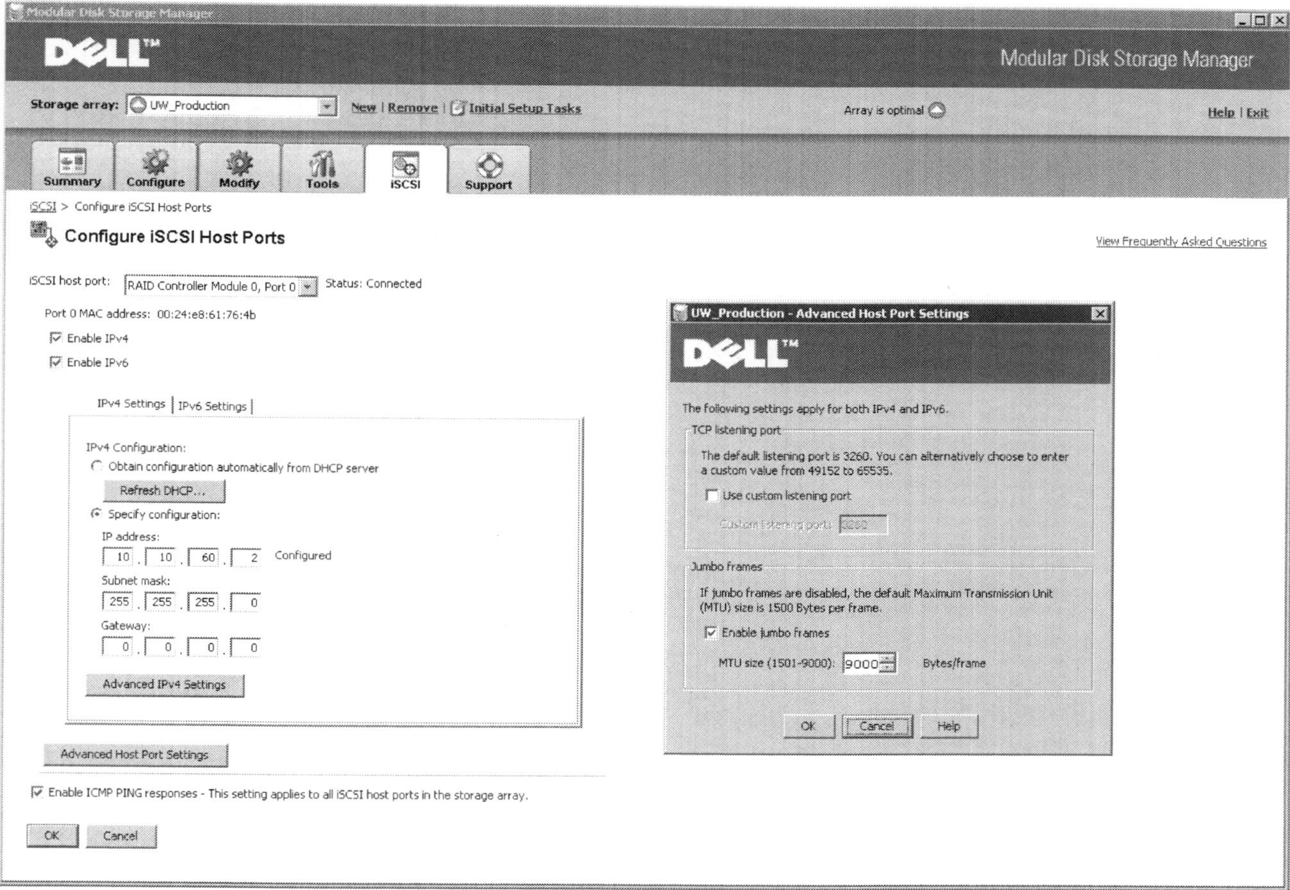


**Figure 4.8**

We are now ready to begin configuring our iSCSI network adapters on the SAN. We will configure them according to our iSCSI topology that we covered earlier in this chapter with the diagram in **Figure 4.1**. We will create two subnets, one for each of our iSCSI redundant switches. In our project, our first iSCSI subnet will be 10.10.60.0/24 and our second iSCSI subnet will be 10.10.70.0/24. We have a dual RAID controller SAN that has a total of four iSCSI host ports, with each controller having two of these iSCSI host ports. We will setup one of each controller's iSCSI host ports for each of our iSCSI subnets making our iSCSI topology fully redundant.

6. In the **MDSM** console, browse to the **iSCSI tab\Configure iSCSI Host Ports**, and then configure your iSCSI ports as follows:

   a. For the **iSCSI Host Port** dropdown field, select the **RAID Controller Module 0, Port 0** option.

i. For the **IPv4 Settings** tab, select the **Specify Configuration** option, and then enter your **IP address** and **Subnet mask** for your first RAID controller's port 0. For our project, we will assign the IP address of **10.10.60.2** with the subnet mask of **255.255.255.0**, as shown in **Figure 4.8**.

ii. Click on the **Advanced Host Port Settings** button, and then select the **Enable jumbo frames** checkbox.

1. For the **MTU size (1501-9000)** field, enter **9000**, and then click on the **OK** button to continue.

b. Return to the **iSCSI Host Port** dropdown field, and select the **RAID Controller Module 0, Port 1** option.

i. For the **IPv4 Settings** tab, select the **Specify Configuration** option, and then enter your **IP address** and **Subnet mask** for your first RAID controller's port 1. For our project, we will assign the IP address of **10.10.70.2** with the subnet mask of **255.255.255.0**.

ii. Click on the **Advanced Host Port Settings** button, and then select the **Enable jumbo frames** checkbox.

1. For the **MTU size (1501-9000)** field, enter **9000**, and then click on the **OK** button to continue.

c. Return to the **iSCSI Host Port** dropdown field, and select the **RAID Controller Module 1, Port 0** option. If you have a single RAID controller SAN, then please disregard the next few of steps and skip to Step G.

i. For the **IPv4 Settings** tab, select the **Specify Configuration** option, and then enter your **IP address** and **Subnet mask** for your second RAID controller's port 0. For our project, we will assign the IP address of **10.10.60.3** with the subnet mask of **255.255.255.0**.

ii. Click on the **Advanced Host Port Settings** button, and then select the **Enable jumbo frames** checkbox.

1. For the **MTU size (1501-9000)** field, enter **9000**, and then click on the **OK** button to continue.

d. Return to the **iSCSI Host Port** dropdown field, and select the **RAID Controller Module 1, Port 1** option.

i. For the **IPv4 Settings** tab, select the **Specify Configuration** option, and then enter your **IP address** and **Subnet mask** for your second RAID controller's port 1. For our project, we will assign the IP address of **10.10.70.3** with the subnet mask of **255.255.255.0**.

ii. Click on the **Advanced Host Port Settings** button, and then select the **Enable jumbo frames** checkbox.

1. For the **MTU size (1501-9000)** field, enter **9000**, and then click on the **OK** button to continue.

e. When finished configuring each of your iSCSI port, click on the **OK** button in the bottom left hand corner to save your changes.

# Chapter 5: Configuring iSCSI Connections on the Servers

In this chapter, you will learn that a significant portion of your iSCSI network configuration involves your servers' network adapters. We will start out with some performance tuning of our iSCSI connections by setting up Jumbo Frames on our network adapters. We'll then cover setting up our logical network configurations such as IP addresses, bindings and metrics. After our basic network topology in place, we'll finish off our configuration by setting up Multi-path Input/Output (MPIO) connections to our SAN from within the Microsoft iSCSI Initiator on each server. Once you've completed this chapter, you'll have your iSCSI network fully in place.

## Creating a Naming Convention for the Network Adapters

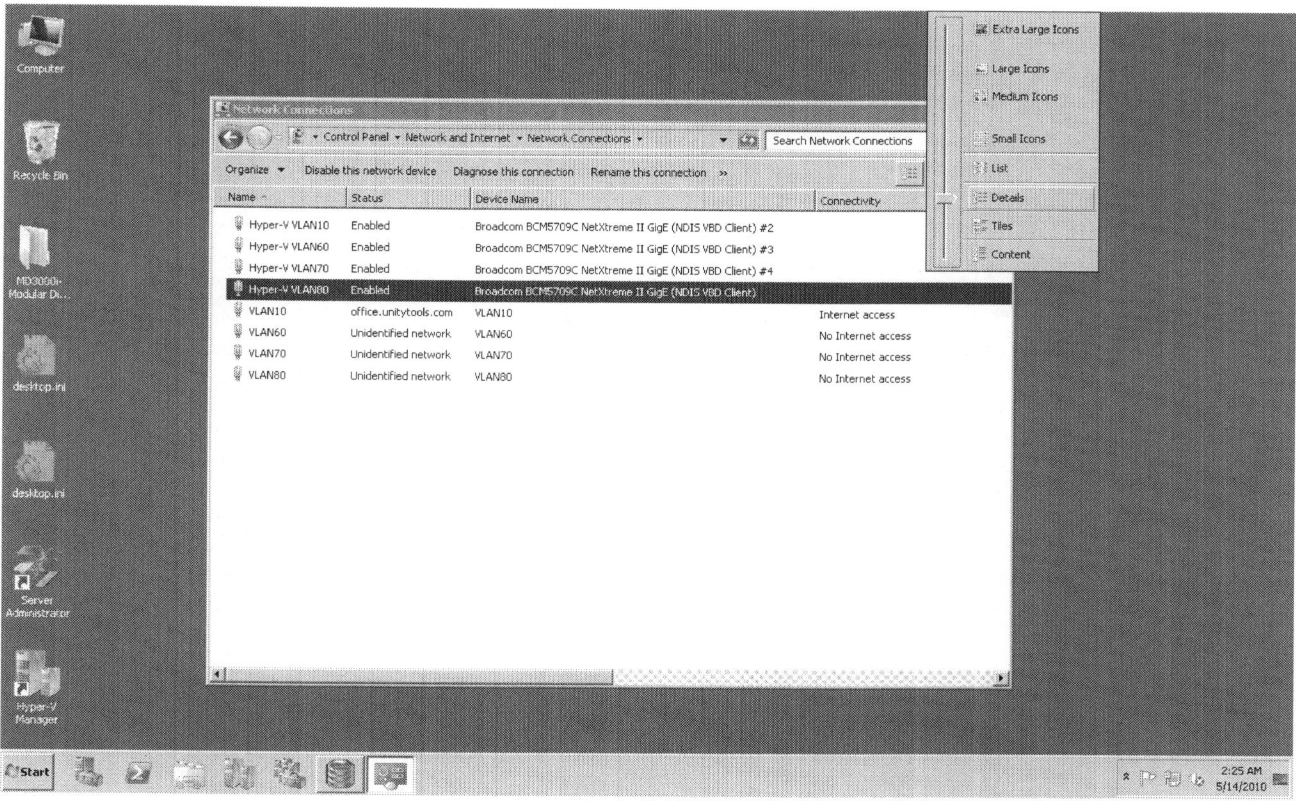


**Figure 5.1**

At this point, you should have your physical topology in place with all your servers, switches and SAN components connected to each other. **Figure 5.1** shows what our network adapters and Hyper-V virtual network adapters will look like from within the Windows Network Connections screen once we've completed the steps in this section. In **Figure 5.1**, you'll notice that we have renamed each of our network adapters to a naming convention. You will want to do the same on each of your servers by following the steps in this section. Our naming convention will become increasingly important as we start creating Hyper-V virtual networks for our failover clusters. If each of our cluster nodes does not have the same network adapter and virtual network names setup, then our clustered resources will not be able to failover successfully between nodes. We will begin by renaming our network adapters followed by configuring our iSCSI network adapters Jumbo Frames. Perform the following steps on each of your physical servers that will be part of the cluster.

1. Click on the **Start** button, and then right click **Network**, and then select the **Properties** option.

    a. Select the **Change adapter settings** option from the upper left hand corner of the **Network and Sharing Center** screen. If you are configuring a Windows Server 2008 vs. an R2 server, then you would select Manage network connections option instead of change adapter settings option.

    b. Change your view to a **Details** view by clicking on the icon with three horizontal lines on the toolbar, as shown in **Figure 5.1**.

    c. Right click on each network adapter and rename it to your naming convention. In our project, we will rename our first iSCSI network adapter for our **10.10.60.0/24** network to **VLAN60**, and then rename our second iSCSI network adapter for the **10.10.70.0./24** network to **VLAN70** and so on for our remaining network adapters.

    d. We want to make note of each iSCSI network adapters' **Device Name**. We will use this information to identify which network adapters we want to set an MTU of 9000 on. Windows Server 2008/R2 is notorious for not numbering these device names the same as the network adapter's physical port number. For example, my **VLAN10** is connected to the first physical network adapter port on the back of the server, however in **Figure 5.1** you can see that the **Device Name** field is named **Broadcom BCM5709C NetXtreme II GigE (NDIC VBD Client) #2**. This can cause confusion, as the physical port is number one; however Windows has given the network adapter a device name with the #2 in it.

# Configuring the iSCSI Network Adapters- Enabling Jumbo Frames

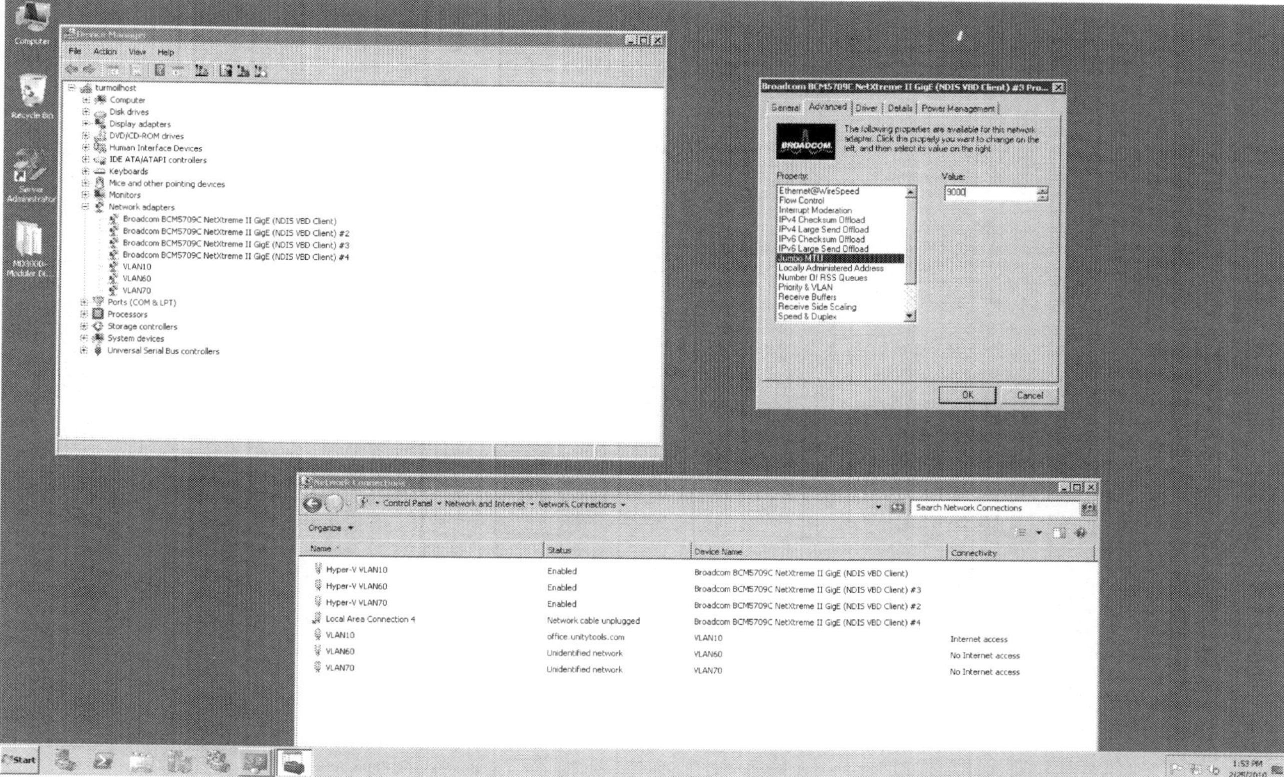


**Figure 5.2**

2. Next we want to enable jumbo frames by setting the Maximum Transfer Unit (MTU) of our iSCSI network adapters to a value of 9000. Click on the **Start** button, and then right click **Computer**, and select the **Properties** option.

   a. Click on the **Device Manager** option in the upper left hand corner, and then expand the **Network adapters** node, as shown in **Figure 5.2**.

   b. Right click on your **first iSCSI network adapter**, and select the **Properties** option. In our project, we will first configure our iSCSI network adapter that is connected to the **10.10.60.0/24** network with the device name of **Broadcom BCM5709C NetXtreme II GigE (NDIC VBD Client) #3**, as shown in the lower window of **Figure 5.2**.

      i. Select the **Advanced** tab, and then highlight the **Jumbo MTU** option in the **Property** field.

         1. Set the **Value** field to **9000** and click the **OK** bottom to exit.

   c. Repeat **Steps a-b** for your server's **second iSCSI network adapter**.

# Configuring the iSCSI Network Adapters- Installing the Broadcom Advanced Control Suite 3 (BACS)

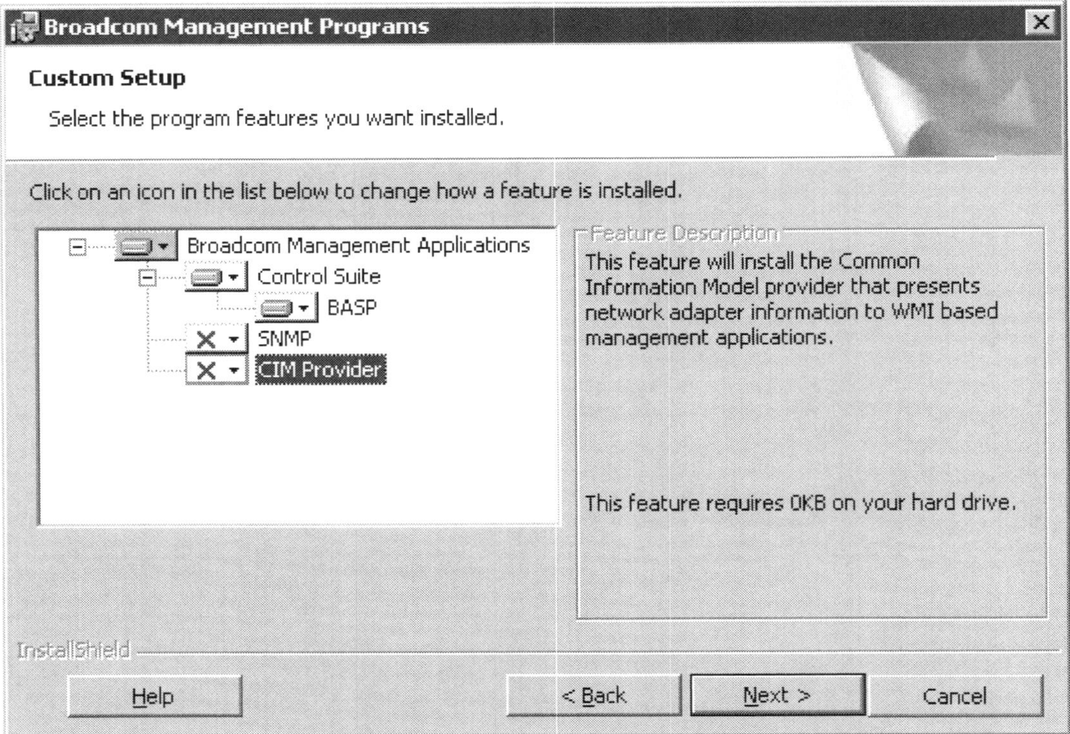


**Figure 5.3**

If your servers have onboard Broadcom BCM5709C NetXtreme II GigE network adapters such as our project's Dell PowerEdge R710's, then you'll need to install the Broadcom Advanced Control Suite 3 for the jumbo frames to work correctly. Even though we have configured our network adapter's properties to use an MTU of 9000 from within the Windows Network Connections screen, our packets will still fragment unless we have Broadcom's management suite installed and configured as well. If your server doesn't use Broadcom network adapters, then please disregard this step and skip to **Step 4**.

3. Download the **Broadcom Advanced Control Suite 3 (BACS)** software named **Broadcom Management Application Installer (x64)** from Broadcom's website at www.broadcom.com.

   a. Unzip and install the **Broadcom Advanced Control Suite 3 (BACS)** software by running the **Setup.exe** from the **Server\MgmtApps\x64** directory of the installation media. If you have any existing Broadcom management software, then your server may require a reboot to complete the installation.

   b. After the install, open the Windows **Control Panel**, and then click on the **Broadcom Advanced Control Suite 3** icon to start the control suite.

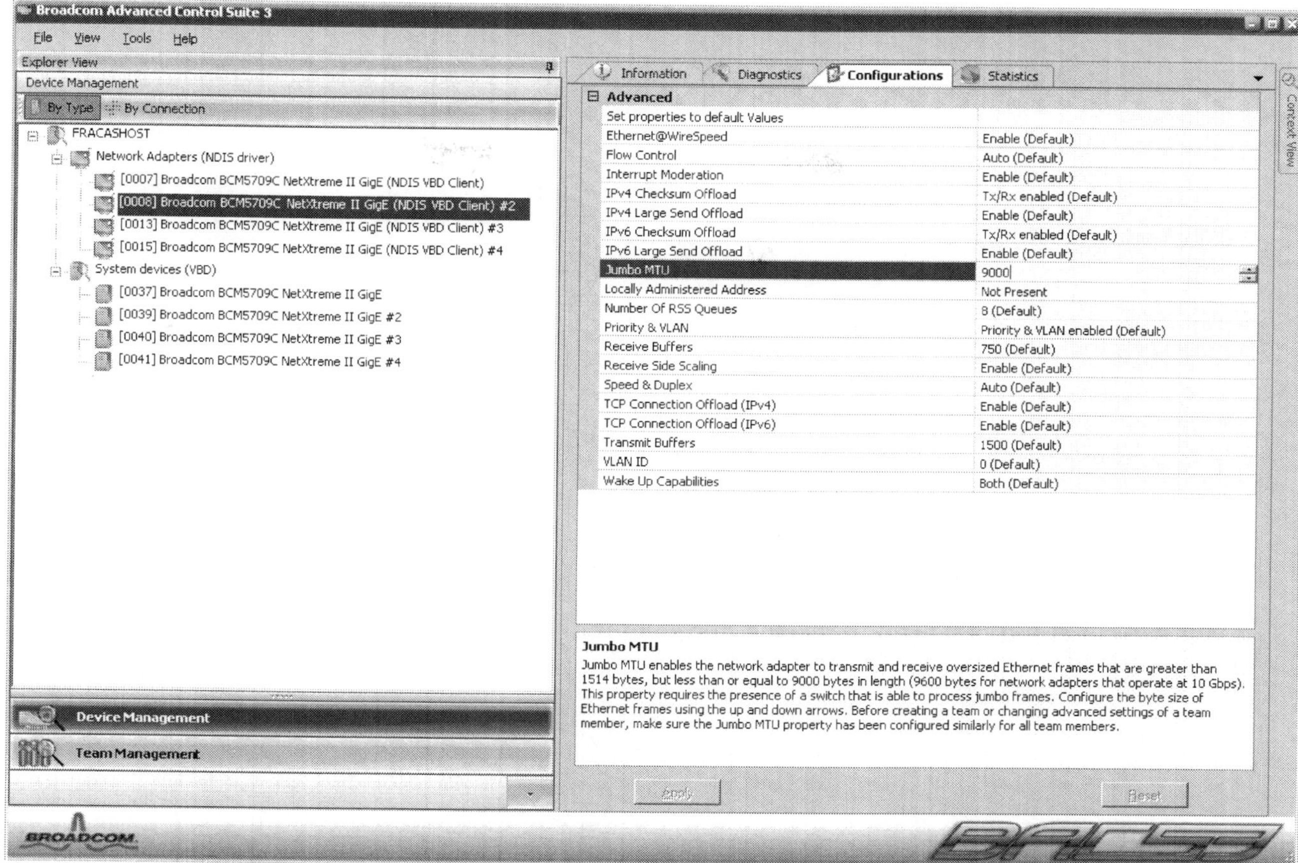


**Figure 5.4**

c. Once the **Broadcom Advanced Control Suite 3** console opens, highlight your iSCSI network adapter in the left pane under the **Network Adapters** node, and then click on the **Configuration** tab in the right pane. If you don't see the **Configuration** tab in the right pane, then click on the **View\Navigate\Device Management\Configurations** from the toolbar at the top of the window for it to appear.

   i. Verify that each of your iSCSI network adapters have their **Jumbo MTU** field value set to **9000**, as shown in **Figure 5.4**. If the iSCSI network adapter isn't already set to a 9000 MTU, verify it's the correct network adapter, and then set its Jumbo MTU field to 9000.

   ii. Once you verify the MTU settings for each of your iSCSI network adapters, you can close the **Broadcom Advanced Control Suite 3** console.

## Configuring the iSCSI Network Adapters- Setting the Sub-interface to use Jumbo Frames

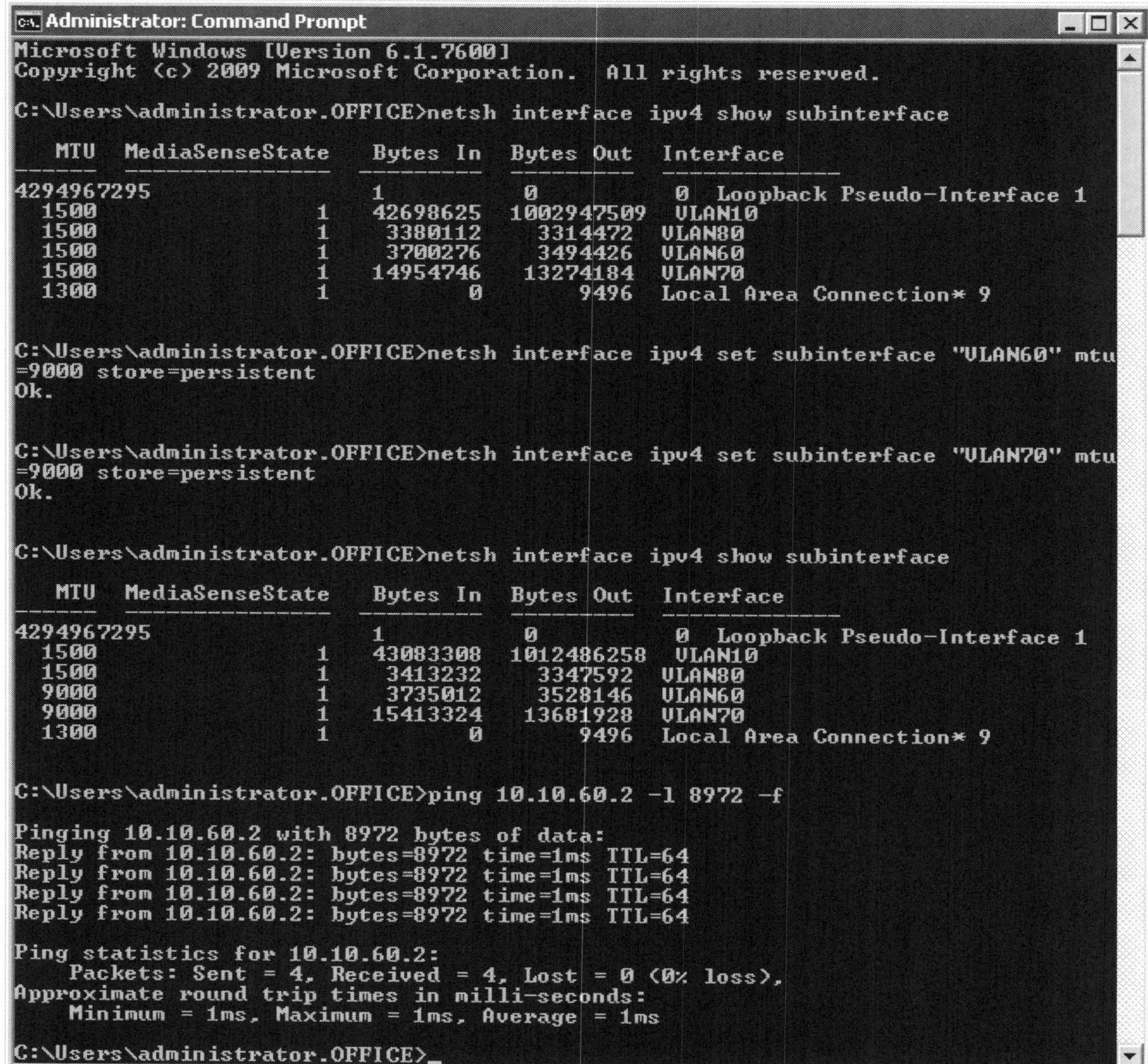

Administrator: Command Prompt
Microsoft Windows [Version 6.1.7600]
Copyright (c) 2009 Microsoft Corporation. All rights reserved.
C:\Users\administrator.OFFICE>netsh interface ipv4 show subinterface
MTU MediaSenseState Bytes In Bytes Out Interface
4294967295 1 0 0 Loopback Pseudo-Interface 1
1500 1 42698625 1002947509 VLAN10
1500 1 3380112 3314472 VLAN80
1500 1 3700276 3494426 VLAN60
1500 1 14954746 13274184 VLAN70
1300 1 0 9496 Local Area Connection* 9
C:\Users\administrator.OFFICE>netsh interface ipv4 set subinterface "VLAN60" mtu=9000 store=persistent
Ok.
C:\Users\administrator.OFFICE>netsh interface ipv4 set subinterface "VLAN70" mtu=9000 store=persistent
Ok.
C:\Users\administrator.OFFICE>netsh interface ipv4 show subinterface
MTU MediaSenseState Bytes In Bytes Out Interface
4294967295 1 0 0 Loopback Pseudo-Interface 1
1500 1 43083308 1012486258 VLAN10
1500 1 3413232 3347592 VLAN80
9000 1 3735012 3528146 VLAN60
9000 1 15413324 13681928 VLAN70
1300 1 0 9496 Local Area Connection* 9
C:\Users\administrator.OFFICE>ping 10.10.60.2 -l 8972 -f
Pinging 10.10.60.2 with 8972 bytes of data:
Reply from 10.10.60.2: bytes=8972 time=1ms TTL=64
Reply from 10.10.60.2: bytes=8972 time=1ms TTL=64
Reply from 10.10.60.2: bytes=8972 time=1ms TTL=64
Reply from 10.10.60.2: bytes=8972 time=1ms TTL=64
Ping statistics for 10.10.60.2:
Packets: Sent = 4, Received = 4, Lost = 0 (0% loss),
Approximate round trip times in milli-seconds:
Minimum = 1ms, Maximum = 1ms, Average = 1ms
C:\Users\administrator.OFFICE>


**Figure 5.5**

The last thing we need to enable on our host servers before the jumbo frames will work is the sub-interface settings of the network adapter.

4. Open the **Command Prompt** with the **Run As Administrator** permissions.

a. To view the current sub-interface MTU settings, type in the **netsh interface ipv4 show subinterface** command, and then hit the **Enter** key, as shown in the first command of **Figure 5.5**. This will list your network adapters and their current MTU settings. Even though we configured our network adapters for a 9000 MTU from within the Windows Network Connections screen, they still show as set to a 1500 MTU. This means that if we tried to ping the SAN with a frame size larger than 1472 that it would become fragmented.

b. To set the sub-interface MTU to 9000 for your server's iSCSI network adapters, type in the **netsh interface ipv4 set subinterface "<Your_iSCSI_Interface_Name>" mtu=9000 store=persistent** command, and then hit the **Enter** key. Replace the **<Your_iSCSI_Interface_Name>** with your first iSCSI network adapter's name and then run the command. You will want to repeat this command for your second iSCSI network adapter as well. For our project, we will run a **netsh interface ipv4 set subinterface "VLAN60" mtu=9000 store=persistent** command for our first iSCSI network adapter, we will then change the interface name, and run the command again for our second iSCSI network adapter, as shown in the second and third commands of **Figure 5.5**.

c. Run the command in **Step a** again, to confirm that your iSCSI network adapters now show their MTU set to 9000, as shown in the fourth command of **Figure 5.5**.

d. To test out the new MTU settings, type in the **ping <Your_SAN's_iSCSI_NIC_IP> -l 8972 –f** command, and then hit the **Enter** key. Replace the **<Your_SAN's_iSCSI_NIC_IP>** with your SAN's first iSCSI network adapter's IP address and then run the command. You will want to repeat this test for all your SAN's iSCSI network adapters to verify jumbo frames are working on each of your SAN's network adapters. It may take a minute or two for the new MTU settings to take affect and allow frames larger than 1472. The –f parameter of the command sets the frame size to 8972, which is the max for a jumbo frame when set to an MTU of 9000. For our project, we will run a **ping 10.10.60.2 -l 8972 –f** command to ping our SAN's first iSCSI network adapter. We will then repeat the command to test our SAN's other three network adapters with the IP addresses of **10.10.60.3**, **10.10.70.2** and **10.10.70.3**.

# Configuring the IP Properties- First iSCSI Network Adapter

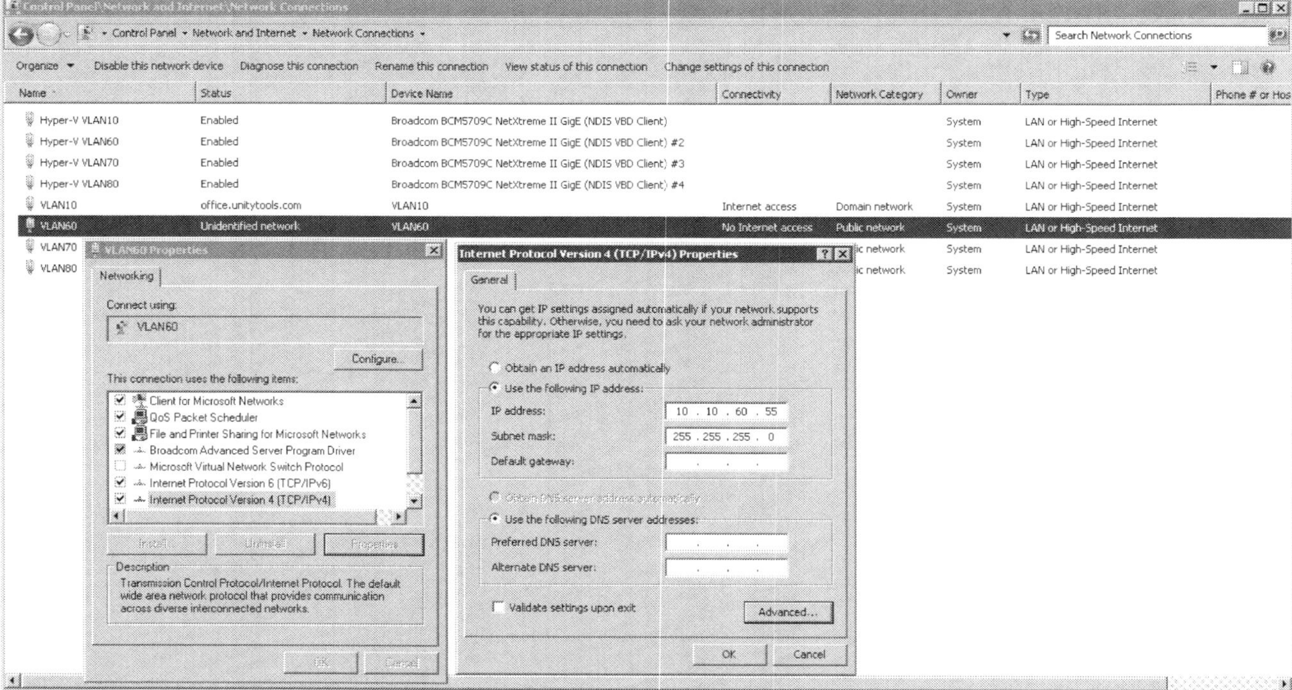


**Figure 5.6**

5. We are now ready to configure the TCP/IPv4 and DNS properties of our iSCSI network adapters. We want to return to the Windows **Network Connections** screen and perform the following steps.

   a. Right click on your **first iSCSI network adapter**, and then select the **Properties** option.

      i. Highlight **Internet Protocol Version 4 (TCP/IPv4)** from the **This connection uses the following items** field, and then click on the **Properties** button.

         1. Select the **Use the following IP address** option, and then enter a static IP address for your server's **first iSCSI network adapter**. For our project, we will assign our first iSCSI network adapter an IP address of **10.10.60.55**, as shown in **Figure 5.6**.

         2. For the **Subnet mask** field, fill in the range that you want to use for your **first iSCSI subnet**. For our project, we will be using a subnet mask of the **255.255.255.0**.

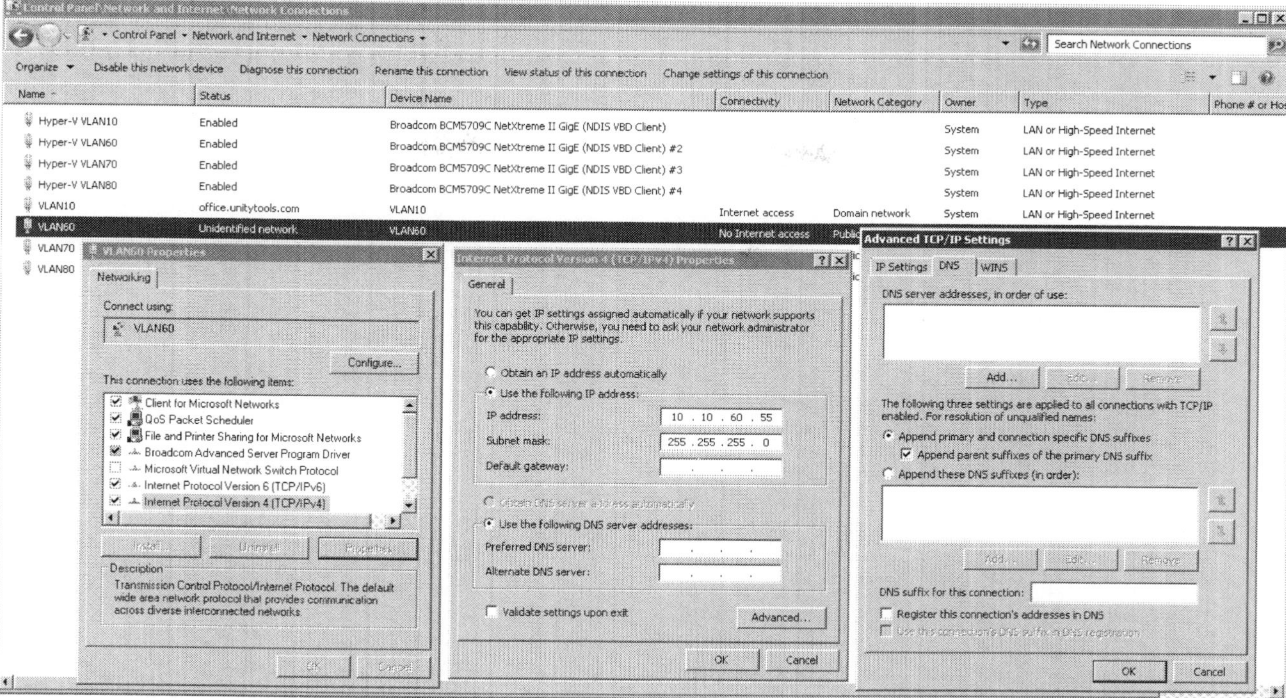

**Figure 5.7**

3. Click on the **Advanced** button, and then select the **DNS** tab on the **Advanced TCP/IP Settings** screen.

4. Unselect the **Register this connection's addresses in DNS** checkbox, and then click on the **OK** button.

ii. Click on the **OK** button two more times to save your changes and to exit the **Properties** screens of this network adapter.

## Configuring the IP Properties- Second iSCSI Network Adapter

6. Next we will repeat these steps for our second iSCSI network adapter. Right click on the **second iSCSI network adapter** and then select **Properties** option.

   a. Highlight **Internet Protocol Version 4 (TCP/IPv4)** from the **This connection uses the following items** field, and then click on the **Properties** button.

      i. Select the **Use the following IP address** option, and then enter a static IP address for your server's **second iSCSI network adapter**. For our project, we will assign our second iSCSI network adapter an IP address of **10.10.70.55**.

      ii. For the **Subnet mask** field, fill in the range that you want to use for your **second iSCSI subnet**. For our project, we will be using a subnet mask of the **255.255.255.0**.

      iii. Click on the **Advanced** button, and then select the **DNS** tab on the **Advanced TCP/IP Settings** screen.

1. Unselect the **Register this connection's addresses in DNS** checkbox, and then click on the **OK** button.

iv. Click on the **OK** button two more times to save your changes and to exit the **Properties** screens of this network adapter.

## Configuring the IP Properties- Heartbeat Network Adapter

For your heartbeat network you could choose to setup it up on one of your client switches, iSCSI switches, or on its own dedicated switch. The important thing is to create a separate subnet for it. You could also choose to create your cluster without this fourth subnet for the heartbeat network; however it's a best practice use a dedicated network when possible. For our project, we will use a separate dedicated switch for our heartbeat network.

7. Right click on the **Heartbeat network adapter**, and then select the **Properties** option.

a. Highlight **Internet Protocol Version 4 (TCP/IPv4)** from the **This connection uses the following items** field, and then click on the **Properties** button.

i. Select the **Use the following IP address** option, and then enter a static IP address for your server's **Heartbeat network adapter**. For our project, we will assign our Heartbeat network adapter an IP address of **10.10.80.55**.

ii. For the **Subnet mask** field, fill in the range that you want to use for your **Heartbeat subnet**. For our project, we will be using a subnet mask of the **255.255.255.0**.

iii. Click on the **Advanced** button and then select the **DNS** tab on the **Advanced TCP/IP Settings** screen.

1. Unselect the **Register this connection's addresses in DNS** checkbox, and then click on the **OK** button.

iv. Click on the **OK** button two more times to save your changes and to exit the **Properties** screens of this network adapter.

## Review of the First Server's Network Connections

| Network Connection | Network Adapter Name | Subnet | IP Address | Subnet Mask | Gateway | DNS | Register in DNS |
|---|---|---|---|---|---|---|---|
| Client | VLAN10 | 10.10.10.0/24 | 10.10.10.55 | 255.255.255.0 | Yes | Yes | Yes |
| First iSCSI | VLAN60 | 10.10.60.0/24 | 10.10.60.55 | 255.255.255.0 | No | No | No |
| Second iSCSI | VLAN70 | 10.10.70.0/24 | 10.10.70.55 | 255.255.255.0 | No | No | No |
| Heartbeat | VLAN80 | 10.10.80.0/24 | 10.10.80.55 | 255.255.255.0 | No | No | No |

**Figure 5.8**

The chart in **Figure 5.8** is a review of the network connections that we have just completed setting up for our first server's configuration. When creating our connections we employed a numbering and naming convention. This will help us eliminate confusion as we add additional host servers and begin configuring our iSCSI Initiators.

## Configuring the Initial Server's iSCSI Initiator

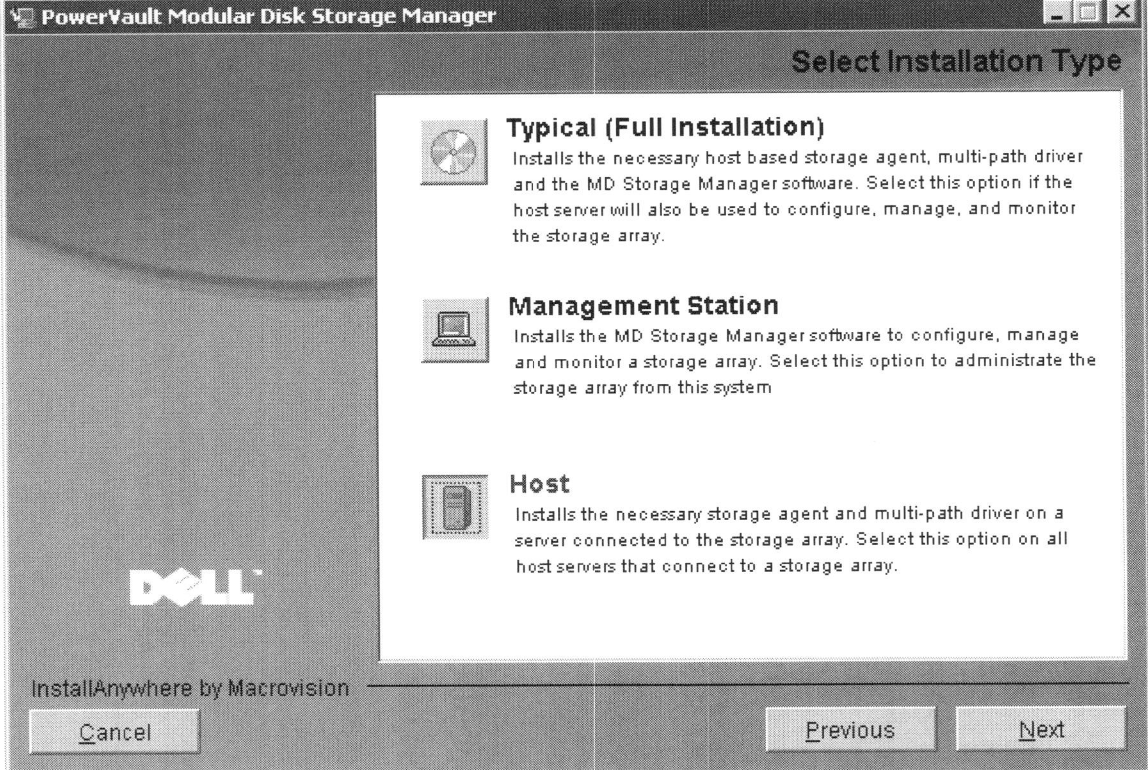


**Figure 5.9**

## Configuring the iSCSI Initiator- Dell Modular Disk Storage Manager (MDSM) Install

For each server that will be connected to our MD3000i SAN we will want to install either the Typical (Full Installation) or the Host installation of the Dell Modular Disk Storage Manager (MDSM) software. On our first server of the project we have already installed the Typical (Full Installation) which allows us to manage our MD3000i's configuration as well as connect to its virtual disks. On any of the subsequent servers you can choose the Host install option, which only installs the minimum components required to connect to the SAN.

**NOTE:** The minimum of the Host option of the Dell Modular Disk Storage Manager (MDSM) software has to be installed on all servers that will connect to the SAN. This includes Hyper-V virtual machines (VM) that will have their Microsoft iSCSI Initiator configured for direct access to any of the shared virtual disks on the SAN. If you do not perform this install you'll experience intermittent and odd connection issues, such as the virtual disks not showing up correctly in Windows Disk Manager and so on.

8. If you haven't already ran the **Dell Modular Disk Storage Manager (MDSM)** software installation on this server, then do so by launching the **Setup.exe** located in the **Windows** folder of the **Dell PowerVault MD 3000i Resource CD** files.

a. On the **Select Installation Type** screen, select the **Host** install option, and then click on the **Next** button, as shown in **Figure 5.9**

b. Continue on through the installation screens and complete the MDSM install.

## Configuring Microsoft iSCSI Initiator- Discovery Portals

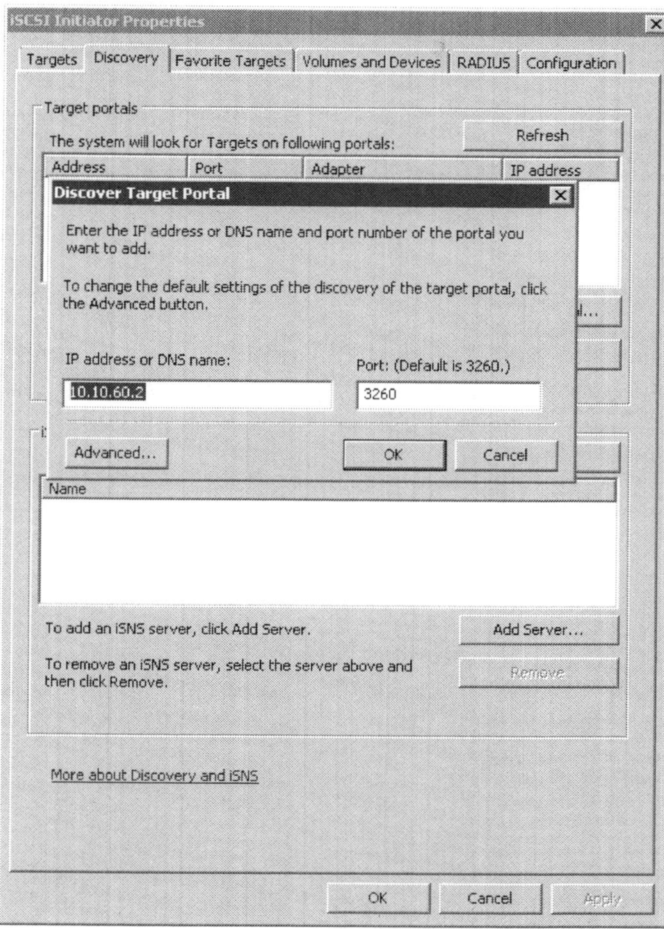


**Figure 5.10**

Once the MDSM installation has completed, we will begin creating our connections to the SAN with our Microsoft iSCSI Initiator. The iSCSI Initiator manages the connections to our SAN and plays a key role in creating our redundant iSCSI network topology.

9. On the first server to be connected to the SAN, browse to the **Start button\Administrative Tools**, and then select the **iSCSI Initiator** option.

   a. Click on the **Yes** button of the **Microsoft iSCSI** pop-up window that asks **Do you want to start the service and have it run automatically each time you start your computer**.

b. Select the **Discovery** tab, and then click on the **Discovery Portal** button. The interface of the iSCSI Initiator is slightly different between Windows Server 2008 and a Windows Server 2008 R2 server. For **Windows Server 2008** you will have an **Add Portal** button vs. a **Discovery Portal** button as with **Windows Server 2008 R2**.

    i. On the **Discover Target Portal** screen, enter your SAN's **first iSCSI Host Port IP address** in the **IP address or DNS name** field. This is the IP address of your SAN's **RAID Controller Module 0, Port 0**. For our project, we will enter the IP address of **10.10.60.2**, as shown in **Figure 5.10**.

    ii. For the **Port** field, we will leave the default of **3260**, and then click on the **OK** to continue.

c. Click on the **Discovery Portal/Add Portal** button again, and then enter your SAN's **second iSCSI Host Port IP address** in the **IP address or DNS name** field. This is the IP address of your SAN's **RAID Controller Module 0, Port 1**. For our project, we will enter the IP address of **10.10.70.2**.

    i. For the **Port** field, we will leave the default of **3260**, and then click on the **OK** to continue.

    **NOTE:** If you have a SAN with a single RAID controller vs. a dual RAID controller, then you will only need to setup these first two host port IP addresses as discovery portals in the iSCSI Initiator.

d. Click on the **Discovery Portal/Add Portal** button again, and then enter your SAN's **third iSCSI Host Port IP address** in the **IP address or DNS name** field. This is the IP address of your SAN's **RAID Controller Module 1, Port 0**. For our project, we will enter the IP address of **10.10.60.3**.

    i. For the **Port** field, we will leave the default of **3260**, and then click on the **OK** to continue.

e. Click on the **Discovery Portal/Add Portal** button again, and then enter your SAN's **fourth iSCSI Host Port IP address** in the **IP address or DNS name** field. This is the IP address of your SAN's **RAID Controller Module 1, Port 1**. For our project, we will enter the IP address of **10.10.70.3**.

    i. For the **Port** field, we will leave the default of **3260**, and then click on the **OK** to continue.

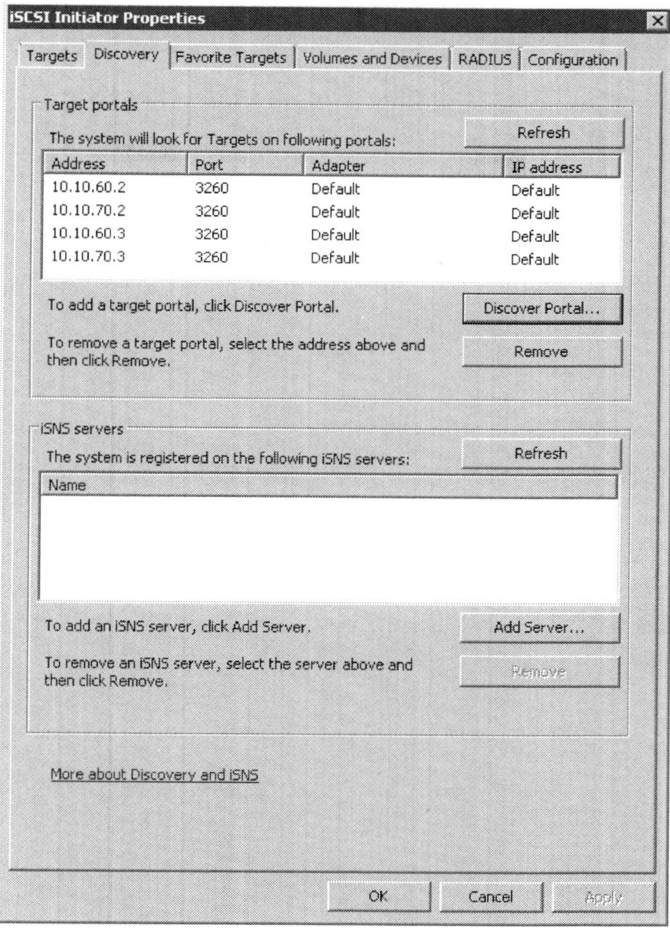


**Figure 5.11**

f. Once done adding your Discovery Portals, the **Target Portals** field should contain your four portals, as shown in **Figure 5.11**. If you are configuring a single RAID controller SAN then you should end up with a total two target portals.

## Configuring Microsoft iSCSI Initiator- Multi-path Connections

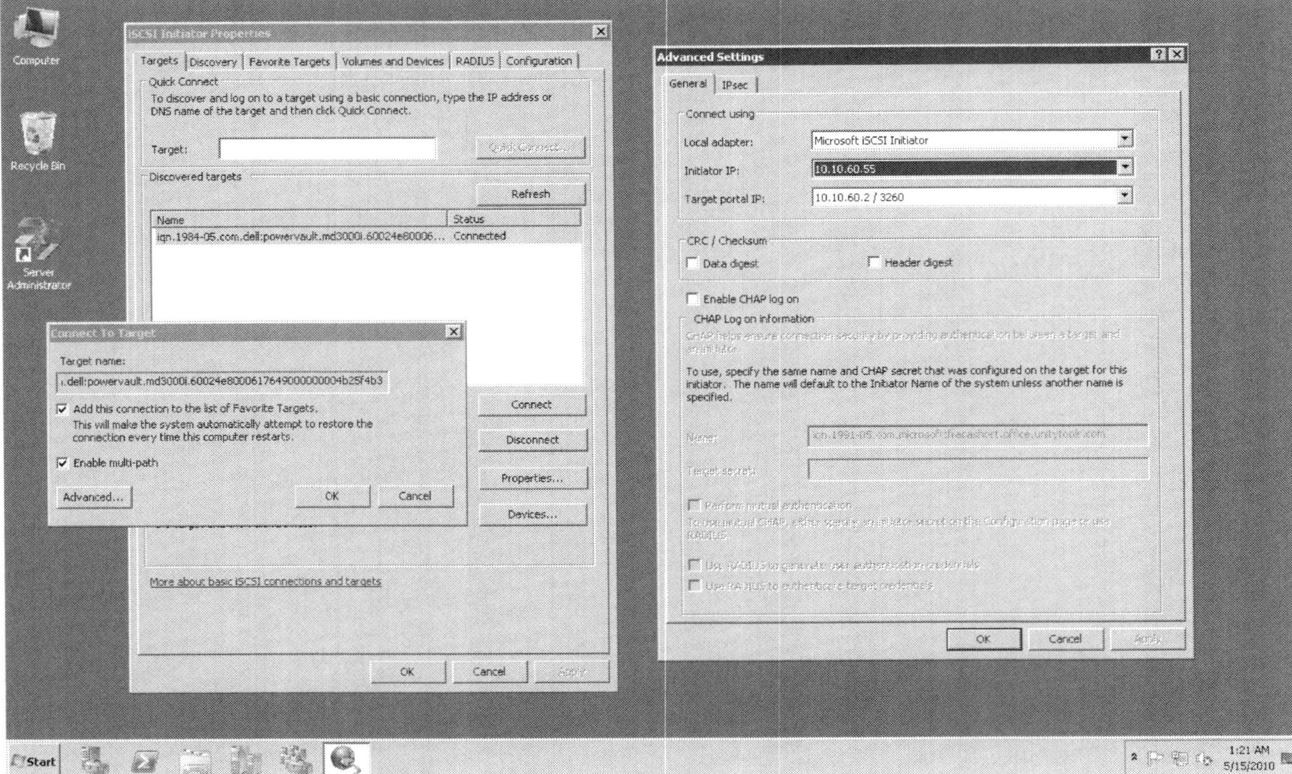

**Figure 5.12**

In this section, we will configure our Microsoft iSCSI Initiator to have multiple connections to our SAN for the best performance and redundancy. To utilize Microsoft and Dell's Multi-path Input/Output (MPIO) technology we will need to setup multiple targets for our Microsoft iSCSI Initiator to use. You can think of each target that we setup as its own pathway or route to the SAN.

## Configuring Microsoft iSCSI Initiator- First iSCSI Target

10. Click on the **Targets** tab of the iSCSI Initiator and you should see a **iqn connection string** for your SAN in the **Discovered Targets** field with the **Status** of **Disconnected**.

    a. Highlight the **iqn connection string**, and then click on the **Connect** button.

        i. On the **Connect To Target** screen, select both the **Add this connection to the list of Favorite Targets** and the **Enable multi-path** checkboxes, as shown in **Figure 5.12**. The **Add this connection to the list of Favorite Targets** option will make the system automatically attempt to restore the connection every time the computer restarts.

        ii. Click the **Advanced** button, and then configure the **Advanced Settings** screen as follows.

1. For the **Local Adapter** dropdown field, select the **Microsoft iSCSI Initiator** option.

2. For the **Initiator IP** dropdown field, select your **first iSCSI network adapter** of the server. For our project, we will select the IP address of **10.10.60.55**, as shown in **Figure 5.12**.

3. For the **Target portal IP** field, select your SAN's **first iSCSI Host Port IP address**. For our project, this is the IP address that we assigned to our **MD3000i's iSCSI Host Port** for the **RAID Controller 0, Port 0**. We will select the IP address of **10.10.60.2/3260** for the target portal field, as shown in **Figure 5.12**.

4. Click on the **OK** button twice to save your changes on the **Advanced Settings** and the **Connect To Target** screens.

## Configuring Microsoft iSCSI Initiator- Second iSCSI Target

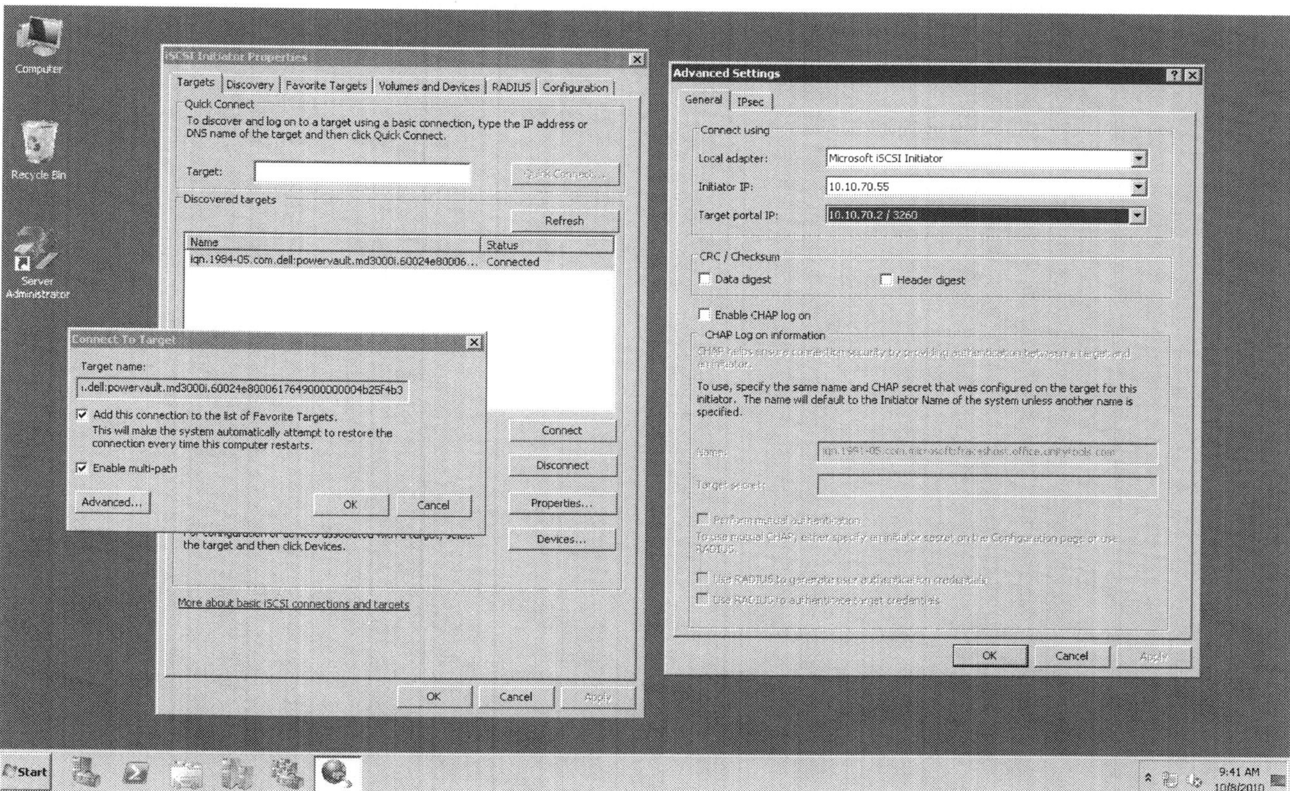


**Figure 5.13**

Here's where the Microsoft iSCSI Initiator interface becomes a little less intuitive. Your iqn connection string in the Discovered Targets field should now have the status of connected; however we still need to use this same iqn connection string to connect our remaining iSCSI Host Ports of the SAN for multi-path redundancy to work. As we add these three remaining targets, you'll notice that only the original iqn connection string appears in the Discovered Targets field even though we have added multiple targets. Once we're finished configuring the remaining targets we'll go over how to confirm that all four multi-path connections are indeed setup.

11. With the same **iqn connection string** still highlighted in the **Discovered Targets** field, click on the **Connect** button again.

    a. On the **Connect To Target** screen, select both the **Add this connection to the list of Favorite Targets** and the **Enable multi-path** checkboxes, as shown in **Figure 5.13**.

    b. Click the **Advanced** button, and then configure the **Advanced Settings** screen as follows.

        i. For the **Local Adapter** dropdown field, select the **Microsoft iSCSI Initiator** option.

        ii. For the **Initiator IP** dropdown field, select your **second iSCSI network adapter** of the server. For our project, we will select the IP address of **10.10.70.55**, as shown in **Figure 5.13**.

        iii. For the **Target portal IP** field, select your SAN's **second iSCSI Host Port IP address**. This is the IP address of your SAN's **RAID Controller Module 0, Port 1**. For our project, we will select the IP address of **10.10.70.2/3260** for the target portal field, as shown in **Figure 5.13**.

        iv. Click on the **OK** button twice to save your changes on the **Advanced Settings** and the **Connect To Target** screens.

        **NOTE:** If your SAN has a single RAID controller, then these first two portal targets is all you need to configure and you can skip **Steps 12-13**.

# Configuring Microsoft iSCSI Initiator- Third iSCSI Target

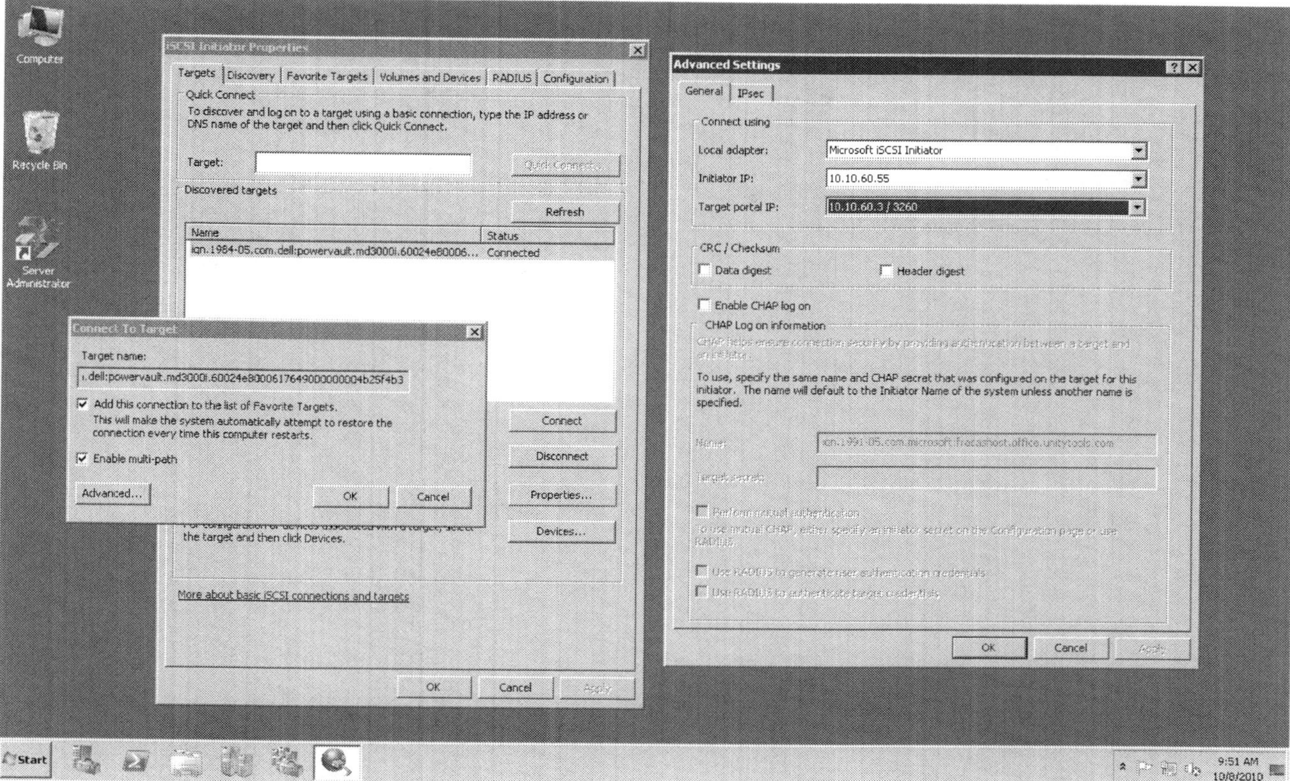

**Figure 5.14**

12. With the same **iqn connection string** still highlighted in the **Discovered Targets** field, click on the **Connect** button again.

    a. On the **Connect To Target** screen, select both the **Add this connection to the list of Favorite Targets** and the **Enable multi-path** checkboxes, as shown in **Figure 5.14**.

    b. Click the **Advanced** button, and then configure the **Advanced Settings** screen as follows.

        i. For the **Local Adapter** dropdown field, select the **Microsoft iSCSI Initiator** option.

        ii. For the **Initiator IP** dropdown field, select your **first iSCSI network adapter** of the server again. For our project, we will select the IP address of **10.10.60.55**, as shown in **Figure 5.14**.

        iii. For the **Target portal IP** field, select your SAN's **third iSCSI Host Port IP address**. This is the IP address of your SAN's **RAID Controller Module 1, Port 0**. For our project, we will select the IP address of **10.10.60.3/3260** for the target portal field, as shown in **Figure 5.14**.

        iv. Click on the **OK** button twice to save your changes on the **Advanced Settings** and the **Connect To Target** screens.

# Configuring Microsoft iSCSI Initiator- Fourth iSCSI Target

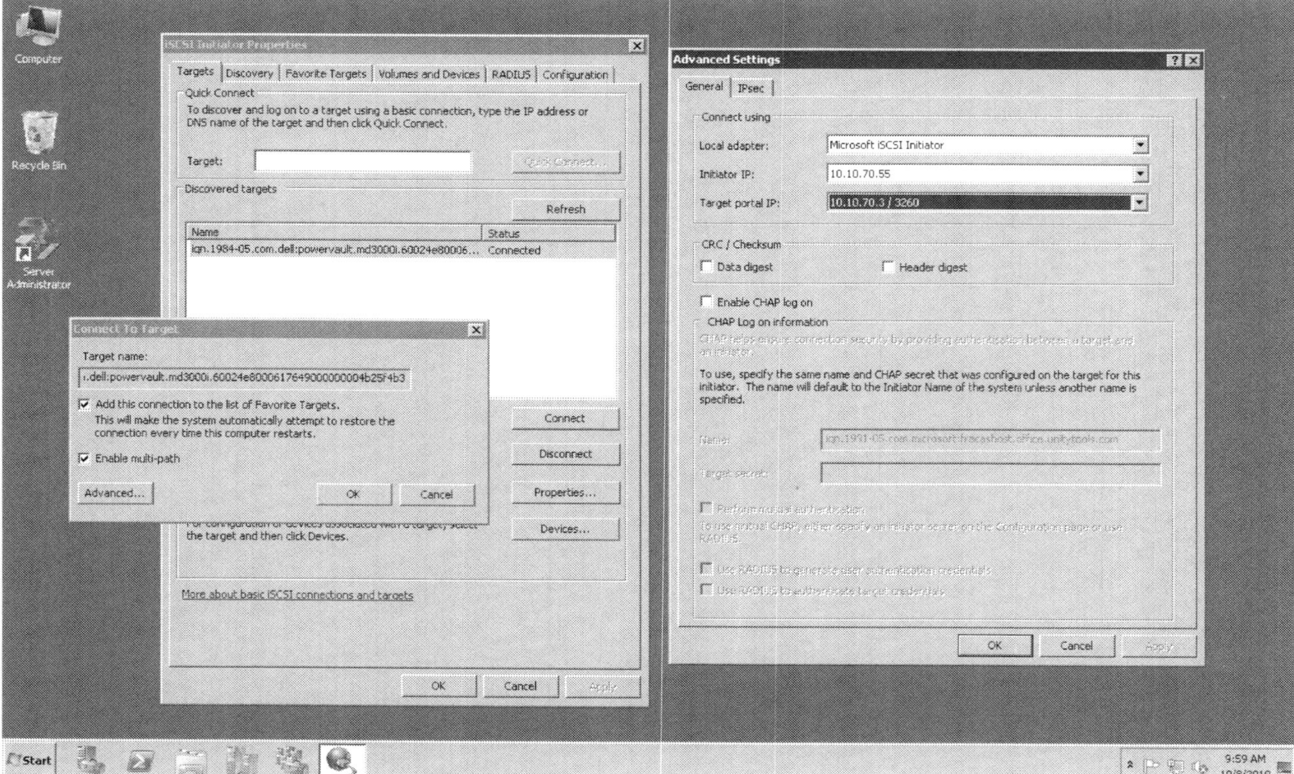

**Figure 5.15**

13. With the same **iqn connection string** still highlighted in the **Discovered Targets** field, click on the **Connect** button again.

    a. On the **Connect To Target** screen, select both the **Add this connection to the list of Favorite Targets** and the **Enable multi-path** checkboxes, as shown in **Figure 5.15**.

    b. Click the **Advanced** button, and then configure the **Advanced Settings** screen as follows.

        i. For the **Local Adapter** dropdown field, select the **Microsoft iSCSI Initiator** option.

        ii. For the **Initiator IP** dropdown field, select your **second iSCSI network adapter** of the server again. For our project, we will select the IP address of **10.10.70.55**, as shown in **Figure 5.15**.

        iii. For the **Target portal IP** field, select your SAN's **fourth iSCSI Host Port IP address**. This is the IP address of your SAN's **RAID Controller Module 1, Port 1**. For our project, we will select the IP address of **10.10.70.3/3260** for the target portal field, as shown in **Figure 5.15**.

        iv. Click on the **OK** button twice to save your changes on the **Advanced Settings** and the **Connect To Target** screens.

# Configuring Microsoft iSCSI Initiator- Verifying the of iSCSI Targets

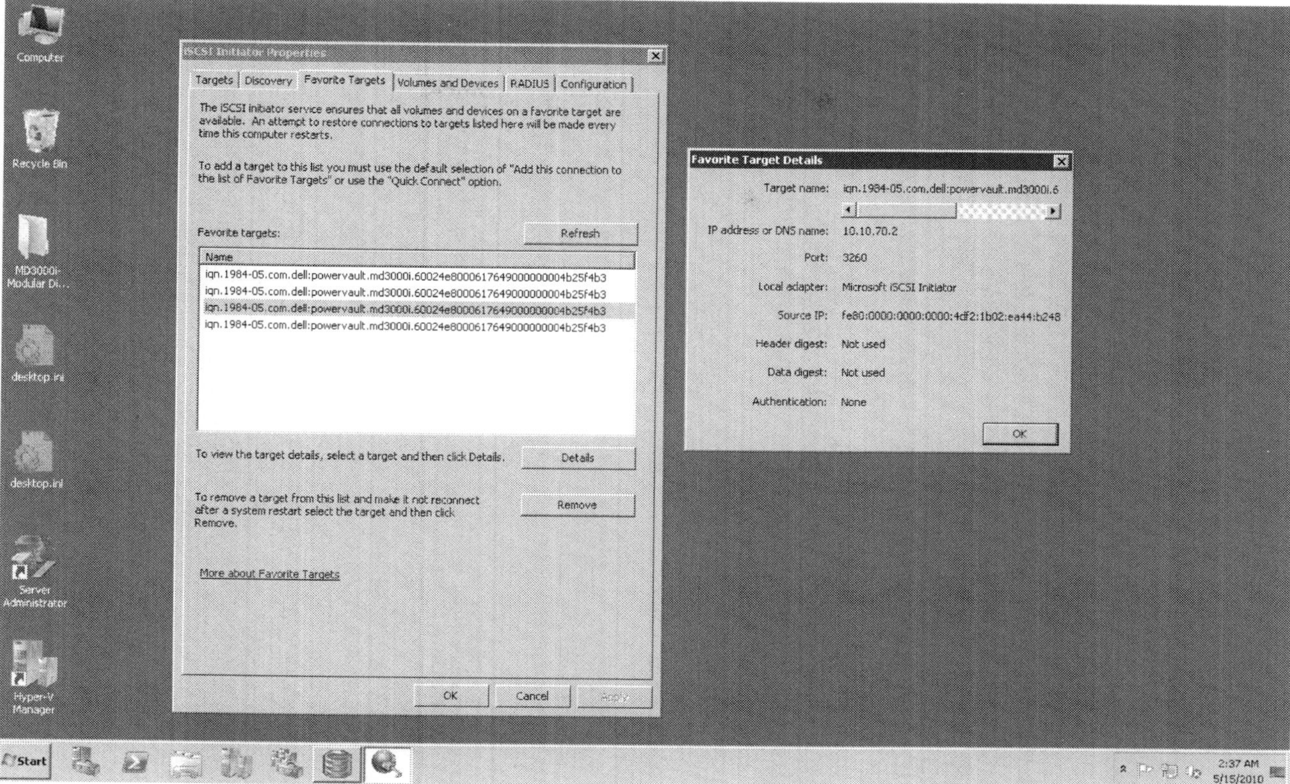


**Figure 5.16**

14. As explained earlier, the four connections won't all appear in the **Discovered Targets** field as you might expect. To confirm that the connections have been created, we'll want to click on the **Favorite Targets** tab and then confirm that there are indeed four connections, as shown in **Figure 5.16**. If you have a single RAID controller SAN then you should see a total of two connections.

    a. To view the properties of each connection, you can highlight the connection you are interested in, and then click on the **Details** button.

## Review of iSCSI Multi-path Topology

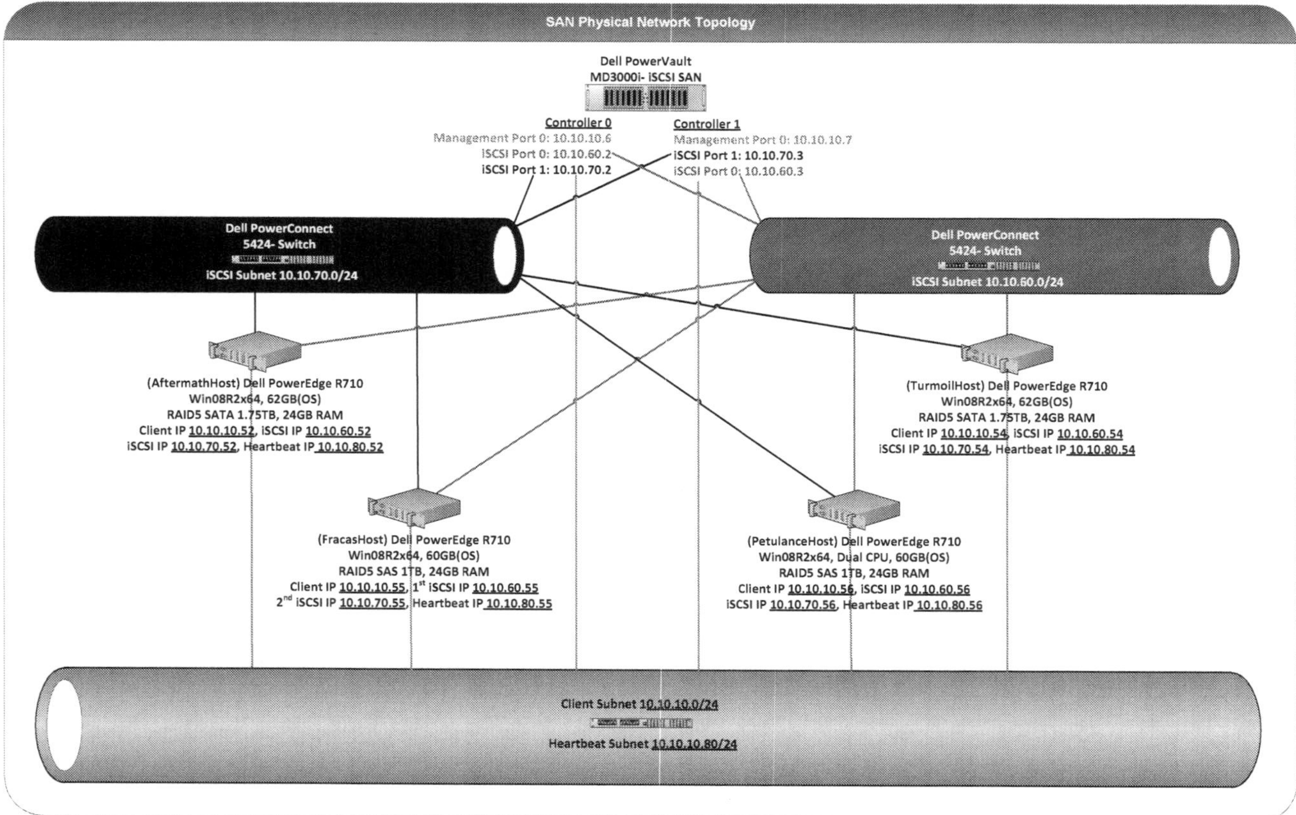


**Figure 5.17**

15. You will need to repeat all the steps outlined in this chapter for each server that you want connected to your SAN. For our project, we will end up with four servers connected to our MD3000i SAN, as outlined in **Figure 5.17**.

## Performance Benefits of TCP/IP Offload Engine (TOE) Network Adapters

Network adapters that have TCP/IP Offload Engine (TOE) capability can significantly reduce the load on your servers CPU. A TOE capable network adapter has the ability to process traffic itself instead of relying on the CPU of the server to do so. If your network adapter's specifications state that its iSCSI-ready, then this most likely means that it is possible to use a hardware based iSCSI Initiator vs. Microsoft's software based iSCSI Initiator. This type of iSCSI adapter can usually share the same physical port of the network adapter that the server's operating system uses, but it would have its own MAC and IP address. Most of the newer Dell PowerEdge servers such as an R710, come with this TOE option already, however you may need to have an additional license key for the feature to be activated.

# Chapter 6: SAN Performance- Planning Disk Layout & Creating Disk Groups

When considering performance, planning out your disk groups and virtual disks is the most important part of your whole SAN setup. This is especially true when you're implementing the SAN to handle heavy applications such as SQL Server 2008, Exchange and/or Cluster Shared Volumes. We will spend considerable time in this area to insure that we have the best setup for our situation. We will discuss why we made the choices that we did with the layout of the disks and what the performance gains specifically are. Another key part of laying out your SAN is to give yourself flexibility where you can dynamically change the size and RAID of your disk groups without having to change your server or application configurations. And to top it all off, we will cover how virtual disk sizes and LUN Id priority can be used to store your more performance hungry data on the fastest part of our physical disks. By the end of this chapter, you will have the answers to all the important questions listed below.

- What type of RAID level to use for each type of application.
- How to partition virtual disks for the best performance.
- What stripe size to use for each type of application.
- How to place I/O intense virtual disks on the fastest part of the physical disks.
- How to assign LUN Id's for the best performance.

Due to different manufactures using their own terminologies, it is important to remember that the following words and terms are synonymous throughout this chapter.

- Virtual disk, partition, LUN
- RAID array, disk group
- Server, node, host

# Overview of the SAN Disk Layout

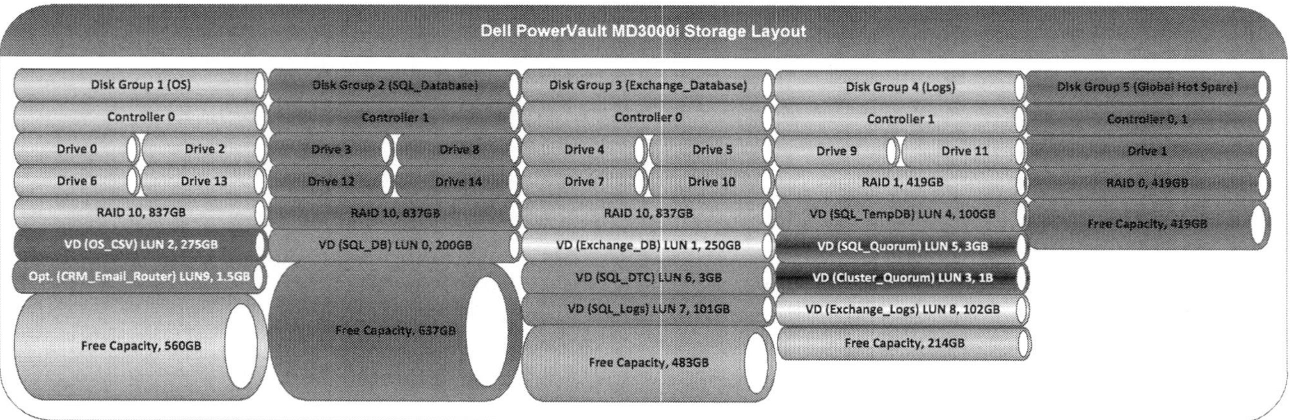


**Figure 6.1**

In **Figure 6.1**, we have a diagram that outlines what our finished disk configuration will look like. Each column in the diagram represents a RAID array created on our project's fifteen disk MD3000i SAN. Each tube within that column represents a property of the RAID array, such as the disk group name, RAID controller, drive numbers, RAID level, virtual disks, and free capacity remaining. If you look closely, you will notice that we have the SQL virtual disks distributed across three of the SAN's RAID arrays. This will provide the best overall performance by placing each of SQL's labor intense components DB, Logs, and TempDB on their own RAID array. The disk groups are distributed across each of the MD3000i's Dual RAID Controllers as well to provide the best possible performance by balancing the workload across both controllers. With this disk layout we end up with a configuration that balances our workload of SQL, CSV virtual disks and Exchange across our SAN's RAID arrays.

**NOTE:** Exchange 2007 is only included among our disk layout to give you an example of how you could distribute other labor intense applications among your SQL and CSV disks.

# Configuring the SAN RAID Arrays for the Best Performance

In our project, we are using a Dell PowerVault MD3000i SAN filled with fifteen 450GB SAS drives with a 15k RPM speed. With most SAN's such as the MD3000i you have the flexibility of choosing to use a mix of SAS and SATA drives within one chassis. In the scenario, where some of your applications are more storage intense vs. performance intense you could choose to run those applications on SATA drives instead of SAS drives. In this book's particular project, we are aiming for the best overall performance of our SAN. You will want to pay close attention to the virtual disk configuration section, as there is a hot tip on how to gain a whopping 30% performance increase. The following information explains why we choose this particular configuration and will help you in deciding if your specific configuration should be the same or different.

# RAID Level Selection

The greatest factor in selecting a RAID level is determined by your Input/Output (I/O) pattern. Since we will be setting up our SAN, to handle multiple applications with many different types of traffic it can be difficult to determine our I/O pattern. In this scenario, RAID 10 becomes the better initial choice for performance as it performs equally or better in most cases then RAID 5, with exception of large and sequential I/O's. The only drawback with RAID 10 vs. RAID 5 is that the disk cost is 50% no matter how many disks you add to your disk group. You will have to determine if you are willing to afford this disk cost for better performance. An important thing to know with most higher end RAID controllers is that you can usually start out with a RAID 10 configuration for performance and then convert it later to a RAID 5 configuration if you need more disk space. This can be done without having to move your data and without having to recreate the RAID array. The following are the main factors concerning performance when selecting a RAID level.

- The principle factor in your RAID level selection should be determined by your Input/Output (I/O) pattern. If the I/O is less than 1/3 of the cache available, then choosing RAID level of 1, 10, 5 or 6 won't make much of a difference as these operations can be handled entirely in cache.
- In a high write I/O scenario-
    - RAID 1 and 10 provide the best overall performance for applications that have a 10% or greater mix of random I/O's. In this scenario RAID 1 and 10 will outperform RAID 5 by more than 20%.
    - RAID 5 and 6 have the worst performance when it comes to an environment that consists of mostly random writes.
- In a low write I/O scenario-
    - RAID 5 provides the approximately the same performance as RAID 1 and 10 for applications that have a 10% or less mix of random I/O's.
- In a sequential I/O scenario-
    - For large I/O's consisting 256KiB or more, RAID 5 and 6 will perform the best
    - For small I/O's of less than 32 KiB, RAID 1, 5 and 10 will perform equally.
- In a mostly read and sequential write scenario-
    - RAID 1, 5 and 10 have similar performance.
- When considering transfers sizes-
    - For small transfer sizes, the RAID level doesn't make much difference
    - For medium transfer sizes, RAID 1/10 tends to outperform RAID 5/6.
    - For large transfer sizes, RAID 1/10 tends to outperform RAID 5/6.
- When considering disk cost-
    - If your main concern is performance and you don't have a clear picture of your I/O pattern, then RAID 10 is your best option.
    - If your main concern is disk cost, then RAID 5 is your best option.

## Virtual Disk Configuration and LUN Id Selections

The following points need to be taken into consideration before we start creating our virtual disks and assigning them priority with LUN Id's.

- The LUN Id assigned to each virtual disk is very important as the lower number will be written on the outer edges of the hard drive where the disk spins the fastest. We will assign the lower LUN Id's to our more labor intense applications, so that the data of these applications is on the fastest part of our disks.

  **HOT TIP:** In our project, we will take advantage of a trick that not known by many, yet it increases your disk performance by a whopping 30% when utilized. If we create our virtual disks of our disk group to use less than 1/3 of the disk group's total available space, then we will be able to take advantage of what's called Short-Stroking the disk. When we configure our disks this way, all the data of the virtual disks will automatically be written on the outer edges of the hard drives where the disks spin the fastest. Of course, the drawback is that you're not using the other 2/3's of the disk group's available disk space. This may sound a little extreme, however if you don't need the space currently, then it's a great option to get the absolute best performance. Another thing to keep in mind is that you can always expand the virtual disk later and use the remaining 2/3's of free space on the disk group. We will cover how to expand an existing virtual disk later in this chapter.

- It is considered a Dell best practice to not create more than four virtual disks per disk group when at all possible.

- When assigning a Stripe/Segment size you need to take into consideration what type of data will be stored on your virtual disk. For file systems and databases a Stripe/Segment size of a 128KB is a good selection, while for larger multimedia files you should select a Stripe/Segment size of a 256KB.

  **NOTE:** The Stripe/Segment size will play a significant role when we are formatting our virtual disks from within Windows Server Manager. In **Chapter 8**, we will be covering something called Partition Alignment/Sector Alignment which relates to aligning the Stripe/Segment size with our operating system's Allocation Unit Size. This is another **HOT TIP** that will gain us a significant performance increase when setup correctly.

## Drive Selection and Number of Spindles

Your drive speed is another principle factor in determining the performance of your RAID arrays. In general, you want to choose faster drives whenever fiscally possible. The basic break down of drive speed and their corresponding I/O performance is as follows.

- If you're comparing a single SAS 10k RPM drive to a single SAS 15k RPM drive, the 15k RPM drive will perform approximately 20% faster than the 10K RPM drive for mixed random and sequential operations.

- A Dell SAS 15k RPM drive has an I/O of 175, while a Dell SATA 7.2k RPM drive has an I/O of 75, making the SAS 15k RPM drive more than twice as fast as the SATA 7.2k RPM drive.

## Creating a Virtual Disk Ownership Balance Between RAID Controllers

We want to distribute our disk groups among the SAN's dual RAID controllers as is shown in the diagram of **Figure 6.1**. By balancing our most disk intense applications across the redundant RAID controllers we will have the best overall performance. In **Figure 6.1**, you can see that we have our Cluster Shared Volumes (CSV) and Exchange virtual disks as primarily owned by Controller 0, while our SQL is primarily owned by Controller 1. If you have a single controller SAN, then you don't have to worry about balancing your RAID controllers and can ignore this section. Our project's Dell PowerVault MD3000i SAN will automatically attempt to balance our virtual disks across the dual RAID controllers for us. This automatic assignment normally would happen when we are creating our virtual disks, however we will assign them manually to insure the best balance.

## Creating Disk Groups and Virtual Disks that Allow Flexibility

An important feature of having a SAN is the flexibility that the RAID controllers give you when managing your disk groups and virtual disks. In this chapter, we cover how configuring our SAN for the performance and flexibility actually are complementary to each other in most cases. We will configure our disk groups in a way that will allow us to add any of our free hard disks an existing disk group without negatively affecting our data or applications. We will also configure our virtual disks in a way that will allow us to add any of our free space to an existing virtual disk without disrupting our data or applications. The following options are what we want to keep in mind for potential future changes.

- You can add free hard disks to a disk group to expand its capacity without needing to move your data or recreate the virtual disks residing in the disk group. The process can take up to 24 hours and once you start it you cannot stop it. Once the process has started, you will not have any options to stop it, even if you just wanted to delete the whole disk group and start over.

- You can convert your high disk cost RAID arrays such as RAID 10 to a RAID 5 or 6 array to gain disk space without needing to move your data or recreate the virtual disks residing on the disk group. Again, the process can take quite a while and cannot be interrupted. If you decide to convert a RAID array, make sure you allot at least 24 hours for it to complete.

- You can always extend a virtual disk, as long as there is free space available within the disk group. The only unfortunate part of this feature for the Dell PowerVault MD3000i SAN is that it's not available from within the management GUI as you would think it would be. Instead, you have to use Dell's Command Line Interface (CLI) to perform this task.

- In our project, we will assign our last available disk as the global hot spare to benefit us in two ways. First, if a RAID array has one of its drives fail then the hot spare will fill the bad drives role and restore the array to its full redundancy. Second, it will allow us flexibility to expand the capacity of an already existing RAID 1 or 10 array, by adding this hot spare to the disk group and converting to a RAID 5 array.

# Disk Layout Considerations for Windows and SQL Cluster Quorum Disks

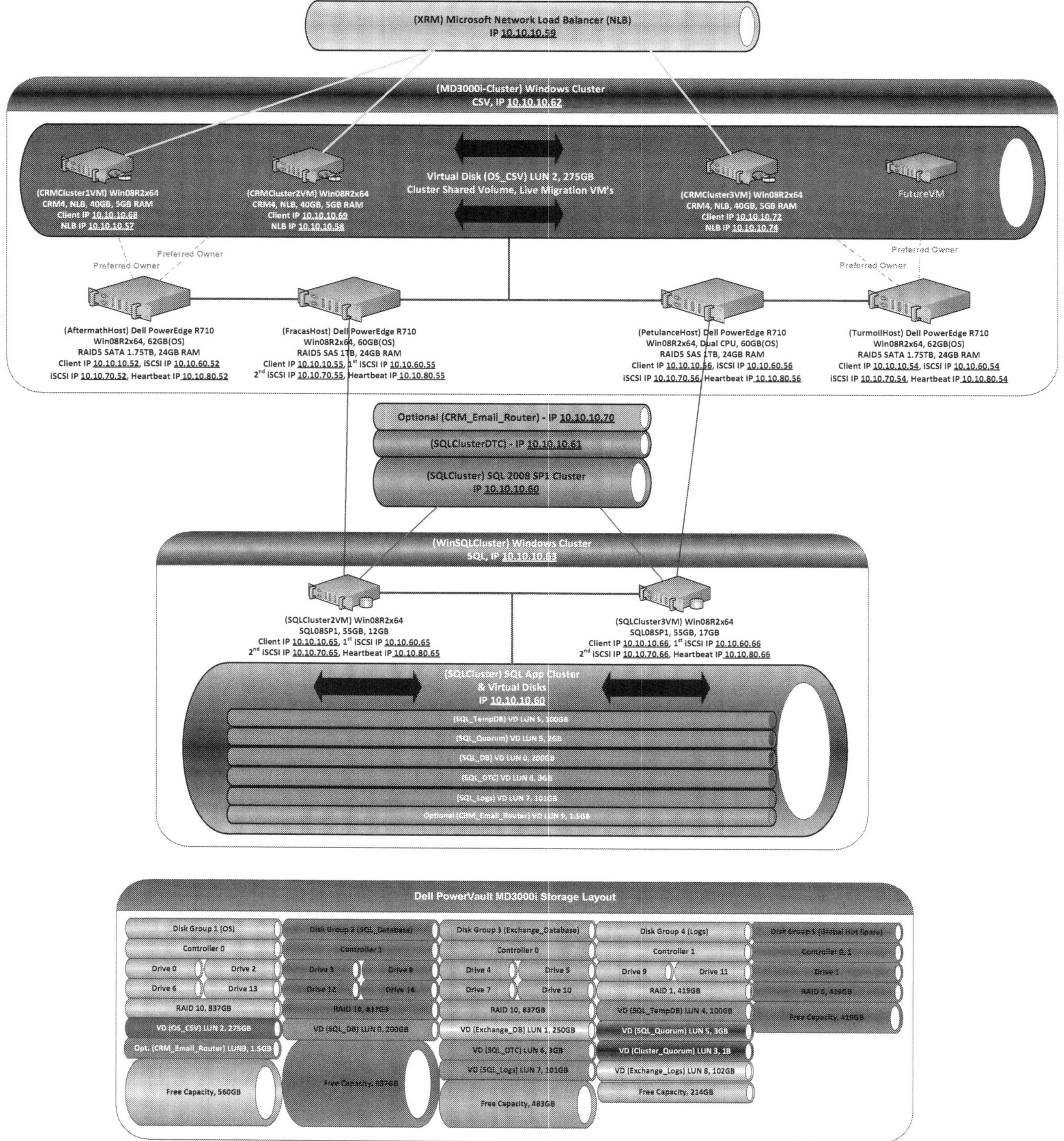


**Figure 6.2**

As a final step before we start creating the disk layout on the SAN, we will need to take into consideration our Windows and SQL clustering topology. In our project, we will be utilizing four physical servers and five virtual machines. Three of the virtual machines will be our front-end application servers running Microsoft Dynamics CRM 4.0 and the other two virtual machines will be our back-end database servers with the Microsoft SQL Server 2008/R2. In **Figure 6.2**, we have our Windows and SQL cluster topologies represented. The following are the disk layout considerations you need to make for your Windows and SQL clusters.

- We need to take into consideration how many nodes are going to be in each cluster. Clusters stay online according to majority vote, which is referred to as a quorum. For a majority vote to exist there always has to be an odd number of voters to avoid any potential tie vote. A cluster node (server) and/or a virtual disk on the SAN can vote. This voting disk is known as the quorum disk in clustering terminology and can be as small as 500MB's in size. A typical failover cluster can consist of two cluster nodes and a quorum disk or simply three cluster nodes without a quorum disk as long as there is an odd number of voters. For example, in our project we will setup two SQL cluster nodes utilizing a quorum disk, so we need include this quorum virtual disk in our disk layout among our other SQL virtual disks.

- If you are planning on having other clustered Services or Applications, such as Microsoft's SQL Distributed Transaction Coordinator (MSDTC) or Microsoft's Dynamics CRM 4.0 E-mail Router service, then you'll need to account for these virtual disks in your disk layout plan as well. In the example project of this book, we will create a virtual disk for both the MSDTC quorum and for the CRM E-mail Router service. The virtual disks required for each of these clustered services are very small with the MSDTC's quorum disk only requiring a minimum of 640MB's, and with the CRM E-mail Router service only requiring 1GB. For our project, we will create the MSDTC virtual disk as part of our initial SAN configuration, however we will leave the creation of the CRM E-mail Router's virtual disk as an option for CRM 4.0 administrators to setup in Chapter 27.

- Keep in mind that your virtual machines are also Services and Applications from within the Windows Failover Cluster Manager. For any additional virtual machines you are planning outside of our project, you'll either need a regular virtual disk dedicated to each additional virtual machine or a shared CSV virtual disk that can host multiple additional virtual machines.

# Configuring the Dell PowerVault MD3000i Storage

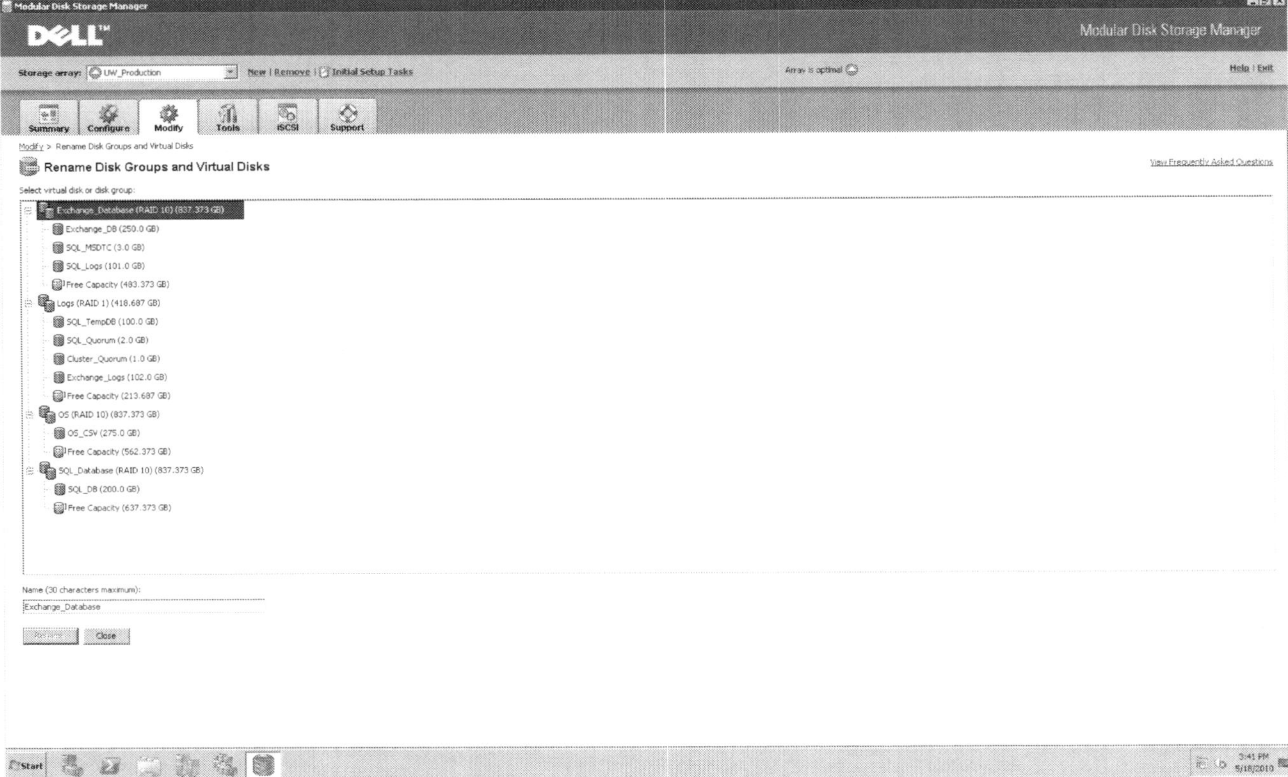


**Figure 6.3**

In **Figure 6.3**, we have a screenshot of what the end result will look like when we our done creating our disk groups and virtual disks with the Dell Modular Disk Storage Manager (MDSM). Changing the disk groups and virtual disks at this point of our setup is very easy, so if you want to play around with your disk layout to get a better understanding of how it all works, now is the time to do so before we start connecting virtual disks to our servers. Just one reminder though, as stated earlier don't try adding a physical disk to an existing disk group or attempting to convert an existing disk group's RAID level to different RAID level unless you're willing to wait 24 hours for the process to complete. The process is very time consuming and blocks you from making any other changes during that time. In our project, we will make each of our virtual disks a unique size, so that later they'll be easily identifiable once we're managing them from within Window's Disk Management.

## Creating Disk Groups with the Dell Modular Disk Storage Manager (MDSM)

| First Disk Group | Disk Group Name | RAID Level | Number of Disks | Capacity | Controller |
|---|---|---|---|---|---|
| | OS | RAID 1/10 | 4 | 837 GB | 0 |
| | **Virtual Disks** | | | | |
| | Virtual Disks | OS_CSV | | | |
| | Capacity | 275 GB | | | |
| | I/O Characteristics | File System | | | |
| | LUN Id | 2 | | | |
| | Host Group | Map Later | | | |

**Figure 6.4**

Now that we covered the basics, we are ready to begin creating our disk groups and virtual disks for our project. We will walk though step by step creating the first disk group and virtual disk. Once we have completed creating our first disk group configuration, you will be able to create the remaining disk groups and virtual disks that we need on your own. We start out by creating the disk group and virtual disk for our Clustered Shared Volumes (CSV) drive. This will be the disk group that hosts our CSV virtual machines for our front-end application servers. For our project, we will create our first disk group and virtual disk with the properties outlined in **Figure 6.4**.

## Creating Disk Groups with MDSM- First Disk Group

1. On the server that you installed the **Dell Modular Disk Storage Manager** on, launch the management interface by going to **Start button\Dell\MD Storage Manager**, and then login.

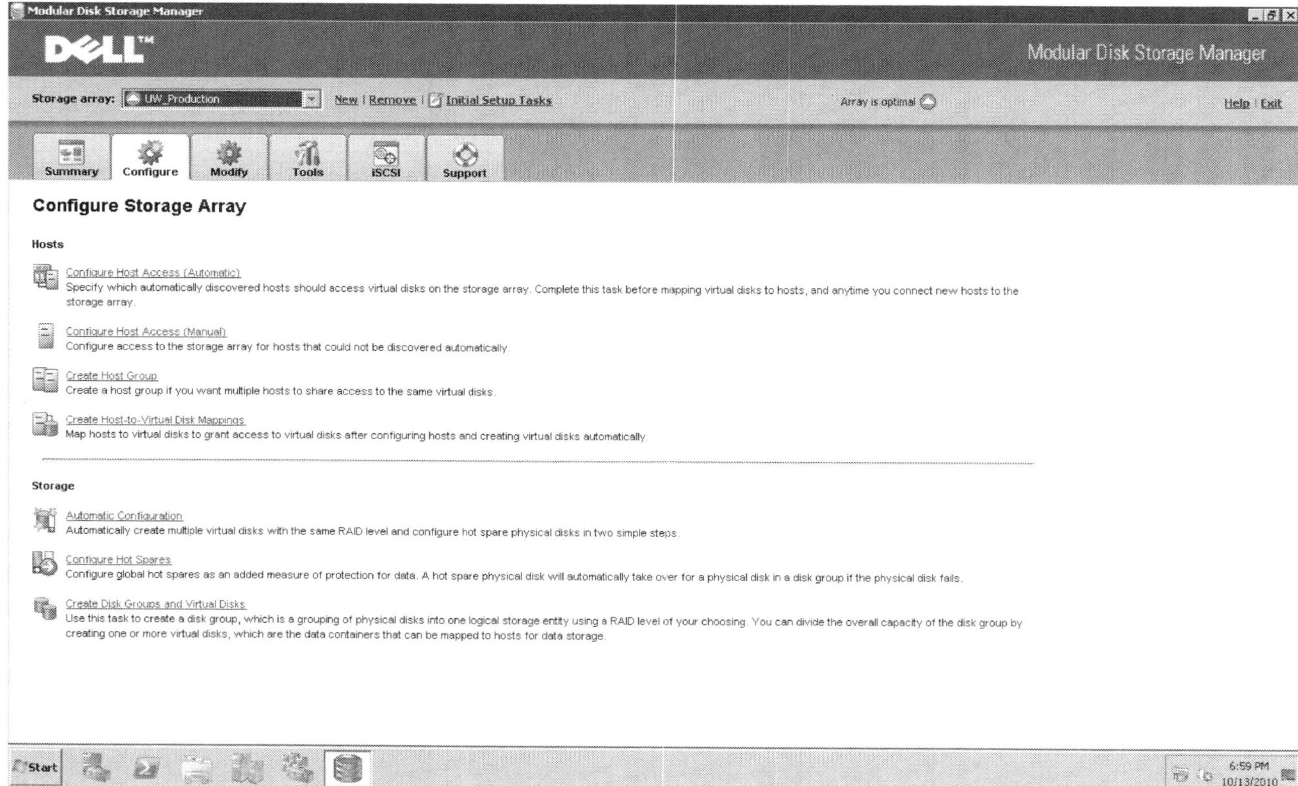


**Figure 6.5**

2. Click on the **Configure** tab, and then select the **Create Disk Groups and Virtual Disks** link, as shown at the bottom of the screen in **Figure 6.5**.

    a. You will most likely receive a pop-up window titled **No Hosts Configured**, click on the **OK** button to continue. We received this message because we haven't configured any of our servers with access to the SAN's virtual disks yet.

    b. On the **Create Disk Groups and Virtual Disks – Select Task** screen, select the bullet next to the **Disk group: Create a new disk group using the un-configured capacity in the storage array** option, and then click on the **Next** button to continue.

    c. On the **Create Disk Groups and Virtual Disks – Specify Disk Group** screen, enter the name that you want for your disk group in the **Disk Group Name** field. For our project, we will name our disk group **OS**. The name OS will help us identity that this is where our virtual machine operating systems will be hosted.

        i. For the **Physical Disk selection choices** section, leave the default of selection of **Automatic (Recommended): Choose from a list of automatically generated physical disk and capacity options**, and then click on the **Next** button to continue. It is recommended that you choose this option initially, so that the MD3000i will intelligently balance of the workload across the RAID controllers and physical disks. We can always manually change the controller assignment later if we need to.

d. On the **Create Disk Groups and Virtual Disks – Disk Group Physical Disk Selection (Automatic)** screen, select the RAID level you want from the **Select RAID level** dropdown field. For our project, we will select the **RAID 1/10** option.

  i. For the **Select capacity** field, choose the number of physical disks to use, and then click on the **Finish** button to continue. For our project, we will choose to use **Four** physical disks.

e. On the **Create Disk Groups and Virtual Disks – Complete** screen, leave the default selection of **Create a virtual disk using the new disk group**, and then click on the **Yes** button to continue. This option will allow you to create a new virtual disk on your disk group.

## Creating Virtual Disks with the Dell Modular Disk Storage Manager (MDSM)

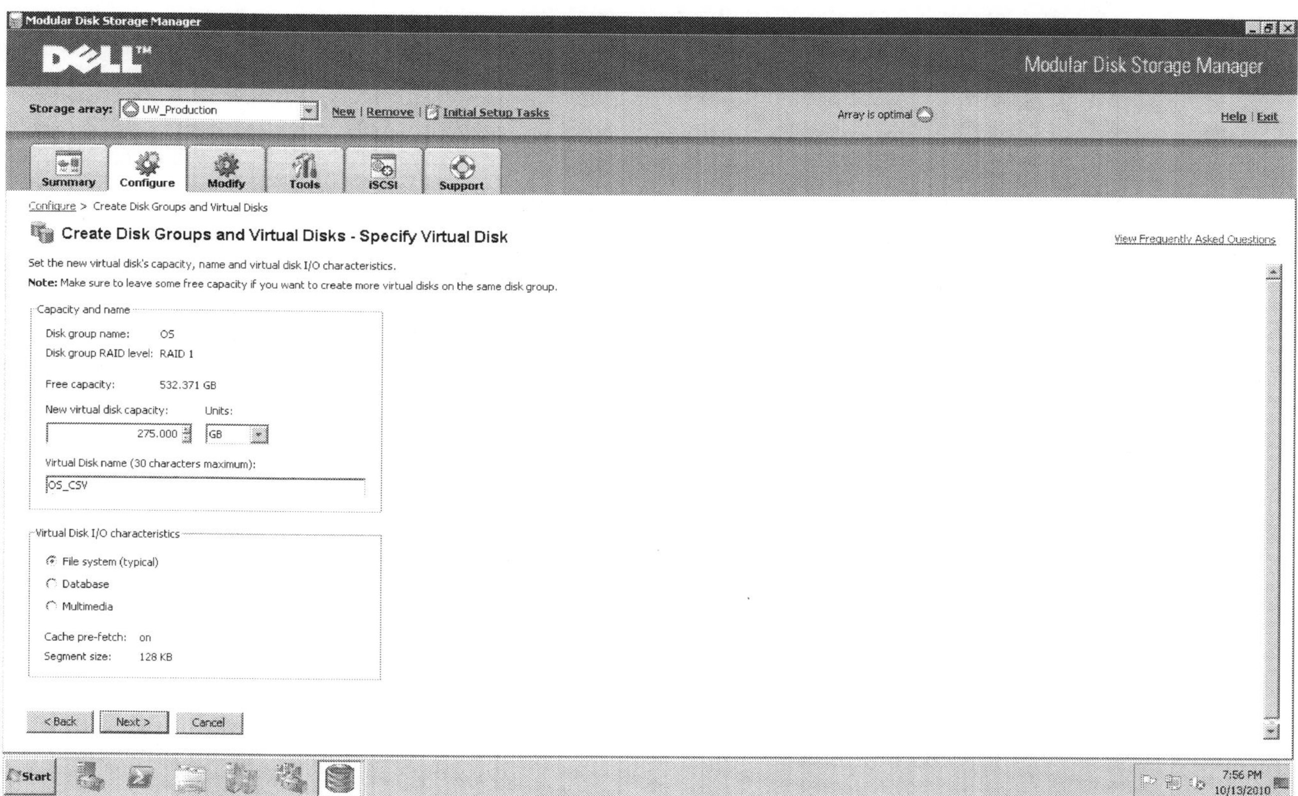


**Figure 6.6**

f. On the **Create Disk Groups and Virtual Disks – Specify Virtual Disk** screen, enter in the capacity you want for the **New virtual disk capacity** field, and then select the unit size for the **Units** dropdown field. For our project, we will enter **275** for our capacity with the **Units** field set to **GB**.

  i. For the **Virtual Disk name** field, enter the name you want for the virtual disk. For our project, we will name our virtual disk **OS_CSV**. The name OS_CSV will help us identity that our virtual machine operating systems are stored on a CSV cluster disk.

  ii. For the **Virtual Disk I/O Characteristics** field, select the type of file system you want, and then click on the **Next** button to continue. For our project, we will select the **File system (typical)** option, as shown in **Figure 6.6**.

g. On the **Create Disk Groups and Virtual Disks – Map Virtual Disk To Host** screen, select the **Logical Unit Number (LUN Id)** that you want from the **Assign logical unit number (LUN)** dropdown field. For our project, we will select the **LUN Id** of **3**.

   **NOTE:** Pay close attention to the **LUN Id** that you assign to your virtual disks, as you want the virtual disks that need the best performance assigned with the lowest LUN Id numbers.

   i. Select the **Map later: Map later using the Create Host-to-Virtual Disk Mappings task under the Configure tab** option at the bottom of the screen, and then click on the **Finish** button. You cannot create a **Host-to-Virtual Disk Mapping** until you have at least one server connected to the SAN and have created a host group, so we will map to our virtual disks to a host group in later steps. If you already have a host group created, then you can select the map now option if you so choose.

h. On the **Create Disk Groups and Virtual Disks – Complete** screen, select either **Create a virtual disk using the new disk group** or the **Create a virtual disk using a different disk group OR create a new disk group** option to continue creating the rest of your disks, and then click on the **Yes** button to continue.

| Second Disk Group | Disk Group Name | RAID Level | Number of Disks | Capacity | Controller |
|---|---|---|---|---|---|
| | SQL_Database | RAID 1/10 | 4 | 837 GB | 1 |
| | **Virtual Disks** | | | | |
| | Virtual Disks | SQL_DB | | | |
| | Capacity | 200 GB | | | |
| | I/O Characteristics | Database | | | |
| | LUN Id | 0 | | | |
| | Host Group | Map Later | | | |

**Figure 6.7**

## Creating Disk Groups with MDSM- Second Disk Group

3. Repeat **Step 2** to create your remaining disk groups and virtual disks. When creating your disk groups, keep in mind that you may want to save one hard disk for a global hot spare, as in our project. We will cover how to configure our global hot spare in **Step 7** of this chapter. For our project, we will create our remaining disk groups and virtual disks as outlined in **Figures 6.7-6.9**. Our second disk group as outlined in **Figure 6.7** will host our project's SQL database virtual disk.

| Third Disk Group | Disk Group Name | RAID Level | Number of Disks | Capacity | Controller |
|---|---|---|---|---|---|
| | Exchange_Database | RAID 1/10 | 4 | 837 GB | 0 |
| | **Virtual Disks** | | | | |
| | Virtual Disks | Exchange_DB | SQL_MSDTC | SQL_Logs | |
| | Capacity | 250 GB | 3 GB | 101 GB | |
| | I/O Characteristics | Database | File System | Database | |
| | LUN Id | 1 | 6 | 7 | |
| | Host Group | Map Later | Map Later | Map Later | |

**Figure 6.8**

## Creating Disk Groups with MDSM- Third Disk Group

4. Our third disk group as outlined in **Figure 6.8** will host our project's Exchange database, SQL logs, and SQL MSDTC's quorum virtual disks.

| Fourth Disk Group | Disk Group Name | RAID Level | Number of Disks | Capacity | Controller |
|---|---|---|---|---|---|
| | Logs | RAID 1/10 | 4 | 837 GB | 1 |
| | **Virtual Disks** | | | | |
| | Virtual Disks | SQL_TempDB | SQL_Quorum | Cluster_Quorum | Exchange_Logs |
| | Capacity | 100 GB | 2 GB | 1 GB | 102 GB |
| | I/O Characteristics | Database | File System | Database | Database |
| | LUN Id | 4 | 5 | 3 | 8 |
| | Host Group | Map Later | Map Later | Map Later | Map Later |

**Figure 6.9**

## Creating Disk Groups with MDSM- Fourth Disk Group

5. Our fourth disk group as outlined in **Figure 6.9** will host our project's SQL temp database, SQL quorum, cluster quorum and Exchange log virtual disks.

6. Once finished creating your disks, you can click the **Summary** tab, and then select the **Disk Groups and Virtual Disks** link to view the disks that you just setup. The summary tab gives you a very condensed view, so you might prefer selecting the **Rename Disk Groups and Virtual Disks** link from the **Modify** tab instead. This will give you a full view of the disk groups and virtual disks that you created. For our project, we should have a configuration that looks similar to **Figure 6.3**.

## Viewing Logical Unit Number (LUN) Id's

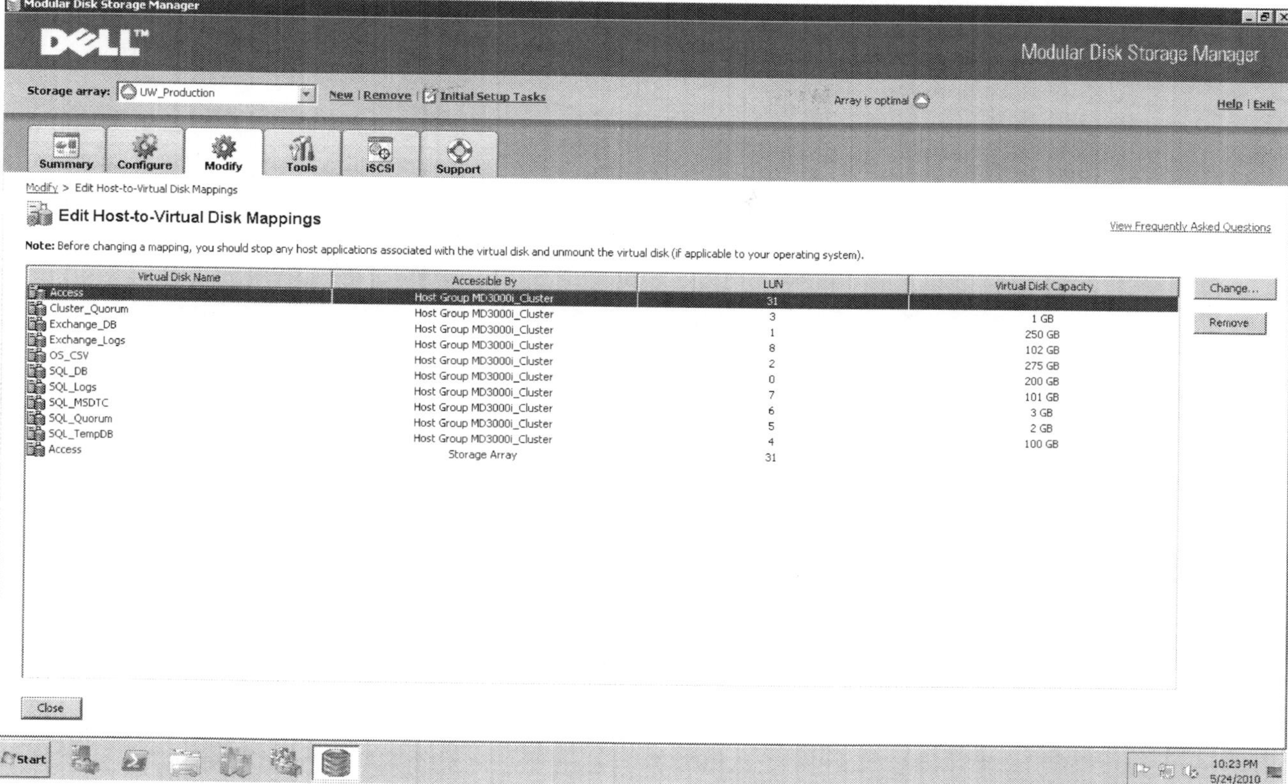


**Figure 6.10**

7. To view the **LUN Id's** that you mapped to your virtual disks, you can click the **Summary** tab, and then select the **Host-to-Virtual Disk Mappings** link to view the LUN Id's that you setup. Once again, the summary tab gives you a very condensed view, so you might prefer selecting the **Edit Host-to-Virtual Disk Mappings** link from the **Modify** tab instead. This will give you a full view as shown in **Figure 6.10**. For our project, we should have a configuration that looks similar to **Figure 6.10**.

## Modifying Logical Unit Number (LUN) Id's

We should already have the LUN Id's configured how we want them, however it is important to review and make any changes to them at this point in the configuration process. Once our virtual disks are brought online using the Window Server Manager our LUN Id's cannot be changed. We would have to take the virtual disk offline to change its LUN Id and then bring it back online once the changed was made. As explained earlier in this chapter, the LUN Id determines the priority of the virtual disk. The lower the LUN Id number the higher the priority, which means a virtual disk with a low LUN Id number will have its data stored towards to the outside edge of your physical disks where the disks spin the fastest. We will cover how to modify our LUN Id's in this chapter's next step. If you already have your LUN Id's configured the way you want them, then please skip **Step 8**.

8. Click on the **Modify** tab, and then select the **Edit Host-to-Virtual Disk Mappings** link option.

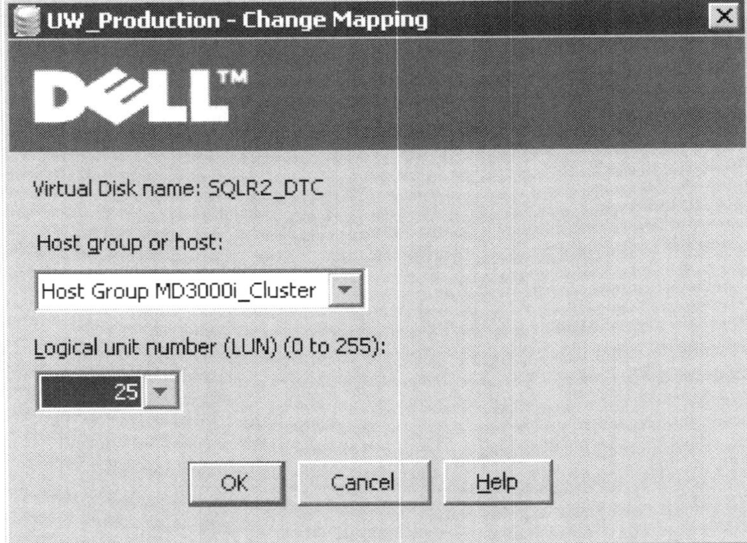


**Figure 6.11**

a. On the **Edit Host-to-Virtual Disk Mappings** screen, select the virtual disk that currently has the **LUN Id** you want assigned to a different disk, and then click on the **Change** button. You first have to free up the LUN Id that you want to use before you can reassign it to a different virtual disk.

   i. On the **Change Mapping** screen, change the **LUN Id** number to a high number that's not currently being used, so that you free up the currently assigned LUN Id, and then click on the **OK** button to continue. For example, **Figure 6.11** shows the LUN Id being reassigned to high number of **25**.

   ii. On the **Change Mapping** warning screen, click on the **Yes** button to make the change.

b. On the **Edit Host-to-Virtual Disk Mappings** screen, select the virtual disk that you want to assign the newly freed up **LUN Id** to, and then click on the **Change** button.

   i. On the **Change Mapping** screen, change **LUN Id** dropdown field to the newly freed up **LUN Id** number, and then click on the **OK** button.

   ii. On the **Change Mapping** warning screen, click on the **Yes** button to make the change.

c. Repeat **Step 8** for any other LUN Id's you would like reassigned.

## Assigning the Global Hot Spare Disk

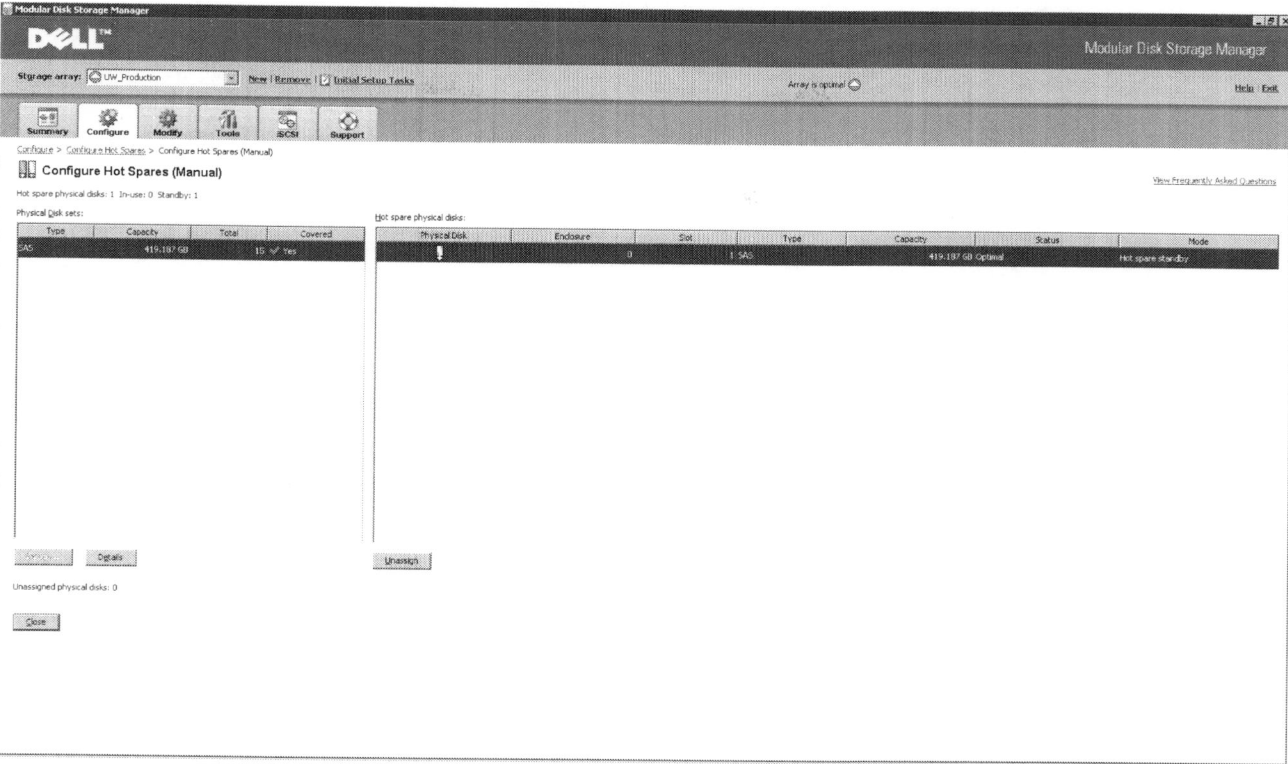


**Figure 6.12**

9. The last disk configuration we want to make is to assign the remaining fifteenth disk as the **Global Hot Spare**. Browse to **Configure tab\Configure Hot Spares\Configure Hot Spares (Manual)**, and then click on the **Assign** button. Once complete, click on the **Close** button to exit.

# Chapter 7: Configuring the Server Access to the Virtual Disks

In this chapter, we will configure our SAN to allow our physical servers access to the shared disks. We have already configured our server side connections to the SAN earlier when we setup the Microsoft iSCSI Initiator connections on each server. We will begin by adding our first physical server's iSCSI connection to our SAN. During this process we will create a host group that will control which servers have access to our virtual disks. The final step will be to map our virtual disks to this new host group. When we are finished, each of our servers will have access to the virtual disks hosted on the SAN.

## Adding the First Physical Server's iSCSI Connection to the SAN

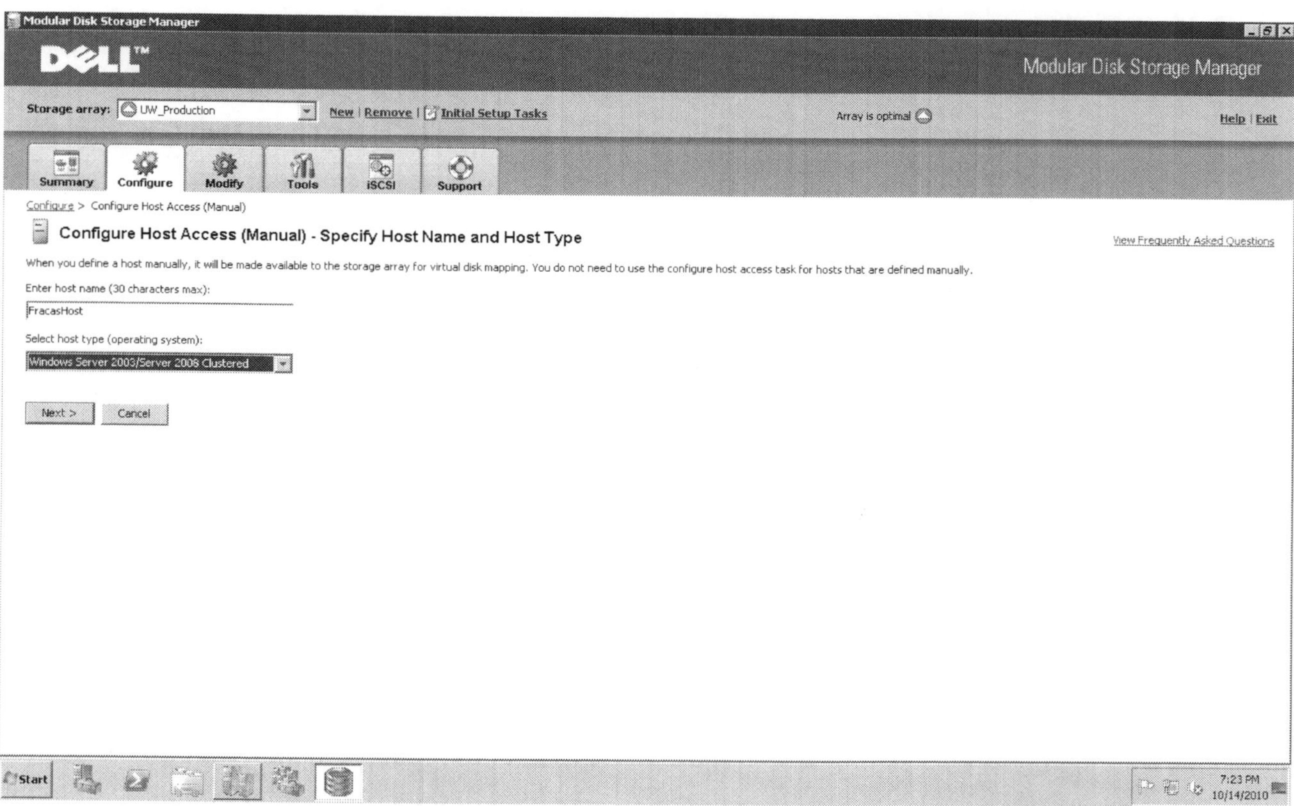


**Figure 7.1**

We will begin by adding our first physical server's iSCSI connection. This process will give us the option to create a new host group on the SAN. For our project, we will only be using one host group for all our servers physical and virtual. You could decide to create multiple host groups, however having all the servers as members of just one group gives us the greatest flexibility with access to our virtual disks. If you are only connecting a small number of servers such as in our project with four physical and two virtual servers then having just one host group will be fine. If you have a larger number of servers then you will want to consider creating multiple host groups with one group for each role that your different servers fulfill. This will make your shared disks more manageable and help reduce confusion when bringing your disks online from within the Windows Server Manager console.

1. Open the **Dell Modular Disk Storage Manager**, click on the **Configure** tab, and then select the **Configure Host Access (Manual)** link.

   a. On the **Configure Host Access (Manual) – Specify Host Name and Host Type** screen, enter your first physical server's name in the **Enter host name** field. For our project, the first server we will add is named **FracasHost**, as shown in **Figure 7.1**.

      i. For the **Select host type** field, select the **Windows Server 2003/Server 2008 Clustered** option, and then click on the **Next** button to continue.

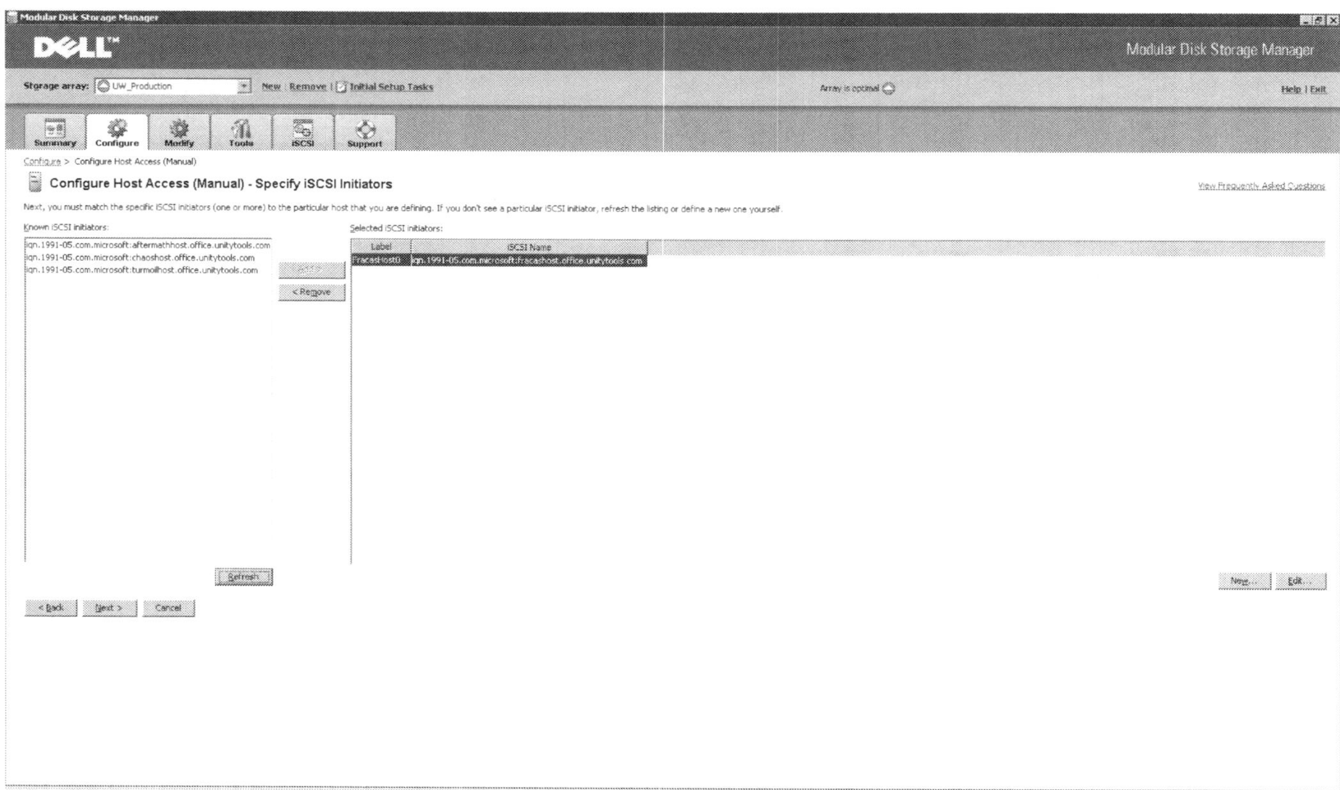


**Figure 7.2**

   b. For the **Known iSCSI Initiator** field on the **Configure Host Access (Manual) – Specify iSCSI Initiators** screen, highlight the **iSCSI iqn connection string** that has your first physical server's name in it. All the physical servers that you configured the Microsoft iSCSI Initiator for should each have an iqn connection string showing in the known iSCSI initiator field.

      i. Click on the **Add** button to move your selected **iqn connection string** into the **Selected iSCSI Initiators** field. For our project, we will select the iqn connection string that contains our first physical server's name of **FracasHost** in it, as shown in **Figure 7.2**.

      ii. Click on the **Next** button to continue.

## Creating the Initial Host Group on the SAN

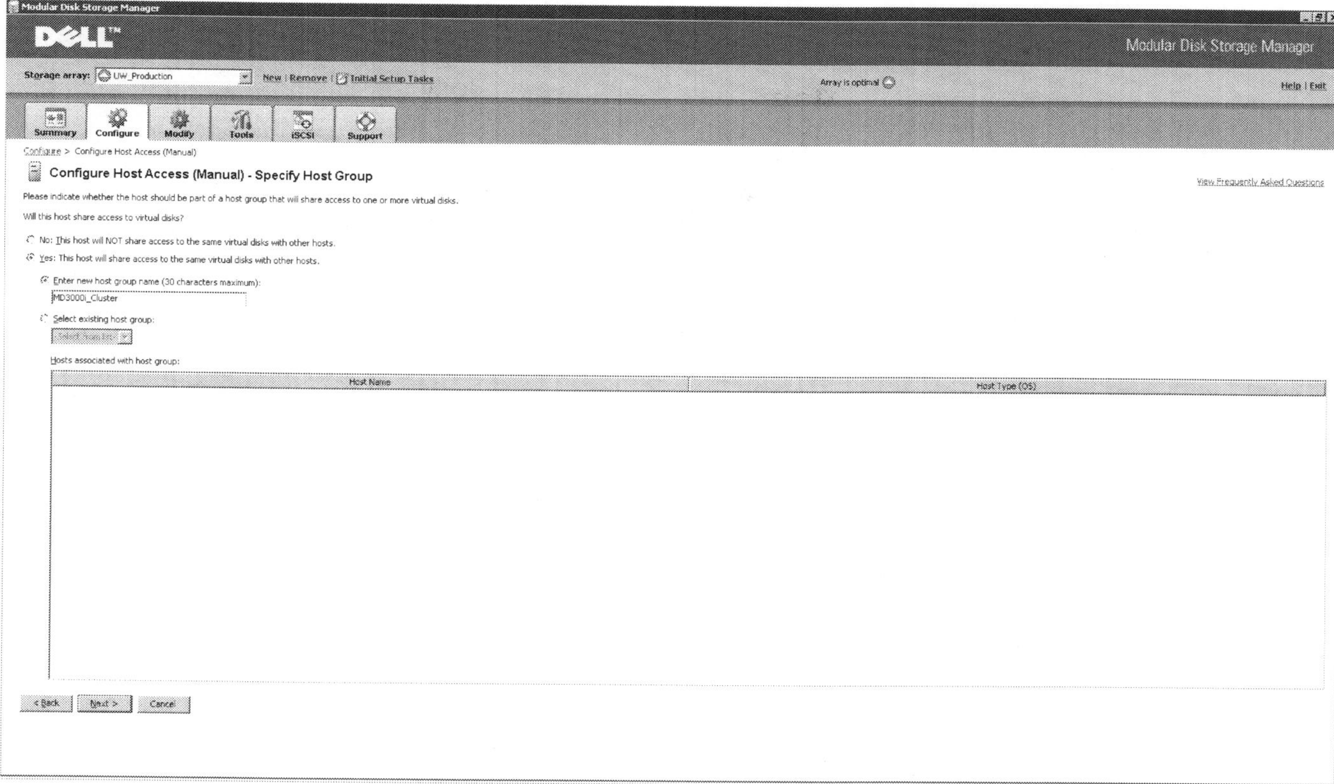


**Figure 7.3**

c. On the **Configure Host Access (Manual) – Specify Host Group** screen, select the **Yes: This host will share access to the same virtual disks with other hosts** option.

   i. For the **Enter host group name** field, enter in the name you'd like your host group to have, and then click on the **Next** button to continue. For our project, we will name our host group **MD3000i-Cluster**.

d. On the **Configure Host Access (Manual) – Confirm Host Definition** screen, click on the **Finish** button.

e. On the **Configure Host Access (Manual) – Complete** screen, click on the **Yes** button for the **Do you want to define another host** question, so that we can continue adding the rest of our servers.

2. Repeat the same basic steps outlined in **Step 1** to add your remaining physical servers, however when you come to the **Configure Host Access (Manual) – Specify Host Group** screen you want to select the **Select existing host group** option instead of the **Enter new host group** option. This will allow you to add your remaining physical servers to the same host group. For our project, we will add our remaining physical servers to our newly created host group named **MD3000i-Cluster**.

## Mapping the Virtual Disks to the Host Group

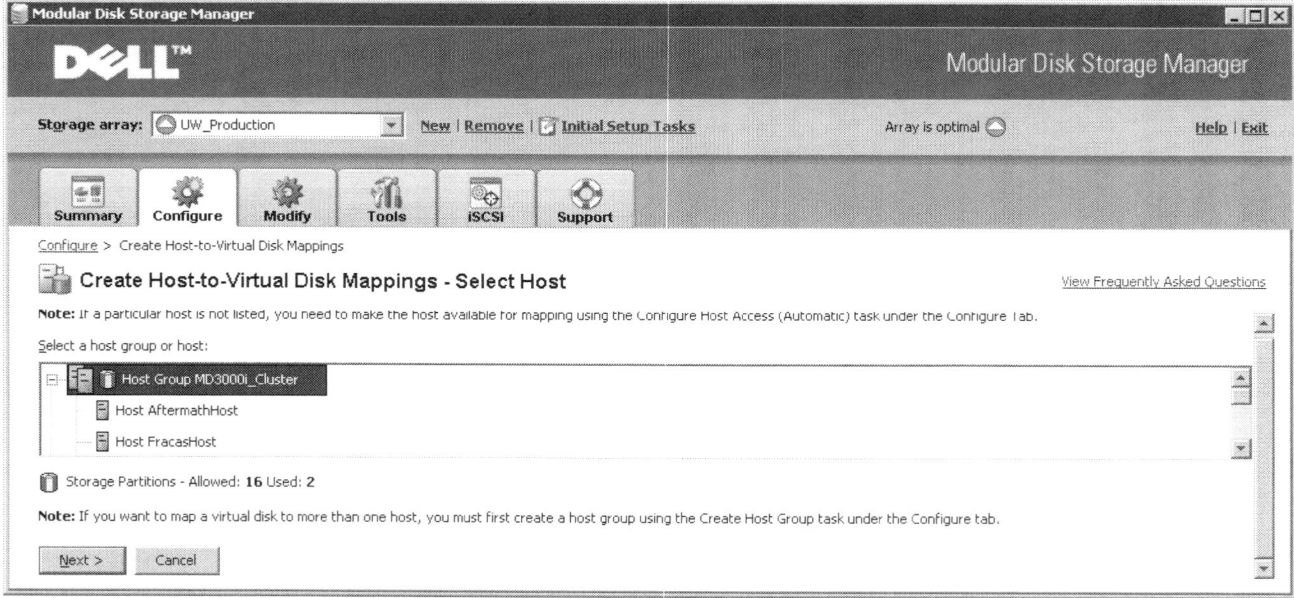


**Figure 7.4**

3. In this section, we will assign our virtual disks to our newly created host group by clicking on the **Configure** tab, and then selecting the **Create Host-to-Virtual Disk Mappings** link.

   a. On the **Create Host-to-Virtual Disk Mappings – Select Host** screen, select your newly created host group from the **Select a group or host** field, and then click on the **Next** button to continue. For our project, we will select the host group named **MD3000i_Cluster**, as shown in **Figure 7.4**.

   b. On the **Create Host-to-Virtual Disk Mappings – Select Virtual Disks** screen, check the **Select all virtual disks** checkbox, and then click on the **Finish** button to continue. If you are using multiple host groups, then make sure to only select the virtual disks that will be part of your first host group.

      i. On the **This operation requires the storage array password** pop-up screen, enter the SAN's password, and then click on the **OK** button to continue.

      ii. On the **Completed** pop-up screen, click on the **OK** button to continue

   c. On the **Create Host-to-Virtual Disk Mappings – Complete** screen, click on the **No** button to exit. For those that are using multiple host groups, select the **Yes** option instead to map your remaining virtual disks to their corresponding host groups.

# Chapter 8: Disk Performance- Configuring Shared Disks and Aligning Partitions

In this chapter, we will bring our shared virtual disks online from within the Windows Server Manager on our initial server. We will cover how shared disks work and appear at different times among the different servers that share them. When bringing our disks online there are crucial configurations that need to be made in order to insure the best possible performance. We will cover how formatting and aligning our disk partitions correctly can give us substantial performance gains of 25-40%. When finished with this chapter, we will have our shared disks online and ready for clustering.

## Overview of Shared Disk Behavior

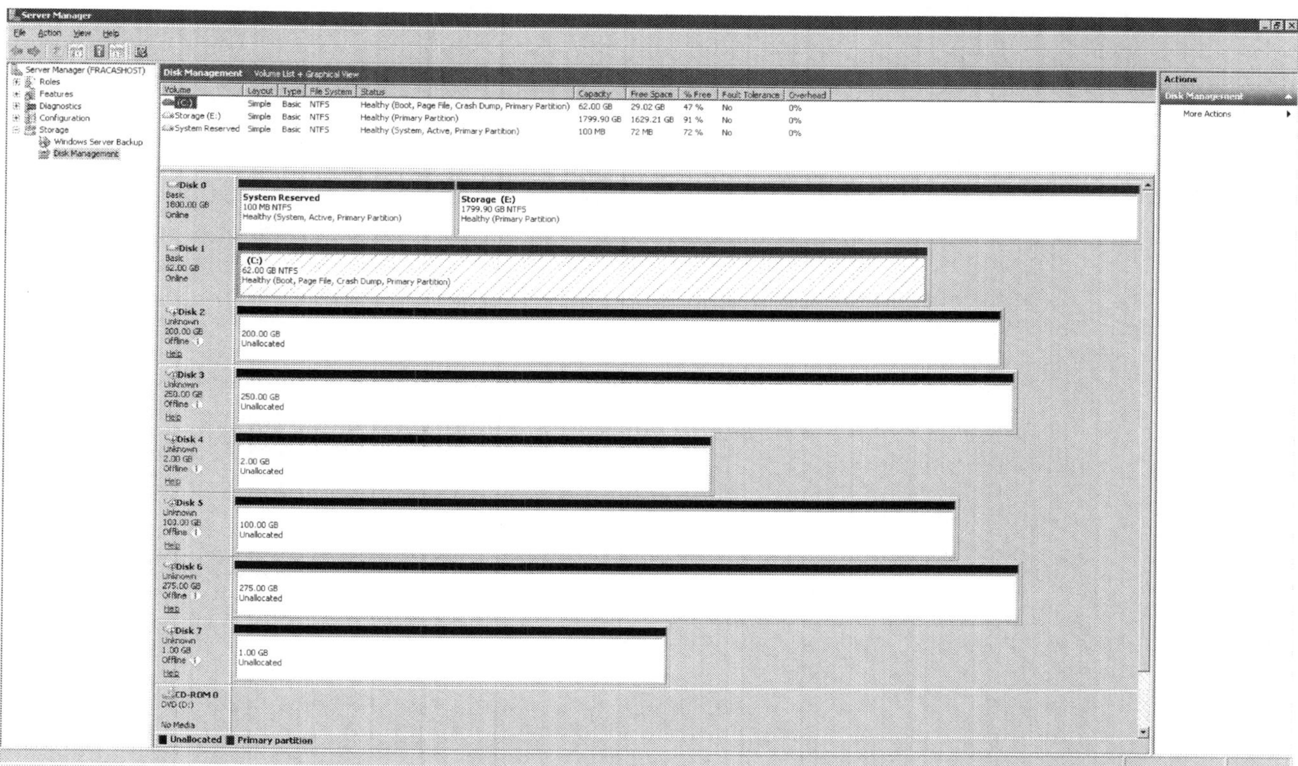


**Figure 8.1**

In this section, we'll cover the basics of how our Windows Server 2008/R2 shared disks look and behave from within the Windows Disk Management console at different times. We will only need to bring our disks online, format and assign drive letters to them from one of our Windows servers that are connected to our shared disks. The number of drives and their size will appear within the Disk Management console of each of our servers, however the drive letters and the status of online will only show on the server that we use initially to format and assign our drive letters with. Each of our other servers should either show the status of reserved with the drive letters appearing or the status of offline without the drive letters appearing. This is due to Windows Server

2008/R2 only allowing one server to be the owner/controller of the shared disk at a time. In general, this is how our Windows 2008/R2 servers will function once clustered as well with the exception of our Cluster Shared Volume (CSV) disk. Our CSV disk will still only be owned/controlled by one server at a time from within the Windows Failover Cluster Manager console, however each of our servers will be able simultaneously access our CSV disk's data. Once we have enabled Cluster Shared Volumes on one of our shared disks its appearance and behavior will differ greatly from within the Windows Disk Management and Windows Explorer consoles then that of a normal cluster disk. The main difference being that our CSV disk's drive letter will no longer appear within the Disk Management console as the disk's path will now be part of our servers' C\: root directory structure. The new path to our CSV disk will be C:\ClusterStorage\Volume1 with a somewhat hidden path whereby you can't browse to it from Windows Explorer unless you manually enter the directory's path in the address field. We will cover more about clustered and CSV clustered disks in **Chapter 9** when we create our first Windows cluster.

## Configuration of the Shared Disks- Initialization

We will start out by bringing our first shared disk online. This disk will eventually become our CSV disk of our first Windows cluster.

1. Go to the server that you want to have initial control of the shared disks. Open **Windows Server Manager** by going to the **Start** button, right clicking on **Computer**, and then selecting the **Manage** option.

    a. Expand the **Storage** node in the left pane, and then select the **Disk Management** node to view your newly attached shared disks. If the disks don't appear right away, then you might have to right click on the **Disk Management** node and select the **Rescan Disks** option a few times before they all show up.

    b. Right click on the **CSV** disk in the gray area where it shows the **Disk** number, and then select the **Online** option. For our project, we want to bring online the **275GB** shared disk that we created for our **CSV** disk.

    c. Repeat this **Step B** to bring to your quorum disk online if you have one. For our project, we have an even number of servers, so we will also bring online our **1GB** shared disk that we created for our **Cluster_Quorum** disk.

    d. The disk(s) that we brought online should now have the **Status** of **Not Initialized**. Right click on one of these disks' gray area where it shows the **Disk** number, and then select the **Initialize Disk** option. For our project, we will select the initialize disk option for our **275GB CSV** shared disk.

        i. On the **Initialize Disk** screen, it's important that unselect all the disk checkboxes, except for your CSV and cluster quorum disks. Once your selection is complete, click on the **OK** button to continue. For our project, we will unselect all other disks, except for our **275GB CSV** and **1GB Cluster_Quorum** disks. We will bring our remaining disks online later from within our initial SQL virtual machine that we will use to create our SQL cluster with. If you're planning on using your physical host servers vs. virtual machines for your SQL cluster, that is absolutely fine. You can follow the same steps for configuring your physical host servers' SQL disks, as we do when setting up our project's SQL virtual machines in a later **Chapter 11**.

## Configuration of the Shared Disks- Formatting

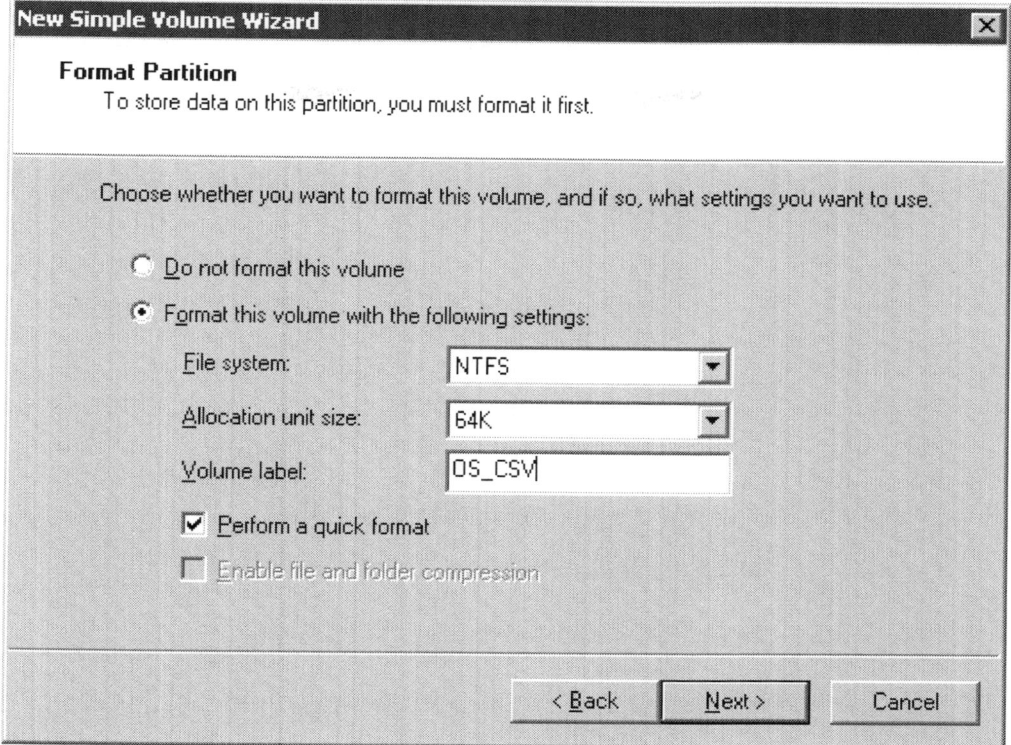


**Figure 8.2**

2. Right click on your first unformatted disk's white area where it says **Unallocated**, and then select the **New Simple Volume** option. For our project, we will select the new simple volume option for our **275GB** disk.

    a. On the **Welcome to the New Simple Volume Wizard** screen, click on the **Next** button to continue.

    b. On the **Specify Volume Size** screen, you can leave the defaults with all available space selected, and then click on the **Next** button to continue.

    c. On the **Assign Drive Letter or Path** screen, we want to assign a drive letter that corresponds to what each disks is. For our project, we will assign drive letter of **O** to our **275GB** disk as this disk will eventually host the operating systems of our CSV virtual machines.

    d. On the **Format Partition** screen, there is a very important change from the defaults that we want to make to increase our performance.

        i. For the **Allocation unit size** field, select the **64K** option from the dropdown.

        **HOT TIP:** Formatting the drives with an allocation unit size of 64K plays a significant role in increasing I/O performance of your disks. We will cover in subsequent steps of this chapter, how to use this 64K allocation unit size to align our partitions for a performance boost of 25-40%.

**NOTE:** If you've already created your partitions, then you will want to check their allocation unit size as outlined in **Step 4** of this chapter.

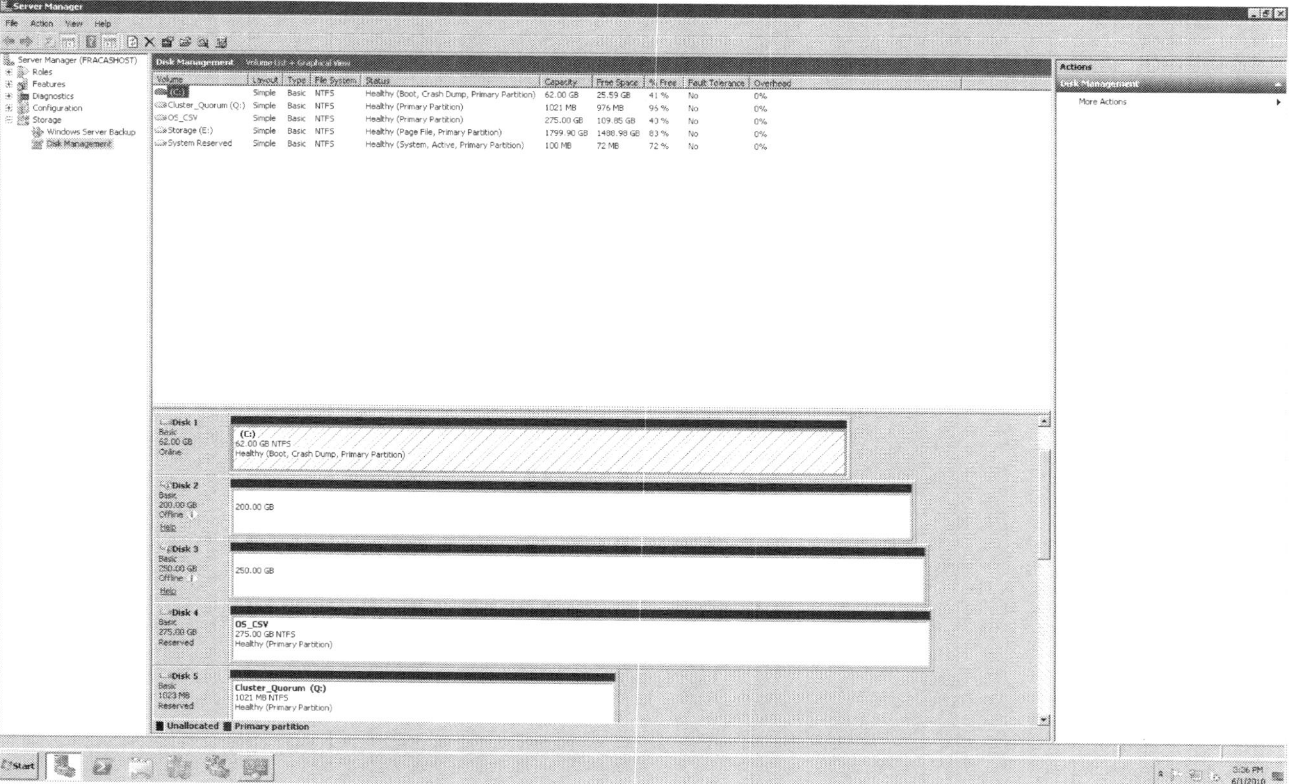


**Figure 8.3**

ii. For the **Volume label** field, give your drive a name that corresponds to what the disk is, and then click on the **Next** button to continue. For our project, we will enter the name of **OS_CSV** for the volume label field, as shown in **Figure 8.2**.

e. On the **Completing the New Simple Volume Wizard** screen, click on the **Finish** button to complete the wizard.

3. Repeat **Step 2** to format your **Quorum** disk if you have one. For our project, we repeat **Step 2** to bring online our **1GB** shared disk for our **Cluster_Quorum**. As we continue to label each of our remaining shared disks we will use the same naming convention as we did when initially creating the virtual disks on our SAN. For example, we will use the name of **OS_CSV** for our **275GB CSV** disk, the name of **Cluster_Quorum** for our **1GB Cluster_Quorum** and so on, as shown in **Figure 8.3**.

## Viewing the Allocation Unit Size of a Previously Formatted Disk

```
Administrator: Command Prompt

C:\Windows\System32>fsutil fsinfo ntfsinfo x:
NTFS Volume Serial Number :       0xd69a5ea09a5e7cc5
Version :                         3.1
Number Sectors :                  0x000000001f3fe7ff
Total Clusters :                  0x000000000003e7fcf
Free Clusters  :                  0x000000000003e7a68
Total Reserved :                  0x0000000000000000
Bytes Per Sector  :               512
Bytes Per Cluster :               65536
Bytes Per FileRecord Segment    : 1024
Clusters Per FileRecord Segment : 0
Mft Valid Data Length :           0x0000000000010000
Mft Start Lcn  :                  0x000000000000c000
Mft2 Start Lcn :                  0x0000000000000001
Mft Zone Start :                  0x000000000000c000
Mft Zone End   :                  0x000000000000cca0
RM Identifier:        CD07A92E-216F-11DF-B3D1-0026B93679E8

C:\Windows\System32>_
```

**Figure 8.4**

If you are planning on using any previously formatted disks for your cluster then you will want to perform the following steps to verify that you have an optimal 64K allocation unit size. If you have freshly formatted your disks as in our project, then please disregard this step.

4. Open the **Command Prompt** on the server that currently controls the shared disk(s).

   a. Type in the command **cd C:\Windows\System32**, and then hit the **Enter** key to change directories.

   b. Type in the command **fsutil fsinfo ntfsinfo <input drive letter here>:**, and then hit the **Enter** key. In **Figure 8.4** for example, the **fsutil fsinfo ntfsinfo x:** command was executed to view drive **X's** allocation unit size. If the **Bytes Per Cluster** field shows a value of **65536** then your allocation unit size is already set to an optimum **64K**. If you receive any other value you should consider reformatting the disk(s) as outlined in **Step 2** of this chapter to take advantage of the better performance a larger allocation unit size offers.

## Configuration of the Shared Disks- Partition Alignment

```
Administrator: Command Prompt
Microsoft Windows [Version 6.1.7600]
Copyright (c) 2009 Microsoft Corporation.  All rights reserved.

C:\Users\administrator.OFFICE>cd..

C:\Users>cd..

C:\>wmic partition get BlockSize, StartingOffset, Name, Index
BlockSize  Index  Name                   StartingOffset
512        0      Disk #6, Partition #0  1048576
512        0      Disk #3, Partition #0  1048576
512        0      Disk #5, Partition #0  65536
512        0      Disk #9, Partition #0  1048576
512        0      Disk #2, Partition #0  1048576
512        0      Disk #4, Partition #0  1048576
512        0      Disk #7, Partition #0  65536
512        0      Disk #8, Partition #0  65536
512        0      Disk #0, Partition #0  1048576
512        1      Disk #0, Partition #1  105906176
512        0      Disk #1, Partition #0  1048576


C:\>_
```

**Figure 8.5**

In this section, we want to confirm that each of our newly created partitions have their 64K allocation unit size aligned optimally with our disk's stripe size. This is known as Partition Alignment/Sector Alignment. When partition alignment is optimally configured it can increase disk performance by 25-40%.

5. To verify your partition alignment, open the **Command Prompt** on the server that you used to format the drives.

    a. Type the **cd..** command, and then hit the **Enter** key. Execute this command again, until you're at the root with only the **C:\>** prompt showing, as shown in **Figure 8.5**.

    b. Type in the command **wmic partition get BlockSize, StartingOffset, Name, Index**, and then hit the **Enter** key.

# Calculating Partition Alignment

c. We will need to run a couple calculations to verify that the partition alignment is optimal. The below is the formula for our calculations.

   i. The result of the following to calculations needs to be an **Integer** value (a whole number, without a decimal point) for your partition to be aligned correctly.

      1. **Partition_Offset ÷ Stripe_Unit_Size** = (**Integer**)

      2. **Stripe_Unit_Size ÷ Allocation_Unit_Size** = (**Integer**)

   ii. In **Figure 8.5**, the first disk listed is **Disk #6** with the **StartingOffset (Partition_Offset)** of **1048576 bytes**, which we need to divide by our **Stripe Size (Stripe_Unit_Size)** of **128K (131072 bytes)**. This makes our first calculation **1048576 ÷ 131072** which results in **8**, and is an **Integer**. Remember, the stripe size we selected when creating our virtual disks on the SAN.

   iii. For the second calculation, we take the **Stripe Size (Stripe_Unit_Size)** of **128K (131072 bytes)** divided by our **Allocation Unit Size** of **64K (65536 bytes)**. Making our calculation **131072 ÷ 65536** which results in **2**, and is an **Integer**. The results of these calculations tell us that Disk #6's partition is correctly aligned.

   **NOTE:** Sometimes the very small partitions like the quorum disks won't meet this partition alignment standard. If this happens on one of the very small and less I/O intense disks like the quorum disks, then don't worry as it's such a small amount of data that it won't make any noticeable performance difference. You can try recreating the disk to resolve the issue. If this happens for one of the I/O intense disks like the CSV, SQL or Exchange disks, then you'll definitely want to resolve the issue before continuing.

   iv. Repeat the calculations in **Step i** for each of your shared disks listed in the command prompt screen to verify that all your disks' partitions are aligned.

# Chapter 9: Creating a Windows Cluster with the Cluster Shared Volumes (CSV) Feature

In this chapter, we will create our first Windows cluster that will host our Cluster Shared Volumes (CSV) disk. A Windows cluster with Cluster Shared Volumes enabled can use Windows Server 2008 R2's new feature of live migration to move and failover virtual machines between physical servers. We will begin by installing and configuring the prerequisites necessary for our servers to be clustered. We will then create, validate, name and assign an IP address to our Windows cluster. Once we have our cluster created, we will cover how to add our shared disks to the cluster. We will utilize one of these disks for our CSV and the other for our quorum. After our disks have been added, we will enable the Cluster Shared Volumes feature on our cluster, and then place our CSV disk within the Cluster Shared Volume. The final step will be to configure our remaining disk as the cluster's quorum. Once we have this initial Windows cluster setup, we will have our first highly available cluster of our topology in place. Our project's finished CSV cluster will consist of four physical servers and a quorum disk. With this configuration, our cluster's resources will remain fully online even if two of our physical servers fail simultaneously.

## Installing the Prerequisites for Windows Clustering and Hyper-V Virtualization

1. On each of our physical servers to be clustered we want to add the following Windows **Features** and **Roles** from within **Windows Server Manager**.
    a. **Failover Clustering** (Feature) (no reboot required)
    b. **Hyper-V** (Role) (reboot required)
2. While the server is rebooting to finish the install of the **Hyper-V** role, we want to enable the CPU **Virtualization Technology (VT)** option from within the **BIOS** of each physical server if you haven't already done so. For our project, we are using **Dell PowerEdge R710** servers, so the following instructions should apply to most of the newer Dell servers. If you have a different brand server, then you'll want to verify that the virtualization technology for the CPU is enabled.
    a. When the server begins to boot up, hit the **F2** key to enter the **BIOS**.
        i. Once in the **BIOS**, select the **Processor Settings** option, and then hit the **Enter** key.
        ii. Select the **Virtualization Technology** option, and then hit the **Space Bar** key to enable it.
        iii. Hit the **Esc** key twice to exit.
        iv. Select the **Save Changes and Exit** option, and then hit the **Enter** key to exit the BIOS.
    b. The server will now reboot with the **VT** option enabled.
    c. Once the server is booted up, login and the Hyper-V installation will complete its final steps.

## Creating the Windows Failover Cluster that will Host the CSV Virtual Machines

3. On one of your physical servers, browse to the **Start button\Administrative Tools\Failover Cluster Manager**.

    a. Right click on the **Failover Cluster Manager** in the upper left hand pane, and select the **Create a Cluster** option.

    b. On the **Before You Begin** screen, click on the **Next** button to continue.

    c. On the **Select Servers** screen, enter each of your physical server names, and then click on the **Next** button to continue. For our project, we will enter our four physical server names of **FracasHost**, **AftermathHost**, **PetulanceHost** and **TurmoilHost**.

## Running the Validate a Cluster Wizard

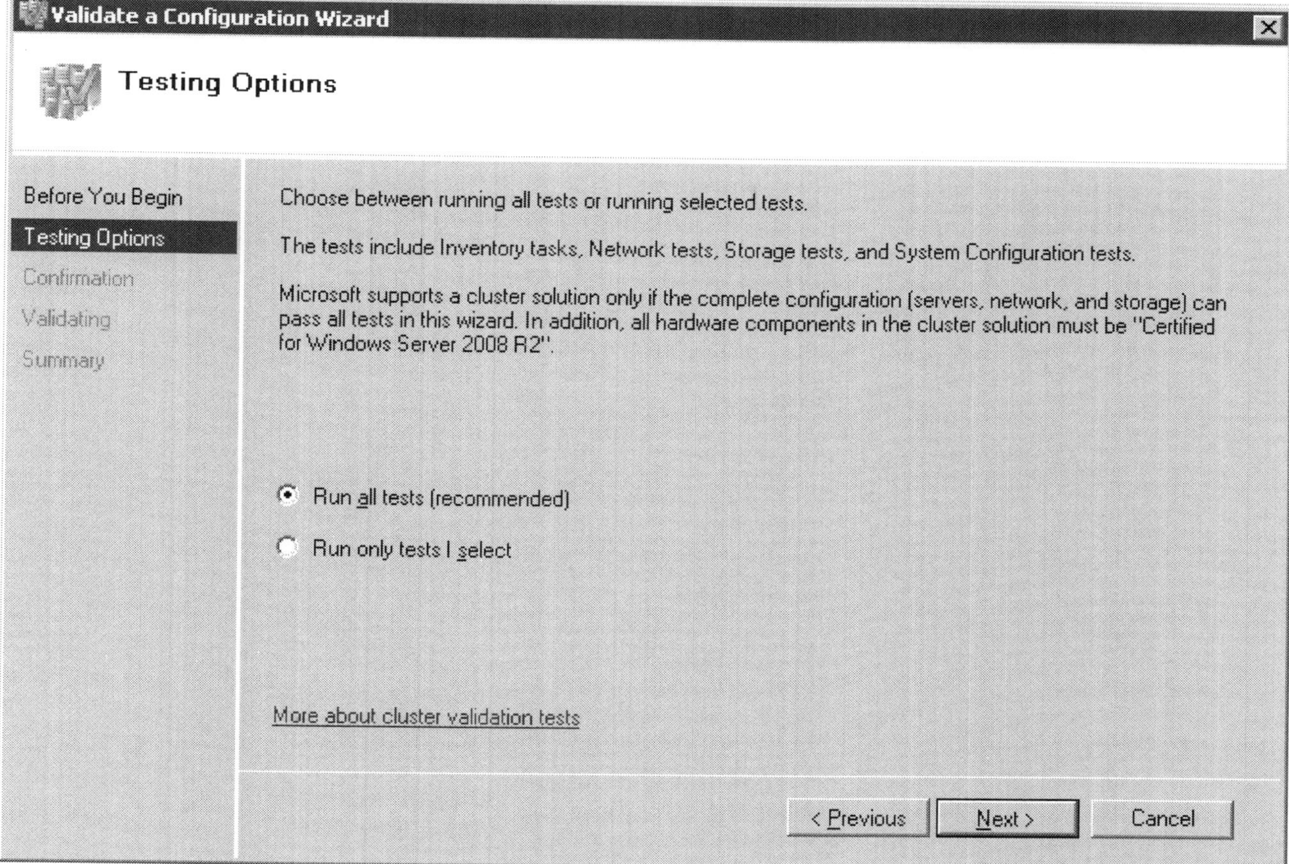


**Figure 9.1**

d. On the **Validate a Configuration Wizard** screen, select the **Run all test (recommend)** option, and then click on the **Next** button to continue. This will verify that the servers are setup correctly for Windows clustering. There are two ways to go about validating your cluster. You can choose to just create the cluster as we are here or you can choose to pre-validate the cluster. If you would like to pre-validate a cluster, then you can use the **Validate a Configuration** option located in the center pane of the **Failover Cluster Management's** console in the **Management** field.

e. Once the validation completes, click on the **View Report** button, and then resolve any issues that are reported.

   **NOTE:** Unfortunately, the configuration validation report may contain warnings that don't truly apply. Do your best at resolving the issues, however if some of the warnings appear to be frivolous then don't let this stop you from continuing with creating your cluster.

f. On the **Validate a Configuration Wizard** screen, click on the **Finish** button to exit and return to the **Create Cluster Wizard** screen.

## Assigning the Cluster Name and IP Address

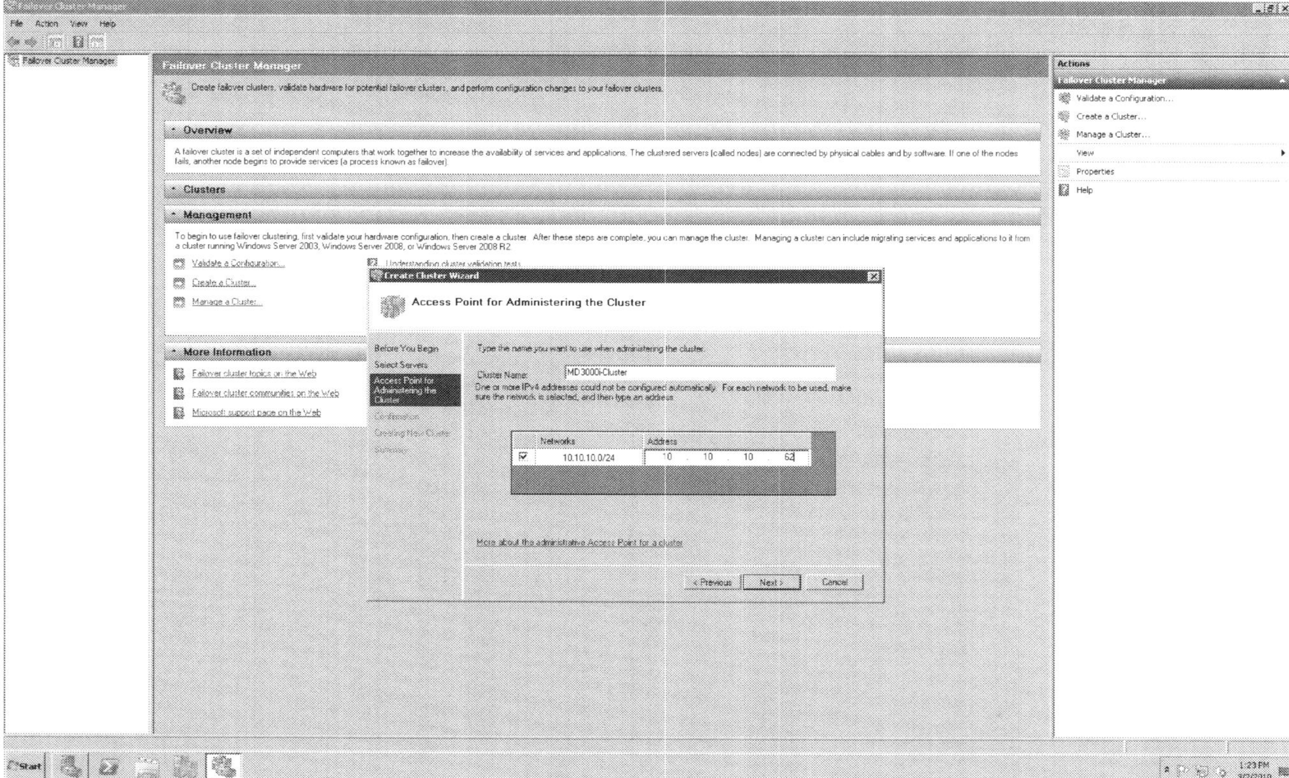

**Figure 9.2**

g. On the **Access Point for Administering the Cluster** screen, enter your cluster name in the **Cluster Name** field. For our project, we will name our cluster **MD3000i-Cluster**.

   i. For the **Networks** field, you want to only have your **Active Directory** client subnet selected. If any other networks are listed here you'll want to unselect their checkboxes. For our project, we will select the **10.10.10.0/24** network which is our Active Directory client subnet.

   ii. For the **Address** field, enter the IP address you want for your Windows cluster, and then click on the **Next** button continue. For our project, we will assign the IP address of **10.10.10.62**, as shown in **Figure 9.2**.

h. On the **Confirmation** screen, click on the **Next** button to create the cluster.

i. On the **Summary** screen, click on the **View Report** button, and then take a quick look at the report to make sure everything looks ok.

j. You can save a copy of the report if you want to have a general summary of the cluster's setup, and then close the Internet Explorer window to return to the **Summary** screen.

k. On the **Summary** screen, click on the **Finish** button to exit the wizard.

## Adding Shared Disks to the Cluster

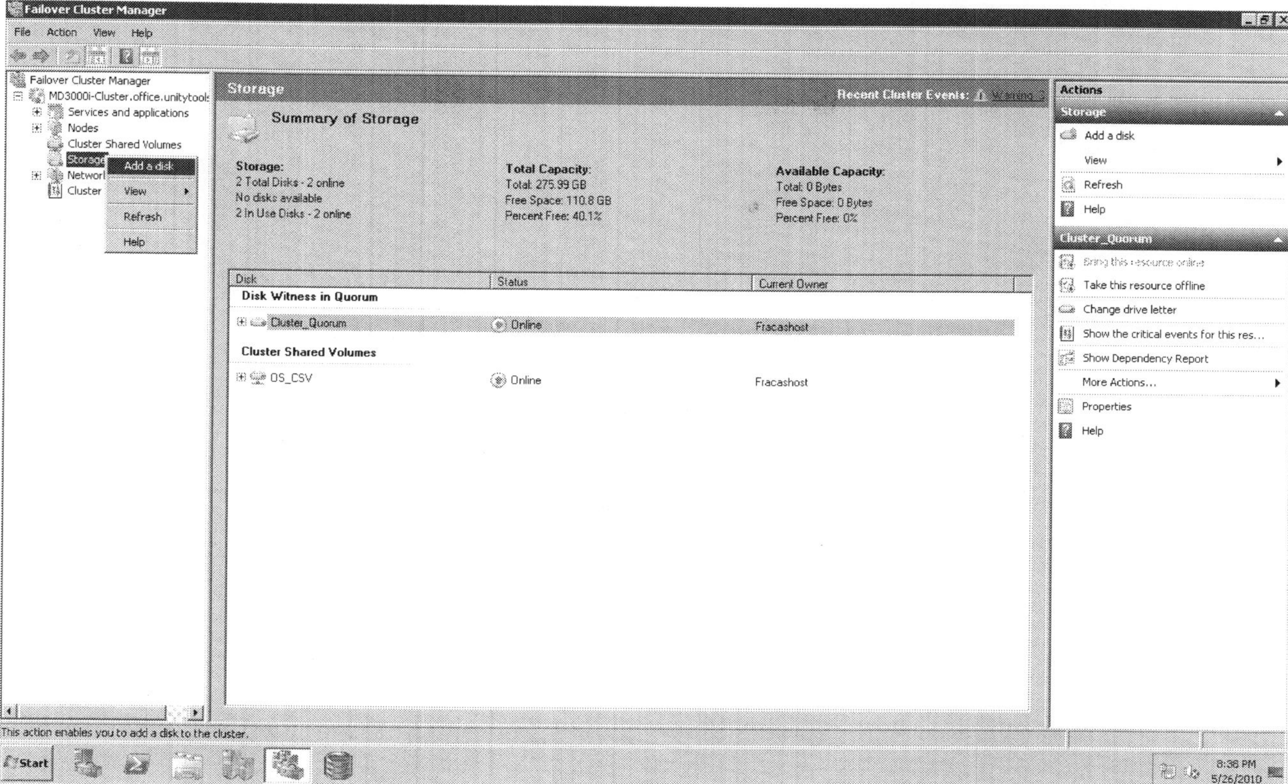


**Figure 9.3**

We will now add the shared disks for our CSV and quorum to the cluster. We will then enable the Cluster Shared Volumes (CSV) feature for the cluster and place our shared disk within the CSV. Ultimately, the CSV disk will host our front-end CRM application virtual machines.

4. In **Failover Cluster Manager**, right click the **Storage** node under your cluster's name in the left pane, and then select the **Add a Disk** option, as shown in **Figure 9.3**.

   a. On the **Add Disks to a Cluster** screen, unselect all disks except for your CSV and quorum disks, and then click on the **OK** button to continue. For our project, we will unselect all disks except for our **275GB OS_CSV** and **1GB Cluster_Quorum** disks.

## Renaming Cluster Disks

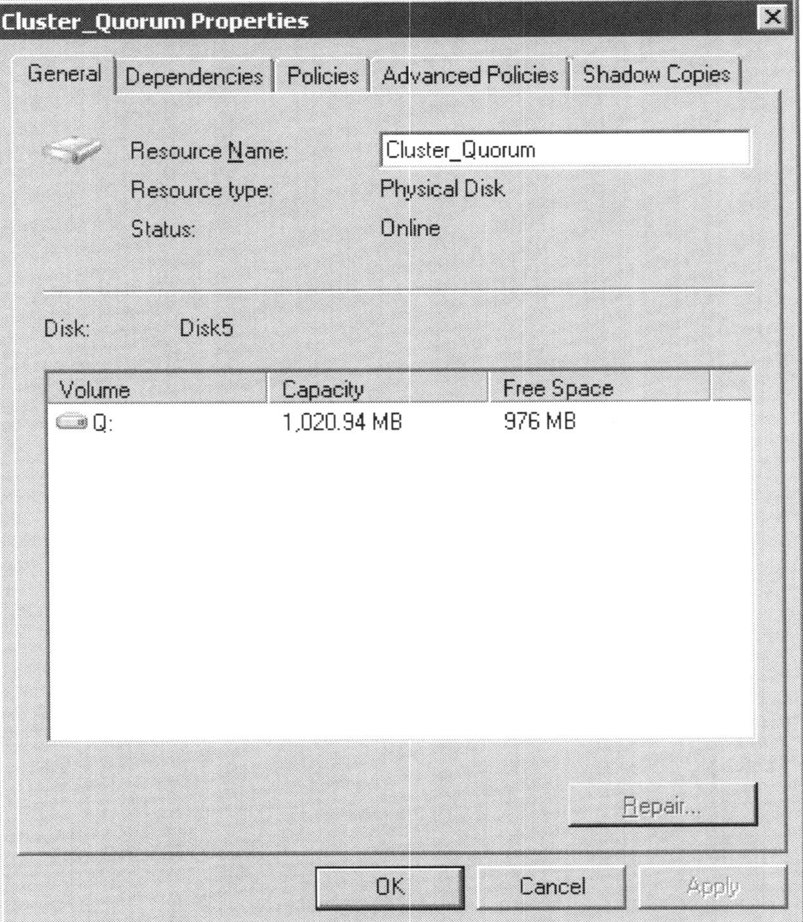


**Figure 9.4**

b. Once your disks are added, highlight on the **Storage** node in the left pane of the **Failover Cluster Manager**.

   i. In the center pane, right click on each of your newly added disk, and then select **Properties** option.

   ii. On the **General** tab, change the name of the **Resource Name** field for each disk to correspond with what the disk actually is, and then click on the **OK** button to save the changes. For our project, we will rename our **275GB** disk to **OS_CSV** and our **1GB** disk to **Cluster_Quorum**, as shown in **Figure 9.4**.

# Enabling the Cluster Shared Volumes (CSV)

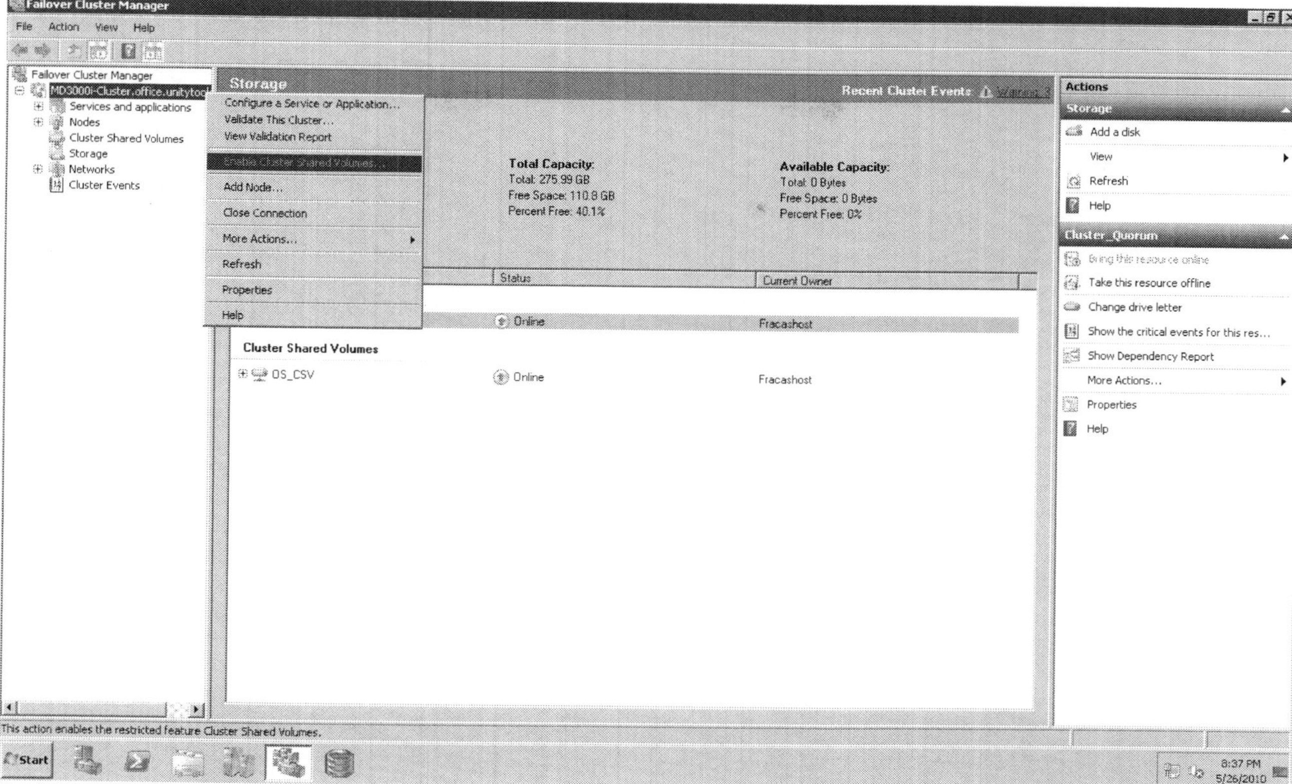


**Figure 9.5**

5. Right click on your clusters name in the left pane, and then select the **Enable Cluster Shared Volumes** option as shown in **Figure 9.5**.

   a. On the pop-up screen, check the **I have read the notice above** checkbox, and then click on the **OK** button to continue. A new node named **Cluster Shared Volumes** will appear in the left navigation pane.

# Adding Disks to the Cluster Shared Volumes (CSV)

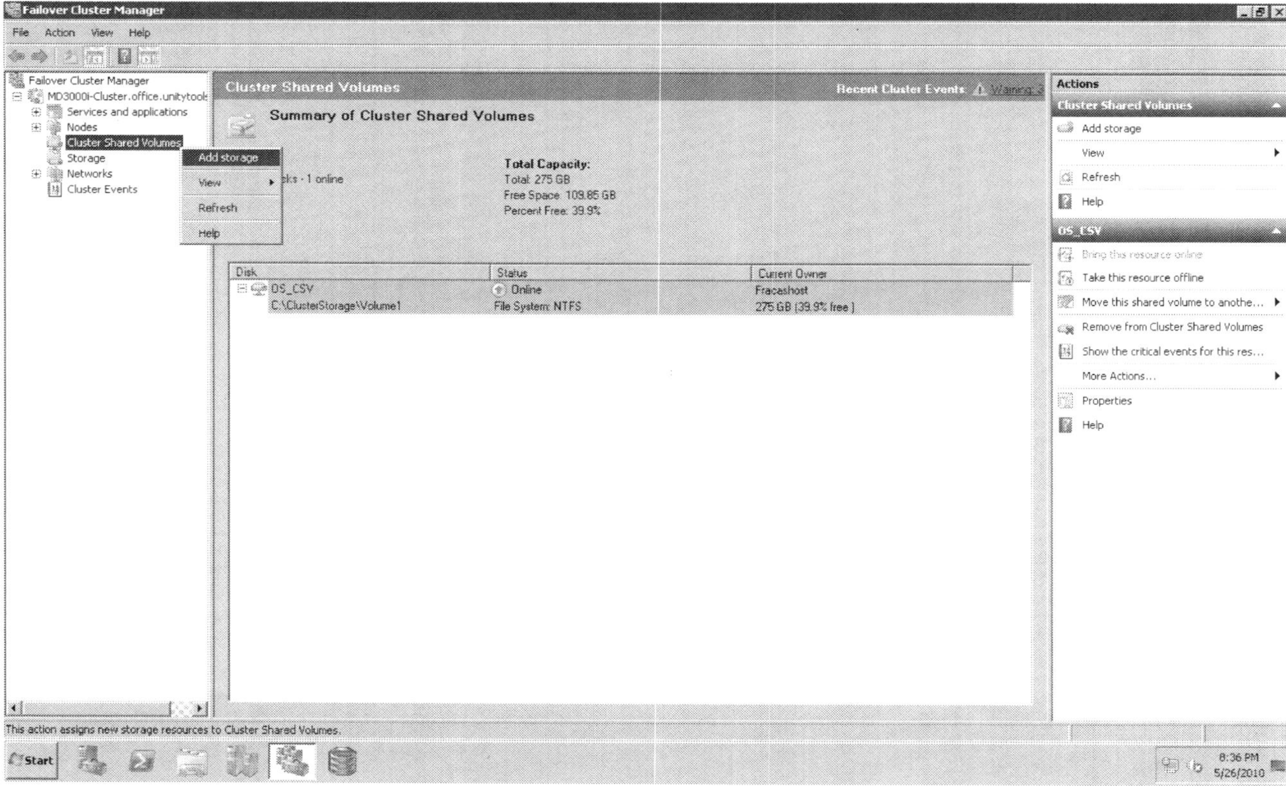


**Figure 9.5**

6. Right click on the **Cluster Shared Volumes** node in the left pane, and then select the **Add Storage** option.

   a. On the **Add Storage** screen, select your disk for the CSV, and then click on the **OK** button to continue. For our project, we will add our **275GB** disk that we named to **OS_CSV**, as shown in **Figure 9.5**.

## Configuring a Quorum Disk for the Cluster

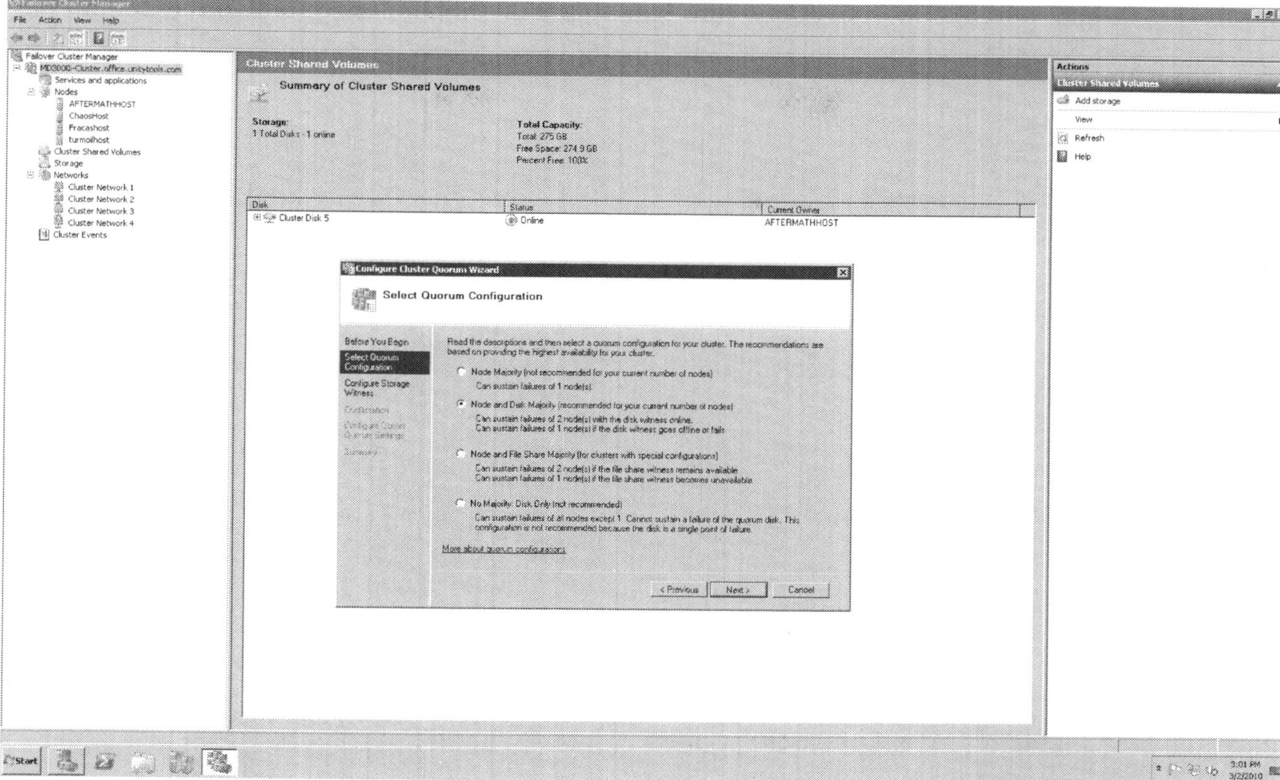


**Figure 9.6**

7. Right click on your cluster's name in the left pane, and then select the **More Actions\Configure Cluster Quorum Settings** option.

   a. On the **Before You Begin** screen of the **Configure Cluster Quorum Wizard**, click on the **Next** button to continue.

   b. On the **Select Quorum Configuration** screen, select the quorum configuration that has the **(recommended for your current number of nodes)** recommendation next to it, and then click on the **Next** button to continue. For our project, we will select the **Node and Disk Majority** option as shown in **Figure 9.6**. In this quorum configuration our cluster resources will remain online even with the failure of two cluster nodes.

      **NOTE:** You should always have an odd number of voting entities in the cluster when everything is fully online. This insures that there will always be a majority vote. If you have an even number of cluster nodes, than you will want to use a quorum disk as an additional voter to give you the odd number of voters required.

   c. On the **Configure Storage Witness** screen, select your quorum disk (if using one), and then click on the **Next** button to continue. For our project, we will select our **1GB** disk that we named **Cluster_Quorum**.

d. On the **Confirmation** screen, click on the **Next** button to continue.

e. On the **Summary** screen, click on the **Finish** button to exit the wizard.

# Chapter 10: Creating the Hyper-V Virtual Networks and Configuring Network Settings

In this chapter, we will begin building our virtual foundation for our CSV and SQL virtual machines. We will start by creating our Hyper-V virtual networks for our four networks to support our iSCSI topology. We will then cover the importance of using a naming convention for our Hyper-V virtual networks in a clustered environment. Next, we will connect our physical network adapters to our new Hyper-V virtual networks and verify their connections. Once we have our virtual networks in place, we'll configure our network adapter binding orders and metric settings. We'll finish off things by configuring our power settings on our network adapters. Once we've completed this chapter, we'll have our virtual network infrastructure optimally configured to support our iSCSI network topology.

## Creating the Hyper-V Virtual Networks

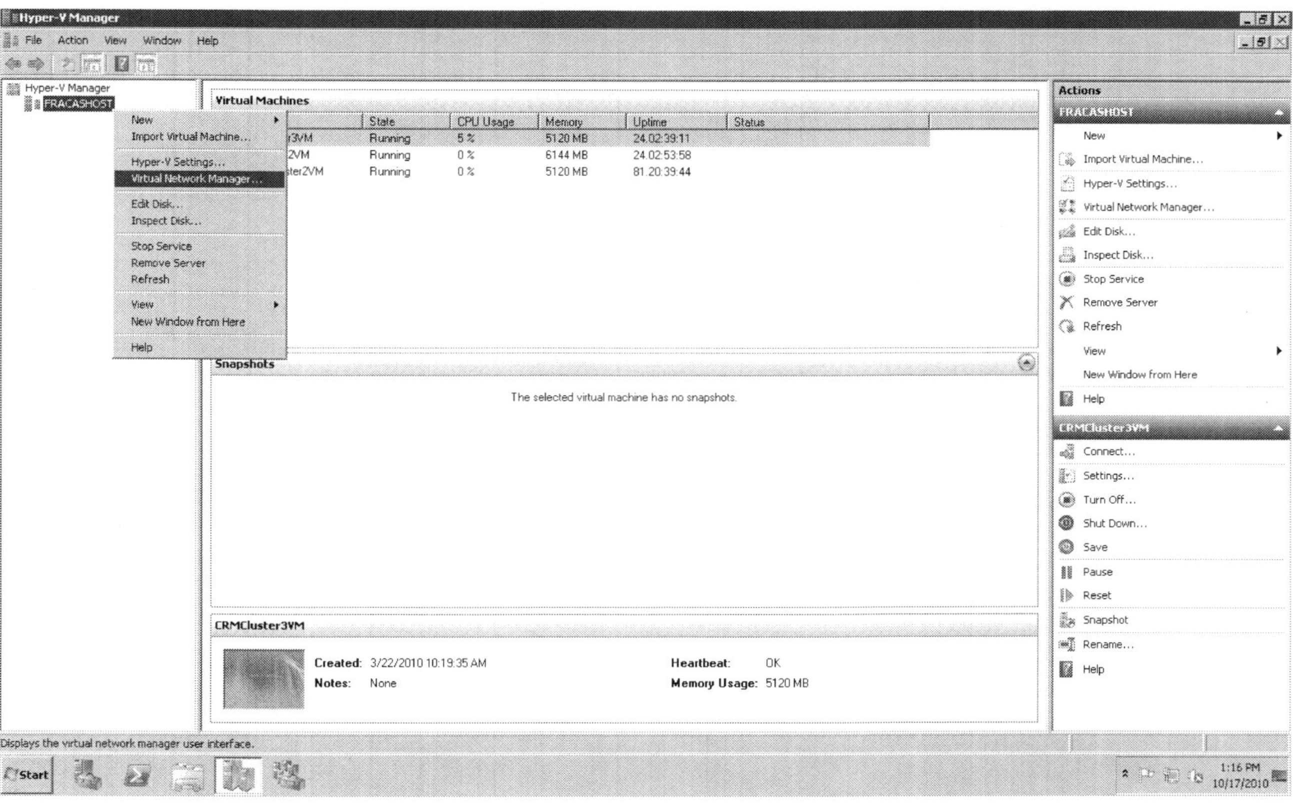

**Figure 10.1**

In this section, we will setup our Hyper-V virtual networks for each of our four network connections. In our project, we are using one network connection for our client Active Directory, one for our heartbeat, and two for our redundant iSCSI connections. We will name our new Hyper-V virtual networks the same on each physical host with a naming convention as we did earlier when setting up our network adapters on each server. When the virtual machines move between physical hosts during the failover process they will attempt to connect to the same virtual network names on the new host. This makes using a naming convention absolutely critical, as our virtual machines will fail to move to the new host during the failover process if the host's virtual networks are named differently than other hosts within the cluster. You will also encounter problems during the Windows cluster validation process. The validation report will have multiple errors listed in it if the virtual networks on each Hyper-V server are not named the same. We will begin by creating a Hyper-V virtual network for each of our physical servers' network adapters.

1. You will need to connect to each of your physical servers and create the following virtual networks. On each of your servers, go to the **Start button\Administrative Tools**, and then select the **Hyper-V Manager** option.

    a. In **Hyper-V Manager**, right click on your server's name in the left pane, and then select the **Virtual Network Manager** option, as shown in **Figure 10.1**.

        i. Highlight the **New Virtual Network** option in the left pane, and then select the **External** option for the **What type of virtual network do you want to create** field.

        ii. Click on the **Add** button to continue.

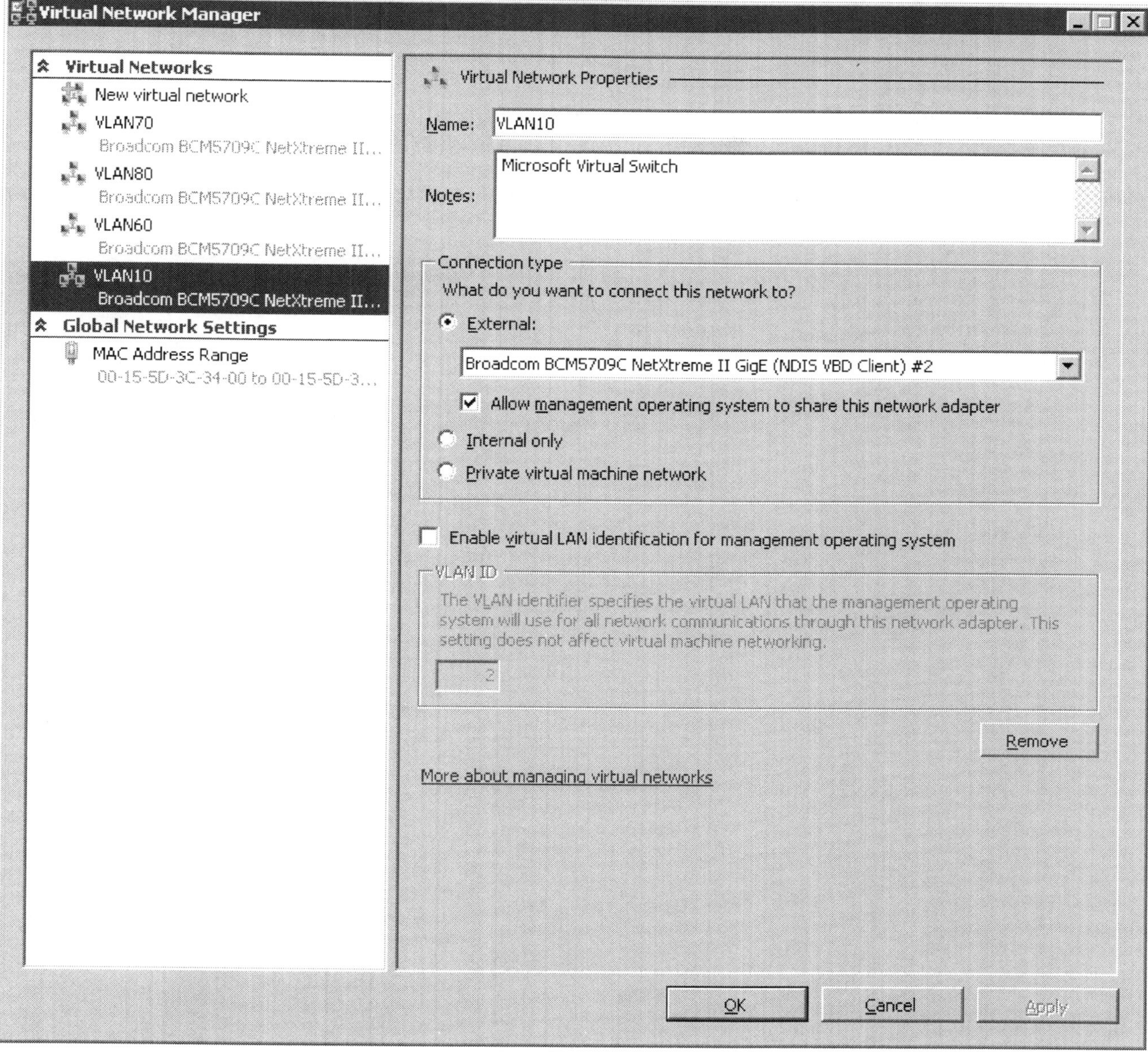


**Figure 10.2**

b. On the **New Virtual Network** screen, enter in the name for your **Client Active Directory** virtual network in the **Name** field. For our project, we will assign our **Client Active Directory** virtual network a name of **VLAN10**, as shown in **Figure 10.2**.

   i. In the **Connection type** section, select the physical network adapter that corresponds to the new virtual network from the **External** dropdown field.

   ii. Click on the **OK** button to continue.

## Verifying the Virtual Network's Connection to their Network Adapter

c. For the **Connection type** dropdown box you'll want to pay close attention to which physical network adapter you select for each network. Windows Server 2008/R2 automatically assigns a **Device Name** and # to each of our server's physical network adapters, such as **Broadcom BCM5709C NetXtreme II GigE (NDIS VBD Client) #2**. Unfortunately, this **#2** in the device name doesn't necessarily mean this is the physical network adapter port number 2 on the back of the server. In our project, this is the case with our first server's network adapter as shown in **Figure 10.2**. Our client network that we labeled **VLAN10** is physically connected to our server's network adapter labeled as number **1** on the back of the server, however Windows assigned a device name of **Broadcom BCM5709C NetXtreme II GigE (NDIS VBD Client) #2** to the network adapter. This makes setting up our Hyper-V virtual networks a little more complicated, as we have to determine which device name actually applies to which physical network adapter port of our server.

| Physical Network Adapter Port | Network |
|---|---|
| 1 | Client Active Directory |
| 2 | First iSCSI |
| 3 | Second iSCSI |
| 4 | Heartbeat |

**Figure 10.3**

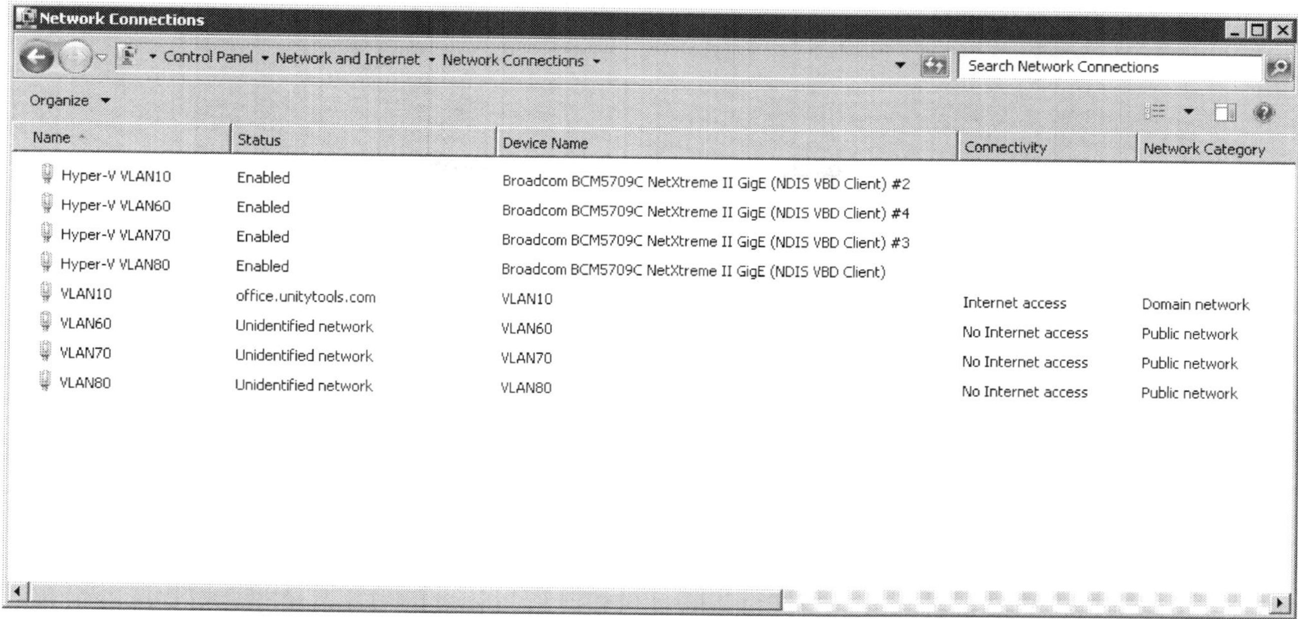


**Figure 10.4**

i. In **Figure 10.3**, we have the order in which all our servers are physically connected, while in **Figure 10.4**, we have the device names that Windows assigned each of our network adapters. As you can see, the physical port numbers and the device name numbers do not line up. This is common on many Windows 2008/R2 servers, so we will have to take this into account when settings up our Hyper-V virtual networks on each server.

## Creating the Remaining Hyper-V Virtual Networks

| Network | Virtual Network Name | Type of Connection | Subnet |
|---|---|---|---|
| Client Active Directory | VLAN10 | External | 10.10.10.0/24 |
| First iSCSI | VLAN60 | External | 10.10.60.0/24 |
| Second iSCSI | VLAN70 | External | 10.10.70.0/24 |
| Heartbeat | VLAN80 | External | 10.10.80.0/24 |

**Figure 10.5**

i. Continue creating all your Hyper-V virtual networks on your first server. For our project, we will create our virtual networks, as outlined in **Figure 10.5**.

## Renaming the New Hyper-V Virtual Networks

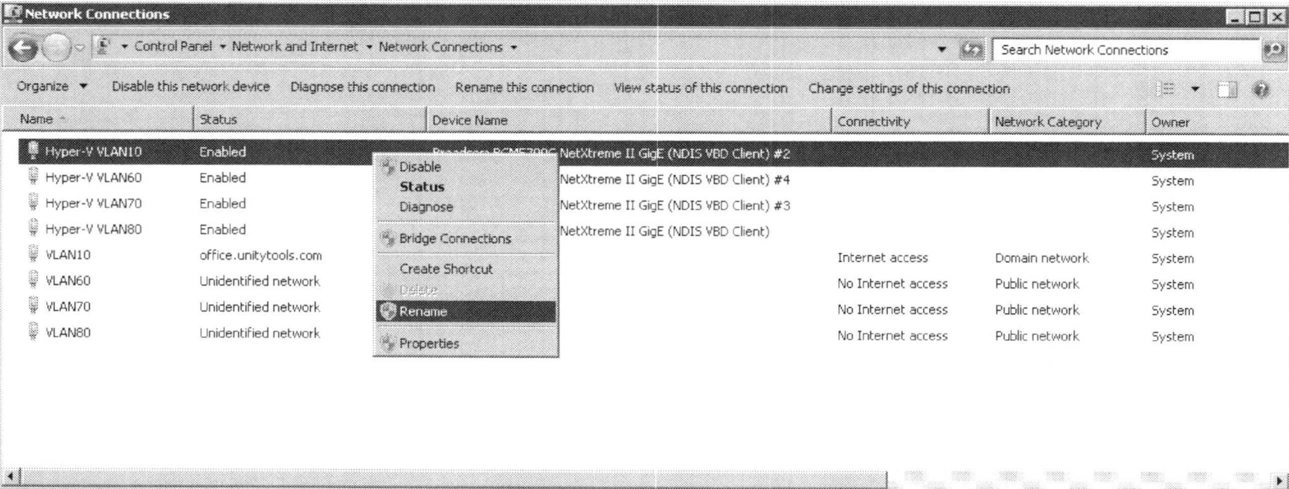

**Figure 10.6**

2. Once we have all our Hyper-V virtual networks created, we want to rename each virtual network from within the Windows **Network Connections** screen. For our project, we will rename our virtual network connections to the name shown in **Figure 10.6**. Again, this may seem trivial, but once you have so many connections it can cause confusion and problems if you don't follow a universal naming convention for all your clustered servers.

## Assigning Network Adapter Binding Orders and Metrics

| Network Connection | Binding Order | Metric Value |
|---|---|---|
| Client AD Network | 1 | 100 - 199 |
| First iSCSI Network | 2 | 200 - 299 |
| Second iSCSI Network | 3 | 200 - 299 |
| Heartbeat Network | 4 | 500 - 599 |
| Client AD Virtual Network | 5 | 7000 – 7999 (Set on VM) |
| First iSCSI Virtual Network | 6 | 8000 – 8999 (Set on VM) |
| Second iSCSI Virtual Network | 7 | 8000 – 9999 (Set on VM) |
| Heartbeat Virtual Network | 8 | 9000 – 9999 (Set on VM) |

**Figure 10.7**

When settings up host servers with multiple physical and virtual networks it is important to configure each server's network adapters with different priorities using binding orders. The binding orders will determine the priority of which network connection is used by the server first, second, third and so on. The settings are especially important for good performance when the servers are part of a Windows cluster and should always be manually set when there are a multitude of connections. We want the physical host servers' network adapters to always take priority over the Hyper-V virtual networks that we create on each server.

Another priority setting that we'll want to configure for each type of connection is called the metric. The metric determines the cost of each network connection. The lower cost connections will always be used first unless unavailable or if they don't route to where the traffic needs to go. Once you are finished with the following few steps you should have your binding orders and metrics configured as outlined in **Figure 10.7**.

## Assigning Network Adapter Binding Orders on the Physical Servers

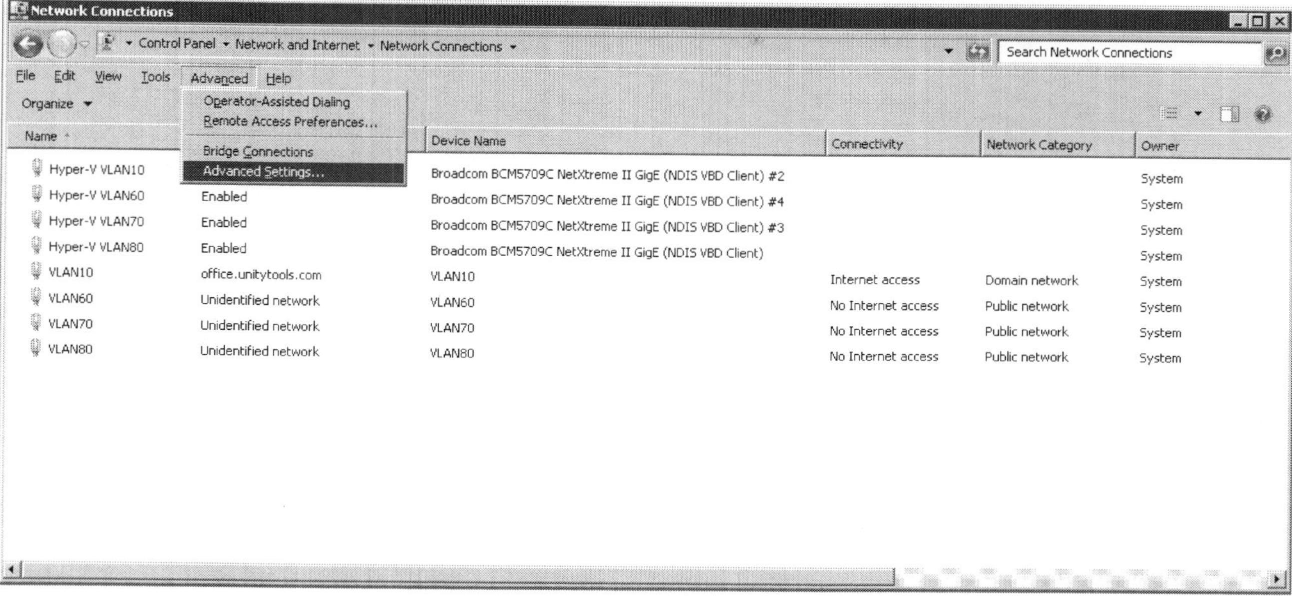


**Figure 10.8**

3. Once we have all our Hyper-V virtual networks created we can adjust our network adapter binding orders for each of our connections. On each on your physical servers, browse to the **Start button\Network properties\Change Adapter Settings** to open the **Network Connections** screen.

    a. In the **Network Connections** screen, hit the key combination of **Alt+N** to bring up the hidden **Advanced** toolbar option, and then select **Advanced Settings** from the dropdown menu, as shown in **Figure 10.8**.

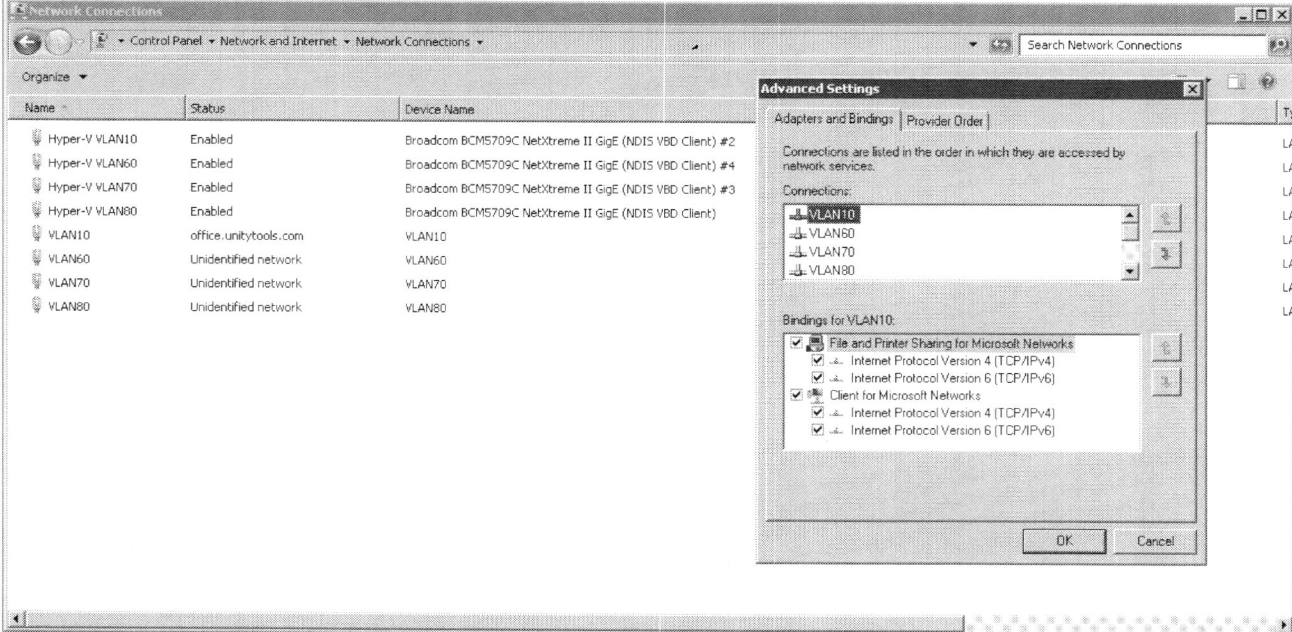


**Figure 10.9**

b. On the **Advanced Settings** screen, with the **Adapters and Bindings** tab selected, use the green up and down arrows to set the priority of your network connections, as shown in **Figure 10.9**. You'll want to make sure that you re-order all your bindings for the physical and virtual connections according to the priority listed in **Figure 10.7**.

c. Click on the **OK** button to save your changes and exit.

## Assigning Network Adapter Metrics on the Physical Servers

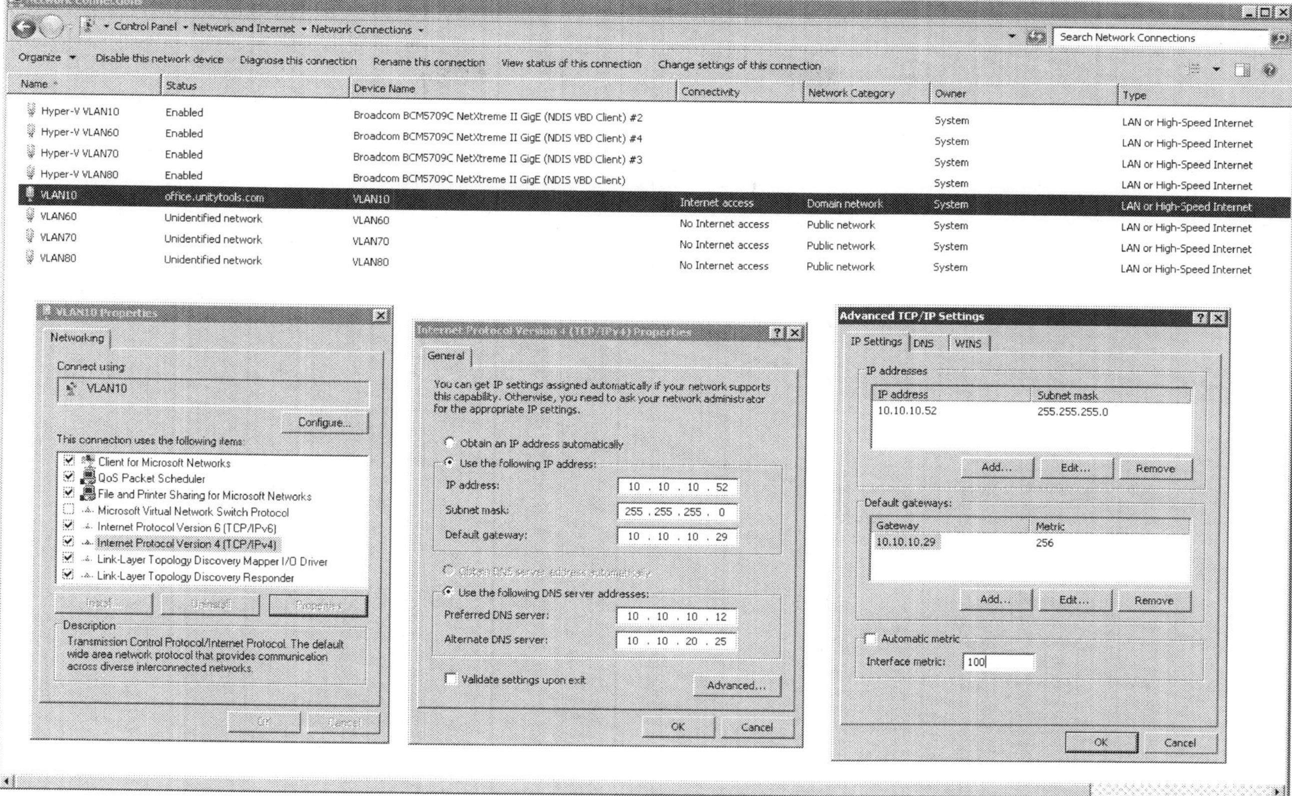


**Figure 10.10**

4. While still in the **Network Connections** screen, right click on each of the physical network adapters, and then select the **Properties** option.

    a. On the **Properties** screen, highlight **Internet Protocol Version 4 (TCP/IPv4)**, and then click on the **Properties** button.

        i. On the **Internet Protocol Version 4 (TCP/IPv4) Properties** screen, click on the **Advanced** button.

            1. While on the **IP Settings** tab, unselect the **Automatic metric** checkbox, and then enter in the value specified for each particular network adapter as outlined in **Figure 10.7**.

               **NOTE:** We will configure the metric values for our virtual network connections from within each virtual machine's network connections.

            2. Click on the **OK** button of each **Property** screen to save your changes and exit.

    b. Repeat **Step 4** for each of your server's physical network adapters.

# Disabling the Network Adapters Power Management

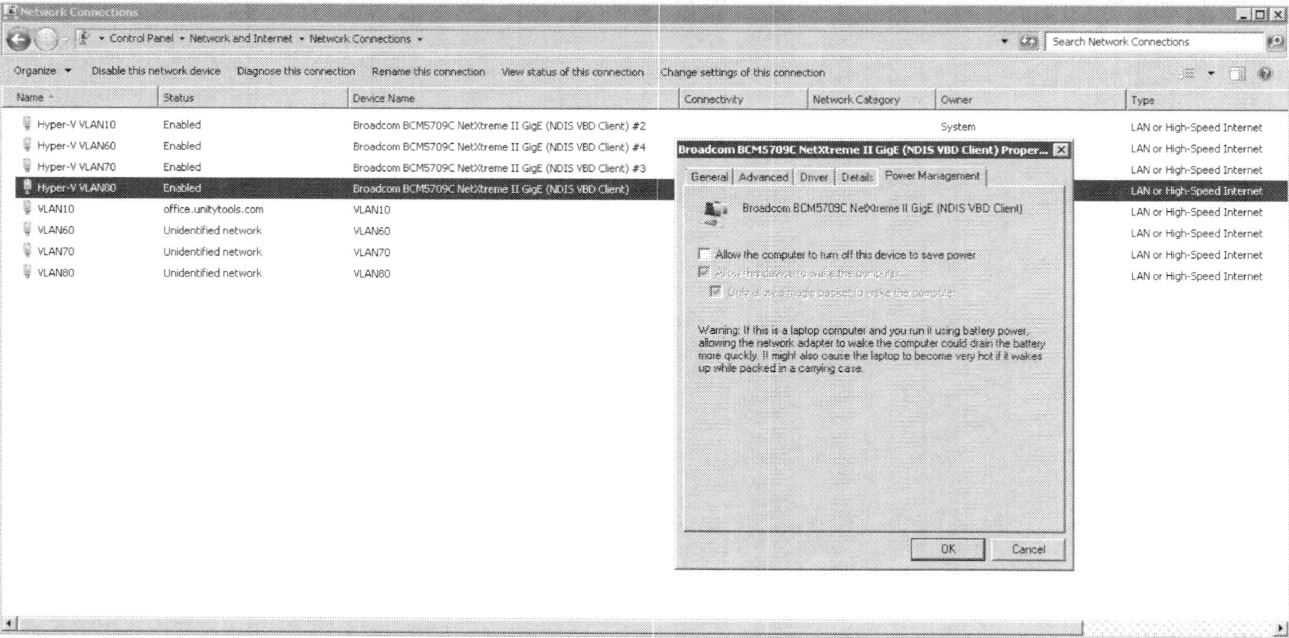

**Figure 10.11**

5. In the **Network Connections** screen, right click on each of the network adapters that we renamed with the **Hyper-V** prefix, and select the **Properties** option.

   a. On the **Properties** screen, click on the **Configure** button.

      i. On the **Device Name Properties** screen, click on the **Power Management** tab, and then unselect the **Allow the computer to turn off this device to save power** checkbox.

         **BEST PRACTICE:** This is a Dell best practice recommendation as outlined in the paper titled "**Dell Networking Solutions Guide for Microsoft Hyper-V**".

      ii. Click on the **OK** button to save your changes and exit.

      iii. Repeat **Step 5** for each of your server's Hyper-V virtual network adapters.

6. Repeat the steps in this chapter for each of your physical servers that will be part of your cluster topology.

# Chapter 11: Preparing the Virtual/Physical Servers for SQL Clustering

In this chapter, we will start with building our back-end SQL virtual machines for our SQL cluster. Most of the steps in preparing our virtual machines for SQL clustering are similar to the steps used earlier when configuring our physical servers for our Windows CSV cluster. For this reason, we will move at a faster pace by referring to previously outlined steps in the book. SQL clustering uses a Windows failover cluster to manage its resources. We will begin by creating our virtual machines and then prepare them for SQL clustering. During this process we will add our network adapters, create a naming convention, add our virtual machines to the Active Directory domain, assign static IP addresses, configure our DNS properties, order our bindings, assign metrics, enable jumbo frames, install the Dell host software, configure the Microsoft iSCSI Initiator connections, add our virtual machines to the SAN's host group, bring our shared disks online, format our disks, align our partitions, and add the prerequisite Windows features and roles required for clustering. As you can see, we will be configuring a great amount of stuff in this chapter to prepare our SQL virtual machines for clustering.

If your SQL cluster nodes will be physical vs. virtual, then you'll want to follow the steps outlined in Chapters 5 & 7 to setup your iSCSI connections between the SAN and each of your physical SQL cluster nodes. Once your iSCSI connections are setup you can jump to Chapter 12 and continue along with the book's steps to build your SQL cluster.

## Connecting to Multiple Servers with Hyper-V Manager

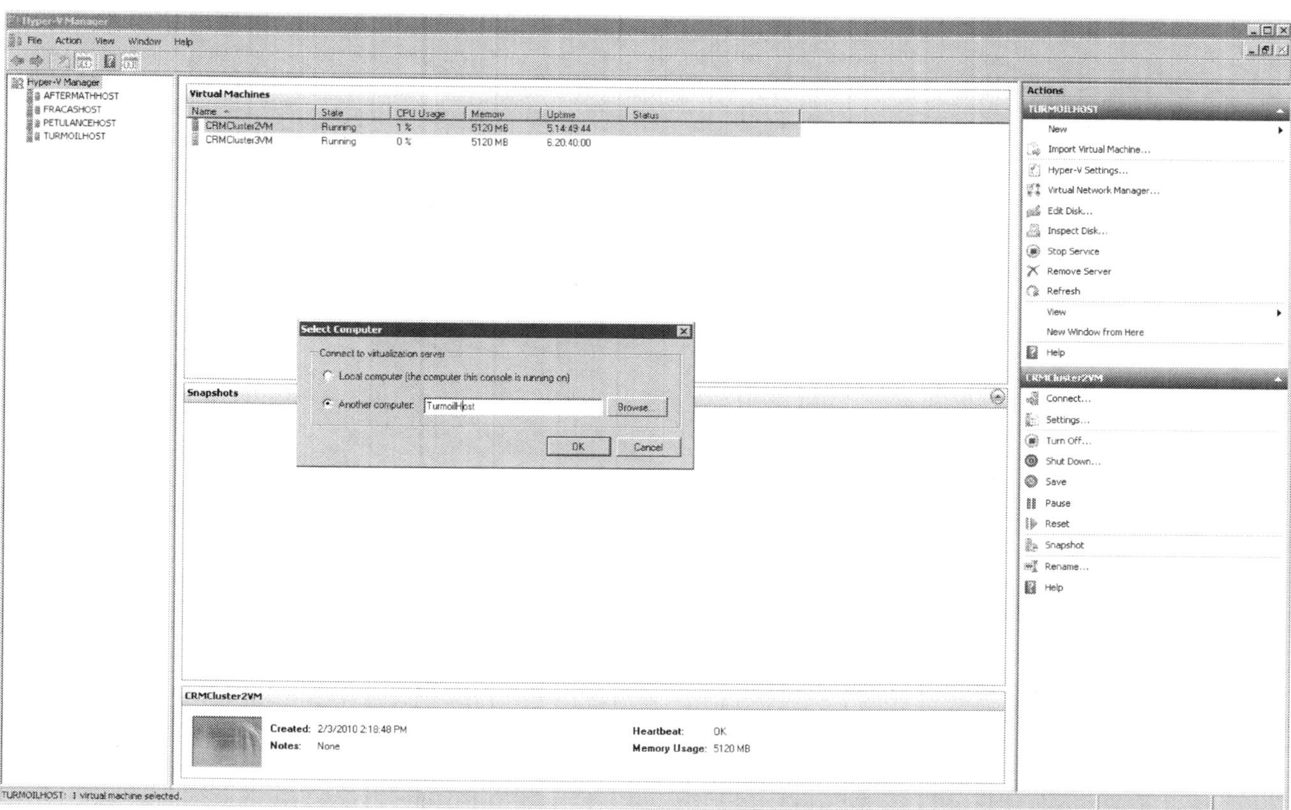


**Figure 11.1**

1. On one of your physical servers launch the **Hyper-V Manager** by going to **Start\Administrative Tools**, and then selecting the **Hyper-V Manager** option.
    a. In the left pane, right click the **Hyper-V Manager** node, and then select the **Connect to Server** option.
        i. On the **Select Computer** screen, select the **Another Server** option, and then enter one of your other physical server's names.
        ii. Click on the **OK** button to connect.
    b. Repeat these steps to add each of your physical servers to your **Hyper-V Manager** console. Once finished adding your servers, you'll be able to manage each of your Hyper-V server's settings from this server.

## Creating the Virtual Machines for the SQL Nodes

We will begin by creating two SQL virtual machines for our SQL cluster nodes. You will want to choose two different physical servers to host one of each of your SQL virtual machines. If you are planning on having a two node Windows cluster, then you have the option of using Windows Server 2008/R2 x64 Standard or Enterprise additions. If you are planning on having a Windows cluster consisting of three to sixteen nodes, then you'll need to use the Enterprise addition of Windows for that functionality. Once both the virtual machines have been created, we will want to setup their network connections in a similar way as we did with the physical servers earlier. These SQL virtual machines will have their own virtual disks and their own iSCSI Initiator connections to the SAN.

2. Open the **Hyper-V Manager** console, and then create a new **Windows Server 2008/R2 x64** virtual machine for each of your SQL cluster nodes. For our project, we will create two virtual machines named **SQLCluster2VM** and **SQLCluster3VM** using the **Windows Server 2008 R2 x64 Enterprise** addition of Windows for our SQL cluster nodes. Unfortunately, I'm already using the name SQLCluster1VM elsewhere on the network, so my naming convention had to start with SQLCluster2VM. You could choose to name your virtual machines as SQLCluster1VM and SQLCluster2VM as it makes more sense.

## Adding the Network Adapters

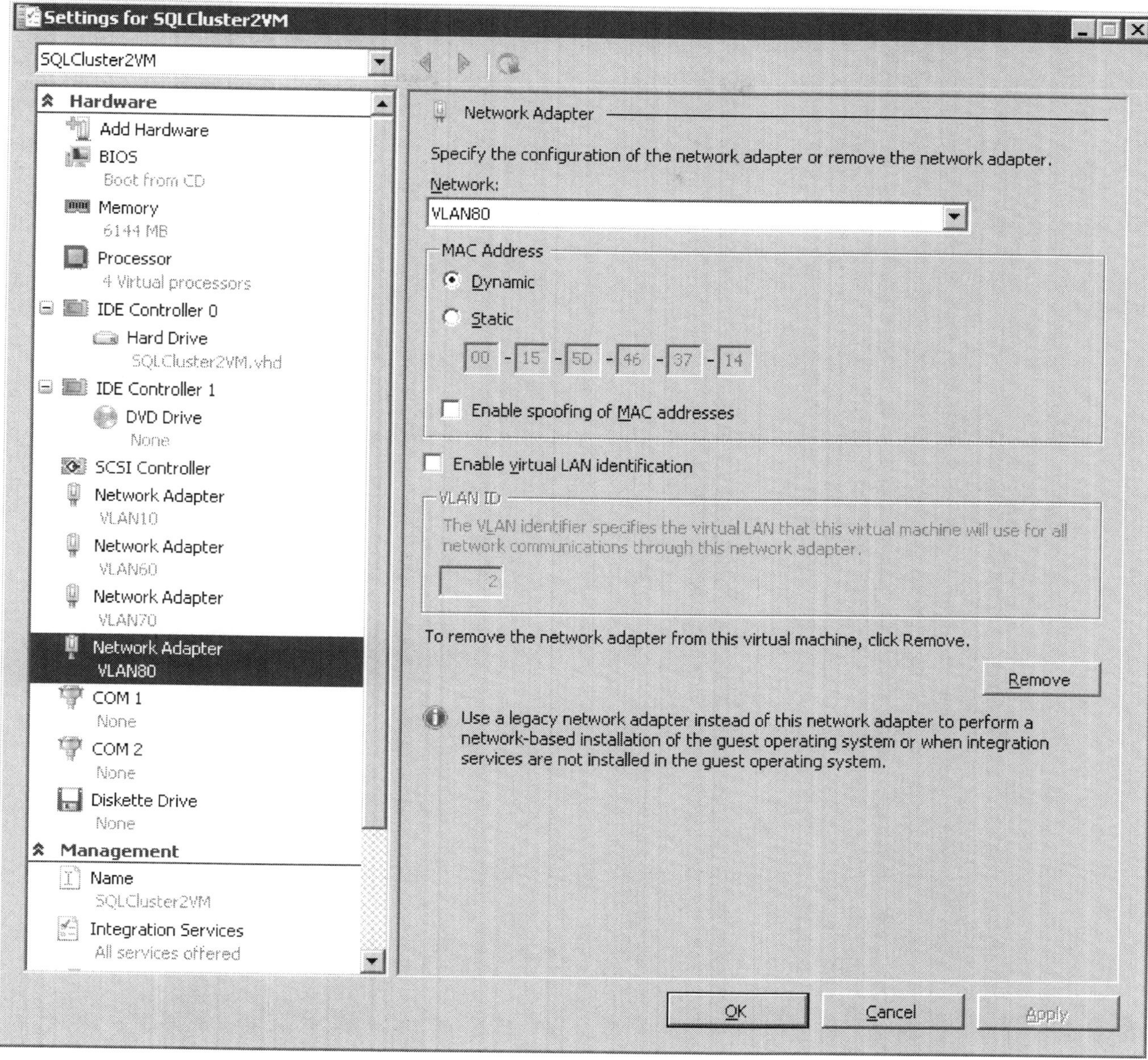


**Figure 11.2**

Next, we want to configure the SQL virtual machines to connect to our Hyper-V virtual networks that we created in the previous chapter. This process will require multiple reboots, as we will want to connect one virtual network at a time so that we can correctly identify and label each network adapter from within the virtual machine's network connections window.

3. Add your Hyper-V virtual networks one at a time, and then start the virtual machine so that you can identify and label each network adapter from within the virtual machine's network connections window. You will want to add the connections in the following order from top to bottom: Client Active Directory, first iSCSI, second iSCSI, and heartbeat. For our project, we will add our Hyper-V virtual networks in the

following: **VLAN10**, **VLAN60**, **VLAN70**, and **VLAN80**, as shown in **Figure 11.2**.

## Configuring the Network Adapters- Assigning a Naming Convention

| Hyper-V Virtual Network | Network Adapter Name | Network Adapter IP Addresses |
|---|---|---|
| VLAN10 | VLAN10 or Client10 | 10.10.10.65 |
| VLAN60 | VLAN60 or iSCSI60 | 10.10.60.65 |
| VLAN70 | VLAN70 or iSCSI70 | 10.10.70.65 |
| VLAN80 | VLAN80 or Heartbeat80 | 10.10.80.65 |

**Figure 11.3**

4. Rename each of the virtual machine's network adapters with the same names as we used for our Hyper-V virtual network names or create a new naming convention specifically for your virtual machines. For our project, we will use a new more specific naming convention of **Client10**, **iSCSI60**, **iSCSI70** and **Heartbeat80** for our virtual machines, as outlined in **Figure 11.3**.

   **NOTE:** If you made copies from one VHD file for your all virtual machines don't be surprised if when you're renaming the network adapters, that the virtual machine won't let you rename the network adapter to a certain name because it thinks that the name already exists. Unfortunately, Hyper-V is notorious for having phantom/ghost network adapters left over from copied VHD images. If you have this problem, then see the below **Steps 4a-4g** on how to remove phantom network adapters, if not then please disregard these steps and move on to **Step 5**.

## Removing Phantom/Ghost Network Adapters from Virtual Machines

```
Administrator: C:\Windows\system32\cmd.exe
Microsoft Windows [Version 6.1.7600]
Copyright (c) 2009 Microsoft Corporation.  All rights reserved.

C:\Users\Administrator>set devmgr_show_nonpresent_devices=1

C:\Users\Administrator>Start DEVMGMT.MSC

C:\Users\Administrator>_
```

**Figure 11.4**

a. To remove phantom/ghost network adapters from the registry, open the **Command Prompt** with the **Run As Administrator** permissions on the virtual machine with the issue.

   i. Type in the **set devmgr_show_nonpresent_devices=1** command, and then hit the **Enter** key, as shown in the first command of **Figure 11.4**.

   ii. Type in the **Start DEVMGMT.MSC** command, and then hit the Enter key, as shown in the second command of **Figure 11.4**. This will launch the Device Manager window.

   **NOTE:** You must run the command in **Step b** first and then also launch the Device Manager from the command in **Step c** vs. just opening the Device Manager normally or the phantom network adapters will not be visible from within the Device Manage console.

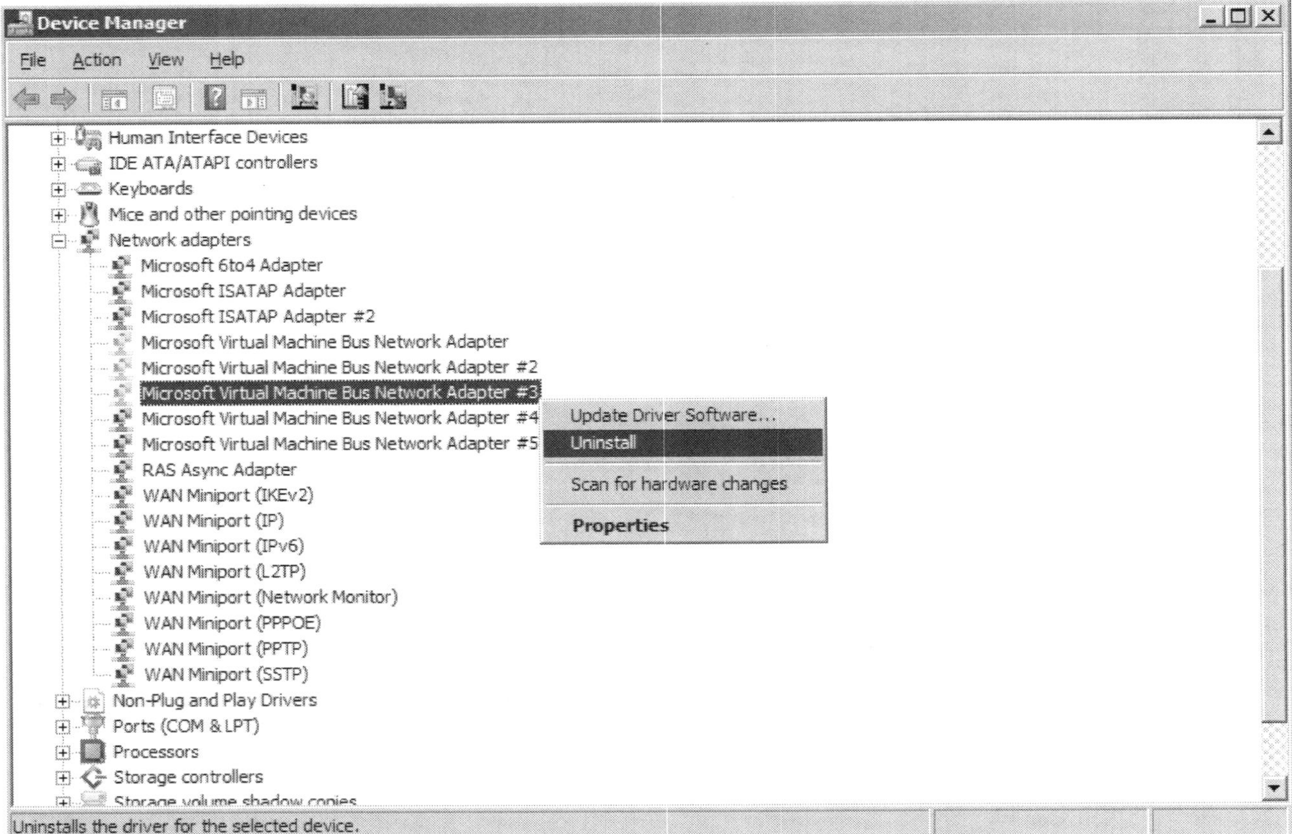


**Figure 11.5**

b. In the **Device Manager** window, click on **View** from the toolbar, and select the **Show Hidden Devices** option.

c. Expand the **Network Adapters** node, and then right click on the dimmed out network adapter, and select the **Uninstall** option, as shown in **Figure 11.5**. Repeat this for any other dimmed out network adapters.

d. On the **Confirm Device Uninstall** screen, click on the **OK** button to complete the removal of the phantom network adapter. Once you have removed any hidden network adapters, you should be able to rename your network adapters to your naming convention from within the **Network Connections** screen.

e. If this doesn't resolve your issue with phantom network adapters, then you could choose to simply create a new naming convention specifically for your virtual machines such as we did for our project in **Step 4**.

## Adding the SQL Virtual Machines to the Active Directory Domain

5. Once you have added the Client Active Directory network connection, rename your SQL virtual machines, and then add them to the domain. Since a reboot is required, you can integrate this step into the process of adding your remaining network connections. For our project, we will name our virtual machines as **SQLCluster2VM** and **SQLCluster3VM**.

## Configuring the Network Adapters- Assigning Static IP Addresses

6. Assign each of your SQL virtual machine network adapters a static IP address for the Client Active Directory, Heartbeat and for both iSCSI connections. For our project, we will use the same numbering convention that we used for the physical servers, as shown in **Figure 11.3**.

## Configuring the Network Adapters- DNS Properties

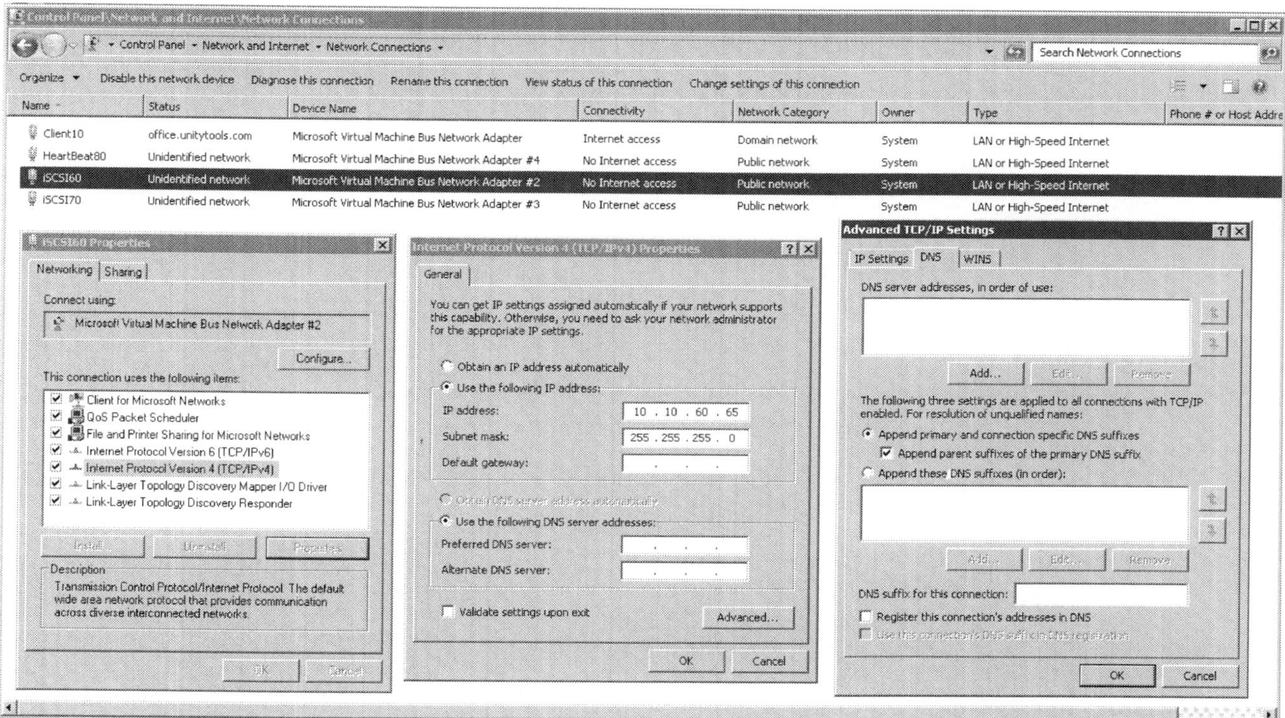


**Figure 11.6**

7. For each of the network adapters, except for the Client Active Directory network, right click on the network adapter, and then select **Properties\Internet Protocol Version 4 (TCP/IPv4)\Properties button\Advanced button\DNS** tab.

   a. On the **DNS** tab, unselect the **Register this connection's addresses in DNS** checkbox, as shown in **Figure 11.6**. Click on the **OK** button to save your changes. We only want the Client Active Directory network adapter of each server to be registered in our DNS. This will prevent multiple IP addresses from being registered in our DNS for the same server name.

# Configuring the Network Adapters- Binding Orders

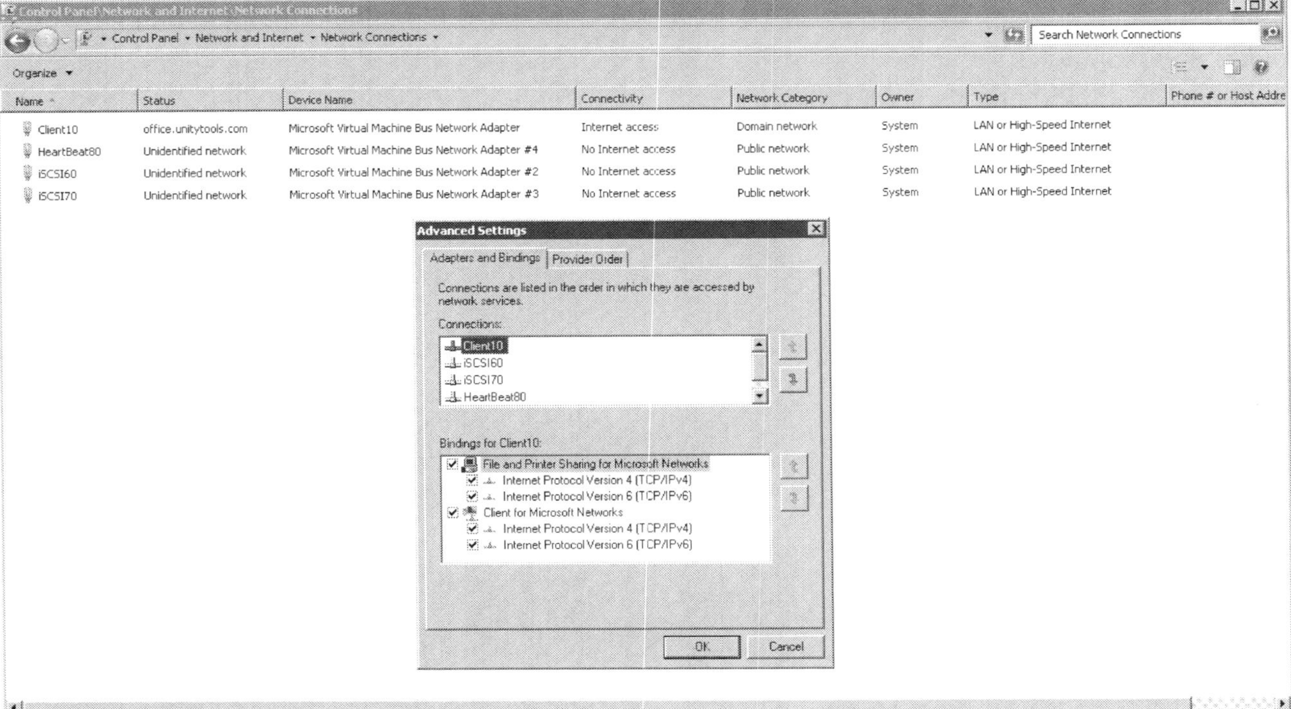


**Figure 11.7**

We want to order our SQL virtual machine network adapter bindings in the same order as we did on our physical servers. The server will attempt connections from top to bottom of the binding order list. Setting the Active Directory client network connection to the top of the list is a prerequisite and requirement of SQL clustering. You'll want to make sure that all the clustered virtual machines have their network adapter bindings in this same order.

8. In the **Network Connections** screen, hit the keys **Alt+N** to bring up the **Advanced** toolbar, and then select the **Advanced Settings** option from the dropdown menu.

    a. On the **Advanced Settings** screen, click on the **Adapters and Bindings** tab, and order your network adapters in the following order from top to bottom: client Active Directory, first iSCSI, second iSCSI, and heartbeat. For our project, we will bind our network adapters in the following order from the top down: **Client10**, **iSCSI60**, **iSCSI70**, and **Heartbeat80**, as shown in **Figure 11.7**.

## Configuring the Network Adapters- Metrics

| Network Connection | Binding Order | Metric Value |
|---|---|---|
| Client AD Virtual Network | 5 | 7000 – 7999 (Set on VM) |
| First iSCSI Virtual Network | 6 | 8000 – 8999 (Set on VM) |
| Second iSCSI Virtual Network | 7 | 8000 – 9999 (Set on VM) |
| Heartbeat Virtual Network | 8 | 9000 – 9999 (Set on VM) |

**Figure 11.8**

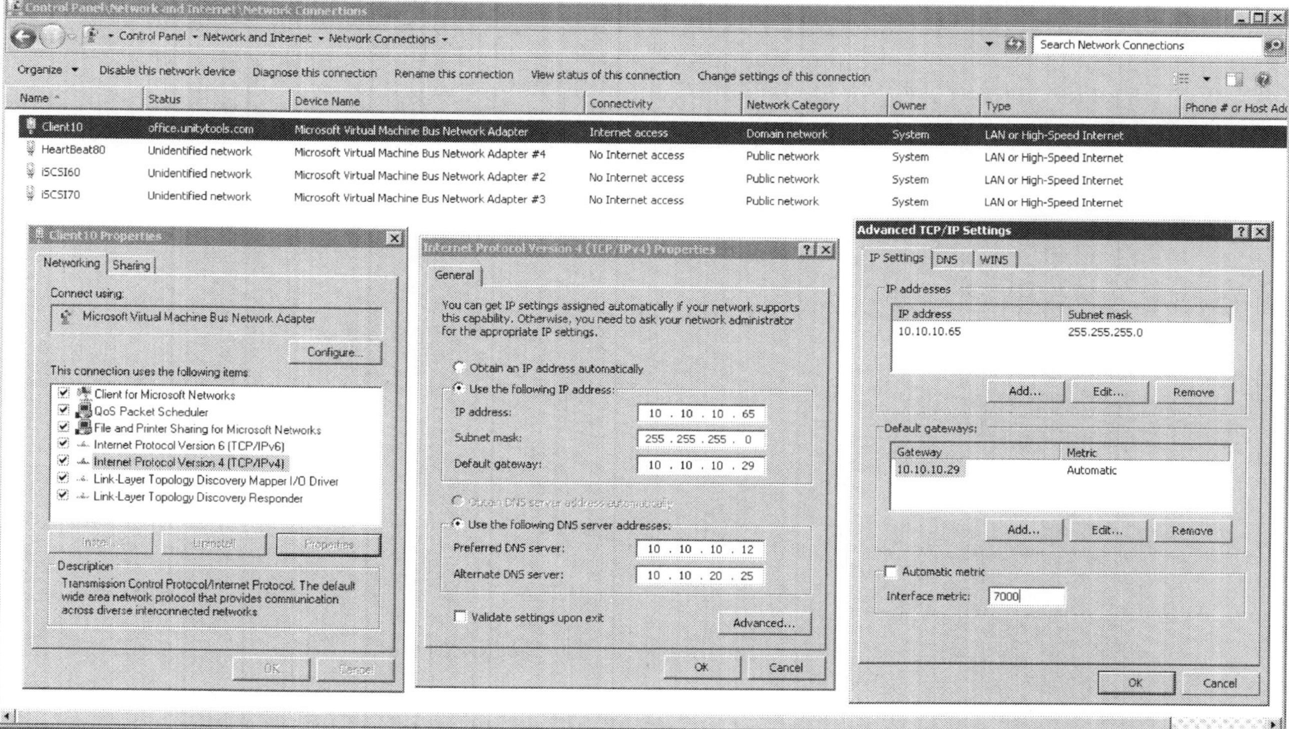


**Figure 11.9**

9. In the **Network Connections** screen, right click on each of the network adapters, and then select the **Properties** option.

    a. On the **Properties** screen, highlight **Internet Protocol Version 4 (TCP/IPv4)**, and then click on the **Properties** button.

        i. On the **Internet Protocol Version 4 (TCP/IPv4) Properties** screen, click on the **Advanced** button.

            1. While on the **IP Settings** tab, unselect the **Automatic metric** checkbox, and then enter in the value specified in **Figure 11.8** for each particular network adapter.

## Configuring the iSCSI Network Adapters- Enabling Jumbo Frames

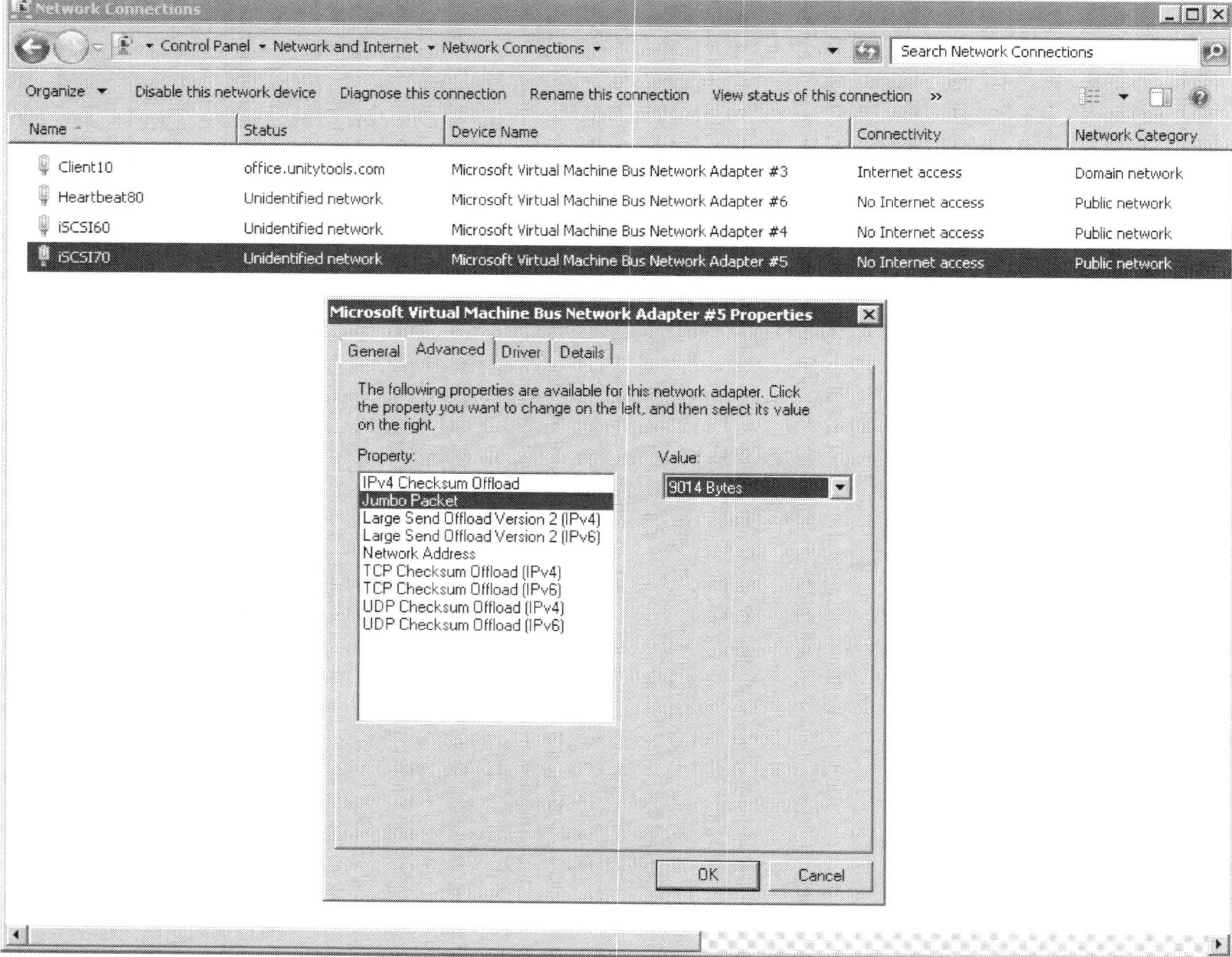


**Figure 11.10**

10. In the **Network Connections** screen, right click on your first iSCSI network adapter, and then select the **Properties** option.

    a. On the **Properties** screen, click on the **Configure** button.

        i. On the **Microsoft Virtual Machine Bus Network Adapter Properties** screen, click on the **Advanced** tab.

        ii. On the **Advanced** tab, highlight the **Jumbo Packet** option in the **Property** field, and then select the **9014 Bytes** option from the **Value** dropdown field, as shown in **Figure 11.10**.

        iii. Click on the **OK** button to save your changes.

## Configuring the iSCSI Network Adapters- Verifying Jumbo Frames are Enabled

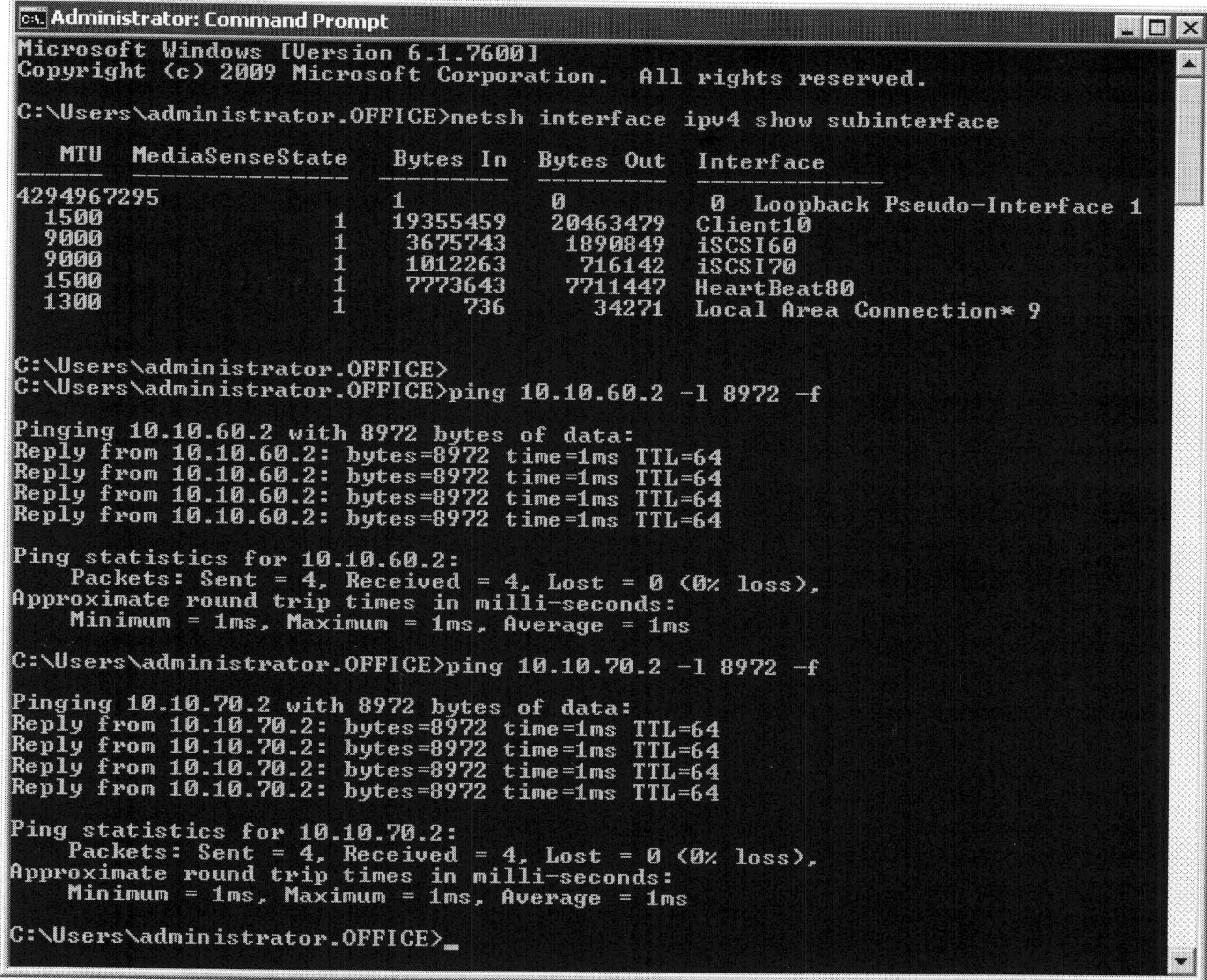
Administrator: Command Prompt
Microsoft Windows [Version 6.1.7600]
Copyright (c) 2009 Microsoft Corporation. All rights reserved.
C:\Users\administrator.OFFICE>netsh interface ipv4 show subinterface
MTU MediaSenseState Bytes In Bytes Out Interface
4294967295 1 0 0 Loopback Pseudo-Interface 1
1500 1 19355459 20463479 Client10
9000 1 3675743 1890849 iSCSI60
9000 1 1012263 716142 iSCSI70
1500 1 7773643 7711447 HeartBeat80
1300 1 736 34271 Local Area Connection* 9
C:\Users\administrator.OFFICE>
C:\Users\administrator.OFFICE>ping 10.10.60.2 -l 8972 -f
Pinging 10.10.60.2 with 8972 bytes of data:
Reply from 10.10.60.2: bytes=8972 time=1ms TTL=64
Reply from 10.10.60.2: bytes=8972 time=1ms TTL=64
Reply from 10.10.60.2: bytes=8972 time=1ms TTL=64
Reply from 10.10.60.2: bytes=8972 time=1ms TTL=64
Ping statistics for 10.10.60.2:
Packets: Sent = 4, Received = 4, Lost = 0 (0% loss),
Approximate round trip times in milli-seconds:
Minimum = 1ms, Maximum = 1ms, Average = 1ms
C:\Users\administrator.OFFICE>ping 10.10.70.2 -l 8972 -f
Pinging 10.10.70.2 with 8972 bytes of data:
Reply from 10.10.70.2: bytes=8972 time=1ms TTL=64
Reply from 10.10.70.2: bytes=8972 time=1ms TTL=64
Reply from 10.10.70.2: bytes=8972 time=1ms TTL=64
Reply from 10.10.70.2: bytes=8972 time=1ms TTL=64
Ping statistics for 10.10.70.2:
Packets: Sent = 4, Received = 4, Lost = 0 (0% loss),
Approximate round trip times in milli-seconds:
Minimum = 1ms, Maximum = 1ms, Average = 1ms
C:\Users\administrator.OFFICE>_

**Figure 11.11**

b. Open the **Command Prompt** with the **Run As Administrator** permissions on each SQL virtual machine.

   i. To view the current MTU settings for each network adapter, type in the **netsh interface ipv4 show subinterface** command into the command prompt, and then hit the **Enter** key, as shown in the first command of **Figure 11.11**. Verify that your two iSCSI network adapters have an MTU value of 9000. For our project, we will verify that both our **iSCSI60** and **iSCSI70** network adapters show an MTU of 9000.

   ii. To test the MTU settings of each iSCSI network adapter by typing in a **ping <Your_SAN's_iSCSI_NIC_IP> -l 8972 –f** command into the command prompt, and then hit the

**Enter** key. Replace the **<Your_SAN's_iSCSI_NIC_IP>** with your SAN's first iSCSI network adapter's IP address and then run the command. You will want to repeat this test for each of your iSCSI network adapters. The –f parameter of the command sets the frame size to 8972, which is the max for a jumbo frame, when set to an MTU of 9000. For our project, we will run a **ping 10.10.60.2 -l 8972 –f** command to test our **iSCSI60** network adapter, by pinging our SAN's first iSCSI network adapter. We will then repeat the command to test our **iSCSI70** network adapter of the server by pinging our SAN's second iSCSI network adapter with the IP address of **10.10.70.2**, as shown in the final command of **Figure 11.11**.

c. Repeat **Step 10** for each of your SQL virtual machines' iSCSI network adapters.

## Installing the Dell Modular Disk Storage Manager (MDSM) software

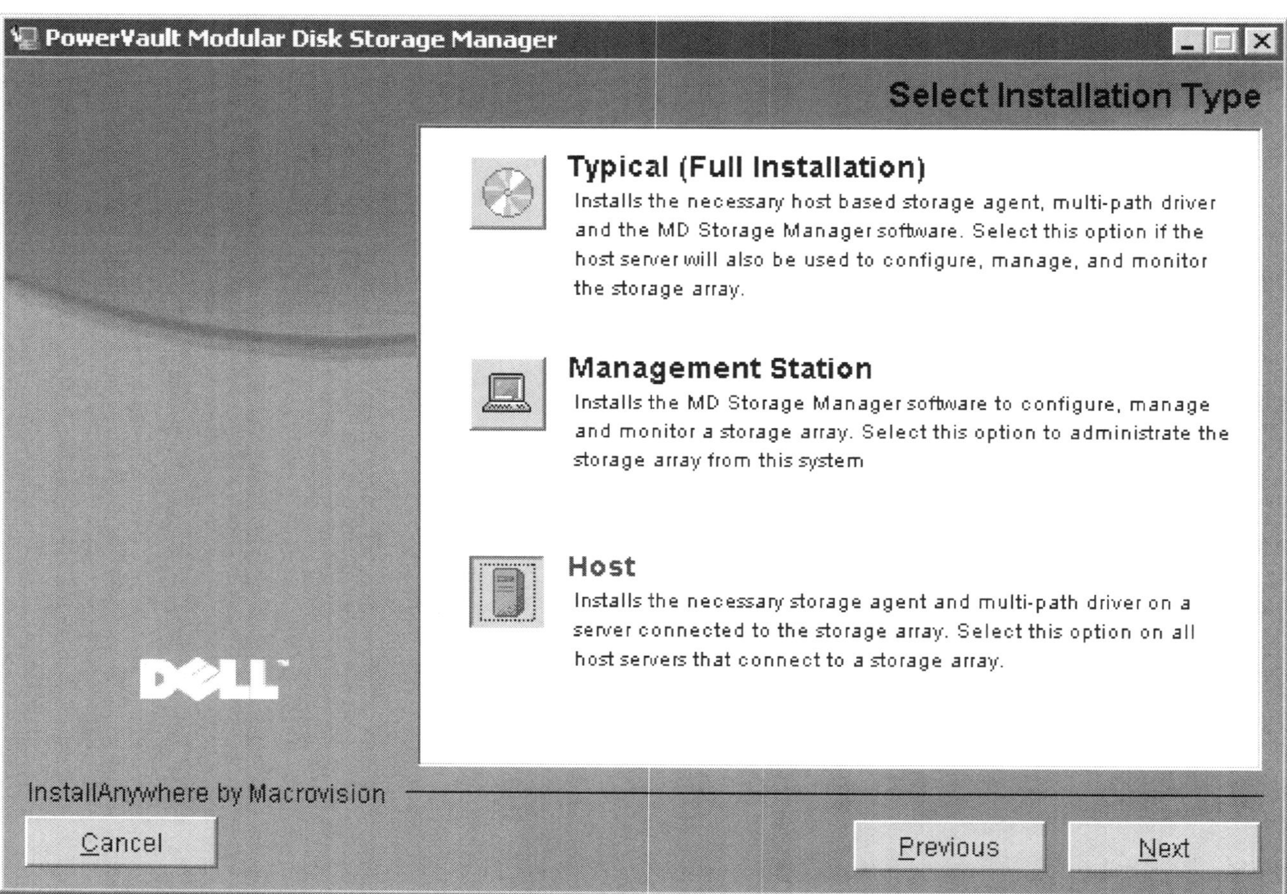


**Figure 11.12**

11. Install the **Dell Modular Disk Storage Manager** software from the **MD3000i Resource CD** with the **Host** type of installation. The minimum of the Host type of installation is required on all servers that will have an iSCSI Initiator connection the MD3000i SAN.

# Configuring the Microsoft iSCSI Initiator Multi-path Connections to the SAN

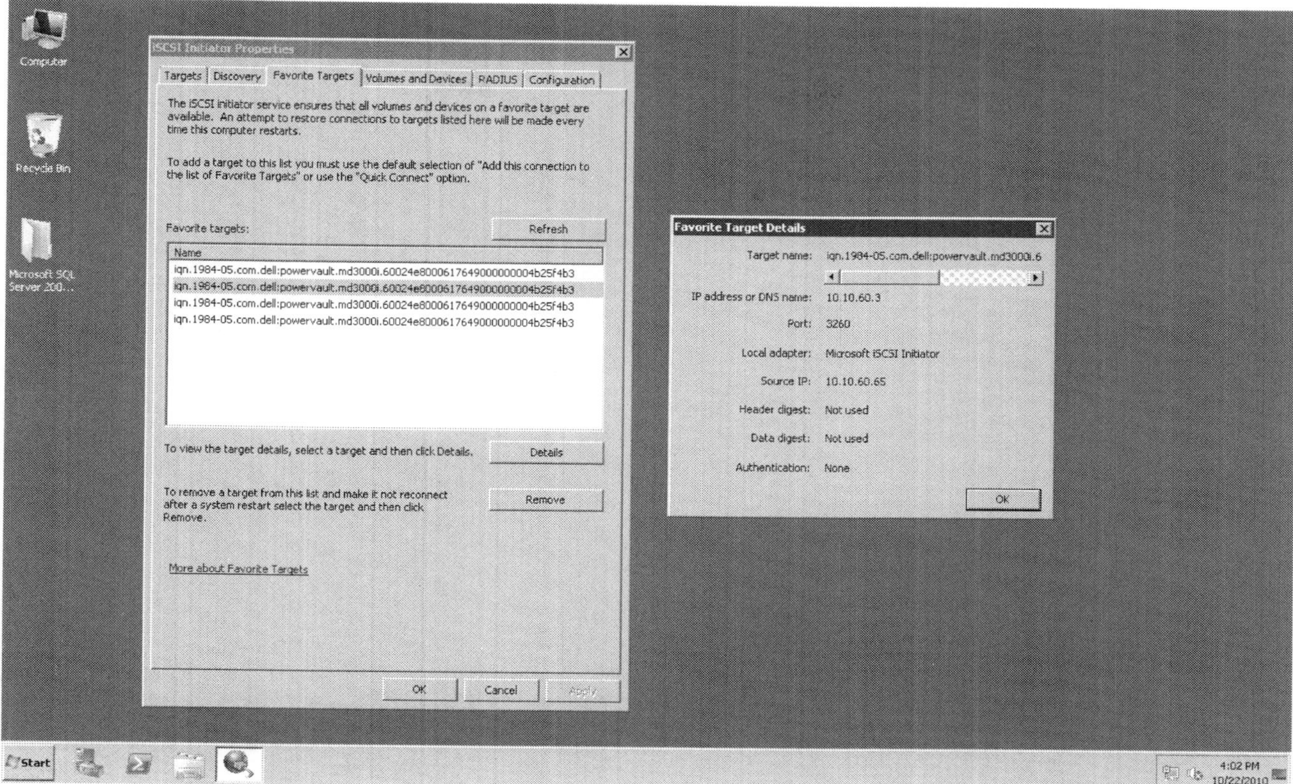


**Figure 11.13**

12. Configure the **Microsoft iSCSI Initiator** for multi-path connections to your SAN as we did for our physical host servers. The detailed steps were previously outlined in **Chapter 5** with **Steps 9-14**. When finished you should have four iSCSI connections to your SAN for a dual controller or two iSCSI connections for single controller, as shown in **Figure 11.13**.

## Adding the SQL Virtual Machines to the SAN's Host Group for Disk Access

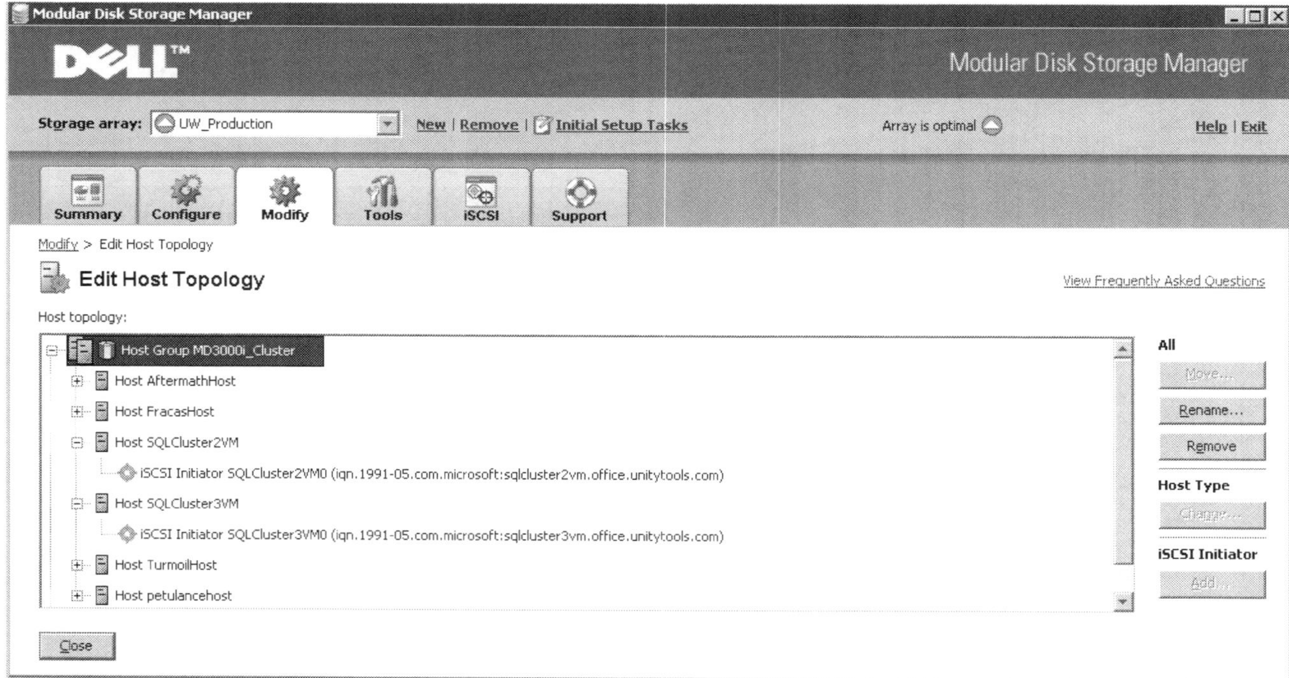


**Figure 11.14**

13. Open the **Dell Modular Disk Storage Manager** console, and then add both of your SQL virtual machines to a host group on your SAN. You can use the existing host group that you created for your physical servers or you can create a new host group, and then map your SQL virtual machine shared disks to this new group. The detailed steps were previously outlined in **Chapter 7, Step 1**. For our project, we will add our SQL virtual machines to our existing **MD3000i_Cluster** host group, as shown in **Figure 11.14**.

## Configuring the SQL Virtual Machine Shared Disks

| Shared Disk Capacity | Shared Disk Name | Assigned Drive Letter |
|---|---|---|
| 200 GB | SQL_DB | S: |
| 101 GB | SQL_Logs | L: |
| 100 GB | SQL_TempDB | T: |
| 3 GB | SQL_MSDTC | M: |
| 2 GB | SQL_Quorum | W: |

**Figure 11.15**

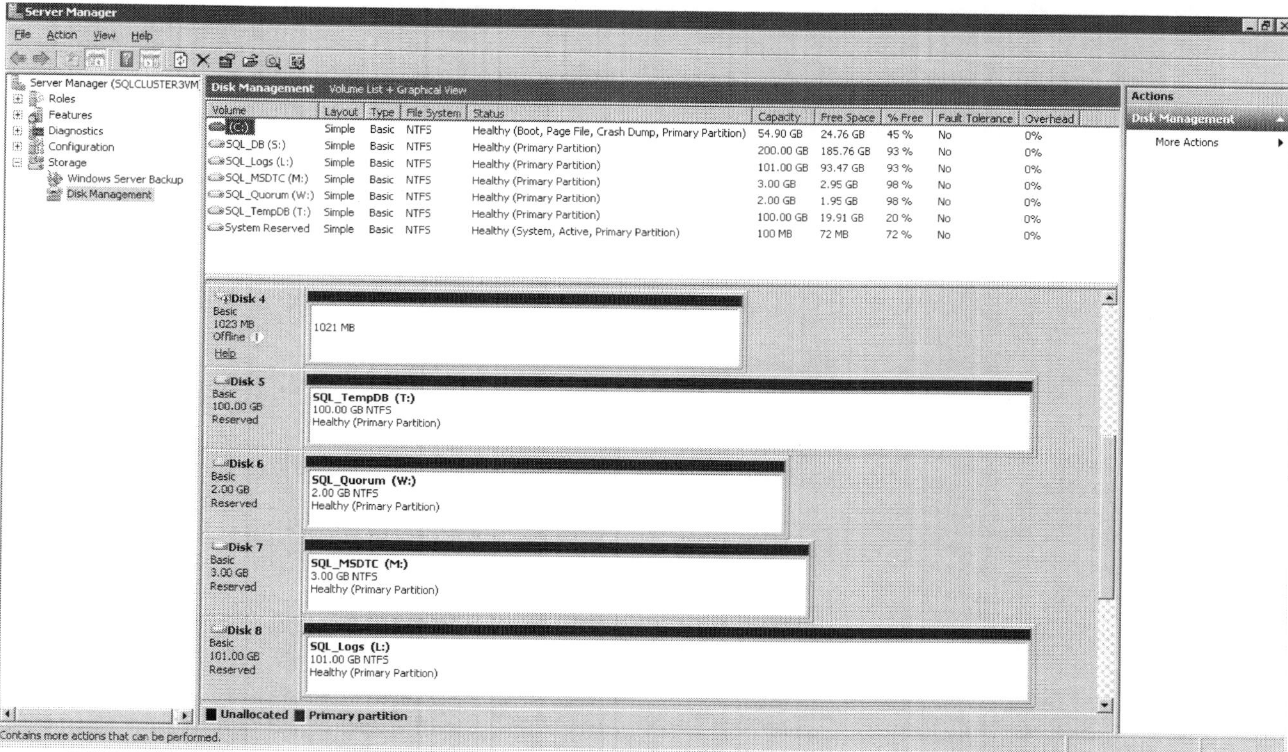

**Figure 11.16**

14. On the virtual machine that you want to be your initial node of the SQL cluster, bring your virtual disks online, format and align their partitions as previously outlined in **Chapter 8, Steps 1-5**. Assign your drive letters and volume labels that correspond to what each disk is. For our project, we will name the drives with the same naming convention that we used when creating the virtual disks on our SAN with the Dell Modular Disk Storage Manager. Using the same naming convention, we will name our shared disks as outlined in **Figure 11.15**. When we are finish, our project's drives should look similar to **Figure 11.16** from within the Windows Server Manager console.

    a. Once done configuring your shared disks, open **Windows Explorer**, and then verify that you can access each of your shared drives from your initial SQL virtual machine.

**NOTE:** If you have already accidentally added your SQL shared disks to the existing Windows cluster, then you'll need to follow these sub-steps before you can give control of the disks to your initial SQL virtual machine.

i. Go to **Failover Cluster Manager**, and then select **Storage** node in the left pane under the Windows cluster that you created earlier.

1. In the center pane where all the SQL shared disks are shown, right click on each disk, and then select the **Delete** option. This will only remove these drives from the existing Windows cluster and will not actually delete them.

## Adding Prerequisites for SQL Clustering- Windows Features

15. Open **Windows Server Manger** console, and then select the **Features** node in the left pane.

a. In the right pane, click the **Add Features** link, and then select the **Failover Clustering** checkbox.

i. Click on the **Next** button, and then click on the **Install** button.

ii. Once the installation is complete, click on the **Close** button to exit.

# Adding Prerequisites for SQL Clustering- Windows Roles

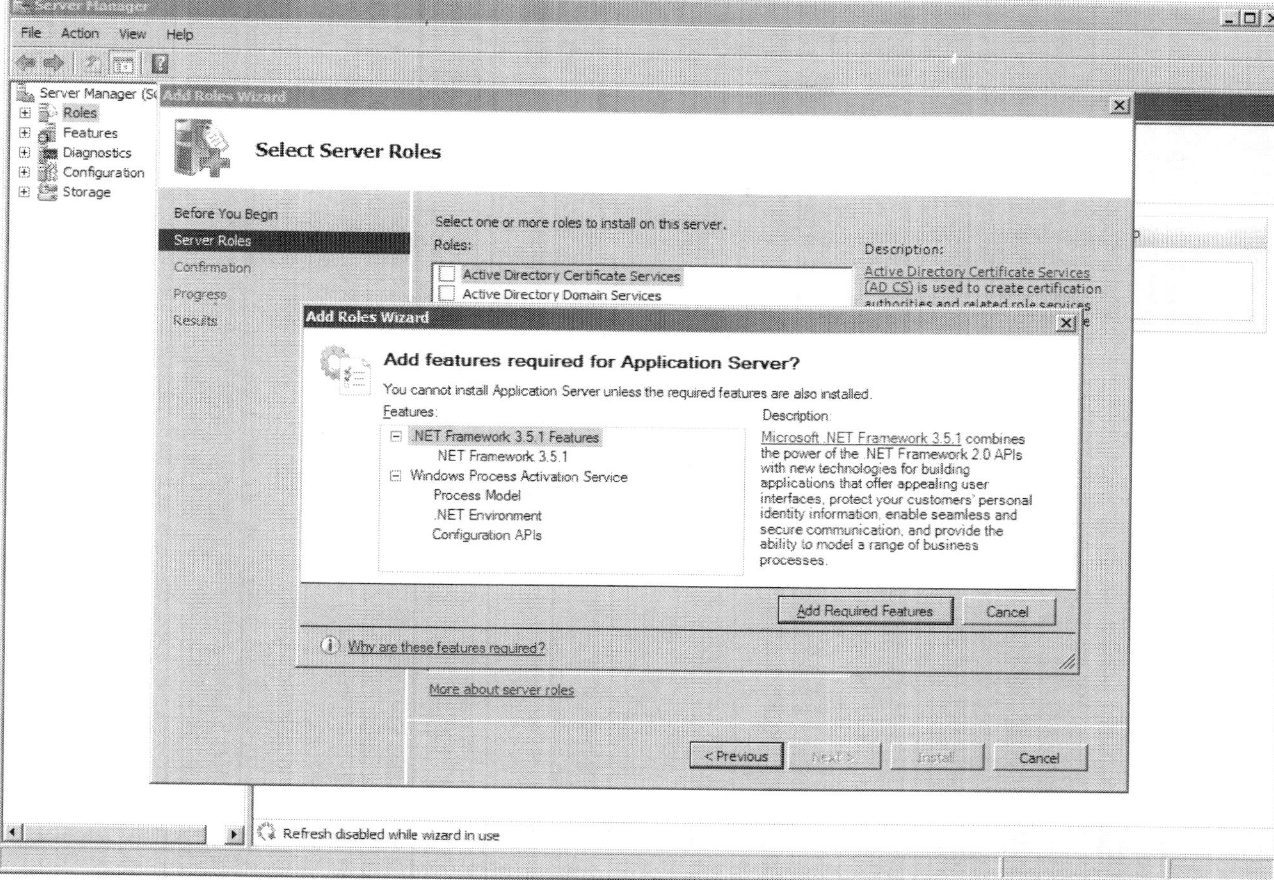


**Figure 11.17**

16. Return to **Windows Server Manager** console, and then select the **Roles** node in the left pane.

    a. In the right pane, click on the **Add Roles** link to launch the **Add Roles Wizard**.

        i. On the **Before You Begin** screen, click on the **Next** button to continue.

        ii. On the **Select Server Roles** screen, select the **Application Server** checkbox.

        iii. On the **Add features required for Application Server** pop-up screen, click on the **Add Required Features** button, as shown in **Figure 11.17**.

        iv. Click on the **Next** button for the next two screens.

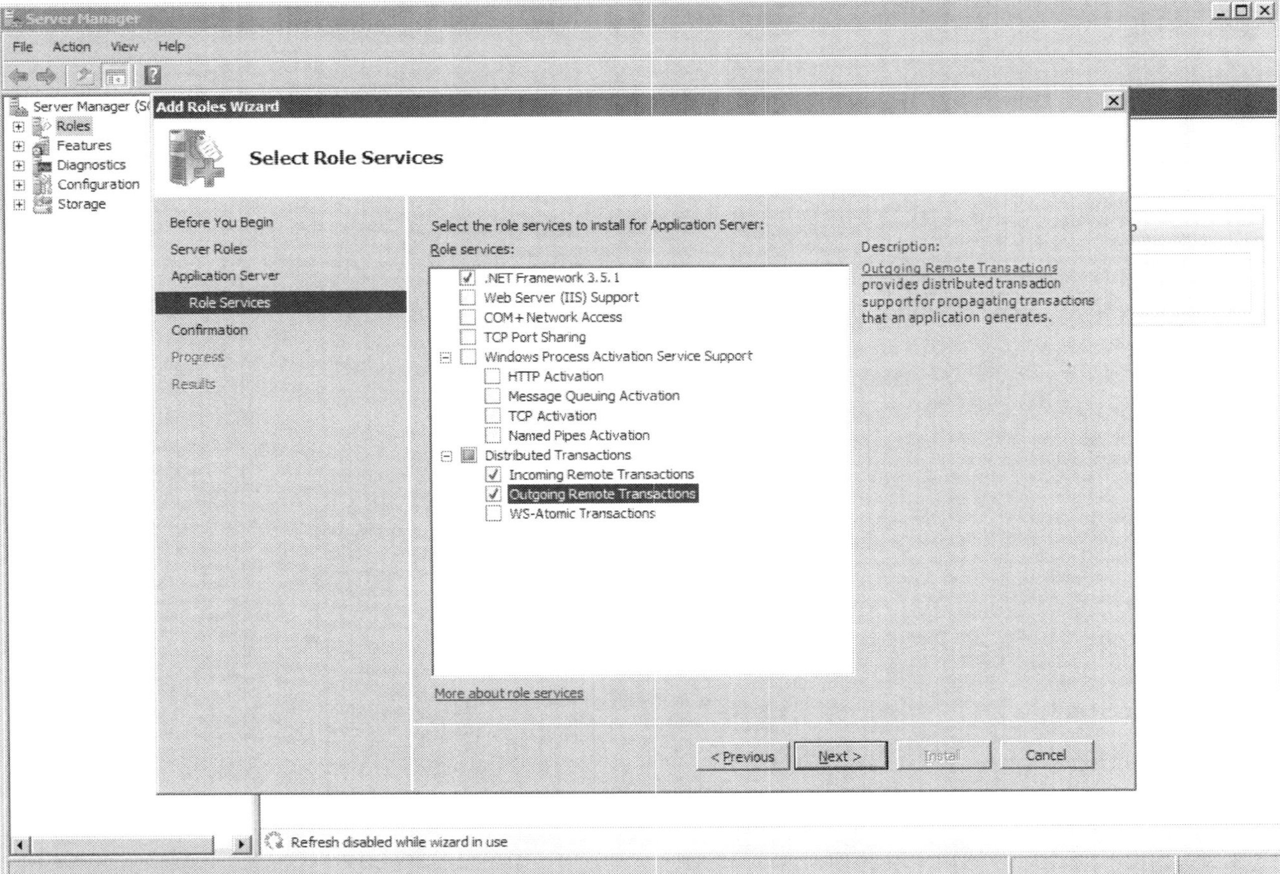


**Figure 11.18**

v. On the **Select Role Services** screen, select the **Incoming Remote Transactions** and the **Outgoing Remote Transactions** checkboxes as shown in **Figure 11.18**, and then click on the **Next** button to continue. These options are required for MSDTC.

vi. On the **Confirm Installation Selections** screen, click on the **Install** button to continue.

vii. On the **Installation Results** screen, click on the **Close** button to complete the installation.

# Chapter 12: Creating the Windows Cluster that will Host the SQL Cluster's Resources

For many of Microsoft's cluster aware applications a Windows Failover Cluster is a prerequisite. This is the case with our SQL clustering whereby our SQL resources are managed from within a Windows Failover Cluster. We will begin by creating a Windows cluster with one of our SQL virtual/physical machines. Once we have the Windows cluster in place, we will configure its resources for the SQL installation. This process will involve adding our shared disks for SQL, renaming the cluster disks to our naming convention, and configuring the quorum disk. Whether you will be installing your SQL cluster on physical or virtual machines the steps are the same. For our project, we will be installing our Windows cluster to host our SQL resources on virtual machines. When finished with this chapter, we will have the prerequisite Windows cluster ready for our SQL software installation.

## Creating the Windows Cluster with the Initial SQL Node

Since we've already went through the steps of creating a Windows cluster when we created our Windows CSV cluster we will move at a faster pace through these steps while focusing on the steps that are different. During this process you can always refer to **Chapter 9** for more detailed steps with screenshots if something is unclear.

1. Open the **Failover Cluster Manager** on the SQL virtual machine that you want to be the initial node, right click the **Failover Cluster Manager** node at the top of the left pane, and then select the **Create a Cluster** option.

    a. On the **Before You Begin** screen, click on the **Next** button to continue.

    b. On the **Select Servers** screen, enter the name of one of your SQL virtual machines that you want to be the initial SQL node, and then click on the **Next** button to continue. For our project, we will enter **SQLCluster2VM** for our initial SQL cluster node.

## Running the Validate a Cluster Wizard

c. On the **Validate a Configuration Wizard** screen, select the **Run all test (recommend)** option, and then click on the **Next** button to continue. This will verify that the server we are adding to the cluster is setup correctly.

d. Once the validation completes, click on the **View Report** button, and resolve any issues that are reported.

   **NOTE:** Unfortunately, the configuration validation report may contain warnings that don't truly apply. Do your best at resolving the issues, however if some of the warnings appear to be frivolous then don't let this stop you from continuing with creating your cluster.

e. On the **Validate a Configuration Wizard** screen, click on the **Finish** button to exit and return to the **Create Cluster Wizard** screen.

## Assigning the Cluster Name and IP Address

f. On the **Access Point for Administering the Cluster** screen, enter your Windows cluster name for the **Cluster Name** field. For our project, we will name our Windows cluster that will host our SQL resources as **WinSQLCluster**.

   **NOTE:** This cluster name is for the Windows Failover cluster that will manage our resources of the SQL cluster and is not the actual name of our SQL cluster that will handle our SQL transactions. We will be assigning the actual SQL cluster name and IP address during the SQL Server 2008/R2 install process. For a visual representation of how these two clusters integrate, please see **Chapter 1**, **Figures 1.1**, **1.4 & 1.5**.

   i. For the **Networks** field, you want to only have your **Client Active Directory** network selected. If any other networks are listed here you'll want to unselect their checkboxes. For our project, we will select our **10.10.10.0/24** network for our Client Active Directory network.

   ii. For the **Address** field, enter the IP address you want for your Windows cluster, and then click on the **Next** button continue. For our project, we will assign the IP address of **10.10.10.63**.

g. On the **Confirmation** screen, click on the **Next** button to create the cluster.

h. On the **Summary** screen, click on the **View Report** button, and then that everything looks ok.

i. Save a copy of the report if you want to have a general summary of the cluster's setup, and then close the Internet Explorer window to return to the **Summary** screen.

j. On the **Summary** screen, click on the **Finish** button to exit the wizard.

# Configuring the Newly Created Windows SQL Cluster

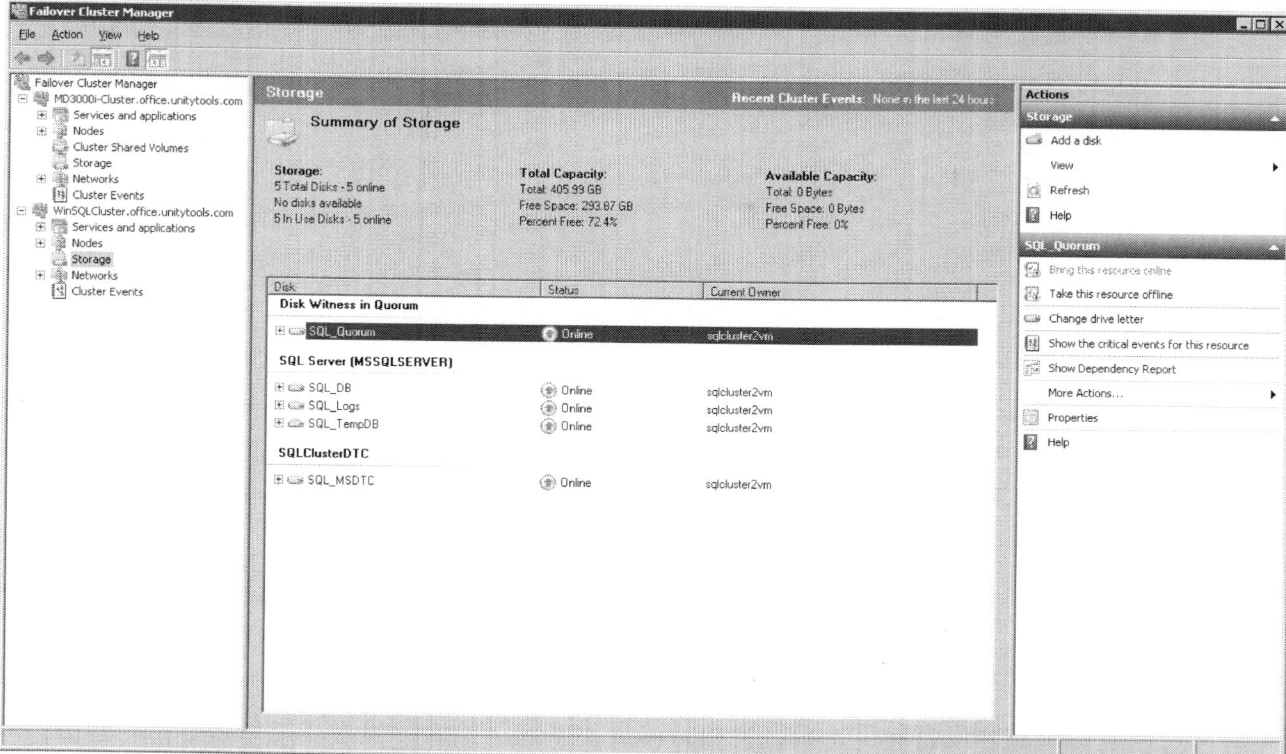


**Figure 12.1**

# Adding Shared Disks to the Windows Cluster

2. In **Failover Cluster Manager**, right click on the **Storage** node under your cluster's name in the left pane, and then select the **Add a Disk** option.

   a. On the **Add Disks to a Cluster** screen, select all the disks that will be used for your SQL cluster, and then click on the **OK** button to continue. For our project, we should have five disks selected, one for each of the following **SQL_MSDTC**, **SQL_DB**, **SQL_TempDB**, **SQL_Logs** and **SQL_Quorum**.

   b. Highlight the **Storage** node in the left pane under your Windows SQL cluster, and then make sure all the disks have a status of **Online**, as shown in **Figure 12.1**.

## Renaming Cluster Disks

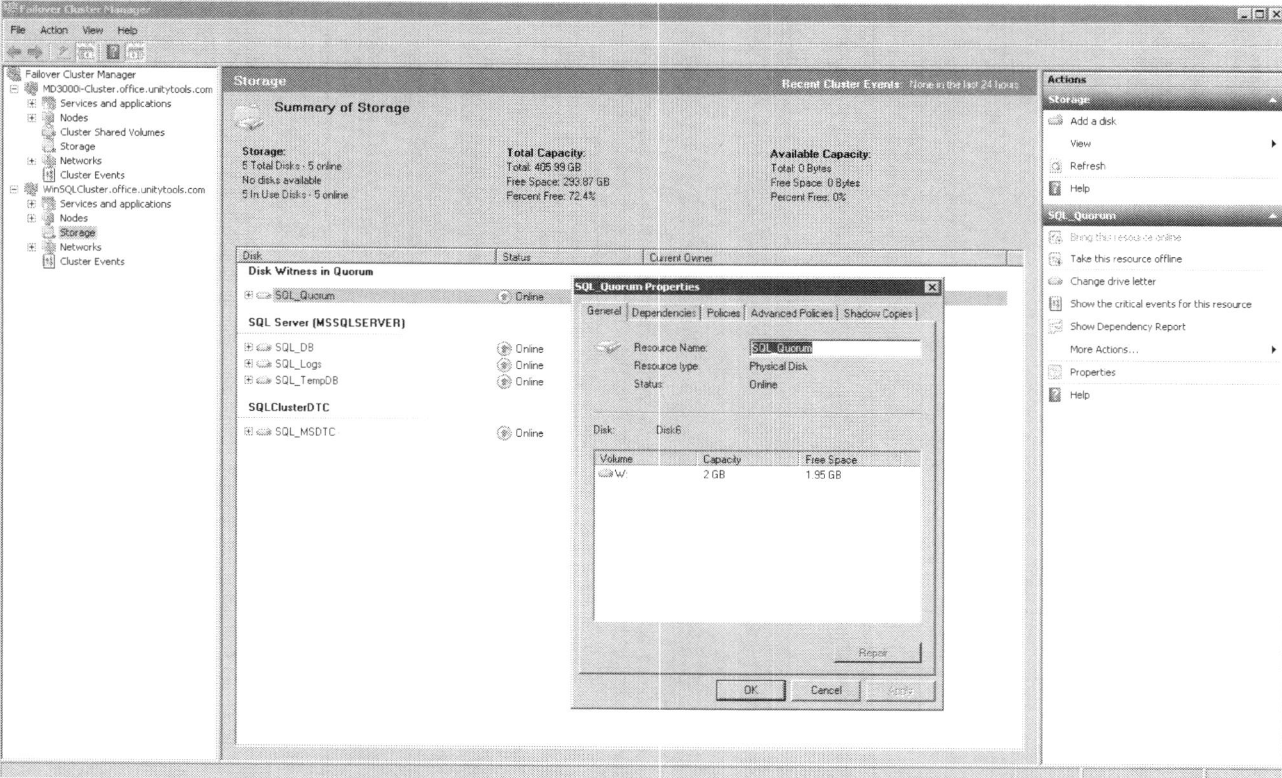

**Figure 12.2**

3. Right click on your first shared disk in the center pane, and then select **Properties** option.

   a. On the **Properties** screen, click on the **General** tab, and then change the **Resource Name** field to a descriptive name of what the disk actually is. Using the same naming convention as you used when creating the shared disk on the SAN keeps it simple.

   b. Repeat **Step 3** to rename each of your Windows SQL cluster disks to descriptive names. For our project, we will rename each of our Windows SQL cluster disks to the same naming convention that we used when creating our disks on the SAN, as shown in the center pane of **Figure 12.2**.

# Configuring a Quorum Disk for the Windows Cluster

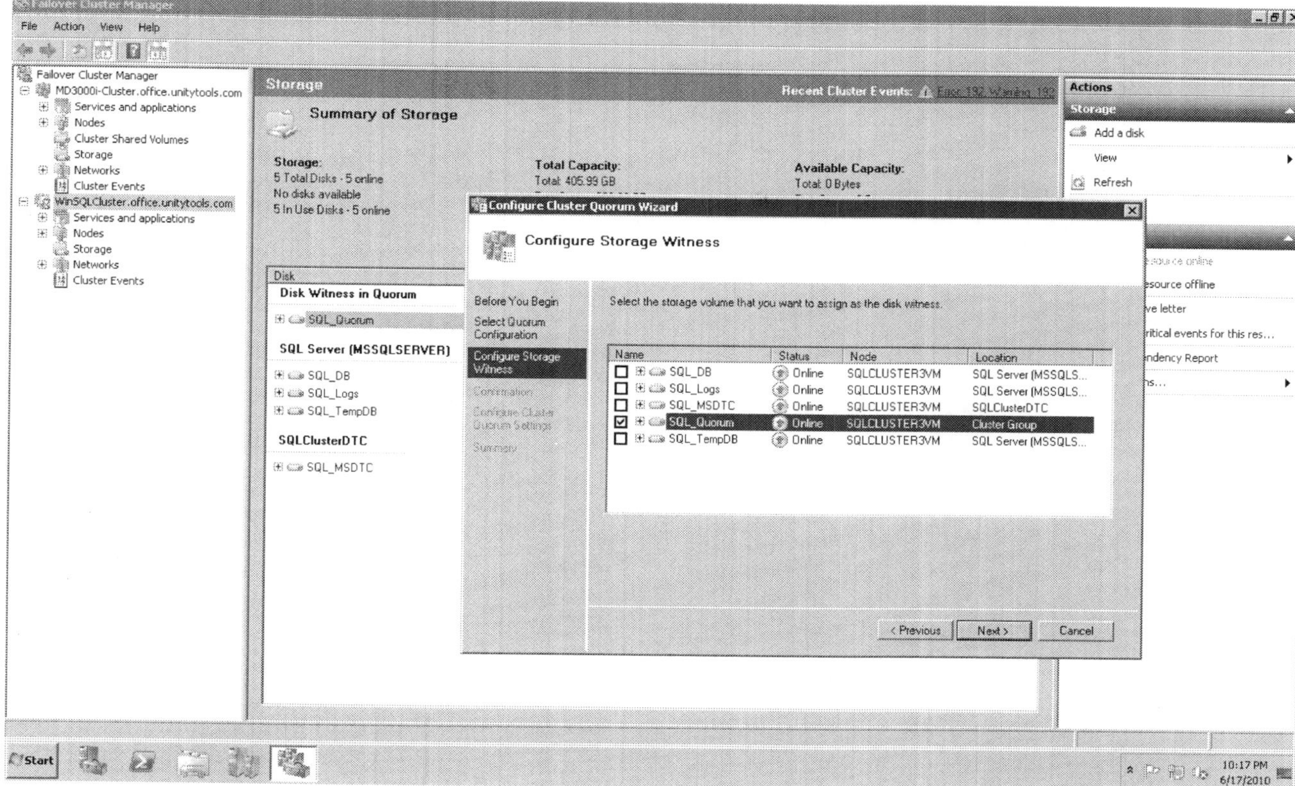


**Figure 12.3**

In this section, we will configure our quorum disk settings for our cluster ahead of time even though we only have one cluster node currently as a member of the cluster. You can change your quorum settings for a Windows cluster at any time. For our project, we will be using a two node cluster, which means we will need to utilize a quorum disk to give us an odd number of voters required.

4. Right click on your Windows cluster name in the left pane, and then select the **More Options\Configure Cluster Quorum Settings** option.

   a. On the **Before You Begin** screen, click on the **Next** button to continue.

   b. On the **Select Quorum Configuration** screen, select the **Node and Disk Majority (not recommended for your current number of nodes)** option, and then click on the **Next** button to continue.

   **NOTE:** You can safely disregard the (not recommended for your current number of nodes) message next to the Node and Disk Majority option, as this issue will be resolved once we add the second SQL virtual machine shortly.

c. On the **Configure Storage Witness** screen, select your quorum disk, and then click on the **Next** button to continue. For our project, we will select our **2GB** shared disk that we labeled **SQL_Quorum**, as shown in **Figure 12.3**.

d. Continue going through the rest of the wizard's screens with the defaults to complete the quorum configuration change.

# Chapter 13: Installing SQL Server 2008/R2 on the Initial SQL Cluster Node

In this chapter, we will make the majority of our application level configurations for our SQL cluster. We will begin with a discussion on the available configuration options for an active/active cluster vs. an active/passive cluster. Following this we will cover the required prerequisites that need to be in place such as service packs to be compatible with different versions of Windows and adding the MSDTC to the cluster as a highly available service. We will then begin our cluster installation by resolving any common warnings and errors that we may receive on the setup support rules screen. Once we have our common issues resolved, we'll cover our high availability options available to us for our Reporting Services installation and how this affects our feature selection during the SQL install process. We will continue through the installation process covering all the critical decisions concerning our setup such as feature selection, assigning cluster and instance names, network selection, assigning security accounts for SQL and Analysis Services, choosing authentication modes, and selecting our disks correctly to insure that our SQL components are distributed across our shared disks for good performance. Once we complete these steps our SQL resources will appear within our Windows cluster that we created earlier and we'll be able to start managing our SQL resources from within the Windows Failover Manager console.

The installation and configuration of our SQL cluster will take place initially on just one of the servers that we want to be the initial node of our cluster. Once we have our initial node in place with our SQL cluster created, we will then cover how to add additional nodes for high availability in Chapter 14. The SQL installation steps are the same whether you are installing your SQL cluster on physical servers or on virtual servers as in the project. Whether you choose to install SQL Server 2008 SP1 or SQL Server 2008 R2 the steps are basically the same and we will cover the few differences that exist during the installation process. For our project, we will install a two node SQL Server 2008 SP1 Enterprise cluster on our Windows Server 2008 R2 virtual machines.

## Understanding SQL Cluster Install Options and Modes

The SQL Server 2008 with SP1 or later is required for installation on a Windows Server 2008 R2 server. The Standard edition of SQL Server 2008 SP1 or higher will allow you to create a two node cluster. If you are planning on three to sixteen nodes then the Enterprise edition of SQL Server is required.

Before we start the installation process we will cover how SQL clustering works when it comes to active/passive vs. active/active clusters. One of the biggest let downs with SQL clustering is Microsoft's constant referrals to active/active clustering even though true active/active clustering doesn't exist. Only one SQL node at a time can control the resources of an SQL instance. This means that you cannot have your SQL cluster nodes load balance the workload of a single instance or share the same disks on the SAN simultaneously. For each SQL instance the only true mode of function is active/passive. What Microsoft refers to as active/active clustering involves two SQL instances installed on the same group of clustered SQL servers. Both of these SQL instances function in an active/passive mode with one SQL node controlling the first instance, while another node controls the second instance. For example, if you were to install two node active/active SQL cluster with the servers named SQLCluster1 and SQLCluster2, then you would first install a default instance of SQL on the server SQLCluster1, and then add the server SQLCluster2 to this first cluster. Next, you would install a second instance of SQL on the server SQLCluster2, and then add the server SQLCluster1 to this second cluster. Both instances have to have their own separate resources, databases, disks on the SAN, and applications that they serve. By having SQLCluster1 as the active node for the first SQL instance, while SQLCluster2 is the active node for the second instance of SQL this makes the cluster an active/active cluster in Microsoft's terminology. In the case of a failover the node remaining online would become the active node for both instances of SQL. There is no true active/active clustering in Microsoft's world yet. If you only have one application that you're hosting such as our project's CRM 4.0 than your cluster can only function in an active/passive mode. Hopefully this issue is close to being resolved seeing that Windows Server 2008 R2's new CSV feature can share SAN disks between hosts and live migrate virtual machines without such an issue.

# Prerequisites- Adding the Microsoft Distributed Transaction Coordinator (MSDTC) to the Windows Cluster as a Service

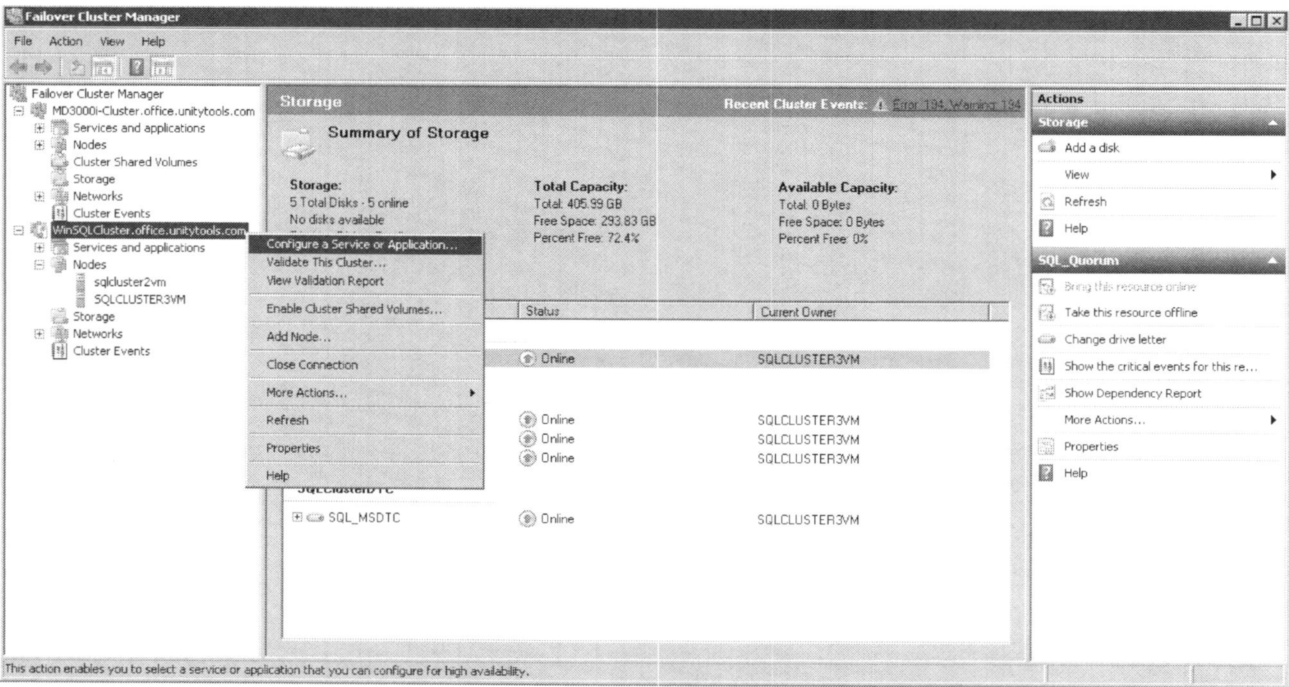


**Figure 13.1**

The Microsoft Distributed Transaction Coordinator (MSDTC) is a transaction coordinator that allows client applications to use several different data sources in one transaction. The Microsoft SQL Server 2008/R2 cluster installation checks for MSDTC as a prerequisite to installing the SQL cluster. Microsoft recommends that you create a highly available MSDTC service on your Windows cluster that will host your SQL resources as a prerequisite. If you do not use distributed transactions, then you can choose to forego setting up MSDTC as a service on your Windows cluster, however the SQL installation will pull a warning. Even though you will receive a warning, the installation will succeed and your SQL cluster will function without issue. For our project, we follow Microsoft's recommendation and setup MSDTC as a highly available service even though our Microsoft Dynamics CRM 4.0 enterprise application does not use distributed transactions.

1. In the **Failover Cluster Management**, right click on your Windows cluster name that you created to host your SQL cluster, and select the **Configure a Service or Application** option, as shown in **Figure 13.1**.

## Selecting the DTC Service

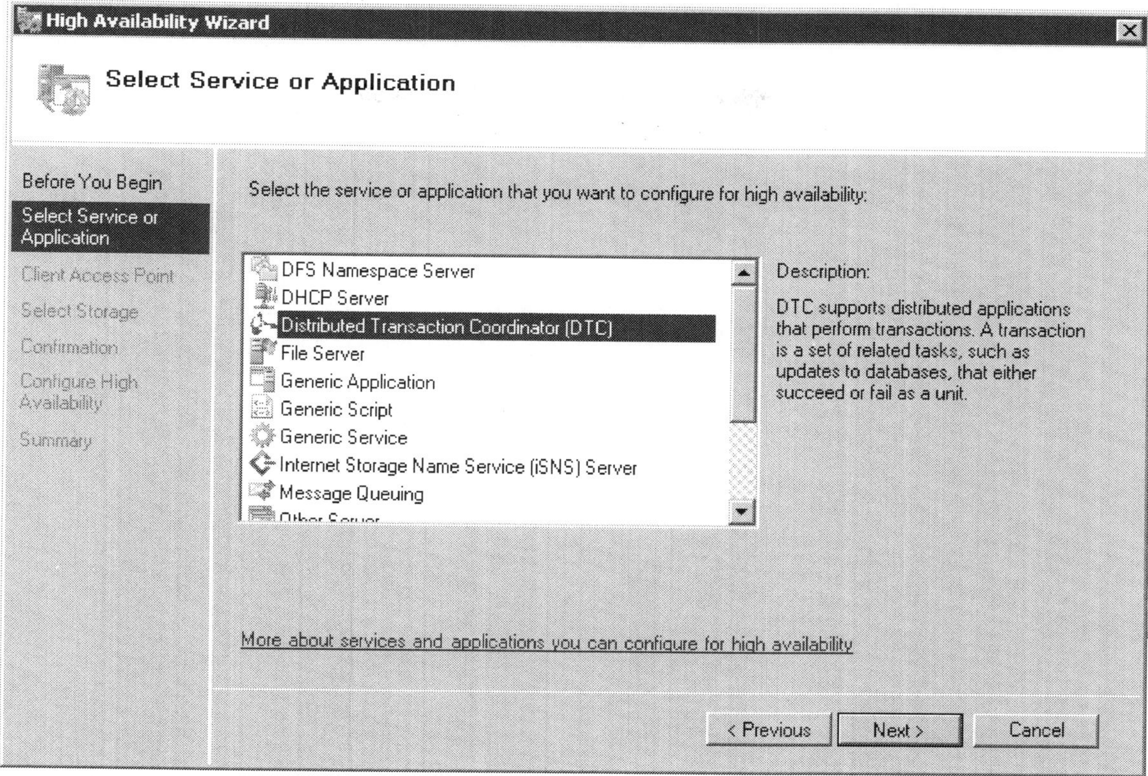


**Figure 13.2**

a. On the **Service or Application** screen, select the **Distributed Transaction Coordinator (DTC)** option as shown in **Figure 13.2**, and then click on the **Next** button to continue.

## Assigning the Client Access Point

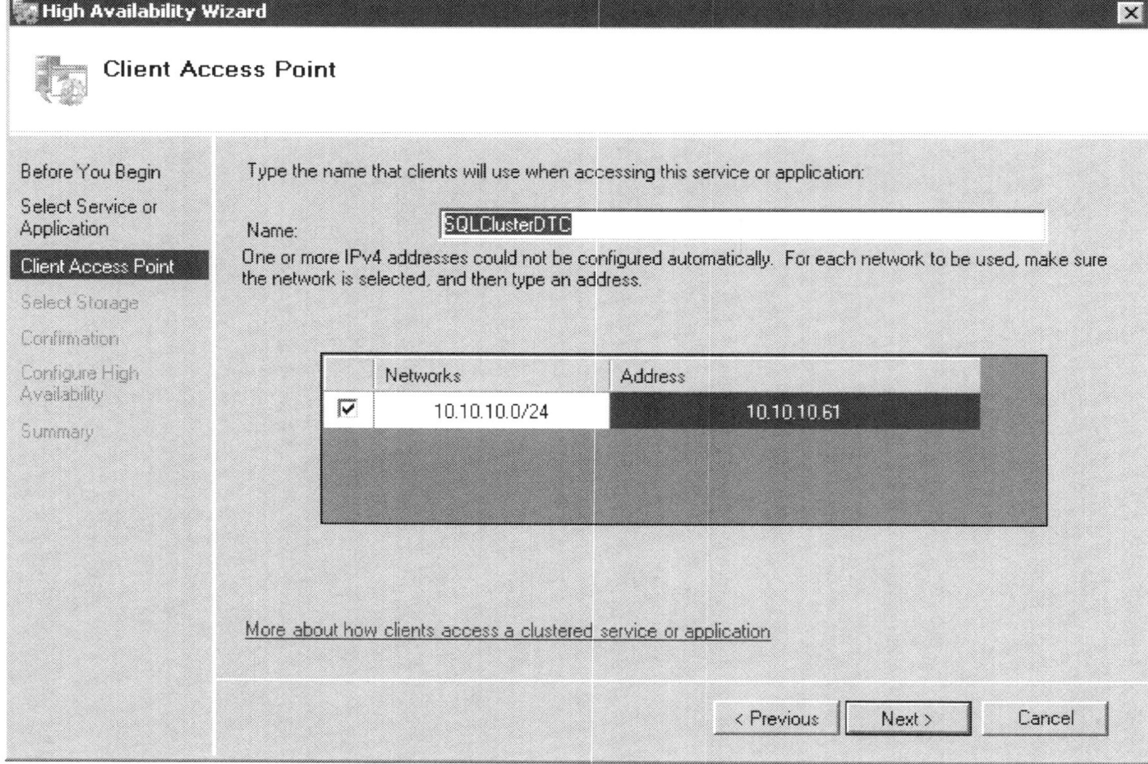


**Figure 13.3**

b. On the **Client Access Point** screen, enter the name you want for your DTC cluster in the **Name** field. This cluster name will only be used for SQL DTC distributed transactions, and not for the actual SQL cluster name that will handle our normal SQL transactions. We will assign the actual SQL cluster's name that will be used by applications for database access later during the SQL Server 2008/R2 software installation process. For our project, we enter the name **SQLClusterDTC** for our MSDTC, as shown in **Figure 13.3**.

   i. For the **Networks** field, make sure that only your Client Active Directory network is selected, and then enter an IP address in the **Address** field for the MSDTC service. Click on the **Next** button to continue. This should be a different IP address and host name from the one that our Windows Server 2008/R2 cluster is already using. For our project, we will select our **10.10.10.0/24** Client Active Directory network, and then enter the IP address of **10.10.10.61** for our MSDTC service's IP address, as shown in **Figure 13.3**.

## Selecting a Shared Disk

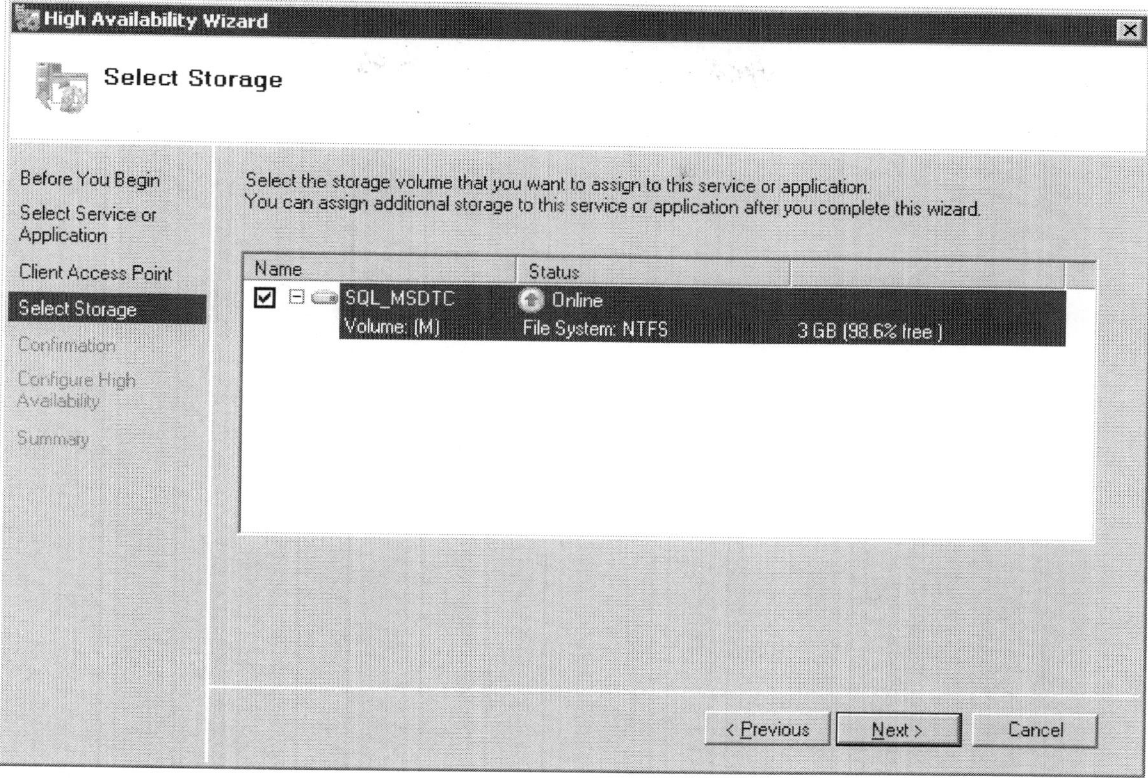


**Figure 13.4**

c. On the **Select Storage** screen, select your shared disk that you created for the MSDTC, and then click on the **Next** button to continue. For our project, we will select our **3GB** disk that we assigned the drive letter of **M:** to and that we named **SQL_MSDTC**.

d. On the **Confirmation** screen, validate your configuration, and then click on the **Next** button to continue.

e. On the **Summary** screen, click on the **Finish** button to create the highly available MSDTC service.

## Installing the SQL Server 2008/R2 on the Initial SQL Cluster Node

2. Copy the SQL Server 2008/R2 installation media onto the local hard disk of server that will be the initial SQL node of the cluster.

   **NOTE:** Make sure to copy the installation media onto the local machine or you may experience weird glitches and/or invalid errors during the install process.

# Prerequisites- When Installing SQL Server 2008 on Windows Server 2008 R2

One of the differences between SQL Server 2008 and SQL Server 2008 R2 when installing on a Windows Server 2008 R2 server is the prerequisites. Windows Server 2008 R2 requires SQL Server 2008 SP1 or later as a prerequisite to installing SQL Server 2008. We will run the SQL Server 2008 Service Pack 1 installation for the shared features on our Windows 2008 R2 servers before performing our SQL Server 2008 installation. If you are installing SQL Server 2008 R2 on Windows Server 2008 R2 or SQL Server 2008 on a Window Server 2008, then please disregard this section and skip to **Step 4**.

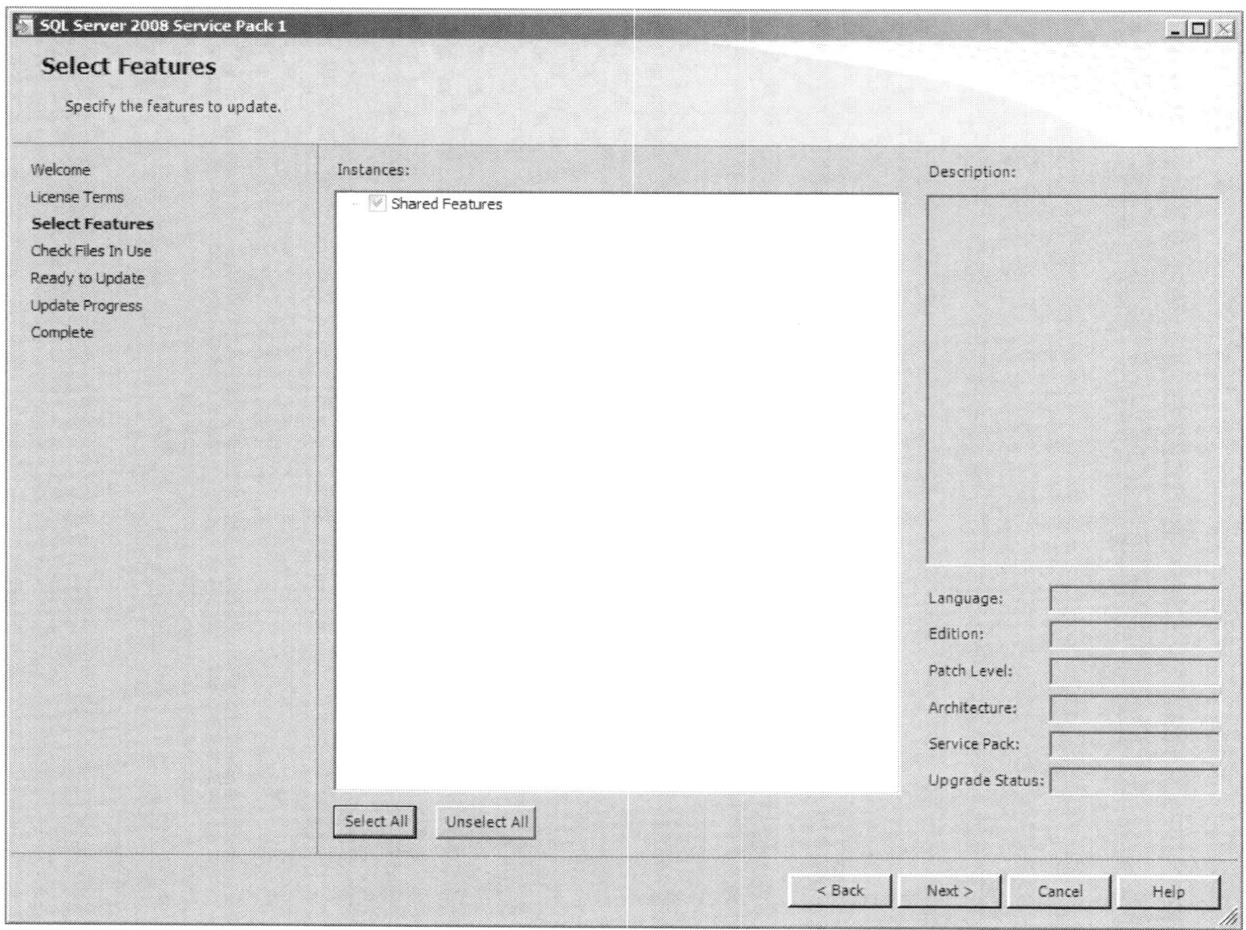


**Figure 13.5**

3. Download and launch the **SQL Server 2008 SP1** or later install on the initial Windows cluster node that will host your SQL resources. For our project, we will run the install on our initial Windows cluster node named **SQLCluster2VM**.

   a. Leave the install options all at their defaults except for when you come to the **Select Features** screen, where you want to click on the **Select All** button, as shown in **Figure 13.5**. Click on the **Next** button to continue.

   b. Finish going through the install screens with the defaults selected to complete the install.

## Launching the SQL Server 2008/R2 Installation

4. Run the SQL Server 2008/R2 **setup.exe** from the installation media to launch **SQL Server Installation Center.**

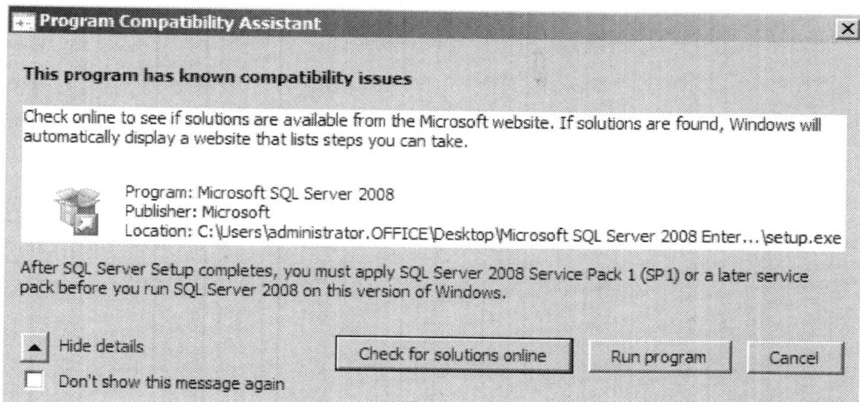


**Figure 13.6**

a. You will most likely receive a **Program Compatibility Assistant** pop-up screen when installing SQL Server 2008 on Windows Server 2008 R2, to which you want to click on the **Run program** button to continue. If you are installing SQL Server 2008 R2 then please disregard this step. This screen is letting you know that for your SQL Server installation to be compatible with Windows Server 2008 R2 you will need to reapply the SQL Server 2008 Service Pack 1 or later after the SQL Server installation has completed.

## Setup Support Rules Screen

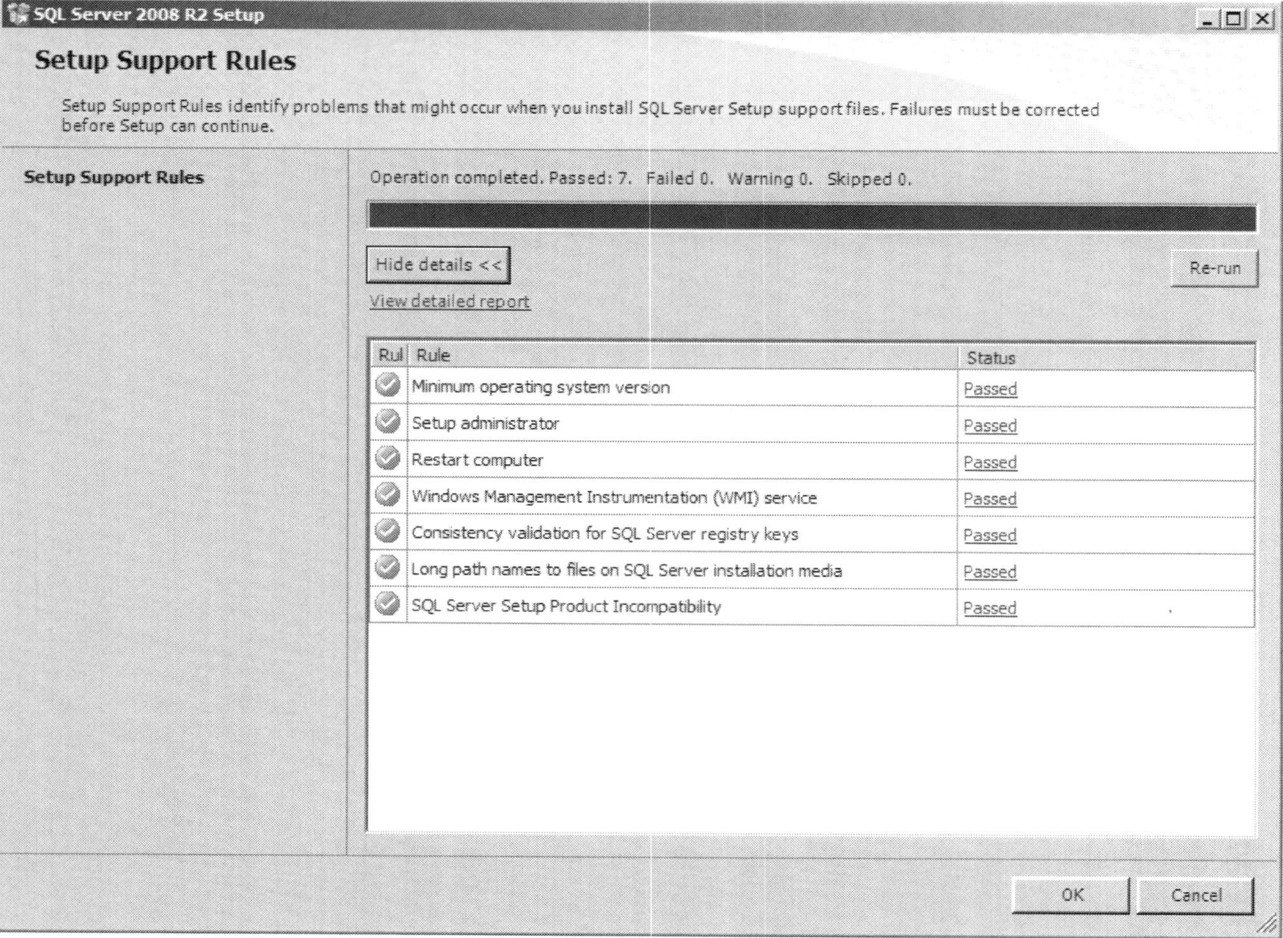


**Figure 13.7**

5. On the **SQL Server Installation Center** screen, click on the **Installation** option in the left pane.

   a. In the right pane, click on the **New SQL Server failover cluster installation** link to launch the **SQL Server 2008/R2 Setup** wizard.

6. You will most likely receive the **Program Compatibility Assistant** pop-up screen again, click on the **Run program** button to continue. If you are installing SQL Server 2008 R2 or on Window Server 2008, then please disregard this step.

7. On the **Setup Support Rules** screen, verify that the results all passed as shown in **Figure 13.7**, and then click on the **OK** button to continue.

8. On the **Product Key** screen, enter your product key, and then click on the **Next** button to continue.

9. On the **License Terms** screen, select the **I accept the license terms** checkbox, and then click on the **Next** button to continue.

10. On the second **Setup Support Files** screen, click on the **Install** button to continue.

## Resolving Common Warnings and Errors of the Setup Support Rules Screen

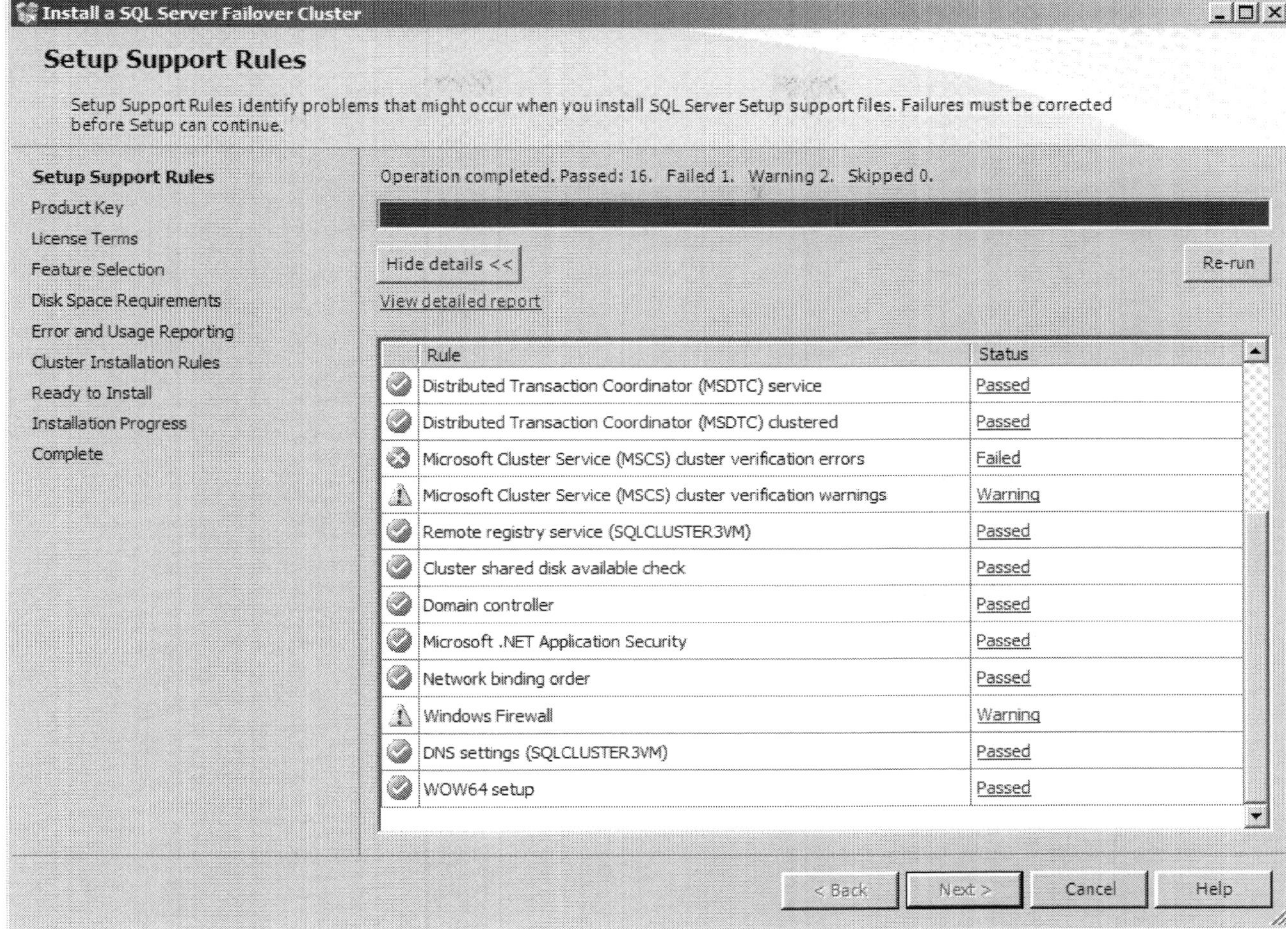


**Figure 13.8**

11. On the third **Setup Support Rules** screen, we will need to resolve some common warnings and errors, as shown in **Figure 13.8**. The following steps will help explain and resolve these commons issues.

## Windows Firewall (Warning)

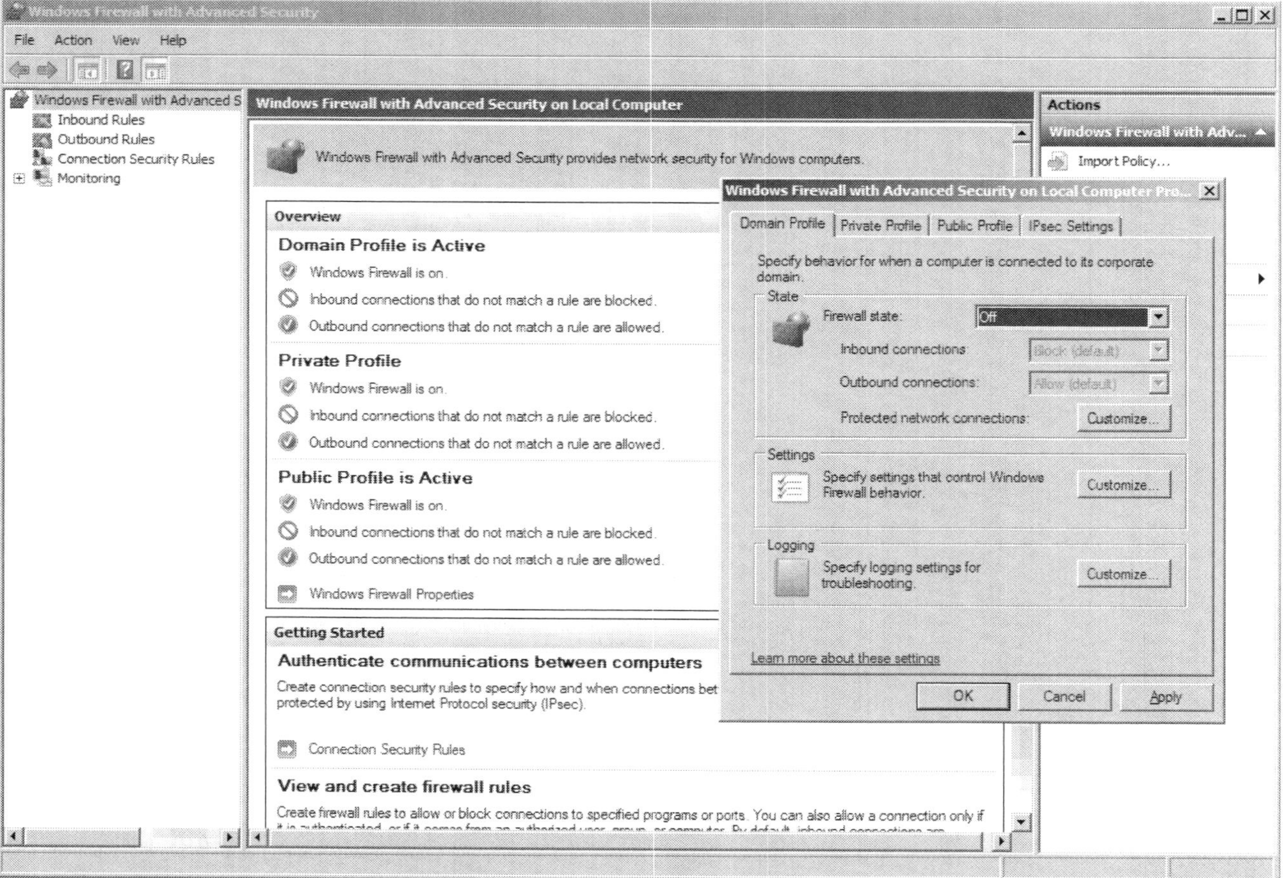


**Figure 13.9**

a. **Windows Firewall (Warning)** result- The easiest way to resolve this is to temporally disable the firewall, and then once our SQL software is installed we will set our SQL Application to be allowed through the firewall. We will cover how to enable and configure the Windows Firewall for our SQL cluster in **Chapter 16**.

   i. Go to **Start\Administrative Tools\Windows Firewall with Advanced Security**, and then in the **Overview** section of the center pane click on the blue text link for the **Windows Firewall Properties** option.

      1. For each tab **Domain Profile**, **Private Profile** & **Public Profile** temporally set the **Firewall State** field to the **Off** option, and then click the **OK** button to save your changes.

## Microsoft Cluster Service (MSCS) cluster verification errors (Failed)

b. **Microsoft Cluster Service (MSCS) cluster verification errors (Failed)** result- If you receive this error, then you will need to return to **Failover Cluster Manager** and manually run the cluster validation. You may just need to manually run the cluster validation or you may have some real issues to resolve.

   i. Right click on your Windows cluster that you created to host your SQL resources, and then select **Validate This Cluster** option.

      1. On the **Before You Begin** screen, click on the **Next** button to continue.

      2. Select the **Run All Tests** option, and click on the **Next** button to continue.

      3. On the **Review Storage Status** screen, select the **Take the listed services or applications offline, so that the associated disks can be tested** option, and then click on the **Next** button to continue.

      4. On the **Confirmation** screen, click on the **Next** button to run the validation.

      5. On the **Summary** screen, verify that the testing completed successfully, and then click on the **Finish** button. If there are issues, click on the **View Report** button, and resolve any issues outlined.

## Microsoft Cluster Service (MSCS) cluster verification warnings (Warning)

c. **Microsoft Cluster Service (MSCS) cluster verification warnings (Warning)** result- If you received any warnings during the initial cluster validation when you created the Windows cluster, then you will receive this error. In our project's particular case, we created our Windows cluster with only one node which causes this warning to appear. If you are following our project's steps, then you can safely ignore this warning when reviewing the validation report and continue on with your SQL installation.

## Network Bindings Order (Warning)

d. **Network Bindings Order (Warning)** result- You will receive this warning if your Client Active Directory network is not set as the first connection in your bindings order. We covered setting the network bindings in **Chapter 10** for our physical host servers, and then in **Chapter 11** for our SQL virtual machines. If you have not yet set your network bindings order with your Client Active Directory network at the top of the priority list, then you'll need to do so by returning to these previous chapters.

## Distributed Transaction Coordinator (Failed)

e. **Distributed Transaction Coordinator (Failed)** result- If you decided to create your SQL cluster without first adding the MSDTC as a highly available service, then you will see failed results for any MSDTC components. Microsoft recommends adding the MSDTC as a highly available service before creating your SQL cluster, however if you don't use distribute transactions then you can choose to continue the install without MSDTC service and your cluster will still function successfully without issues. If this is your scenario, then you can safely ignore this error and continue with the installation.

12. Returning to the **Setup Support Rules** screen, click on the **Re-Run** button, and then verify that the issues have been resolved. Once the test results pass successfully, click on the **Next** button to continue.

## SQL Feature Selection and How It Relates to a Reporting Services Scale-Out Deployment

SQL Server Reporting Services (SSRS) is not supported in a clustered SQL environment. This means that in the event of a failover the reporting services will stop functioning due to this particular resource not being able to migrate to other node(s) of the cluster. Fortunately, this issue can easily be overcome by installing the SQL Reporting Services feature on our front-end application servers, and then utilizing a Reporting Services Scale-out Deployment.
The SQL Reporting Services Scale-Out Deployment connects each instance of Reporting Services on our front-end application servers together. This will allow our front-end application servers to deliver reports seamlessly from our SQL cluster no matter which cluster node currently hosts our SQL resources. We only want SQL Reporting Services installed on servers that will point at our SQL cluster for reports and that are actively part of our Scale-out Deployment. This is important, because any server that has SQL Reporting Services installed on it will automatically show up in our Scale-Out Deployment regardless of being configured as part of the deployment or not. If you have instances of SQL Reporting Services showing up in your Scale-out deployment that aren't actively part of your cluster, then your reports may sporadically malfunction.

If you absolutely cannot have the SQL Reporting Services installed on your front-end application servers, then there is an option to install it on your SQL cluster nodes by utilizing a second instance of SQL on your passive cluster node(s). We will not cover this setup step by step in this book, however you should be able to follow the same basic steps outlined for our front-end application servers Scale-out Deployment to accomplish this. Since in the next step of the installation you have to make decision of what SQL features/components to install, we will cover a quick summary of what would be involved in setting up a Scale-out Deployment with your SQL cluster nodes vs. on your front-end application servers. If you are planning on following our project's recommended setup by installing your SQL Reporting Services on your front-end application servers, then please disregard this section and skip to **Step 13**.

In this configuration, you want your initial/active SQL cluster node to have only one default instance of SQL installed with all SQL features. Then for any of your passive nodes would need to install two instances of SQL with the default instance having all of the SQL features installed except for the SQL Reporting Services, while the second instance of SQL would only have the SQL Reporting Services feature installed. Your passive nodes default instance of SQL has to be a member of your SQL cluster, while your passive nodes second instance of SQL with Reporting Services has to be a member of your Scale-out Deployment. If you try using just one default instance on your passive nodes, then your reporting will work fine when the initial/active SQL cluster node controls your SQL cluster's resources, however once a failover occurs to one of the passive nodes then your reporting services will cease to function.

# Selecting SQL Features for Installation

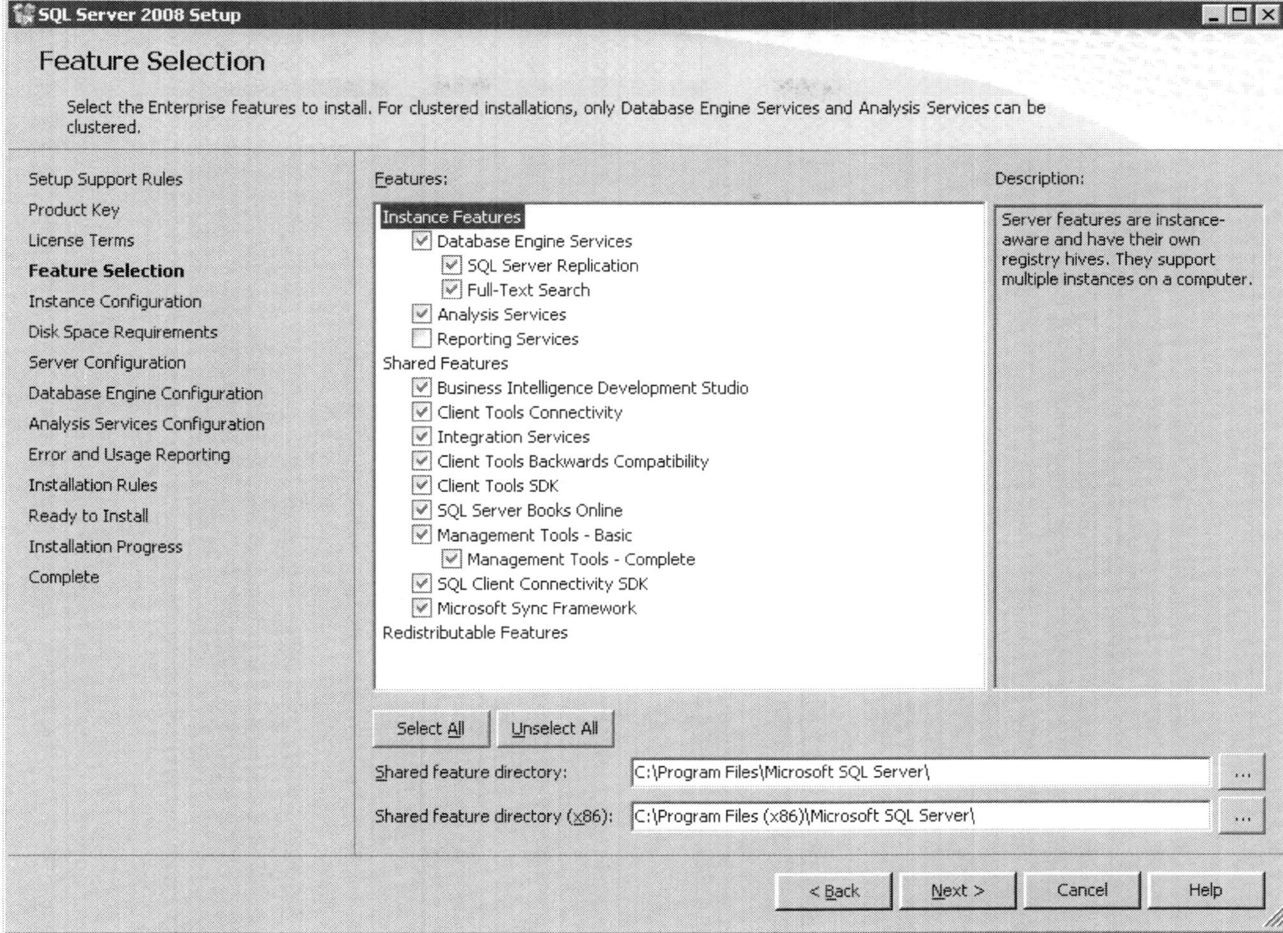


**Figure 13.10**

13. On the **Feature Selection** screen, select the SQL features that you want to install. For our project, we will select all the features except for the **Reporting Services**, as shown in **Figure 13.10**. We will create our highly available reporting in **Chapter 20** by installing our SQL Reporting Services in a Scale-out Deployment on our front-end application servers.

    a. For the **Shared feature directory** field, we will leave default path to the local C: drive with the path of **C:\Program Files\Microsoft SQL Server**, and then click the **Next** button to continue. If do not have sufficient disk space on your C: drive, then you will want to place the shared feature directory on another local disk. In later steps of the install process we will specify our different paths to each our shared disks for our databases, database logs and temp database directories.

## Assigning the SQL Cluster and Instance Names

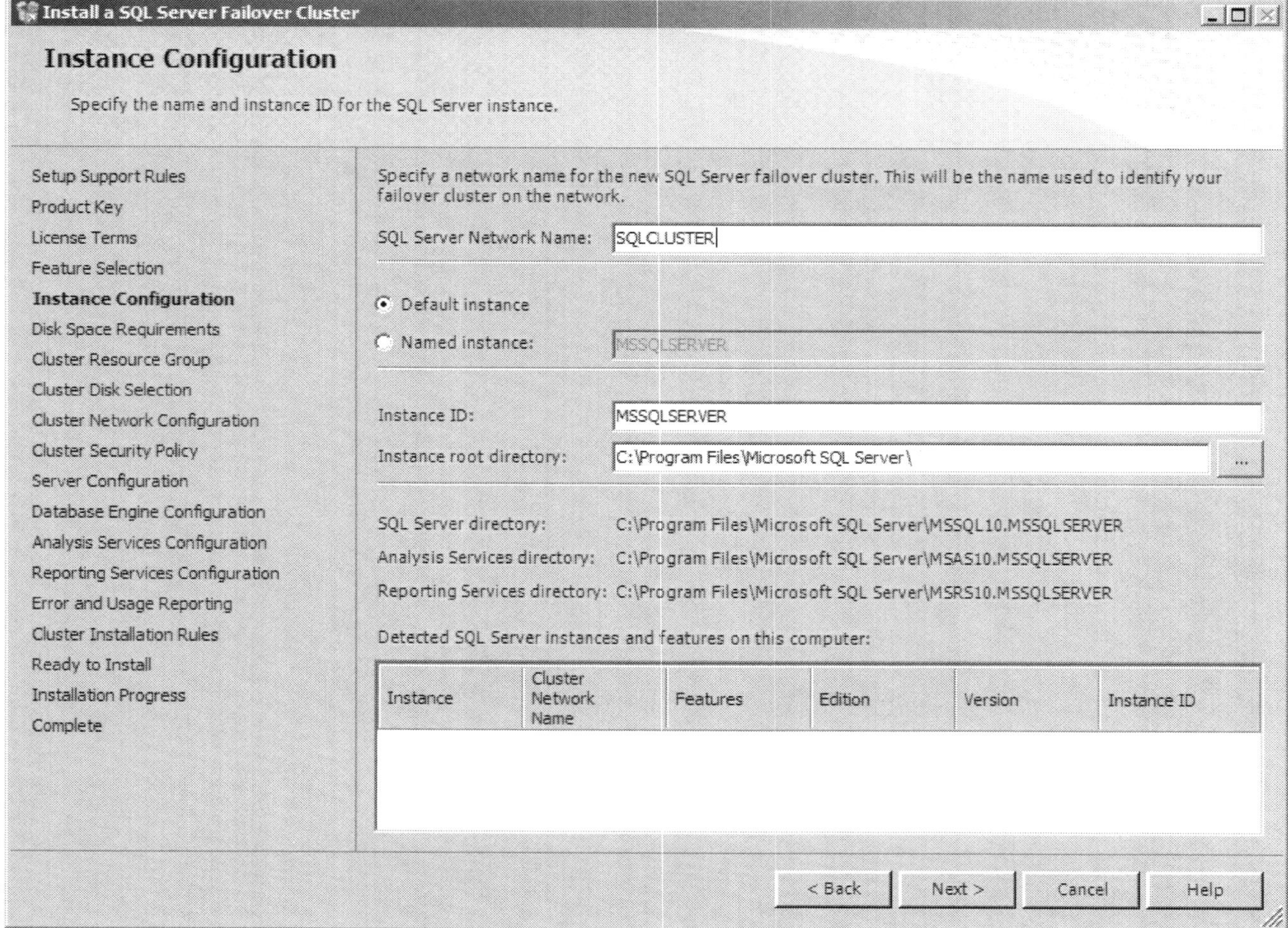


**Figure 13.11**

14. On the **Instance Configuration** screen, enter the name you want for your SQL cluster in the **SQL Server Network Name** field. This is the actual name of your SQL cluster that will be available on the network, and that all your applications will point to for access to your databases. You will also use this name when connecting to your database engine with the SQL Server Management Studio program. For our project, we will enter **SQLCLUSTER** for our SQL cluster's name, and then leave the remaining fields at their defaults, as shown in **Figure 13.11**.

    a. We will leave the type of instance set to the **Default Instance** option. The Named Instance option is usually only chosen when installing a second instance on an already existing SQL Server.

    b. We will leave the **Instance ID** field set to its default of **MSSQLSERVER**. The Instance ID is the name of your SQL instance and will also be used to identify installation directories and registry keys for each installation/instance of SQL Server you have on each server.

    c. We will also leave the default set for the **Instance Root Directory** field with the path of **C:\Program Files\Microsoft SQL Server**. This is where SQL will install its files referred to as binaries. In later steps of the install process we will specify different our paths to each of our shared disks for our databases, database logs and temp database directories.

15. On the **Disk Space Requirements** screen, verify that you have enough space, and then click on the **Next** button to continue.

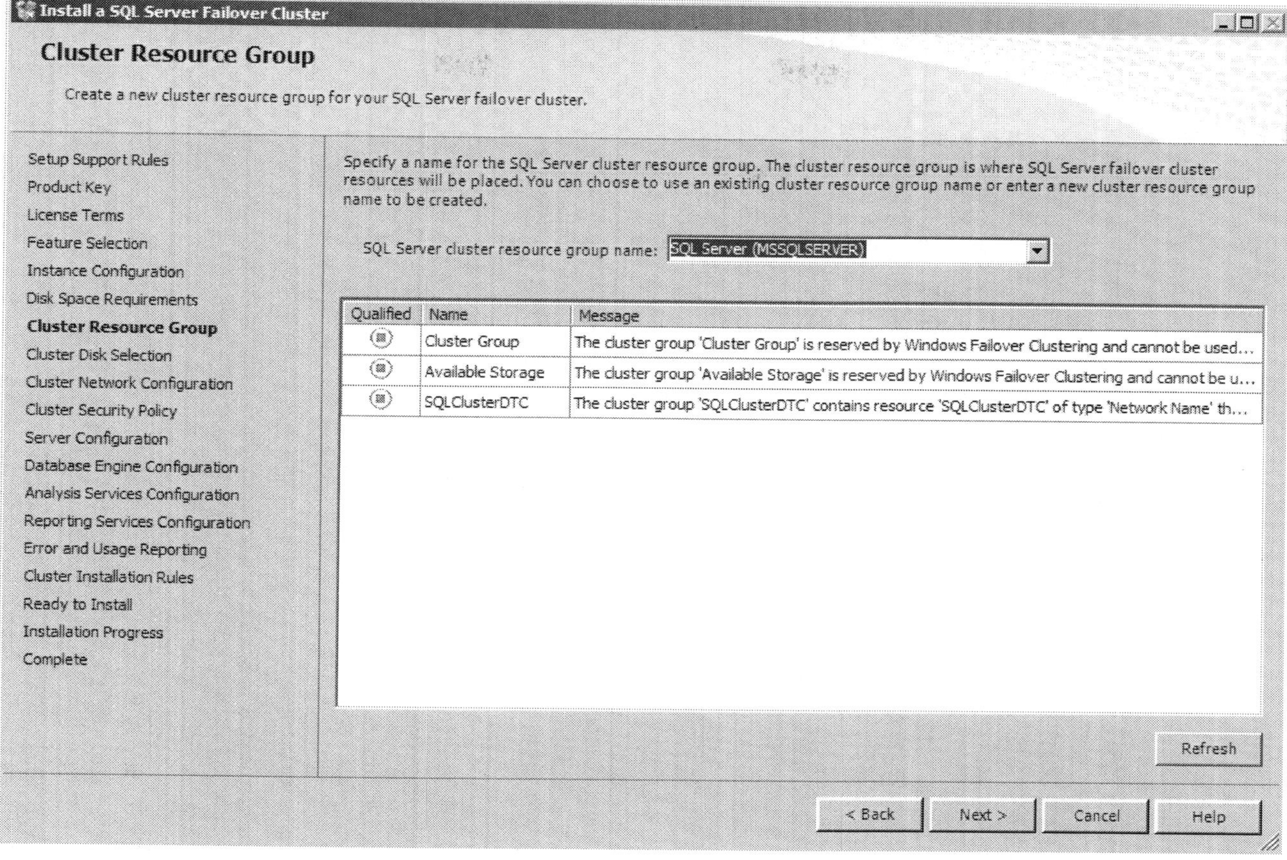


**Figure 13.12**

16. On the **Cluster Resource Group** screen, leave the defaults as shown in **Figure 13.12**, and then click on the **Next** button to continue.

## Selecting the Shared Disks to be Included in the SQL Cluster

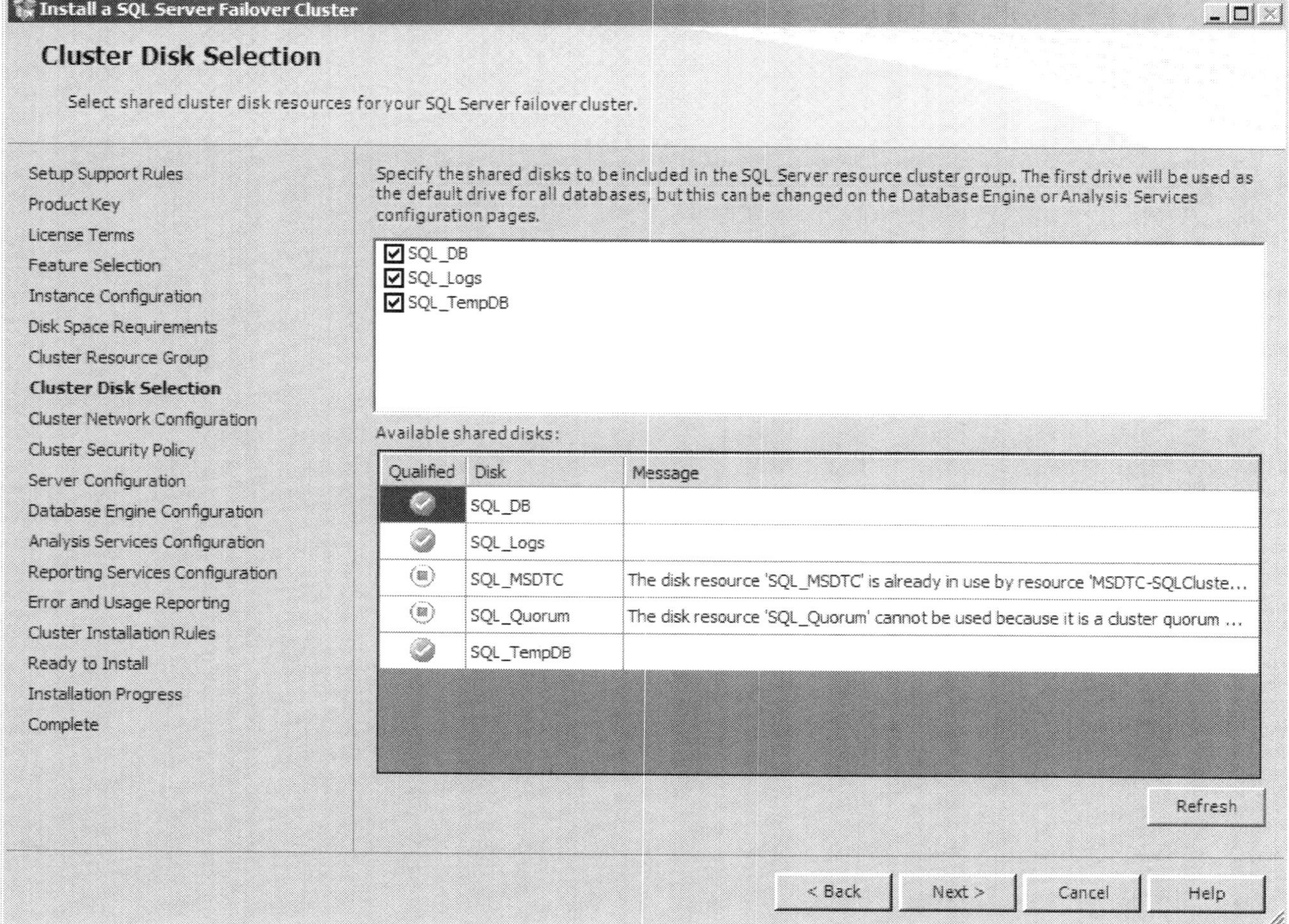


**Figure 13.13**

17. On the **Cluster Disk Selection** screen, you want to select the shared disks that you will use for your databases, database logs and temp databases, and then click on the **Next** button to continue. For our project, we will select our three shared disks that we labeled **SQL_DB**, **SQL_Logs** and **SQL_TempDB**, as shown in **Figure 13.13**.

## Assigning the Client Active Directory Network as the Cluster's Network

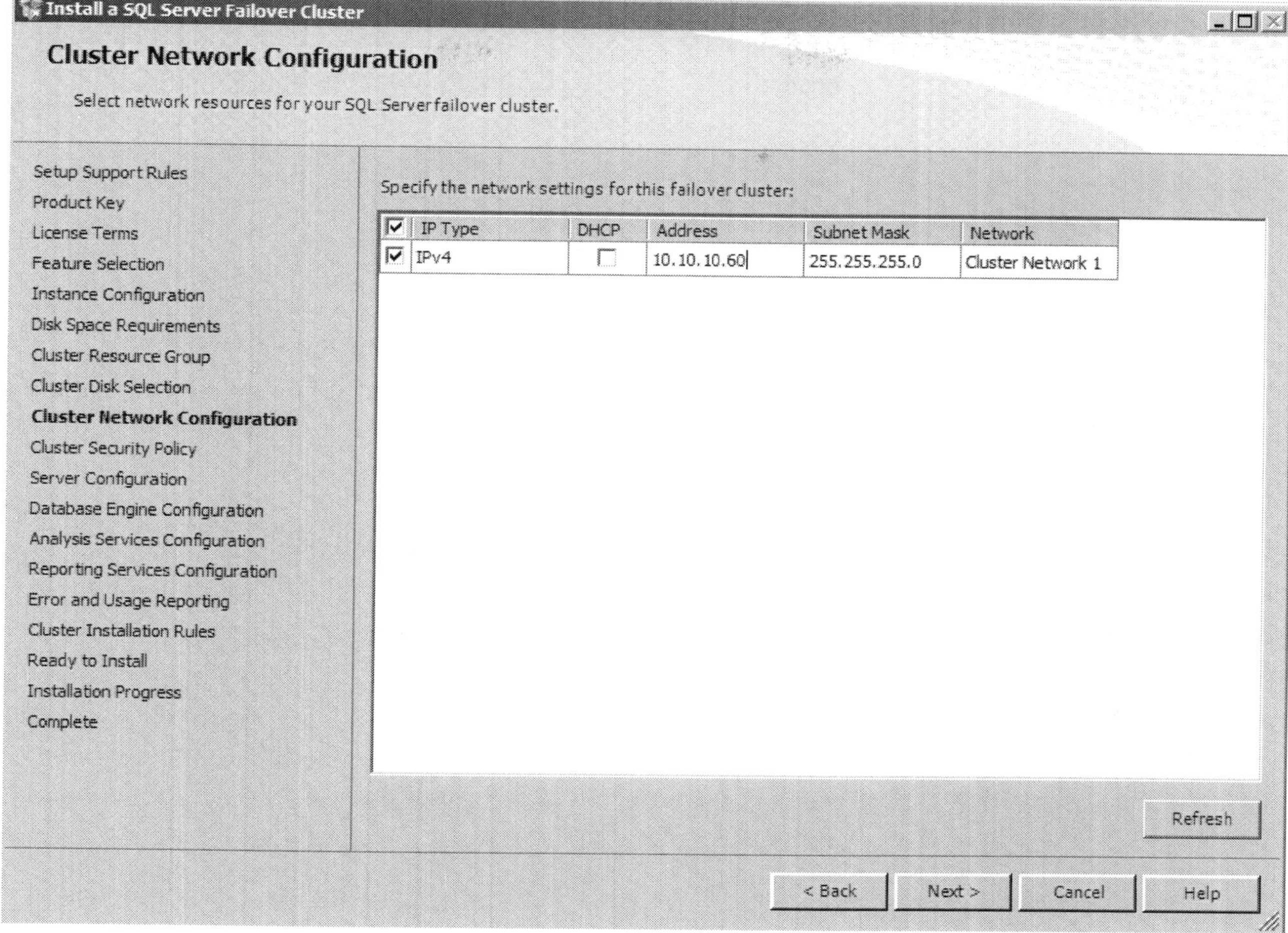


**Figure 13.14**

18. For the **IPv4** row of the **Cluster Network Configuration** screen, unselect the **DHCP** checkbox, and then enter the IP address and subnet mask you want for your SQL cluster in the **Address** and **Subnet Mask** fields. This is the actual IP address of your SQL cluster that will be available on the network. The IPv4 network settings you assign here should be part of your Client Active Directory network. If you have any other networks listed here such as an IPv6 network, then you'll want to unselect them, and then click on the **Next** button to continue. For our project, we will assign our SQL cluster an IP address of **10.10.10.60** with a subnet mask of **255.255.255.0**, as shown in **Figure 13.14**.

19. On the **Cluster Security Policy** screen, accept the default value of **Use service SIDs (recommended)**, and then click on the **Next** button to continue. Previously for Windows Server 2003 you would have specified domain groups for all your SQL Server services, but for Windows Server 2008 or later is recommended that you to use service SIDs. For more information on using service SIDs with SQL Server 2008, please refer to this MSDN article at http://msdn.microsoft.com/en-us/library/ms143504.aspx#Service_SID.

## Assigning User Accounts to SQL Services

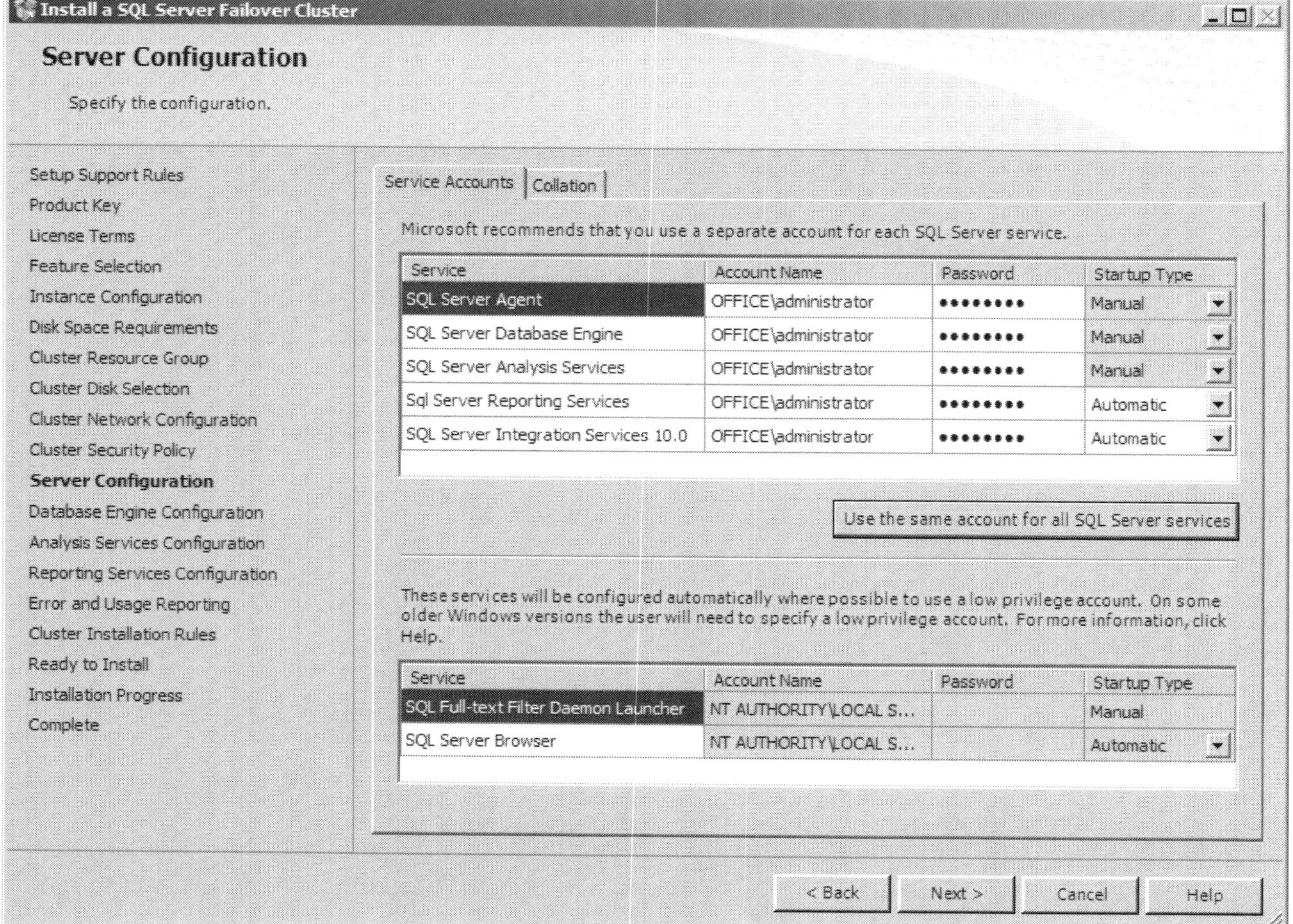


**Figure 13.15**

20. On the **Server Configuration** screen under the **Service Accounts** tab, click on the **Use the same account for all SQL Server services** button, and then enter the user account that you want to use for your SQL Server service accounts. User accounts and security are usually a complicated endeavor, so unless you have a firm understanding of the user account(s) that you want your SQL services to run under, it is recommended that you use an administrator level account. In **Chapter 22** we will cover how to secure our Microsoft Dynamics CRM 4.0 front-end application servers access to our SQL cluster. For our project, we will use the **Domain Administrator** account for our SQL services, as shown in **Figure 13.15**.

    **NOTE:** You may have noticed that the startup type fields are set to manual and that they cannot be changed during the SQL cluster install process. This is because the SQL cluster will stop or start these services depending on which server is given control of the SQL resources. Be aware of this when viewing the services from within the Services console of your server, as it is perfectly normal for the startup type to be set to manual for services that belong to your SQL cluster.

    a. If you want your SQL install to use a different language then English, then click on the **Collation** tab, and select the language you want.

b. Once you're done configuring the **Server Configuration** screen, click on the **Next** button to continue.

## Selecting the Authentication Mode

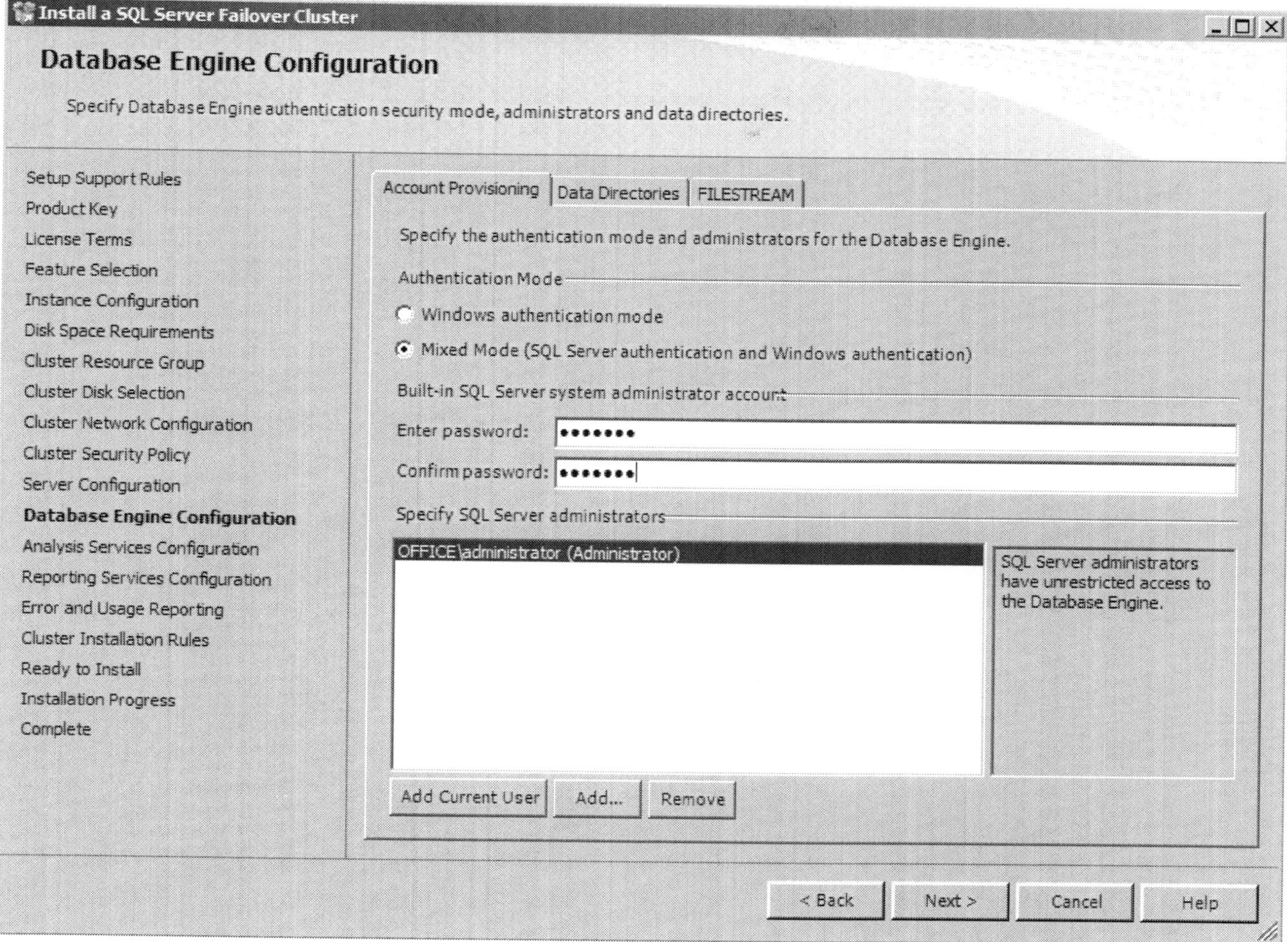


**Figure 13.16**

21. On the **Database Engine Configuration** screen, select the appropriate **Authentication Mode** for your environment. If you have applications that need to use SQL server authentication, then choose the **Mixed Mode** authentication option, and entered a password for the default SQL administrator account of **sa**. You can always enable the mixed mode authentication later by enabling the sa account from within the SQL Server Studio Management console's logins node. For our project, we will choose the **Mixed Mode** option, as shown in **Figure 13.16**.

    a. Click on the **Add Current User** button to add the account that you're currently using install SQL with. For our project this will add the **Domain Administrator** to the **SQL Server Administrators Group**.

# Distributing SQL Directories Across the Shared Disks

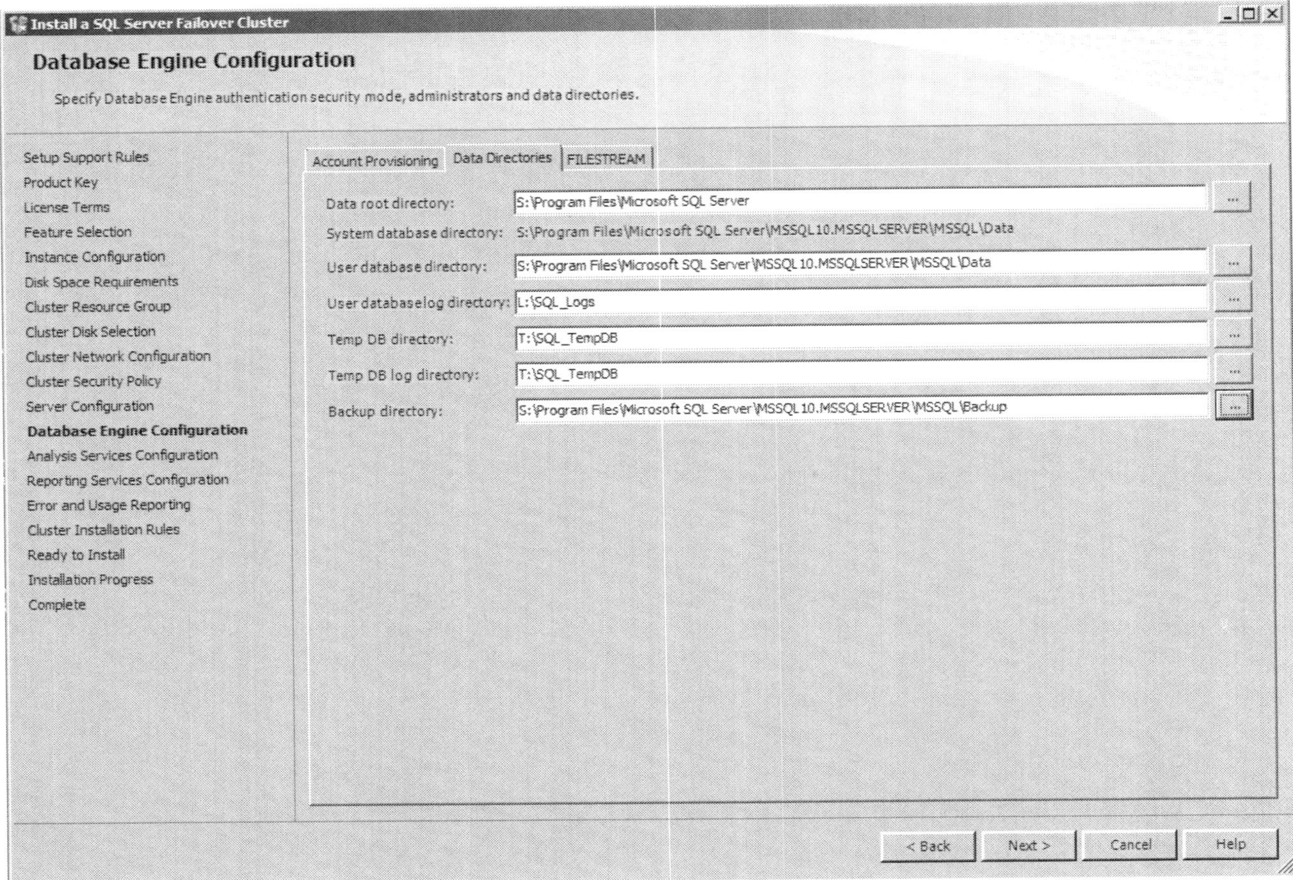


**Figure 13.17**

22. While still on the **Database Engine Configuration** screen, click on the **Data Directories** tab. You'll notice by default that the install sets the directory paths to our first shared disk of the cluster. We want to enter our paths manually for the field of each SQL component, so that we distribute our SQL directories across our shared disks for better performance. For our project, we will manually enter the different paths listed below for each component.

    a. **User Database Directory** field- We will enter the path of **S:\Program Files\Microsoft SQL Server\MSSQL10.MSSQLSERVER\MSSQL\Data**, which SQL will then create this directory structure on our **SQL_DB** shared disk for our user databases. If you are installing an **SQL Server 2008 R2** cluster, then the default paths are a little different by having the addition of **_50** in the folders name. For example, the folder **MSSQL10.MSSQLSERVER** in **SQL Server 2008 SP1** would be **MSSQL10_50.MSSQLSERVER** in **SQL Server 2008 R2**. You can enter the directory paths of your choice for each component, however keep in mind that the important thing is to distribute your SQL components across your SAN's RAID arrays for optimum performance. For our project, we will mirror the directory structure of a default SQL installation for the data directory. The benefits of doing so are listed below.

i. The SQL install creates this basic directory structure anyway for its **System Database Directory** field as shown in **Figure 13.17**, so it only makes sense to place our **Data** folder in the same directory structure.

ii. You eliminate any potential upgrade or third party software issues that could be arise due to using different paths then the defaults.

iii. Most likely your IT staff is already familiar with SQL's default directory structure, thus making the new SQL cluster easy to use for your co-workers by them not having to learn new paths to data.

b. **User Database Log Directory**, **Temp DB Directory**, and **Temp DB Log Directory** fields- For these directories you can choose to simply create a single folder on the root of the corresponding shared disk for your path. These directories will host data specific only to their own individual SQL component, so there is no benefit to creating a more complex directory structure as we did for our user database directories. For our project, we will enter our directory paths as shown in **Figure 13.17**

c. **Backup Directory** field- We can choose to either enter the SQL's default installation path for this directory or we can choose to place this directory on its own shared disk on the SAN. For our project, we will enter SQL's default installation path of **S:\Program Files\Microsoft SQL Server\MSSQL10.MSSQLSERVER\MSSQL\Backup**, which will create this directory structure on our **SQL_DB** shared disk. This local backup directory shouldn't be used for any significant amount of backup operations, as we should always be backing up our data to a location outside of our cluster for disaster recovery purposes. This makes the local backup directory of little significance, thus SQL's default location is fine.

d. Once you are finished entering your paths, click on the **Next** button to continue.

## Assigning a User Account to the Analysis Services

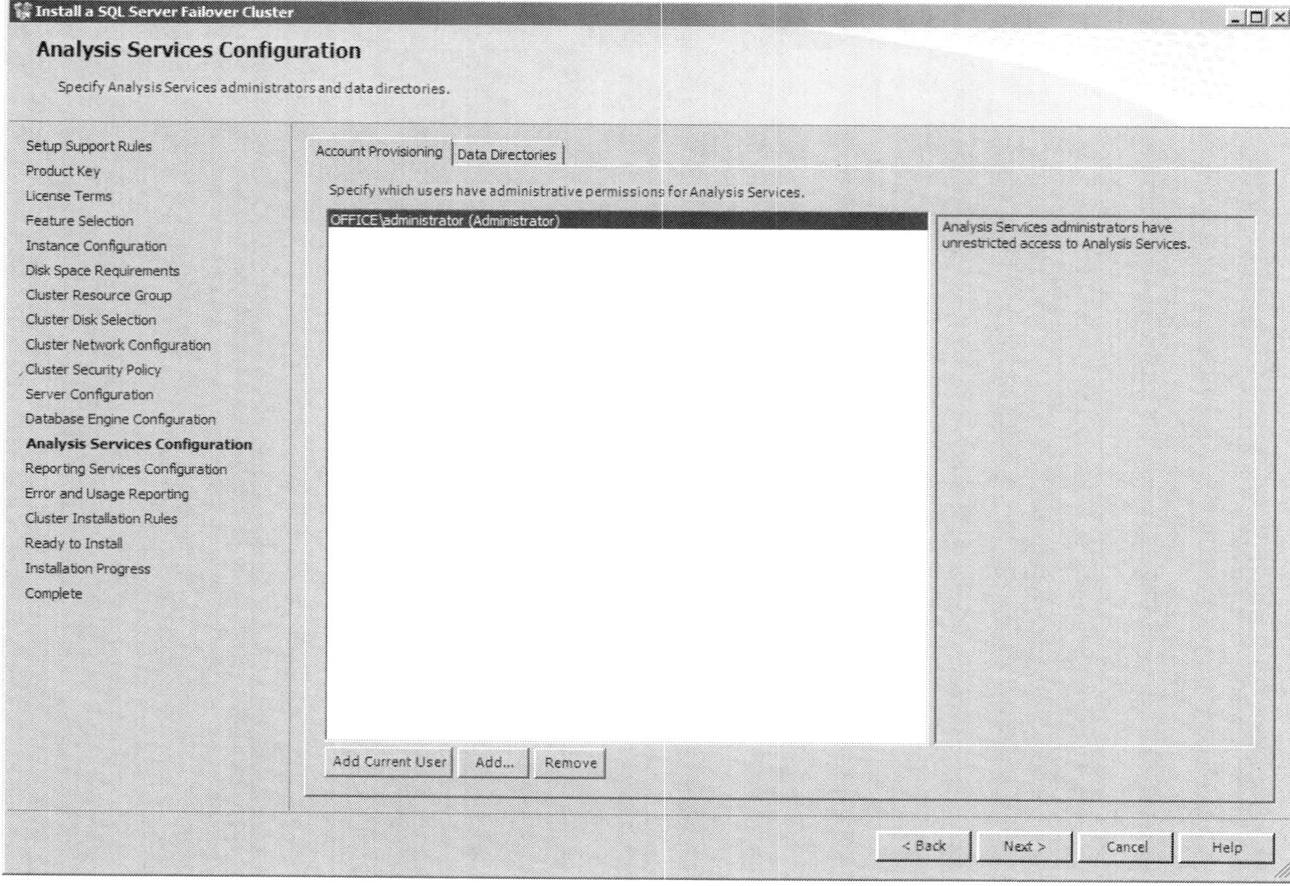


**Figure 13.18**

23. On the **Analysis Services Configurations** screen under the **Account Provisioning** tab, add the user account that you want to have administrative permissions for Analysis Services. For our project, we will click on the **Add Current User** button, which will add the **Domain Administrator** account to have administrative rights. If you didn't select the Analysis Services feature for installation, then you can ignore this step and the next as you continue.

# Distributing Analysis Services Directories Across the Shared Disks

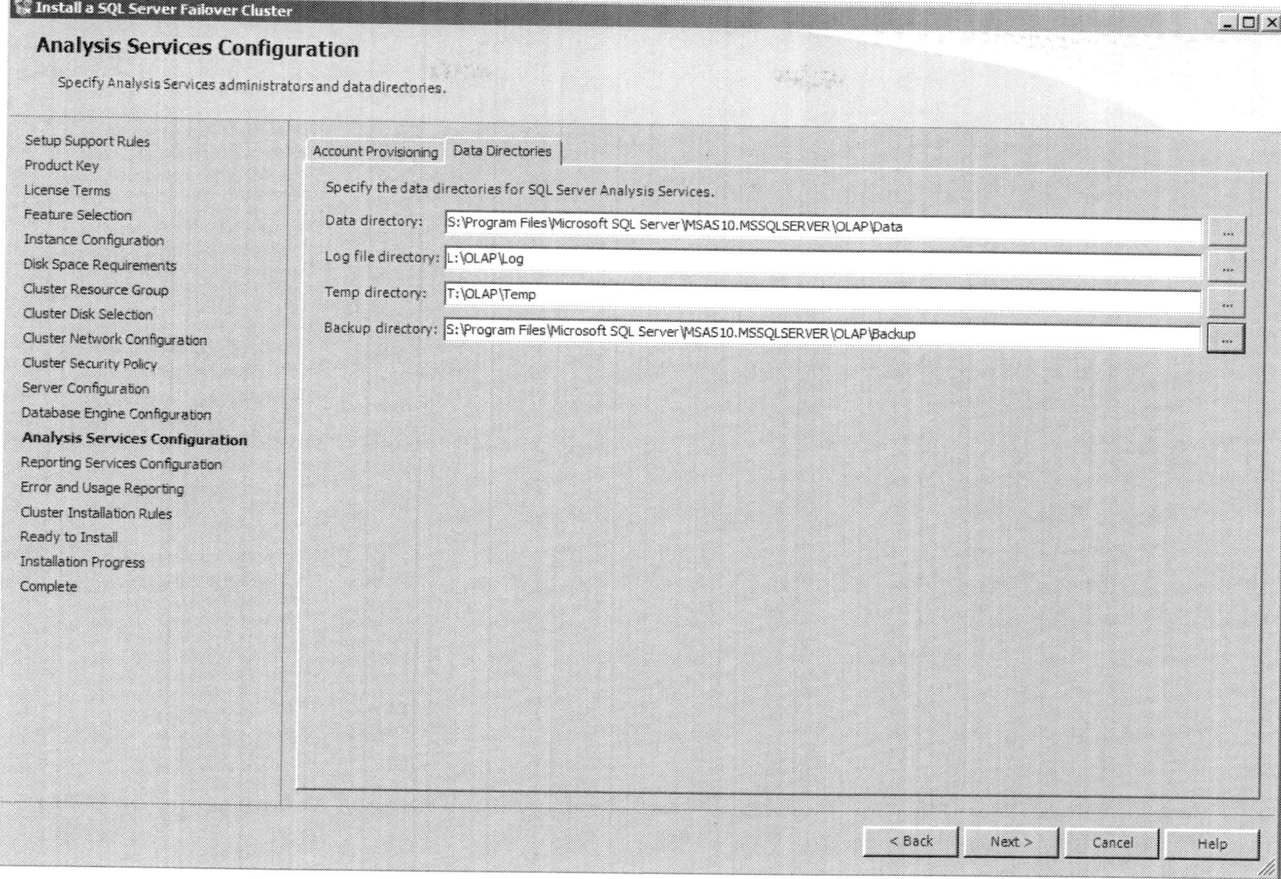


**Figure 13.19**

24. While still on the **Analysis Services Configuration** screen, click on the **Data Directories** tab. You'll notice by default that the install sets the directory paths to our first shared disk of the cluster. We want to enter our paths manually for the field of each SQL component, so that we distribute our Analysis Services directories across our shared disks for better performance. For our project, we will manually enter the different paths listed below for each component.

    a. **Data Directory** field- We will enter the path of **S:\Program Files\Microsoft SQL Server\MSAS10.MSSQLSERVER\OLAP\Data**, which SQL will then create this directory structure on our **SQL_DB** shared disk for our Analysis Services data. Again, if you are installing an **SQL Server 2008 R2** cluster, then the default paths are a little different by having the addition of **_50** in the folders name. For example, the folder **MSSQL10.MSSQLSERVER** in **SQL Server 2008 SP1** would be **MSSQL10_50.MSSQLSERVER** in **SQL Server 2008 R2**.

    b. **Log File Directory** and **Temp Directory** fields- For these directories you can choose to simply create a single folder on the root of the corresponding shared disk for your path. These directories will host data specific only to their own individual SQL component, so there is no benefit to creating a more complex directory structure as we did for our user database directories. For our project, we will enter our directory paths as shown in **Figure 13.19**.

    c. **Backup Directory** field- We can choose to either enter the SQL's default installation path for this directory or we can choose to place this directory on its own shared disk on the SAN. For our project, we will enter SQL's default installation path of **S:\Program Files\Microsoft SQL Server\MSSQL10.MSSQLSERVER\ OLAP\Backup**, which will create this directory structure on our **SQL_DB** shared disk. Again, this local backup directory shouldn't be used for any significant amount of backup operations as we should always be backing up our data to a location outside of the cluster for disaster recovery purposes. This makes the local backup directory of little significance, thus SQL's default location is fine.

   d. Once you are finished entering your paths, click on the **Next** button to continue.

25. On the **Error Reporting** screen, click on the **Next** button to continue.
26. On the **Cluster Installation Rules** screen, verify that all checks passed, and then click on the **Next** button to continue.
27. On the **Ready to Install** screen, verify the features to be installed, and then click on the **Install** button to continue.
28. On the **Complete** screen, verify that the installation was successful, and then click on the **Close** button to finish.

## Re-Applying the SQL Server 2008 Service Pack when Installing on Windows Server 2008 R2

29. If you installed the prerequisite **SQL Server 2008 SP1** or later to be compatible with **Windows Server 2008 R2** then you'll need to re-apply that version of service pack to complete the installation. If you installed **SQL Server 2008 R2**, then please disregard this step. This concludes the installation of the initial SQL cluster node.

# Verifying that the SQL Cluster is Online

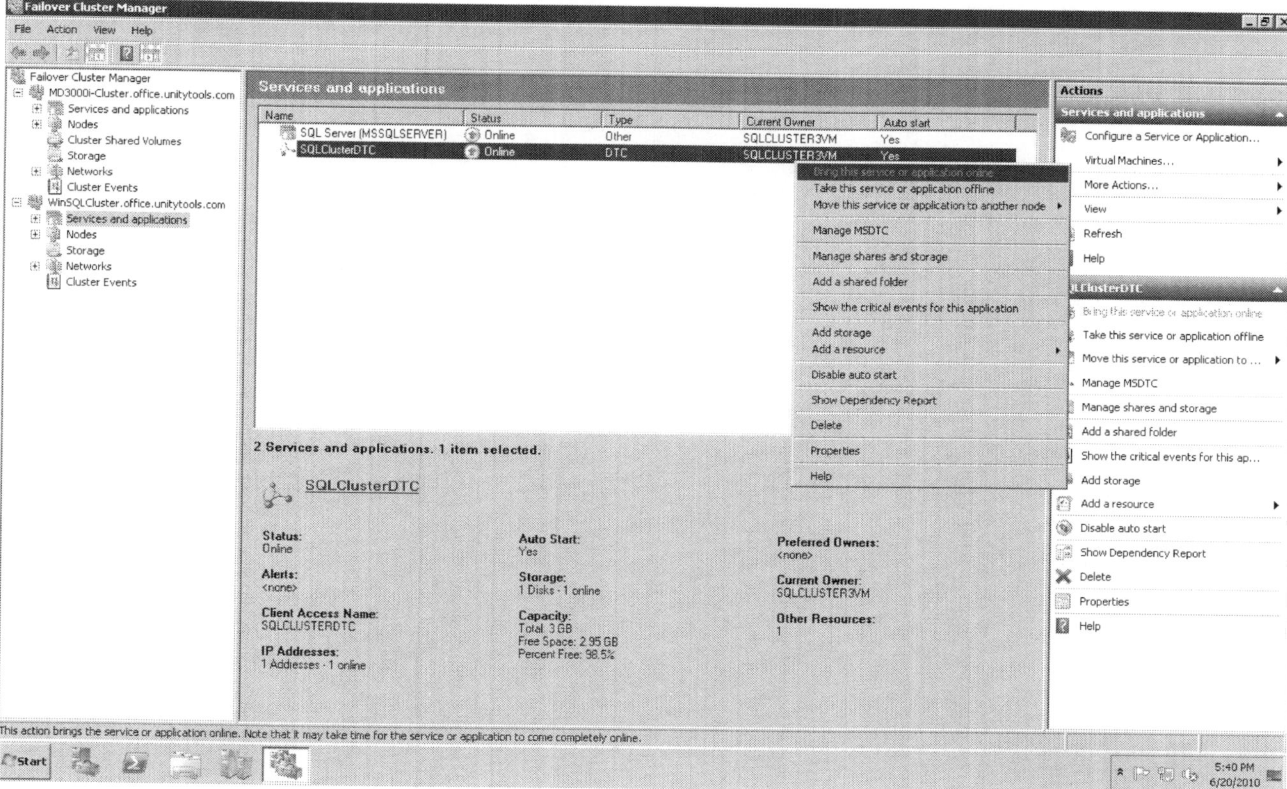


**Figure 13.20**

30. Return to **Failover Cluster Manager** and under the Windows cluster that you created for your SQL resources, click on the **Services and Applications** node, and then verify that your SQL server instance appears with the status of **Online**. You may have to give SQL a few minutes after the install for it to show up in the Windows cluster. For our project, we should see the SQL server instance of **SQL Server (MSSQLSERVER)**, as shown in **Figure 13.20**.

    a. If the SQL resources show up but don't have the status of **Online**, then you'll want to verify that the SQL services on the SQL virtual/physical machine are started. If your SQL resources are online, then please disregard this step and skip to **Step 31**. On the SQL virtual/physical machine go to **Administrative Tools\Services,** and then verify that the services are started. If the SQL services aren't started, then manually start them.

        i. Once you confirm that the SQL services are started, return to the **Failover Cluster Manager** console, and then highlight the **Services and Applications** node in the left pane.

        ii. Right click on your **SQL Server** application in the center pane, and then select the **Bring this service or application online** option to start the SQL cluster resource.

        iii. Repeat **Step i** to bring online your **MSDTC** service.

# Connecting to the SQL Cluster with SQL Server Management Studio

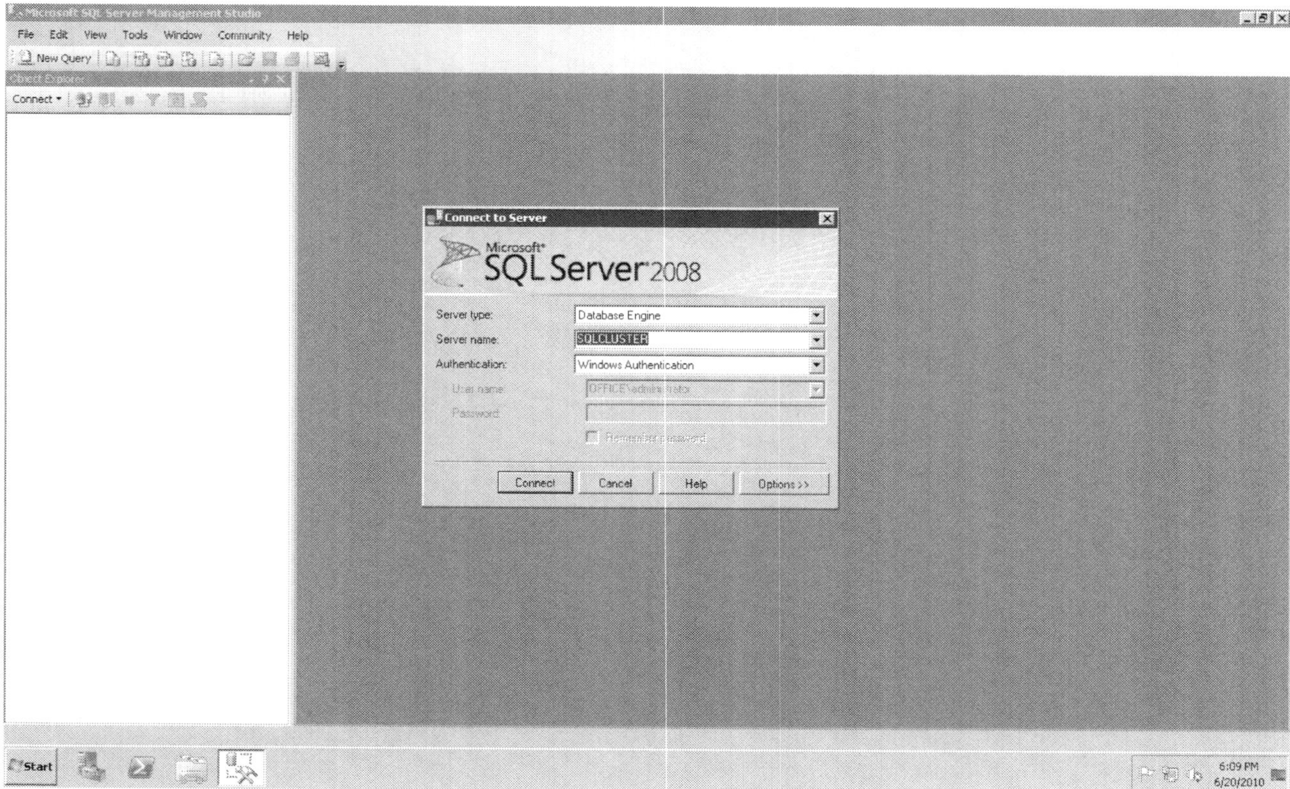


**Figure 13.21**

31. Open the **Microsoft SQL Server Management Studio** console on the SQL virtual/physical machine, and then make sure you can connect to your SQL cluster using the cluster's name that you created during the install. For our project, we will connect with our cluster's name of **SQLCLUSTER** with **Windows Authentication** selected for the **Authentication** field, as shown in **Figure 13.21**. Once connected, you should be able to browse all SQL components in the left pane as you would with any other SQL installation. When connecting to the cluster via the SQL Server Management Studio console, you always want to connect using your cluster's name and never by the name of one of your individual cluster nodes. This will insure that you're always connected to the active node of the cluster.

# Chapter 14: Installing SQL Server 2008/R2 on Additional Nodes to Make the Cluster Highly Available

In this chapter, we will go through the steps of making our SQL cluster highly available by adding a secondary node(s). We will begin by adding a second node to our Windows cluster that hosts our SQL resources. Once we have the new node added to our Windows cluster we will cover the necessary prerequisites for installing the SQL Server 2008/R2 software. Following this we will add our new Windows cluster node to our SQL cluster for high availability. This is done through the SQL Server 2008/R2 software installation process. During the install we will verify that the new node is being added to our same SQL instance as our initial SQL node belongs to. We will also verify that our service account logins match our initial SQL nodes configuration. Once the SQL Server 2008/R2 software installation has been completed, we will bring our SQL version up to the same patch level as our initial node by applying any necessary service packs. After the SQL software installation is complete, we will test out our new redundancy by failing over our SQL resources to our newly added cluster node. In the final steps we will cover how to safely shut down our cluster nodes to avoid the system detecting them as being down or offline. We will move through the steps at a faster pace, as there is significantly less configuration when adding additional nodes then when creating the SQL cluster with the initial node.

As explained earlier in Chapter 13, the SQL installation steps are the same whether you are installing your SQL cluster on physical servers or on virtual servers as in the project. Whether you choose to install SQL Server 2008 SP1 or SQL Server 2008 R2 the steps are basically the same and we will cover the few differences that exist during the installation process. The number of nodes you can add to your failover cluster depends on which editions of SQL Server you choose to use. The Standard edition of SQL Server 2008/R2 can support up to two nodes in a failover cluster while the Enterprise edition can support up sixteen nodes. For our project, we will install a second node to give us our two node SQL Server 2008 SP1 Enterprise cluster running on our Windows Server 2008 R2 virtual machines.

## Adding Additional Nodes to the Windows SQL Cluster

In **Failover Cluster Manager**, right click on the **Nodes** node in the left pane, and then select the **Add a Node** option. For our project, we will add our second SQL virtual machine named **SQLCluster3VM** to our Windows cluster named **WinSQLCluster**.

1. Run through **Add Node Wizard**, and then run all the **Validation Tests**.

   a. Complete the **Add Node Wizard**, then and verify that the new node is online within the Windows cluster.

## Installing the SQL Server 2008/R2 on the Additional SQL Cluster Nodes

2. Copy the SQL Server 2008/R2 installation media onto the local hard disk of virtual/physical machine that will be added to the SQL cluster.

   **NOTE:** Make sure to copy the installation media onto the local machine or you may experience weird glitches and/or invalid errors during the install process.

## Prerequisites- Temporally Disabling the Windows Firewall

3. Turn off the **Windows Firewall** temporally until the SQL install is complete. Once complete with the install, we will turn our firewall back on, and then allow our SQL application through the firewall.

## Prerequisites- When Installing SQL Server 2008 on Windows Server 2008 R2

Again, one of the differences between SQL Server 2008 and SQL Server 2008 R2 when installing on a Windows Server 2008 R2 server is the required prerequisites. Windows Server 2008 R2 requires SQL Server 2008 SP1 or later as a prerequisite to installing SQL Server 2008. We will run the SQL Server 2008 Service Pack 1 installation for shared features on our Windows 2008 R2 servers before performing our SQL Server 2008 installation. If you are installing SQL Server 2008 R2 on Windows Server 2008 R2 or SQL Server 2008 on a Window Server 2008, then please disregard this section and skip to **Step 5**.

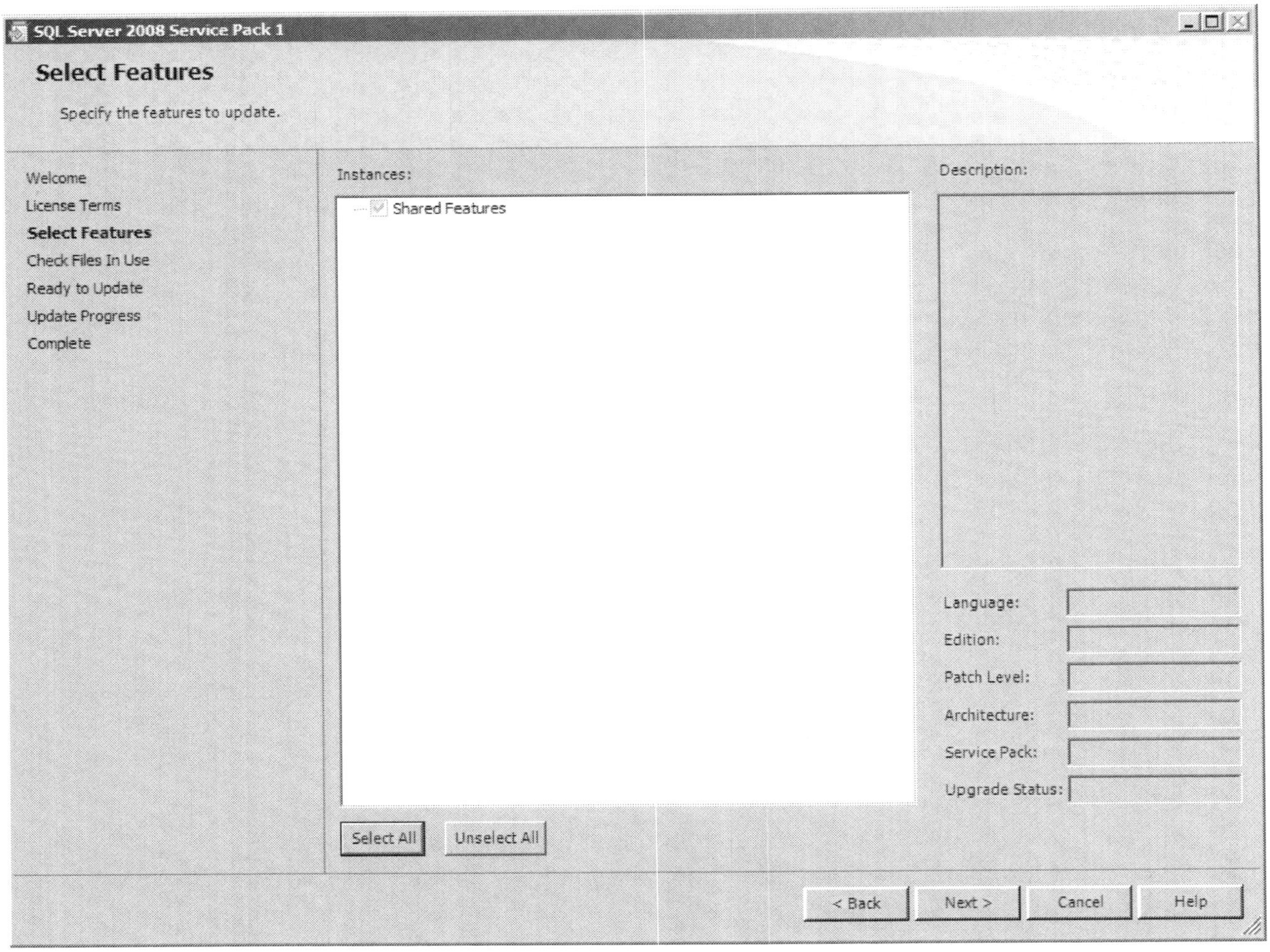

**Figure 14.1**

4. Download and launch the **SQL Server 2008 SP1** install on your second Windows cluster node that will host your SQL resources. For our project, we will run the install on our second Windows cluster node named **SQLCluster3VM**.

    a. Leave the install options all at their defaults except for when you come to the **Select Features** screen, where you want to click on the **Select All** button, as shown in **Figure 14.1**. Click on the **Next** button to continue.

    b. Finish going through the install screens with the defaults to complete the install.

## Launching the SQL Server 2008/R2 Installation

5. Run the SQL Server 2008/R2 **setup.exe** from the installation media to launch **SQL Server Installation Center.**

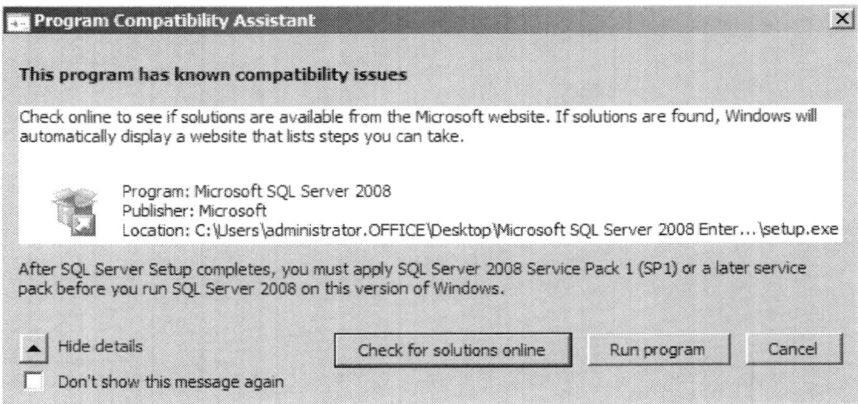


**Figure 14.2**

    a. You will most likely receive a **Program Compatibility Assistant** pop-up screen when installing SQL Server 2008 on Windows Server 2008 R2, to which you want to click on the **Run program** button to continue. If you are installing SQL Server 2008 R2 then please disregard this step. This screen is letting you know that for your SQL Server installation to be compatible with Windows Server 2008 R2 you will need to reapply the SQL Server 2008 Service Pack 1 or later after the SQL Server installation has completed.

    b. On the **SQL Server Installation Center** screen, click on the **Installation** option in the left pane.

        i. In the right pane, click on the **Add node to a SQL Server failover cluster** link to launch the **SQL Server 2008/R2 Setup** wizard.

            1. You will most likely receive the **Program Compatibility Assistant** pop-up screen again, click on the **Run program** button to continue. If you are installing SQL Server 2008 R2 or on Window Server 2008, then please disregard this step.

    c. On the **Setup Support Rules** screen, verify that the results all passed, and then click on the **OK** button to continue.

    d. On the **Product Key** screen, enter your product key, and then click on the **Next** button to continue.

e. On the **License Terms** screen, select the **I accept the license terms** checkbox, and then click on the **Next** button to continue.

## Selecting the SQL Instance for Additional SQL Cluster Nodes

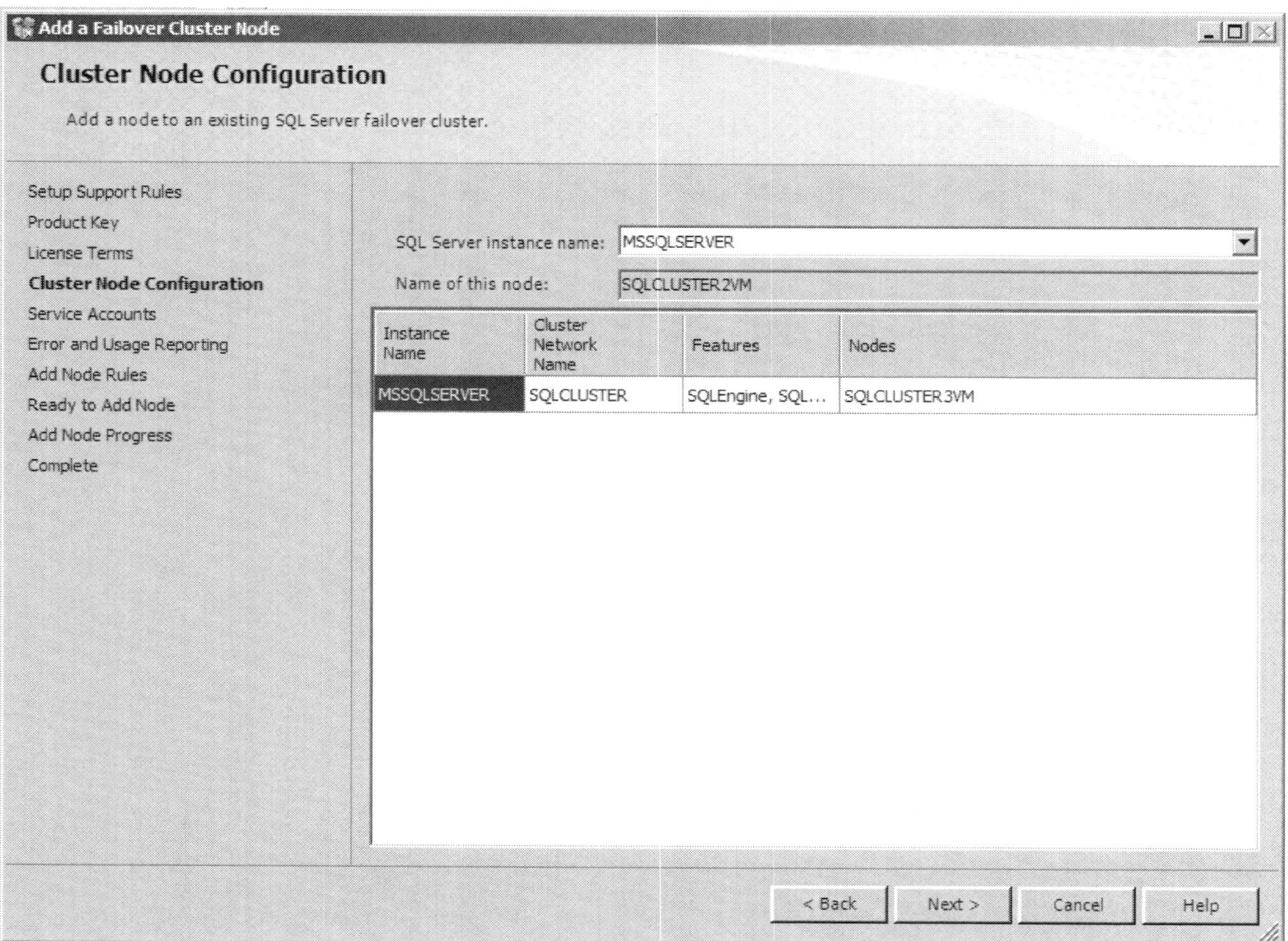


**Figure 14.3**

f. On the **Cluster Node Configuration** screen, verify that the information for the existing SQL Server 2008/R2 cluster is correct, and then click on the **Next** button to continue. For our project, the **SQL Server instance name** field should have the default instance name of **MSSQLSERVER** specified, as shown in **Figure 14.3**.

## Selecting the SQL Service Accounts for Additional SQL Cluster Nodes

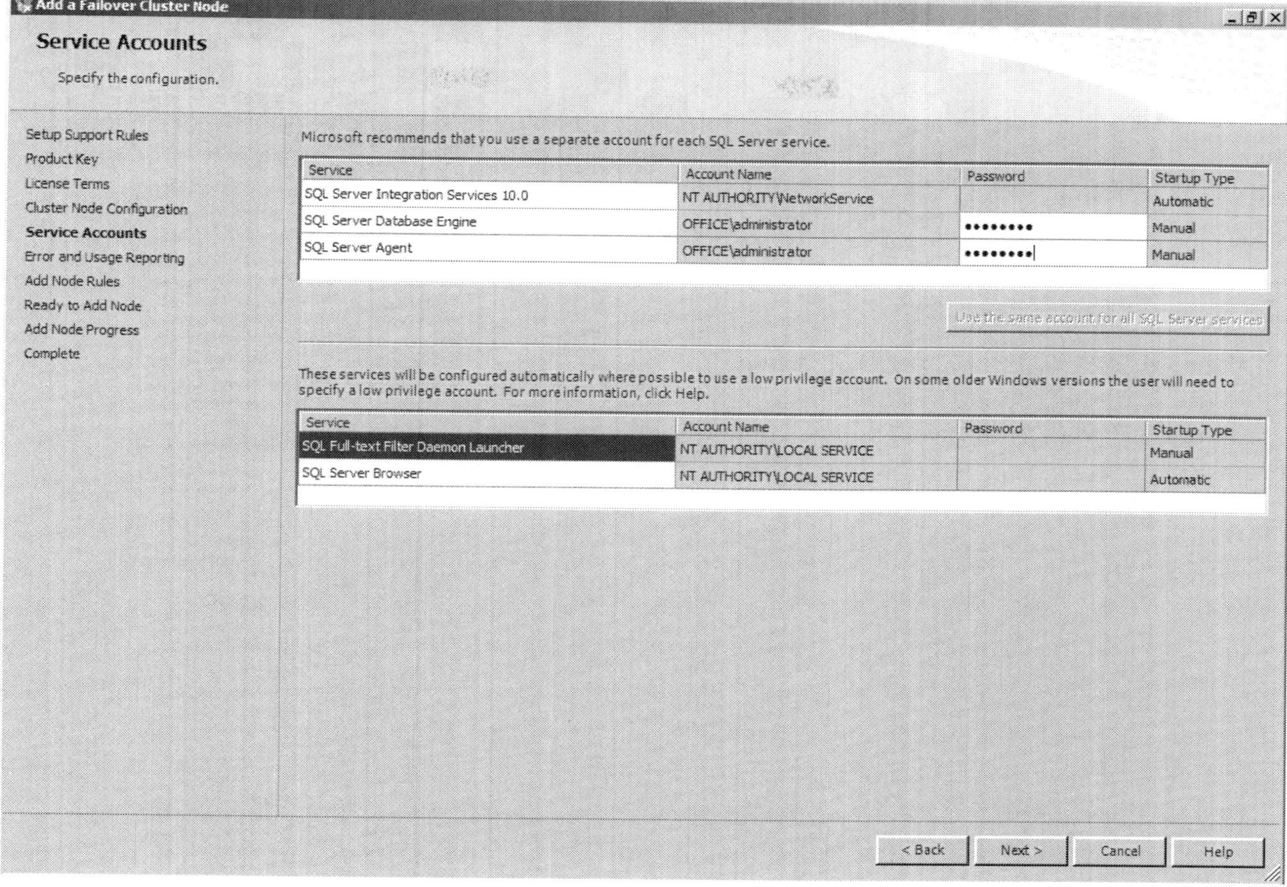


**Figure 14.4**

g. On the **Service Accounts** screen, verify that the information is the same as what you used when configuring the initial SQL cluster node, and then enter your user account's password for the **Password** fields. Click on the **Next** button to continue.

h. On the **Error Reporting** screen, click on the **Next** button to continue.

i. On the **Add Node Rules** screen, verify that all checks are successful, and then click on the **Next** button to continue.

j. On the **Ready to Add Node** screen, make sure that all your configurations are correct, and then click on the **Install** button to continue.

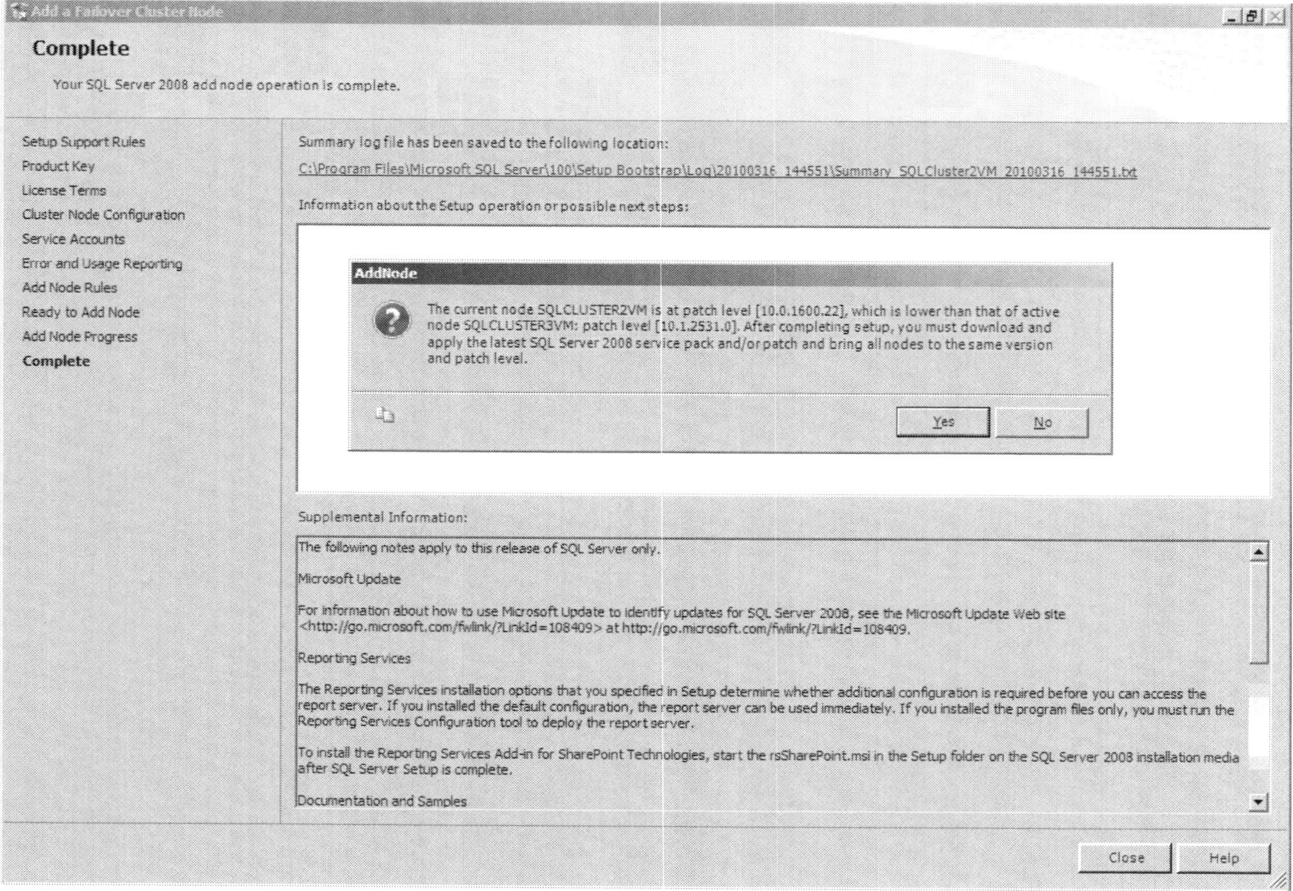


**Figure 14.5**

k. On the **Complete** screen, you will most likely receive an **AddNode** pop-up screen concerning the new SQL node's patch level being lower the active node. Click on the **Yes** button of the **AddNode** pop-up screen to continue. We will run the full install of SP1 or later after the SQL add node installation is complete. If you are installing SQL Server 2008 R2 or using Windows Server 2008 as your operating system, then please disregard this step.

l. On the **Complete** screen, click on the **Close** button to finish the installation.

## Re-Applying the SQL Server 2008 Service Pack when Installing on Windows Server 2008 R2

6. If you installed the prerequisite **SQL Server 2008 SP1** or later to be compatible with **Windows Server 2008 R2**, then you'll need to re-apply that version of service pack to complete the installation. If you installed SQL Server 2008 R2, then please disregard this section. All the nodes in your SQL cluster should be on the same version of SQL Server. This concludes the installation of the secondary SQL cluster node for high availability.

a. If you have any additional nodes beyond the two nodes of the project, then you'll want to repeat the steps in this chapter to add each of them to your SQL cluster.

## Testing High Availability of the Newly Completed SQL Cluster

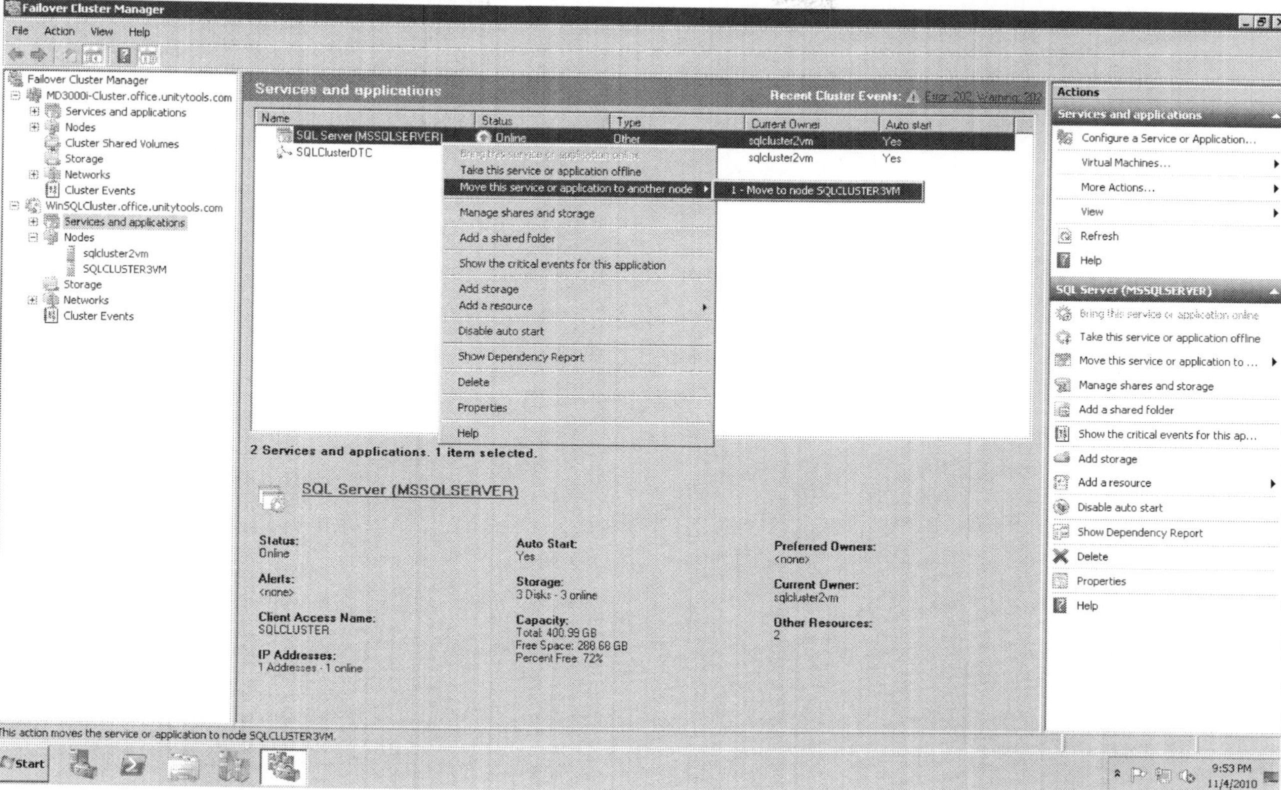


**Figure 14.6**

## Testing Failover- Moving the SQL Application to a Different Cluster Node

7. Return to the **Failover Cluster Manager**, and then highlight the **Services and Applications** node under your Windows cluster with the SQL resources.

    a. Right click on the **SQL Server** application in the center pane, and then select the **Move this service or application to another node** option to failover to the newly added node. For our project, we will move our SQL Server application named **SQL Server (MSSQLSERVER)** to our newly added node with the name of **SQLCluster3VM**, as shown in **Figure 14.6**.

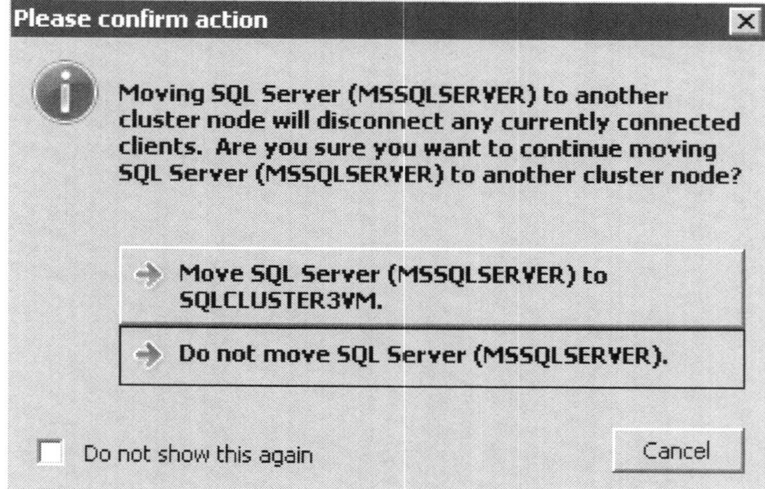


**Figure 14.7**

b. On the **Please confirm action** pop-up screen, select the **Move <Your_SQL_Server_Instance_Name> to <Your_Newly_Added_Node's_Name>** option to failover. For our project, we will select the **Move SQL Server (MSSSQLSERVER) to SQLCLUSTER3VM** option of the **Please confirm action** screen, as shown in **Figure 14.7**.

## Testing Failover- Moving the SQL DTC to a Different Cluster Node

8. We will repeat the failure process for your MSDTC service as well by right clicking on your SQL cluster's DTC service name, and then selecting the **Move this service or application to another node** option to failover. Once complete, you should now have all your SQL services and applications on your newly added SQL cluster node. For our project, we will move our MSDTC service named **SQLClusterDTC** to our newly added node **SQLCluster3VM**.

   a. On the **Please confirm action** pop-up screen, select the **Move <Your_SQL_DTC_Service_Name> to <Your_Newly_Added_Node's_Name>** option to failover. For our project, we will select the **Move SQLClusterDTC to SQLCLUSTER3VM** option of the **Please confirm action** screen.

# Testing Failover- Testing Connections to the New Active Cluster Node

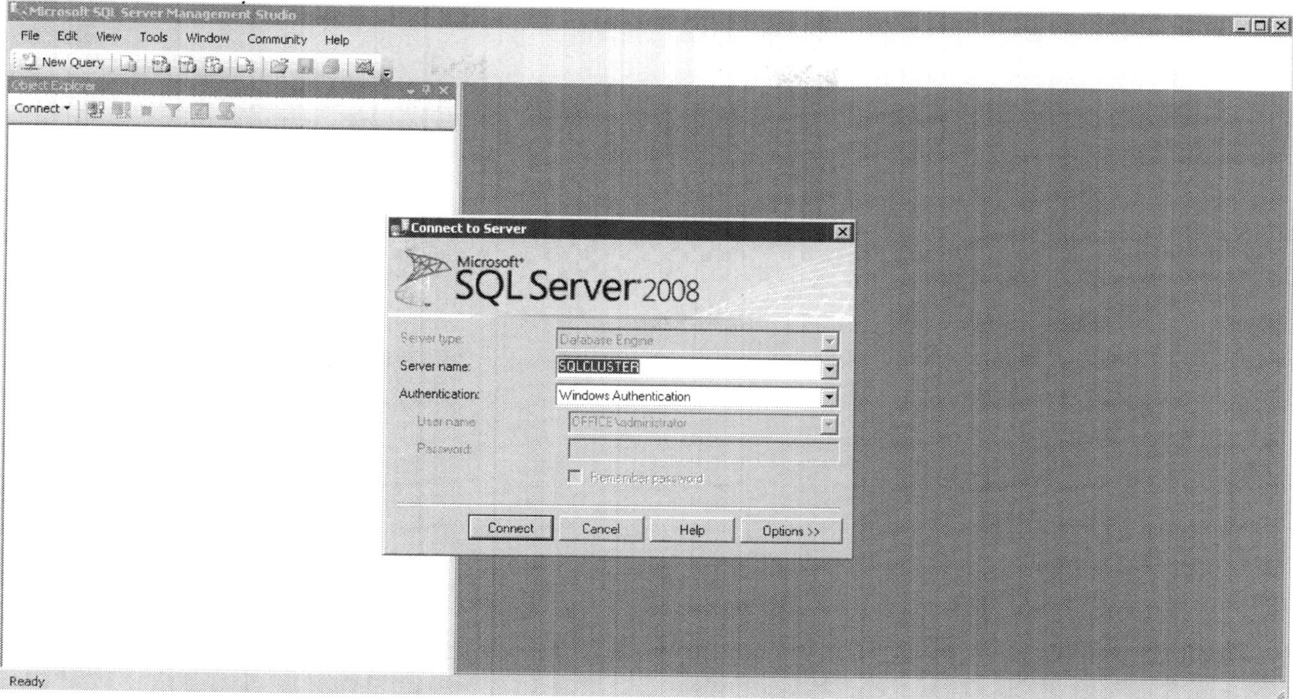


**Figure 14.8**

9. Open the **Microsoft SQL Server Management Studio** console on the new active cluster node and make sure you can connect to the SQL cluster using the cluster's name that you created during the install. For our project, we will connect with our cluster's name of **SQLCLUSTER** with **Windows Authentication** selected for the **Authentication** field, as shown in **Figure 14.8**. Once connected, you should be able to browse all your SQL components in the left pane as with any other SQL installation. When connecting to the cluster via the SQL Server Management Studio console, you always want to connect using your cluster's name and never by the name of one of your individual cluster nodes. This will insure that you're always connected to the active node of the cluster.

## Testing Failover- Stopping the Cluster Service on the Passive Node

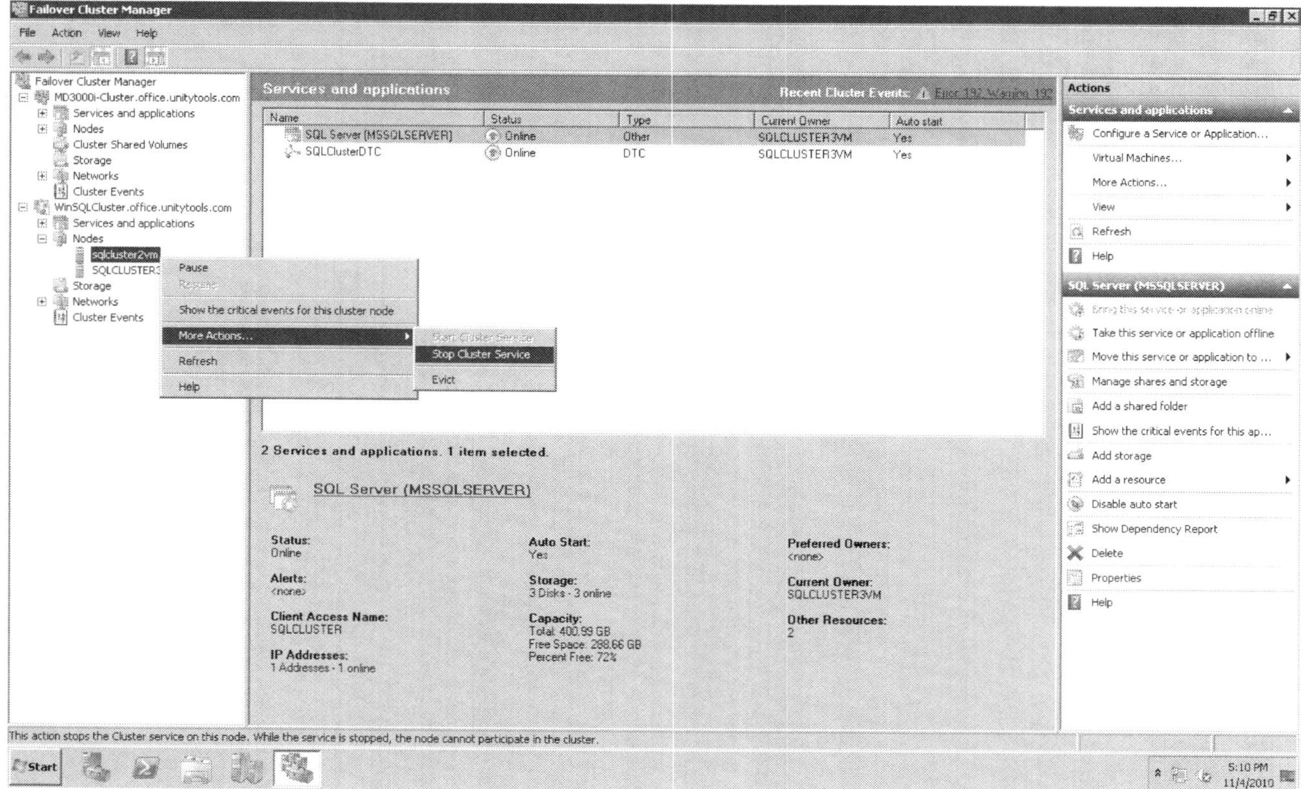


**Figure 14.9**

10. Once you have verified that all your SQL resources are available on your new active node from within the SQL Server Management Studio console then you are ready to test shutting down your passive node. In the left pane of the **Failover Cluster Manager** console, expand the **Nodes** node under your Windows SQL cluster name, as shown in **Figure 14.9**.

    a. Right click on the passive node, and then select the **More Actions\Stop Cluster Service** option. For our project, we will stop our cluster service on our node named **SQLCluster2VM**, as shown in **Figure 14.9**. Once the cluster service has stopped on the passive node a small red icon will appear on the passive node's name.

## How to Safely Shutdown the Passive SQL Cluster Node

With a highly available redundant system it is important to follow a specific process to move and shutdown resources so that you avoid the system as detecting the resource as down or offline.

11. The process to safely shutdown your passive SQL cluster node(s) are as follows.

    a. Make sure that all your SQL resources are moved off the cluster node that you want to shut down, as outlined in **Step 7**.

b. Stop the cluster service on the passive node to be shut down, as outlined in **Step 10**.

c. Shutdown or reboot the passive node as you normally would by using the Windows start button. When rebooting or shutting down a cluster node it is always preferable to first use the Failover Cluster Manager to stop the cluster service. Once the server is started up again it will automatically come back online within the cluster as the passive node and thus restore redundancy to the cluster.

# Chapter 15: Optimizing SQL Server's Performance by Adding Additional TempDB Files

In this chapter, we will cover how to increase our SQL Server 2008/R2's performance by creating additional temp database files. We will begin by covering the role that the TempDB files play during SQL transactions. Once we understand how the TempDB files are used by SQL, we will then cover some performance best practices that should always be followed. We will learn how the number of cores on our server's CPU plays a key role in deciding the number of additional TempDB files that we want to create. We will then add and configure our TempDB files accordingly. Once we have completed this chapter we will have all our SQL configurations optimized for high end performance.

## Overview of the Optimum Configuration for SQL Temporally Database Files

Many times the database administrator may not realize the performance implications that their TempDB files play with their overall SQL Server 2008/R2 performance. SQL server uses temporally database files called TempDB files, to store intermediate results as part of executing a query. For example, the TempDB files would be used for building a hash table, or for query results that use order sorting. Microsoft recommends creating at least one TempDB file per server CPU core for performance optimization. The TempDB files created should all be of equal size, as this will cause SQL to automatically balance its temporally database workload across all the files simultaneously. If you create TempDB files of different sizes, then SQL will automatically write all temporally database transactions to the current file with the most available space, and thus cause a performance bottleneck. Your largest gain in performance is to have at least one TempDB file per CPU core, you can have more TempDB files than CPU cores, however it doesn't necessarily guarantee that you will have additional performance above the initial one file per core. You can also choose to spread your TempDB files across multiple RAID arrays to increase your I/O bandwidth performance. The TempDB files should be treated similarly to your user databases when it comes to performance, workload, and the measuring of I/O bandwidth. Placing your TempDB files on their own fast RAID array when possible is a best practice.

Determining your TempDB file sizes should be based on your query plan and length of transactions. In this regard your TempDB's are different than estimating your user database sizes which are based on a simple rate of overall growth. If you have a test environment that mirrors your production environment then you should be able to determine your optimum TempDB file size needed. Creating larger than needed TempDB files has no negative impact on your SQL performance, so it is recommend to simply create rather large TempDB files if you have the available disk space. For our project, we have plenty of disk space available on our SAN so we will start out with rather large TempDB files and then monitor our production environment after the fact to insure they are sufficient in size.

## Summary of Best Practices for TempDB Configurations

Microsoft recommends creating at least one TempDB file for each CPU Core of the server. For example, if you have a server with two Quad Core CPU's then you would want to create a minimum of eight TempDB files. Your TempDB files should have the following properties for best overall performance.

- All TempDB files created should be the same size. If they are not created equally, SQL will automatically write more data to the TempDB files that are larger in size, and thus cause slower I/O performance.

- You should create at least one TempDB file per CPU core. You can always create more than one TempDB file per core, however it doesn't guarantee an additional performance gain beyond the initial file per core.

- All TempDB files should be set to a fixed size and never left to auto-grow. If the size of the TempDB files are allowed to auto-grow, then the files will become different in size, which will result slower I/O performance over time.

- The TempDB is a write intense database and therefore should be placed on a dedicated RAID 1 or RAID 10 array whenever possible. If a separate RAID array from your SQL database and log arrays isn't available, then choosing to place your TempDB on the same array as your logs is the next best option.

## Configuring the Initial TempDB's Properties

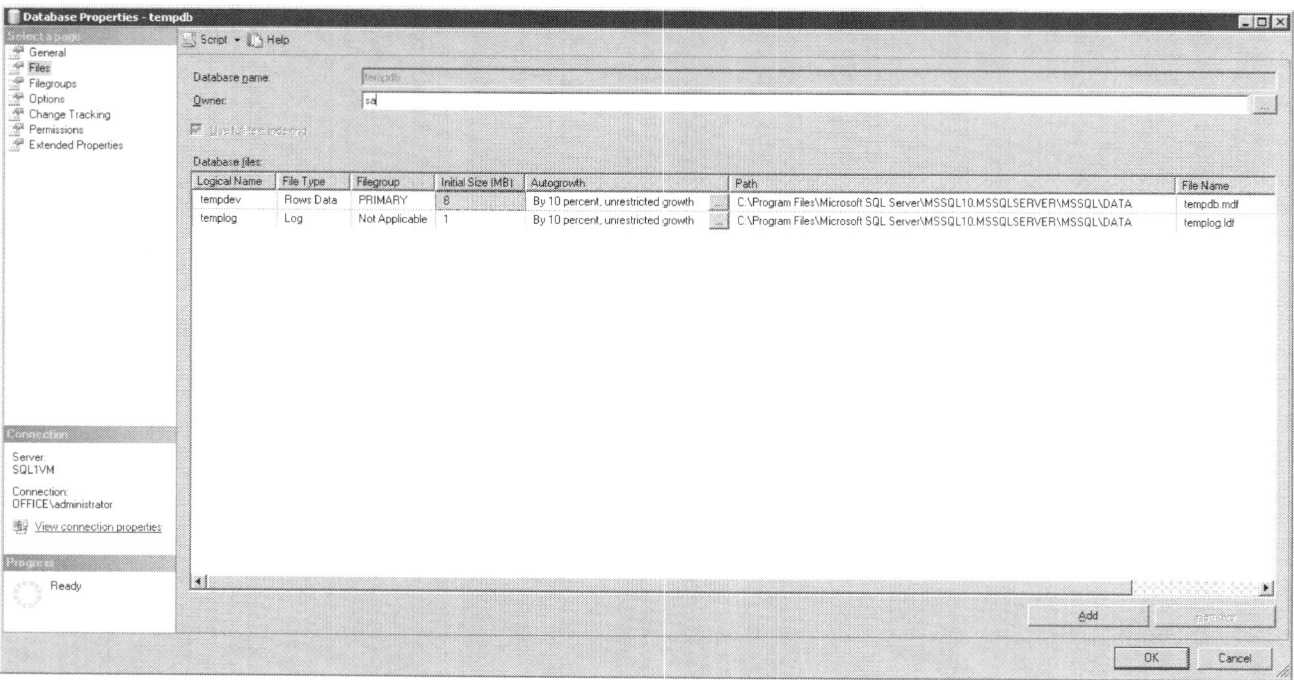


**Figure 15.1**

As shown **Figure 15.1**, the SQL server installation by default only creates one file for the TempDB, so in the next steps we will create additional TempDB files for our SQL cluster to use. If your SQL cluster is installed on virtual machines, then you'll want to create at least one TempDB file per virtual processor assigned to the virtual machine. For our project, we created a 100GB shared disk with drive letter T: and then labeled it as SQL_TempDB for our TempDB files. We will utilize the majority of this shared disk's space by creating each TempDB file at 10GB's to insure that our SQL won't have any initial bottlenecks. This may be rather large for some SQL environments, so if your environment is limited on disk space you could easily choose to create your TempDB files with a much smaller initial size such as 500MB or 1GB. Since our project's SAN has plenty of disk space, we will choose to start with a rather large initial size for each of our TempDB files. This will give us time to monitor our TempDB's performance and growth in a production environment, than if need be we can grow or shrink them accordingly. In the following steps, we will create and configure our TempDB files.

1. Open **Microsoft SQL Server Management Studio**, and then connect to your SQL cluster's name. For our project, we connect to our SQL cluster's name of **SQLCLUSTER** with **Windows Authentication** selected for the **Authentication Type** field.

   a. In the **Object Explorer** pane on the left side of the screen, expand the **Databases\System Databases** node.

b. Right click on the **TempDB** database, and then select the **Properties** option.

c. Select the **Files** option in the left pane to view the current TempDB file. You should see a **tempdev** and a **templog** file that the SQL installation created for you during the install, as shown in **Figure 15.1**.

   i. In the right pane under the **Database files:** section, change the value of the **Initial Size (MB)** field of the **tempdev** file to the size you want for your initial TempDB file. For our project, we will set the **Initial Size (MB)** field of **tempdev** file to a value of **10240**.

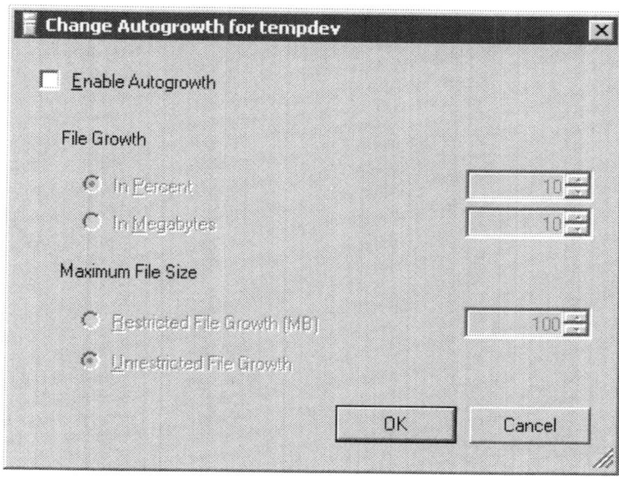


**Figure 15.2**

   ii. For the **Autogrowth** field of the **tempdev** file, click on the **... ellipsis** button, and then unselect the **Enable Autogrowth** checkbox as shown in **Figure 15.2**. Click on the **OK** button to save your changes.

# Creating Additional TempDB Files with an SQL Script

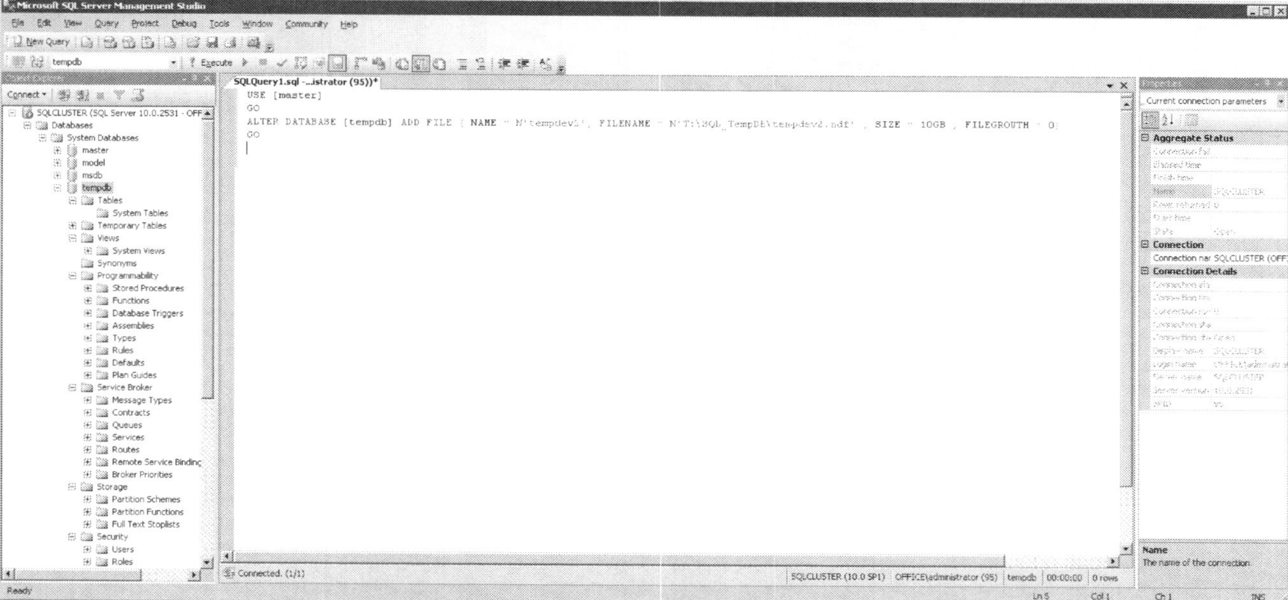


**Figure 15.3**

2. Next, we will run a SQL query to create the additional tempdev (TempDB) files that we need. Click on the **New Query** button on the top left of **SQL Server Management Studio's** toolbar to launch the **SQL Query** pane.

   a. Type the below script syntax into the **SQL Query** pane, and then modify the parts in bold for your particular environment. The script creates one new TempDB file every time you run it, so you will have to edit and run it multiple times depending on how many TempDB files you need to create. The explanation of each command and what has to be modified each time you run the script is explained in detail. When you're finished entering the script into the SQL Query pane it should look similar to what is shown in **Figure 15.3**.

   **NOTE:** When copying and pasting the SQL Query Intellisense doesn't always pickup on each snippet of code, so it is always better to just manually type in the script in the query editor. The code in between the **GO** commands should all be on the same line as shown in **Figure 15.3**, and not as the syntax appears below with the word wrap breaking it into multiple lines.

   **<u>Script Syntax:</u>**

   USE [master]
   GO
   ALTER DATABASE [tempdb] ADD FILE ( NAME = N'**<Your_New_TempDB_File_Name>**', FILENAME = N'**<Location_&_Name_On_Disk>**' , SIZE = **<Your_TempDB_File_Size_In_MB's_Or_GB's>**, FILEGROWTH = 0)
   GO

For our project, we will run the following script to create our second TempDB file named **tempdev2**, with a size of **10GB**, and **Autogrowth** disabled, as shown in **Figure 15.3**.

**Project Example:**

```
USE [master]
GO
ALTER DATABASE [tempdb] ADD FILE ( NAME = N'tempdev2', FILENAME =
N'T:\SQL_TempDB\tempdev2.ndf' , SIZE = 10GB , FILEGROWTH = 0)
GO
```

b. Once you have the script entered into the **SQL Query Editor** pane, click on the **Blue Checkmark** from the toolbar to verify the syntax is correct.

c. After the syntax verification is successful, click on the **! exclamation** button from the toolbar to create the new TempDB file.

## Modifying the Script to Create Multiple TempDB Files

3. To continue creating additional TempDB files, simply modify the number after the **tempdev** filename for the **NAME** and **FILENAME** parameters. For our project, we will modify our script as shown below by changing the number that follows the tempdev filename from **tempdev2** to **tempdev3** and so on for each subsequent TempDB file we create. We will repeat this process until we have a total of eight uniquely named TempDB files, as shown in **Figure 15.4**.

**Project Example:**

```
USE [master]
GO
ALTER DATABASE [tempdb] ADD FILE ( NAME = N'tempdev3', FILENAME =
N'T:\SQL_TempDB\tempdev3.ndf' , SIZE = 10GB , FILEGROWTH = 0)
GO
```

a. Once you have modified the number that follows the tempdev filename, click on the **Blue Checkmark** from the toolbar to verify the syntax is correct.

b. After the syntax verification is successful, click on the **! exclamation** button from the toolbar to create your new TempDB file.

## Verifying the Newly Created TempDB Files

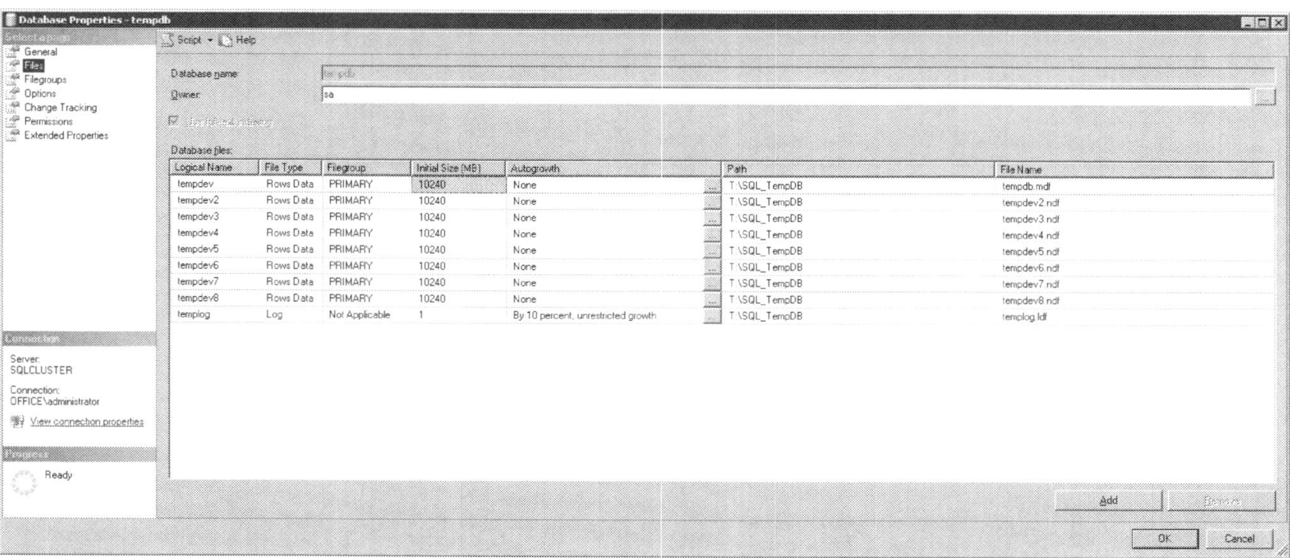

**Figure 15.4**

4. Once complete, close the **SQL Query Editor** screen, and then return to **Properties** screen of your **tempdb** database.

   a. On the **Database Properties – tempdb** screen, click on the **Files** node in the left pane, and then verify that your TempDB files were created successfully. For our project, our TempDB files should look similar to **Figure 15.4**.

# Chapter 16: Enabling the SQL Server 2008/R2 Program through the Windows Firewall

In this is chapter, we will enable and configure our Windows firewall to allow our SQL traffic. During the SQL install process we disabled our Windows firewall to avoid having to manually configure each SQL port number through our firewall for SQL traffic. Now that our SQL installation is complete, we will configure our firewall to allow our SQL programs through the firewall. The firewall will then automatically allow traffic through on any ports needed for our SQL traffic. Once complete with this chapter, we will have our servers protected by our Windows firewall.

## Allowing Traffic Through the Firewall- SQL Server Management Studio

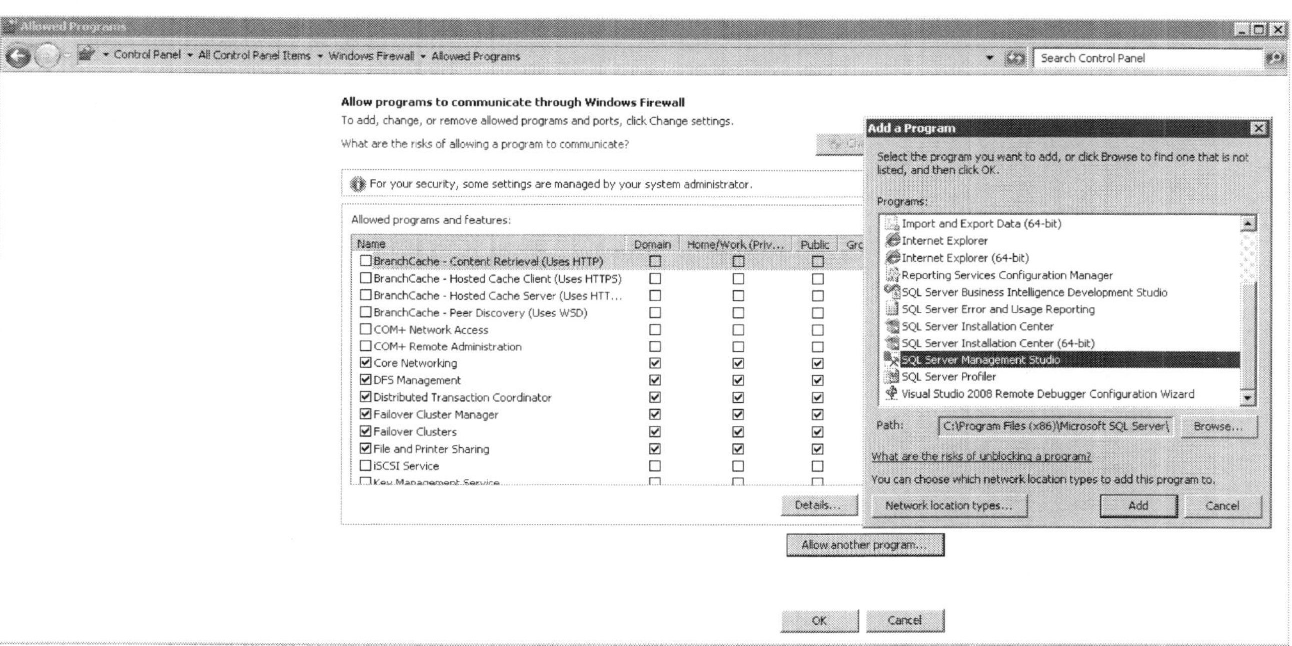

**Figure 16.1**

1. Open the Windows **Control Panel** on each of your SQL nodes, and then select the **Windows Firewall** icon.

    a. In the left pane, click on the **Allow a program of feature through the Windows Firewall** option, and then click on the **Allow another program** button.

        i. On the **Add a Program** screen, select the **SQL Server Management Studio** program from the **Programs** field, as shown in **Figure 16.1**. Click on the **Add** button to continue.

## Allowing Traffic Through the Firewall- SQL Instance

b. To allow our SQL instance through the firewall, we need to browse to its executable. Click on the **Allow another program** button, and then click on the **Browse** button on the **Add Program** screen.

   i. Browse to the **sqlservr.exe** file of your SQL instance, and then click on the **Open** button. The default location of the sqlservr.exe file is in the **C:\Program Files\Microsoft SQL Server\MSSQL10.MSSQLSERVER\MSSQL\Binn** folder for **SQL Server 2008** and the **C:\Program Files\Microsoft SQL Server\MSSQL10_50.MSSQLSERVER\MSSQL\Binn** folder for **SQL Server 2008 R2**. If you are using multiple instances of SQL, then keep in mind that each instance has its own sqlservr.exe executable file and that you'll want to repeat these steps to allow each of your sqlservr.exe files through the firewall. For our project, we will browse to our default instance's **sqlservr.exe** file located in default directory of **C:\Program Files\Microsoft SQL Server\MSSQL10.MSSQLSERVER\MSSQL\Binn**.

   ii. On the **Add Program** screen, click on the **Add** button to add the SQL Server program.

## Allowing Traffic Through the Firewall- Selecting Networks

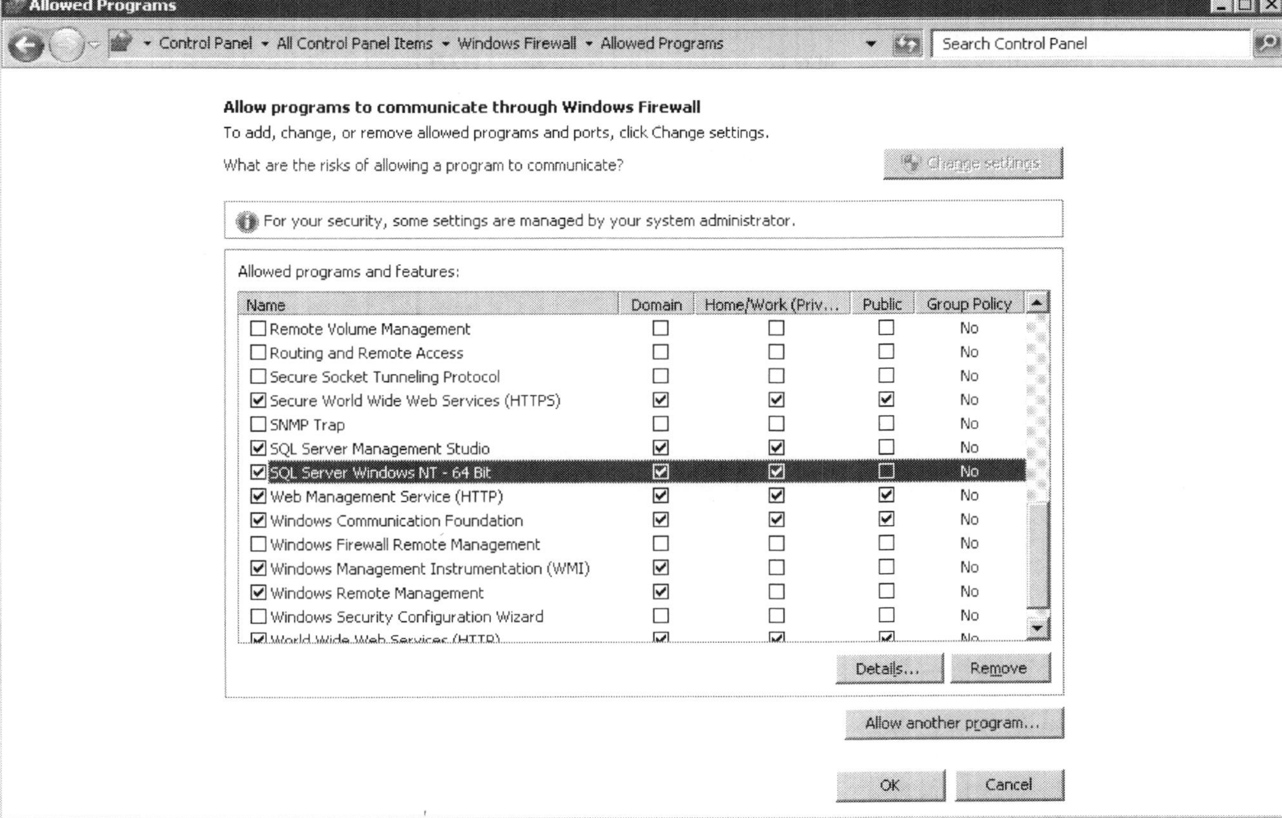


**Figure 16.2**

c. Depending on your network setup you can choose which networks are allowed. Check the boxes for each network you want to be allowed, and then click on the **OK** button. For our project, we will allow the **Domain** and **Home/Work (Private)** networks for both our **SQL Server Management Studio** and our **SQL instance**, as shown in **Figure 16.2**.

## Enabling the Firewall and Testing Communications

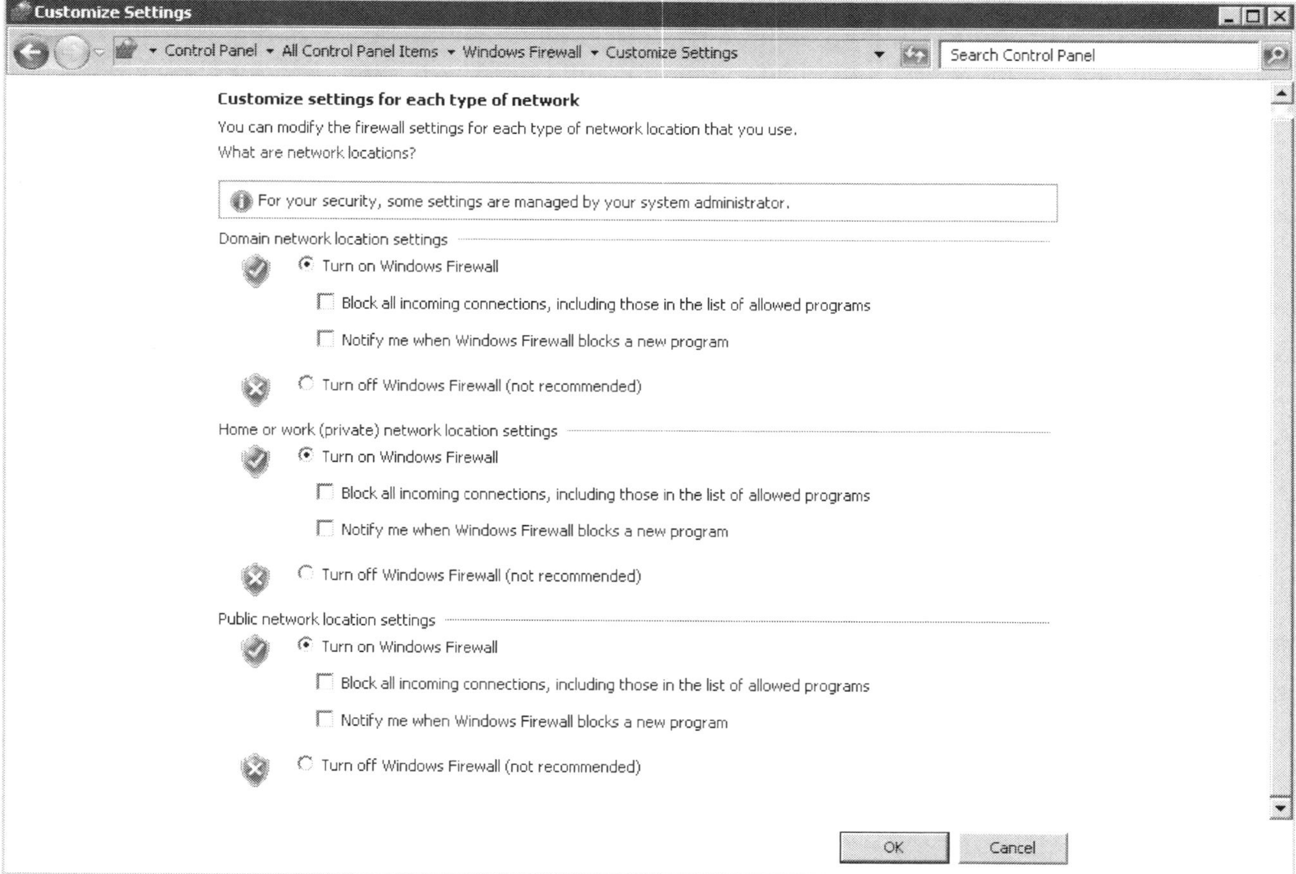


**Figure 16.3**

Now that we have our SQL Server programs allowed through the Windows Firewall, we will turn back on the firewall, and then test that our SQL communications and failovers are working correctly.

2. Click on the **Turn Windows Firewall on or off** option in the left pane, and then select the **Turn on Windows Firewall** option for all three networks **Domain**, **Home/Work (Private)** and **Public**, as shown in **Figure 16.3**.

3. Test out your SQL cluster's communications by connecting to your cluster with the SQL Server Management Studio and then also by failing over the cluster once or twice.

   **NOTE:** If you enable these settings for a SQL Server 2008 SP1 installation, but then later decide to upgrade to SQL Server 2008 R2 then you will most likely need to dis-allow and then re-allow the SQL Server program components through your server's firewall. This is necessary for your server's firewall to pick-up on the different ports that SQL Server 2008 R2 uses vs. the previous SQL Server 2008 SP1 installation.

4. For a detailed listing of Microsoft's SQL Server 2008's components and the specific port numbers they use see the MSDN article titled "Configuring the Windows Firewall to Allow SQL Server Access".

# Chapter 17: Applying Updates to an SQL Server 2008/R2 Cluster

You have probably noticed by now, that when it comes to Windows and SQL clustering that most things have to be done in a chronological order. The same is true when applying updates to your SQL cluster nodes. When applying patches or service packs to an SQL Server 2008/R2 cluster you must always apply the update to the passive node first. After the installation is complete on the passive node(s), you will then want to failover all your SQL Server 2008/R2 cluster resources to one of the passive node(s). Once all your clustered resources are online on the new active node, you can then proceed with the updates on the previously active node. You will also want to make sure that your firewall settings are configured correctly to work with the new version of SQL. It is common for different versions to use different port numbers for communication, and therefore you'll want to re-enable your firewall settings for the new version SQL, as outlined in **Chapter 16**, **Step 5**.

# Chapter 18: Creating the CSV Virtual Machines to Host the Front-end Application Servers

Earlier in Chapter 9, we created our Windows CSV cluster to host our front-end application servers. In this chapter, we will begin utilizing our Windows CSV cluster by placing our virtual machines into the Cluster Shared Volume. When you create or import a virtual machine into your Windows CSV cluster it gains high availability at the host level by being able to live migrate between different hosts in the event of a failure or for maintenance.

We will begin by covering how to place our front-end application virtual machines into the Cluster Shared Volume of our Windows CSV cluster. After we have our CSV virtual machines in place, we will go over some important management procedures including how to safely shutdown, live migrate, set preferred owners and set possible owners of our CSV virtual machines. Once finished with this chapter, we will have our CSV high availability clustering complete. Our completed Windows CSV cluster will be the foundation that we'll build our final layer of high availability on with an active/active Network Load Balancing (NLB) cluster in Chapter 19.

## Creating New Virtual Machines on the Cluster Shared Volume (CSV) Disk

In this section, we will cover how to bring our CSV virtual machines online. For our project, these CSV virtual machines will host our front-end CRM 4.0 application servers. We will create and host our three CSV virtual machines on different physical hosts, as outlined in **Figure 1.1** of **Chapter 1**. As the figure outlines, we will host two of our CSV virtual machines named **CRMCluster1VM** and **CRMCluster2VM** on our physical host named **AftermathHost**, while our third CSV virtual machine named **CRMCluster3VM** will be hosted on our physical host named **TurmoilHost**.

1. Create at least two fresh Windows Server 2008/R2 images for your front-end application virtual machines. If you already have virtual machines that you'd like to use, then please skip to **Step 2** where copying your exported virtual machines or their .vhd files onto the Cluster Shared Volume disk is outlined. For our project, we will create three new Windows Server 2008 R2 virtual machines with the names **CRMCluster1VM**, **CRMCluster2VM** and **CRMCluster3VM**.

   a. Open the **Hyper-V Manager** console on at least two of your different physical nodes, and then create at least one virtual machine on each of physical nodes. Go through the steps of creating your new virtual machines and selecting the options you want, however when you come to screens that required paths, you want to make sure to enter your Cluster Shared Volume's path, as outlined in the steps below.

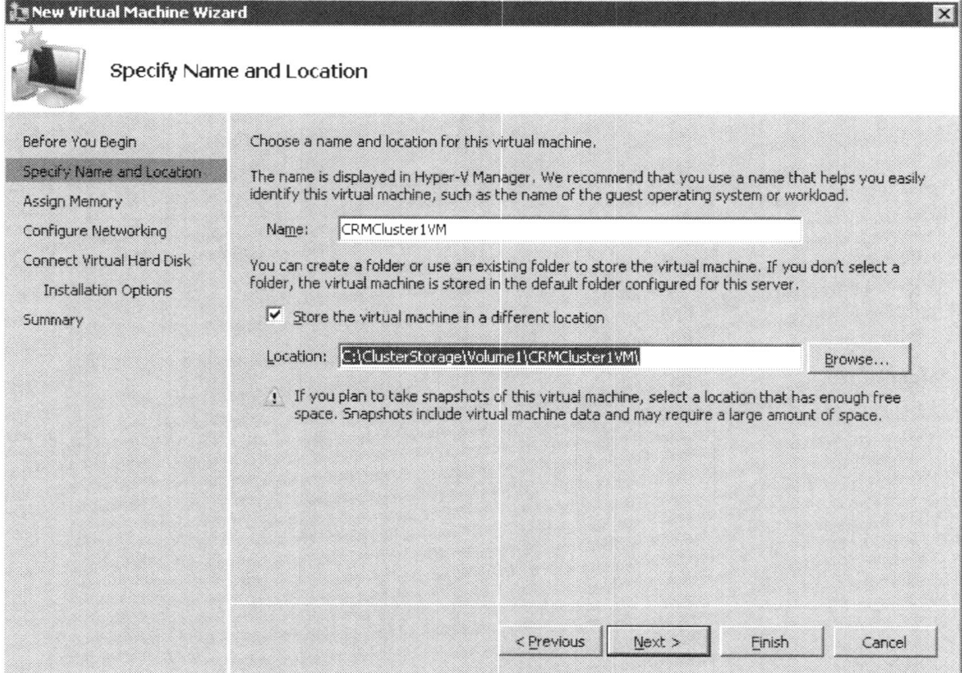


**Figure 18.1**

i. When you come to the **Specify Name and Location** screen, select the **Store the virtual machine in a different location** checkbox, and then browse to your CSV directory of **C:\ClusterStorage\Volume1\<Your_Folder_For_The_VM>**. For our project, we will enter the path of **C:\ClusterStorage\Volume1\CRMCluster1VM** for our first CSV virtual machine named **CRMCluster1VM**, as shown in **Figure 18.1**.

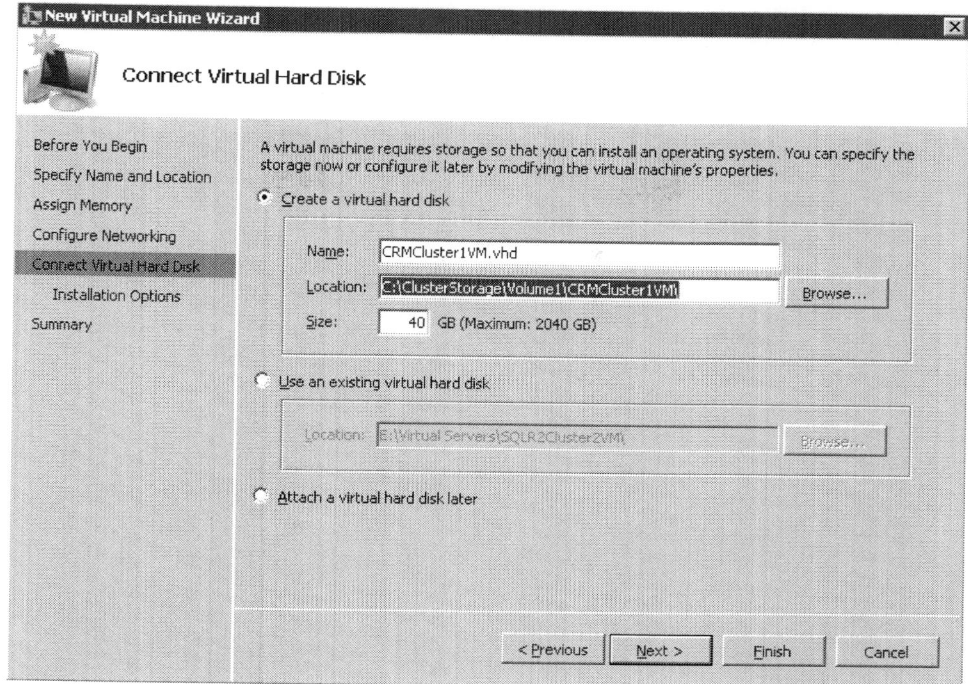


**Figure 18.2**

ii. When you come to the **Connect Virtual Hard Disk** screen, browse to your CSV directory of **C:\ClusterStorage\Volume1\<Your_Folder_For_The_VM>** for the **Location** field. For our project, we will enter the path of **C:\ClusterStorage\Volume1\CRMCluster1VM** for the **Location** field, as shown in **Figure 18.2**.

## Copying Existing Virtual Machines into the Cluster Shared Volume (CSV)

2. If you already have virtual machines that you'd like to use, then follow the below steps to copy them into your CSV volume. If you created your virtual machines in **Step 1** above, then please disregard this section and skip to **Step 4**. Open **Windows Explorer** on one of your physical nodes of the CSV Windows cluster, and then browse to the CSV shared disk by going to **C:\ClusterStorage\Volume1**.

   a. Paste your virtual machines into the **C:\ClusterStorage\Volume1** directory.

# Importing Existing Virtual Machines into the Cluster Shared Volume (CSV)

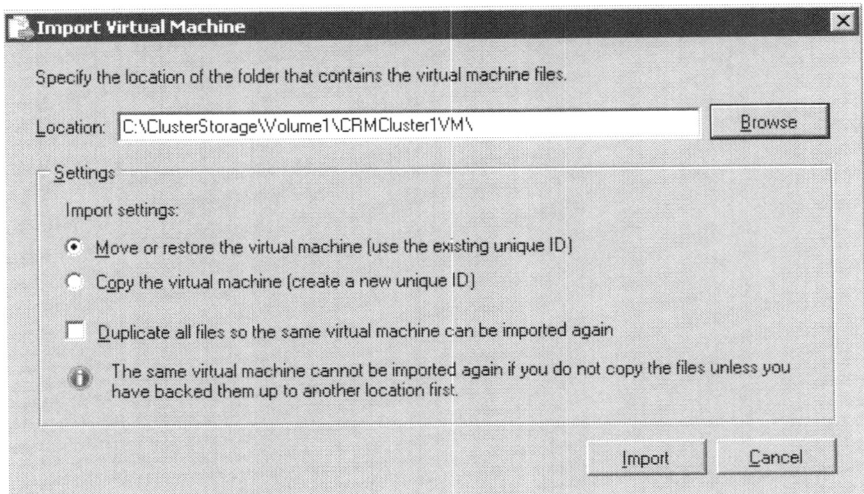


**Figure 18.3**

3. Once you have all your CSV virtual machine images copied onto your CSV shared disk, you want to import the virtual machines into Hyper-V on your different physical nodes of your CSV Windows cluster. Open the **Hyper-V Manager** console on at least two of your different physical nodes, and then import at least one virtual machine on each of physical nodes.

    a. On the **Import Virtual Machine** screen, browse to the **C:\ClusterStorage\Volume1** directory, and then select the virtual machine to import, as shown in **Figure 18.3**.

# Verifying the CSV Virtual Machines in Hyper-V Manager

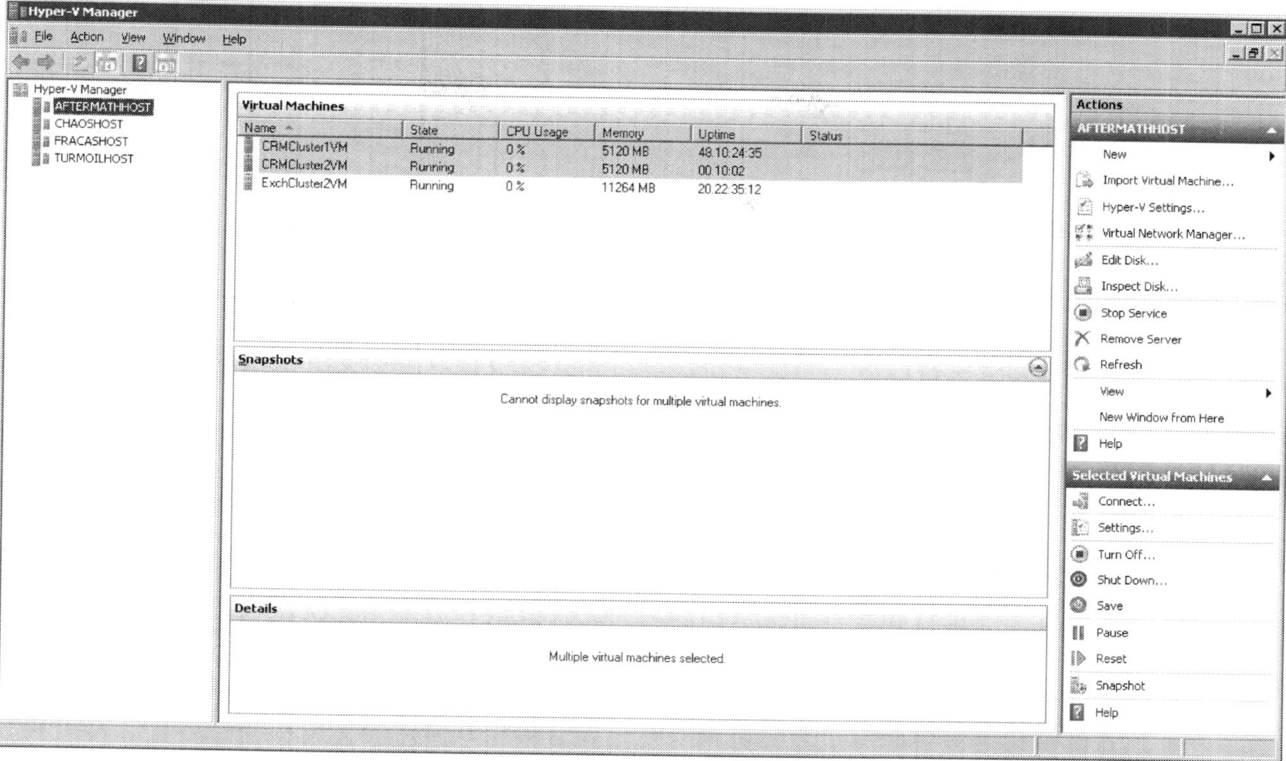


**Figure 18.4**

4. You should now have at least one CSV virtual machine on at least two different physical nodes of your CSV Windows cluster. For our project, we will now have two of our CSV virtual machines **CRMCluster1VM** and **CRMCluster2VM** hosted on our physical node **AftermathHost**, while we have our third CSV virtual machine **CRMCluster3VM** hosted on our physical node **TurmoilHost** for redundancy. You can see our CSV virtual machines hosted on **AftermathHost** in **Figure 18.4**.

# Adding Virtual Machines to the Windows CSV Cluster with the High Availability Wizard

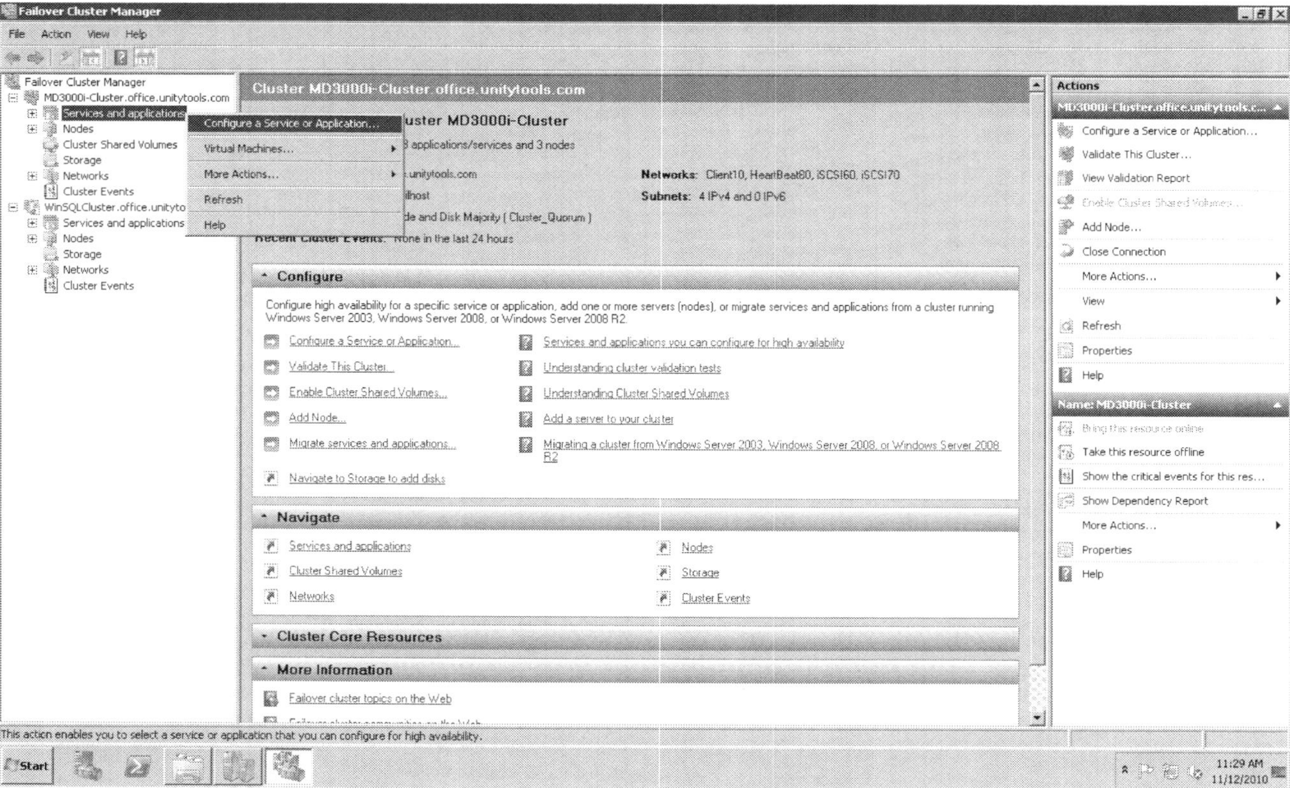


**Figure 18.5**

In this section, we will add our virtual machines that we created/imported to our Windows CSV cluster as highly available applications. When adding virtual machines to the Windows CSV cluster it is required that they be either turned off or in a saved state from within the Hyper-V Manager console.

5. Open the **Hyper-V Manager** console, right click on each of your virtual machines to be added to the Windows CSV cluster, and then select the **Shut Down** or **Save** option. For our project, we will shut down our three virtual machines named **CRMCluster1VM**, **CRMCluster2VM** and **CRMCluster3VM**.

6. Open the **Failover Cluster Manager** console, right click on the **Services & Applications** node under your Windows CSV cluster name, and then select the **Configure a Service or Application** option, as shown in **Figure 18.5**. This will launch the High Availability Wizard.

   a. On the **Before You Begin** screen, click on the **Next** button to continue.

## High Availability Wizard- Selecting the Virtual Machine Application

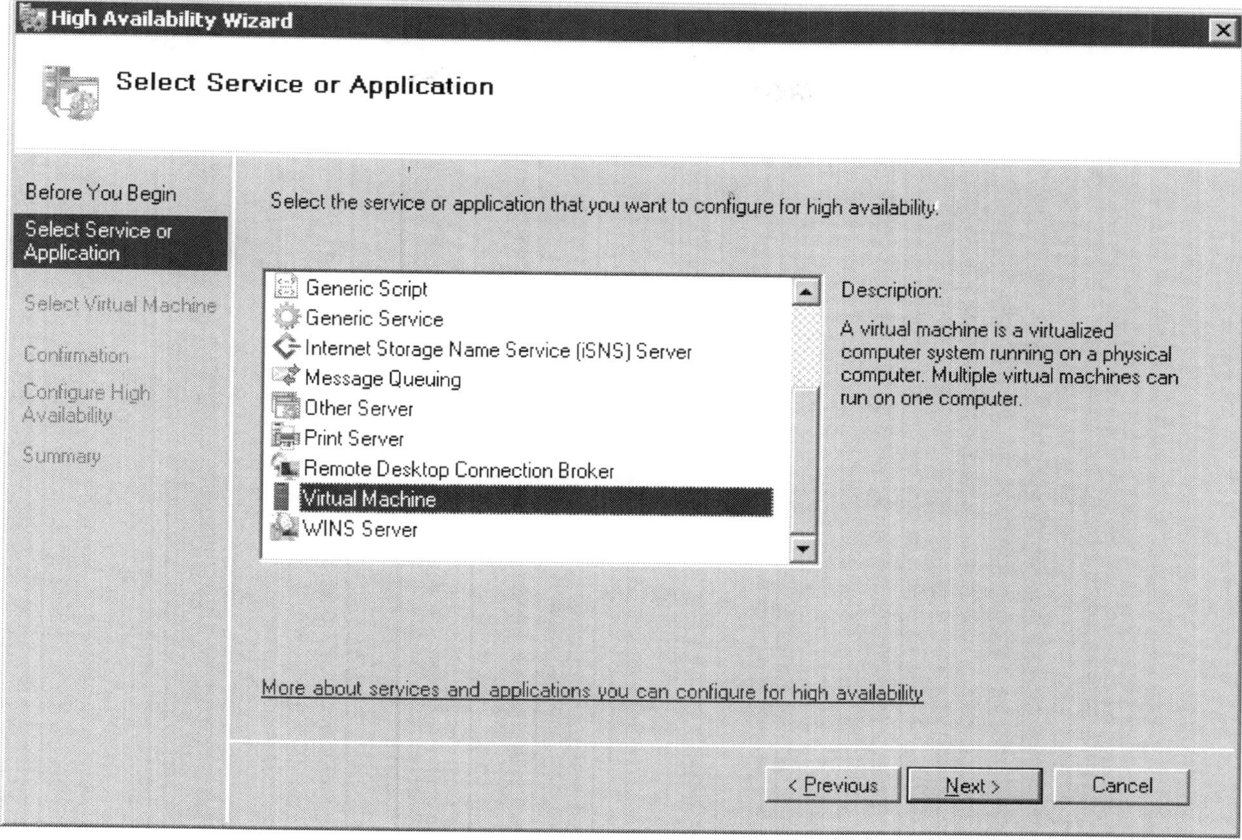


**Figure 18.6**

b. On the **Select Service or Application** screen, select the **Virtual Machine** option, and then click on the **Next** button, as shown in **Figure 18.6**.

## High Availability Wizard- Selecting the Virtual Machines

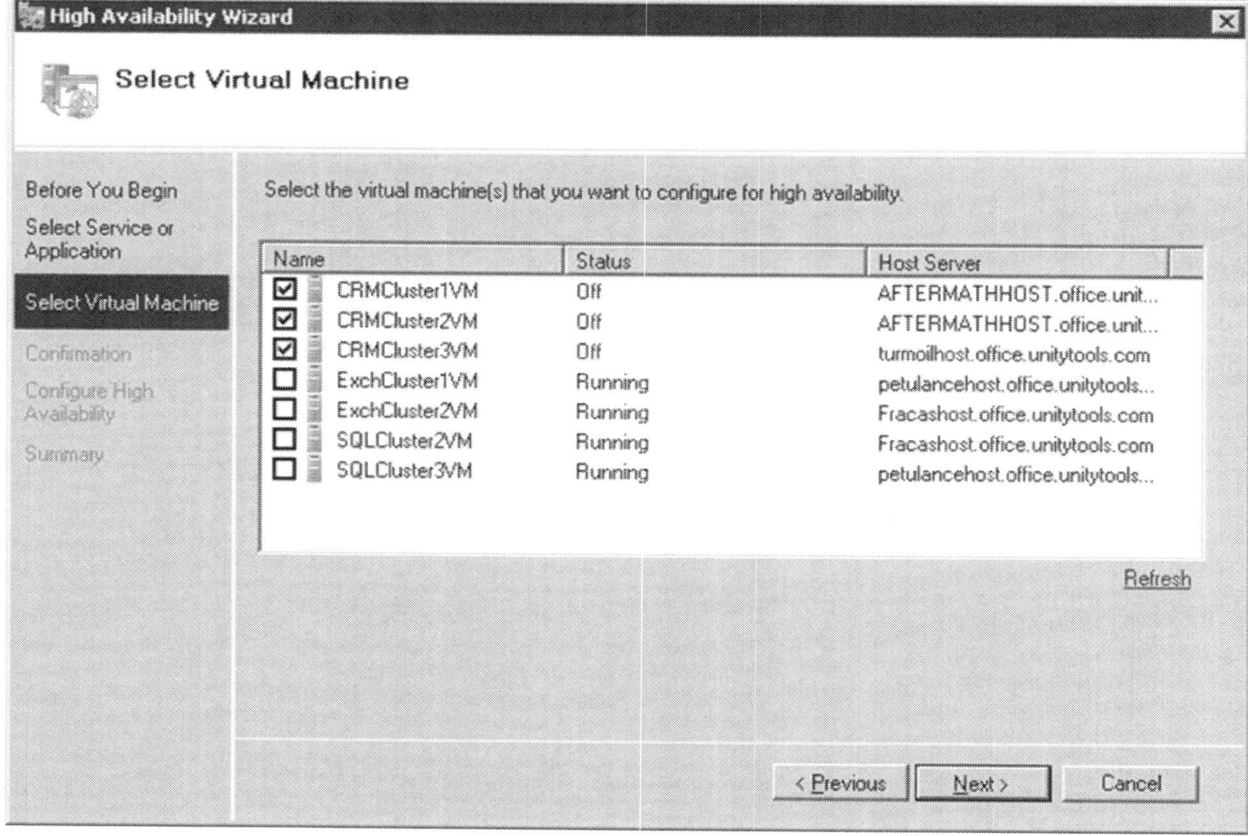


**Figure 18.7**

c. On the **Select a Virtual Machine** screen, select each of your virtual machines that will be part of the Windows CSV cluster. For our project, we will select our virtual machines **CRMCluster1VM**, **CRMCluster2VM** and **CRMCluster3VM**, as shown in **Figure 18.7**.

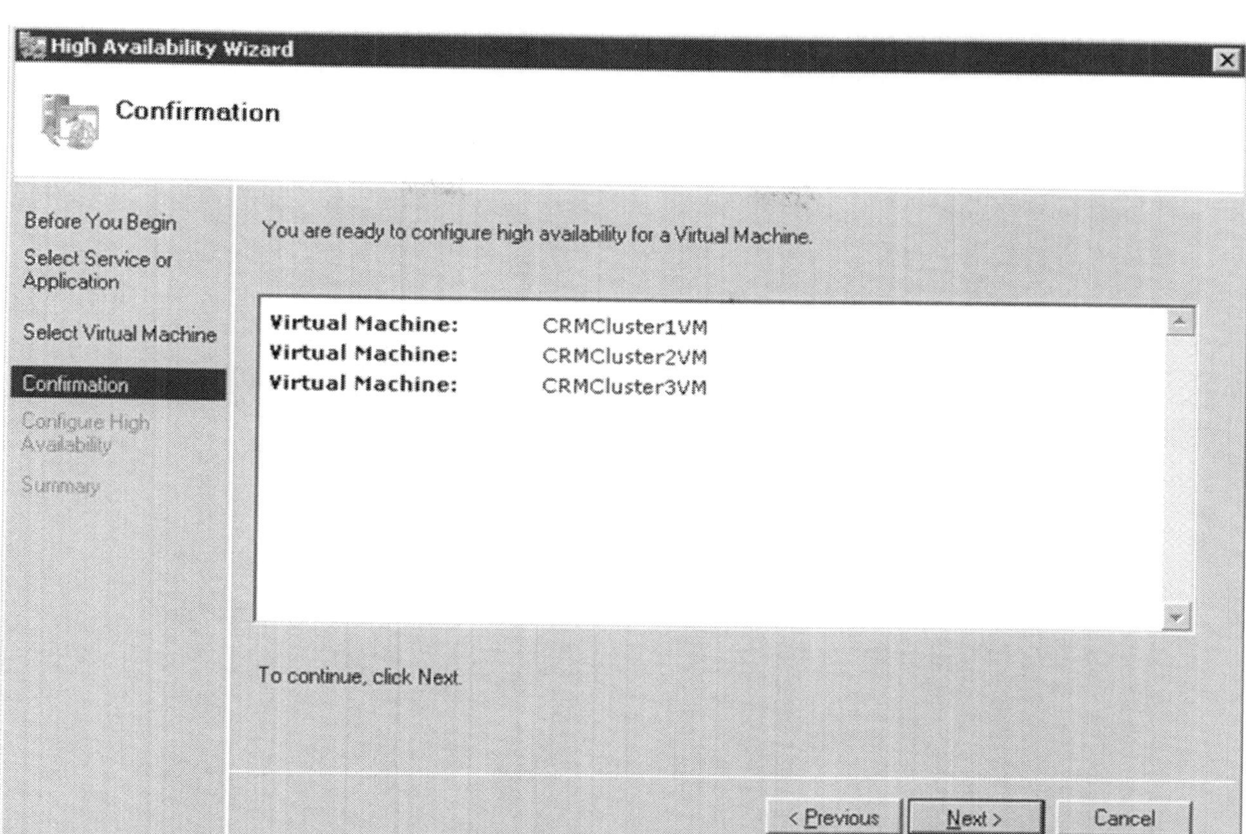


**Figure 18.8**

d. On the **Confirmation** screen, verify that the correct virtual machines are selected, and then click on the **Next** button to continue.

e. On the **Summary** screen, click on the **Finish** button to add your virtual machines. If you receive any **Errors** or **Warnings** on this screen, then click on the **View Report** button and resolve any issues that might exist.

# Verifying the Virtual Machines were Added to the Windows CSV Cluster

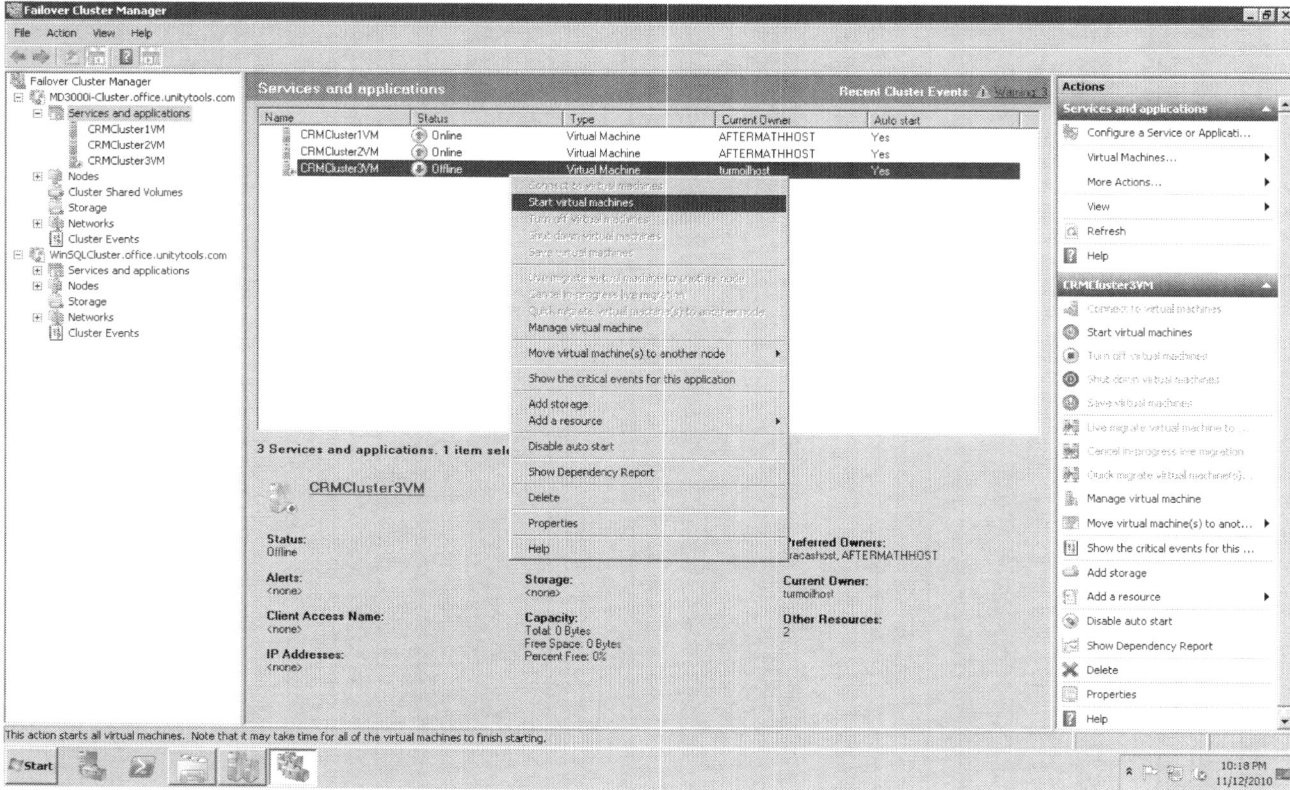


**Figure 18.9**

7. In the **Failover Cluster Manager** console, click on the **Services & Applications** node in the left pane under your Windows CSV cluster's name.

   a. In the **Services & Applications** center pane, verify that all your virtual machines were added, and then right on each and select the **Start virtual machines** option, as shown in **Figure 18.9**. Once our CSV virtual machines are started they will be online within our Windows CSV cluster.

# Managing the New CSV Virtual Machines

In this section, we will cover how to manage our new CSV virtual machines safely. With a highly available system we have to be careful as to how we shutdown and/or modify cluster resource settings to avoid the cluster from assessing the change as a failure.

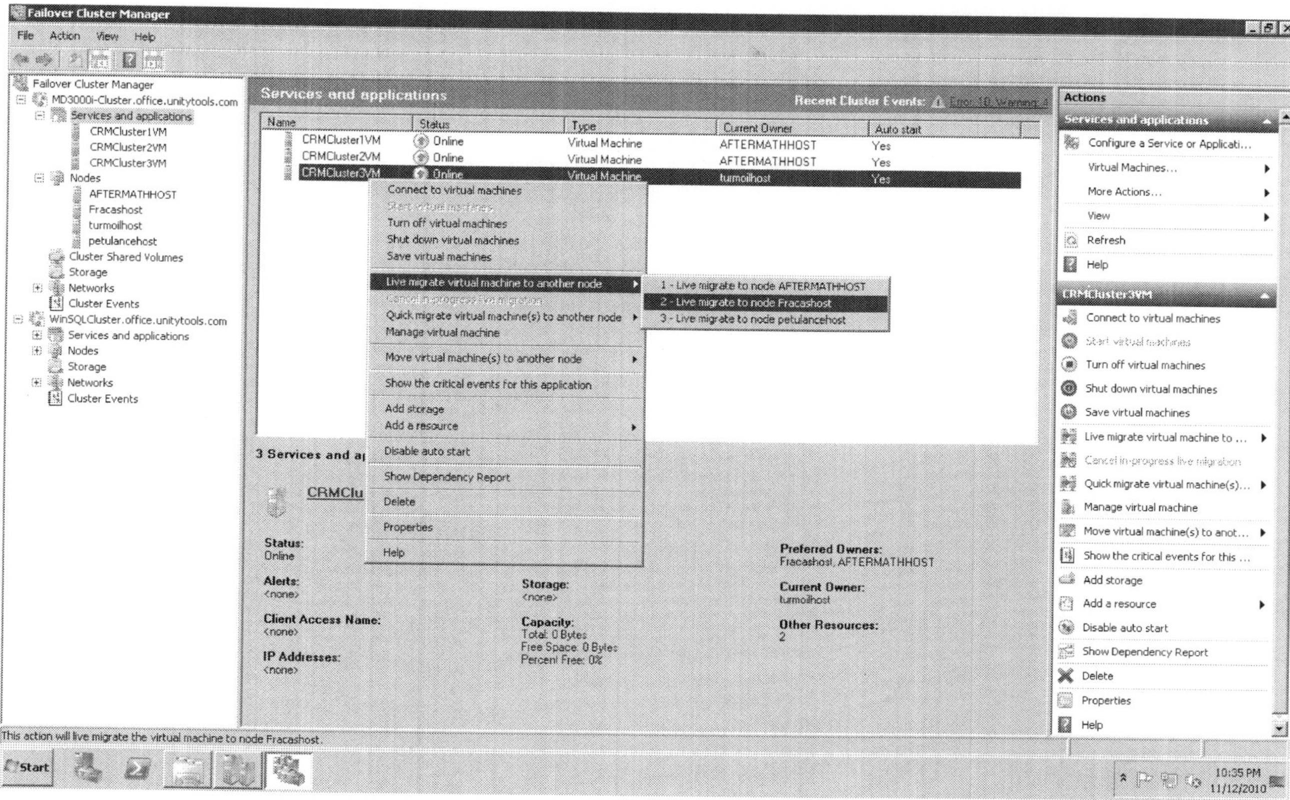


**Figure 18.10**

# Managing the New CSV Virtual Machines- Live Migration

8. In the **Services and Applications** center pane, right click on one of your new CSV virtual machines, and then select the **Live migrate the virtual machine to another node** option, as shown in **Figure 18.10**. We want to live migrate each of our CSV virtual machines between our different physical hosts to confirm that the live migration is working correctly. Make sure that the physical host that you're migrating to has enough memory to support your CSV virtual machine's migration. The live migration feature of Windows Server 2008 R2 allows us to move our CSV virtual machines between physical hosts without causing any interruptions to our clients accessing the resources on those virtual machines.

# Managing the New CSV Virtual Machines- Shutting Down

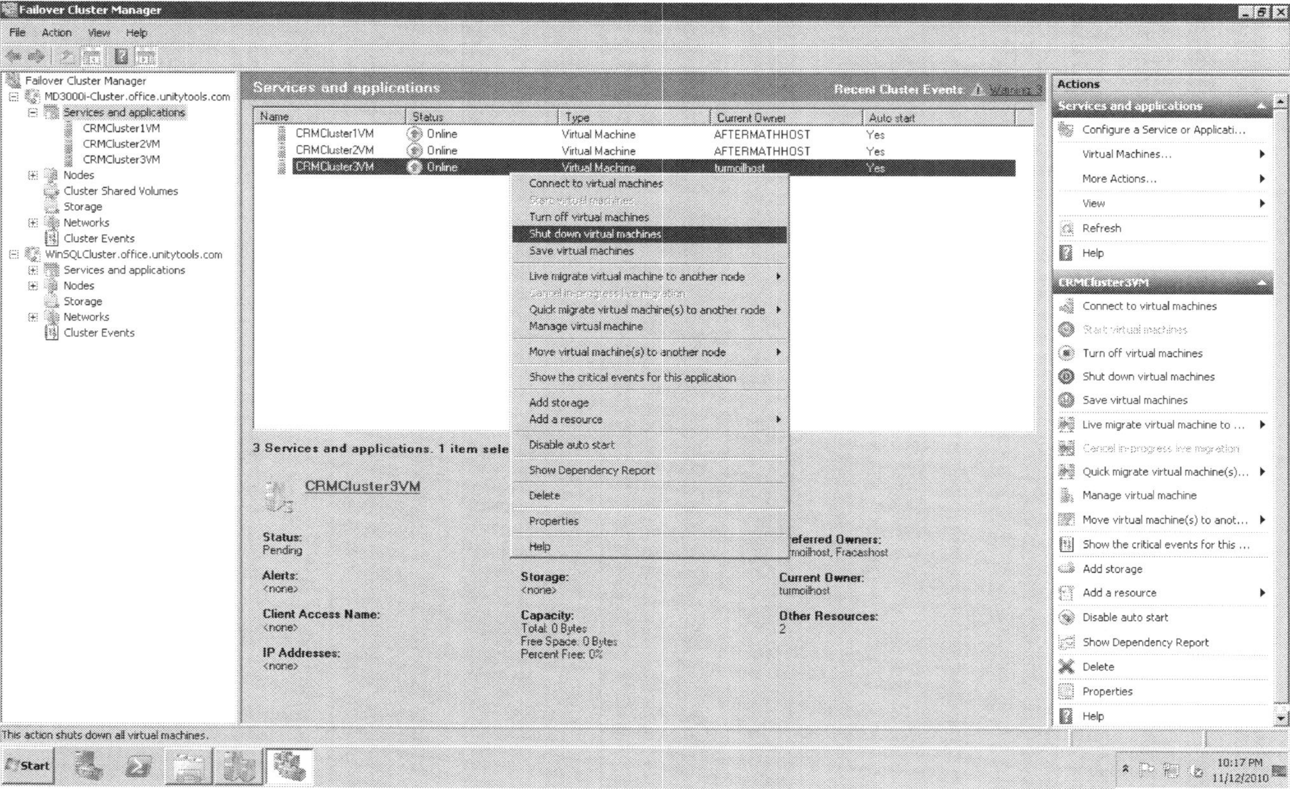


**Figure 18.11**

9. In the **Services and Applications** center pane, right click on one of your new CSV virtual machines, and then select the **Shutdown virtual machines** option, as shown in **Figure 18.11**. Any time you need to shutdown one of your CSV virtual machines it should always be perform in this manner from within the **Failover Cluster Manager** console. You can highlight multiple virtual machines, and then select the shutdown option, to shutdown multiple virtual machines at the same time. When turning your virtual machines back on, you can choose to start them from either within Hyper-V Manager or the Failover Cluster Manager console. Once the virtual machine's operating system is online, it will automatically come on online within the cluster.

# Managing the New CSV Virtual Machines- Setting Preferred Owners

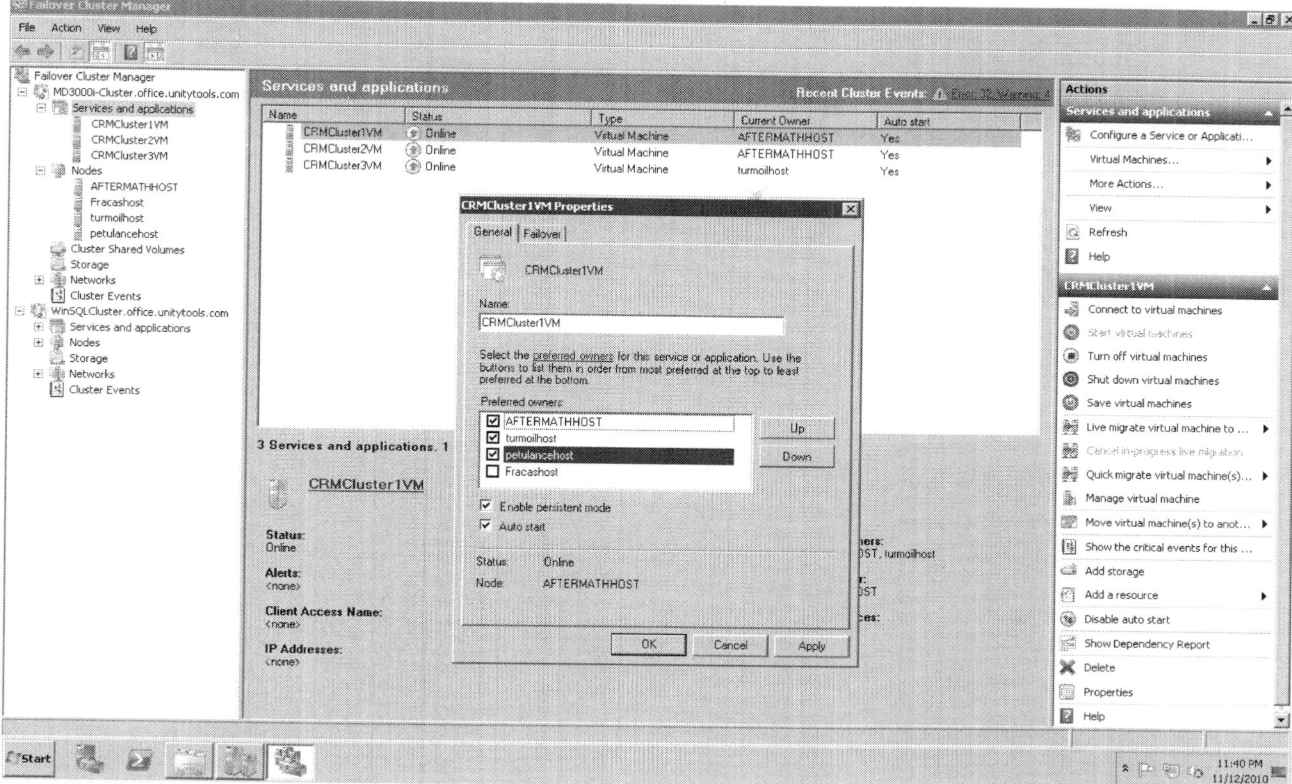


**Figure 18.12**

10. In the **Services and Applications** center pane, right click on one of your new CSV virtual machines, and then select the **Properties** option.

    a. In the **Preferred owners** field of the **General** tab, set your preferred owners of the **CSV virtual machine**, as shown in **Figure 18.10**. The preferred owners field sets the order of which physical hosts the CSV virtual machine is will failover to. You can use the preferred owners setting in conjunction with the **Failover** tab settings to allow your CSV virtual machine to automatically failback to the preferred owner at the top of list once that host becomes available again.

    **NOTE:** Even if you unselect a physical host's checkbox in the preferred owners field a failover to that physical host could still occur in the event that none of the preferred owners are currently available. We will cover how to completely prevent a virtual machine from moving to certain physical hosts by using advanced policies in the next couple steps.

# Managing the New CSV Virtual Machines- Virtual Machine Advanced Policies

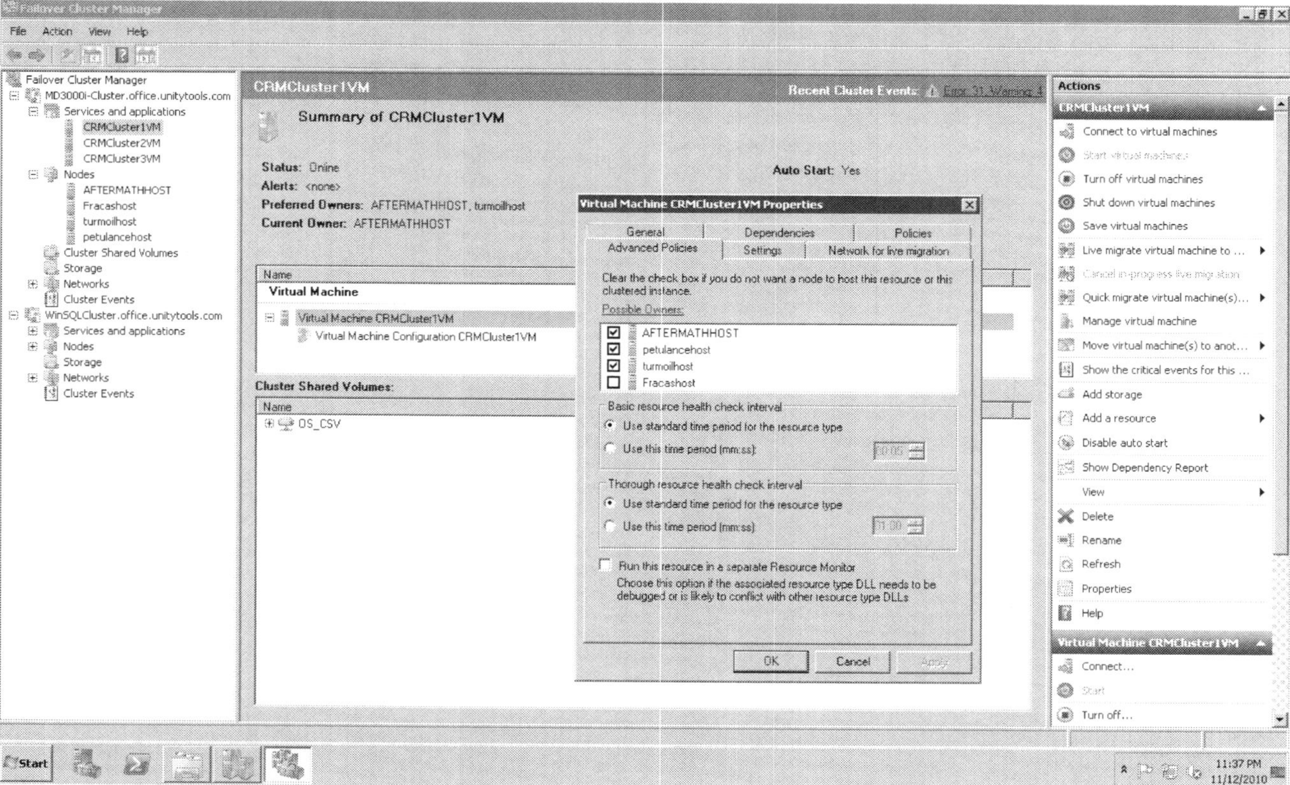


**Figure 18.13**

11. Under the **Services and Applications** node of the left pane, highlight one of your CSV virtual machines.

    a. In the center pane, right click on your virtual machine's name in the **Name** field, and then select the **Properties** option, as shown in **Figure 18.13**.

        i. Click on the **Advanced Policies** tab, and then for the **Possible Owners** field set which physical hosts can be owners of your **CSV virtual machine**. The possible owners field sets which physical hosts the CSV virtual machines can be hosted by. This allows you to prevent the cluster from attempting to move a CSV virtual machine to physical host without enough resources to support the virtual machine. By using the possible owners and preferred owners settings together you can configure your cluster for the best possible outcome in the event of a failure. For our project, we will set our possible owners primarily based on the amount of free memory each of our physical hosts has available.

        **NOTE:** If you don't configure these settings, then your cluster may attempt to failover your CSV virtual machines to physical hosts that don't have enough resources to support failover. This will cause the failover itself to fail and usually results in the virtual machine going into a saved state on its new host.

# Managing the New CSV Virtual Machines- Virtual Machine Configuration Advanced Policies

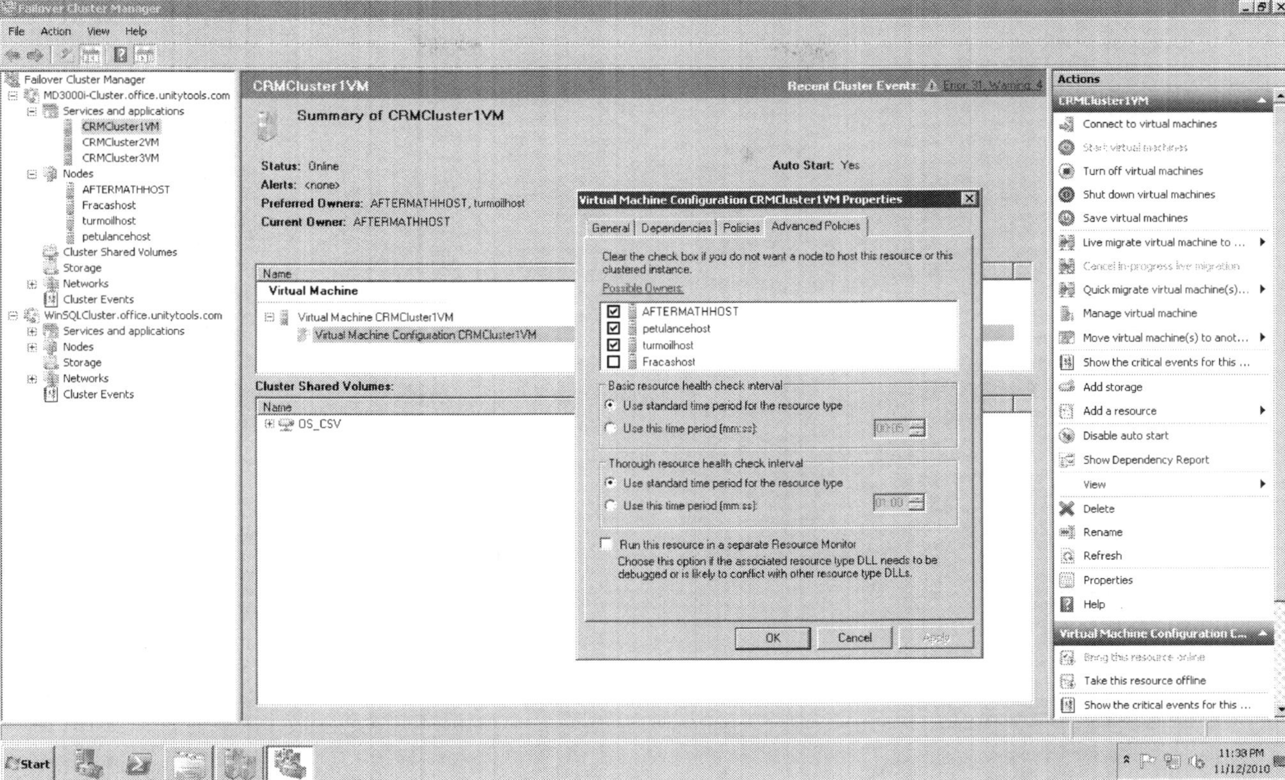


**Figure 18.14**

b. In the center pane, right click on your virtual machine's configuration in the **Name** section, and then select the **Properties** option, as shown in **Figure 18.14**.

   i. Click on the **Advanced Policies** tab, and then for the **Possible Owners** field set which physical hosts can be owners of your **CSV virtual machine's configuration** to match that which you set in **Step A** for your CSV virtual machine. Your virtual machine's configuration files can hosted by a different physical host then your CSV virtual machine's virtual hard disk (.vhd) files. For our project, we will keep our setup simple by setting our virtual machine and virtual machine configuration's possible owners the same.

# Chapter 19: Installing and Configuring the Microsoft Network Load Balancer (NLB) in an Active/Active Cluster

In this chapter, we will utilize another great built-in high availability feature of Windows Server 2008/R2 called the Network Load Balancer (NLB). The NLB can provide active/active clustering for traffic coming in on any ports specified. Whether you're interested in building a NLB cluster between CSV virtual machines, regular virtual machines, or with physical servers the steps in this chapter are basically the same. For regular virtual machines and CSV virtual machines the steps are equal, and if you're using physical servers you'll want to disregard some of the beginning parts of this chapter dealing with configuration of the virtual machines, and then follow the same basic steps outlined for setting up your NLB cluster. In our project, we will use an active/active NLB cluster to provide the final level of redundancy for our front-end application(s). When using Windows Network Load Balancer (NLB) feature in conjunction with Windows Server 2008 R2's new feature of Cluster Shared Volumes (CSV) we are able to build a true highly available environment. In this configuration, we have protection at the hardware level by using multiple physical hosts for our Windows CSV cluster while also having protection at the operating system and application levels by having an active/active NLB cluster configured between our CSV virtual machines. We will begin by covering some key information about the NLB feature that isn't highly publicized, and then we'll get started with configuring our CSV virtual machines for network load balancing. Once we have our network load balancing prerequisites in place, we will create our NLB cluster with one initial node, and then add our secondary node(s) to make the cluster highly available. We'll finish up by covering how to manage our new NLB cluster with the Network Load Balancer Manager console for such things as failovers and taking resources offline. When finished with this chapter, we will have a highly available infrastructure in place and ready for the deployment of our front-end application(s).

## Four Key Things to Know About Configuring the Microsoft Network Load Balancer (NLB) that Aren't Highly Publicized

There are four key things you need to know for Microsoft Network Load Balancer (NLB) to work correctly and they're not highly published by Microsoft documentation.

- The NLB requires two network adapters on each server to be connected to the same Client Active Directory network to work correctly. If you are using virtual machines or CSV virtual machines as in our project, then you will need to add a second virtual network adapter to each of your CSV virtual machines that will be part of the NLB cluster. If you are using physical servers you choose to add either virtual network adapter or a another physical network adapter to give you the required second network adapter. This second network adapter will have its MAC address spoofed by the NLB and therefore will be dedicated only to NLB communications.

- When adding the second network adapter from within Hyper-V, you have to enable spoofing of the MAC address.

- For Windows Server 2008 or later you need to enable WeakHostReceive and WeakHostSend from within the command prompt for your NLB network adapter.

- For better performance you will want to disable IPv6 on all of your NLB cluster node network adapters. The NLB servers will try to resolve traffic to IPv6 addresses first by default, so if you leave the IPv6 enabled you will see poor performance.

## Configuring the Prerequisites for the Microsoft Network Load Balancer on the CSV Virtual Machines

In this section, we'll move at a fast pace configuring some basic virtual machine and Windows prerequisites. If you already have some of these settings configured or if they don't apply to your particular setup, then please skip the non-applicable steps.

1. From within the **Hyper-V Manager**, right click on each of your CSV virtual machines, and then select the **Settings** option. Modify your virtual machine settings as follows.

    a. If you haven't already added your initial Client Active Directory network adapter, then you'll want to do so at this time. When adding your virtual network adapter in Hyper-V make sure to connect the network adapter to your Hyper-V's virtual network that you created for your Client Active Directory network. For our project, we will add the **Hyper-V Virtual Network** named **VLAN10** to each of our CSV virtual machines.

    b. Set the **Number of logical processors** that you want for each of your CSV virtual machines. For our project, we will set each of our CSV virtual machines to the max available of **4**.

    c. Set the each of your CSV virtual machines **Automatic Start Action** field to **Always Start**.

2. From within the **Hyper-V Manager**, right click on each of your CSV virtual machines, and then select the **Start** option.

    a. Once your CSV virtual machines are online, configure each of their network adapters with a static IP, and then name each of their network adapters according to your naming convention. For our project, we will assign static IP's to our Client Active Directory network adapters within the **10.10.10.0/24** network range, and then name each of our CSV virtual machines network adapters with the name of **Client10**.

3. Open the **Windows Server Manager** console on each of your CSV virtual machines, and then select the option to install a new Windows **Feature**.

    a. When running through the **Add Features Wizard**, select the **Windows Network Load Balancing** checkbox to install the NLB feature.

4. If you haven't already done so, Activate the Windows Server license on each of your CSV virtual machines.

5. Change the computer name of each of your CSV virtual machines to your chosen naming convention, and then add each virtual machine to the Active Directory domain.

    a. When prompted to restart the computer for the changes to take effect, select the **Restart Later** option, and then shutdown the CSV virtual machine manually. This will allow us to add the required second network adapter for our NLB from within Hyper-V Manager.

## Adding and Configuring the Network Load Balancer (NLB) Network Adapter

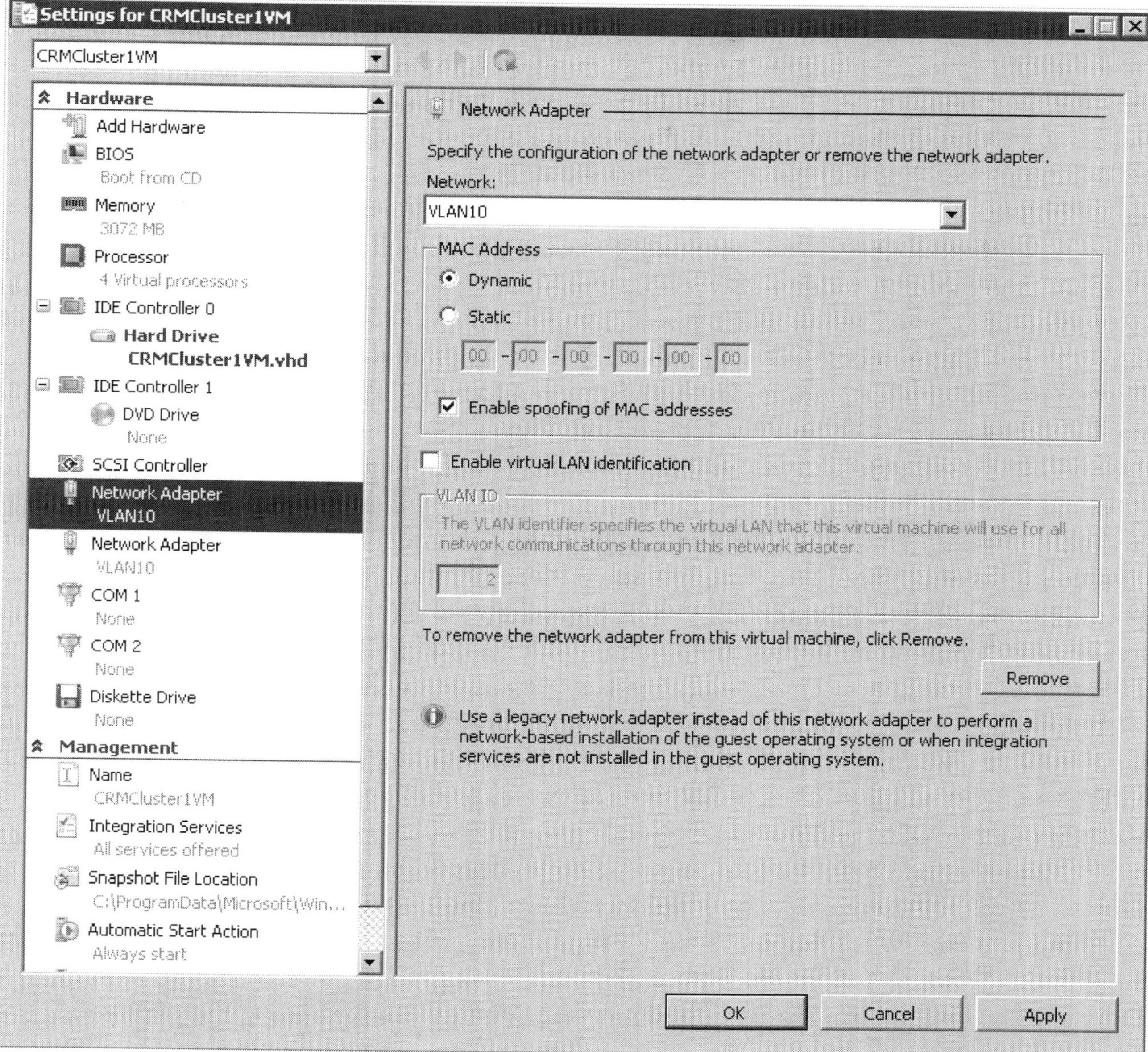


**Figure 19.1**

6. Once your CSV virtual machines are shutdown, return to the **Hyper-V Manager** console,.

   a. Right click on each of your CSV virtual machines, and then select the **Settings** option.

   b. Add a second network adapter for your Client Active Directory network to each of your CSV virtual machines. It is required to have two network adapters on the Active Directory domain when using Windows NLB. The first network adapter will handle all your normal Active Directory network communications, while your second adapter will be dedicated solely to your NLB traffic. For our project, we will add a second network adapter attached to our **Hyper-V Virtual Network** named **VLAN10**, as shown in **Figure 19.1**.

      i. On the Settings screen of your newly added NLB network adapter, select the **Enable spoofing of MAC addresses** checkbox, as shown in **Figure 19.1**. Click on the **OK** button to complete the configuration of your new NLB network adapter.

7. Start the virtual machine, and then logon with an account that has **Administrator** level privileges. For our project, we will logon with the **Domain Administrator** user account.

8. Turn on/allow **Network Discovery** and **File and Printer Sharing** through the **Windows Firewall** each of your servers.

9. Set the **Windows Updates** from within the **Control Panel** to the **Download updates, but let me choose whether to install them** option. It is a good practice to manually choose when Windows updates are applied, as we do not want our NLB server's configuration to change without our knowledge.

## Configuring the NLB Network Adapter's Properties

10. Rename your newly connected NLB network adapter to your naming convention for each of your CSV virtual machines that will be part of the NLB cluster. For our project, we will rename our newly connected network adapters to **Client10 NLB** on each of our CSV virtual machines.

    a. Right click on the new NLB network adapter, and then select the **Properties** option.

# Disabling IPv6 on the NLB Network Adapters

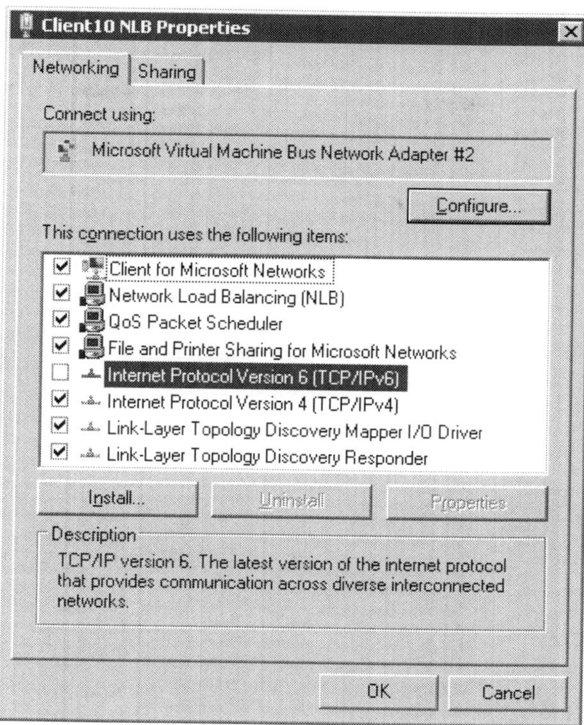


**Figure 19.2**

b. On the network adapter's **Properties** screen, unselect the **Internet Protocol Version 6 (TCP/IPv6)** checkbox, as shown in **Figure 19.2**.

## Configuring the IPv4 Properties on the NLB Network Adapters

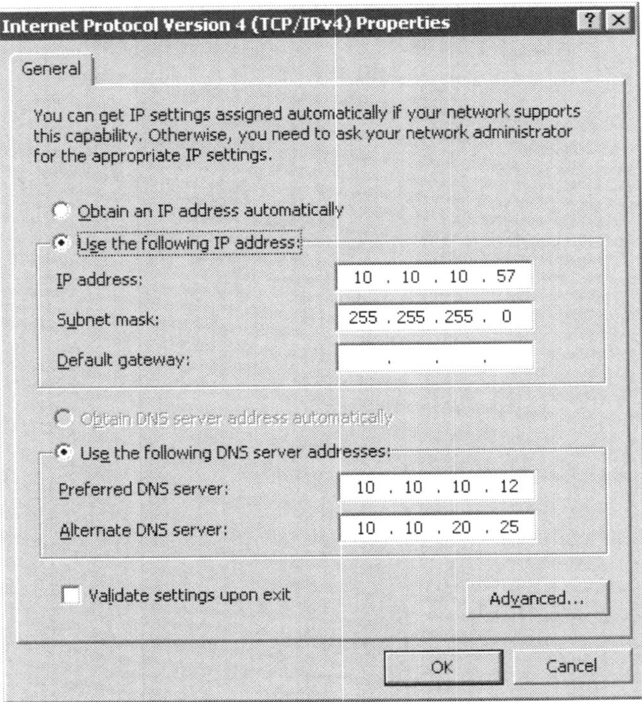


**Figure 19.3**

c. While still on the networks adapter's **Properties** screen, highlight the **Internet Protocol Version 4 (TCP/IPv4)** option, and then click on the **Properties** button. We want to assign the following properties to each of our NLB network adapters.

   i. Assign a **Static IP** and **Subnet Mask** for each of your NLB network adapters. The IP address needs to be within your Active Directory network's range. For our project, we will assign our IP addresses within our Client Active Directory's **10.10.10.0/24** network range, as shown in **Figure 19.3**.

   ii. Leave the **Default gateway** field blank. Only one of our network adapters can have a default gateway assigned to it and in our setup we want that network adapter to be our initial Client Active Directory network adapter and not our NLB network adapter.

   iii. Assign **DNS** servers for your Client Active Directory network.

## Configuring the Advanced IPv4 Properties on the NLB Network Adapters

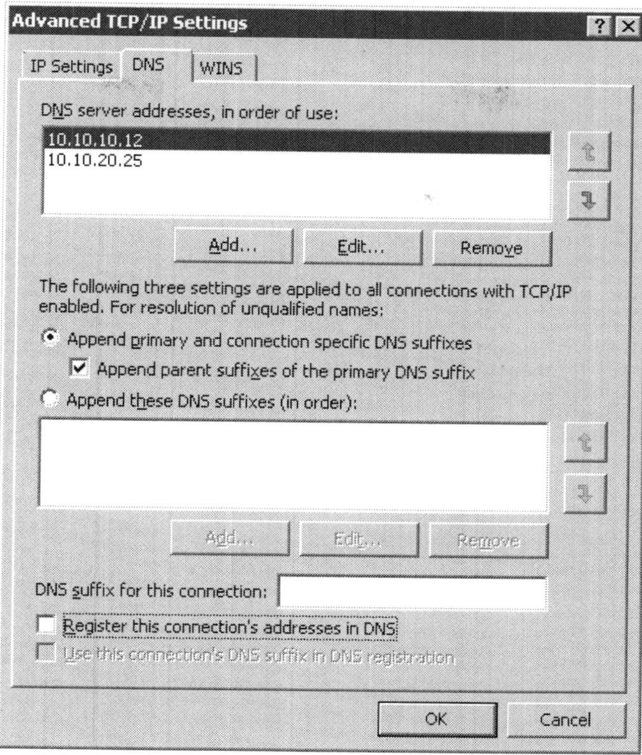


**Figure 19.4**

1. On the **Internet Protocol Version 4 (TCP/IPv4) Properties** screen, click on the **Advanced** button at the bottom of the screen, and then select the **DNS** tab on the **Advanced TCP/IP Settings** screen.

2. Unselect the **Register this connection's addresses in DNS** checkbox as shown at the bottom of **Figure 19.4**, and then click on the **OK** button of each screen to save and exit the properties of the NLB network adapter.

## Configuring the Network Adapters to Route Traffic Between Each Other on Windows Server 2008 or Later

Before we continue configuring the network settings on our soon to be NLB cluster nodes, we will first cover how our network load balancing functions in regard to each node routing traffic its two network adapters. For our project, we have our first network adapter named Client10 to will handle our normal Client Active Directory network traffic, while our second network adapter named Client10_NLB will handle all of our incoming NLB traffic. If the incoming traffic from the NLB cluster necessitates a response from a NLB cluster node, then the node will respond to the client computer with its Client10 network adapter and not its Client10_NLB network adapter. The reason for this is that as back and forth communication between the client and server is initiated the client will automatically respond to the network adapter on the server that sent it the initial reply, and therefore it is necessary that the Client10 network adapter of the server handle the continued back and forth communication to avoid the client computer from attempting to respond to the server's Client10_NLB network adapter. If the client computer responded to the server's Client10_NLB network adapter instead of the server's Client10 network adapter, then the client computer's traffic would be routed through the NLB cluster again, and the NLB cluster could end up redistributing the client computer's return traffic to a different NLB cluster node then the client computer was conducting a transaction with. It is important to understand that even though the Client10_NLB network adapter on each NLB cluster node has its own static IP address that the MAC address of the Client10_NLB network adapter it is being spoofed by the NLB cluster. This means that if the Client10_NLB network adapter of the server were to respond to a client computer, then the client computer would see the response as coming from the NLB cluster's IP address and not as from the IP address of the server's Client10_NLB network adapter.

Due to new security on Windows Server 2008/R2 a multi-homed server will not automatically route traffic between multiple network adapters on the same subnet as was the case with previous versions of Windows Server. When using Windows Server 2003, if you had two network adapters on the same subnet, one with a gateway and one without, then you were able to point traffic from outside the local subnet to the network adapter without the gateway and the server would respond back to the non-local subnet by routing the traffic through the network adapter with the default gateway. Currently, the only way to route traffic between multiple network adapters of a Windows Server 2008 or later is to disable these new security features.

## Changing the Network Adapter Security Settings of Windows 2008 or Later for Multi-homed Servers

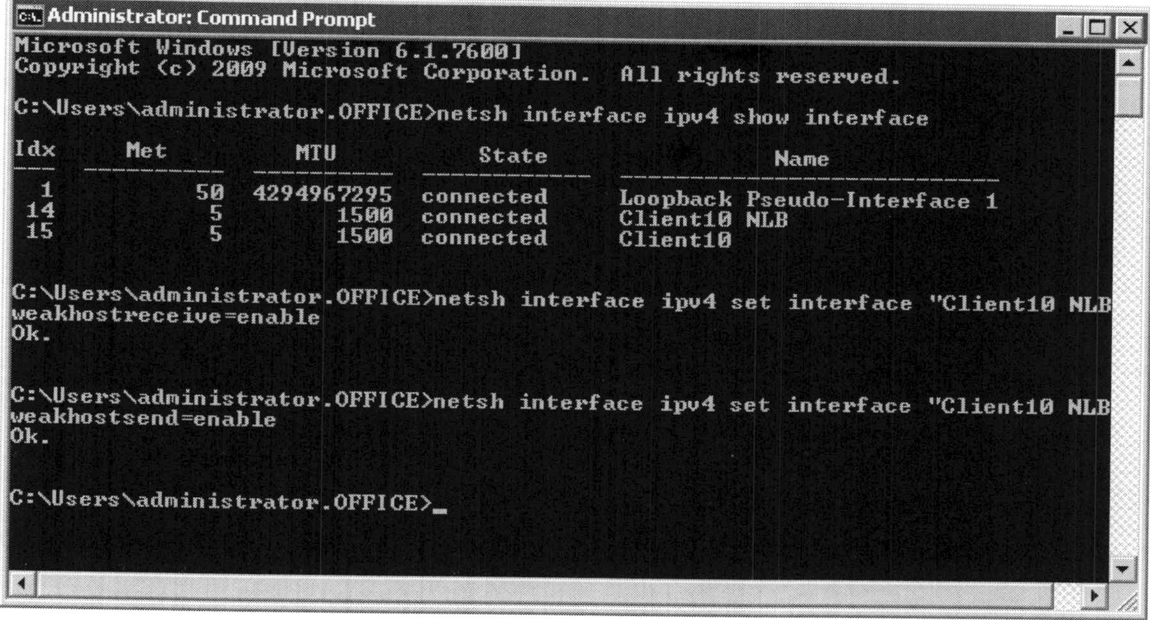
Administrator: Command Prompt
Microsoft Windows [Version 6.1.7600]
Copyright (c) 2009 Microsoft Corporation. All rights reserved.
C:\Users\administrator.OFFICE>netsh interface ipv4 show interface
Idx Met MTU State Name
1 50 4294967295 connected Loopback Pseudo-Interface 1
14 5 1500 connected Client10 NLB
15 5 1500 connected Client10
C:\Users\administrator.OFFICE>netsh interface ipv4 set interface "Client10 NLB
weakhostreceive=enable
Ok.
C:\Users\administrator.OFFICE>netsh interface ipv4 set interface "Client10 NLB
weakhostsend=enable
Ok.
C:\Users\administrator.OFFICE>_

**Figure 19.5**

11. Open the **Command Prompt** with the **Run as administrator** permissions, and then manually type the in following commands for your NLB network adapter. For our project, we will run these commands for our **Client10 NLB** network adapter, as shown in **Figure 19.5**.

    a. Manually type in **netsh interface ipv4 show interface**, and then hit the **Enter** key. This will display all your network adapters, as shown in the first command of **Figure 19.5**.

    b. Manually type in **netsh interface ipv4 set interface "Client10 NLB" weakhostreceive=enable**, and then hit the **Enter** key. You will need to replace the **Client10 NLB** with your NLB network adapter's name.

    c. Manually type in **netsh interface ipv4 set interface "Client10 NLB" weakhostsend=enable**, and then hit the **Enter** key. Once again, you will need to replace the **Client10 NLB** with your NLB network adapter's name.

    d. Type in **Exit**, and then hit the **Enter** key to exit the command prompt.

## Creating the Network Load Balancer (NLB) Cluster

12. Launch the **Network Load Balancing Manager** console, by going to **Start button\Administrative Tools**, and then selecting the **Network Load Balancing Manager** program. You can also launch the **Network Load Balancing Manager** by typing the command **Nlbmgr** into the **Run** line.

    a. Right click on the **Network Load Balancing Clusters** node in the left pane, and then select the **New Cluster** option.

## Creating the NLB Cluster- Adding the Initial Node

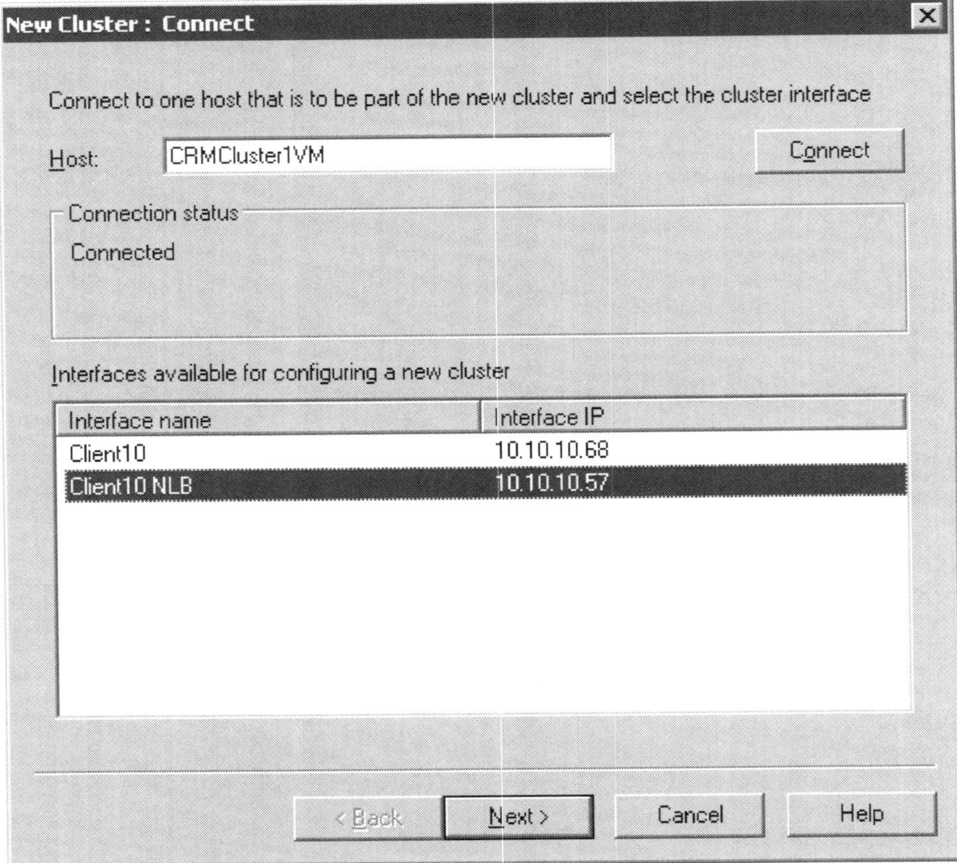


**Figure 19.6**

b. On the **New Cluster: Connect** screen, enter one of your CSV virtual machine names in the **Host** field, and then click on the **Connect** button. For our project, we will enter **CRMCluster1VM** for our CSV virtual machine.

c. Highlight your server's NLB network adapter, and then click on the **Next** button to continue. This network adapter will host the virtual IP address of your NLB cluster, and thus will handle your incoming NLB cluster traffic. For our project, we will select our **Client10 NLB** network adapter, as shown in **Figure 19.6**.

## Creating the NLB Cluster- Configuring Host Parameters

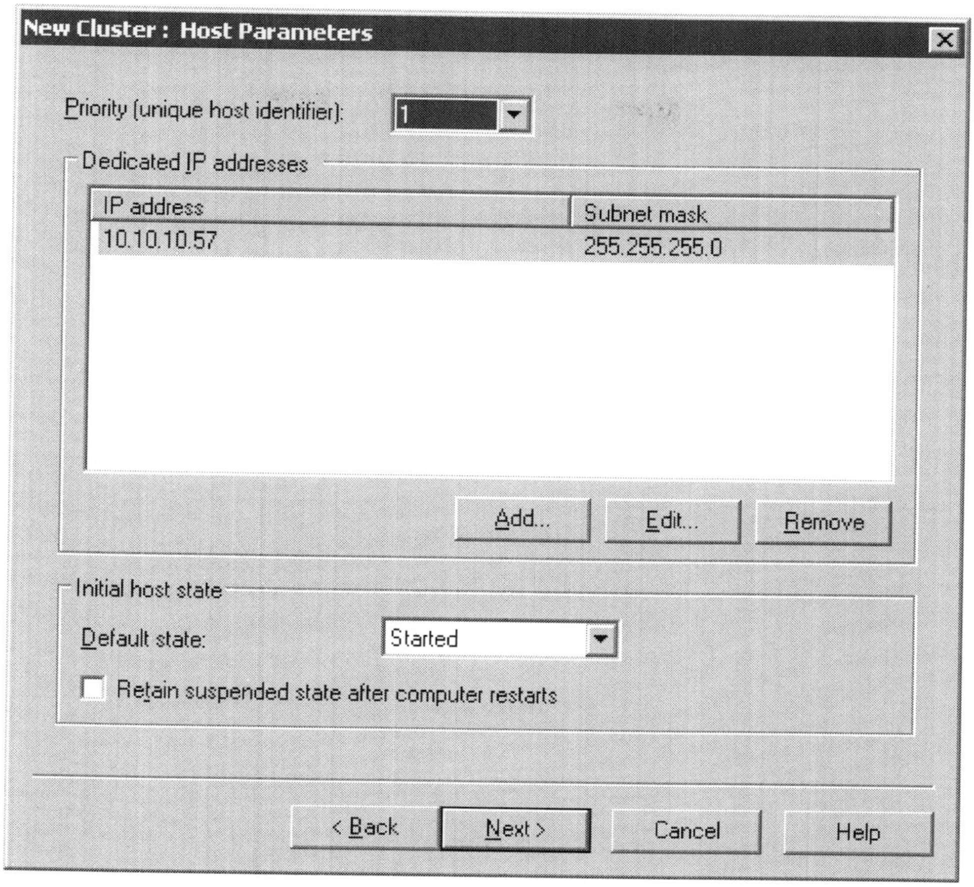

**Figure 19.7**

d. On the **New Cluster: Host Parameters** screen, you can leave the defaults, and then click on the **Next** button to continue. The **Priority (unique host identifier)** field of this screen specifies a unique ID for the host. The host with the lowest numerical priority among the members of the NLB cluster will handle all of the cluster's network traffic that is not covered by a port rule. You can override these priorities by configuring load balancing for specific ranges of ports on the **Port Rules** tab of the network load balancing's **Properties** screen. When you choose to load balance all the ports across all your cluster nodes as in our project, then your NLB cluster will function in an active/active mode distributing the workload evenly across all member nodes. For our project, we will be load balancing all ports across all our NLB cluster nodes, so the priority number doesn't play a role other than being the NLB cluster node's ID number within the cluster.

## Creating the NLB Cluster- Assigning the Cluster IP Address

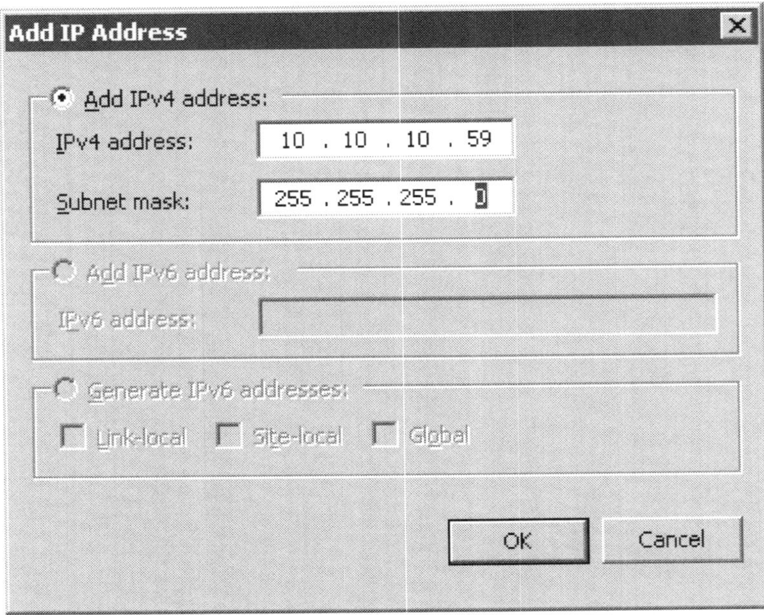


**Figure 19.8**

f. On the **New Cluster: Cluster IP Addresses** screen, click on the **Add** button to continue.

   i. On the **Add IP Address** screen, enter the **IP Address** and **Subnet mask** that you want to use for your NLB cluster, and then click on the **OK** button to continue. This IP address will be shared by each host in the cluster and will be the IP address that all your clients use when accessing the resources of the NLB cluster. The NLB will add this IP address to the TCP/IP stack on the selected interface of each host that is part of your NLB cluster. The NLB cluster does not support Dynamic Host Configuration Protocol (DHCP) and therefore will automatically disable DHCP on each network interface that is part of the cluster. For our project, we will enter **10.10.10.59** for our IP address and then **255.255.255.0** for our subnet mask of our NLB cluster, as shown in **Figure 19.8**.

g. On the **New Cluster: Cluster IP Addresses** screen, verify the **Cluster IP address** field is correct, and then click the on the **Next** button to continue.

## Creating the NLB Cluster- Configuring Cluster Parameters

h. On the **New Cluster: Cluster Parameters** screen, leave the defaults, and then click on the **Next** button to continue. The below is some additional information explaining the fields of this screen for your reference.

   i. On this screen you've probably notice the **Full internet name** field. This field is only used for reference within the **Network Load Balancing Manager** itself, so if you feel like entering the name for this field then feel free to do so. Our name resolution on the LAN for the NLB cluster's IP address will be handled by adding a Host (A) record to our internal DNS server.

ii. The **Cluster operation mode** field specifies the type of **Media Access Control (MAC)** address that will be used for cluster operations. In unicast mode the MAC address of the NLB cluster is assigned to each cluster node's NLB network adapter, while the node's built-in MAC address of the network adapter is no longer used.

## Creating the NLB Cluster- Configuring Port Rules

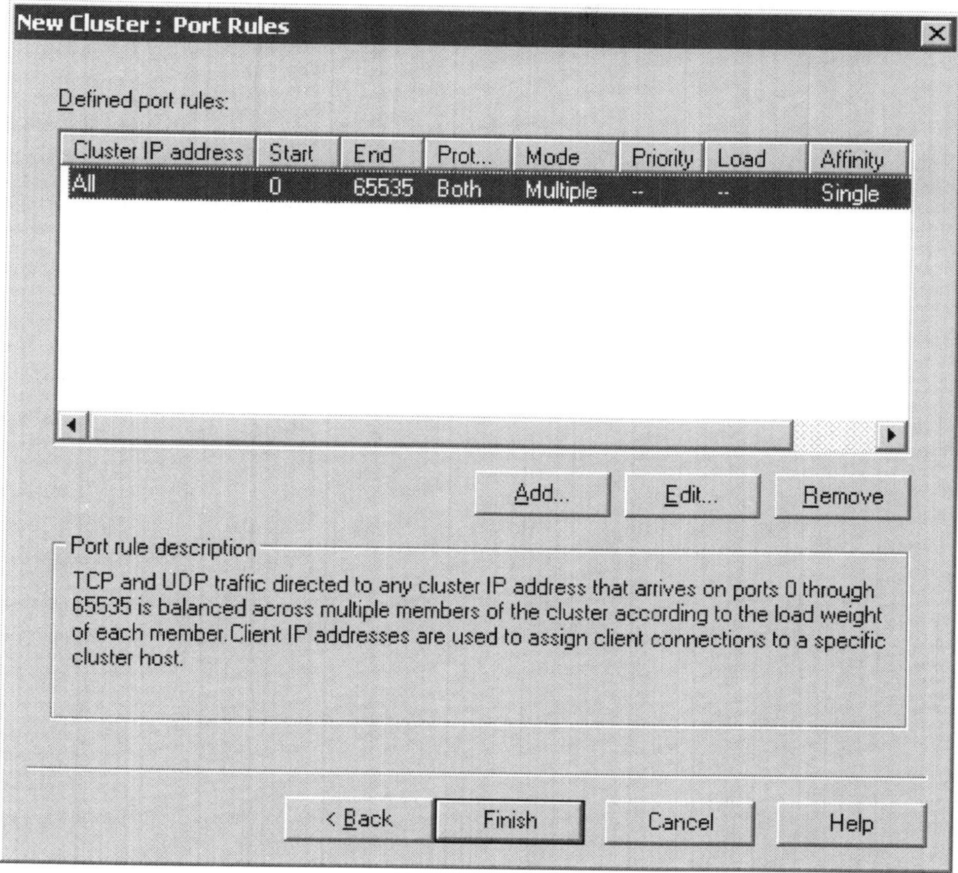


**Figure 19.9**

i. On the **New Cluster: Port Rules** screen, click on the **Edit** button to view the details of the port rules that you've chosen to use for your cluster.

## Creating the NLB Cluster- Reviewing the Port Rules

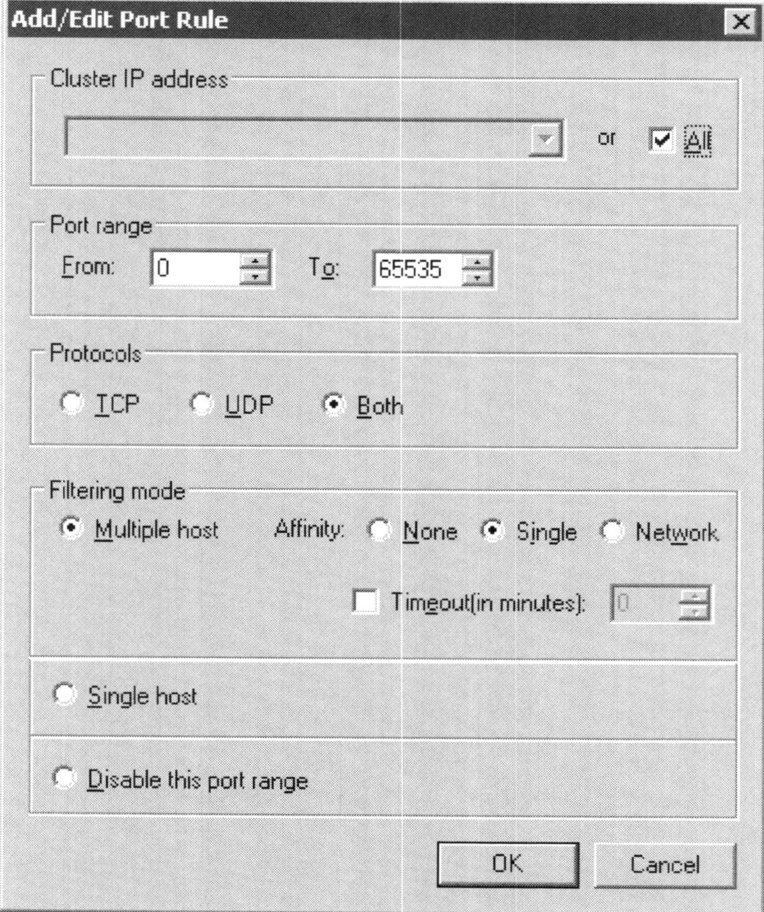


**Figure 19.10**

For our project, our load balanced front-end application will be Microsoft Dynamics CRM 4.0, which requires the same settings as the NLB's cluster creation wizard's defaults. The below information explains the different fields of the **Add/Edit Port Rule** screen.

i. For the **Port Range** fields, we will use the default range of **0** to **65535**. This sets the NLB cluster to load balance traffic coming in on any port.

ii. For the **Protocols** field, we will use the default option of **Both**. This works in conjunction with the port range that we specified and sets the NLB cluster to handle all TCP and UDP traffic for those ports. This also sets all incoming traffic to be active/active load balanced across all the member nodes of the NLB cluster.

iii. For the **Filtering mode** field, we will use the default of **Multiple host** with the **Affinity** field set to **Single**. Using a single affinity means that once the client initially hits the NLB cluster and begins transacting with one of the cluster nodes that it will continue to talk to this same server during the whole session unless interrupted by outage/failover. In the event of an outage/failover the NLB cluster will re-route the current client traffic from the failed node to other cluster nodes that remain available.

iv. Click on the **OK** button to return to the **New Cluster: Port Rules** screen.

j. On the **New Cluster: Port Rules** screen, click on the **Finish** button to complete your NLB cluster's creation.

## Adding Additional Nodes to Make the NLB Cluster Highly Available

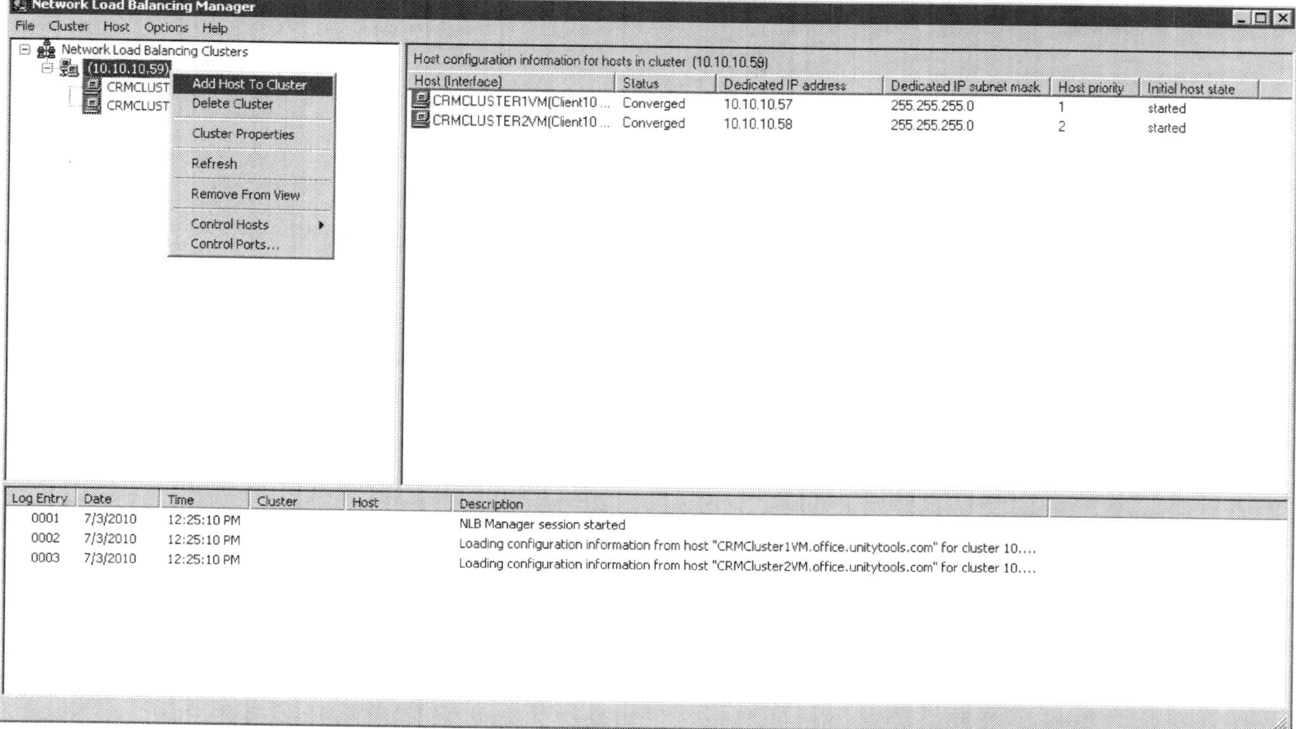


**Figure 19.11**

Adding additional nodes to an existing NLB cluster is a very easy process. Once we have at least two or more member nodes joined to our cluster it becomes a highly available solution. When adding additional members to the cluster, we will use the same configuration settings that we used when creating the cluster with the initial node.

13. In the **Network Load Balancing Manager** console, right click on your NLB cluster's IP in the left pane, and then select the **Add Host To Cluster** option. For our project, we will right click on our IP of **10.10.10.59** that assigned to our NLB cluster, as shown in **Figure 19.11**.

## Adding Additional Nodes- Second Node

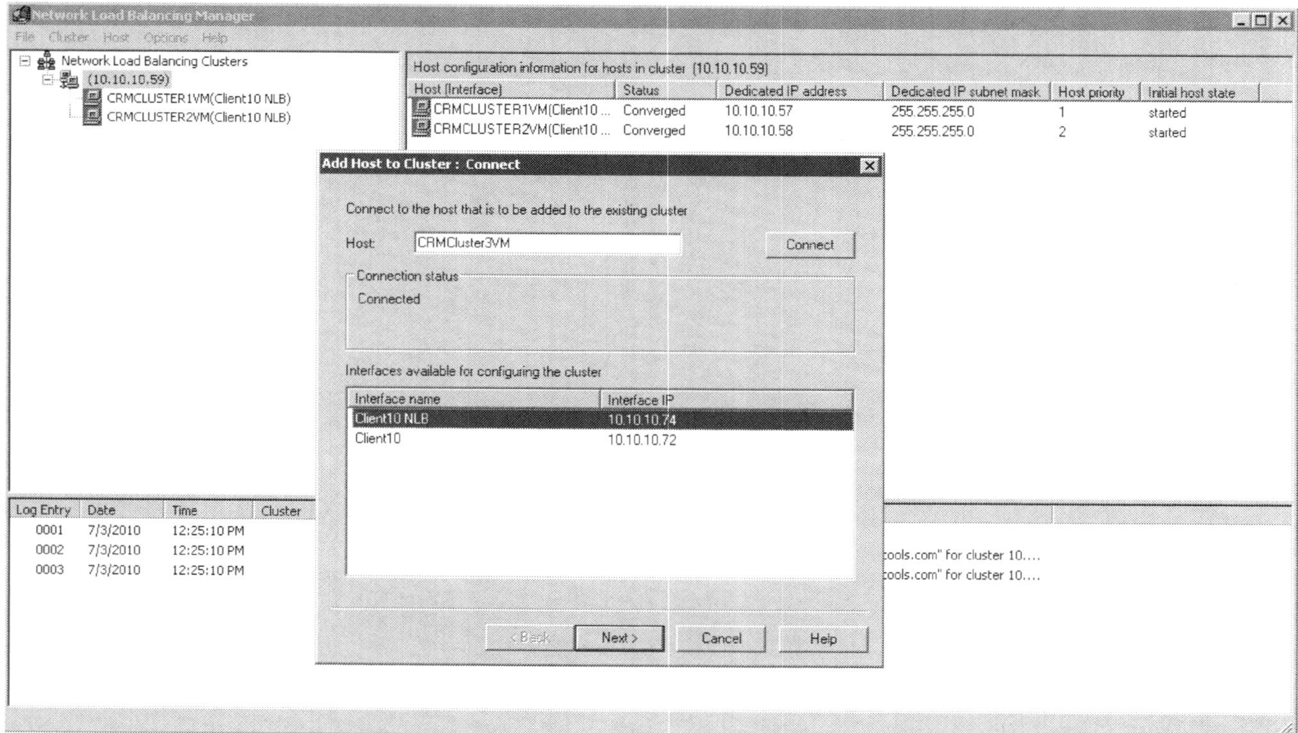

**Figure 19.12**

a. On the **Add Host to Cluster: Connect** screen, enter your second CSV virtual machine's name in the **Host** field, and then click on the **Connect** button. For our project, we have two additional CSV virtual machines **CRMCluster2VM** and **CRMCluster3VM** that we will be adding to our NLB cluster.

b. Highlight your server's NLB network adapter, and then click on the **Next** button to continue. For our project, we will select our **Client10 NLB** network adapter, as shown in **Figure 19.12**.

# Adding Additional Nodes- Configuring Host Parameters

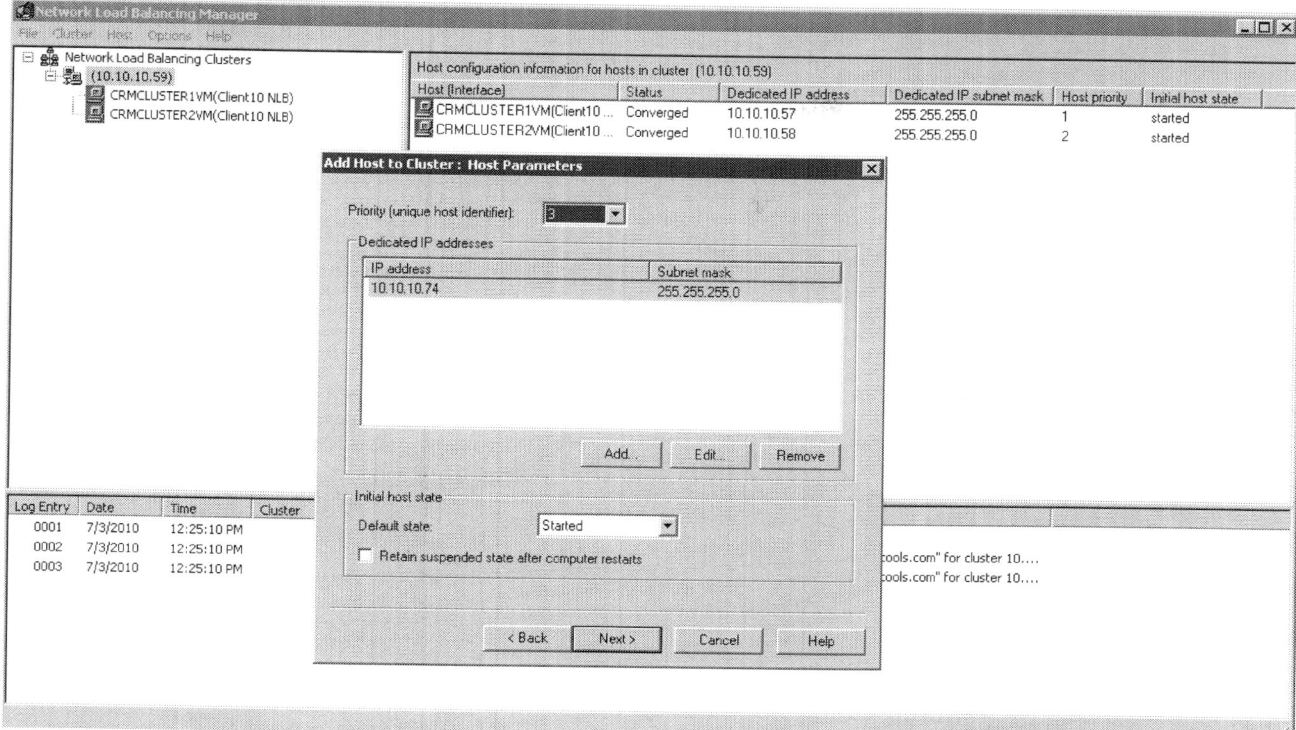

Figure 19.13

c. On the **Add Host to Cluster: Host Parameters** screen, leave the defaults, and then click on the **Next** button to continue. The **Priority (unique host identifier)** field of this screen specifies the unique ID for each host and will increment by one for each additional node we add. For our project, we have chosen to load balance all our ports, so the priority number does not actually set a priority in our case and is only used as the host's ID within the cluster itself.

## Adding Additional Nodes- Configuring Port Rules

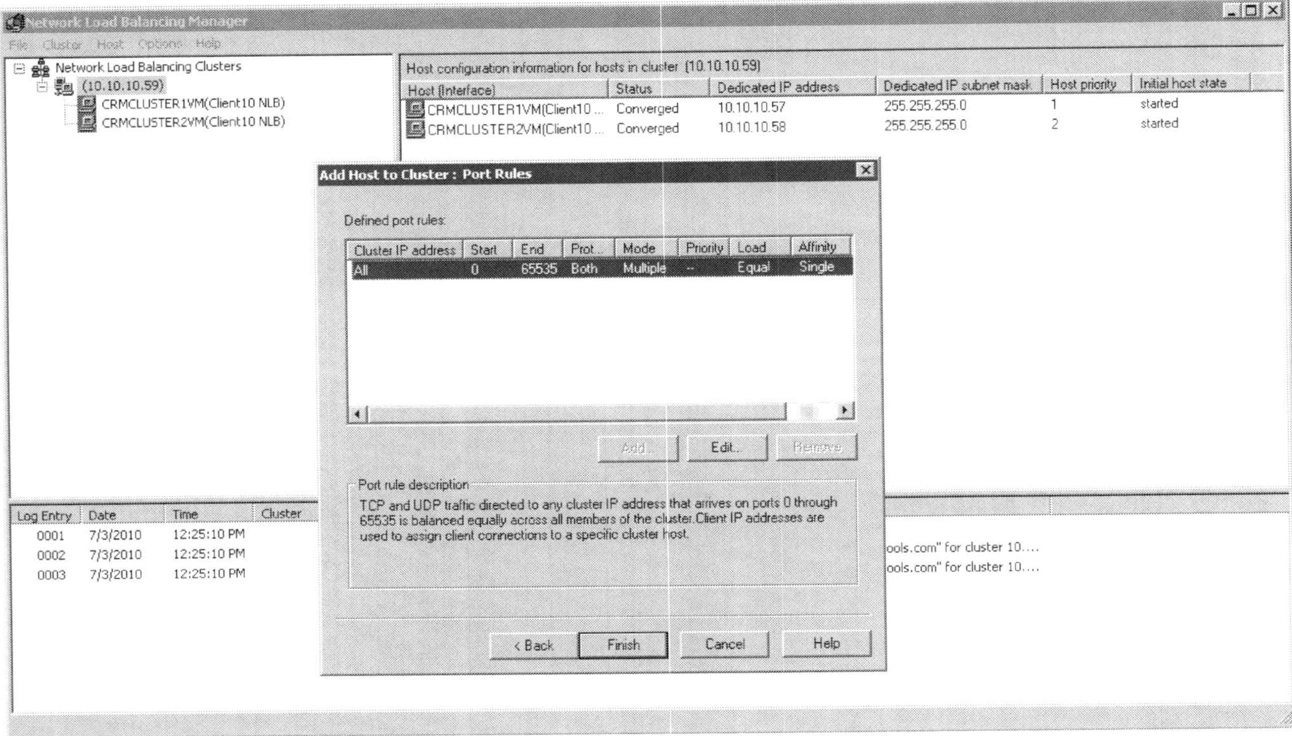


**Figure 19.14**

d. On the **Add Host to Cluster: Port Rules** screen, leave the defaults, and then click on the **Finish** button to complete adding the node.

## Verifying the Network Load Balancer's Final Configuration

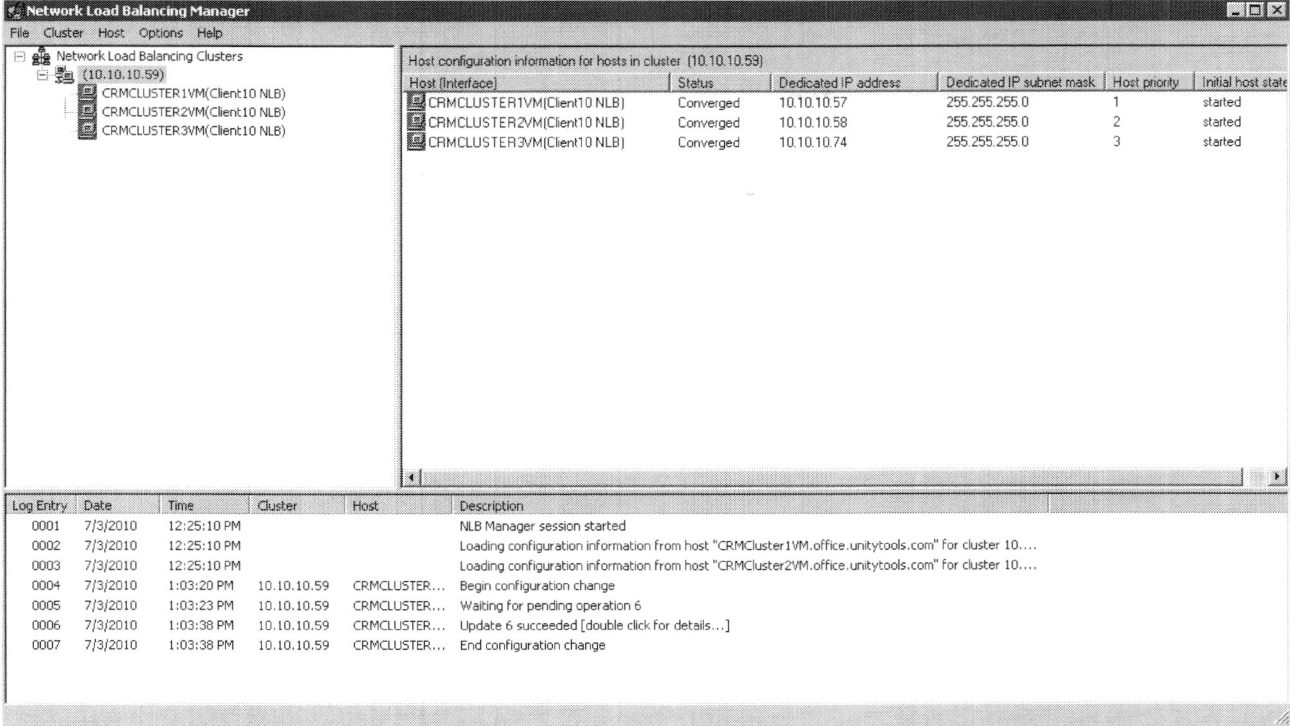


**Figure 19.15**

14. Once you're done adding each of your nodes to the cluster your **Network Load Balancing Manager** console should appear similar to **Figure 19.15**. Each of your nodes should have a green computer icon next to their name and the **Status** column of each should show the status of **Converged**. If any of your cluster nodes have a yellow computer icon or errors, then most likely you missed a network adapter configuration step. If this is your scenario, then you should run through the beginning of this chapter again to verify your network adapter's configuration.

15. Repeat **Step 13** for each additional NLB cluster node you want to add.

16. The final step is to create an internal DNS **Host (A)** record for your NLB's cluster IP address so that the cluster's IP address will resolve to a DNS name on your Client Active Directory network. For our project, we will add a **Host (A)** record to our DNS with the name of **xrm** for our NLB cluster's IP address of **10.10.10.59**.

## Managing the NLB Cluster

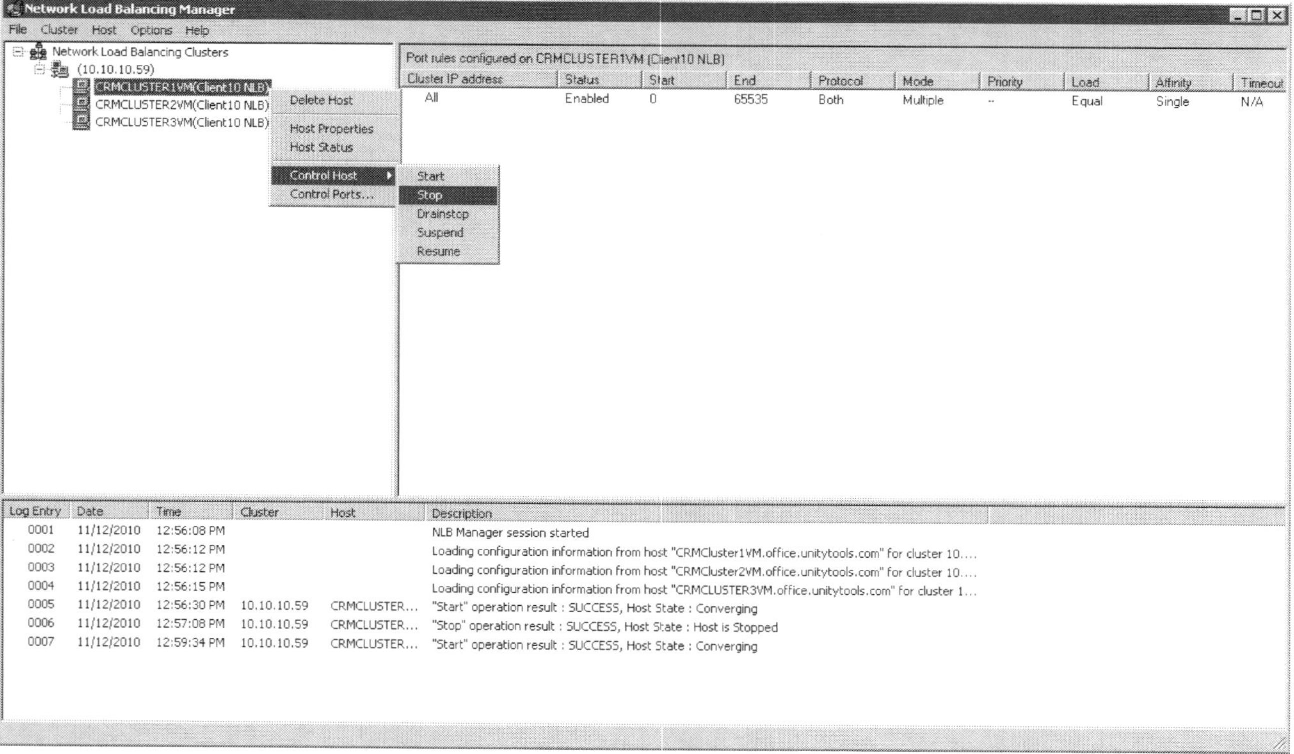

**Figure 19.16**

## Managing the NLB Cluster- Stopping Traffic to a Node

If you want to prevent traffic from going to one of your NLB cluster nodes such as before a shutdown or virtual machine quick migration, than you can simply stop the node from receiving traffic with the following below steps. You do not need to manually stop traffic from going to the cluster node before a reboot, however it's recommend as the transition of traffic to the other nodes will always be smoother when you manually stop the node from receiving traffic first.

17. In the **Network Load Balancing Manager** console, right click on your cluster node that you want to stop receiving traffic, and then select the **Control Host\Stop** option, as shown in **Figure 19.16**. From the control host option you can start and stop the node manually as you please. The active connections to the NLB cluster node will be interrupted and all traffic to the node will be immediately transitioned to the remaining active node(s). Even though the **Stop** option interrupts active client connections the transition is fast and fairly smooth without your end users usually even noticing. If you need to insure that no active user connections are interrupted then you should select the **Control Host\Drainstop** option instead. The **Drainstop** option allows the host to continue servicing active connections but won't accept any new incoming connections, and thus gives you the smoothest possible transition. Keep in mind that this option can take quite some time from hours to days to transition all the traffic off the host as the server has to continue servicing active connections until the client machine disconnects. When making changes to your cluster nodes you'll want to right click on your NLB cluster's IP in the left pane, and then select the refresh option a couple times after each change so that the Network Load Balancing Manager console will refresh each nodes status. It is normal to see the cluster node icons change to a yellow or red color during the converging of changes.

# Managing the NLB Cluster- Setting the Default State

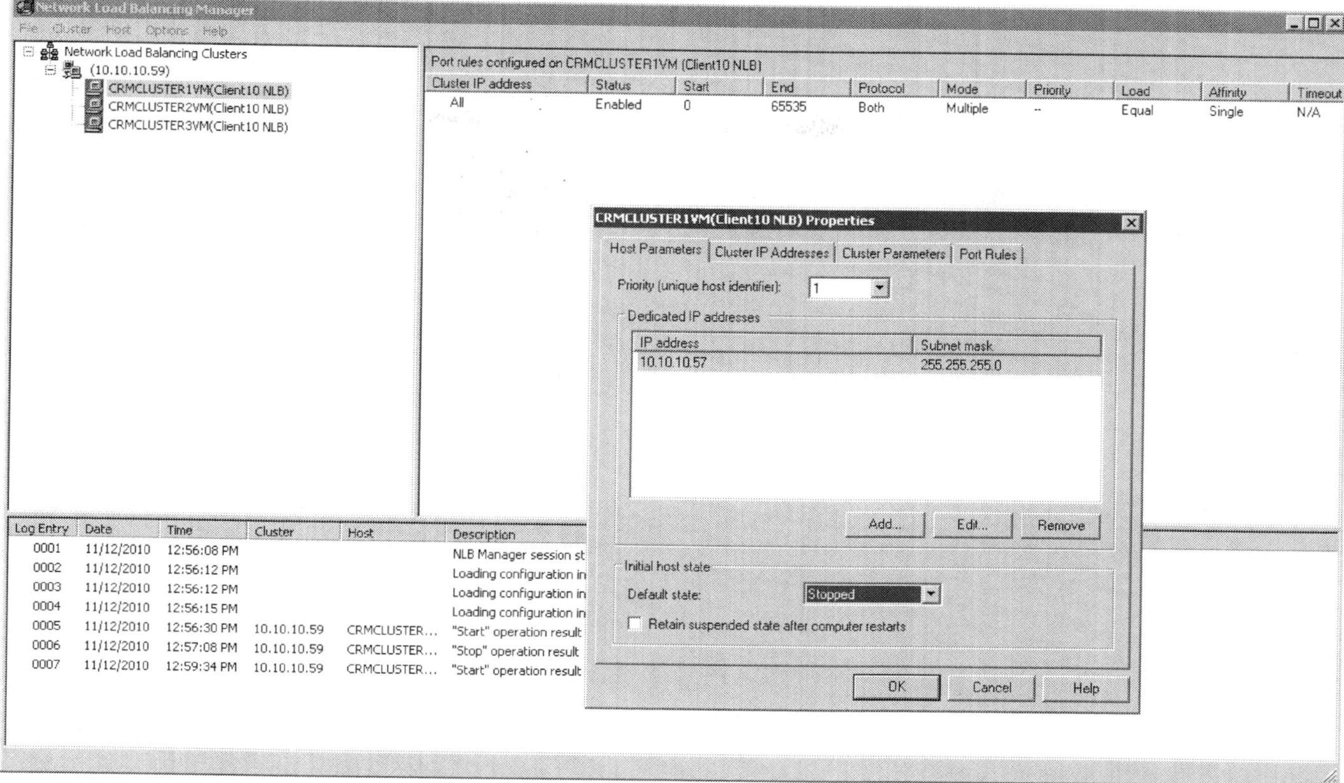


**Figure 19.17**

The NLB cluster node's default state determines what state the server will be in once it is restarted. If you reboot the cluster node it will automatically come back online, when the default state is set to started.

18. In the **Network Load Balancing Manager** console, right click on the cluster node that you want to change the default state of, and then select the **Host Properties** option.

    a. On the **Host Properties** screen, select the **Host Parameters** tab, and then select the default state that you want from the **Default State** dropdown box, as shown in **Figure 19.17**. If you set the default state to Stopped, then your cluster node will remain inactive after a reboot unless you manually start the node from within the Network Load Balancing Manager console.

# Chapter 20: Installing and Configuring SQL Server 2008/R2 Reporting Services Scale-Out Deployment on Load Balanced Servers

In this chapter, we will cover all the intricacies of how to setup Microsoft's SQL Server Reporting Services (SSRS) between our network load balanced servers for high availability. Earlier in Chapter 13 when we installed our SQL server, we choose not to install the SQL Reporting Services feature due to it not being compatible with SQL clustering during a failover. This means that SQL Reporting Services will work on the initial SQL cluster node, however once a failover to a different cluster node occurs the SQL Reporting Services will cease to work until failed back to the initial node. We will overcome this limitation by placing our SQL Reporting Services on our front-end application servers, and then configuring an SQL Reporting Services Scale-out Deployment between our servers.

Whether you are deploying your SQL Reporting Services on physical or virtual servers, on cluster nodes behind a physical or software load balancer, or whether you are installing SQL Server 2008 SP1 or SQL Server 2008 R2 Reporting, you will find that the SQL installation steps are pretty the same. There are a few exceptions that exist between the different SQL Server 2008 versions, which we will cover during the installation process.

For our project, we will setup our SQL Reporting Services Scale-out Deployment between our front-end application servers that are members of our Microsoft Network Load Balancer (NLB) cluster. Once completed with this chapter, we will have true high availability for our SQL Reporting Services with our reports working successfully from any of our NLB cluster nodes that clients are directed to by the load balancer.

## Installing SQL Reporting Services on the Initial NLB Cluster Node

We will go through the SQL server installation similarly to as we did earlier, however this time we will only be installing the Reporting Services component on each of our NLB cluster nodes.

1. Copy the **SQL Server 2008/R2** installation media onto the local hard disk of one of your NLB cluster nodes that you want to be the initial node of the **SQL Reporting Services Scale-out Deployment**.

   **NOTE:** Make sure to copy the installation media onto the local machine or you may experience weird glitches and/or invalid errors during the install process.

## Prerequisites- Creating the Active Directory Service Account

As a prerequisite to installing our SQL Reporting Services we will first need to create Active Directory user account that will be used for our SQL Reporting Services service to run under. This user account will become a very important piece of our security as build our SQL Reporting Services Scale-out Deployment. It will insure that our SQL Reporting Services can authenticate from any node of the NLB cluster. We will also use this account to setup the Service Principle Names (SPN) for our NLB cluster. And finally, if your front-end application will be Microsoft Dynamics CRM 4.0 as in our project, then we will also be using this account to secure our application.

2. On one of your domain controllers, open the **Active Directory Users and Computers** console, and then create a new user account in the **Domain Users** group for your **SQL Reporting Services service** to run under. For our project, we will create a user account named **CRMService**.

## Prerequisites- Temporally Disabling the Windows Firewall

3. The SQL installation will pull a warning concerning the **Windows Firewall**, so temporally we want to disable the Windows Firewall on our NLB cluster nodes until after the SQL installation is complete at which point we will set the SQL program to be allowed through the Windows Firewall.

## Prerequisites- When Installing SQL Server 2008 on Windows Server 2008 R2

One of the differences between SQL Server 2008 and SQL Server 2008 R2 when installing on a Windows Server 2008 R2 server is the prerequisites. Windows Server 2008 R2 requires SQL Server 2008 SP1 or later as a prerequisite to installing SQL Server 2008. We will run the SQL Server 2008 Service Pack 1 installation for the shared features on our Windows 2008 R2 servers before performing our SQL Server 2008 installation. If you are installing SQL Server 2008 R2 on Windows Server 2008 R2 or SQL Server 2008 on a Window Server 2008, then please disregard this section and skip to **Step 5**.

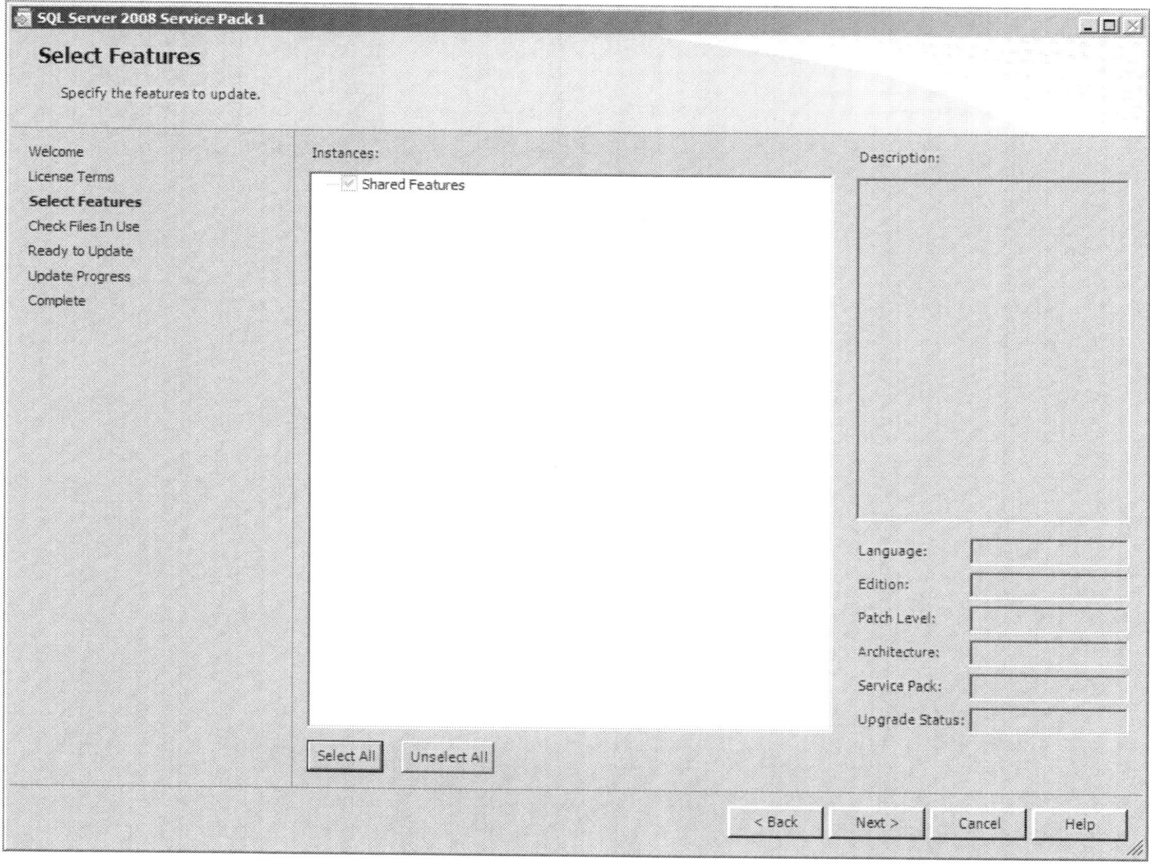


**Figure 20.1**

4. Launch the **SQL Server 2008 SP1** or later on the NLB cluster node that you want to be your initial node of the SQL Reporting Services Scale-out Deployment. For our project, we will install SQL Reporting Services on our NLB cluster node named **CRMCluster1VM**.

    a. Leave the install options all at their defaults except for when you come to the **Select Features** screen, where you want to click on the **Select All** button, as shown in **Figure 20.1**. Click on the **Next** button to continue.

    b. Finish going through the install screens with the defaults to complete the install.

## Installing SQL Reporting Services- Launching the Install

5. Run the SQL Server 2008/R2 **setup.exe** from the installation media to launch the **SQL Server Installation Center** screen. If you are installing SQL Reporting Services 2008 R2 on a Windows Server 2008 R2, then please disregard the next couple of steps and skip to **Step 7**.

    a. If you receive the **Program Compatibility Assistant** pop-up screen, click on the **Run program** button to continue. This screen is letting you know, that for your SQL Server installation to be compatible with Windows Server 2008 R2 you will have to re-apply the SQL Server 2008 Service Pack 1 or later after your SQL Server installation has completed.

## Prerequisites- When Installing SQL Server 2008/R2 on Windows Server 2008

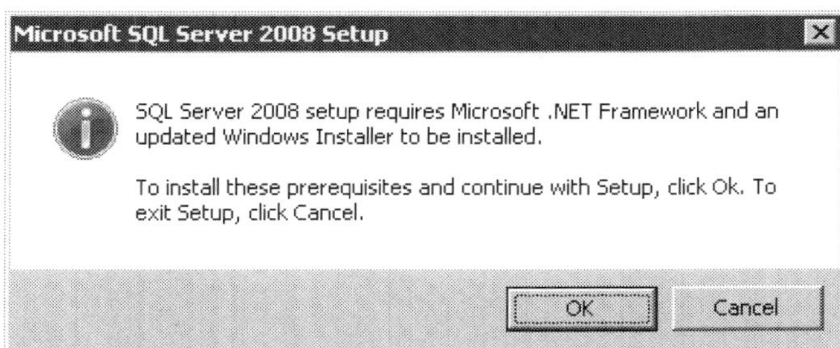


**Figure 20.2**

6. If you're installing Microsoft SQL Server 2008/R2 on a Windows Server 2008 then the setup will automatically prompt you to install the needed prerequisites of the .NET Framework and the Windows Installer. If installing SQL Server 2008/R2 on Windows Server 2008 R2, then please disregard this step and skip to **Step 7**. On the **Microsoft SQL Server 2008/R2 Setup** pop-up screen asking if it's ok to install the **.NET Framework** and **Windows Installer** applications, click on the **OK** button to continue.

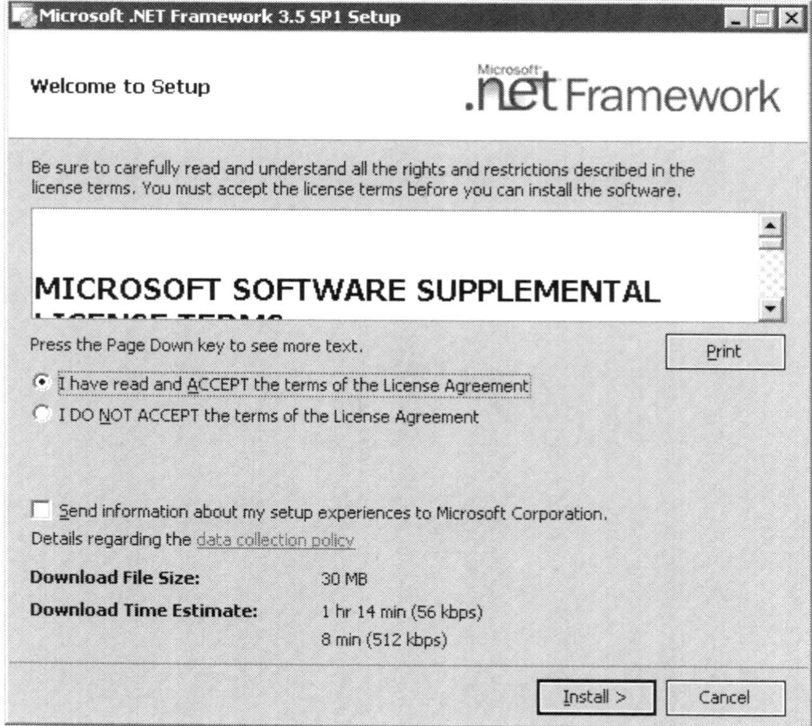


**Figure 20.3**

a. On the **Welcome to Setup** screen, select the **I have read and ACCEPT the terms of the License Agreement** bullet, and then click on the **Install** button to continue.

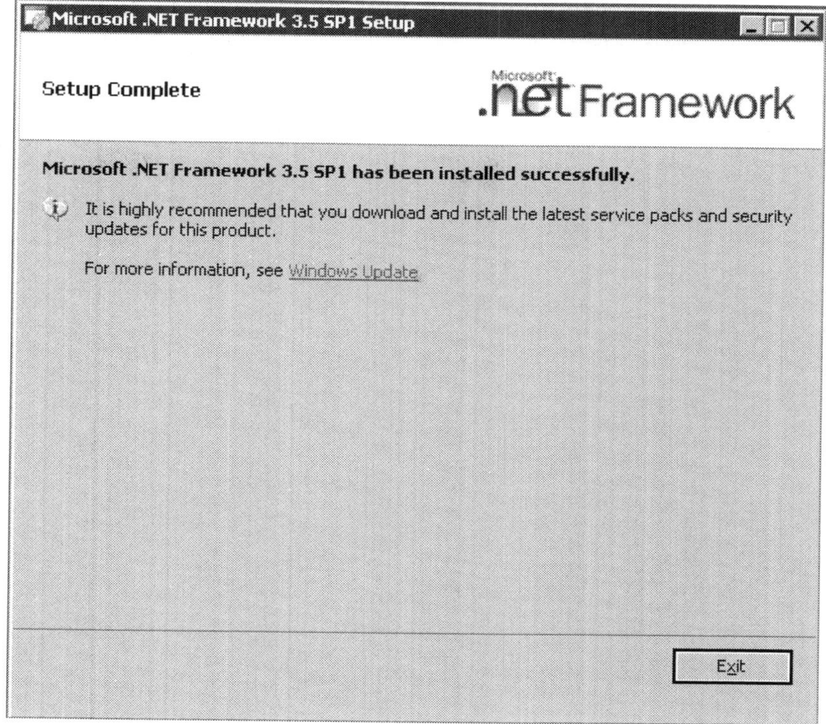


**Figure 20.4**

b. On the **Setup Complete** screen, click on the **Exit** button to continue the SQL install.

## Installing SQL Reporting Services- Selecting Install Type

7. On the **SQL Server Installation Center** screen, click on the **Installation** option in the left pane.

   a. Click on the **New SQL Server Stand-Alone Installation or Add Features to an Existing Installation** link to launch the **SQL Server 2008/R2 Setup** wizard.

   b. If you are installing SQL Server 2008 SP1 on Windows Servers 2008 R2, then you will most likely receive the **Program Compatibility Assistant** pop-up screen again. Click on the **Run program** button to continue. If you are installing **SQL Server 2008 R2**, then please disregard this step.

8. Continue going through the SQL setup wizard screens with their defaults until you come to the specific screens noted in the next steps.

# Installing SQL Reporting Services- Feature Selection

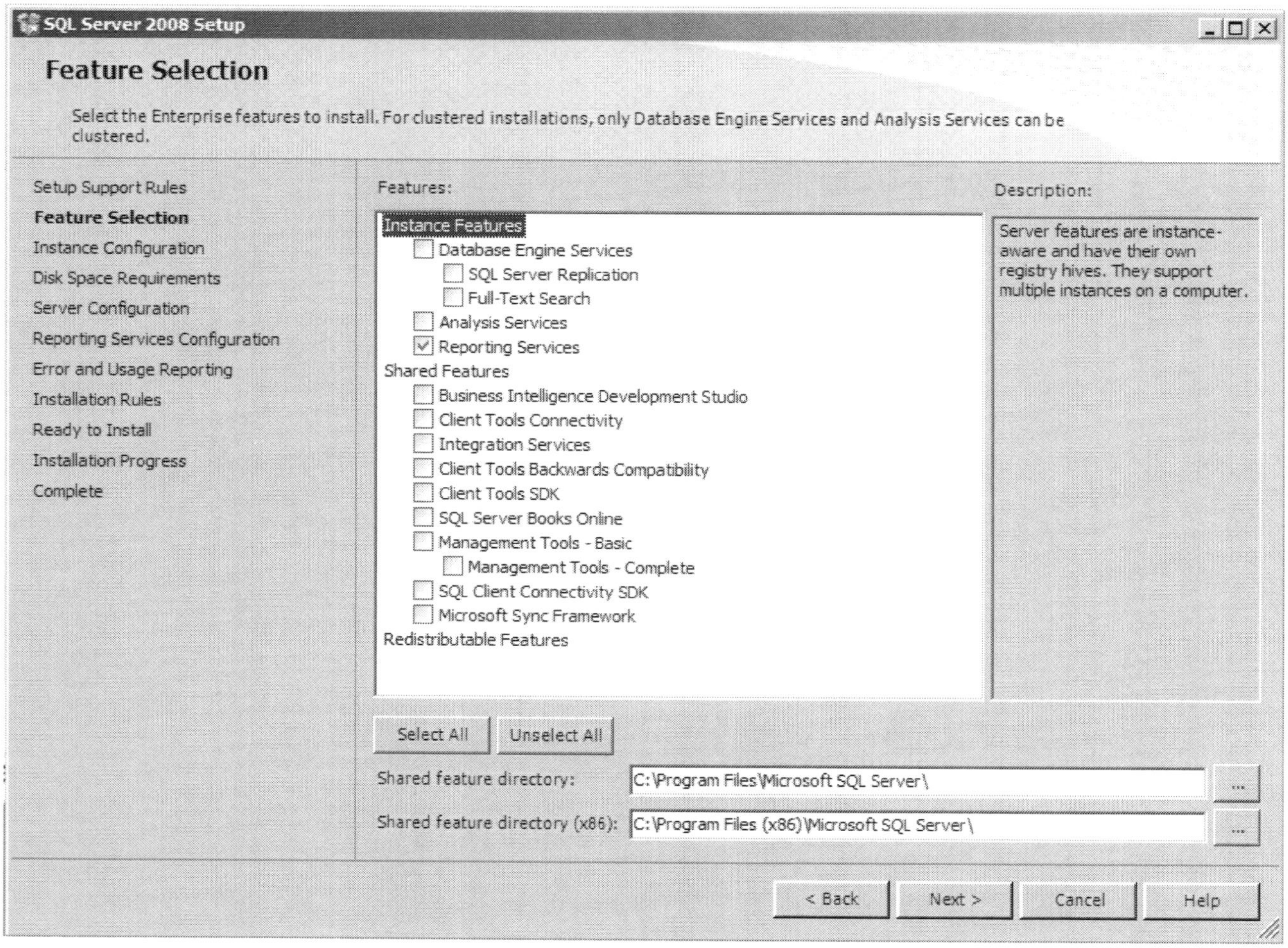

Figure 20.5

a. On the **Feature Selection** screen, select only the **Reporting Services** checkbox as shown in **Figure 20.5**, and then click on the **Next** button to continue.

# Installing SQL Reporting Services- Instance Configuration

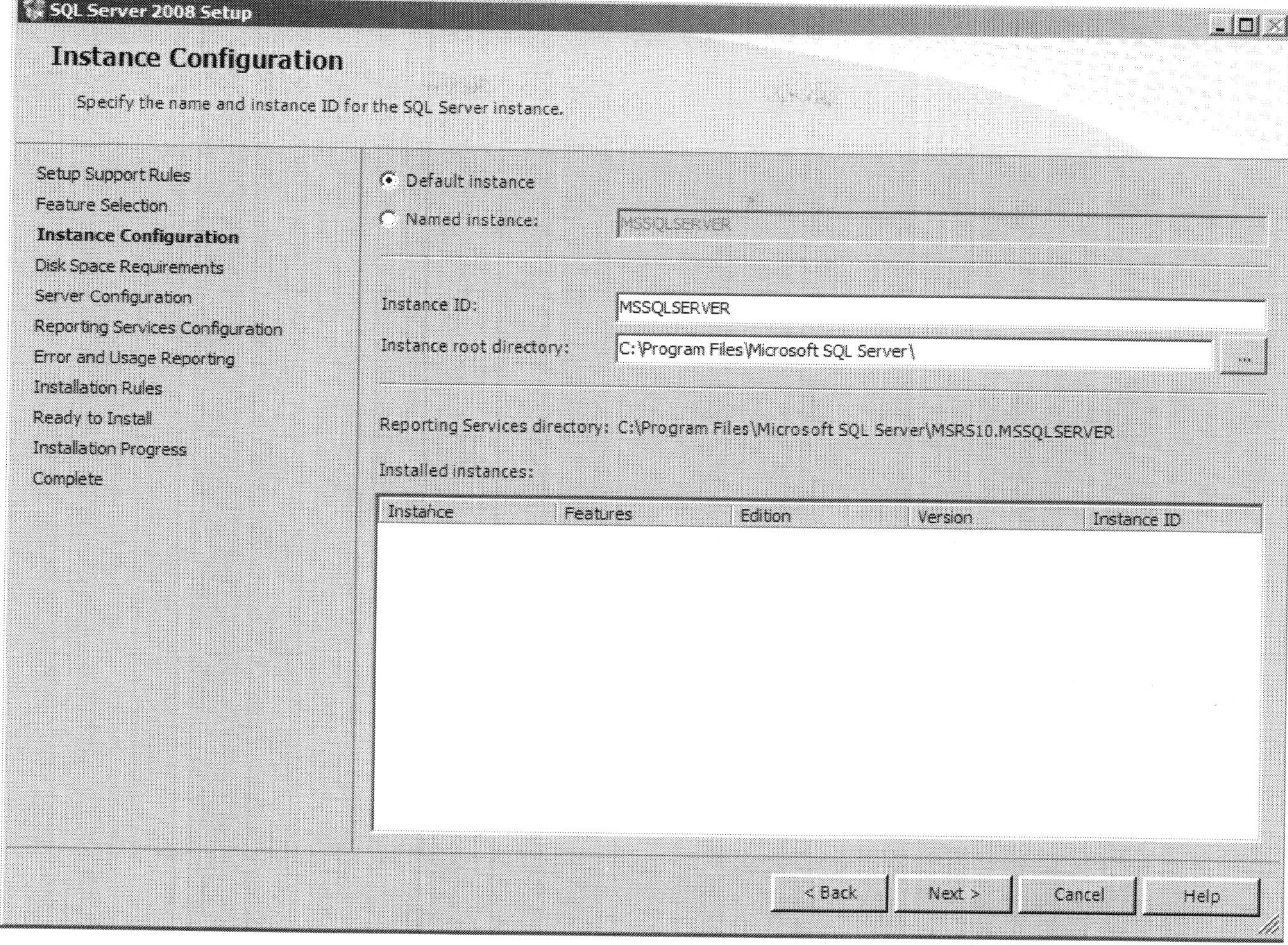


**Figure 20.6**

b. On the **Instance Configuration** screen, leave the defaults, and then click on the **Next** button to continue.

# Installing SQL Reporting Services- Service User Account

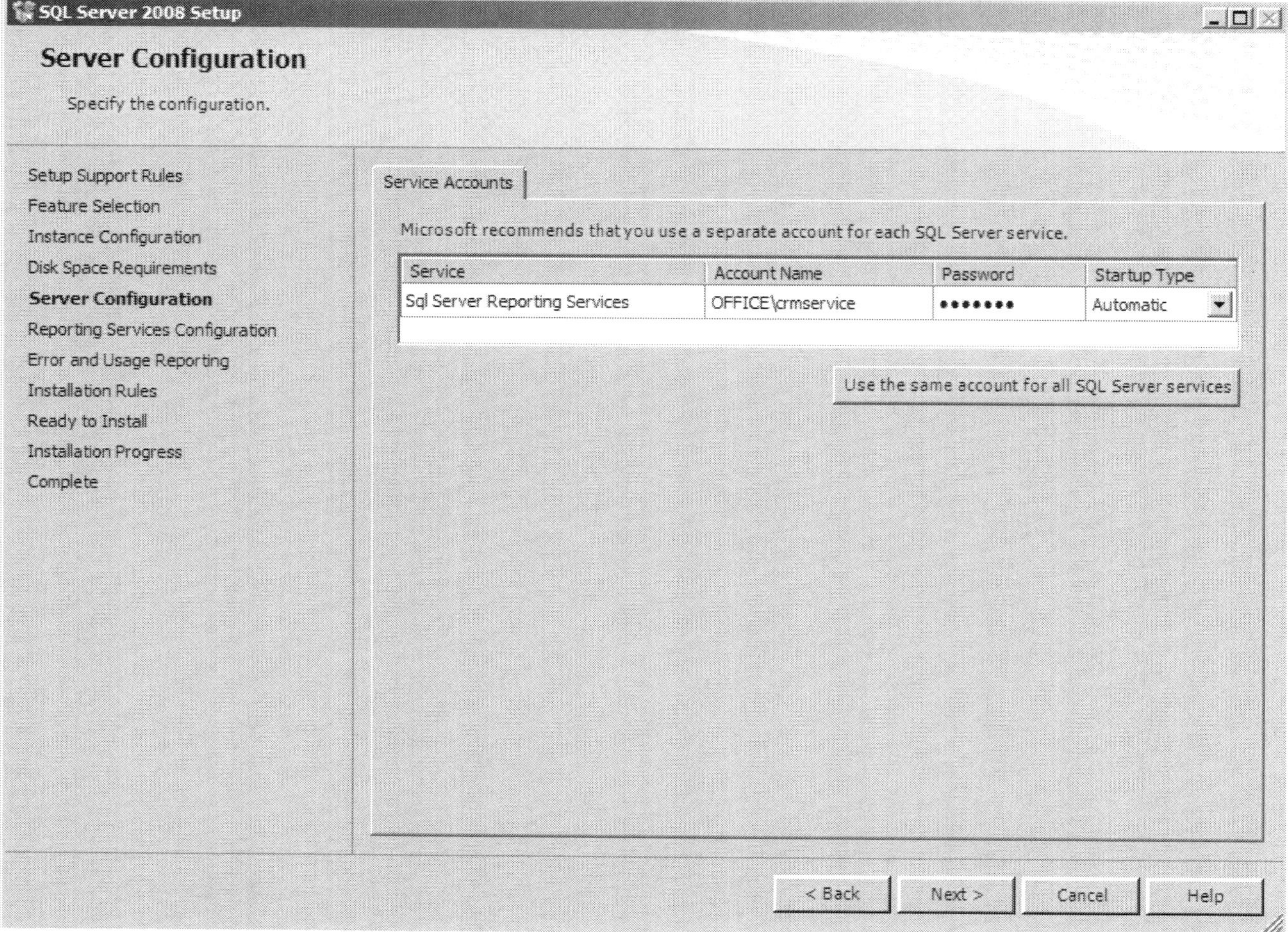


**Figure 20.7**

c. Continue going through the SQL setup wizard screens with their defaults until you come to the **Server Configuration** screen.

d. On the **Server Configuration** screen, click on the **Use the same account for all SQL Server services** button.

   i. Enter your Active Directory domain user account and password that you created earlier to run your **SQL Server Reporting Services** service, and then click on the **Next** button to continue. For our project, we will enter our user account **CRMService** that we created earlier, as shown in **Figure 20.7**.

e. On the **Reporting Services Configuration** screen, we will leave the default option of **Install, but do not configure the report server**, and then click on the **Next** button to continue.

f. Continue going through the SQL setup wizard screens with their defaults and complete the installation.

9. If you applied an **SQL Server 2008 Service Pack** as a prerequisite, then you'll want to re-apply the same version to update your newly installed SQL components. If you installed SQL Reporting Services on a Windows 2008 server or if you installed SQL Server 2008 R2 Reporting Services, then please disregard this step.

10. Repeat the above **Steps 1-9** for all your additional NLB cluster nodes following the same SQL Reporting Services install process.

## Configuring SQL Server Reporting Services (SSRS) on the Initial NLB Node

The SQL Reporting Services installation steps are equal for each of our NLB cluster nodes, however the configuration part of our SQL Reporting Services Scale-out Deployment will differ between our initial NLB cluster node that we will use to create our ReportServer database and any subsequent NLB cluster node(s) that we add to our Scale-out Deployment. On this initial NLB cluster node we will use the Reporting Services Configuration Manager to create our reporting database. You can choose any one of your NLB cluster nodes to be your initial node of your Scale-out Deployment. For our project, we will keep things simple by using SQL Reporting Services default name of ReportServer for our project's reporting database. If you are planning on installing the Microsoft Dynamics CRM 4.0 Server component on your front-end NLB cluster nodes as in our project, then you'll need to have your SQL Reporting Services and database setup as a prerequisite before you begin the CRM 4.0 install.

11. Launch the **Reporting Services Configuration Manager** by going to **Start button\All Programs\Microsoft SQL Server 2008\Configuration Tools**, and then selecting the **Reporting Services Configuration Manager** option. For our project, we will use our NLB cluster node named **CRMCluster1VM** as the initial node in our SQL Reporting Service Scale-out Deployment.

# Configuring SSRS on the Initial NLB Node- Connecting to the Instance

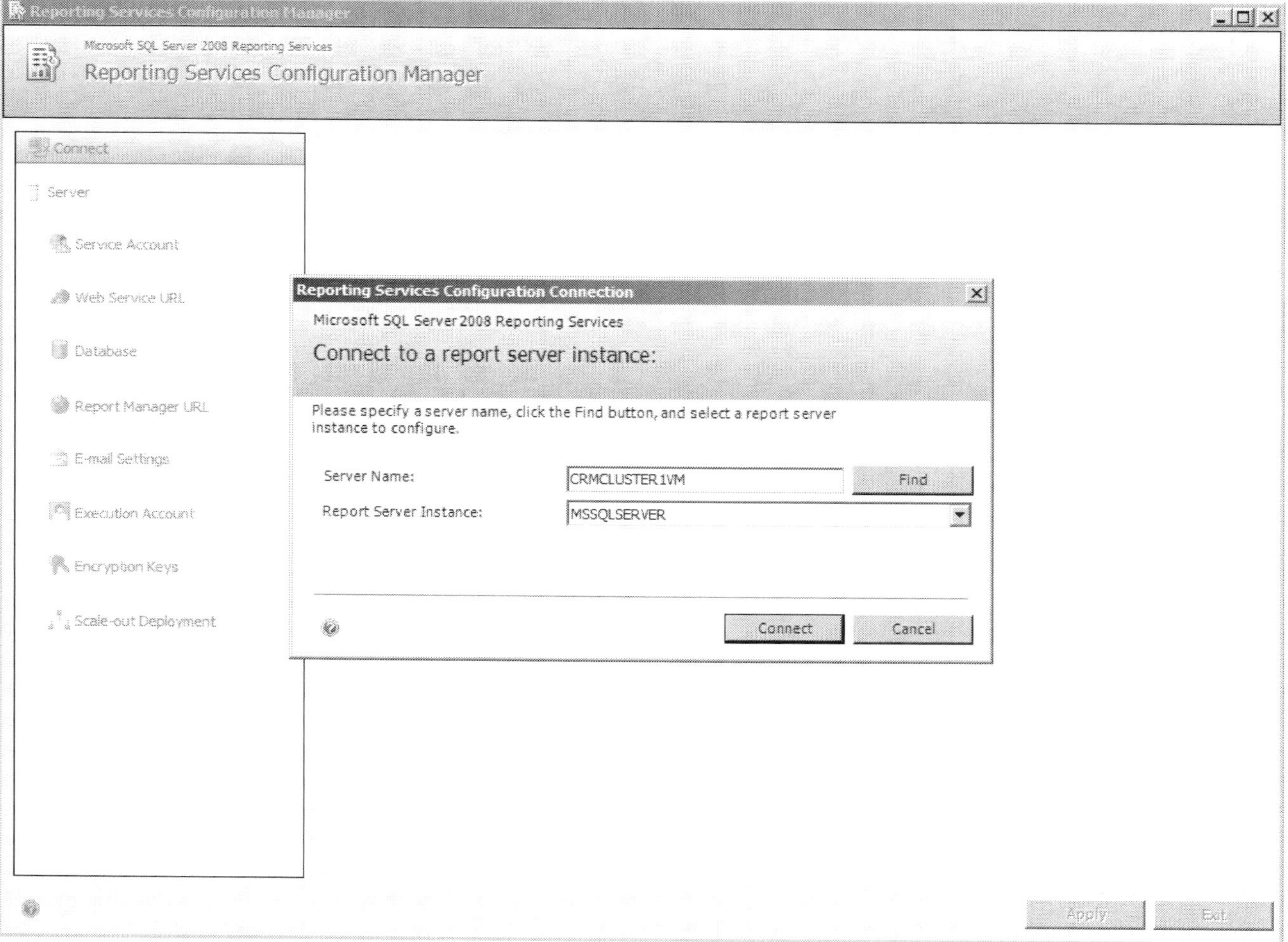


**Figure 20.8**

12. On the **Connect to a report server instance** screen, verify that your NLB cluster node's name is in the **Server Name** field and that the correct SQL Reporting Services instance name is in the **Report Server Instance** field, and then click on the **Connect** button. For our project, we will connect to our NLB cluster node named **CRMCluster1VM** with the default SQL instance name of **MSSQLSERVER**, as shown in **Figure 20.8**.

13. In the **Reporting Services Configuration Manager** console, click on the **Database** node in the left pane, which will open the **Report Server Database** screen in the right pane.

    a. On the **Report Server Database** screen in the right pane, click on the **Change Database** button to launch the **Report Server Database Configuration Wizard**.

## Configuring SSRS on the Initial NLB Node- Creating the Report Server Database

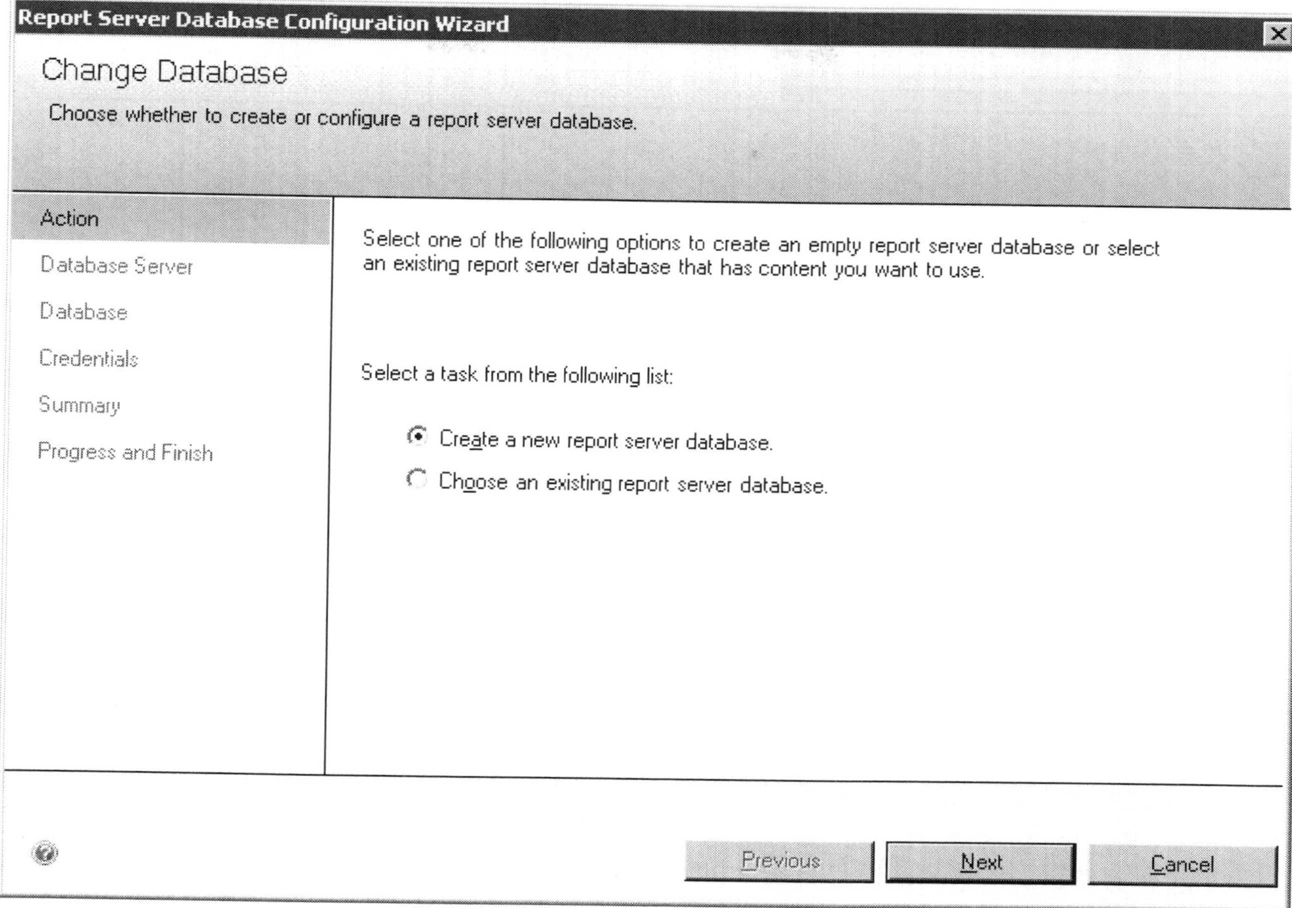


**Figure 20.9**

b. On the **Change Database** screen, select the **Create a new report server database** option, and then click on the **Next** button to continue.

## Configuring SSRS on the Initial NLB Node- Connecting to the SQL Cluster

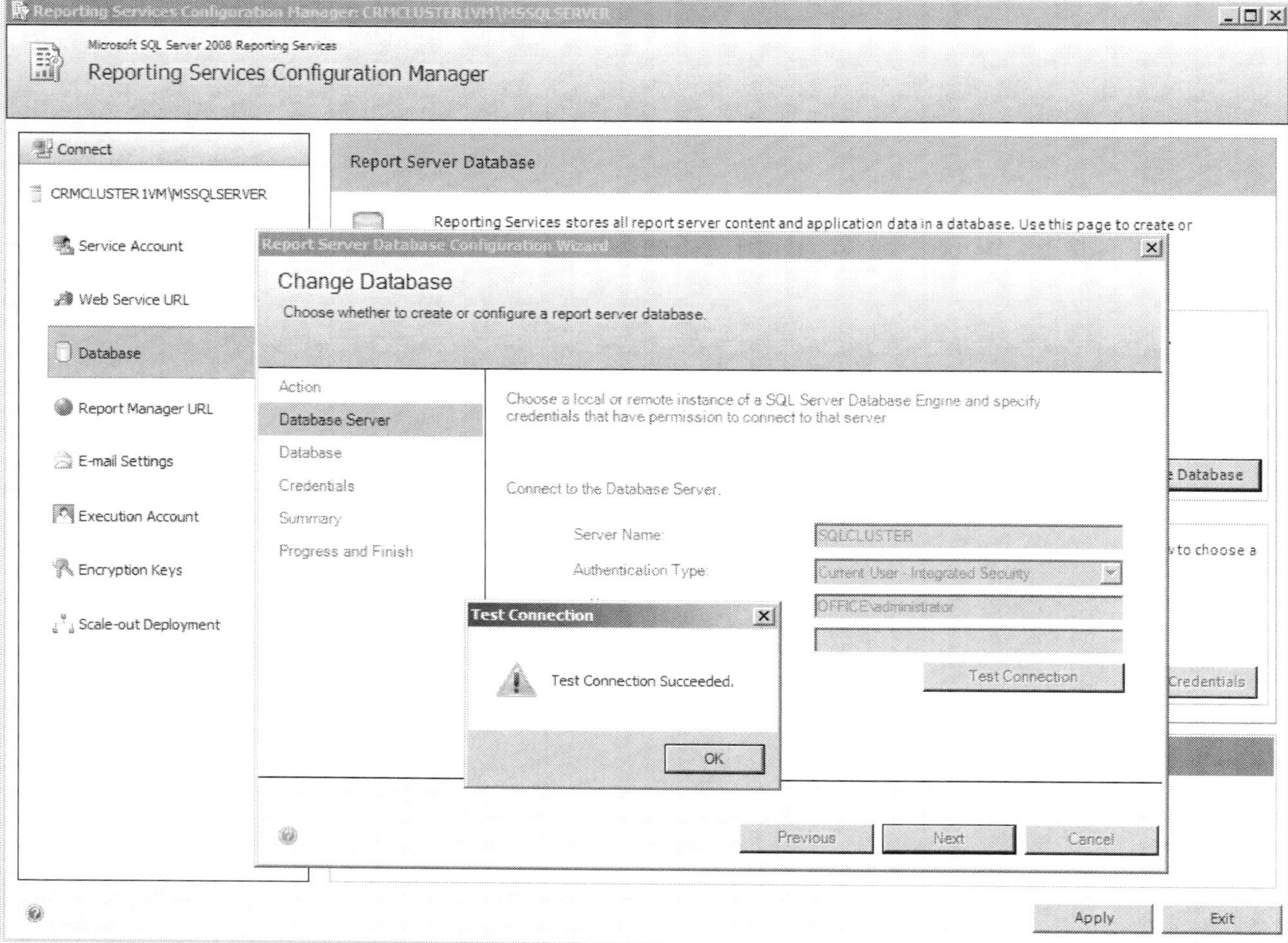


**Figure 20.10**

c. On the **Connect to the Database Server** screen, enter your SQL cluster's name in the **Server Name** field, and then verify that the **Authentication Type** field is set to **Current User – Integrated Security**. When selecting the Current User – Integrated Security option the wizard will automatically use the user account that you are currently logged onto the server with. For our project, we will enter our SQL cluster's name of **SQLCLUSTER** in the **Server Name** field, and then leave the **Authentication Type** field set to the **Current User – Integrated Security** option. The Current User – Integrated Security option will log us on with the **Domain Administrator** account, as shown in **Figure 20.10**.

   i. Click on the **Test Connection** button to verify the connection is successful, and then click on the **Next** button to continue.

## Configuring SSRS on the Initial NLB Node- Assigning Database Name

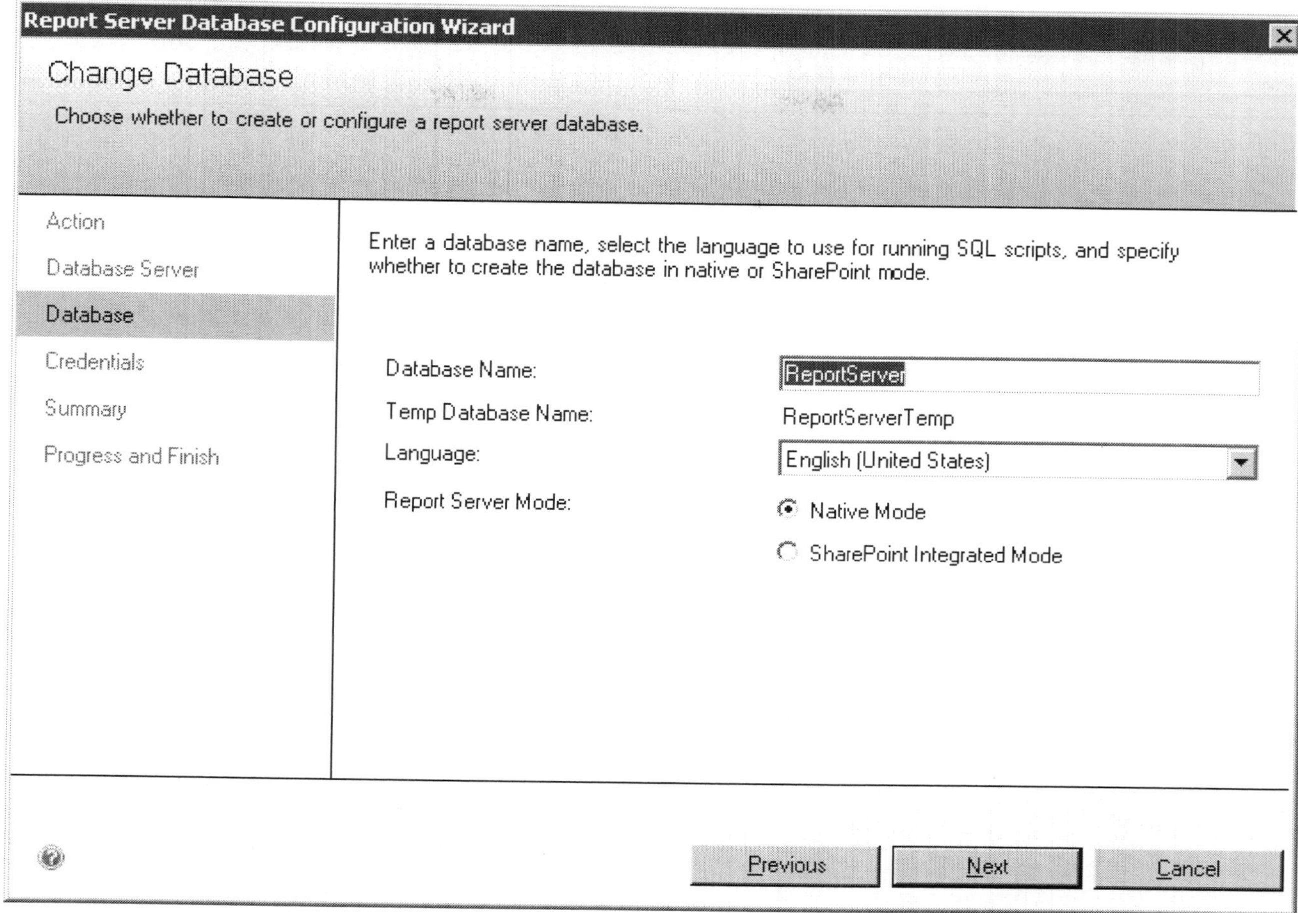


**Figure 20.11**

d. On the **Enter database name, Language and Mode** screen, you can leave all the defaults, and then click on the **Next** button to continue. For our project, we will leave the default database name of **ReportServer** for the **Database Name** field, as shown in **Figure 20.11**.

## Configuring SSRS on the Initial NLB Node- Assigning Database Credentials

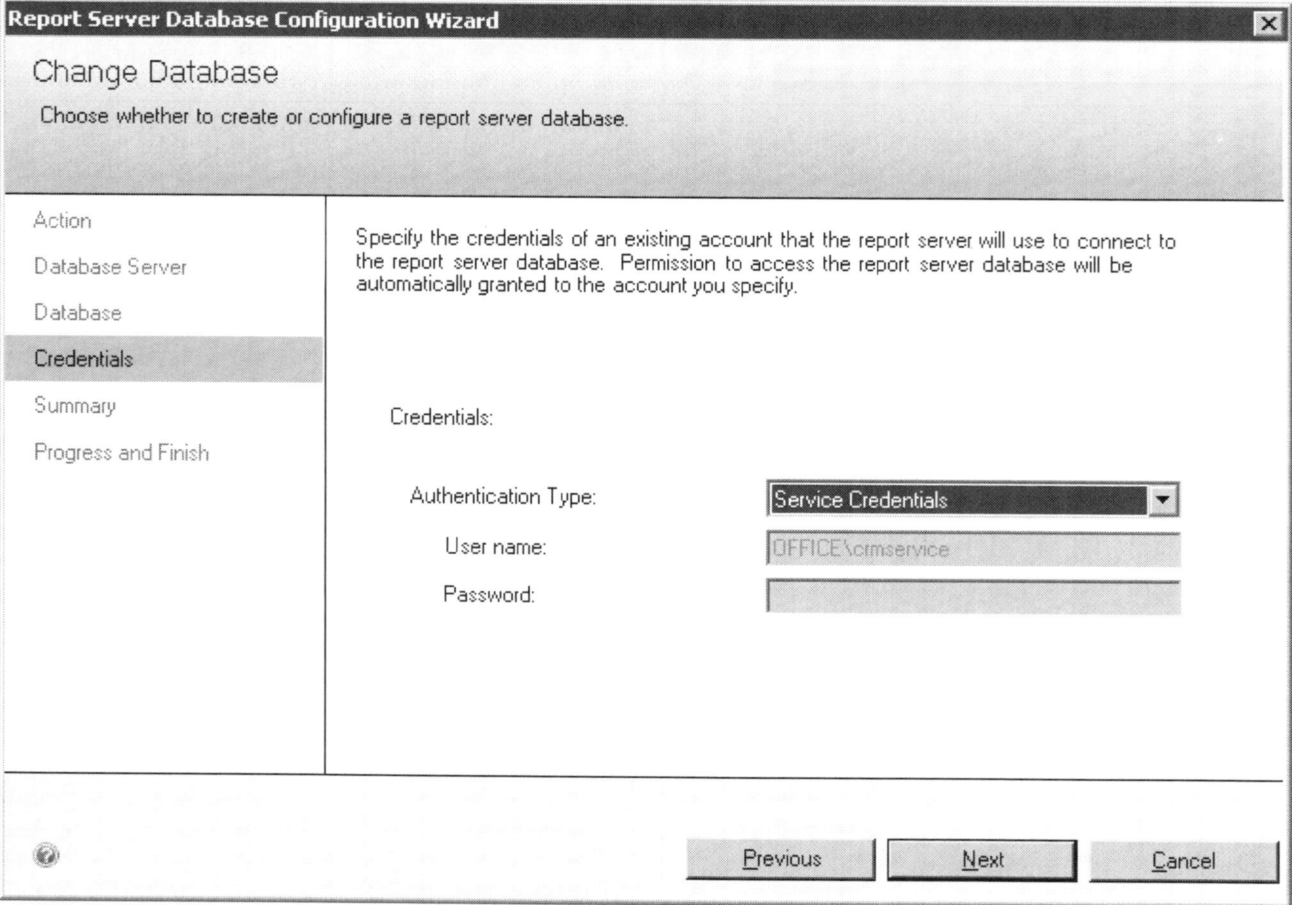


**Figure 20.12**

e. On the **Credentials** screen, you can leave the default of **Service Credentials** selected for the **Authentication Type** field, and then click on the **Next** button to continue. The service credentials were configured during the SQL Reporting Services install when you selected a user account for SQL Reporting Services to run under. For our project, we created a domain user account named **CRMService** for our service credentials during the SQL Reporting Services install, as shown **Figure 20.12**.

f. On the **Summary** screen, verify your configuration, and then click on the **Next** button to continue.

## Configuring SSRS on the Initial NLB Node- Completing the Database Configuration

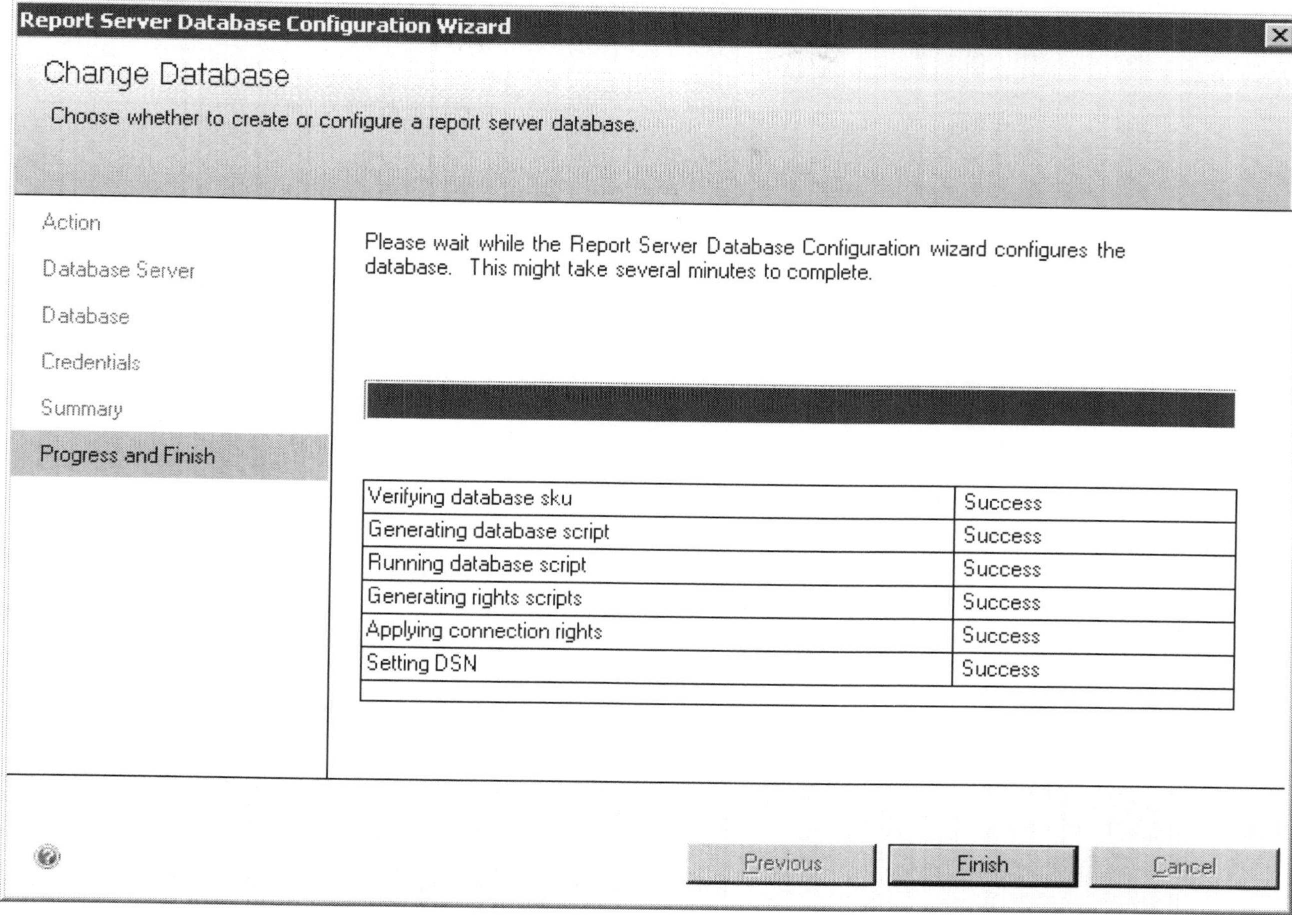


**Figure 20.13**

g. On the **Progress and Finish** screen, click on the **Finish** button to complete the database configuration process.

# Configuring SSRS on the Initial NLB Node- Creating the Web Service URL

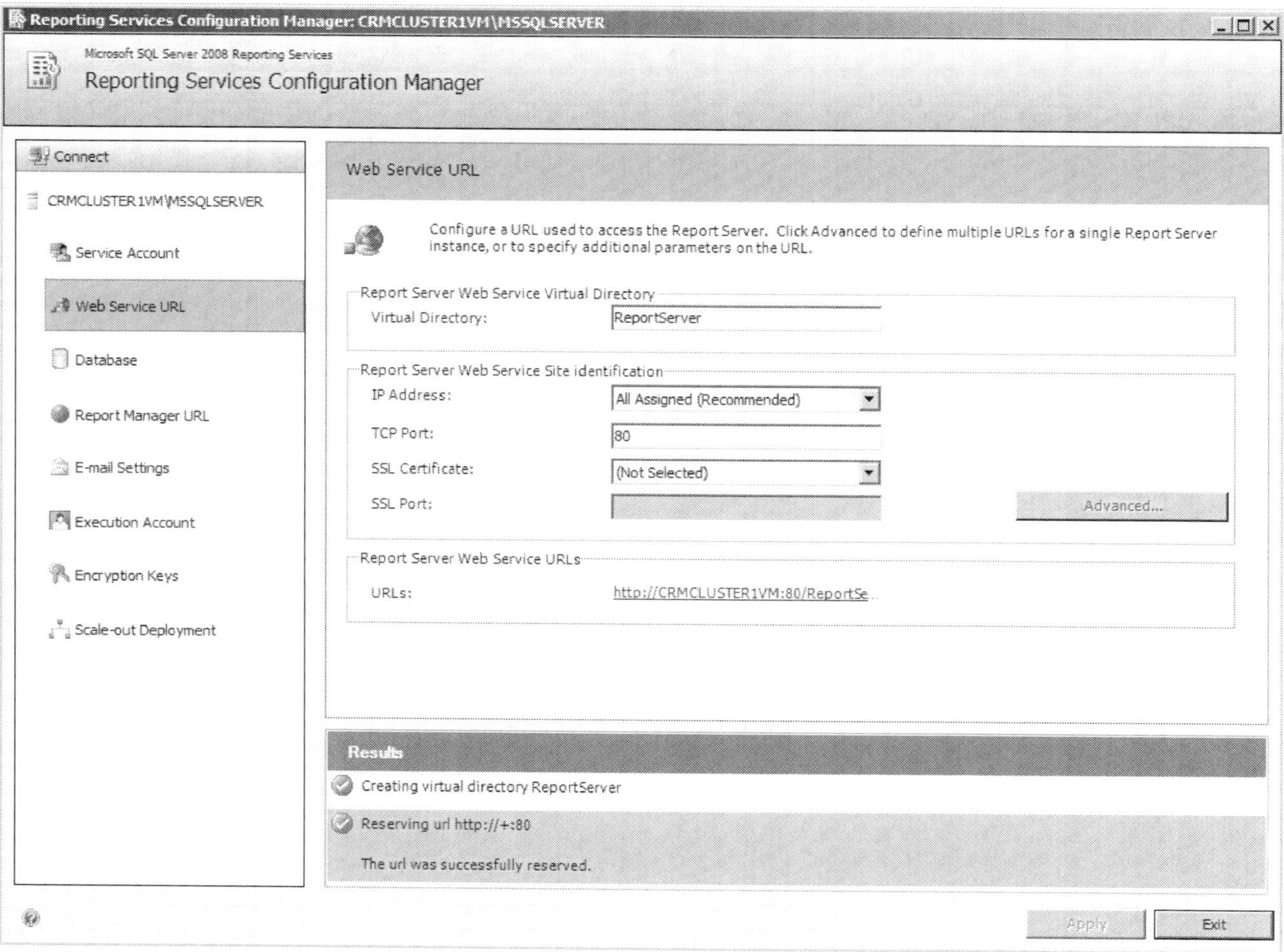


**Figure 20.14**

14. In the **Reporting Service Configuration Manager** console, click on the **Web Service URL** node in the left pane, which will open the **Web Service URL** screen in the right pane.

    a. On the **Web Service URL** screen in the right pane, choose the settings that you want, and then click the **Apply** button. If your SQL Reporting Services will use an SSL certificate, then you will want set the **TCP Port** field to a value of **443**, and then select your certificate for the **SSL Certificate** dropdown field. The web service virtual directory specified on this screen will be created in IIS on the local server. For our project, we will use the **Web Service URL** screen's defaults, as shown in **Figure 20.14**.

## Configuring SSRS on the Initial NLB Node- Creating the Report Manager URL

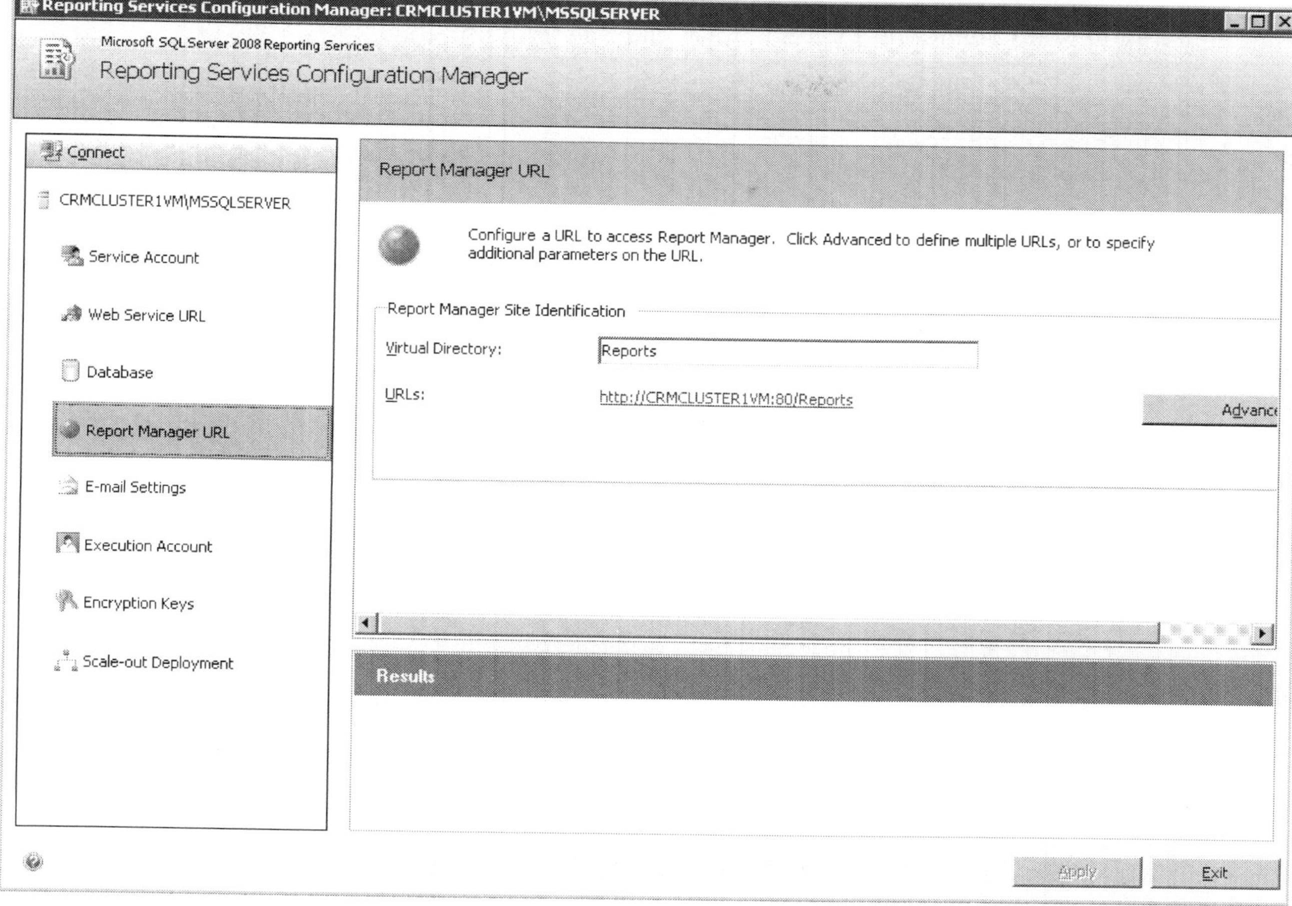


**Figure 20.15**

15. In the **Reporting Service Configuration Manager** console, click on the **Report Manager URL** node in the left pane, which will open the **Report Manager URL** screen in the right pane.

    a. On the **Report Manager URL** screen in the right pane, enter the name you want for the **Virtual Directory** field, and then click the **Apply** button. The report manager virtual directory specified on this screen will be created in IIS on the local server. For our project, we will use the **Report Manager URL** screen's default virtual directory named **Reports**, as shown in **Figure 20.15**.

16. Click on the **Exit** button in the lower right hand corner of the **Report Manager URL** screen to exit the **Reporting Services Configuration Manager** console.

# Configuring SQL Server Reporting Services (SSRS) on Additional NLB Nodes to Create a Scale-out Deployment

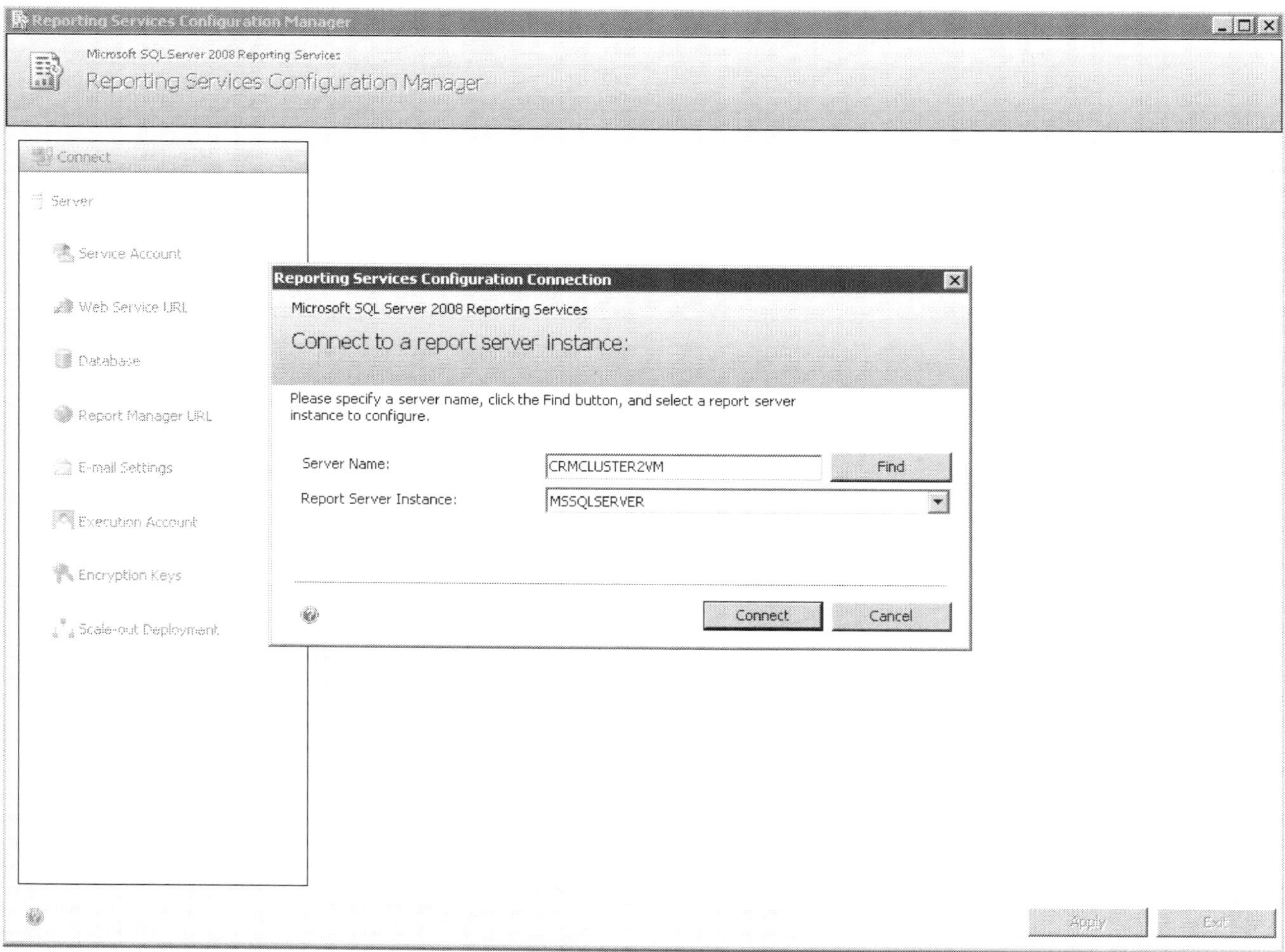


**Figure 20.16**

In this section, we will configure the SQL Reporting Services on our remaining NLB cluster node(s). You should have already installed SQL Server 2008/R2 Reporting Services component on each of your NLB cluster nodes as outlined in the beginning of this chapter. If you haven't done so, then you'll want to return to the beginning of this chapter and then follow the steps to install SQL Reporting Services on each of your NLB cluster nodes before continuing.

17. Logon to your second NLB cluster node, and then launch the **Reporting Services Configuration Manager** by going to **Start button\All Programs\Microsoft SQL Server 2008\Configuration Tools**, and selecting the **Reporting Services Configuration Manager** option.

18. On the **Connect to a report server instance** screen, verify that your second NLB cluster node's name is in the **Server Name** field and that the correct SQL Reporting Services instance name is in the **Report Server Instance** field, and then click on the **Connect** button. For our project, we will connect to our

second NLB cluster node named **CRMCluster2VM** with the default SQL instance name of **MSSQLSERVER**, as shown in **Figure 20.16**.

## Configuring SSRS on Additional NLB Nodes- Connecting to an Existing Database

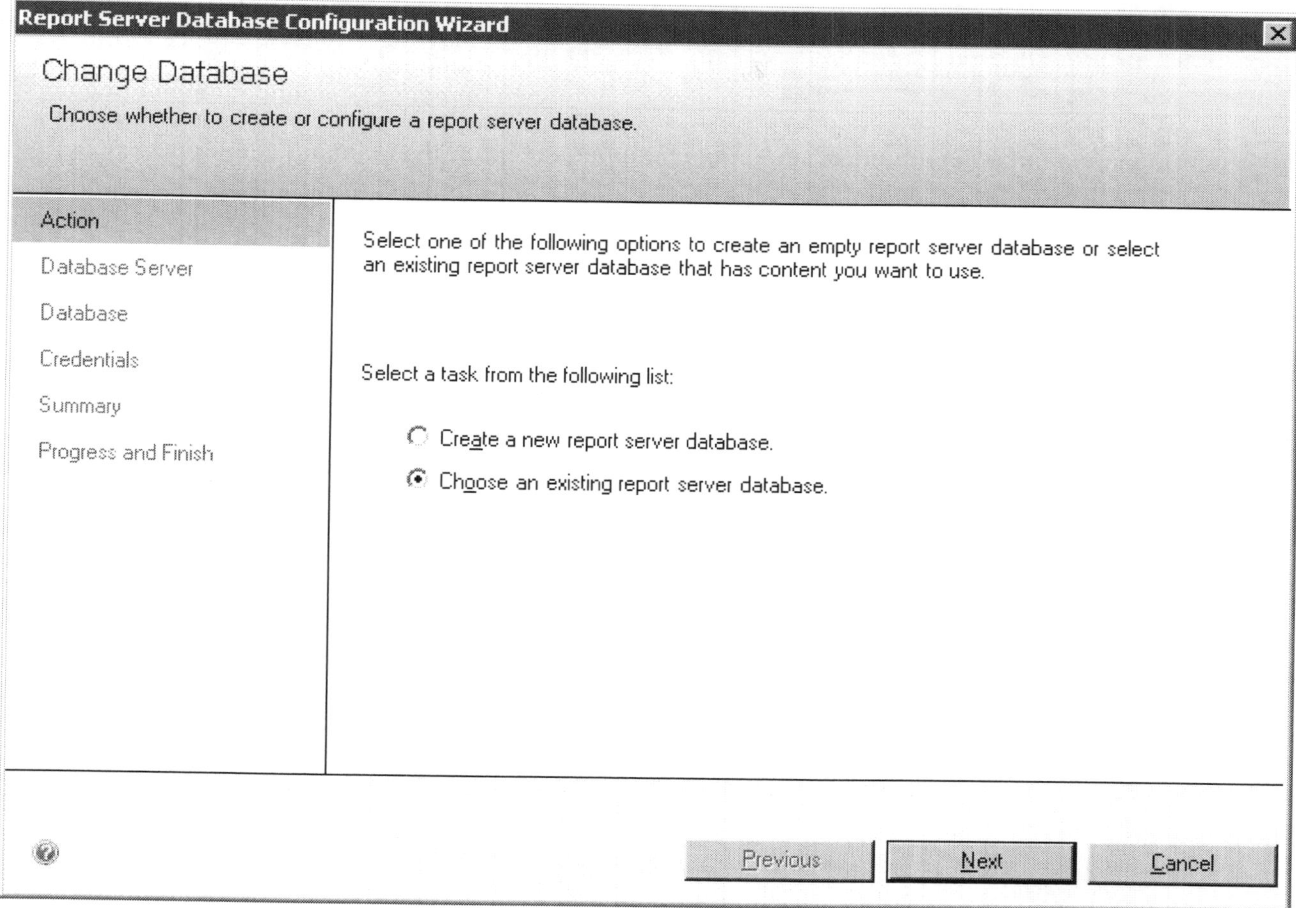


**Figure 20.17**

19. In the **Reporting Services Configuration Manager** console, click on the **Database** node in the left pane, which will open the **Report Server Database** screen in the right pane.

    a. On the **Report Server Database** screen in the right pane, click on the **Change Database** button to launch the **Report Server Database Configuration Wizard**.

        i. On the **Change Database** screen, select the **Choose an existing report server database** option, and then click on the **Next** button to continue.

## Configuring SSRS on Additional NLB Nodes- Connecting to the SQL Cluster

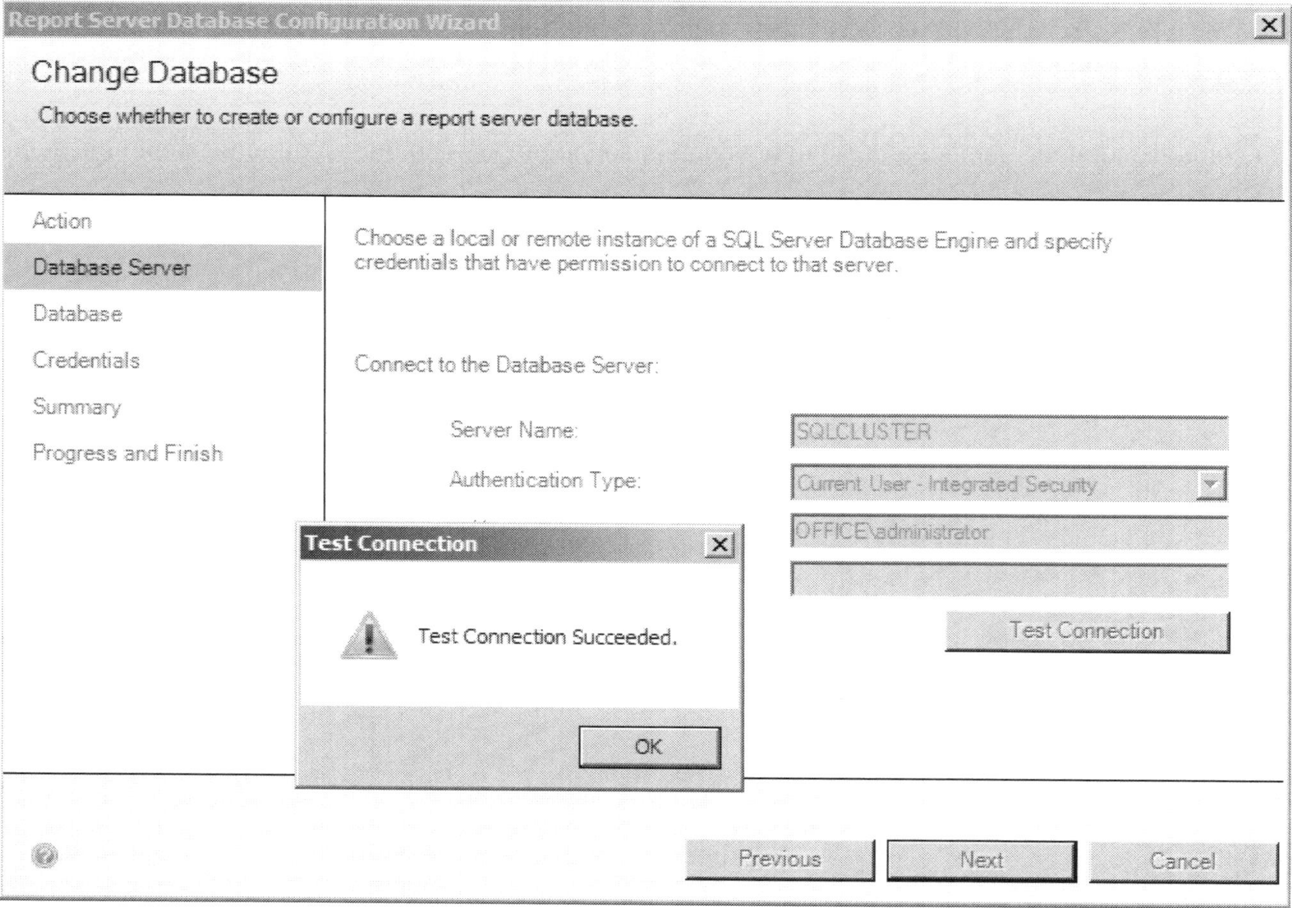


**Figure 20.18**

b. On the **Connect to the Database Server** screen, enter your SQL cluster's name in the **Server Name** field, and then verify that the **Authentication Type** field is set to **Current User – Integrated Security**. When selecting the Current User – Integrated Security option the wizard will automatically use the user account that you are currently logged onto the server with. For our project, we will enter our SQL cluster's name of **SQLCLUSTER** in the **Server Name** field, and then leave the **Authentication Type** field set to the **Current User – Integrated Security** option. The Current User – Integrated Security option will log us on with the **Domain Administrator** account, as shown in **Figure 20.18**.

   i. Click on the **Test Connection** button to verify the connection is successful, and then click on the **Next** button to continue.

## Configuring SSRS on Additional NLB Nodes- Selecting the Existing ReportServer Database

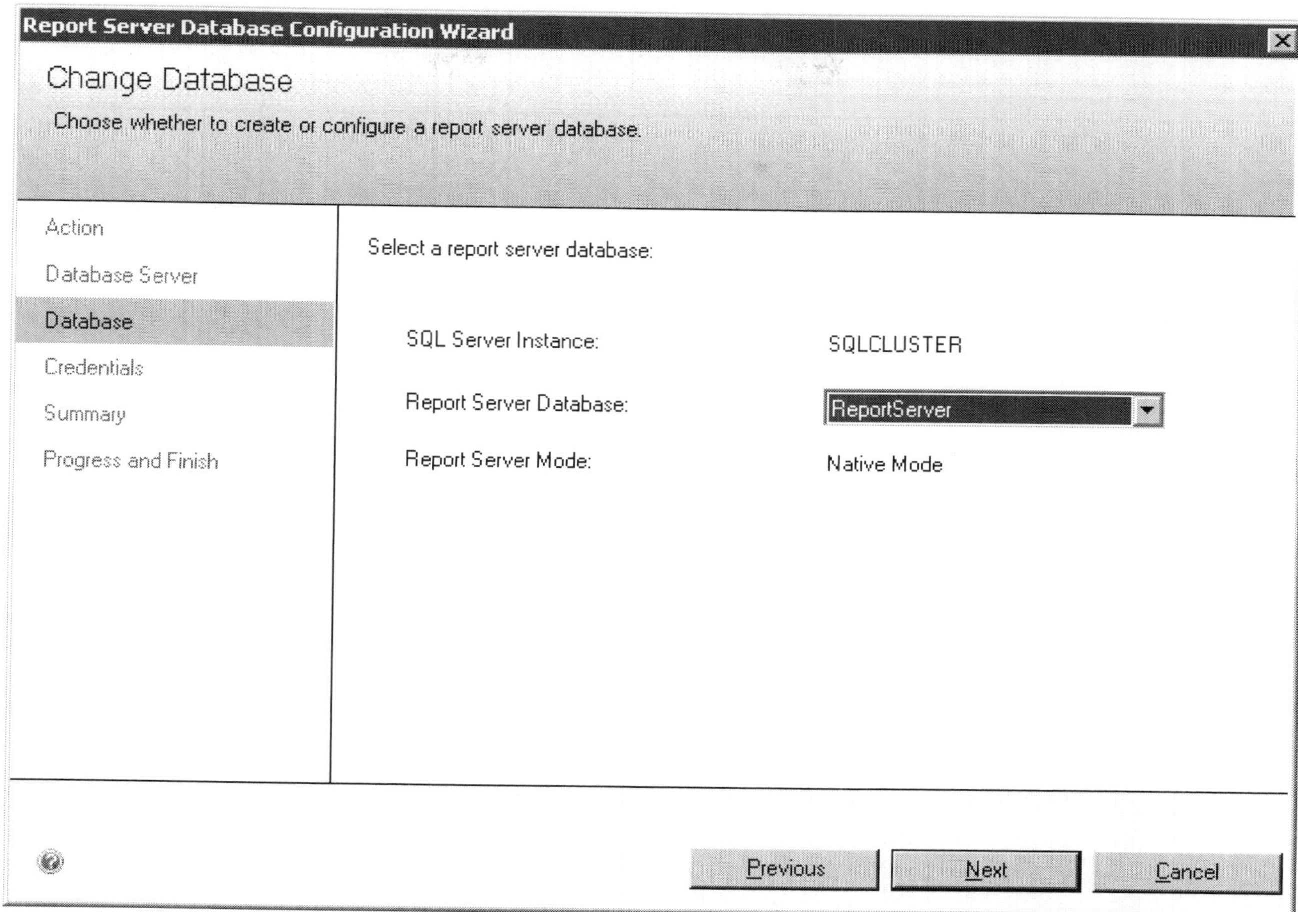


**Figure 20.19**

c. On the **Select a report server database** screen, select your existing report server database from the **Report Server Database** dropdown field, and then click on the **Next** button to continue. This is the report database that you created earlier when configuring your initial NLB cluster node for the SQL Reporting Services. For our project, we will select our database named **ReportServer**, as shown in **Figure 20.19**.

## Configuring SSRS on Additional NLB Nodes- Assigning Database Credentials

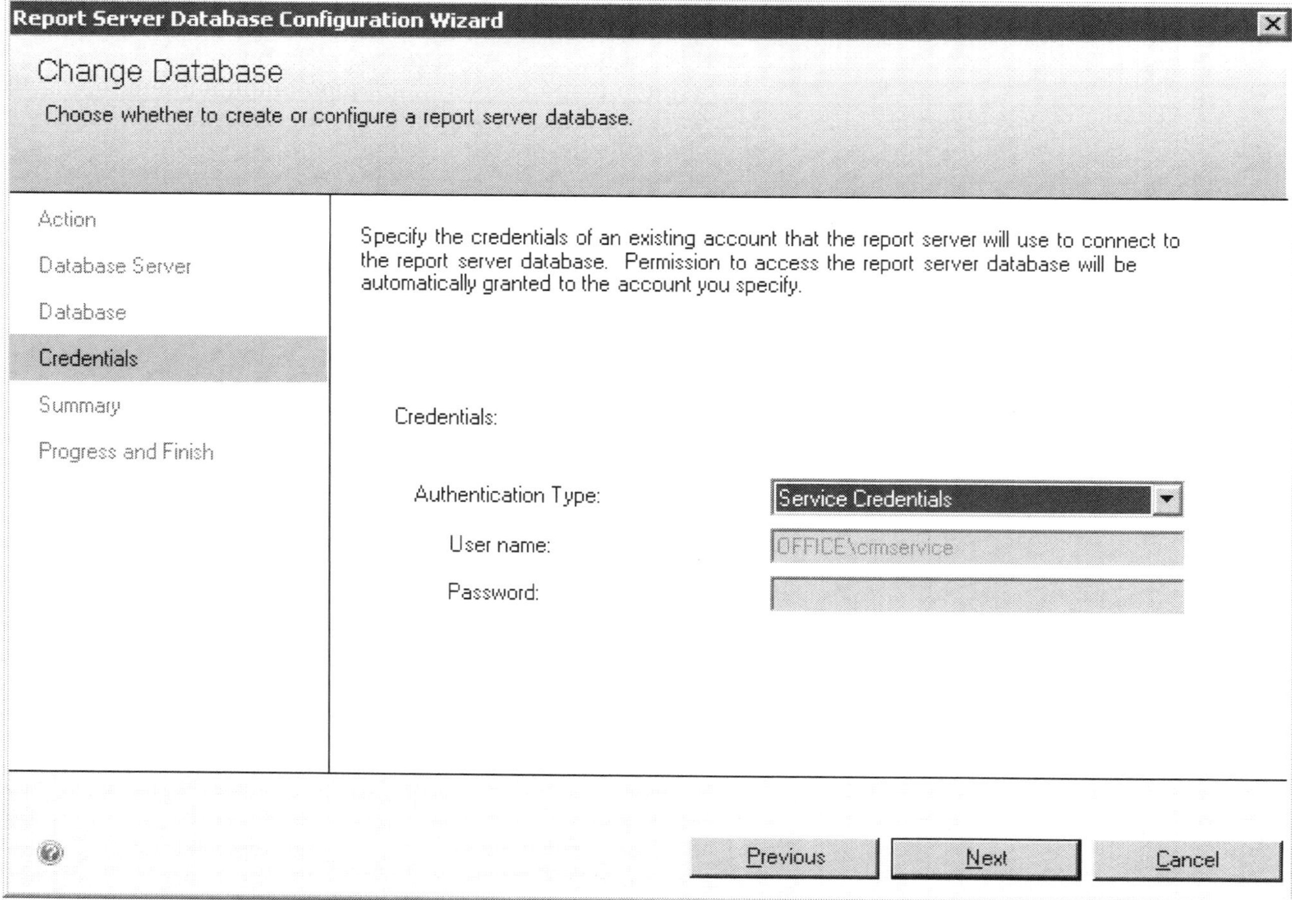


**Figure 20.20**

d. On the **Credentials** screen, you can leave the default of **Service Credentials** selected for the **Authentication Type** field, and then click on the **Next** button to continue. The service credentials were configured during the SQL Reporting Services install when you selected a user account for SQL Reporting Services to run under. For our project, we created a domain user account named **CRMService** for service credentials during the SQL Reporting Services install, as shown **Figure 20.20**.

e. On the **Summary** screen, verify your configuration, and then click on the **Next** button to continue.

## Configuring SSRS on Additional NLB Nodes- Completing the Database Configuration

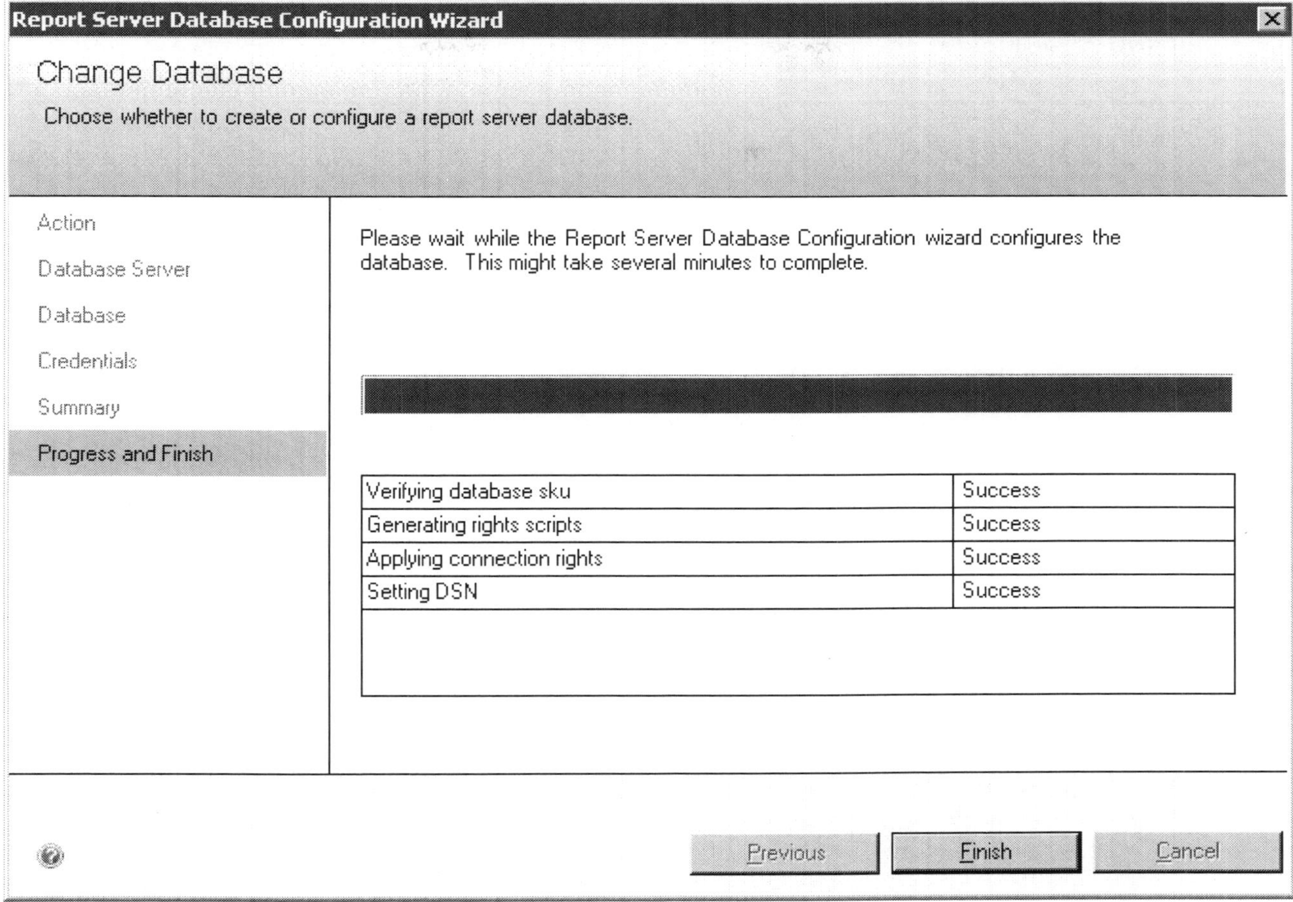


**Figure 20.21**

f. On the **Progress and Finish** screen, click on the **Finish** button to complete the database configuration process.

# Configuring SSRS on Additional NLB Nodes- Creating the Web Service URL

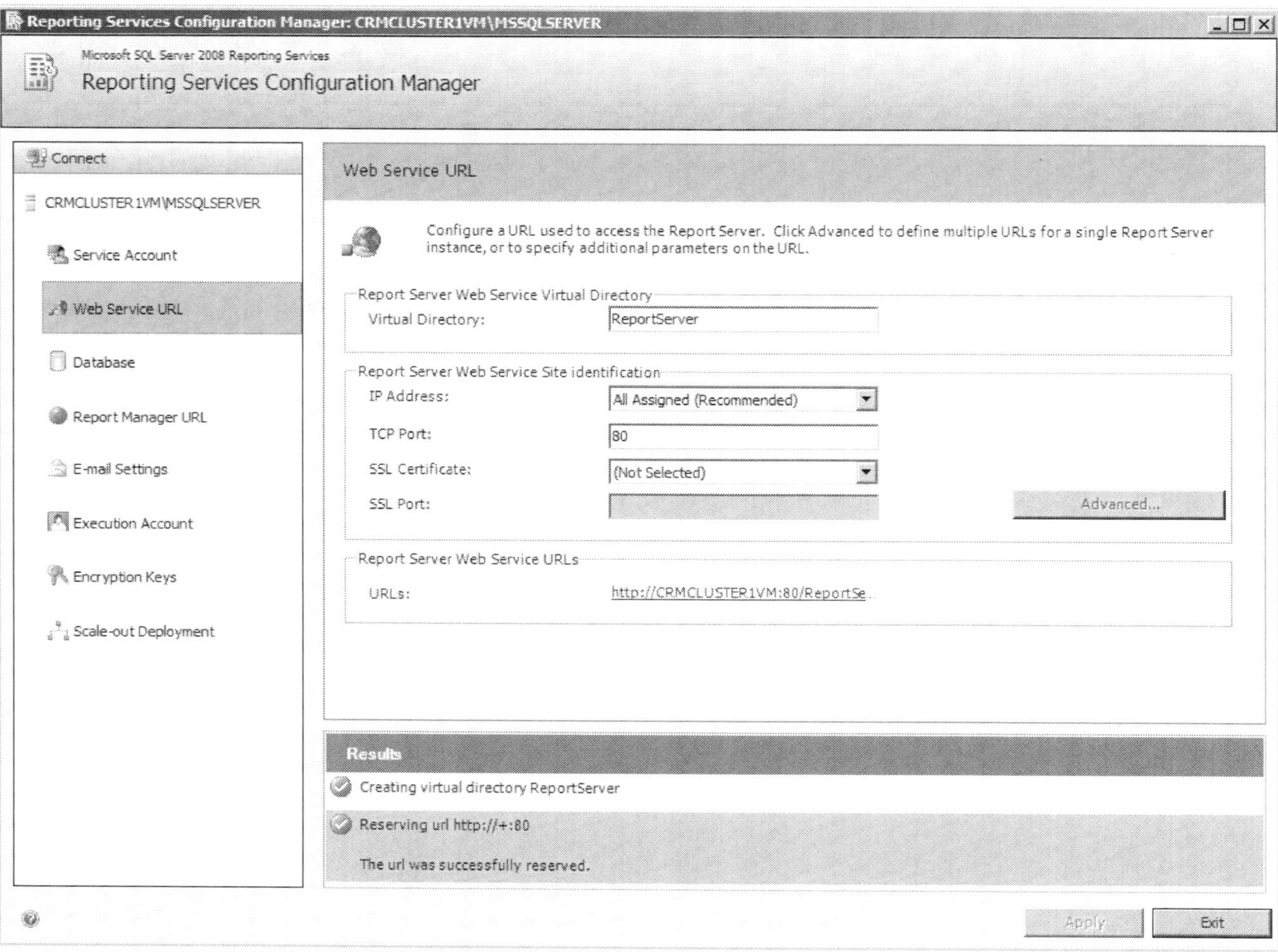


**Figure 20.22**

20. In the **Reporting Service Configuration Manager** console, click on the **Web Service URL** node in the left pane, which will open the **Web Service URL** screen in the right pane.

    c. On the **Web Service URL** screen in the right pane, choose the settings that you want, and then click the **Apply** button. If your SQL Reporting Services will use an SSL certificate, then you will want set the **TCP Port** field to a value of **443**, and then select your certificate for the **SSL Certificate** dropdown field. The web service virtual directory specified on this screen will be created in IIS on the local server. For our project, we will mirror the Web Service URL settings of our initial SQL Reporting Services node by using the **Web Service URL** screen's defaults, as shown in **Figure 20.22**.

# Configuring SSRS on Additional NLB Nodes- Creating the Report Manager URL

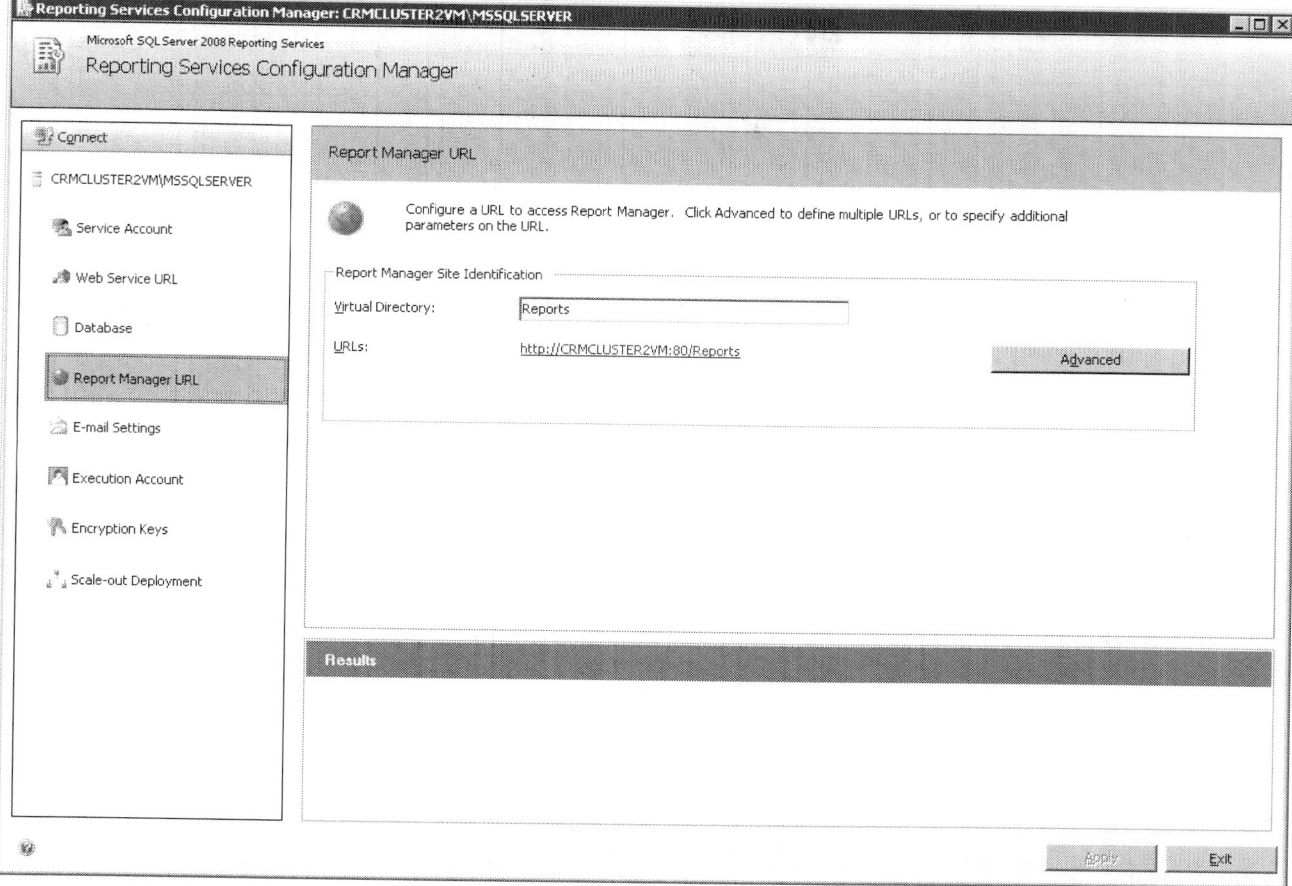


**Figure 20.23**

21. In the **Reporting Service Configuration Manager** console, click on the **Report Manager URL** node in the left pane, which will open the **Report Manager URL** screen in the right pane.

    a. On the **Report Manager URL** screen in the right pane, enter the name you want for the **Virtual Directory** field, and then click the **Apply** button. The report manager virtual directory specified on this screen will be created in IIS on the local server. For our project, we will mirror the Report Manager URL settings of our initial SQL Reporting Services node by using the **Report Manager URL** screen's defaults, as shown in **Figure 20.23**.

22. Click on the **Exit** button in the lower right hand corner of the **Report Manager URL** screen to exit the **Reporting Services Configuration Manager** console.

23. Repeat **Steps 17-22** for each of your remaining NLB cluster nodes. For our project, we will repeat these steps for our third and final NLB cluster node named **CRMCluster3VM**.

## Creating the SQL Reporting Services Scale-out Deployment

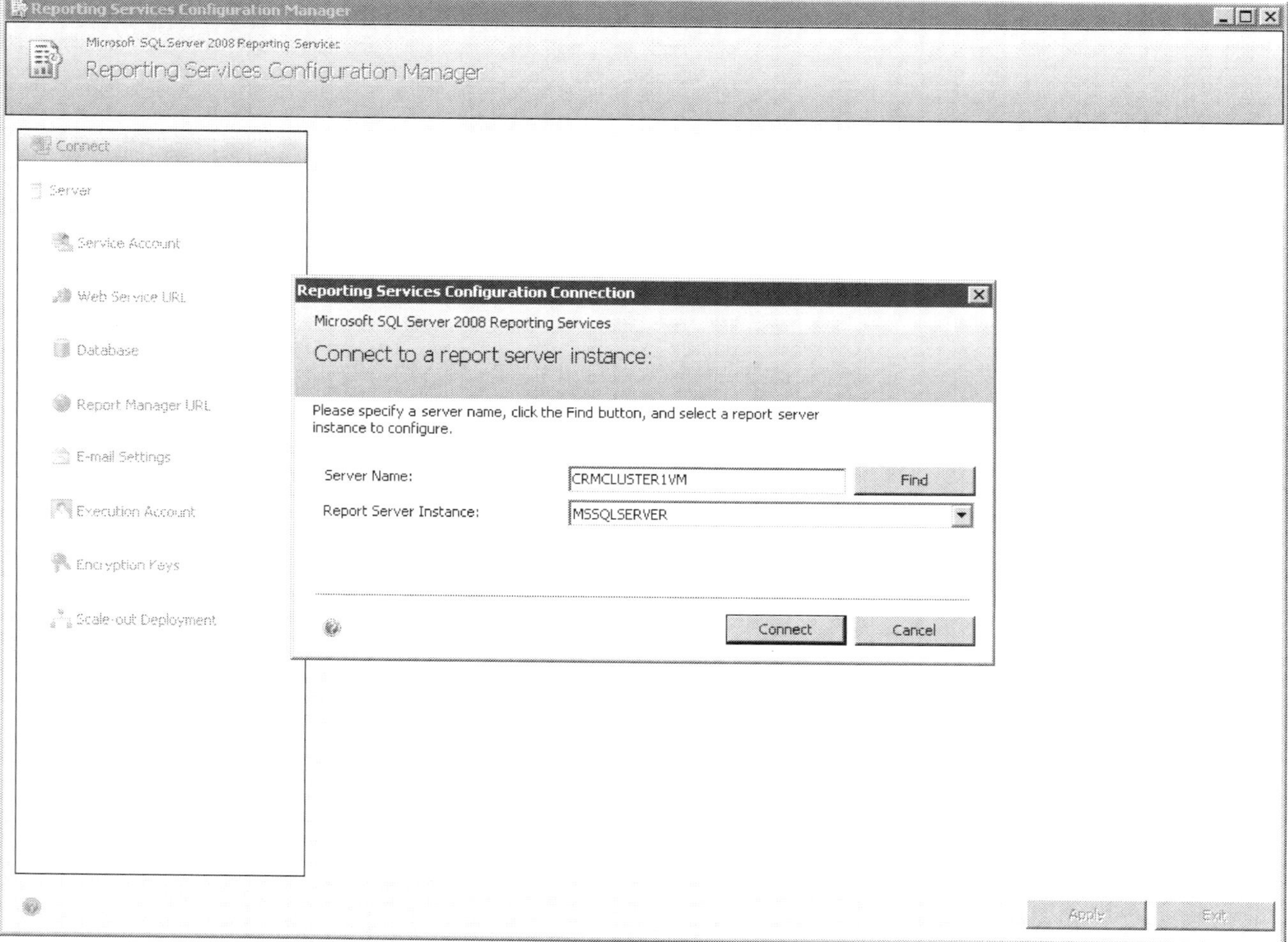


**Figure 20.24**

Once the SQL Reporting Services has been configured on each of our NLB cluster nodes, we will then join each node's instance of SQL Reporting Services to our Scale-out Deployment. This will allow our servers to work in unison when serving up reports to clients accessing the load balancer.

## SSRS Creating the Scale-out Deployment- Connecting to the Instance

24. Return to the initial NLB cluster node that you used to create the **ReportServer** database, and then open the **Reporting Services Configuration Manager** console. For our project, we will return to our initial NLB cluster node named **CRMCluster1VM**, and then launch the **Reporting Services Configuration Manager** console.

    a. On the **Connect to a report server instance** screen, verify that your initial NLB cluster node's name is in the **Server Name** field and that the correct SQL Reporting Services instance name is in the **Report Server Instance** field, and then click on the **Connect** button. For our project, we will connect to our initial NLB cluster node named **CRMCluster1VM** with the default SQL instance name of **MSSQLSERVER**, as shown in **Figure 20.24**.

## SSRS Creating the Scale-out Deployment- Joining the NLB Cluster Nodes

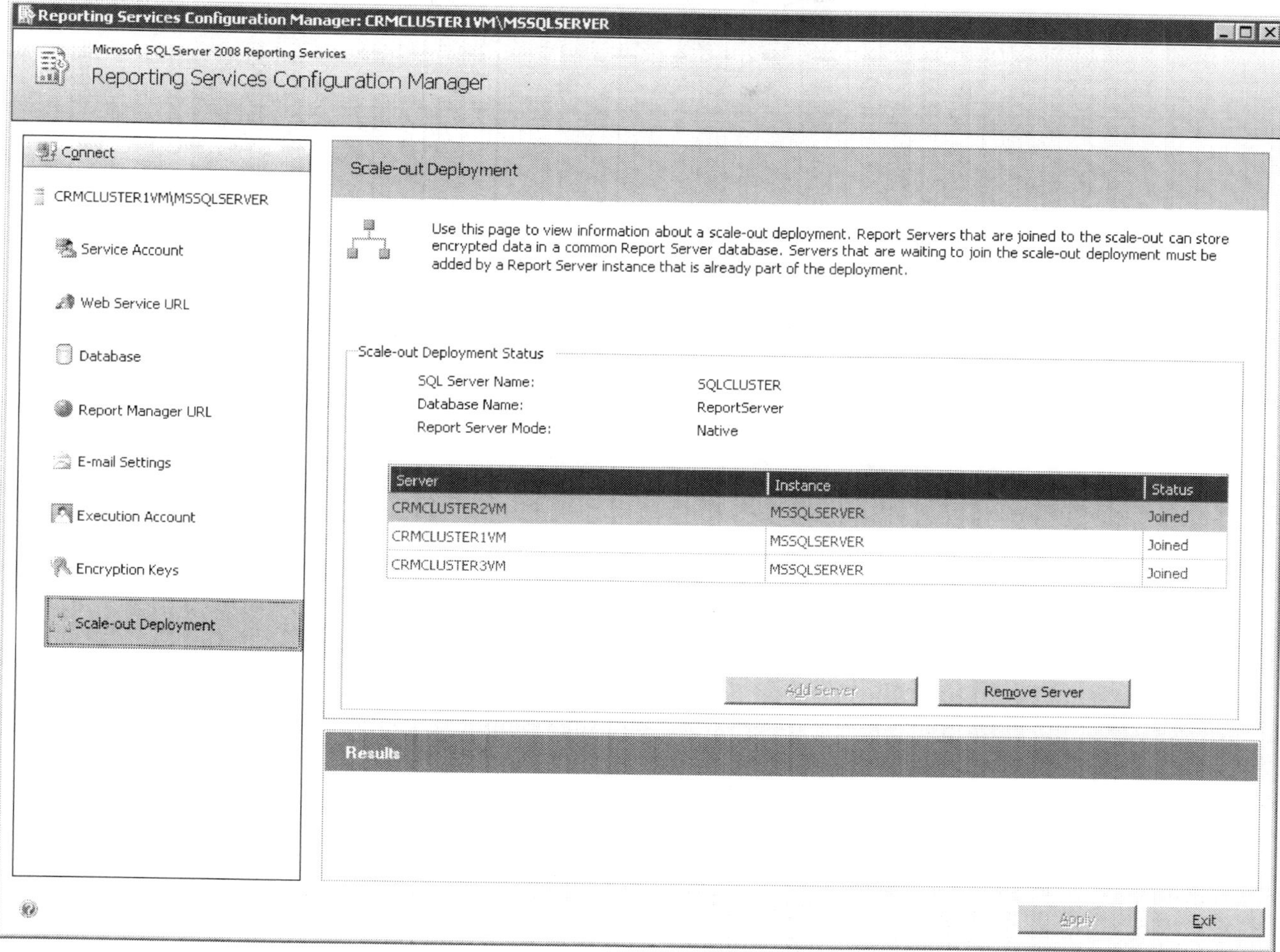


**Figure 20.25**

b. In the **Reporting Services Configuration Manager** console, click on the **Scale-out Deployment** node in the left pane to open the **Scale-out Deployment** screen. You should see each of your NLB cluster nodes that you installed SSRS on listed in the server column of the Scale-out Deployment screen. For the status column your initial NLB cluster node should show the status of Joined, while each of your secondary NLB cluster nodes that were installed after should show the status of Waiting to Join. If you don't see any servers listed in the Scale-out Deployment screen, then you'll want to verify that you're connected to your initial NLB cluster node and that its SQL Reporting Services has been configured to use your report server database. Only your initial NLB cluster node that you used to create your report server database with should already be joined to the Scale-out Deployment. Once this initial node has the status Joined, then it will be able to perform reversible encryption operations and thus enable the rest of your NLB cluster node(s) to be joined to your Scale-out Deployment.

**NOTE:** We only want SQL Reporting Services installed on servers that will point at our SQL cluster's reports database and that are part of our Scale-out Deployment. This is important, because if you have SQL Reporting Services installed on other servers that point at your SQL cluster's reports database then those servers will automatically show up within your Scale-out Deployment. Any servers that show up within your Scale-out Deployment but that are not joined to the deployment can cause your SQL Reporting Services to function sporadically.

i. For each of your NLB cluster nodes with the **Waiting to join** status, highlight the server name, and then click on the **Add Server** button to join each server to your Scale-out Deployment. For our project, we will join our two remaining NLB cluster nodes named **CRMCluster2VM** and **CRMCluster3VM** to our Scale-out Deployment, as shown in **Figure 20.25**.

ii. Once all your NLB cluster nodes have been joined to the SQL Reporting Services Scale-out Deployment, click on the **Exit** button in the lower right hand corner of the **Scale-out Deployment** screen to exit the **Reporting Services Configuration Manager** console.

## Synchronizing Encryption Keys of the SSRS Scale-out Deployment Nodes

For the SQL Reporting Services Scale-out Deployment nodes to function in unison we need to synchronize our encryption keys between the nodes. We will accomplish this by backing up the encryption key on our initial Scale-out Deployment node, and then importing the key to our other members of the deployment.

25. Return to the initial Scale-out Deployment node that you used to create the **ReportServer** database with, and then open the **Reporting Services Configuration Manager** console. For our project, we will return to our initial NLB cluster node named **CRMCluster1VM**, and then launch the **Reporting Services Configuration Manager** console.

    a. On the **Connect to a report server instance** screen, verify that your initial NLB cluster node's name is in the **Server Name** field and that the correct SQL Reporting Services instance name is in the **Report Server Instance** field, and then click on the **Connect** button. For our project, we will connect to our initial NLB cluster node named **CRMCluster1VM** with the default SQL instance name of **MSSQLSERVER**.

# SSRS Synchronizing Encryption Keys- Backing Up the Initial Node's Key

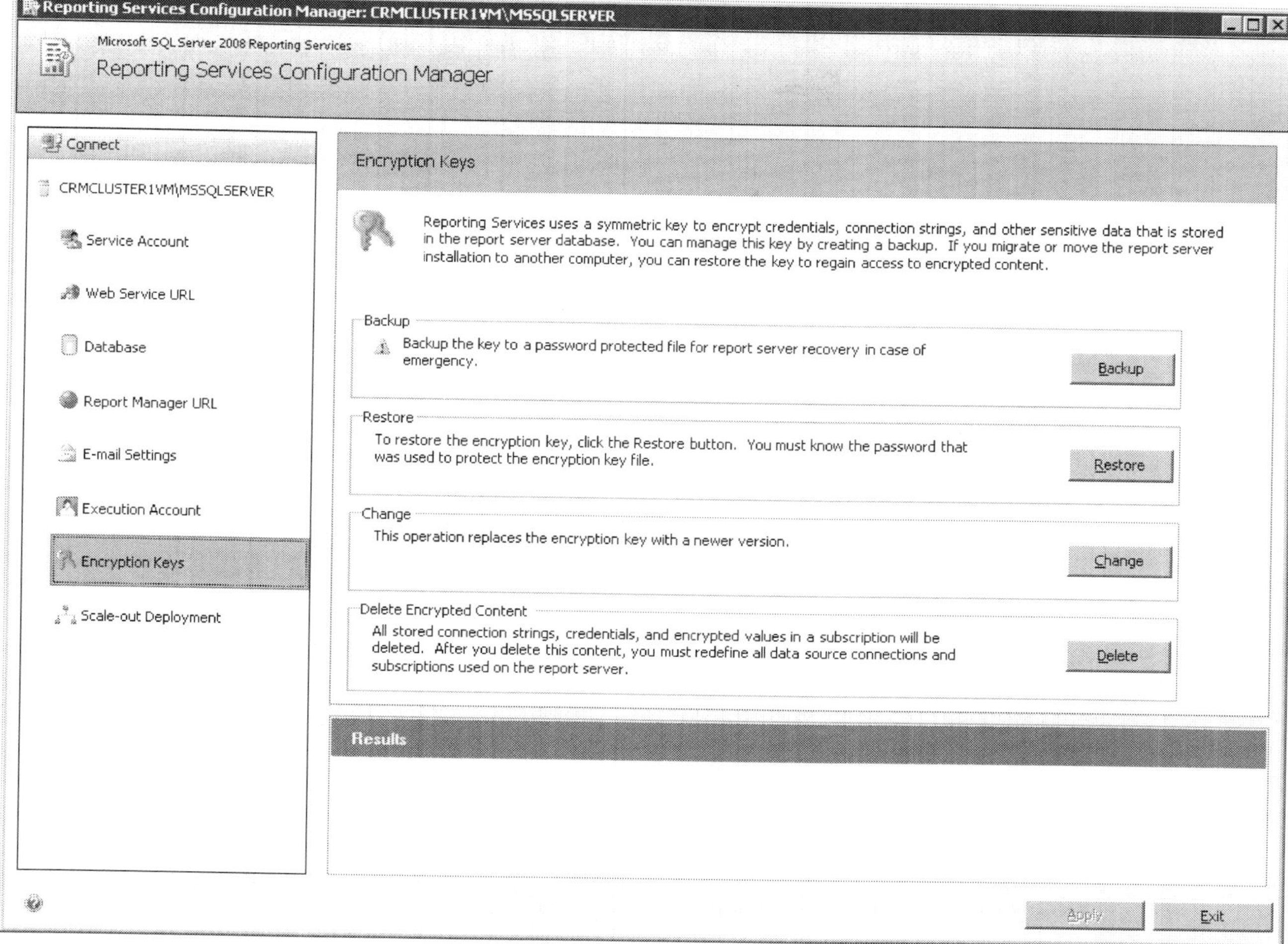


**Figure 20.26**

b. In the **Reporting Services Configuration Manager** console, click on the **Encryption Keys** node in the left pane, which will open the **Encryption Keys** screen in the right pane.

   i. On the **Encryption Keys** screen, click on the **Backup** button.

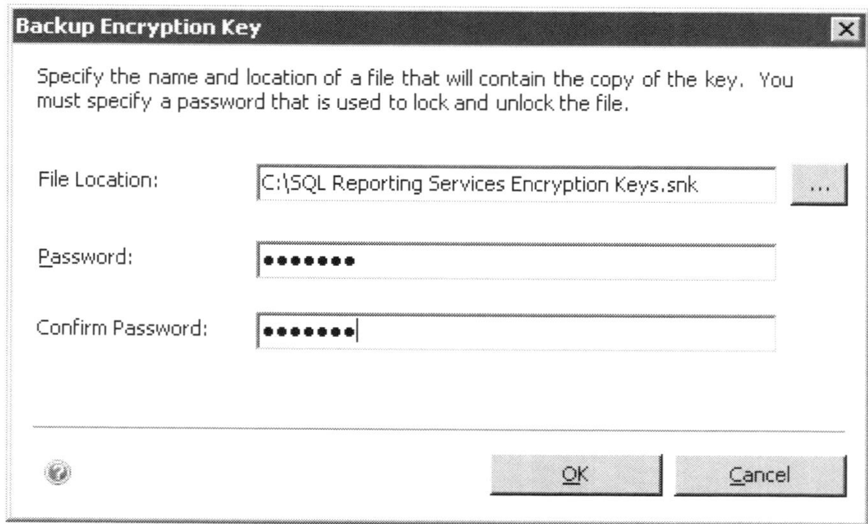


**Figure 20.27**

ii. On the **Backup Encryption Key** screen, fill in **File Location** and **Password** fields, and then click on the **OK** button to backup the encryption key file. This process will create a **.snk** file that contains your encryption information. For our project, we will save our encryption key as **SQL Reporting Services Encryption Keys.snk** on the local **C:** drive, as shown in **Figure 20.27**.

iii. On the **Encryption Keys** screen you should receive a green checkmark icon stating **Creating Encryption Key Backup** in the **Results** pane. This means the encryption key file was created successfully and that you can click on the **Exit** button to exit the **Reporting Services Configuration Manager** console.

c. Copy your encryption key **.snk** file onto the local disk of each your secondary node(s) of your Scale-out Deployment.

## SSRS Synchronizing Encryption Keys- Importing the Key on Member Nodes

26. On each of your remaining nodes of the Scale-out Deployment launch the **Reporting Services Configuration Manager** console.

a. On the **Connect to a report server instance** screen, verify that your secondary NLB cluster node's name is in the **Server Name** field and that the correct SQL Reporting Services instance name is in the **Report Server Instance** field, and then click on the **Connect** button. For our project, we will connect to our second NLB cluster node named **CRMCluster2VM** with the default SQL instance name of **MSSQLSERVER**.

i. In the **Reporting Services Configuration Manager** console, click on the **Encryption Keys** node in the left pane, which will open the **Encryption Keys** screen in the right pane.

ii. On the **Encryption Keys** screen, click on the **Restore** button.

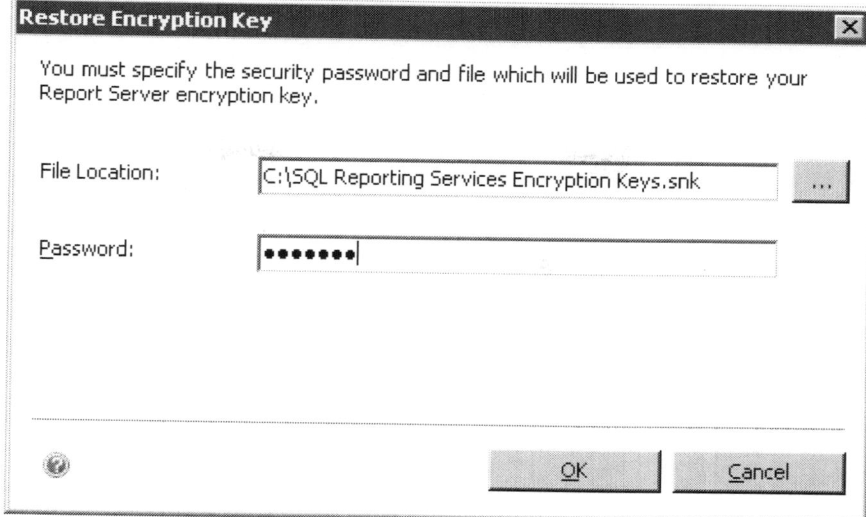


**Figure 20.28**

iii. On the **Restore Encryption Key** screen, fill in the **File Location** and **Password** fields, and then click on the **OK** button to restore the encryption key.

iv. On the **Encryption Keys** screen you should receive a green checkmark icon stating **Restoring Encryption Key** in the **Results** pane. This means the encryption key file was restored successfully and that you can click on the **Exit** button to exit the **Reporting Services Configuration Manager** console.

b. Repeat **Step 26** to restore the encryption key on each of your remaining Scale-out Deployment members. For our project, we will repeat the process to restore the encryption key on our third and final NLB cluster node named **CRMCluster3VM**.

## Modifying the SQL Reporting Services (SSRS) .Config File for the NLB Cluster Configuration

**Figure 20.29**

In this section, we will modify our SQL Reporting Services configuration file so that each of our Scale-out Deployment nodes will work correctly with our network load balancer configuration. This will involve hardcoding our network load balancer's hostname, URL root, and authentication method to our SQL Reporting Services configuration file.

27. On each of your NLB cluster nodes that have SQL Reporting Services installed browse, to the following directory **C:\Program Files\Microsoft SQL Server\MSRS10.MSSQLSERVER\Reporting Services\ReportServer**, and then open the **rsreportserver.config** file with **Notepad**. If you are configuring **SQL Server 2008 R2 Reporting Services**, then you want to browse to the **C:\Program Files\Microsoft SQL Server\MSRS10_50.MSSQLSERVER\Reporting Services\ReportServer** directory to edit the file.

## Modifying the SSRS .Config File- Adding the NLB Cluster's Hostname

a. Find the **<service>** tag, and then add an XML tag **<Hostname>Your_NLB_Cluster_Name</Hostname>** below the **<service>** tag for your NLB cluster's DNS name. This will force the SQL Reporting Services instance on each NLB cluster node to always resolve to the NLB cluster's name vs. the individual NLB cluster node's name. For our project, we created a DNS Host (A) record named **xrm** for our NLB's cluster IP of **10.10.10.59**, we will need to add the XML hostname tag of **<Hostname>xrm</Hostname>**, as shown in **Figure 20.29**.

# Modifying the SSRS .Config File- Adding the NLB Cluster's URL Root

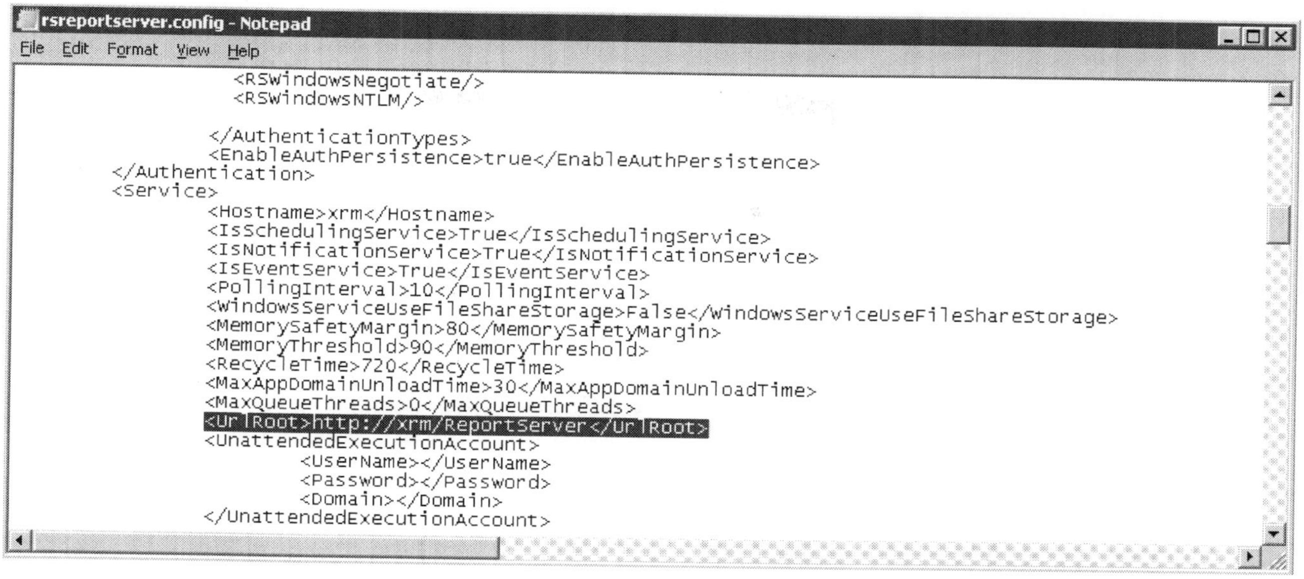

rsreportserver.config - Notepad

File Edit Format View Help

```
            <RSWindowsNegotiate/>
            <RSWindowsNTLM/>

        </AuthenticationTypes>
        <EnableAuthPersistence>true</EnableAuthPersistence>
    </Authentication>
    <Service>
        <Hostname>xrm</Hostname>
        <IsSchedulingService>True</IsSchedulingService>
        <IsNotificationService>True</IsNotificationService>
        <IsEventService>True</IsEventService>
        <PollingInterval>10</PollingInterval>
        <WindowsServiceUseFileShareStorage>False</WindowsServiceUseFileShareStorage>
        <MemorySafetyMargin>80</MemorySafetyMargin>
        <MemoryThreshold>90</MemoryThreshold>
        <RecycleTime>720</RecycleTime>
        <MaxAppDomainUnloadTime>30</MaxAppDomainUnloadTime>
        <MaxQueueThreads>0</MaxQueueThreads>
        <UrlRoot>http://xrm/ReportServer</UrlRoot>
        <UnattendedExecutionAccount>
            <UserName></UserName>
            <Password></Password>
            <Domain></Domain>
        </UnattendedExecutionAccount>
```

**Figure 20.30**

b. In this same general area below the **<service>** tag find the already existing XML tag **<urlRoot></urlRoot>**, and then add your NLB cluster's **ReportServer URL** in between the start and end tags. For our project, our NLB cluster's ReportServer URL is **http://xrm/ReportServer**, so we will modify the tag to **<urlRoot>http://xrm/ReportServer</urlRoot>**, as shown in **Figure 20.30**.

## Modifying the SSRS .Config File- Adding the NLB Cluster's Authentication Type

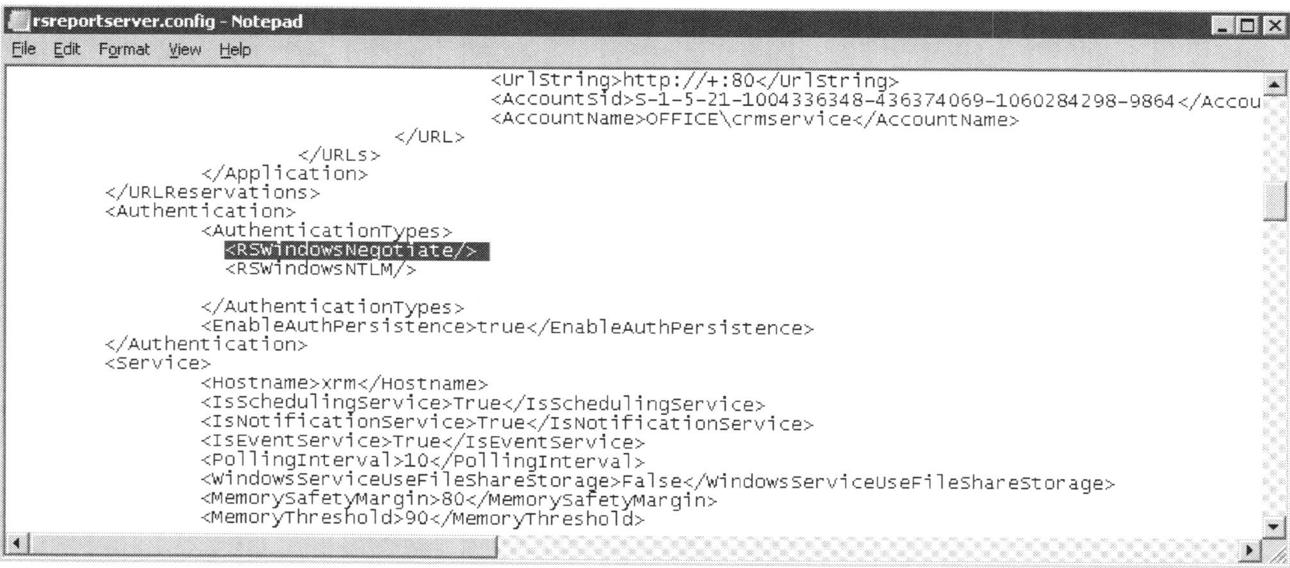

```
rsreportserver.config - Notepad
File Edit Format View Help
                                        <UrlString>http://+:80</UrlString>
                                        <AccountSid>S-1-5-21-1004336348-436374069-1060284298-9864</Accou
                                        <AccountName>OFFICE\crmservice</AccountName>
                                </URL>
                        </URLs>
                </Application>
        </URLReservations>
        <Authentication>
                <AuthenticationTypes>
                  <RSWindowsNegotiate/>
                  <RSWindowsNTLM/>

                </AuthenticationTypes>
                <EnableAuthPersistence>true</EnableAuthPersistence>
        </Authentication>
        <Service>
                <Hostname>xrm</Hostname>
                <IsSchedulingService>True</IsSchedulingService>
                <IsNotificationService>True</IsNotificationService>
                <IsEventService>True</IsEventService>
                <PollingInterval>10</PollingInterval>
                <WindowsServiceUseFileShareStorage>False</WindowsServiceUseFileShareStorage>
                <MemorySafetyMargin>80</MemorySafetyMargin>
                <MemoryThreshold>90</MemoryThreshold>
```

**Figure 20.31**

c. Next, we will give our SQL Reporting Services the ability to use Kerberos authentication. While still in the **rsreportserver.config** file find the **<Authentication>** tag, and then add the following XML tag **<RSWindowsNegotiate/>** right below the **<AuthenticationTypes>** tag, but before the **<RSWindowsNTLM/>** tag, as shown in **Figure 20.31**.

# Modifying the SSRS .Config File- Saving the Changes

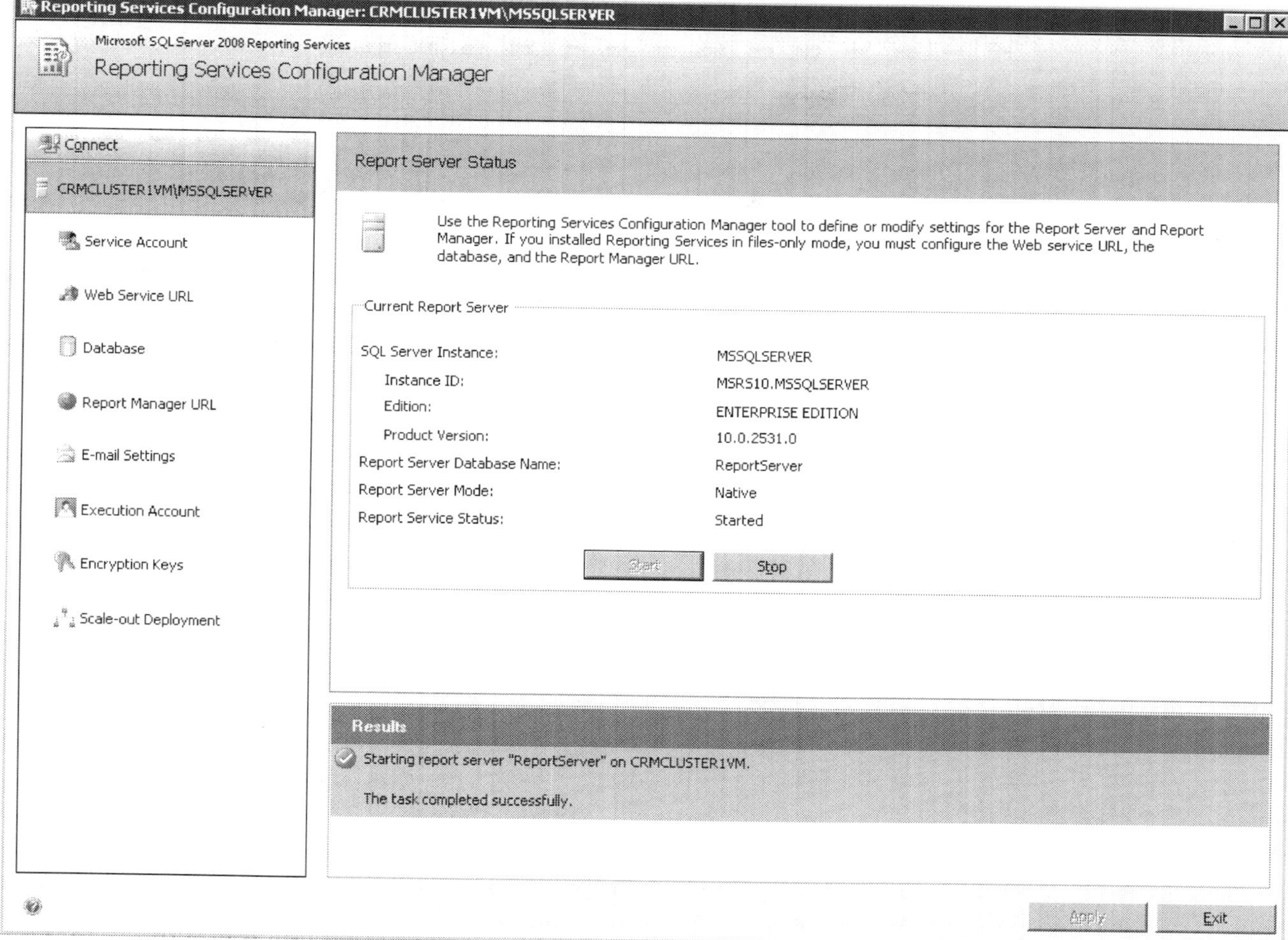


**Figure 20.32**

d. Save your changes and then close the **rsreportserver.config** file.

e. For the changes to take effect we need to restart the SQL Reporting Services service. Login to the **SQL Reporting Services Configuration Manager** console, and then on the **Report Server Status** screen click on the **Stop** button. Once the service has stopped, click on the **Start** button to restart the SQL Reporting Services service, as shown in **Figure 20.32**. You can also accomplish this by going to **Administrative Tools\Services**, and then restarting the **SQL Server Reporting Services (MSSQLSERVER)** service.

f. Repeat **Step 27** to modify the same tags in the **rsreportserver.config** file of each of your remaining Scale-out Deployment nodes.

## Configuring Internet Explorer Security on the NLB Cluster Nodes

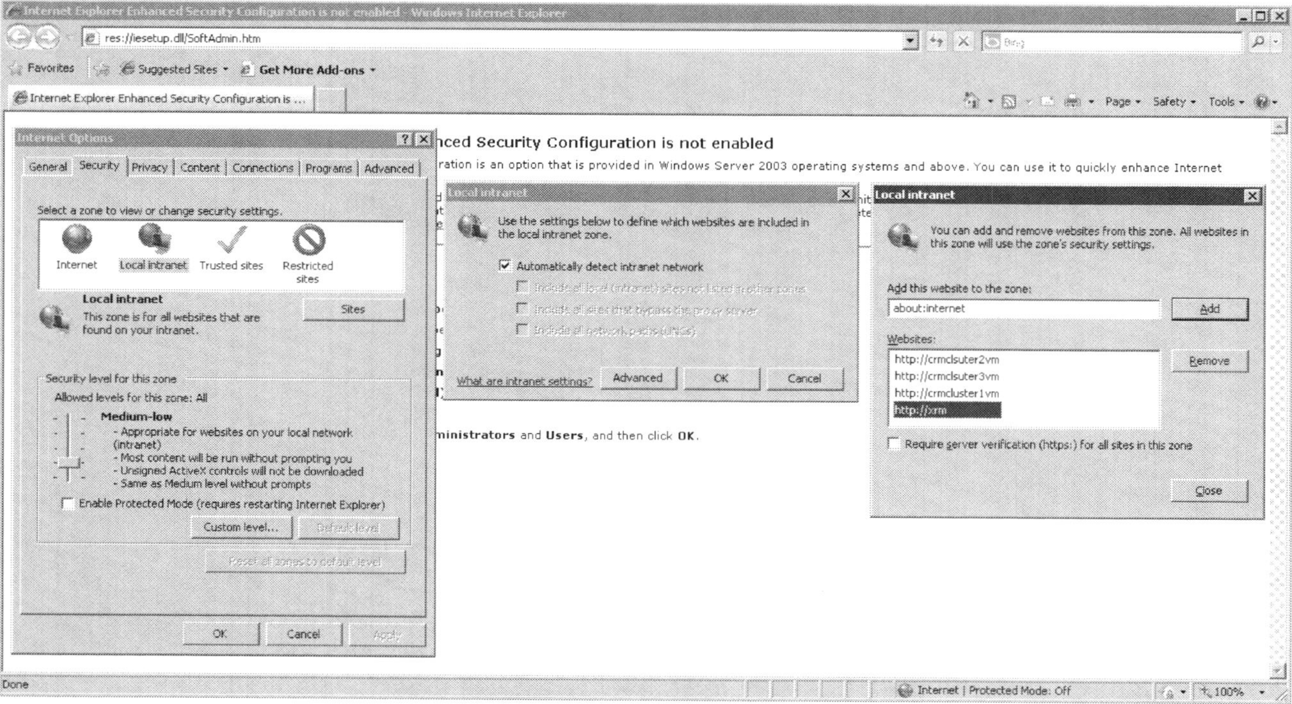


**Figure 20.33**

Before we are able to test our SQL Reporting Services configuration, we need to make some security changes to each of our NLB cluster nodes Internet Explorer.

28. Open **Internet Explorer** on each of your NLB cluster nodes, and then browse to the **Tools\Internet Options\Security** tab.

## Configuring Internet Explorer Security- Disabling Protected Mode

a. Highlight the **Local intranet** icon, and then in the **Security level for site zone** field, unselect the **Enable Protected Mode (requires restarting Internet Explorer** checkbox option.

## Configuring Internet Explorer Security- Adding Nodes to Local Intranet Zone

b. Click on the **Sites** button to open the **Local intranet** screen.

   i. On the **Local intranet** screen, verify that the **Automatically detect intranet network** option is selected, and then click on the **Advanced** button. If you are using Windows Server 2008 vs. Windows Server 2008 R2 then you won't have this screen, but instead will be brought directly to the screen in the next step.

ii. On the second **Local intranet** screen with the **Websites** field, click on the **Add** button, and then enter each of your NLB cluster nodes URL's along with your NLB cluster URL's. For our project, we will add **http://crmcluster1vm**, **http://crmcluster2vm**, **http://crmcluster3vm** for our NLB cluster node URLs, and then **http://xrm** for our NLB cluster's URL, as shown in **Figure 20.33**.

## Configuring Internet Explorer Security- Moving Sites to the Local Intranet

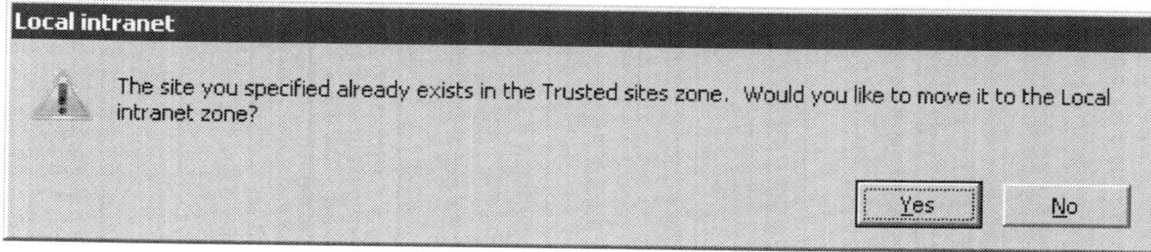


**Figure 20.34**

iii. If receive a **Local intranet** warning pop-up screen as shown in **Figure 20.34** when adding your websites, then click on the **Yes** button to move the sites into the local intranet zone.

**NOTE:** If you don't add your NLB cluster nodes and your NLB cluster's URL's to the websites field of the local intranet zone, then you will most likely receive a login pop-up screen later on when we are testing our SQL Reporting Services configuration.

iv. Save all your changes and then close **Internet Explorer**.

## Configuring Internet Explorer Security- Disabling Protected Mode Warnings

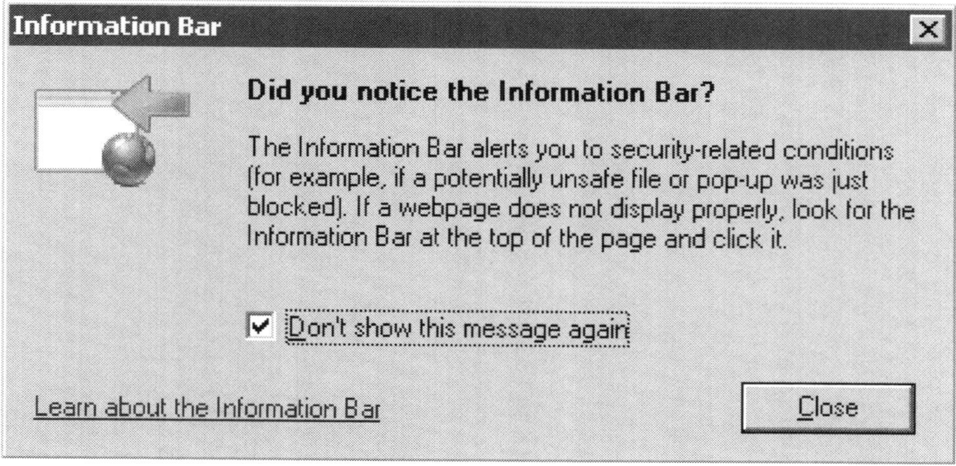


**Figure 20.35**

v. Restart **Internet Explorer** on each of your NLB cluster nodes, so that we can disable any warnings about the protected mode being turned off. When restarting Internet Explorer you will most likely receive a warning about the protected mode being turned off with a beige **Information Bar** toolbar at the top of Internet Explorer stating **Protected mode is currently turned off for the Local intranet zone. Click here to open security settings**. If you did not receive this warning, then please disregard this step and the next.

1. If you received the **Information Bar** toolbar, then you also most likely received an **Information Bar** pop-up screen, as shown in **Figure 20.35**. On this **Information Bar** pop-up screen, select the **Don't show this message again** checkbox, and then click **Close** button. This will stop any further messages from appearing in regard to the protect mode for the local intranet zone being shut off.

# Disabling the LoopbackCheck in the Registry of Each NLB Cluster Node

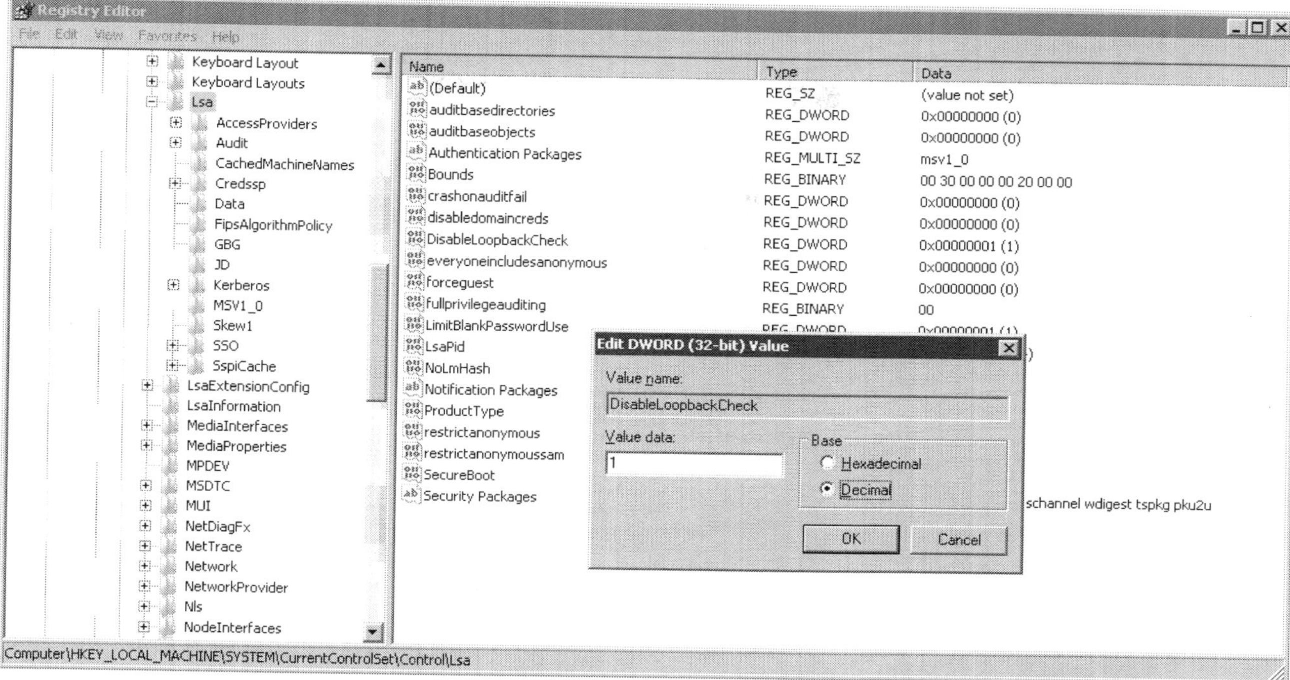


**Figure 20.36**

We will test our SQL Reporting Services and CRM 4.0 application on each NLB cluster node by browsing with Internet Explorer to web pages hosted on the node itself. By default, Windows Server 2008 and later prevents most of this type of browsing with the LoopbackCheck registry key, so we will need to disable the LoopbackCheck key from within the registry of each of our nodes. Once you're done testing, then you can decide if you want to re-enable this feature or not.

29. On each of your NLB cluster nodes, click the on Windows **Start** button, and then select the **Run** program.
    a. Type in the command **regedit** in the **Run** field, and then hit the **Enter** key.
    b. In the **Registry Editor** console, browse to the **HKEY_LOCAL_MACHINE\SYSTEM\CurrentControlSet \Control\Lsa** directory.
    c. Right click the **Lsa** folder, and then select the **New\DWORD (32-bit) Value** option.
        i. Name the new key **DisableLoopbackCheck** and make sure the case of letters is the same as shown here.
        ii. Right click on the newly created **DisableLoopbackCheck** value, and then select the **Modify** option.
            1. Set **Value data** field to **1**, and then select the **Decimal** option for the **Base** field, as shown in **Figure 20.36**. Click on the **OK** button to save your changes.

d. Close the **Registry Editor** console, and then reboot each of the NLB cluster nodes for the registry changes to take effect.

## Testing the SQL Reporting Services Scale-out Deployment on each NLB Cluster Node

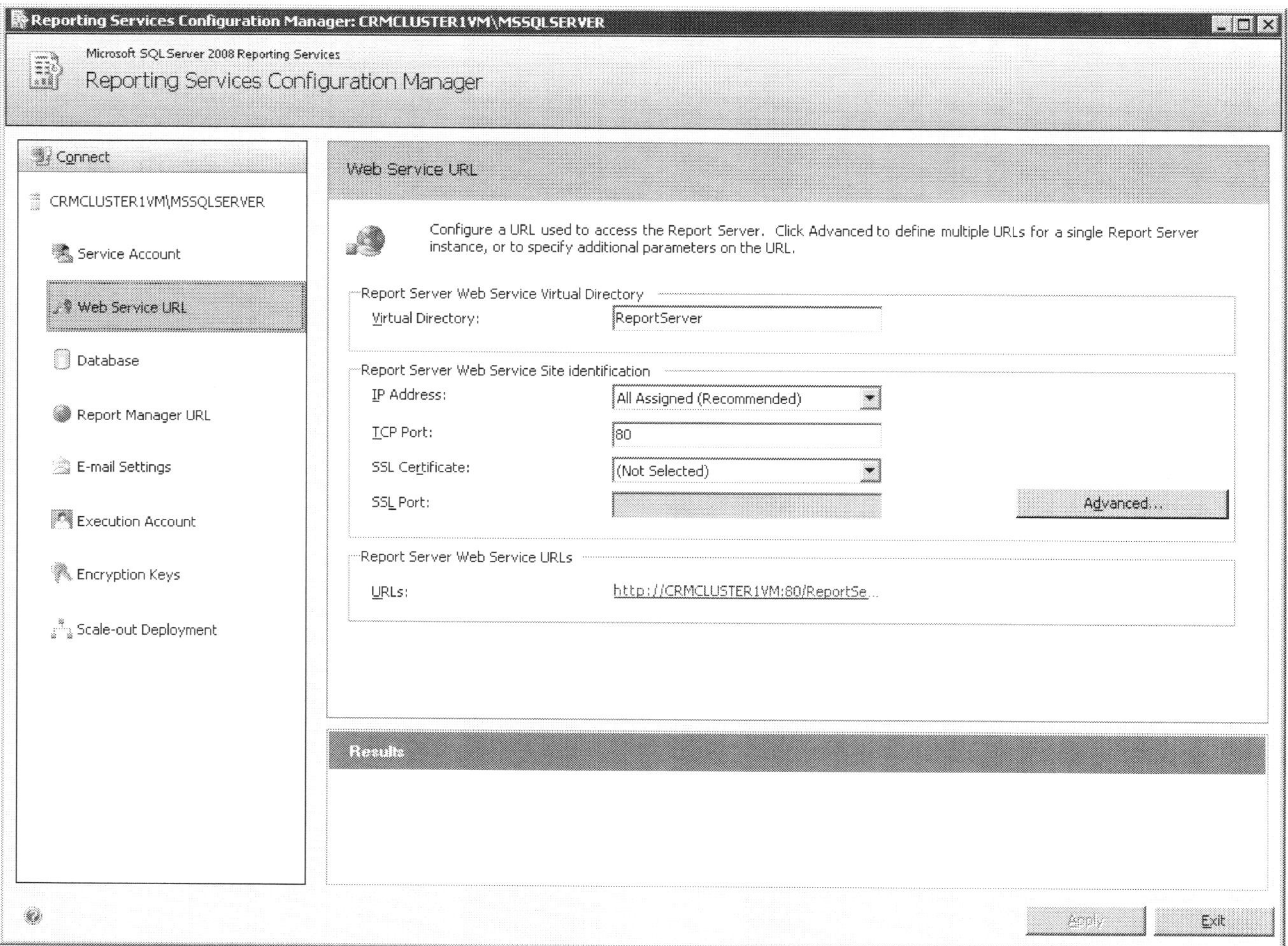


**Figure 20.37**

We are now ready to test our SQL Reporting Services configuration on each of our NLB cluster nodes. We will verify that both our report server and our reports virtual directories on each of our NLB cluster nodes are working correctly by querying our reportserver database that's hosted on our SQL cluster.

30. Open the **Reporting Services Configuration Manager** console, and then on each NLB cluster node perform the following steps.

   a. On the **Connect to a report server instance** screen, verify that your NLB cluster node's name is in the **Server Name** field and that the correct SQL Reporting Services instance name is in the **Report Server Instance** field, and then click on the **Connect** button. For our project, we will connect to our first NLB cluster node named **CRMCluster1VM** with the default SQL instance name of **MSSQLSERVER**.

## Testing the SSRS Scale-out Deployment- Web Service URL

i. Click the **Web Service URL** node in the left pane, which will open the **Web Service URL** screen in the right pane, and then click on the blue URL link located in the **Report Server Web Service URLs** field. This will launch Internet Explorer to view the local NLB cluster node's **ReportServer URL**. For our project, the URL for our NLB cluster node should be **http://CRMCLUSTER1VM:80/ReportServer**, as shown in **Figure 20.37**.

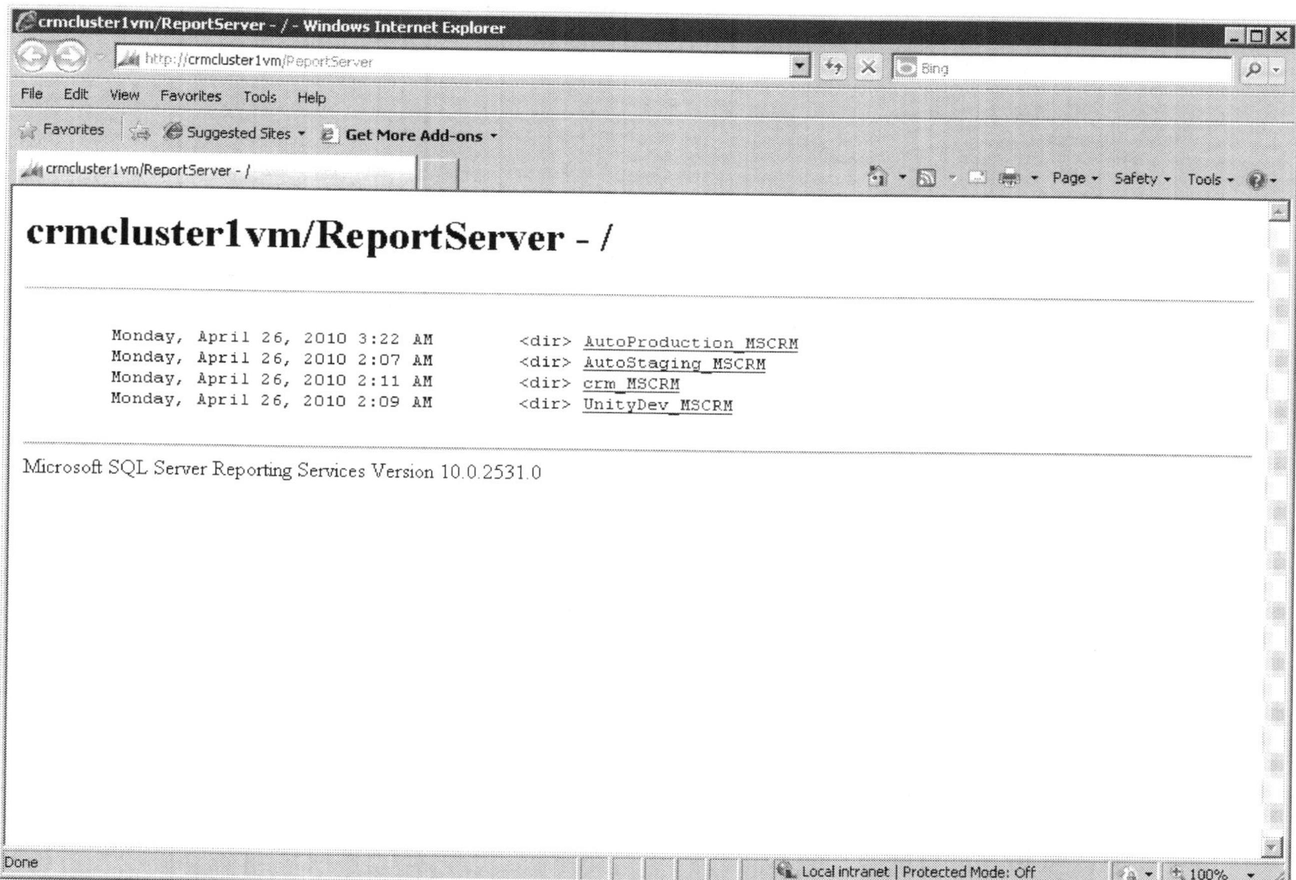


**Figure 20.38**

1. Most likely your reports listed will be different than **Figure 20.38**, which is fine as long as the URL resolves without errors and that the webpage shows the **Microsoft SQL Server Reporting Services Version** that you have setup. This verifies that your **ReportServer** virtual directory in IIS for this NLB cluster node's SQL Reporting Services is setup correctly.

## Testing the SSRS Scale-out Deployment- Report Manager URL

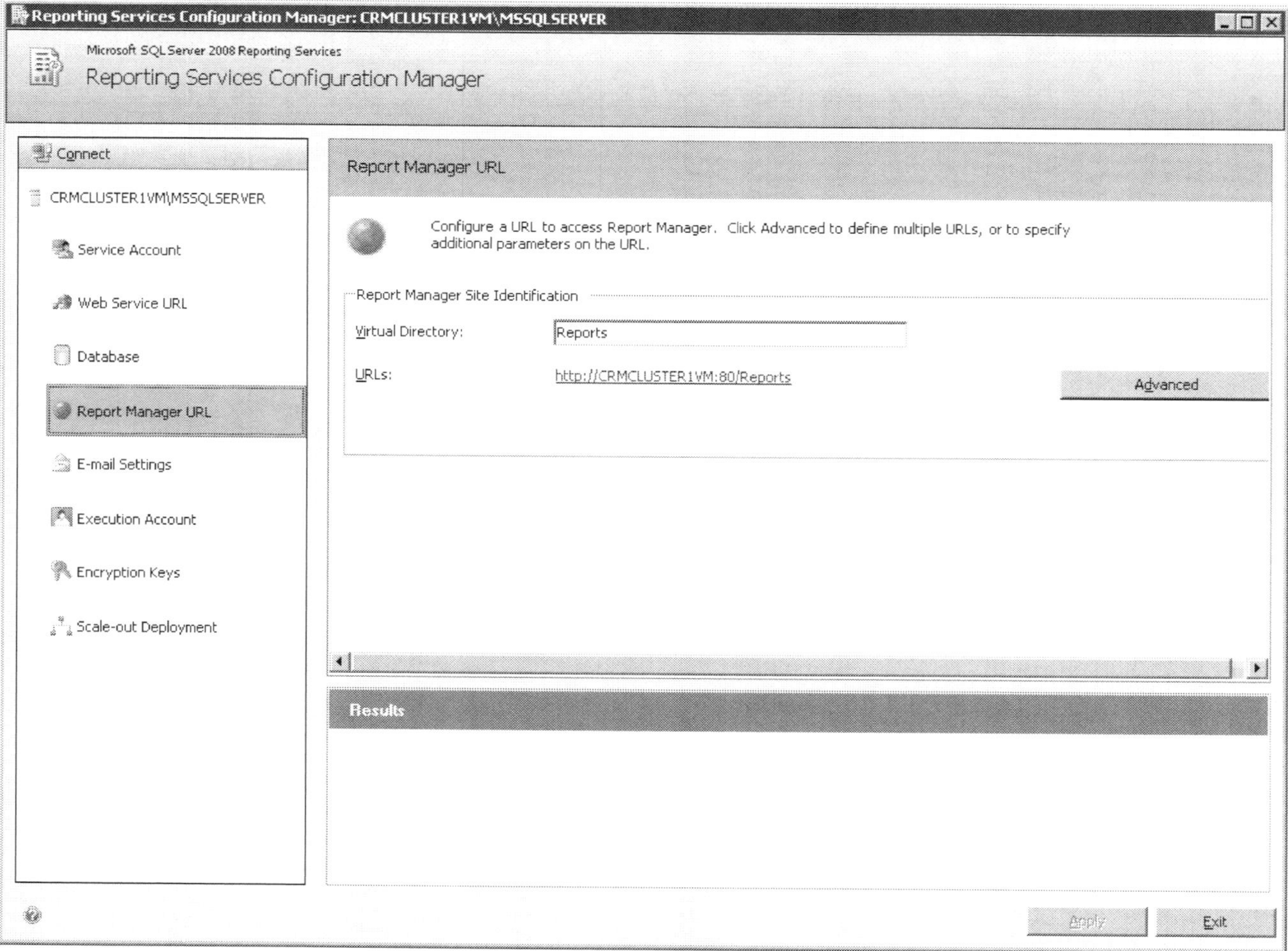


**Figure 20.39**

ii. Click the **Report Manager URL** node in the left pane, which will open the **Report Manager URL** screen in the right pane, and then click on the blue URL link located in the **Report Manager Site Identification** field. This will launch Internet Explorer to view the local NLB cluster node's **Reports** URL. For our project, the URL for our NLB cluster node should be **http://CRMCLUSTER1VM:80/Reports**, as shown in **Figure 20.39**.

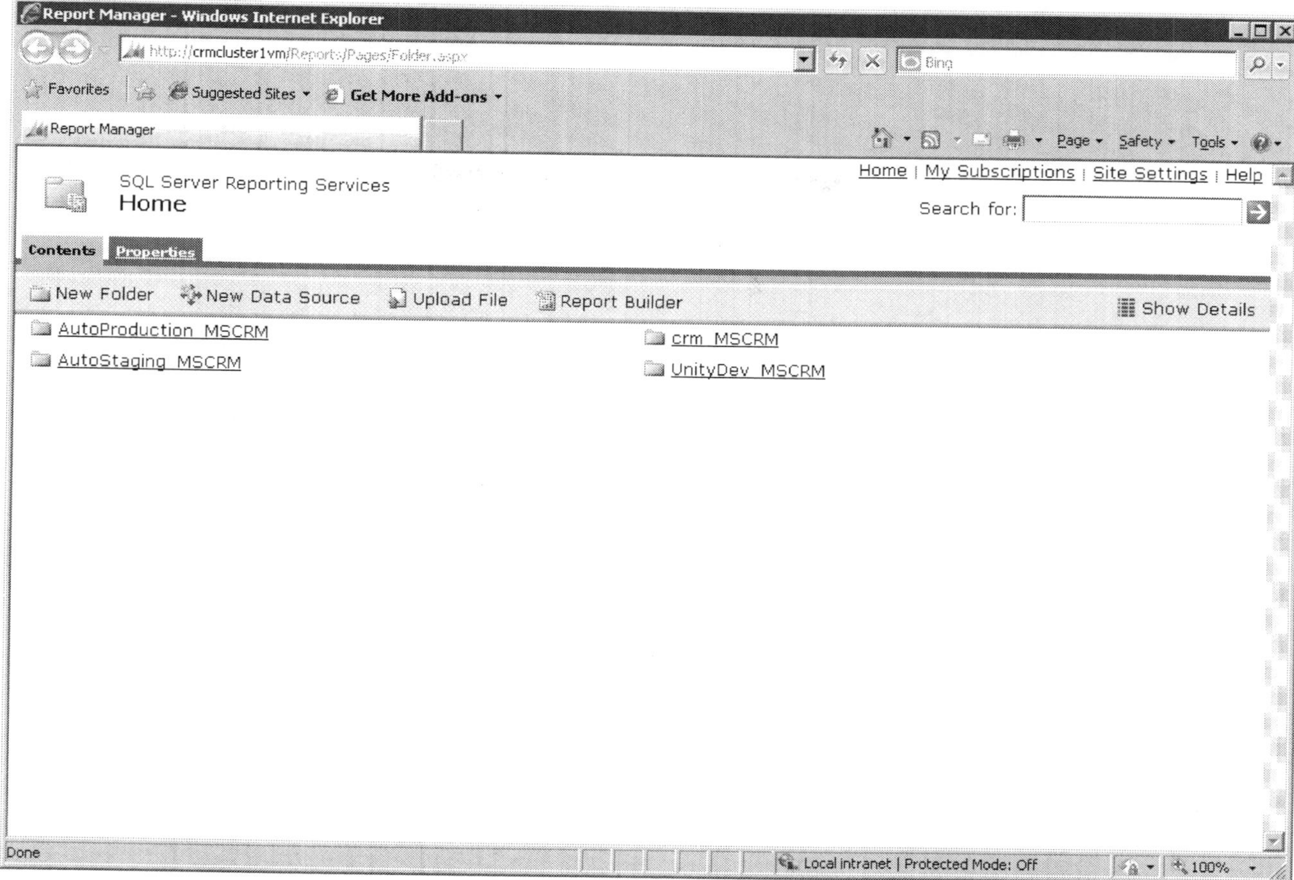


**Figure 20.40**

1. Most likely your reports listed will be different than **Figure 20.40**, which again is fine as long as the URL resolves without errors to the **SQL Server Reporting Services Home** webpage. This verifies that your **Reports** virtual directory in IIS for this NLB cluster node's SQL Reporting Services is setup correctly.

b. Repeat **Step 30** for each of your NLB cluster nodes to verify that your SSRS Scale-out Deployment is setup correctly.

# Chapter 21: Installing Microsoft Dynamics CRM 4.0 on the NLB Cluster

Microsoft Dynamics CRM 4.0 is an enterprise level application with multiple components that can be distributed across many servers for high availability. Setting up your enterprise level applications can be quite complex with many components ranging from the database, to web servers, email, reports and security. In this chapter, we will be installing the first component of our front-end application across our NLB cluster nodes. We will start with installing the CRM Server role on our initial NLB cluster node to create a new CRM deployment in our clustered environment. During the install we will configure CRM to use a new Organizational Unit that we'll create in our Active Directory for its security accounts. Following this we will configure our CRM deployment to place its databases in our SQL cluster and to use our NLB cluster's SQL Reporting Services for our CRM reporting. After this we will set our CRM deployment to use our highly available CRM Email Router service that we'll create in Chapter 27. Whether you plan on migrating an existing CRM organization into your new clustered environment or if you will be creating brand new CRM deployment the installation steps in this chapter are the same with only the exception of CRM organization names. We will cover how to avoid CRM organization name conflicts when importing CRM organizations from previous deployments. Once we've completed the steps in this chapter we will have our base CRM installation in place.

## Prerequisites- Installing Windows Roles

1. Log on to one of your NLB cluster nodes that will host your front-end application. The logon account used to install Microsoft Dynamics CRM 4.0 account has to be a domain user account with domain administrator level privileges. This domain user account also has to be a member of the local computer's administrators group on each server that the CRM Server role will be installed on. In addition, the user account has to be from the local domain as you cannot install the application as a member from a trusted domain. For our project, we will install CRM when logged on as the **Domain Administrator**. Then in Chapter 22 we will cover all the aspects of our CRM security and how to tighten down our CRM service accounts.

    a. Open Windows **Server Manager**, right click on the **Roles** node in the left pane, and then select the **Add Roles** option.

    b. On the **Before You Begin** screen, click on the **Next** button to continue.

    c. Select the checkbox for the following roles, and then click on the **Next** button to continue.

        i. **Application Server**

        ii. **File Services**

    d. On the **Application Server** screen, click on the **Next** button to continue.

    e. On the **Select Roles Services** for the **Application Server** screen, select the checkbox next to **Web Server (IIS) Support** to launch the **Add Roles Wizard**.

    f. On the **Add Roles Wizard** screen, click on the **Add Required Role Services** button to continue

    g. On the **Select Roles Services** screen, click on the **Next** button to continue.

h. On the **Select Roles Services** for the **Web Server (IIS)** screen, leave all the existing checkboxes, and then select the checkbox next to **IIS 6 Management Compatibility**. Click on the **Next** button to continue.

i. On the **File Services** screen, click on the **Next** button to continue.

j. On the **Select Roles Services** for the **File Services** screen, select the checkbox next to **Indexing Service**, and then click on the **Next** button to continue.

k. On the **Confirm Installation Selections** screen, click on the **Install** button to continue.

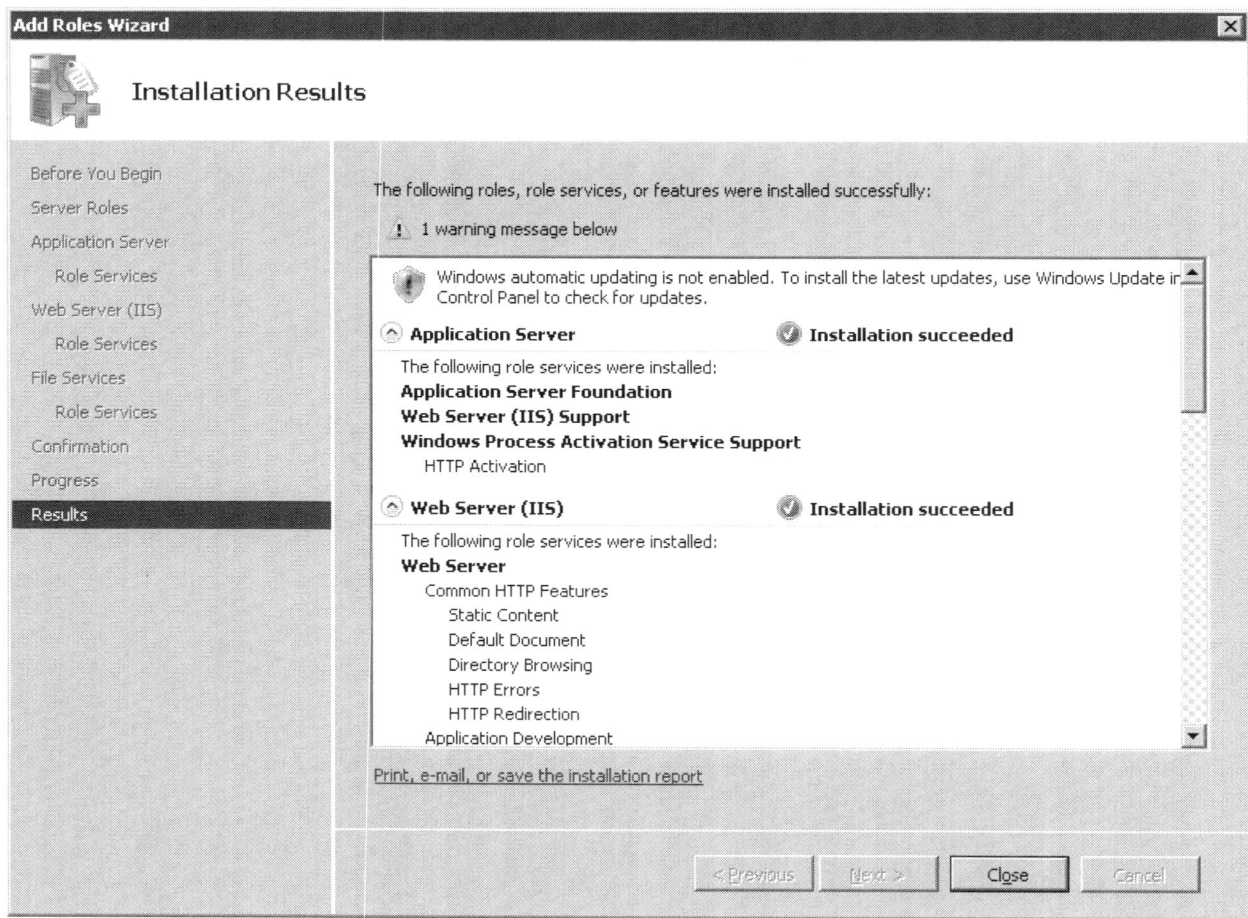


**Figure 21.1**

l. On the **Installation Results** screen, verify that all the components were successfully installed, and then click on the **Close** button to complete the installation.

## Prerequisites- Creating an Active Directory Organizational Unit (OU) for the CRM Security Accounts

Creating an OU for CRM 4.0 security accounts is a prerequisite to installing the CRM Server role. During the CRM Server install process we will have to select an OU for CRM to create its security accounts in.

2. Go to one of your **Windows Domain Controllers (DC)**, browse to the **Start\Administrative Tools**, and then select the **Active Directory Users and Computers** option.

    a. Right click on your domain's name node in the left pane, and then select the **New\Organizational Unit** option. Name the new Organizational Unit (OU) with a descriptive name for your CRM cluster setup. For our project, we will create an **OU** named **CRM_Cluster** for our CRM security accounts.

## Installing Microsoft Dynamics CRM 4.0 Server Role on the Initial NLB Cluster Node

3. Copy the **Microsoft Dynamics CRM 4.0** installation media onto a local drive of one of your NLB cluster nodes.

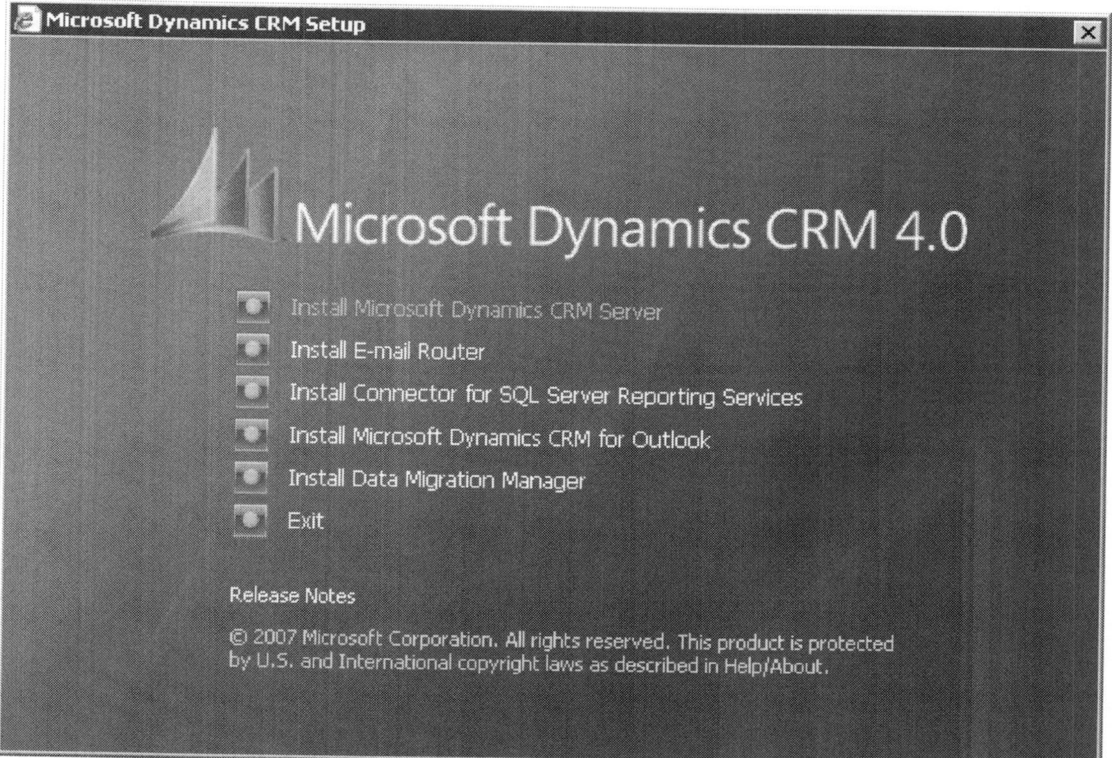


**Figure 21.2**

4. Launch the CRM 4.0 install by inserting the DVD or by double clicking on the **Splash.exe** in the root of the install files.

5. On the **Microsoft Dynamics CRM Setup** screen, select the **Install Microsoft Dynamics CRM Server** option, as shown in **Figure 21.2**.

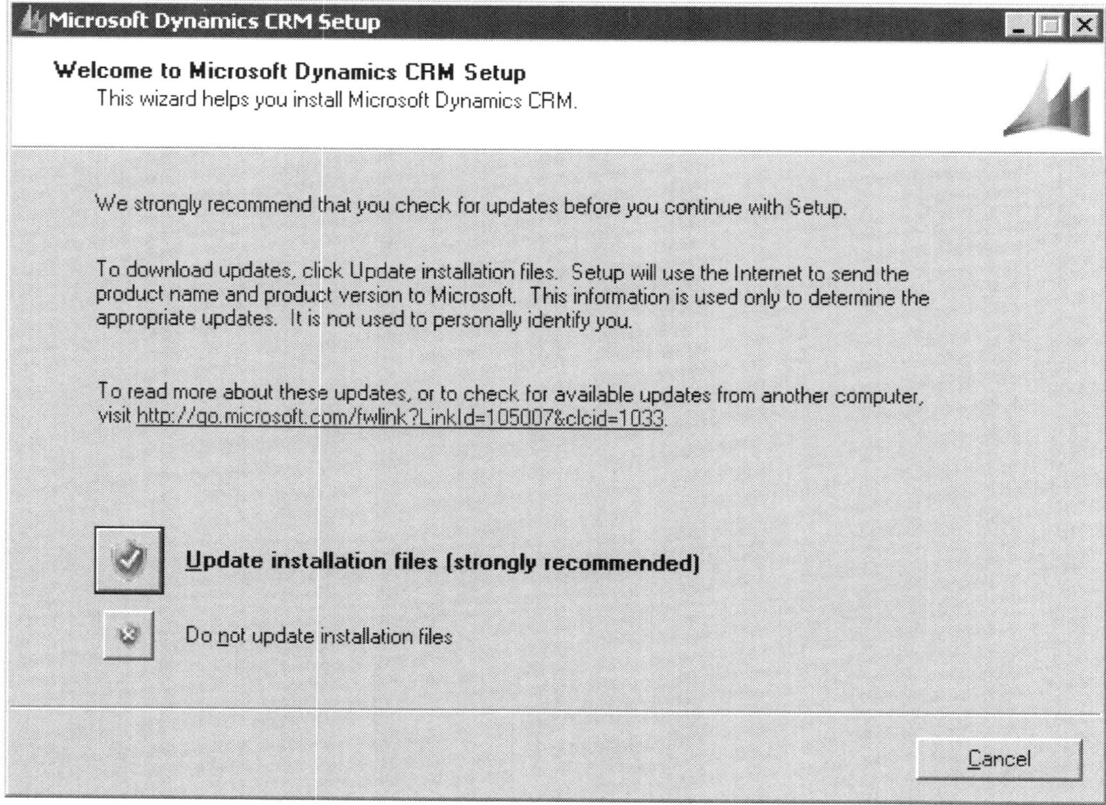


**Figure 21.3**

6. On the **Welcome to Microsoft Dynamics CRM Setup** screen, click on the **Update installation files (strongly recommended)** button.

7. On the **Checking for Update** screen, click on the **Next** button to continue.

8. On the **License Code Information** screen, enter your license number, and then click on the **Next** button to continue.

9. On the **License Agreement** screen, select the **I accept this license agreement** option, and then click on the **I Accept** button to continue.

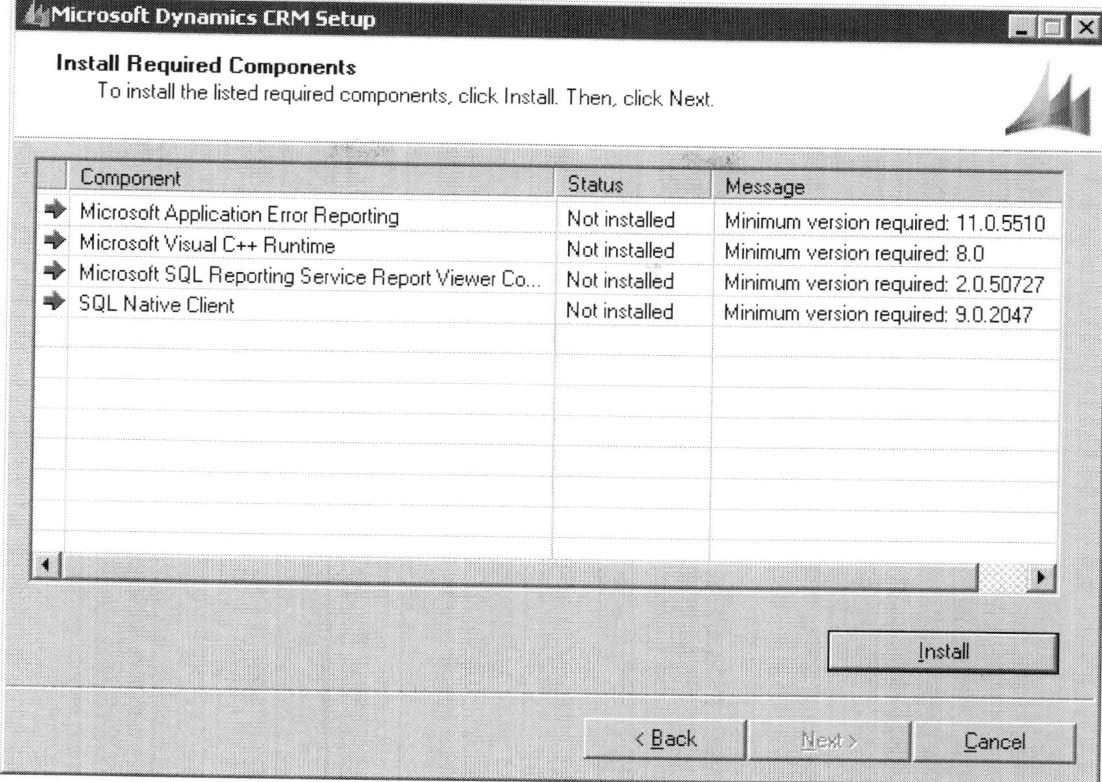


**Figure 21.4**

10. On the **Install Required Components** screen, click on the **Install** button to continue.

    a. Verify that all the components installed successfully, and then click on the **Next** button to continue.

## Installing the CRM Server Role- Specifying Install Type

11. If you are installing the **Enterprise** version of **Microsoft Dynamics CRM 4.0**, then a **Specify Setup Type** screen will appear, where you can select either a **Typical** or **Custom** install type. If you are installing the **Standard** version of CRM 4.0, then please disregard this step. When you select the Typical option all the components of the CRM Server role will be installed. When you select the Custom install option there are two server role groups available to select. The first is Application Server role which installs the services that provide users access to data and content, and the second is the Platform Server role which installs services that process data. For additional information about server roles, see the Microsoft's Planning Deployment chapter in the Microsoft Dynamics CRM 4.0 Planning Guide. For our project, we will select the **Typical** install option to install all components of the CRM Server role.

## Installing the CRM Server Role- Selecting the SQL Cluster to Host the Database

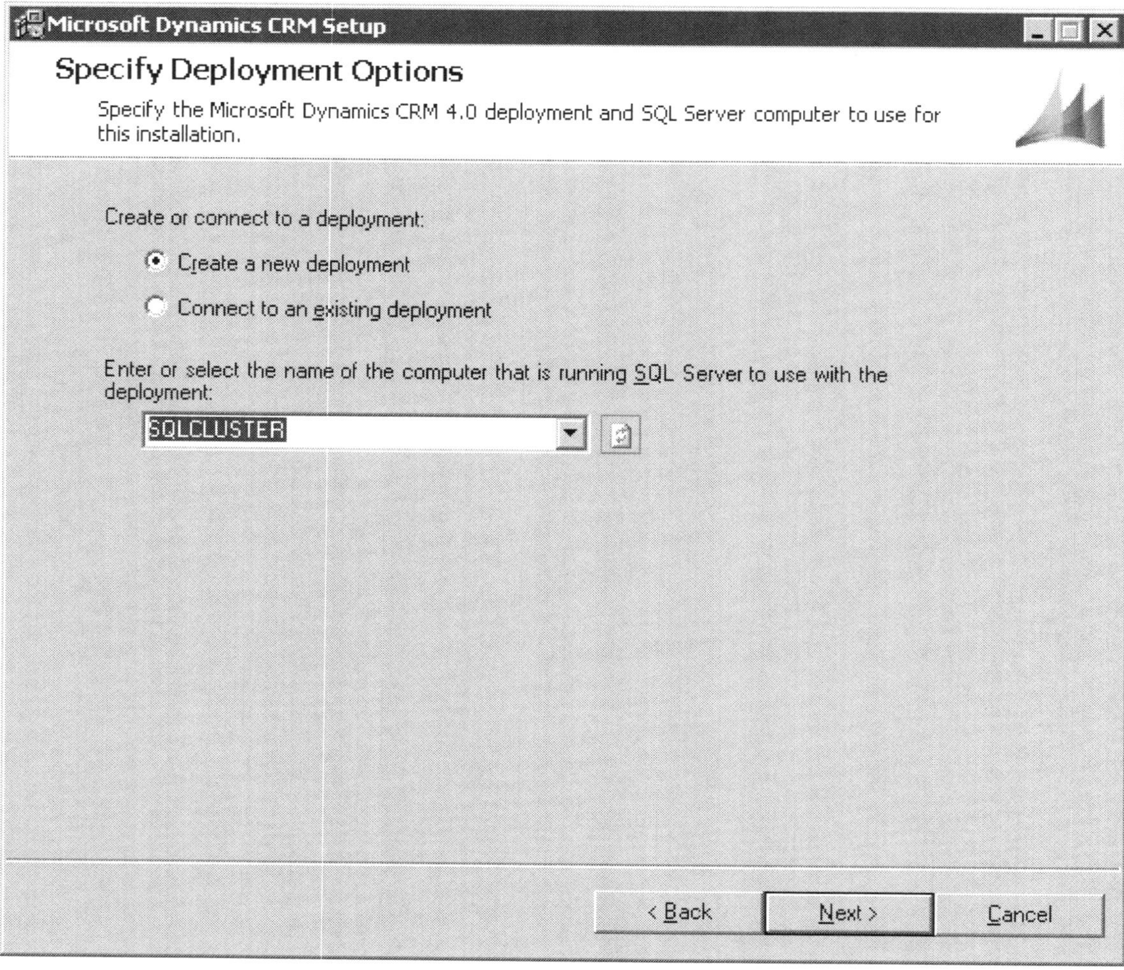


**Figure 21.5**

12. On the **Specify Deployment Options** screen, leave the default option of **Create a new deployment** selected. Whether you plan on migrating an existing CRM organization into your new CRM cluster or if you will be creating brand new CRM organization, you want to select the Create a new deployment option here. In Chapter 24 we will cover how to import an existing CRM organization into our new CRM cluster.

    **NOTE:** When you select the Create a new deployment option the setup will create a new organization database using the name that you specify along with creating a new configuration database named MSCRM_CONFIG. If you receive an error stating that this MSCRM_CONFIG database already exists, then you will need to remove this existing configuration database from the SQL cluster before you can continue. As a good practice, it is always recommended that you backup your databases before deleting them off the database server.

    a. For the **Enter or select the name of the computer that is running SQL Server to use with the deployment** field, enter your SQL cluster's name or click on the **Browse** button to select your SQL cluster's name, and then click the on **Next** button to continue. This SQL Server will be where all the Microsoft Dynamics CRM databases stored. For our project, we will enter our SQL cluster's name of **SQLCLUSTER**, as shown in **Figure 21.5**.

## Installing the CRM Server Role- How the Organization Name and CRM URL's Relate

When choosing a name for your CRM organization you will want to take into consideration that your CRM organization name has to be part of both your internet and internal URLs for your CRM authentication to work correctly. If you are creating a brand new CRM installation, then it is recommended that choose a user friendly organization name such as simply **crm**. As an example, let's assume your CRM organization name is simply **crm** as suggested in which case your URL would have to be **http://crm.<YourDomain>.com** or **https://crm.<YourDomain>.com** with the organization name of **crm** on front of your internet domain's URL. For your internal URL you should have already created an internal DNS Host (A) record for your NLB cluster's IP address. As an example, let's assume your NLB cluster's name is simply **xrm** as in our project, then your internal URL would have to be **http://xrm/crm** or **https://xrm/crm** with a forward slash and the organization name for **crm** after your NLB cluster's URL. Unfortunately, when setting up an internet facing deployment of CRM you have to use have a different URL internally vs. from the internet or your internal users will receive a login prompt the same as internet users do for authentication. We will cover how to setup our URLs in **Chapter 26** when configuring the **CRM Internet Facing Deployment (IFD) Tool**.

## Installing the CRM Server Role- Specifying the CRM Organization Name

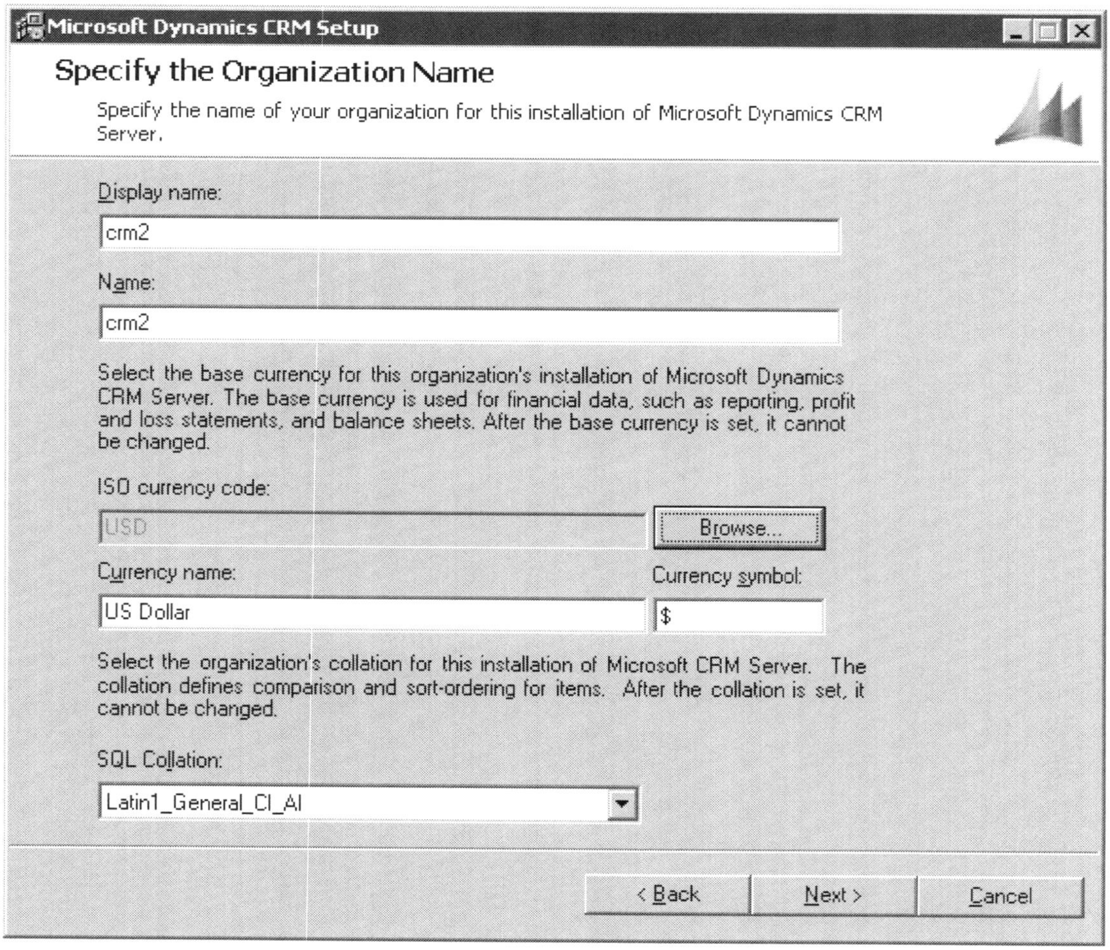

**Figure 21.6**

13. On the **Specify the Organization Name** screen, enter the name of your CRM organization in the **Display name** field, and then hit the **Tab** key so that the **Name** field will automatically be populated with the same name as the display name.

    **NOTE:** If you are planning on importing an existing organization into your SQL cluster then you will want to enter a different CRM organization name here than the name of the organization that you will be importing. When importing an organization from a previous CRM deployment you will want to maintain the organization's name. The CRM importation process does allow you to rename the organization that you're importing, however the process is problematic as it does not rename the actual database name and thus can still cause you to have a name conflict with other CRM organizations. If for some reason you already have an organization name conflict, then you can always disable and delete the conflicting organization from within the CRM cluster before importing an organization as long as you create or already have another organization within the CRM cluster that can be assigned as the default organization first. For our project, we will be importing our previous organization already named **crm**, so to avoid any organization name conflicts we will enter **crm2** for the both the **Display name** and **Name** fields, as shown in **Figure 21.6**.

    a. For the **ISO currency code** field, click on the **Browse** button, and then select the base currency for your CRM organization.

b. For the **SQL collation** field, you can leave at the default unless you have a different language to select, and then click on the **Next** button to continue.

14. On the **Help Us Improve the Customer Experience** screen, click on the **Next** button to continue.

15. On the **Select Installation Location** screen, you can leave the default location of **C:\Program Files\Microsoft Dynamics CRM** or enter the directory of your choice, and then click on the **Next** button to continue. For our project, we will leave the default location for our CRM install location.

## Installing the CRM Server Role- Selecting the Website

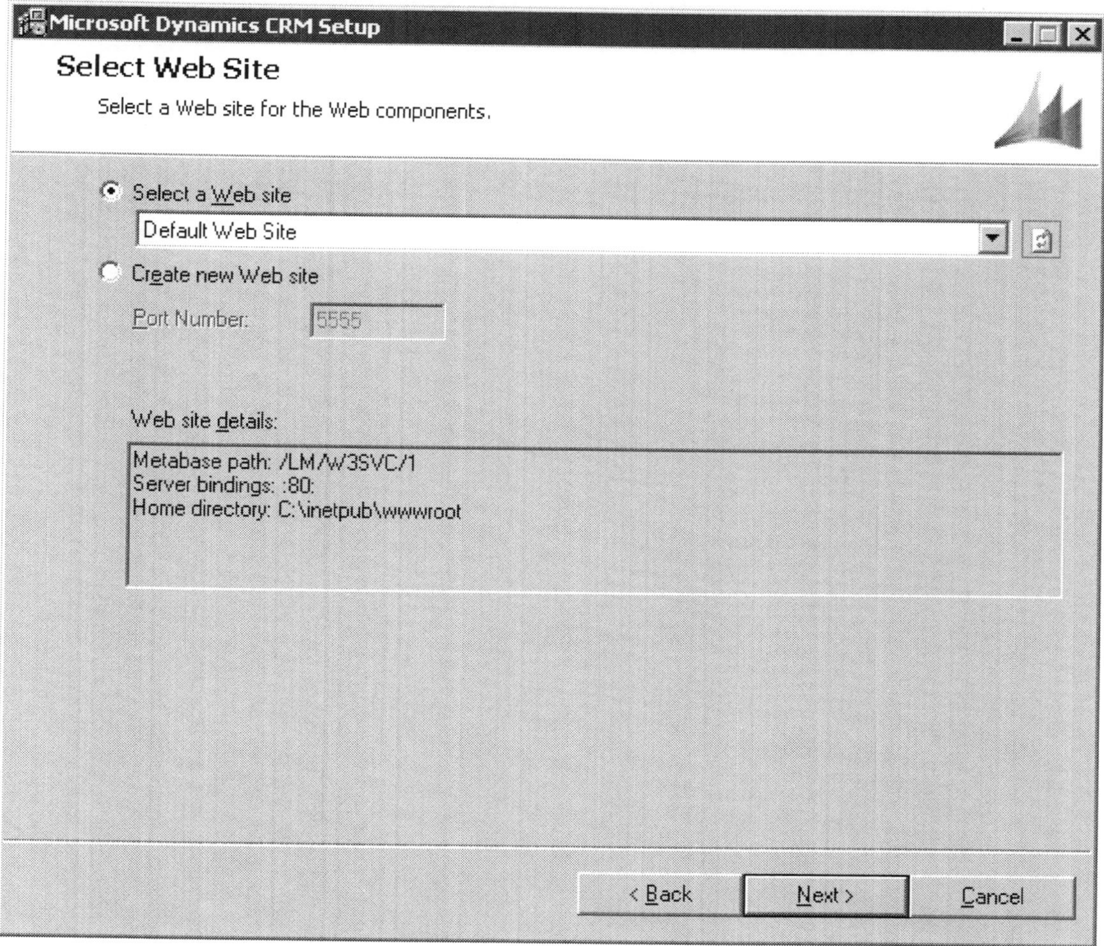


**Figure 21.7**

16. On the **Select Web Site** screen, you can leave the defaults or select the option to create a new website, and then click the **Next** button to continue. When selecting an existing site the CRM installation will overwrite the selected web site with CRM's configuration. If you're already using the default web site, then you will want to select the **Create new Web site** option. When selecting the **Create new Web site** option, it is recommended that you leave the default port number of **5555** unless you have a specific reason for changing it. For our project, we will select the **Default Web Site**, as shown in **Figure 21.7**.

## Installing the CRM Server Role- Specifying the Report Server URL

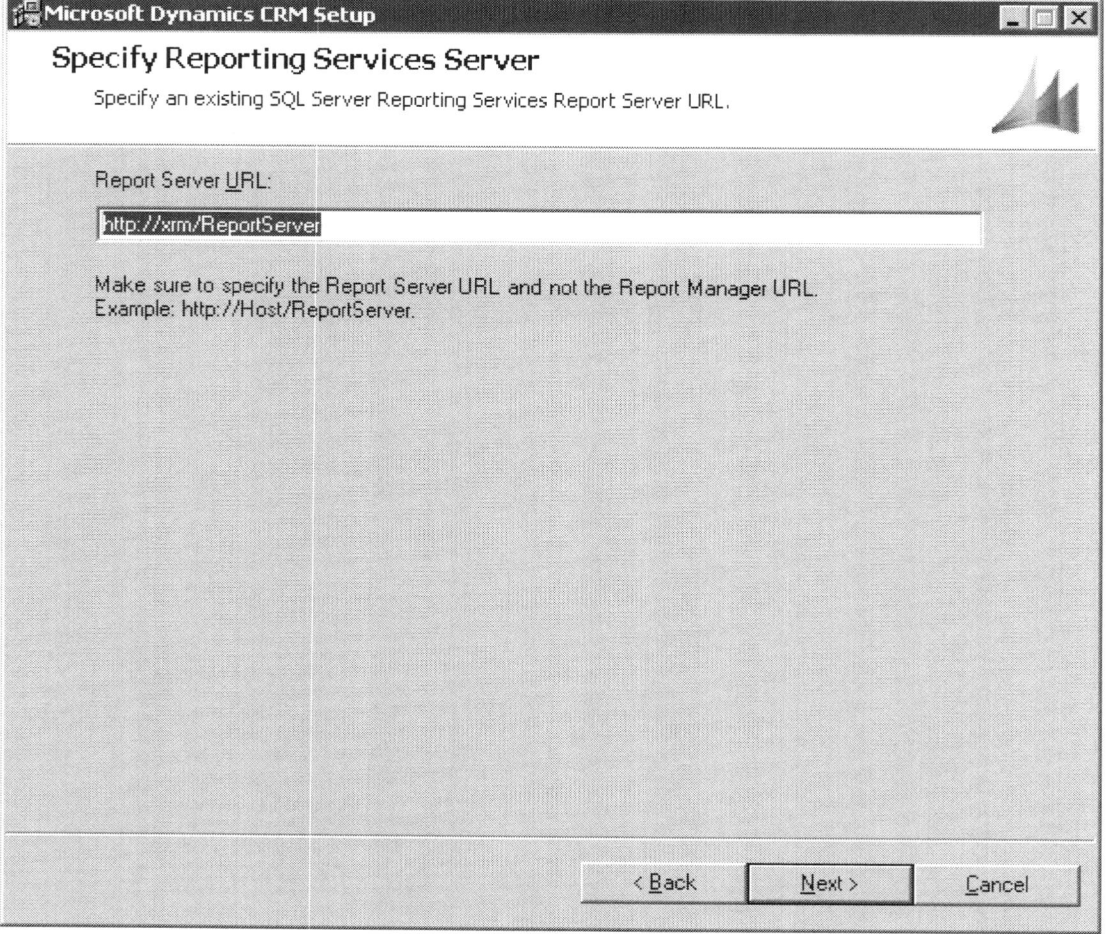


**Figure 21.8**

17. On the **Specify Reporting Services Server** screen, enter the URL for your **NLB Cluster's Report Server**, and then click on the **Next** button to continue. For our project, we will enter our NLB cluster's report server URL of **http://xrm/ReportServer**, as shown in **Figure 21.8**.

18. On the **Select the Organizational Unit** screen, click on the **Browse** button, and then select the **Organizational Unit (OU)** that you created earlier as a prerequisite. Click on the **Next** button to continue. CRM will create all its security accounts in this OU during the installation process. For our project, we will select the **OU** named **CRM_CLUSTER** that we created earlier in the prerequisites section of this chapter.

## Installing the CRM Server Role- Specifying the Security Account

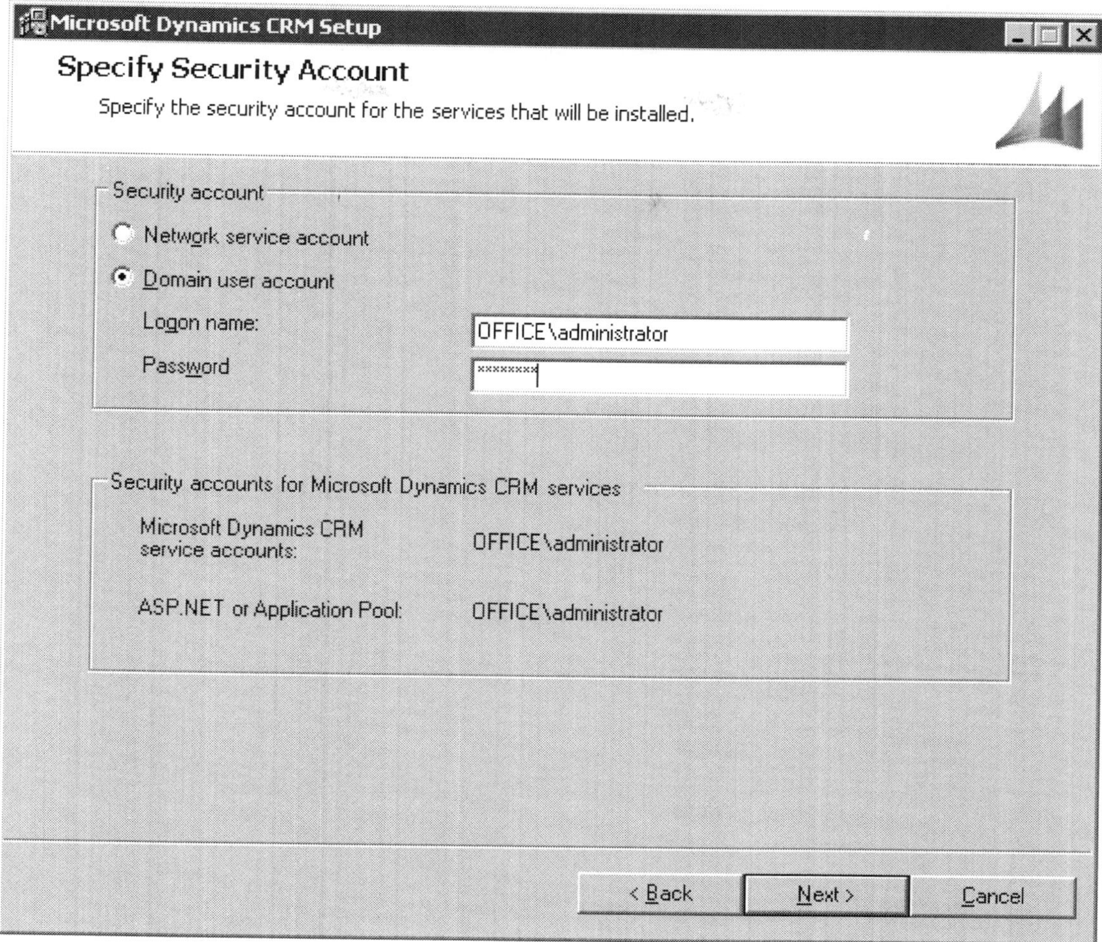


**Figure 21.9**

19. On the **Specify Security Account** screen, select the security account that your **Microsoft Dynamics CRM Service Accounts** and that your **ASP.NET Application Pool** will run under, and then click on the **Next** button to continue. For our project, we will initially use the **Domain Administrator** user account due to the complexity of using a different account for the ASP.NET application pool, as outlined in Microsoft's Knowledge Base Article# 329290. In Chapter 22 we will cover all the aspects of our CRM security including how to change our CRM services and ASP.NET Application Pool accounts to run under our CRM Service user account that we created in Chapter 20, Step 2.

## Installing the CRM Server Role- Understanding the CRM Email Router Role

Before specifying the CRM Email Router server name during the CRM Server role install there are some things to consider in the below bullet points concerning the router and its email functionality.

- The CRM Email Router role is a separate install from the CRM Server role install that we are running currently and can be installed on any server of your choice including servers that don't host any other CRM components.

- Once the CRM Email Router has been configured it will give you the ability to send emails directly from within CRM as well as providing you with three different upload options for CRM to upload your users email messages from their Microsoft Outlook and/or Exchange Web Mail.

- The CRM Email Router role does not support high availability out of the box, however we'll easily overcome this limitation in our project by utilizing a generic clustered service. We will cover all the steps in setting up our CRM E-mail Router in Chapter 27.

- The CRM Server role install only allows you to specify one server's name during the install process, however you can always specify a different server and/or add additional servers by adding the new server(s) computer account(s) to the PrivUserGroup CRM security group.

## Requirements for Clustering the CRM Email Router Service

- Requires a Windows active/passive cluster, this means that your CRM Email Router service cannot be installed on your CRM front-end CSV virtual machines as this is a different type of cluster. For our project, we will install our clustered CRM Email Router on our back-end SQL servers. This details of this decision are explained in Chapter 27.

- Requires a very small but dedicated shared disk on your SAN. Any Windows active/passive clustered application or service requires its own dedicated disk on the SAN.

## Installing the CRM Server Role- Specifying the CRM Email Router Server

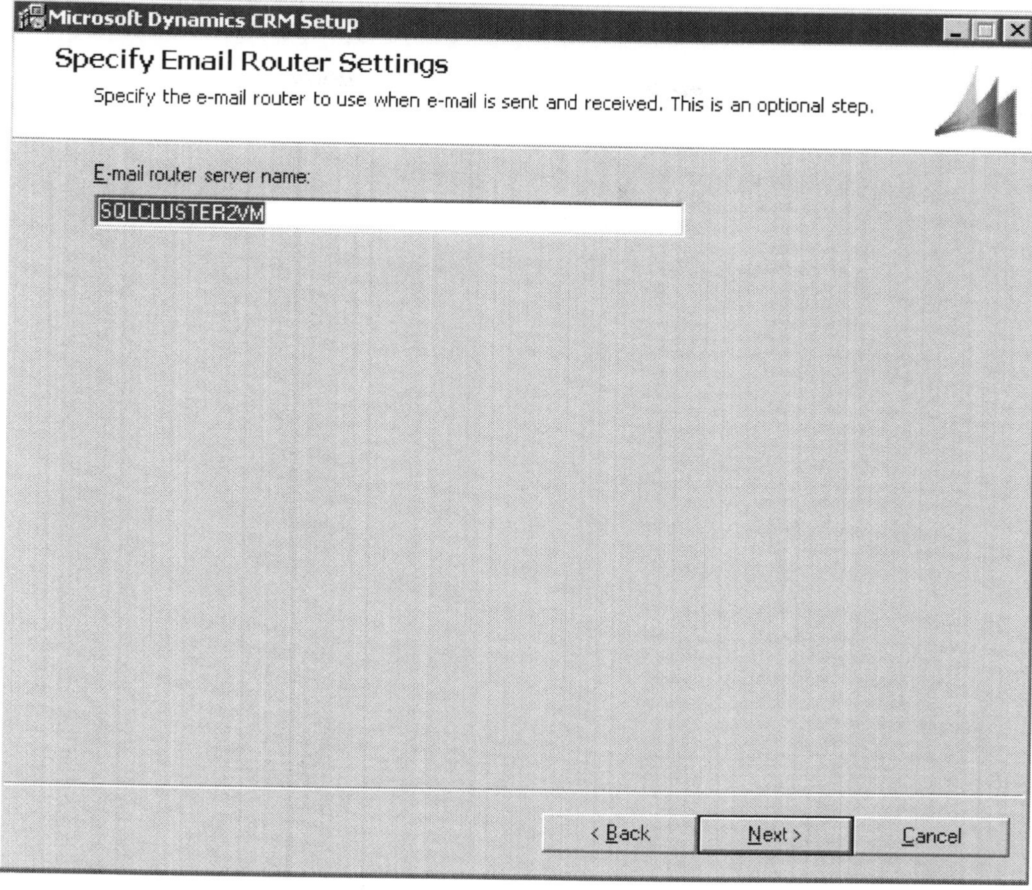


**Figure 21.10**

20. On the **Specify Email Router Settings** screen, enter your server's name that you will install the **CRM Email Router role** on, and then click on the **Next** button to continue. If don't plan on utilizing the CRM Email Router, then you can leave this field blank. For our project, we will enter our **WinSQLCluster** node's name of **SQLCLUSTER2VM** into the **E-mail router server name** field, as shown in **Figure 21.10**.

# Installing the CRM Server Role- Verifying System Requirements

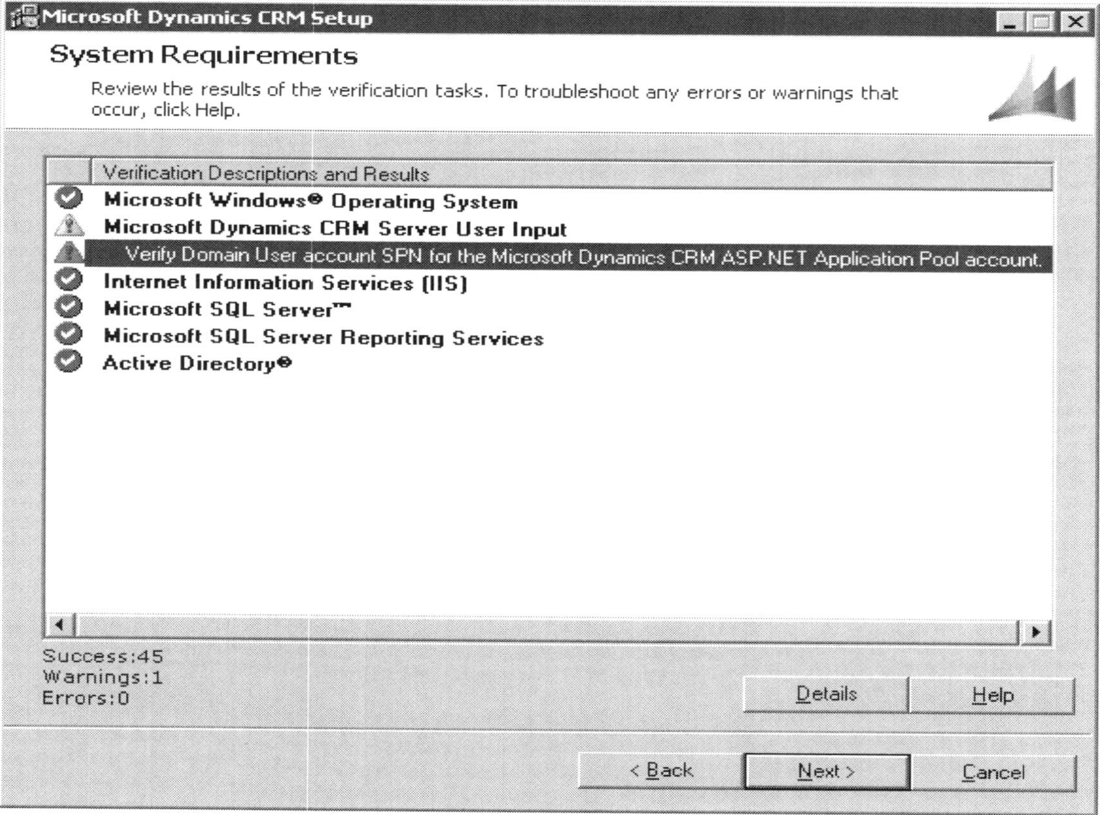


**Figure 21.11**

21. On the **System Requirements** screen, verify that there are no **Red X Errors**, and then click on the **Next** button to continue. You may notice that we received a **Warning** stating **Verify Domain User account SPN for the Microsoft Dynamics ASP.NET Application Pool account**. This warning simply references that our SPNs still need to be setup, which we will configure in Chapter 22 with the rest of our CRM security settings. If you already have your SPNs setup don't be surprised if you receive this warning anyway, as Microsoft's install unfortunately seems to pull this warning regardless. If you receive any other warnings at this screen you can safely disregard them and continue on with the installation, however you will have to resolve the warnings shown here after your installation has completed. If you receive any red X errors on this screen, then you will need to cancel out of the installation and resolve the errors before attempting to re-run the installation.

22. On the **Ready to Install Microsoft Dynamics CRM** screen, verify your configuration, and then click on the **Install** button to continue. You can always click on the **Back** button you if you need to correct any errors.

23. On the **Microsoft Dynamics CRM Server install Completed** screen, click on the **Finish** button to complete the install, and then restart the server. This concludes the CRM Server install on the initial NLB cluster node.

# Installing Microsoft Dynamics CRM 4.0 Server Role on the Remaining NLB Cluster Nodes

Now that we have completed our Microsoft Dynamics CRM 4.0 Server role installation on our initial NLB cluster node we can proceed to install CRM on our remaining NLB cluster nodes to make our CRM application highly available. During the initial install of CRM we created a CRM deployment that we now will connect our remaining NLB cluster nodes to. You'll want to pay close attention to the next steps, as they are quite a bit different from the steps we followed during the initial NLB cluster node's install.

# Prerequisites- Installing Windows Roles

24. Logon to each of your remaining NLB cluster nodes that will host the **Microsoft Dynamics CRM 4.0 Server Role**. You want to logon with the same user account that you did on the initial CRM cluster node.
    a. Open Windows **Server Manager**, right click on the **Roles** node in the left pane, and then select the **Add Roles** option.
    b. On the **Before You Begin** screen, click on the **Next** button to continue.
    c. Select the checkbox for the following roles, and then click on the **Next** button to continue.
        i. **Application Server**
        ii. **File Services**
    d. On the **Application Server** screen, click on the **Next** button to continue.
    e. On the **Select Roles Services** for the **Application Server** screen, select the checkbox next to **Web Server (IIS) Support** to launch the **Add Roles Wizard**.
    f. On the **Add Roles Wizard** screen, click on the **Add Required Role Services** button to continue
    g. On the **Select Roles Services** screen, click on the **Next** button to continue.
    h. On the **Select Roles Services** for the **Web Server (IIS)** screen, leave all the existing checkboxes, and then select the checkbox next to **IIS 6 Management Compatibility**. Click on the **Next** button to continue.
    i. On the **File Services** screen, click on the **Next** button to continue.
    j. On the **Select Roles Services** for the **File Services** screen, select the checkbox next to **Indexing Service**, and then click on the **Next** button to continue.
    k. On the **Confirm Installation Selections** screen, click on the **Install** button to continue.

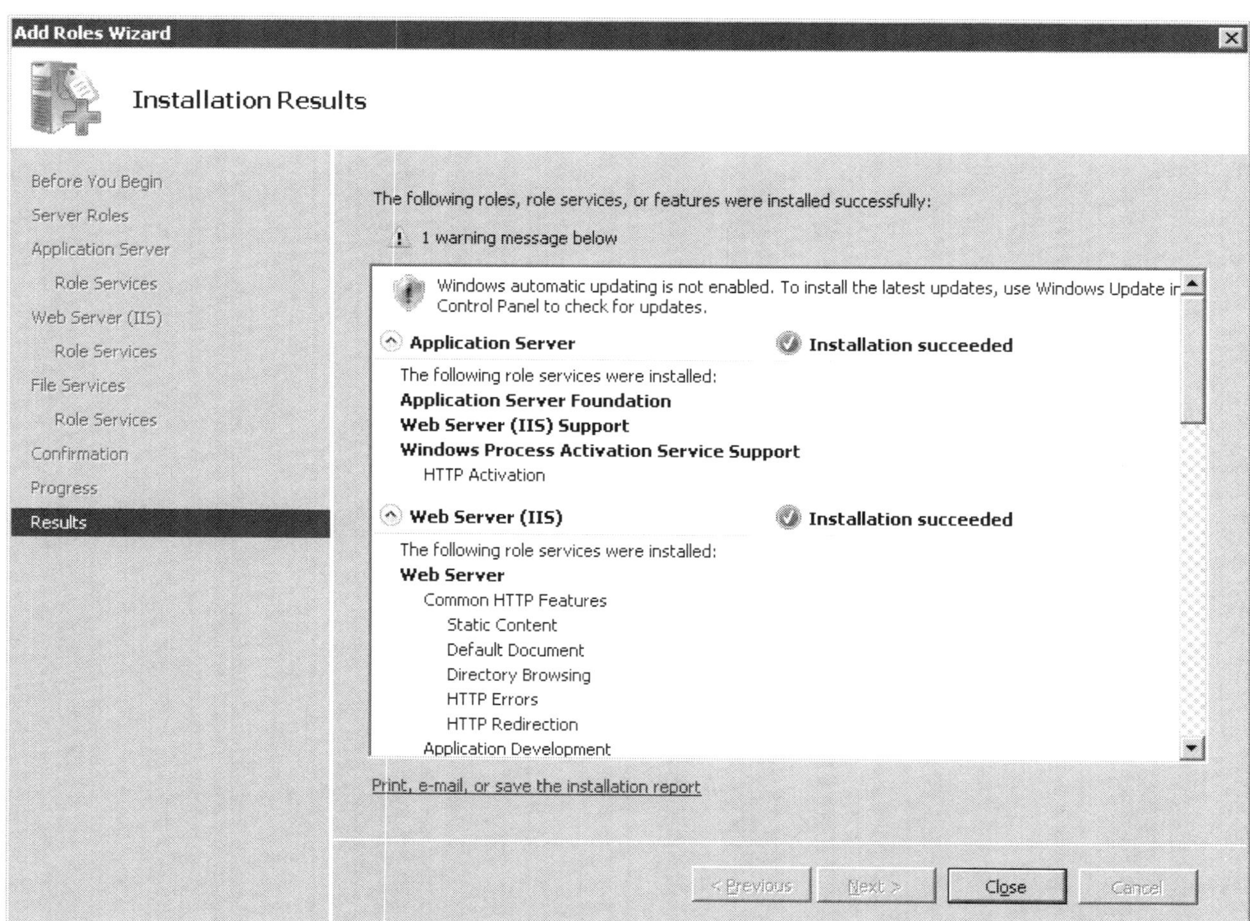


**Figure 21.12**

1. On the **Installation Results** screen, verify that all the components were successfully installed, and then click on the **Close** button to complete the installation.

## Installing the CRM Server Role- Launching the Install

25. Copy the **Microsoft Dynamics CRM 4.0** installation media onto a local drive of your remaining NLB cluster node(s).

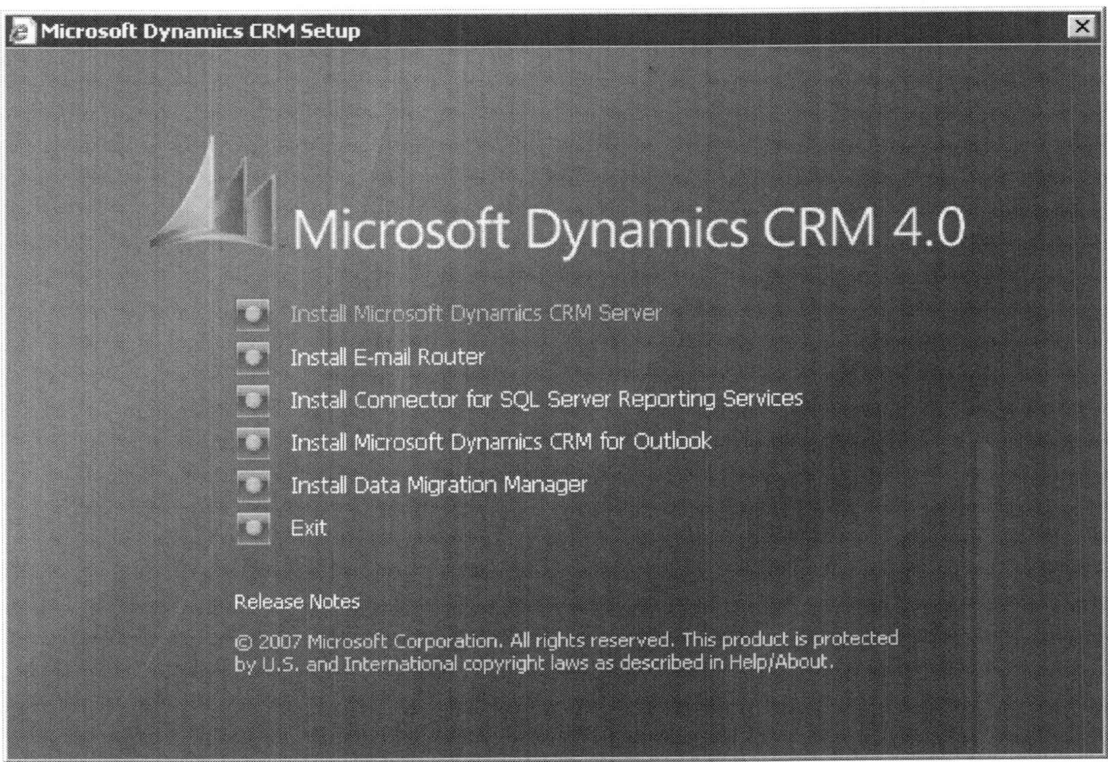


**Figure 21.13**

26. Launch the CRM 4.0 install by inserting the DVD or by double clicking on the **Splash.exe** in the root of the install files.

27. On the **Microsoft Dynamics CRM Setup** screen, select the **Install Microsoft Dynamics CRM Server** option, as shown in **Figure 21.13**.

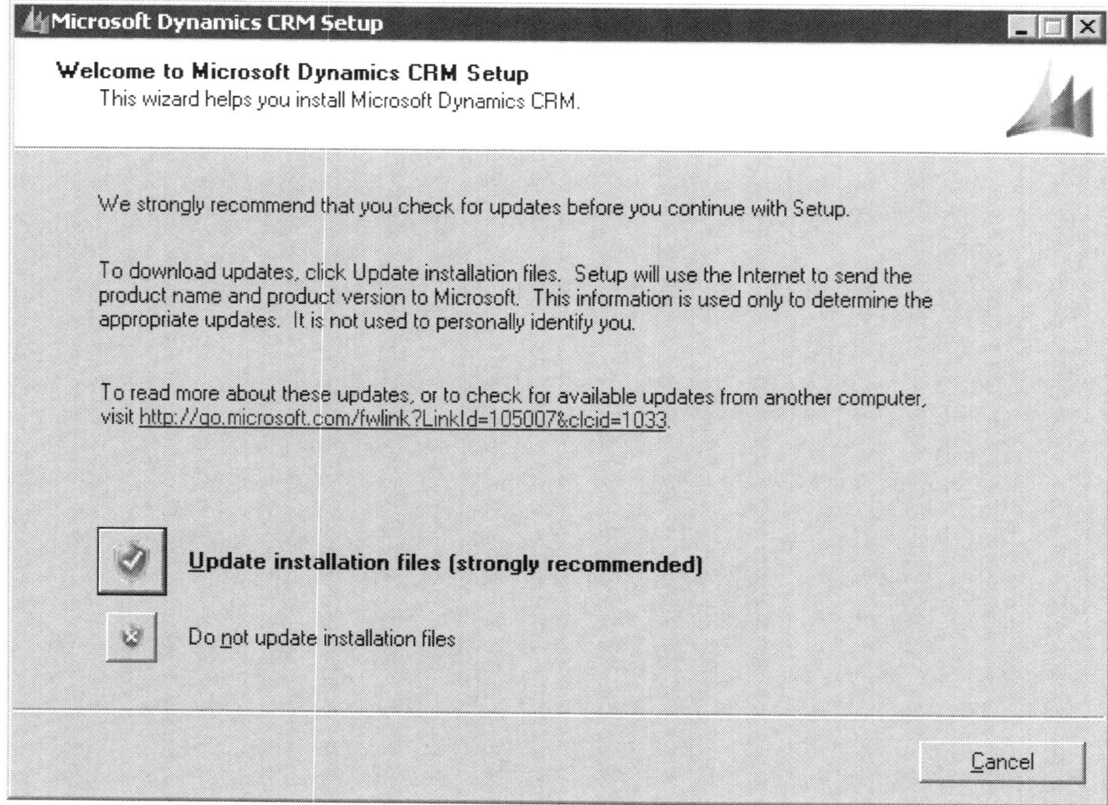


**Figure 21.14**

28. On the **Welcome to Microsoft Dynamics CRM Setup** screen, click on the **Update installation files (strongly recommended)** button.

29. On the **Checking for Update** screen, click on the **Next** button to continue.

30. On the **License Code Information** screen, enter your license number, and then click on the **Next** button to continue.

31. On the **License Agreement** screen, select the **I accept this license agreement** option, and then click on the **I Accept** button to continue.

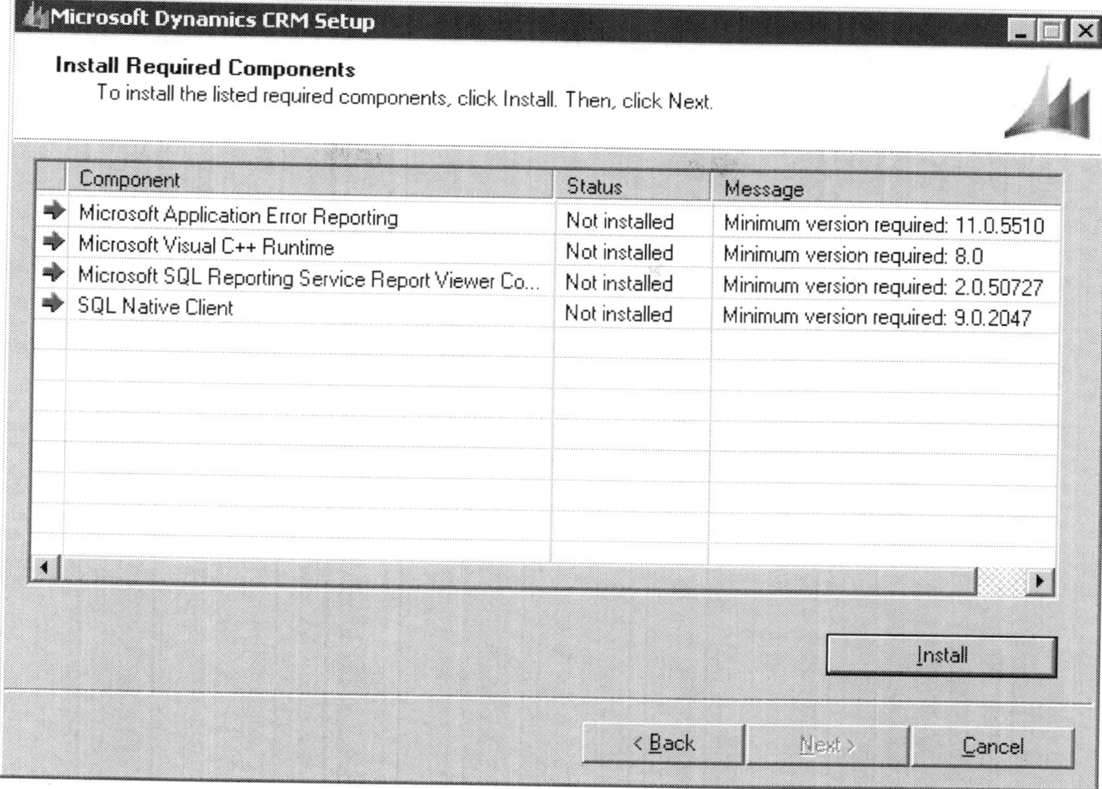


**Figure 21.15**

32. On the **Install Required Components** screen, click on the **Install** button to continue.

33. Verify that all the components installed successfully, and then click on the **Next** button to continue.

## Installing the CRM Server Role- Specifying Install Type

34. If you are installing the **Enterprise** version of **Microsoft Dynamics CRM 4.0**, then a **Specify Setup Type** screen will appear where you can select either a **Typical** or **Custom** install type. If you are installing the **Standard** version of CRM 4.0, then please disregard this step. For our project, we will select the **Typical** install option to install all components of the CRM Server role.

# Installing the CRM Server Role- Connecting to an Existing Deployment

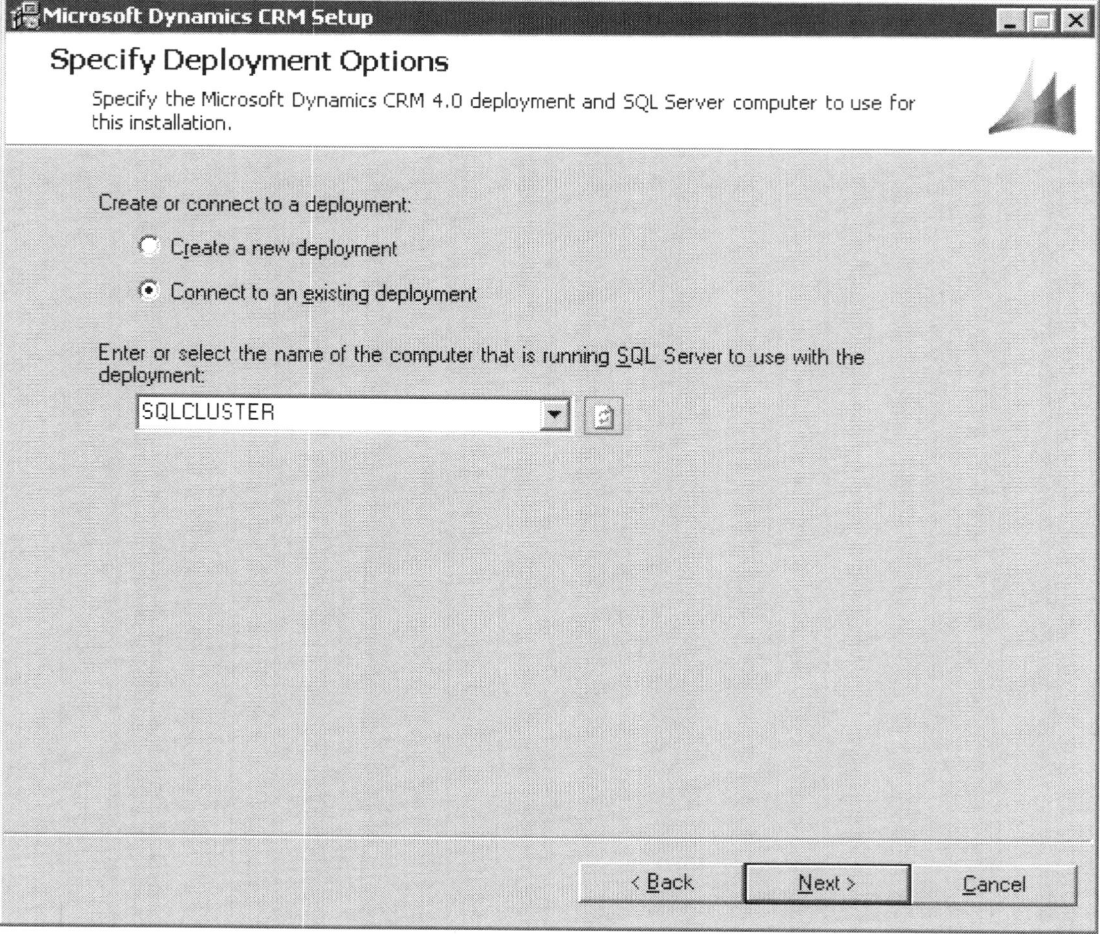


**Figure 21.16**

35. On the **Specify Deployment Options** screen, select the **Connect to an existing deployment** option.

    a. For the **Enter or select the name of the computer that is running SQL Server to use with the deployment** field, enter your SQL cluster's name or click on the **Browse** button to select your SQL cluster's name, and then click the on **Next** button to continue. For our project, we will enter our SQL cluster's name of **SQLCLUSTER**, as shown in **Figure 21.16**.

36. On the **Help Us Improve the Customer Experience** screen, click on the **Next** button to continue.

37. On the **Select Installation Location** screen, leave the default location of **C:\Program Files\Microsoft Dynamics CRM** or enter the directory of your choice, and then click on the **Next** button to continue. For our project, we will leave the default location for our CRM install location.

# Installing the CRM Server Role- Selecting the Website

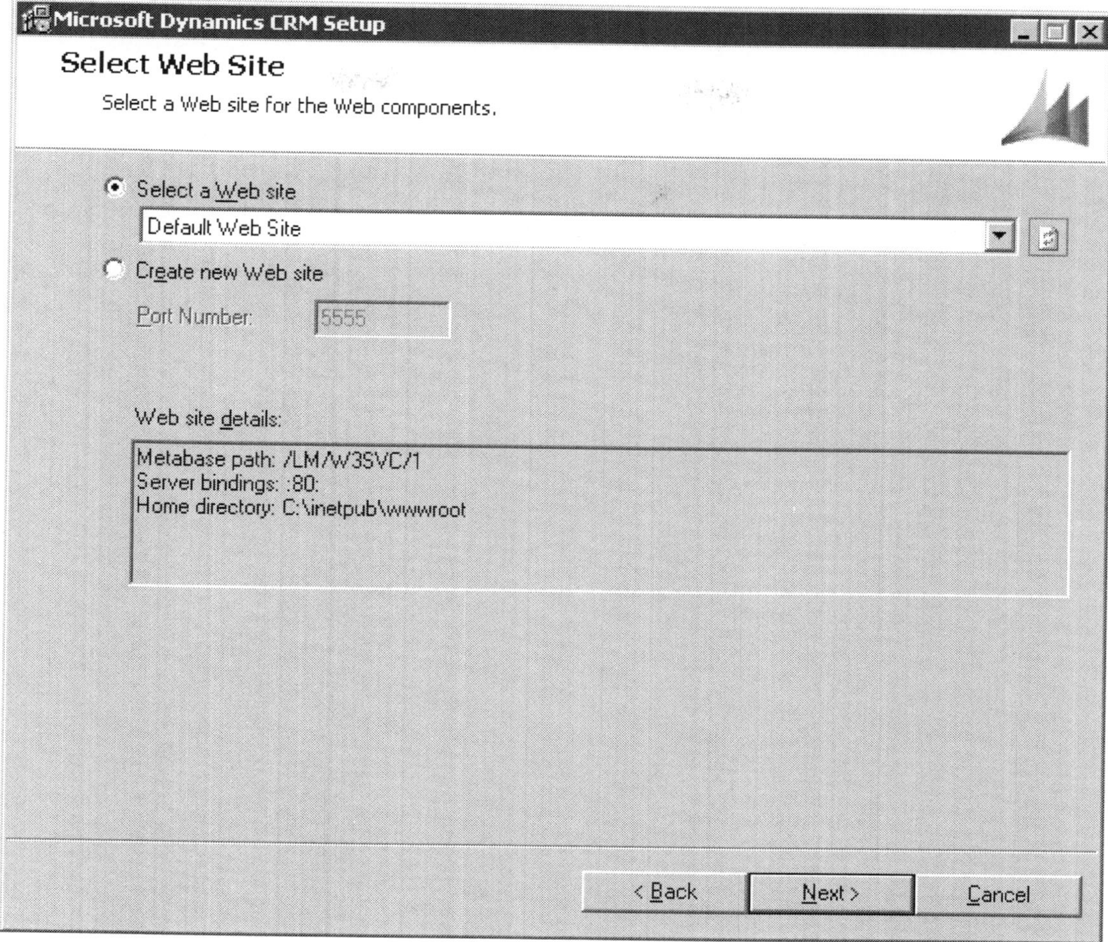


**Figure 21.17**

38. On the **Select Web Site** screen, you can leave the defaults or select the option to create a new website, and then click the **Next** button to continue. When selecting an existing site the CRM installation will overwrite the selected web site with CRM's configuration. If you're already using the default web site, then you will want to select the **Create new Web site** option. When selecting the **Create new Web site** option it is recommended that you leave the default port number of **5555** unless you have a specific reason for changing it. For our project, we will select the **Default Web Site**, as shown in **Figure 21.17**.

## Installing the CRM Server Role- Specifying the Report Server URL

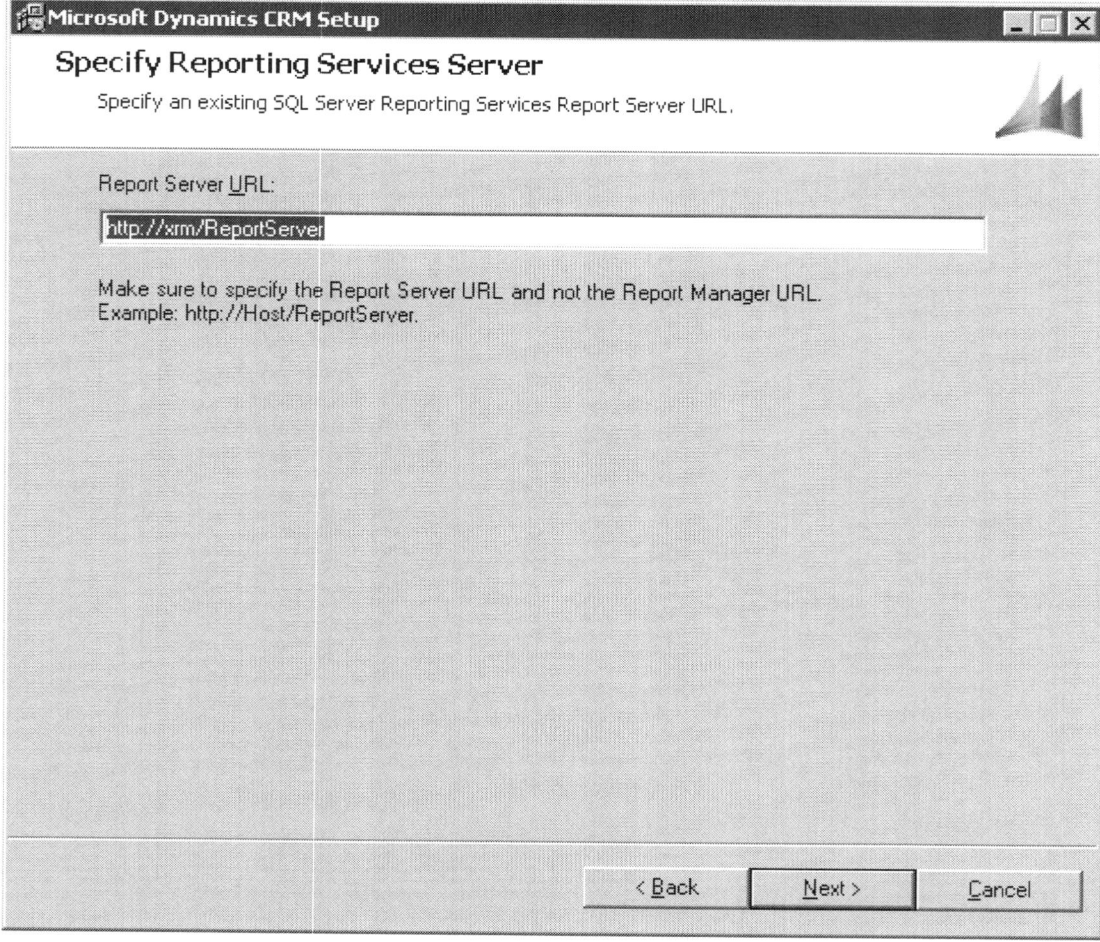


**Figure 21.18**

39. On the **Specify Reporting Services Server** screen, enter the URL for your **NLB Cluster's Report Server**, and then click on the **Next** button to continue. For our project, we will enter our NLB cluster's report server URL of **http://xrm/ReportServer**, as shown in **Figure 21.18**.

# Installing the CRM Server Role- Specifying the Security Account

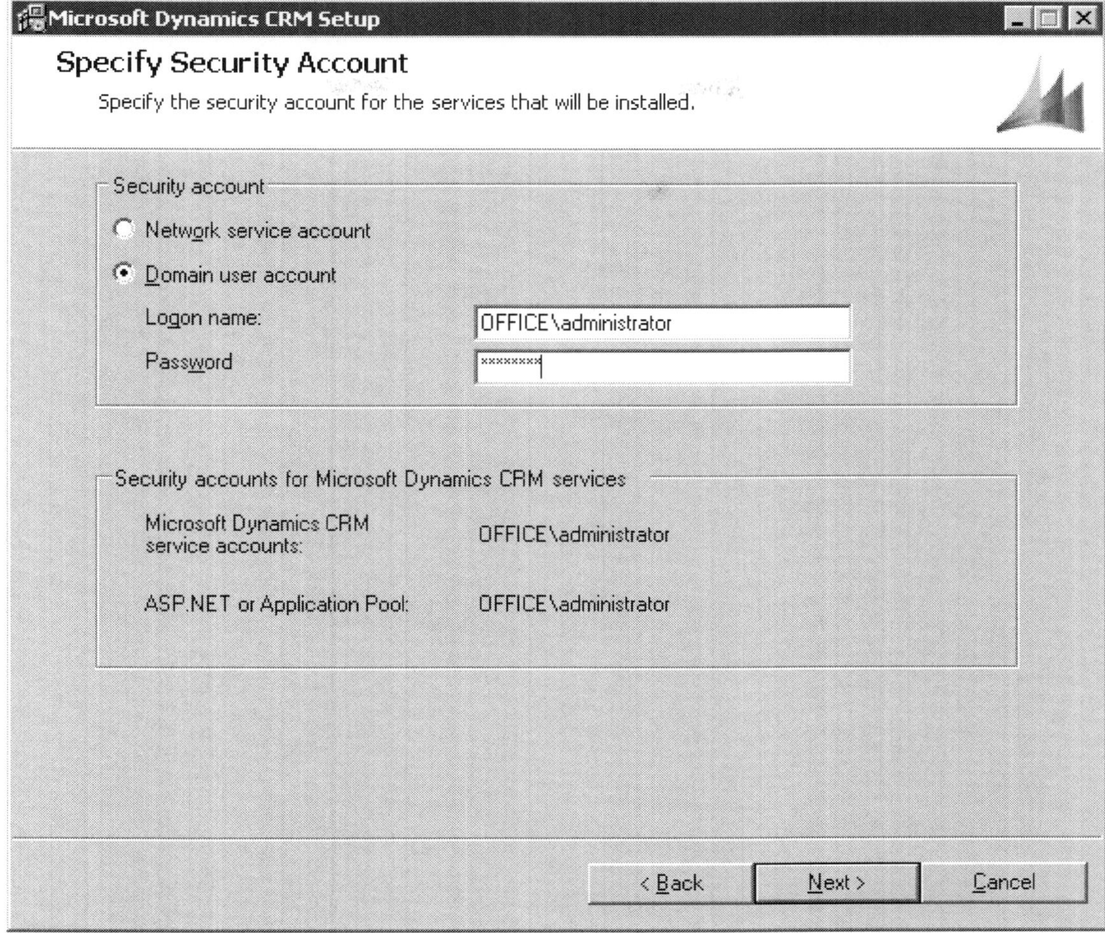


**Figure 21.19**

40. On the **Specify Security Account** screen, select the security account that your **Microsoft Dynamics CRM Service Accounts** and that your **ASP.NET Application Pool** will run under, and then click on the **Next** button to continue. For our project, we will initially use the **Domain Administrator** user account due to the complexity of using a different account for the ASP.NET application pool, as outlined in **Microsoft's Knowledge Base Article# 329290**. In Chapter 22 we will cover all the aspects of our CRM security including how to change our CRM services and ASP.NET Application Pool accounts to run under our CRM Service user account that we created in Chapter 20, Step 2.

## Installing the CRM Server Role- Specifying the CRM Email Router Server

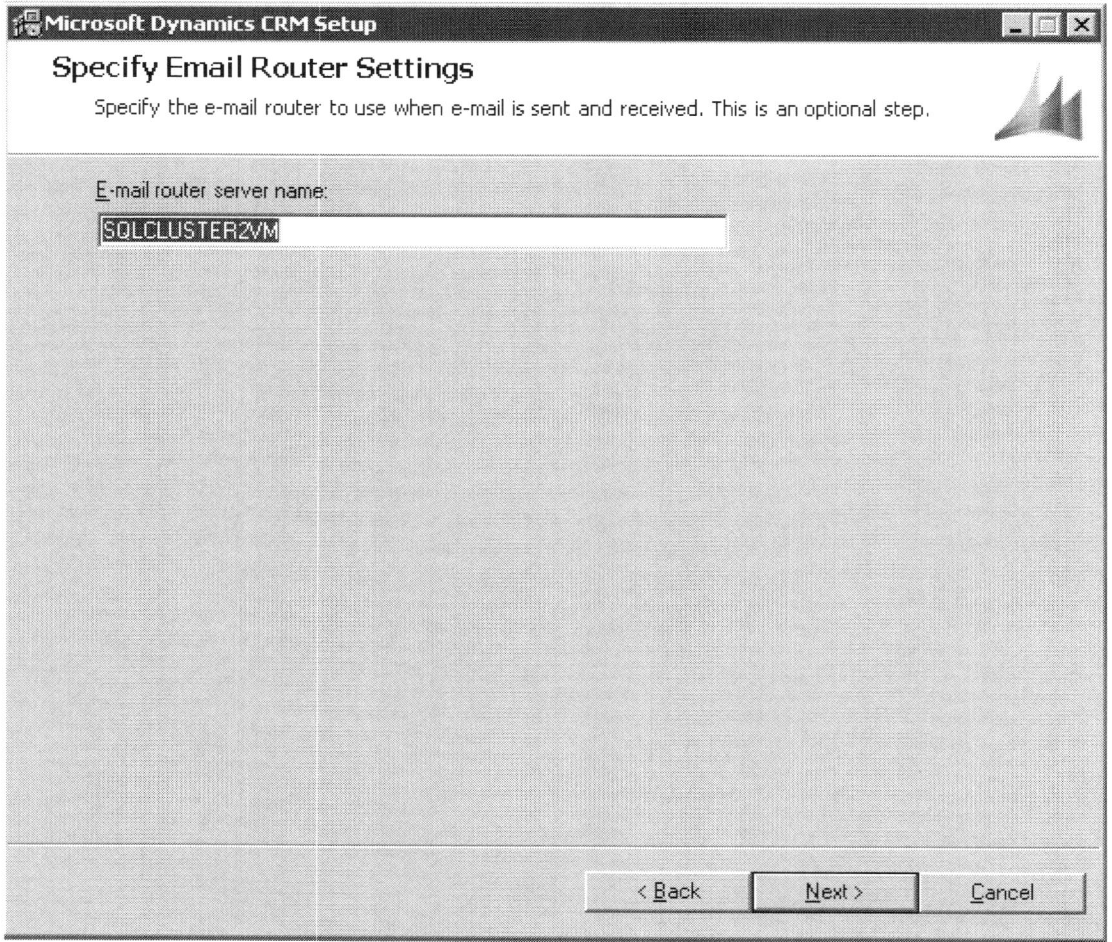


**Figure 21.20**

41. On the **Specify Email Router Settings** screen, enter your server's name that you will install the **CRM Email Router role** on, and then click on the **Next** button to continue. If don't plan on utilizing the CRM Email Router, then you can leave this field blank. For our project, we will enter our **WinSQLCluster** node's name of **SQLCLUSTER2VM** into the **E-mail router server name** field, as shown in **Figure 21.20**.

# Installing the CRM Server Role- Verifying System Requirements

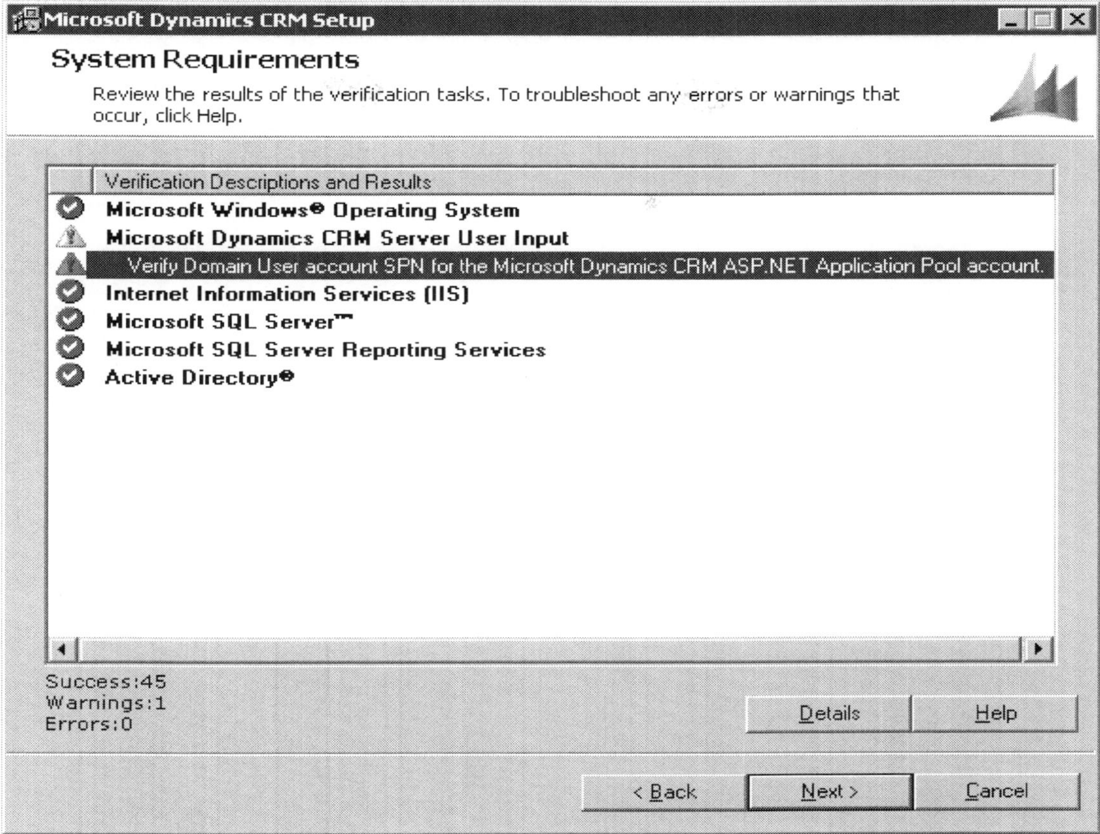


**Figure 21.21**

42. On the **System Requirements** screen, verify that there are no **Red X Errors**, and then click on the **Next** button to continue. If you receive any **Warnings** on this screen you can safely disregard them for now and continue on with the installation, however you will want to resolve any warnings listed here after the installation has completed. If you receive any **Red X Errors** on this screen, then you will need to cancel out of the installation and resolve any errors listed here before attempting to re-run the installation.

43. On the **Ready to Install Microsoft Dynamics CRM** screen, verify your configuration, and then click on the **Install** button to continue. You can always click on the **Back** button you if you need to correct any errors.

44. On the **Microsoft Dynamics CRM Server install Completed** screen, click on the **Finish** button to complete the install, and then restart the server. This concludes the CRM Server install on the second NLB cluster node.

45. Repeat **Steps 25-44** for any remaining NLB cluster nodes that you'd like the CRM 4.0 installed on. For our project, we will repeat these steps for our third and final NLB cluster node named **CRMCluster3VM**. For high availability you only technically need to have two front-end application servers, however adding additional nodes further distributes the workload and increases redundancy.

## Verifying the Install from within the CRM Deployment Manager

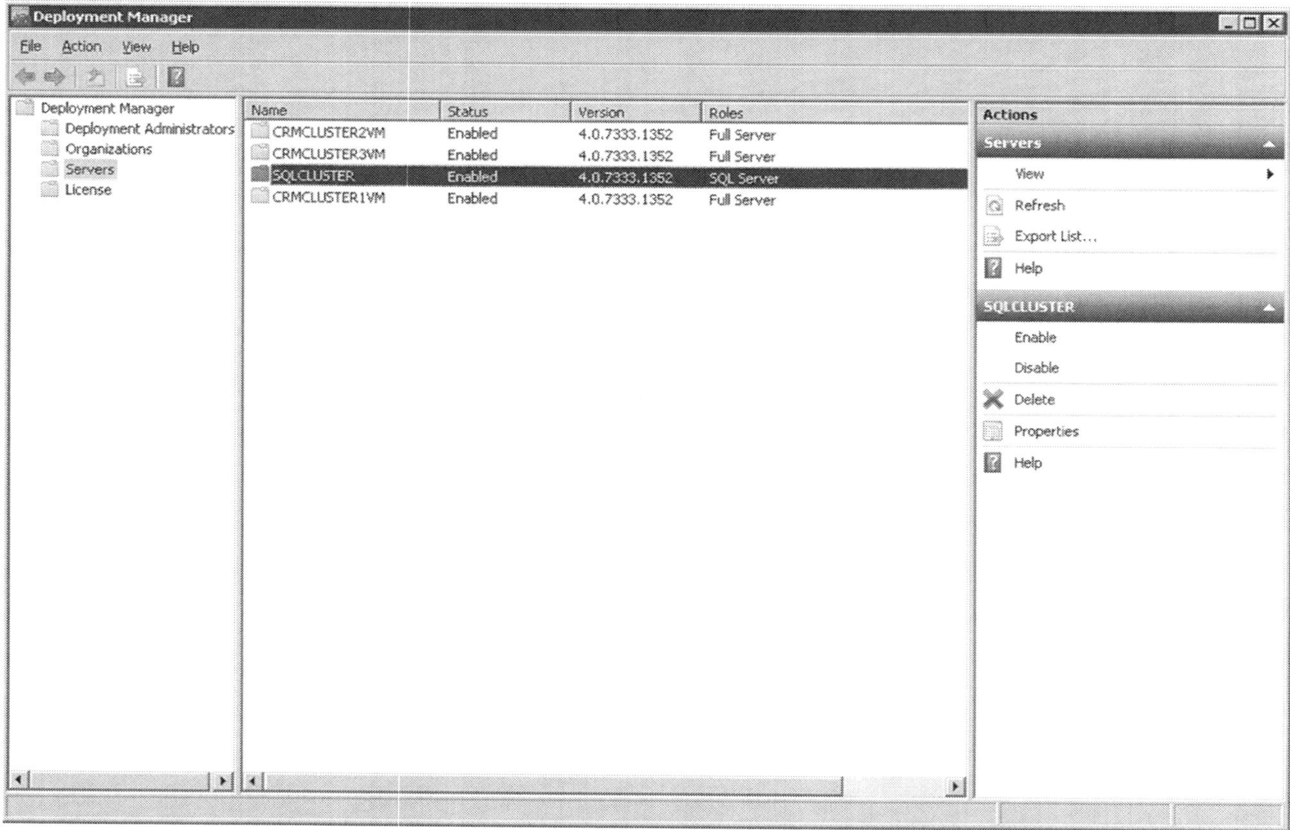


**Figure 21.22**

46. Once you have the CRM installed on each of your NLB cluster nodes, go to **Start\All Program\Microsoft Dynamics CRM\Deployment Manager** on each of your CRM NLB cluster nodes, and then verify that each of your servers show the **Status** of **Enabled**. If any of your servers listed don't show as enabled, then right click on the server, and select the **Enable** option to bring it online. Once complete with this chapter, your CRM **Deployment Manager** console should appear similar to **Figure 21.22**. You may have noticed that only the active SQL cluster node along with the SQL cluster's name appears in the CRM Deployment Manager console. The SQL cluster node shown in the CRM Deployment Manager console depends on which node is currently active. If you failed over your SQL cluster to your passive node then that node's name would appear within the console once refreshed.

# Chapter 22: Configuring Microsoft Dynamics CRM 4.0 Security Settings

Learning how to configure the security settings on an enterprise application with multiple servers involved can be one of the most challenging parts of your deployment. For this reason, we will dedicate this full chapter to configuring the security of our Microsoft Dynamics CRM 4.0 deployment. During most of our project's CRM deployment process we used the domain administrator user account. By using the domain administrator user account in our project's previous steps it gives us an opportunity to explain how to tighten the security on each of our CRM components. Once you are finished with this chapter, your CRM application will be secure and you will have a significantly better overall understanding of your CRM deployment's security settings.

## Overview of the CRM 4.0 Active Directory Security Groups Created During the Installation

Before we begin tightening the security on our CRM 4.0 application, we will cover the roles that each CRM security group plays. The following will give you a better understanding of each security group that CRM created in your Active Directory Organizational Unit (OU).

- **PrivReportingGroup**- Privileged Microsoft Dynamics CRM user group for reporting functions. This group is created during Server role install and is configured during SRS Data Connector setup.

- **PrivUserGroup**- This group is for special administrative functions of CRM. Users who need to be able to configure the Microsoft Dynamics CRM Server must be part of this group, as well as the user accounts that CRM Application Pool (CRMAppPool) identity and that the CRM Email Router service run under.

- **SQLAccessGroup**- All service accounts and server processes that require access to SQL server need to be part of this group. This includes the domain user or Network Service account that the CRMAppPool identity runs under. Full access to the Microsoft CRM database is granted to members of this group. This group is used by the Microsoft CRM platform layer and your CRM end users should never be part of this group.

- **ReportingGroup**- All Microsoft Dynamics CRM users are part of this group. The users in this group are updated automatically as users are added or removed from Microsoft Dynamics CRM. By default, this group has browse permissions for all Microsoft Dynamics CRM reports and read only access to filtered views in the Microsoft CRM database.

- **UserGroup**- All Microsoft Dynamics CRM users are part of this group. The users in this group are updated automatically as users are added or removed from Microsoft Dynamics CRM.

## Configuring Active Directory User and Computer Accounts for CRM 4.0

Earlier in our project we installed the CRM 4.0 Server role on each of our NLB cluster nodes while logged on with the Domain Administrator account. We will now tighten our CRM 4.0 security by further utilizing our CRM service user account that we created earlier in Chapter 20 when installing our SQL Server Reporting Services (SSRS). For our project, we called this account CRMService, and then set our SSRS service to run under this account. We will use this same user account to tighten the security in our CRM deployment.

## Moving the CRM Service User Account into the CRM Organizational Unit (OU)

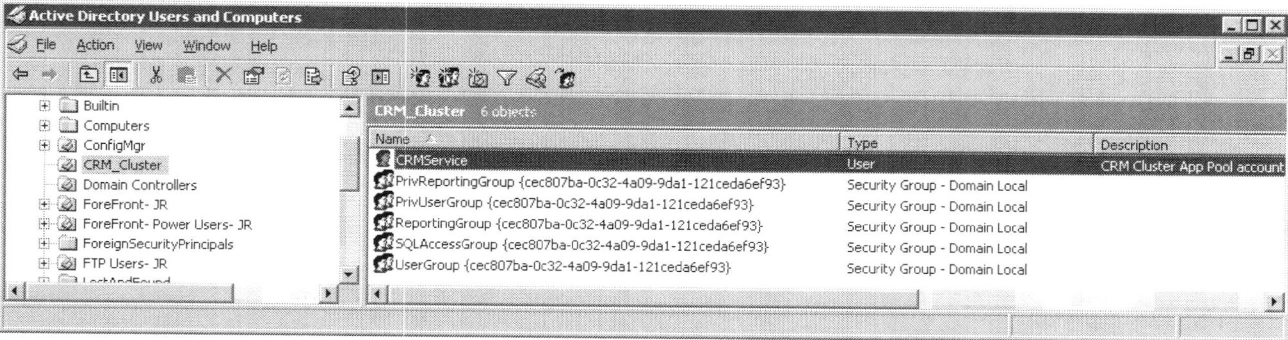


**Figure 22.1**

1. Go to your domain controller, open the **Active Directory User and Computers** console, and then highlight the **Users** Organizational Unit in the left pane.

    a. In the right pane find your CRM service user account that you created earlier for our **SQL Reporting Services**, and then right click on it and select the **Move** option.

        i. Browse to the **Organizational Unit** that you created for your CRM security groups, and then click on the **OK** button to move the user account. For our project, we will move our user account named **CRMService** into our CRM Organizational Unit named **CRM_CLUSTER**, as shown in **Figure 22.1**.

## Assigning Group Membership to the CRM Service User Account

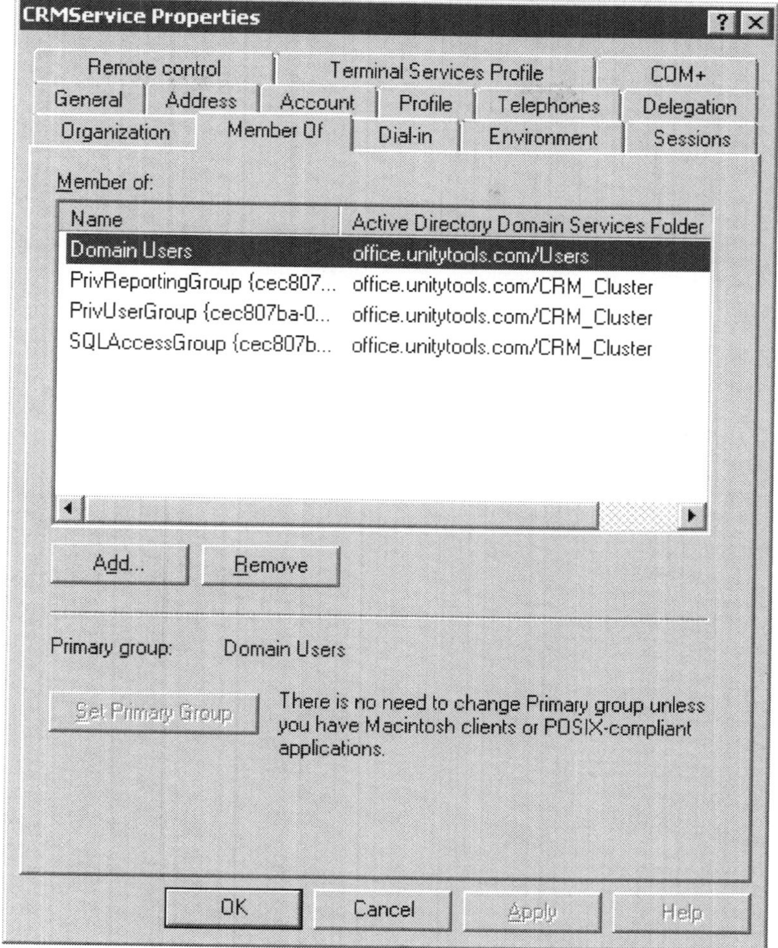


**Figure 22.2**

2. While still in the **Active Directory User and Computers** console, browse to your **CRM Organizational Unit** in the left pane, and then highlight it to view its members. For our project, we will highlight our CRM **Organizational Unit** named **CRM_CLUSTER**.

   a. Double click on your CRM service user account to open its **Properties** screen.

      i. Select the **Member Of** tab, and then click on the **Add** button. Add or verify that your CRM service account is a member of the following groups listed below. For our project, we will verify and/or add our **CRMService** user account as member of the following groups listed below, and as shown in **Figure 22.2**.

         - **Domain Users**
         - **PrivReportingGroup**
         - **PrivUserGroup**
         - **SQLAccessGroup**

# Adding and Verifying Members of the Active Directory CRM Security Groups

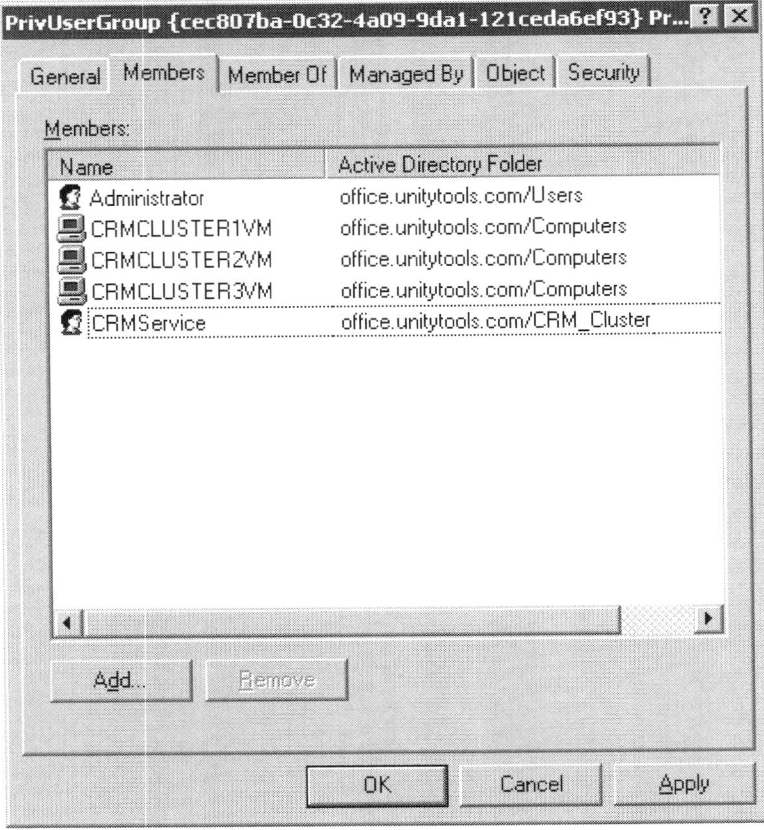


**Figure 22.3**

3. While still in your CRM's Organizational Unit, double click on the **PrivUserGroup** group, and then select the **Members** tab. Verify and/or add your **Domain Administrator's** user account, your **CRM Service** user account, and each of your NLB cluster node's **Computer Accounts** as members of your CRM **PrivUserGroup**. For our project, we verify and/or add our **Domain Administrator** user account, **CRMService** user account, **CRMCluster1VM** computer account, **CRMCluster2VM** computer account, and our **CRMCluster3VM** computer accounts as members of our CRM's **PrivUserGroup**, as shown in **Figure 22.3**.

## Adding and Verifying Members of the CRM NLB Cluster Node Local Groups

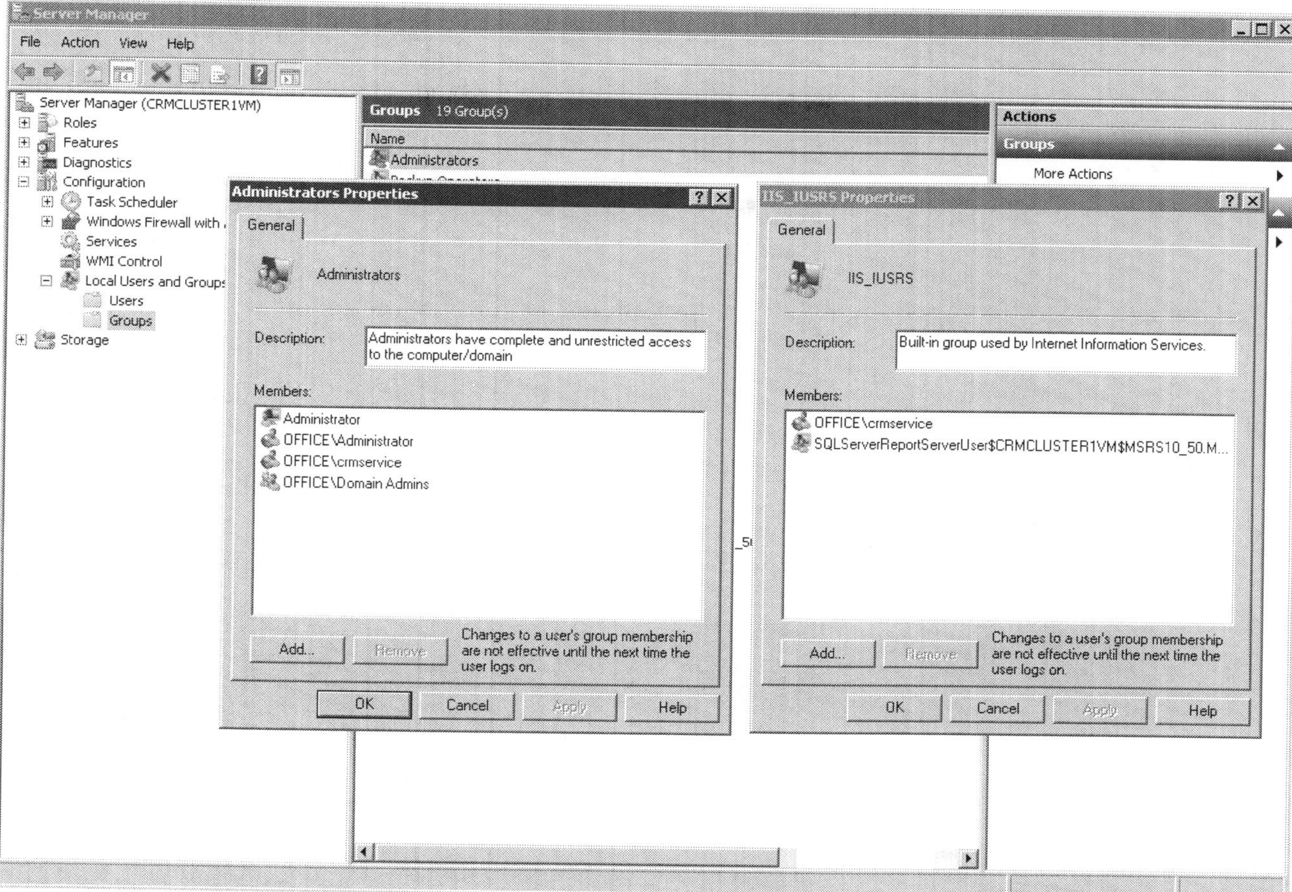


**Figure 22.4**

4. On each of your CRM NLB cluster nodes, open the Windows **Server Manager** console, and then add your **CRM service** user account to the local **Administrators** and **IIS_IUSRS** groups. For our project, we will add our CRM service user account named **CRMService** to both local groups, as shown in **Figure 22.4**.

## Configuring CRM 4.0 Services- Understanding the Roles of each Service

Before we begin tightening the security of our CRM services we will cover the role that each service plays for different CRM functions. There are different services that will be installed depending on what CRM roles are installed on each server. The Microsoft Dynamics CRM Asynchronous Processing Service is installed with the CRM Server role, while the Microsoft CRM Email Router service is installed with the CRM Email Router role. The following will give you a better understanding of the functions that each CRM service performs.

- **Microsoft Dynamics CRM Asynchronous Processing Service**- Handles asynchronous processes such as workflow, bulk email and database clean up.

- **Microsoft CRM Email Router**- Sends out email and tracks CRM related emails. The CRM email router filters through CRM users' Exchange and POP email in order to upload CRM related email based on the criteria you set.

## Configuring CRM 4.0 Services- User Accounts

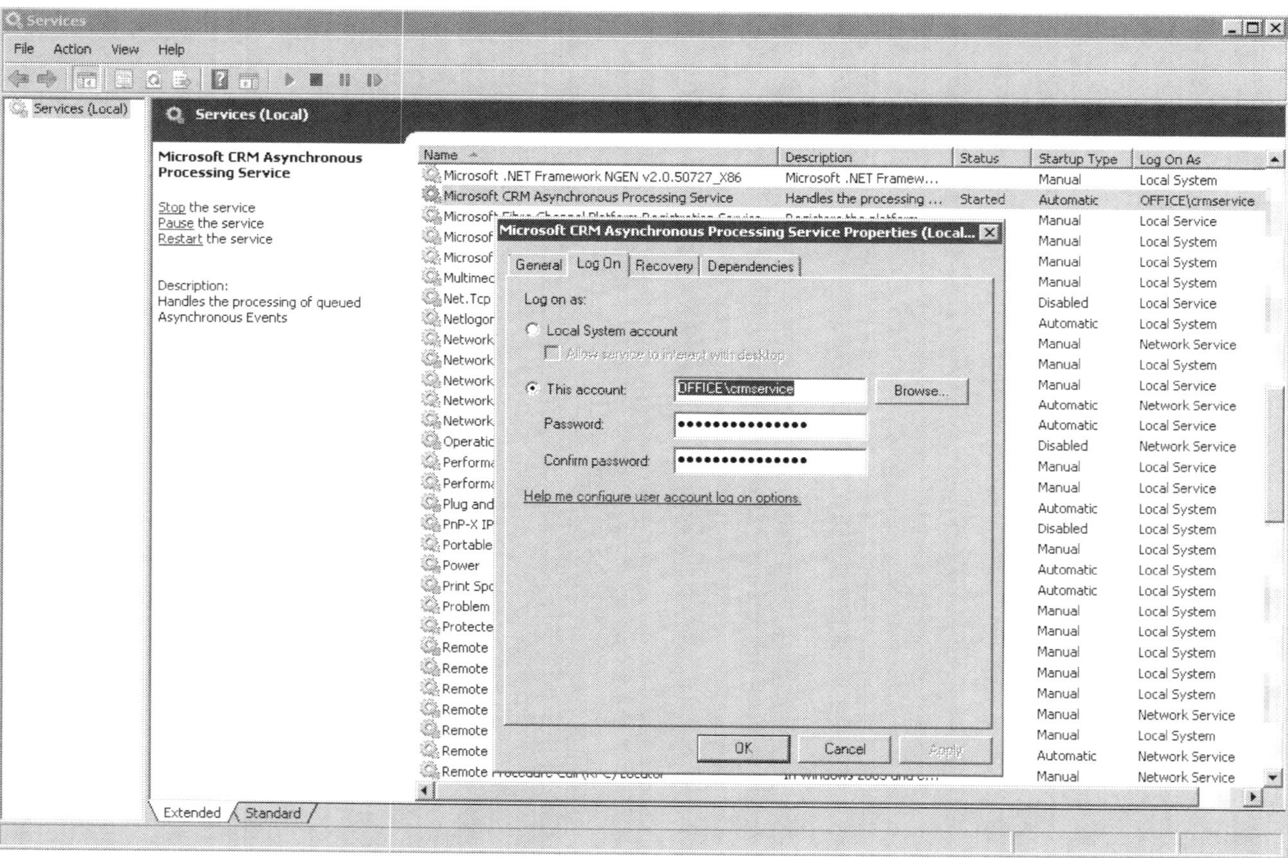


Figure 22.5

We will continue to tighten our security by changing the log on user account that our CRM services run under. When we initially installed CRM we used the domain administrator user account for our project. To tighten our security we will change our services from running under the domain administrator user account to our CRM service account. If you already have installed or are planning on installing the CRM Email Router role, then you will also want to set its service named Microsoft CRM Email Router service to run under the your CRM service user account as well. We will cover the installation, configuration, and security of the CRM Email Router in depth in **Chapter 27**.

5. On each of your CRM NLB cluster nodes, browse to **Start\Administrative Tools\Services**, and then right click the **Microsoft CRM Asynchronous Processing Service**, and select the **Properties** option.

    a. On the **Properties** screen, click on the **Log On** tab, and then set the **This account** field to your CRM service user account. Enter the password, and then click on the **OK** button to save your changes. For our project, we will enter our domain name and user account as **OFFICE\CRMService**, as shown in **Figure 22.5**.

        i. When prompted to restart the service for the changes to take effect, click on the **OK** button, and then right click on the service and select the **Restart** option.

    b. Repeat **Step 5** for each of your CRM NLB cluster nodes.

## Overview of the IIS Application Pool Account Used for CRM's Web Components

Before we begin tightening the security of our IIS application pool, we will cover the role that the CRM application pool plays within IIS. The IIS application pool for CRM is named CRMAppPool and the user account that it runs under is often referred to as the CRM ASP.NET account. The following bullet point will give you a better understanding of CRM application pool.

- **CRMAppPool**- Microsoft Dynamics CRM Server installation creates its own ASP.NET application pool for CRM 4.0 to run under. The Active Directory user account that the CRMAppPool account runs under needs to be a member both the PrivUserGroup and SQLAccessGroup CRM security groups.

## Configuring the CRM Application Pool Identity in Internet Information Services (IIS) 7.5 to use the CRM Service User Account

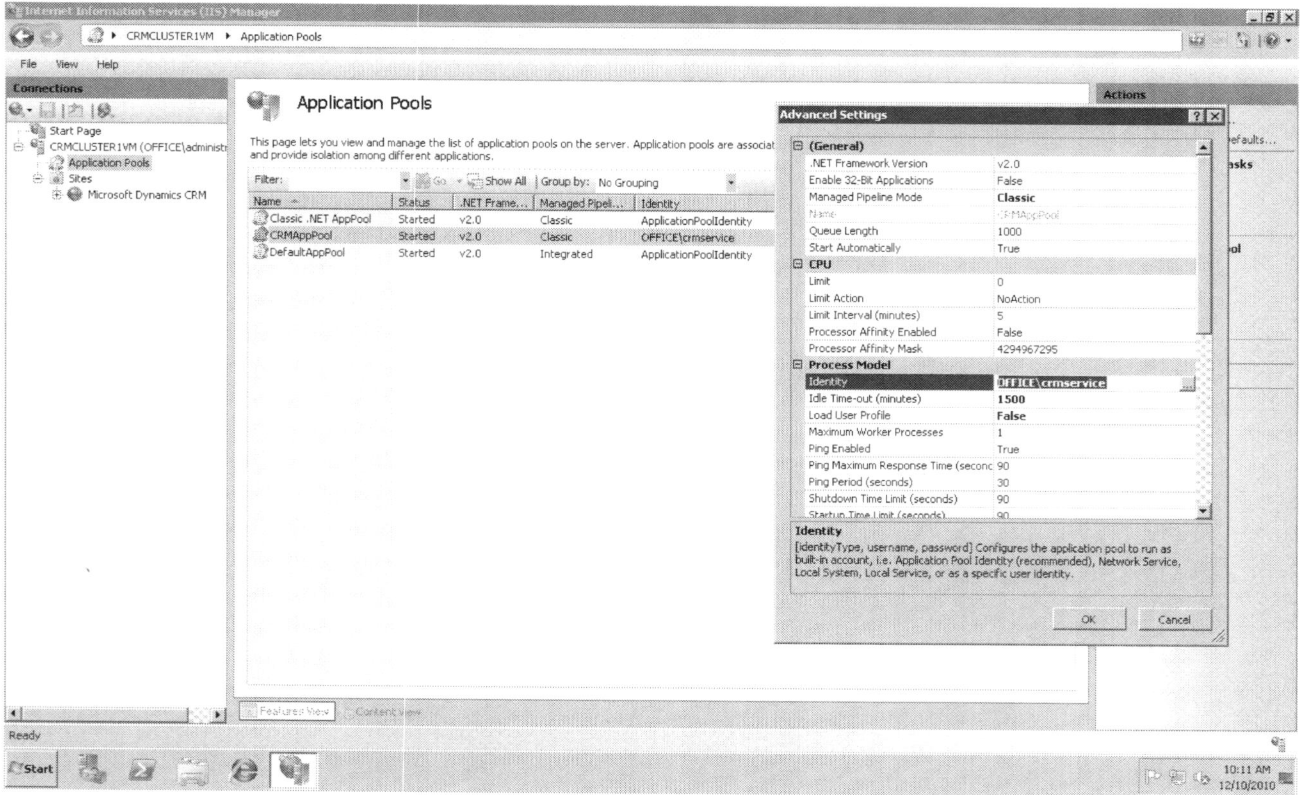


**Figure 22.6**

6. On each of your CRM NLB cluster nodes, launch the **Internet Information Services (IIS) Manager** console by going to **Start/Administrative Tools**, and then click on the **Internet Information Services (IIS) Manager** option.

   a. In the **Internet Information Services (IIS) Manager** console, click on the plus signs in the left pane to expand the available nodes.

   b. Under your CRM NLB cluster node's name, highlight the **Application Pools** node.

      i. In the right pane, right click on the **CRMAppPool** from the list of application pools, and then select the **Advanced Settings** option.

      ii. Under the **Process Model** section, change the **Identity** field to use your CRM service user account, and then click on the **OK** button to save the changes. For our project, we will set the identity field to our CRM service user account named **CRMService,** as shown in **Figure 22.6**.

## Disabling Internet Information Services (IIS) 7.5 Kernel-mode Authentication for Windows Server 2008 R2

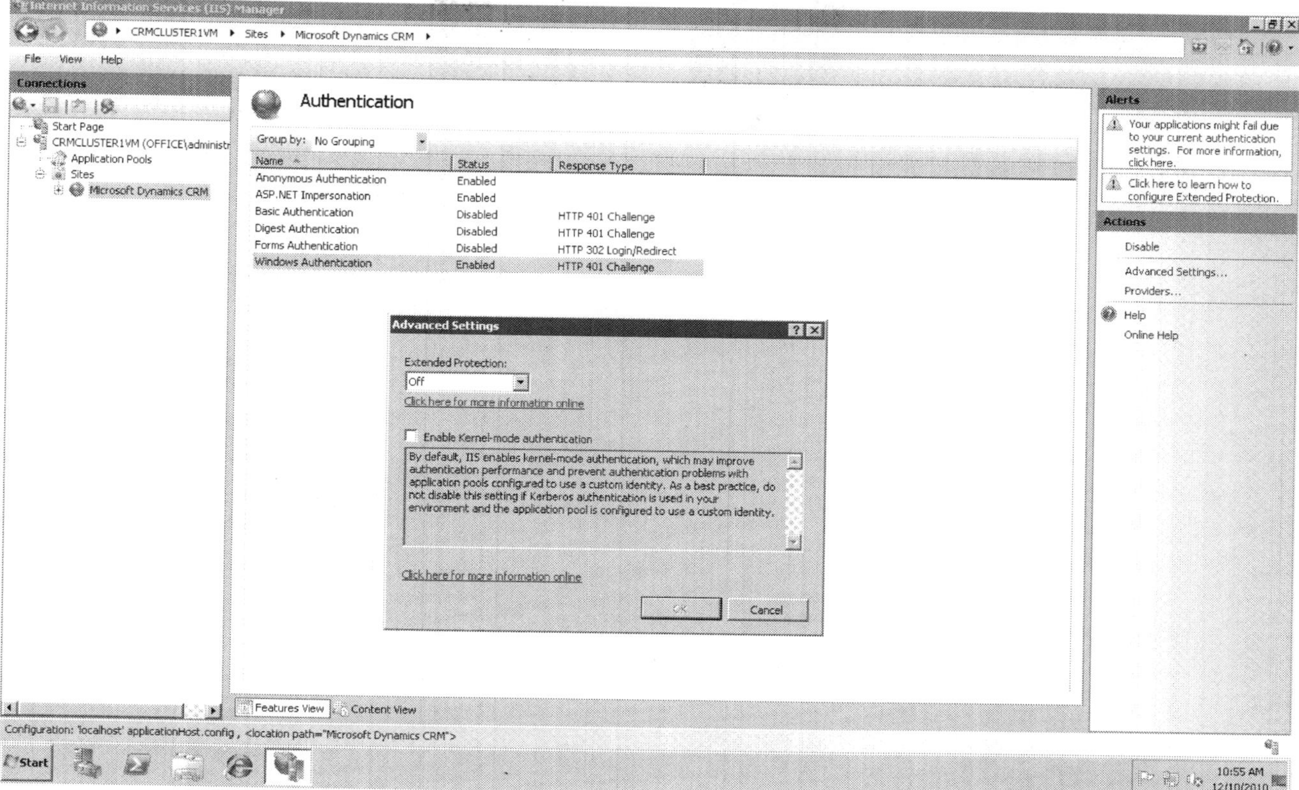


**Figure 22.7**

If your CRM NLB cluster nodes are running Windows Server 2008 R2 with IIS 7.5, then for CRM authentication to function correctly with Microsoft's Network Load Balancer (NLB) software you will need to disable the Kernel-mode Authentication. If you're not using Windows Server 2008 R2 with IIS 7.5, then please disregard this step and skip to **Step 9**. For our project, we our using Windows Server 2008 R2 with IIS 7.5, so we will need to disable the Kernel-mode Authentication as outlined below.

7. While still in the **Internet Information Services (IIS) Manager** on each of your CRM NLB cluster nodes, browse to your **Microsoft Dynamics CRM** website under the **Sites** node in the left pane.

    a. In the center pane, double click on the **Authentication** icon under the **IIS** section. If you don't see icons in the center pane but instead folders, then you most likely need to select the **Features View** button at the bottom of the center pane to change your view.

        i. Right click on the **Windows Authentication** option from the list, and then select the **Advanced Settings** option.

        ii. On the **Advanced Settings** screen, unselect the **Enable Kernel-mode authentication** checkbox, and then click on the **OK** button to save your changes.

8. Repeat **Steps 4-7** for each of your CRM NLB cluster nodes.

## Configuring Service Principle Names (SPN) Security for the Microsoft Network Load Balancer Cluster

Microsoft's Network Load Balancer clusters and Microsoft Dynamics CRM 4.0 require Service Principle Names (SPN) to be configured when you are running Internet Information Services (IIS) 6.0, IIS7.0 or IIS7.5. The SPNs identify an instance of a service. The Active Directory is then able to use this identification for authentication when accessing resources located across the different NLB cluster nodes.

## Using the ADSI Edit Tool to Edit the Service Principle Names (SPN)

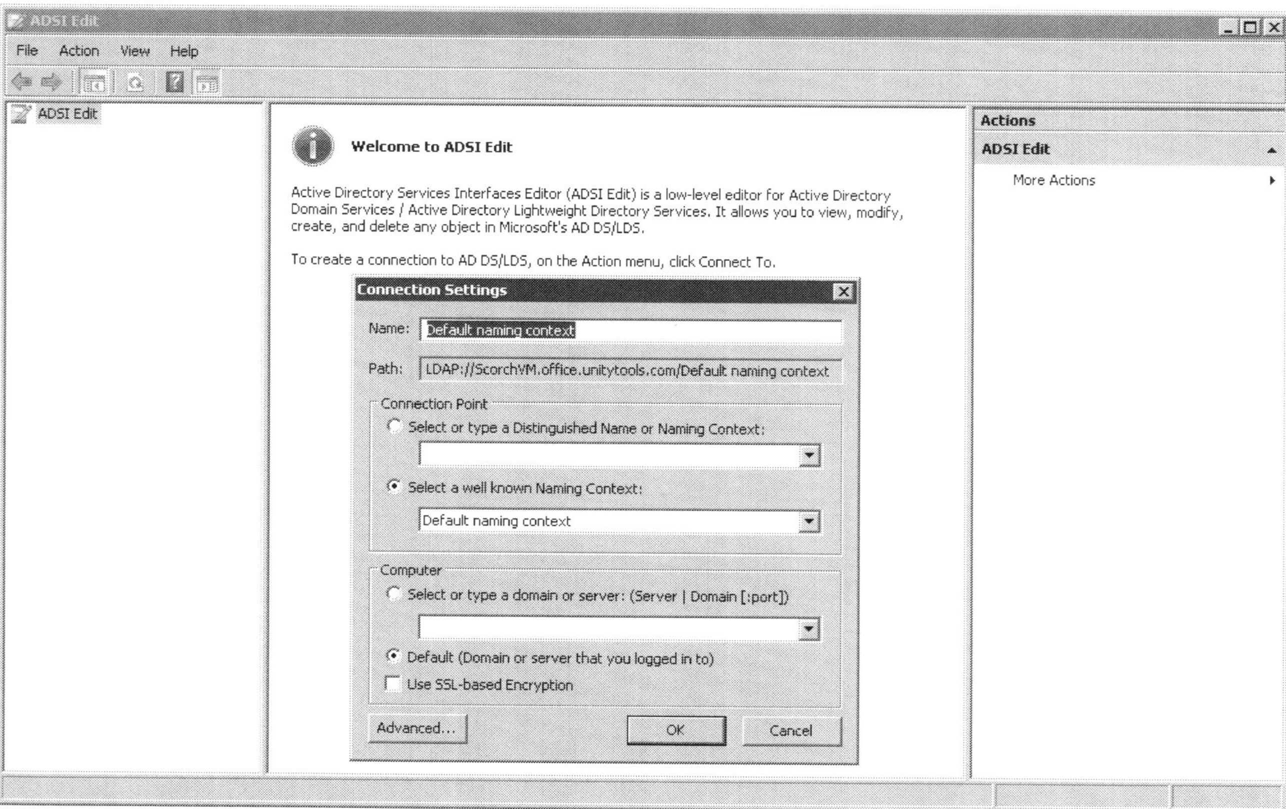


**Figure 22.8**

9. We will be using the Windows support tool called adsiedit.msc on our Windows domain controller to create our SPNs. If your domain controller is Windows Server 2008, then the adsiedit.msc tool is already installed. For a Windows Server 2003 domain controller you will have to install the adsiedit.msc tool from the Support\Tools folder of the Windows Server 2003 installation media.

   a. Launch the adsiedit.msc tool by going to **Start\Run**, and then typing in the command **adsiedit.msc**, which will launch the ADSI Edit snap-in for the Microsoft Management Console (MMC).

b. If this is the first time you have used the ADSI Edit tool on your domain controller, then you will first need to make a connection to your domain. Right click on the **ADSI Edit** node in the left pane of the console, and then select the **Connect to** option. If you have used the tool previously, then please disregard these steps and skip to **Step 10**.

   i. On the **Connection Settings** screen, leave the defaults, and then click on the **OK** button to connect, as shown in **Figure 22.8**.

## Adding the CRM NLB Cluster's Information to the Service Principle Names (SPN) of the CRM Service User Account

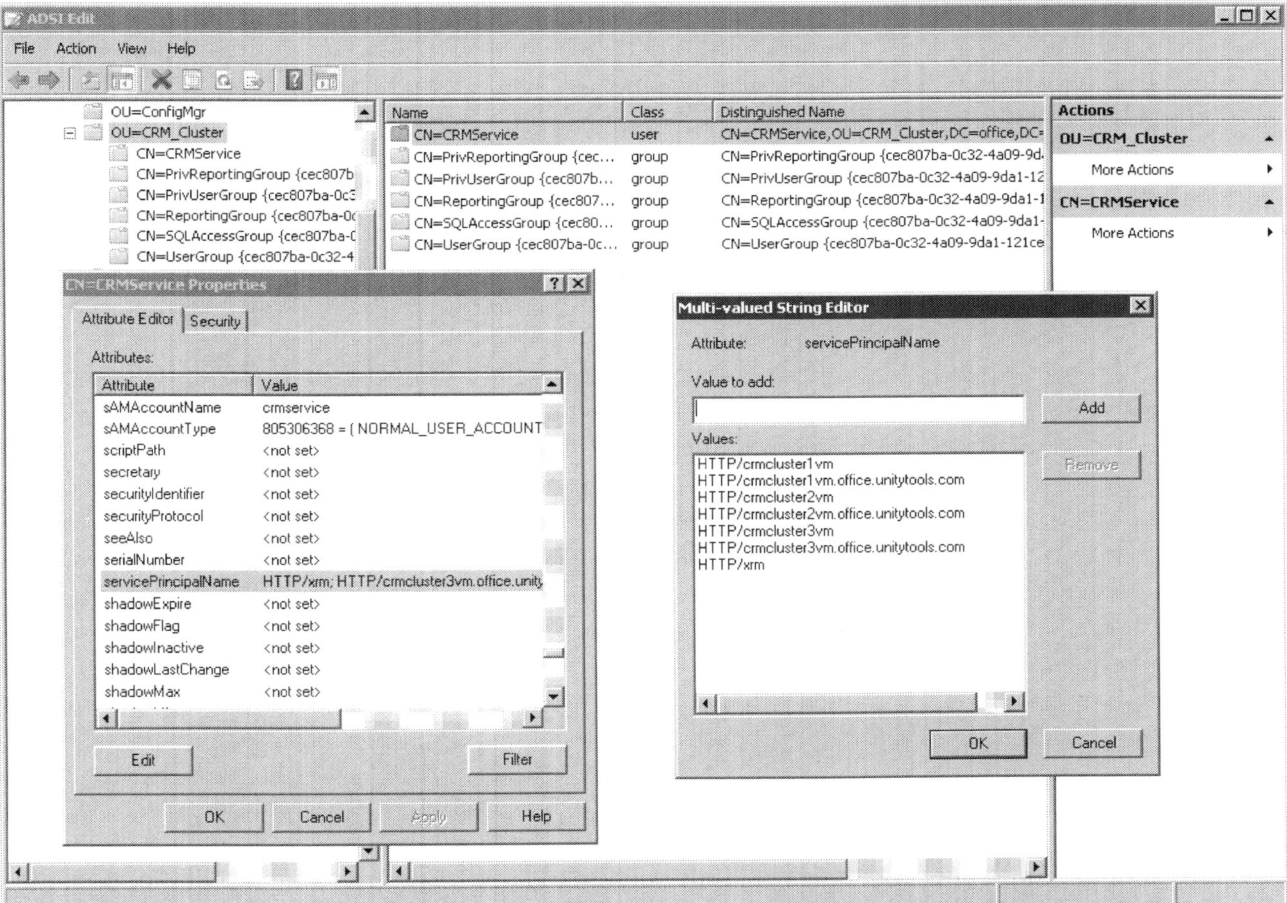


**Figure 22.9**

10. In the left pane of the **ADSI Edit** console, click on the plus signs to expand your **Active Directory domain**, and then highlight your **Organizational Unit** that you created for CRM.

    a. Right click on your **CRM service** user account, and then select the **Properties** option. For our project, we will open the properties of our CRM service user account named **CRMService**, as shown in **Figure 22.9**.

b. On the user account **Properties** screen, click on the **Attribute Editor** tab, and then browse the **Attributes** field for the **servicePrincipalName** attribute in the list.

c. Highlight the **servicePrincipalName** attribute from the list, and then click on the **Edit** button.

i. On the **Multi-valued String Editor** screen, enter each of your CRM NLB cluster node names and protocols being used in the following format for the **Value to add** field, and then click on the **Add** button. When entering your NLB cluster node's information, you want to enter the protocol and name in the following format **HTTP/<Your_CRM_NLB_Node_Name>** and **HTTP/<CRM_NLB_Node.FQDN>**. You will also need to add an entry for your NLB cluster's internal DNS name. For our project, we will add the following **servicePrincipalName** attributes for each of our CRM NLB cluster nodes and for our CRM NLB cluster. You have to add your cluster's **HTTP/NetBIOS** names first and then your cluster's **HTTP/FQDN** names. When you're done adding your setup it should appear similar to **Figure 22.9**.

- **HTTP/crmcluster1vm**
- **HTTP/crmcluster2vm**
- **HTTP/crmcluster3vm**
- **HTTP/xrm**
- **HTTP/crmcluster1vm.office.unitytools.com**
- **HTTP/crmcluster2vm.office.unitytools.com**
- **HTTP/crmcluster3vm.office.unitytools.com**

ii. Click on the **OK** buttons to save your changes, and then exit out of the **ADSI Edit** tool.

## How to Troubleshoot Service Principle Name (SPN) Conflicts

```
C:\WINDOWS\system32\cmd.exe
Microsoft Windows [Version 5.2.3790]
(C) Copyright 1985-2003 Microsoft Corp.

C:\Documents and Settings\administrator.OFFICE> ldifde -f c:\spn_out.txt -d "DC=
office,DC=unitytools,DC=com" -l serviceprincipalname -r "(serviceprincipalname=*
/*)" -p subtree
Connecting to "monsoon.office.unitytools.com"
Logging in as current user using SSPI
Exporting directory to file c:\spn_out.txt
Searching for entries...
Writing out entries.............................................................
................................................................................
................................................................................

221 entries exported

The command has completed successfully

C:\Documents and Settings\administrator.OFFICE>_
```

**Figure 22.10**

The SPNs for your CRM NLB cluster can only assigned to one user account in your Active Directory domain. If you're having trouble creating your SPNs because they already exist for another user account, then you'll want to use the following command to determine which user account the SPNs are currently assigned to. If you were successful in creating your SPNs in the previous step, then please disregard this step and skip to **Step 12**.

11. On your **Domain Controller**, browse to **Start\Run**.

    a. In the **Run** field, type in the command **cmd**, and then hit the **Enter** key to launch the **Command Prompt** console.

    b. Type in the below command, replacing the **<sub-domain>**, **<domain>**, and **<internet domain>** names with your domain's information, and then hit the **Enter** key to run the command. The command will create an output file named **spn_out.txt** on the root of the **C:** drive. Once you have found the SPNs set for a different Active Directory user account, use the ADSI Edit tool to delete them from the current user account, and then add them to your CRM service user account. As an example, the command ran in **Figure 22.10** logs all the SPNs for the active directory domain **office.unitytools.com** to a file named **spn_out.txt**. The command syntax is as follows:

    **ldifde -f** c:\spn_out.txt **-d "DC=<sub-domain>,DC=<domain>,DC=<internet domain>" -l serviceprincipalname -r "(serviceprincipalname=*/*)" -p subtree**

**NOTE:** If you are having syntax issues, then try manually typing in the command vs. copying and pasting it. You can also try copying and pasting the command into the Windows Notepad session to strip away any potentially hidden characters.

## Enabling Trust Delegation for the CRM Service User Account

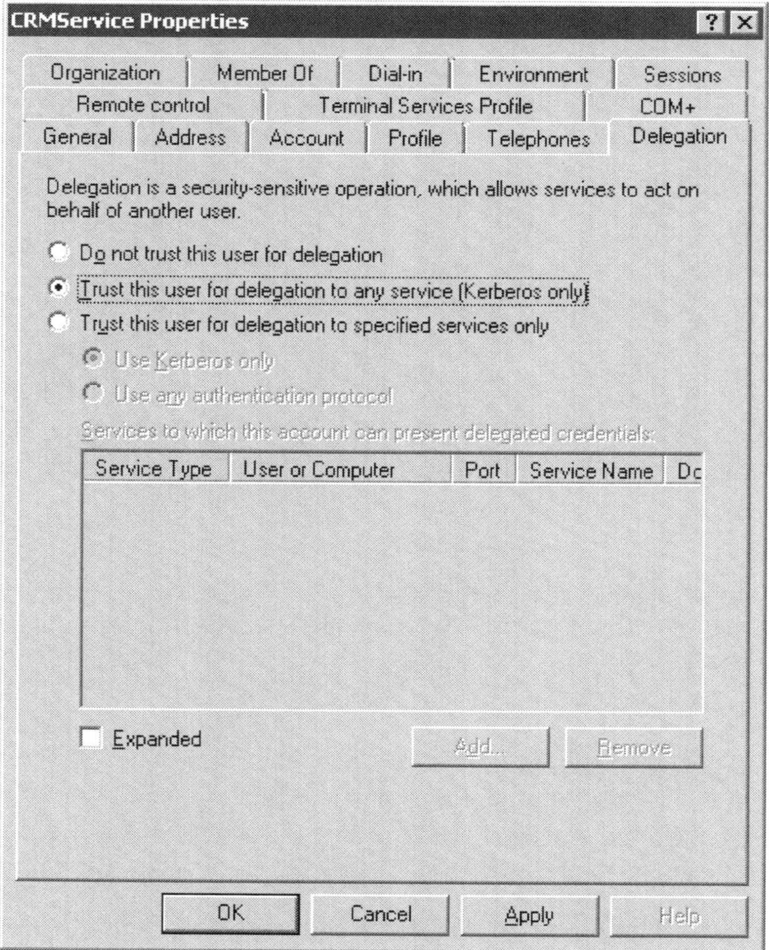


**Figure 22.11**

If you plan on having your CRM 4.0 deployment accessible from the internet for your users, then you will need to enable trust delegation for your CRM service user account. If your users will not be accessing CRM from the internet, then you can skip this step and simply install the CRM SRS Data Connector as outlined in the Chapter 25. To make your CRM deployment accessible for the internet as well as highly available with Microsoft's Network Load Balancer you will have to utilize Active Directory's Trust Delegation along with both CRM's SRS Data Connector and CRM's Internet Facing Deployment (IFD) Tool for your deployment. We will cover the installation and configuration of CRM's SRS Data Connector in Chapter 25 followed by CRM's Internet Facing Deployment (IFD) Tool in Chapter 26. For our project, we will configure all three of these components to make our CRM highly available as well as available from the internet.

12. On your **Domain Controller**, open the **Active Directory Users and Computers** console, and then browse to your **CRM service** user account.

   a. Right click on your **CRM service** user account, and then select the **Properties** option. On the **Properties** screen, click on the **Delegation** tab, and then select the **Trust this user for delegation to any service (Kerberos only)** option. Click on the **OK** button to save your changes. If the delegation tab isn't available, then most likely it's due to you not having set the SPNs for your CRM service user account. For our project, we will select the **Trust this user for delegation to any service (Kerberos only)** option for our CRM service user account named **CRMService**, as shown in **Figure 22.11**.

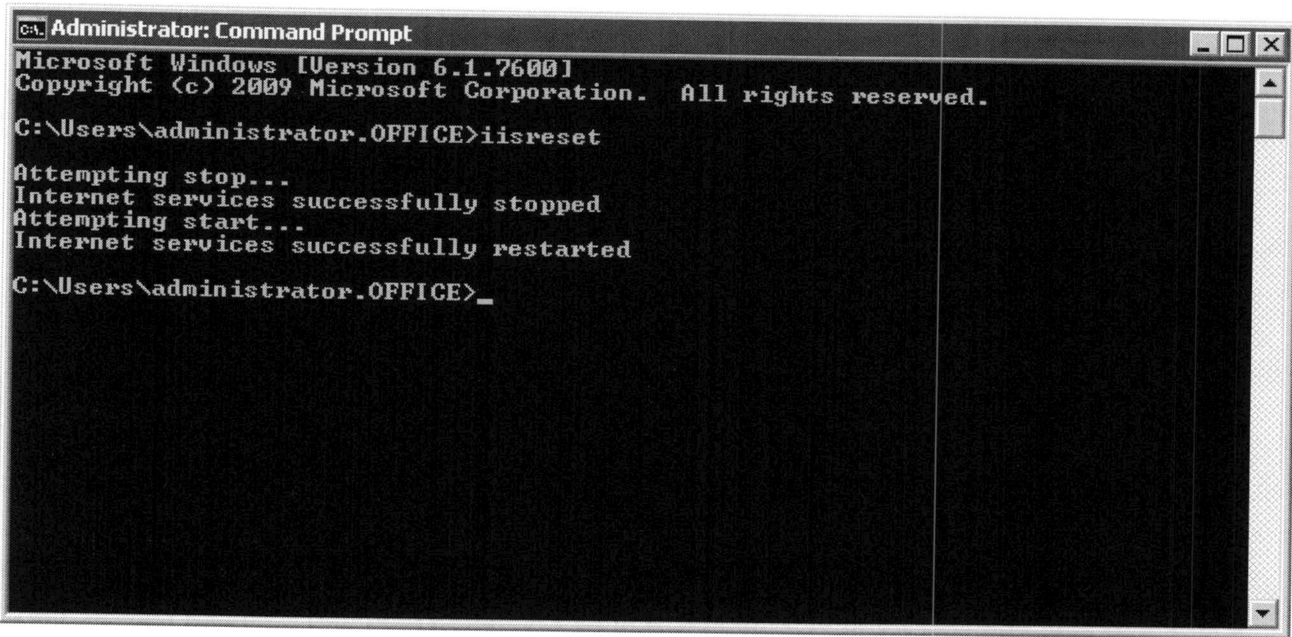

Administrator: Command Prompt
Microsoft Windows [Version 6.1.7600]
Copyright (c) 2009 Microsoft Corporation. All rights reserved.
C:\Users\administrator.OFFICE>iisreset
Attempting stop...
Internet services successfully stopped
Attempting start...
Internet services successfully restarted
C:\Users\administrator.OFFICE>_

**Figure 22.12**

After you have set the Trust Delegation to your CRM service user account you need to run the iisreset command or reboot each of your CRM NLB cluster nodes for the security changes to take effect.

   b. On each of your CRM NLB cluster nodes, open the **Command Prompt**, and then type in the command **iisreset** and hit the **Enter** key. The command will restart the web server service on each of CRM NLB cluster nodes that it's ran on. For our project, we will run the **iisreset** command on each of our CRM NLB cluster nodes **CRMCluster1VM**, **CRMCluster2VM** and **CRMCluster3VM**, as shown in **Figure 22.12**.

# Chapter 23: Applying Microsoft Dynamics CRM 4.0 Update Rollups

In this quick chapter, we will make sure our new CRM 4.0 cluster has the correct Update Rollups applied for our particular situation. The version of Update Rollup that you should apply depends largely on if you're importing data from a previous CRM deployment, or if you are deploying a brand new CRM deployment. Another determining factor depends on the version of SQL Server 2008 that you are using. The below outline of the three different scenarios will help you make the decision as to which version of CRM Update Rollups you should apply to your deployment.

- **Importing Data from Previous CRM Deployment**- If you will be importing data from a previous CRM 4.0 deployment into your new CRM cluster then you will want to only apply CRM Update Rollups to the same level as the CRM deployment that you're importing the data from. This will eliminate any potential version conflicts during the data importation process. Once you have all your data imported into your new CRM cluster then you can apply Microsoft's latest CRM Update Rollups.

- **Starting Fresh with a New CRM Deployment**- If you are just beginning to use CRM 4.0, and don't have data to import from previous CRM 4.0 deployments, then you will want to apply Microsoft's latest CRM Update Rollups.

- **SQL Server 2008 R2**- If your CRM cluster is deployed in a SQL Server 2008 R2 environment, then you will need to apply Update Rollup 7 or higher to be compatible. If you are importing organizations from a previous CRM 4.0 deployment into your new CRM cluster, then you will want to upgrade the previous deployment to Update Rollup 7 or higher before importing your organizations. You will only need to update the Server role component of your previous deployment before importing your organizations. For any CRM for Outlook users you can wait to update their rollups until you are ready to repoint their CRM for Outlook's configuration to your new CRM cluster's name. The CRM Update Rollups are usually cumulative, however there is an exception to this for the CRM for Outlook installations as you first have to upgrade CRM for Outlook to Update Rollup 7 and only then can you apply Update Rollups 8 or higher.

## How and When to Apply Update Rollups to Each Different CRM Component

Each of CRM 4.0 components Server, SRS Data Connector, Email Router and CRM for Outlook have their own Update Rollups that need to be applied. The Update Rollup packages released from Microsoft are usually cumulative with a rare exception, so you can simply apply Microsoft's latest release and all of the previous versions are included. It is recommended to update all CRM components to the same CRM Update Rollup level, but is not a requirement. When importing previous CRM organizations into our new CRM cluster, we will have different CRM 4.0 components installed and configured at different points during the CRM deployment process. We currently only have the CRM Server component installed, so we will begin by applying its Update Rollup first. After the CRM Server component is updated we will be able to import our previous CRM organization(s) into our CRM cluster. Once we have our previous organization(s) imported, we will be able to install and configure our remaining CRM components which depend on data and user accounts being present to be configured.

1. Browse to Microsoft's download website at www.microsoft.com/downloads on the internet, and then enter **Microsoft Dynamics CRM 4.0 Update Rollup** in the search field to find the different Update Rollups available for download.

a. Download each CRM component's **Update Rollup** version that applies to your environment.

b. Apply the same version of the **CRM Server Update Rollup** to each of your CRM NLB cluster nodes.

# Chapter 24: Importing a Previous Microsoft Dynamics CRM 4.0 Organization into the New CRM Cluster

In this chapter, we will cover step by step how to import our previous CRM 4.0 organization(s) into our new CRM cluster. We will begin at the database level with backing up our pre-cluster CRM databases and then restoring them into our SQL cluster. Once we have all our previous CRM organizational databases restored onto our SQL cluster we will then be ready to perform the CRM importation process from within the CRM Deployment Manager console. During the CRM importation process, we will cover what settings to specify for our CRM organizational names, SQL cluster, and for our SQL Report Server. In the last steps of the process, we will cover how to map our previous CRM organization's user accounts to our current Active Directory accounts. Once finished with this chapter, we will have our CRM servers up and running in our new clustered environment.

## Backing Up the Previous CRM 4.0 Database(s) for Migration to the New CRM 4.0 Cluster

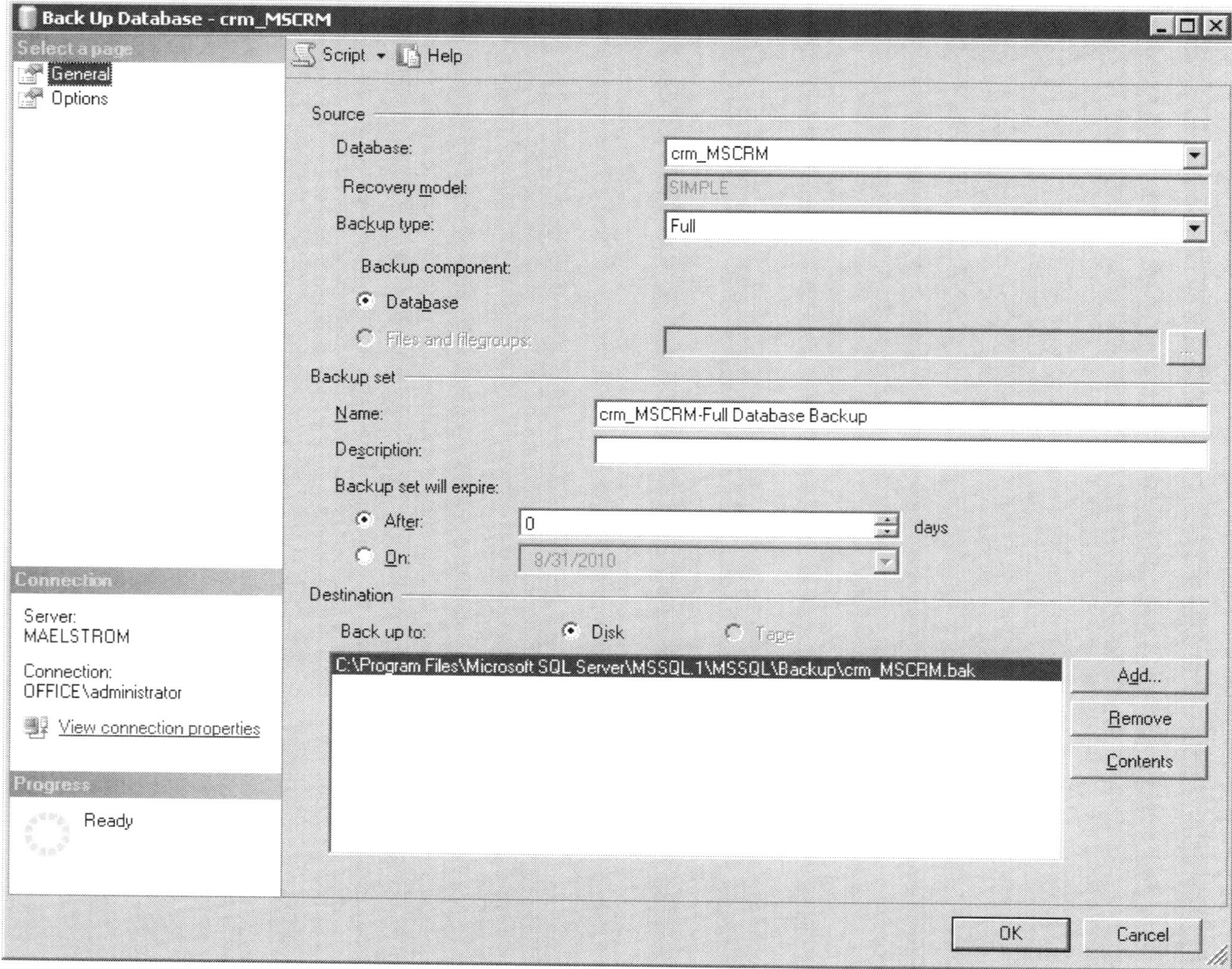


**Figure 24.1**

1. Go to the database server that hosts your pre-cluster CRM 4.0 database(s), and then launch the **Microsoft SQL Server Management Studio**. We want to backup each of our CRM databases that are labeled in the following format **<Your_Organization>_MSCRM**. For our project, we will backup our pre-cluster database named **crm_MSCRM**, as shown in **Figure 24.1**.

   a. Right click on your CRM database, and then select the **Tasks\Back up** option.

   b. On the **Back Up Database** screen, select the **Disk** option for the **Destination** field at the bottom of the screen, and then click on the **Add** button to select the location where the backup file will be created. Make sure to add the **.bak** extension to the end of your backup file name, and then click on the **OK** button to save the location.

c. On the **Back Up Database** screen, verify that the **Backup Type** dropdown field towards the top of the screen is set to **Full**, and then click on the **OK** button to backup your CRM database.

d. Repeat these SQL backup steps for each of your CRM organization database(s) that you want to import into your CRM cluster.

**NOTE:** You do not need to backup the **MSCRM_CONFIG** database, as only the CRM organization databases(s) with the naming convention of **<Your_Organization>_MSCRM** are needed to import your organizations into the CRM cluster.

## Restoring the Previous CRM 4.0 Database(s) into the New CRM 4.0 Cluster

2. Using **Windows Explorer**, copy your CRM database backup file(s) into your SQL cluster's **Backup** directory. For our project, we will copy our **crm_MSCRM.bak** file into our SQL cluster's **Backup** directory located at **\\SQLCluster\S$\Program Files\Microsoft SQL Server\MSSQL10.MSSQLSERVER\MSSQL\Backup**.

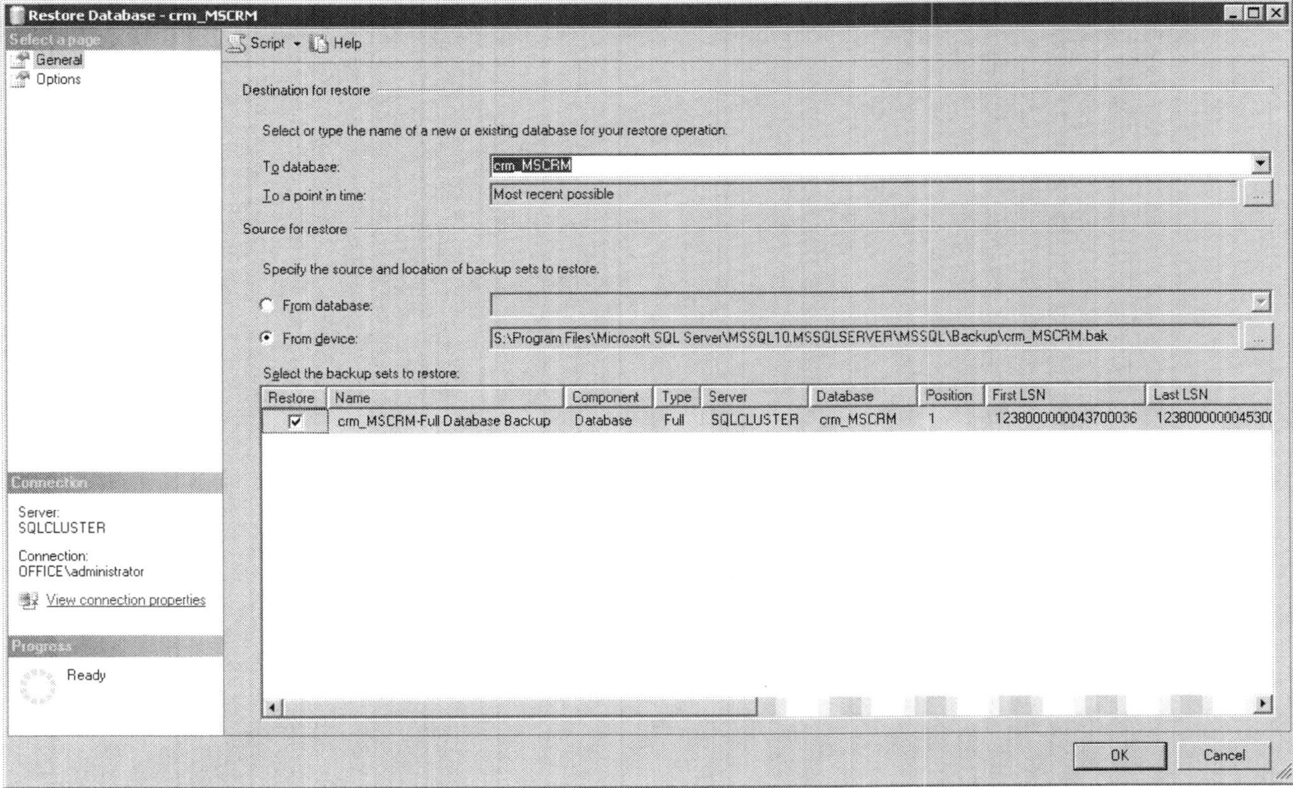


**Figure 24.2**

3. Go to the active SQL node of your CRM cluster, and then launch the **Microsoft SQL Server Management Studio**.

a. In the left **Object Explorer** pane, right click on the **Databases** node under your SQL cluster's name, and then select the **Restore Database** option.

b. On the **Restore Database** screen under the **Destination to restore** section, enter in the name of your **<Organization>_MSCRM** database into the **To database** field. For our project, we will restore our **crm_MSCRM** database backup, as shown in **Figure 24.2**.

c. Under the **Source for restore** section, select the **From device** option, and then click on the **ellipsis ...** button to select your CRM database.

d. For the **Select the backup sets to restore** field, select the **Restore** checkbox next to the database you just added, and then click on the **OK** button to restore the database.

e. Repeat these **Steps 1-3** for any additional CRM organizations you want to bring into your new CRM cluster.

## Importing Previous CRM 4.0 Organizations- Deployment Manager

4. Go to one of your CRM NLB cluster nodes, and then launch the CRM Deployment Manager by going to **Start\All Programs\Microsoft Dynamics CRM** and selecting the **Deployment Manager** option.

   a. Right click on the **Organizations** node in the left pane, and then select the **Import Organization** option.

   b. If you are using the **Professional** edition of **Microsoft Dynamics CRM 4.0**, then you will be prompted to delete the existing organization. Click on the **OK** button to delete the organization that was created during the CRM server installation. If you are using the **Enterprise** edition as in our project, then please disregard this step as you can have multiple organizations in a single deployment. This action won't delete the physical database from your SQL server but will simply remove the current organization from your CRM deployment. This is necessary for the Professional edition of Microsoft Dynamics CRM 4.0 as you can only have one organization.

# Importing CRM Organizations- Selecting the CRM Database

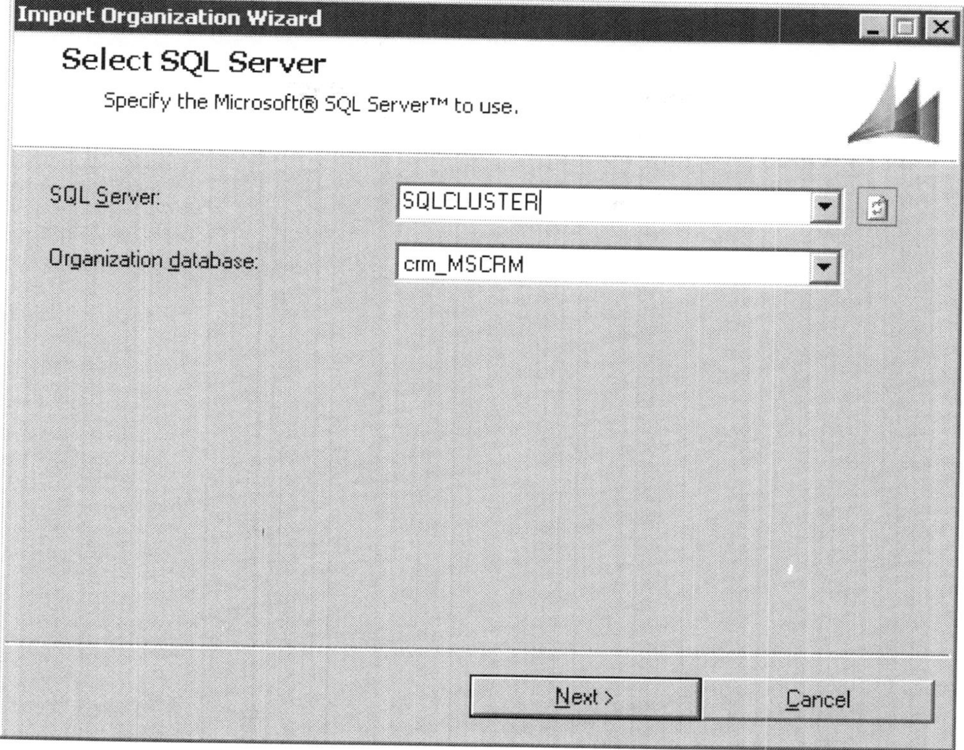


**Figure 24.3**

c. On the **Select SQL Server** screen of the **Import Organization Wizard**, enter in your SQL cluster's name in the **SQL Server** field. For our project, we will enter our SQL cluster's name of **SQLCLUSTER**, as shown in **Figure 24.3**.

   i. For the **Organization database** field, select the CRM database that you restored, and then click on the **Next** button to continue. If the Organization database field doesn't populate, then click on the white and green folder icon next to the SQL Server field to populate the Organization database field by querying the SQL cluster. For our project, we will select the **crm_MSCRM** organization for the **Organization database** field, as shown in **Figure 24.3**.

# Importing CRM Organizations- Specifying the Organization Name

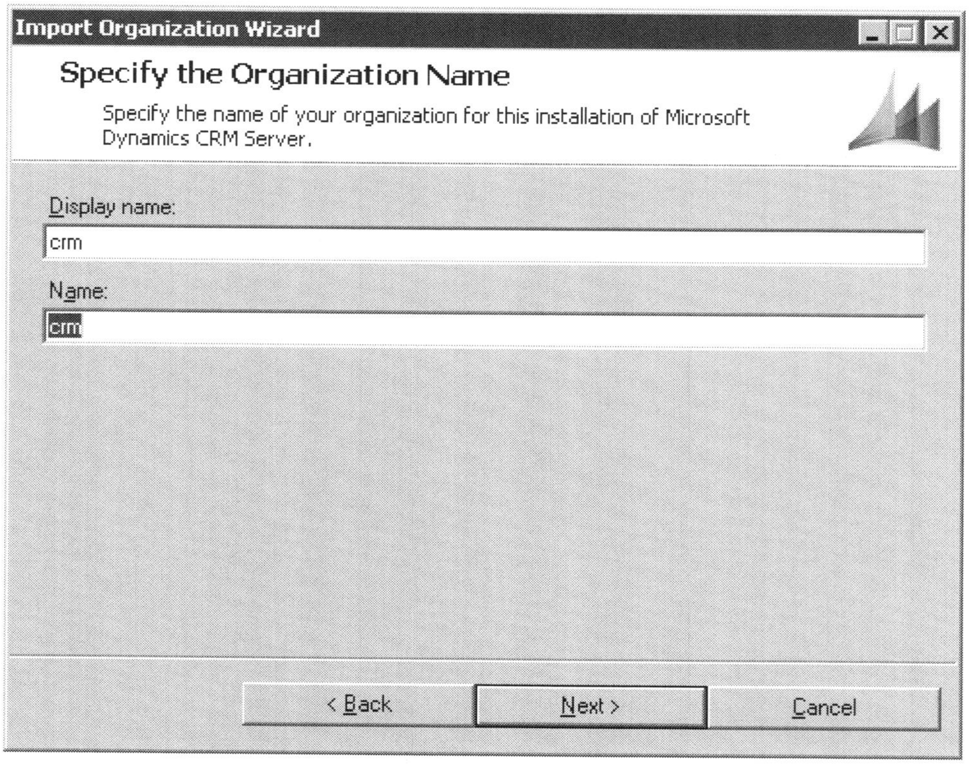

Figure 24.5

d. On the **Specify the Organization Name** screen, fill in the **Display name** and **Name** fields with the name of your CRM organization that you're importing, and then click on the **Next** button to continue. For our project, we will keep the same name as our previous CRM's organization of **crm**, as shown in **Figure 24.5**.

**NOTE:** When importing an organization from a previous CRM deployment you will want to maintain the organization's name. The CRM importation process does allow you to rename the organization that you're importing, however the process is problematic as it does not rename the actual database name and thus can still cause you to have a name conflict with other CRM organizations. If for some reason you already have an organization name conflict, then you can always disable and delete the conflicting organization from within the CRM cluster before importing an organization as long as you create or already have another organization within the CRM cluster that can be assigned as the default organization first.

# Importing CRM Organizations- Specifying the Report Server

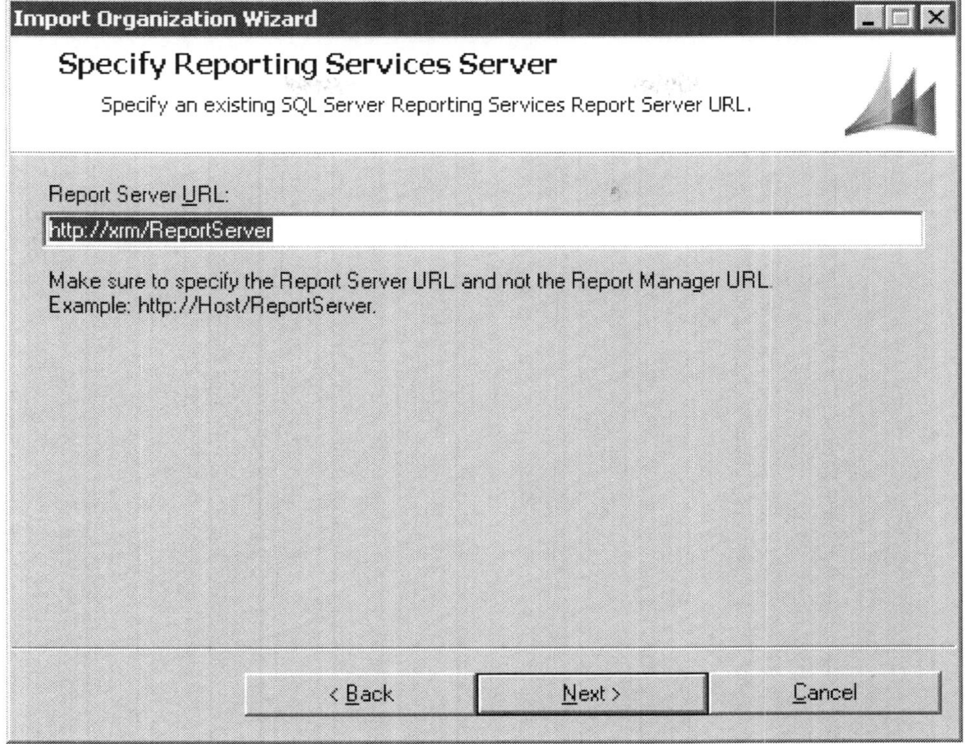


**Figure 24.6**

e. On the **Specify Reporting Services Server** screen, enter your NLB cluster's reporting services URL for the **Report Server URL** field, and then click on the **Next** button to continue. For our project, we named our NLB cluster **xrm** and used Microsoft's default SQL Reporting Services URL of **ReportServer**, which results in our report server's URL being **http://xrm/ReportServer**, as shown in **Figure 24.6**.

## Importing CRM Organizations- Selecting a Method for Mapping Users

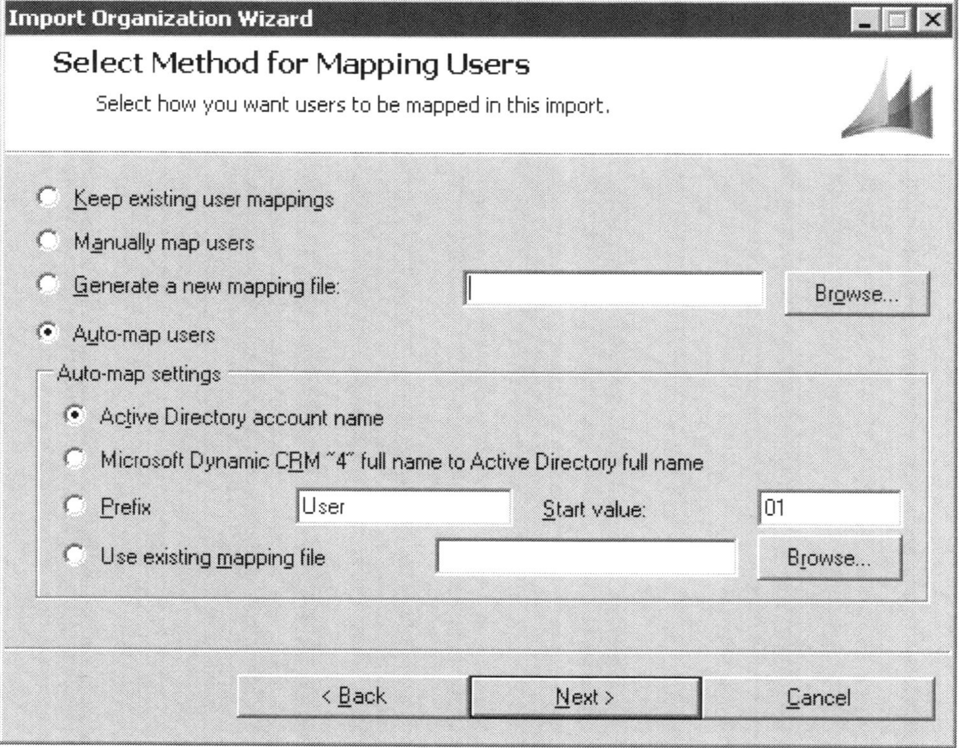


**Figure 24.7**

f. On the **Method for Mapping Users** screen, select the method for mapping users, and then click on the **Next** button to continue. When selecting the default setting of **Auto_map users** the system will automatically map your CRM user accounts to your Active Directory user accounts. Then on the next screen you'll have the opportunity manually map any CRM user accounts that the system couldn't map automatically. For our project, we will leave the screen defaults, as shown in **Figure 24.7**.

## Importing CRM Organizations- Edit User Mappings

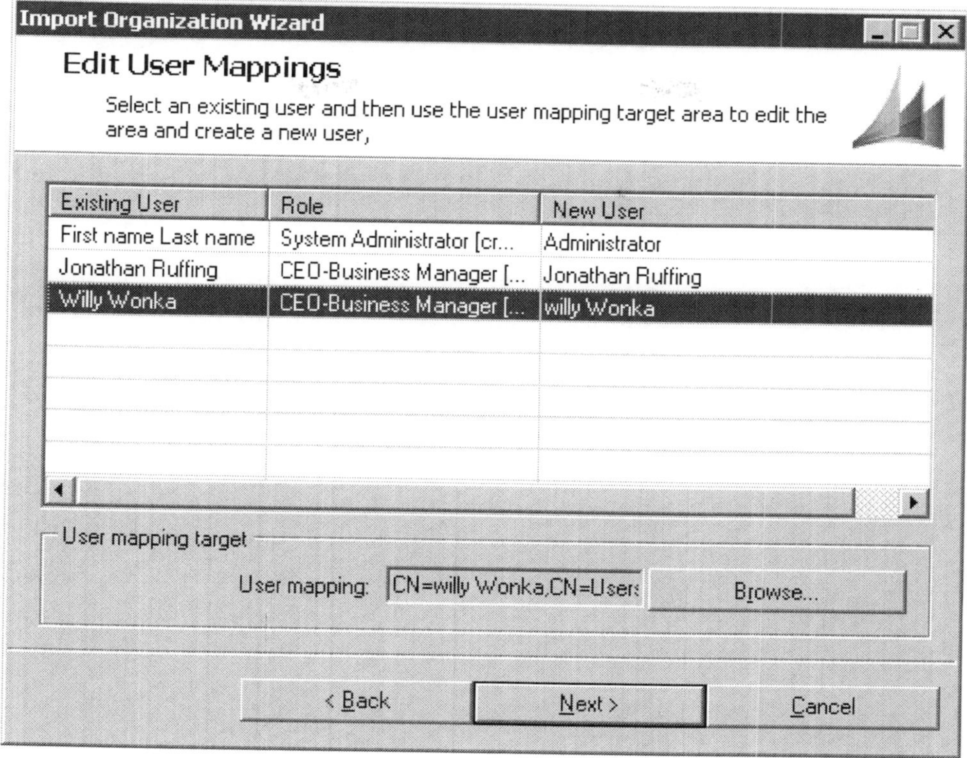


**Figure 24.8**

g. On the **Edit User Mappings** screen, manually map any users that didn't automatically map to your Active Directory. Simply highlight an unmapped user, and then click on the **Browse** button to select an Active Directory user account to be associated with the CRM user account. Once complete with your changes, click on the **Next** button to continue. For example, you may have a former employee/CRM user whose Active Directory user account was deleted when they left the company. In this case you could recreate the Active Directory user account, set the account to disabled within the Active Directory, and then map the CRM user account to this disabled Active Directory account.

# Importing CRM Organizations- System Requirements

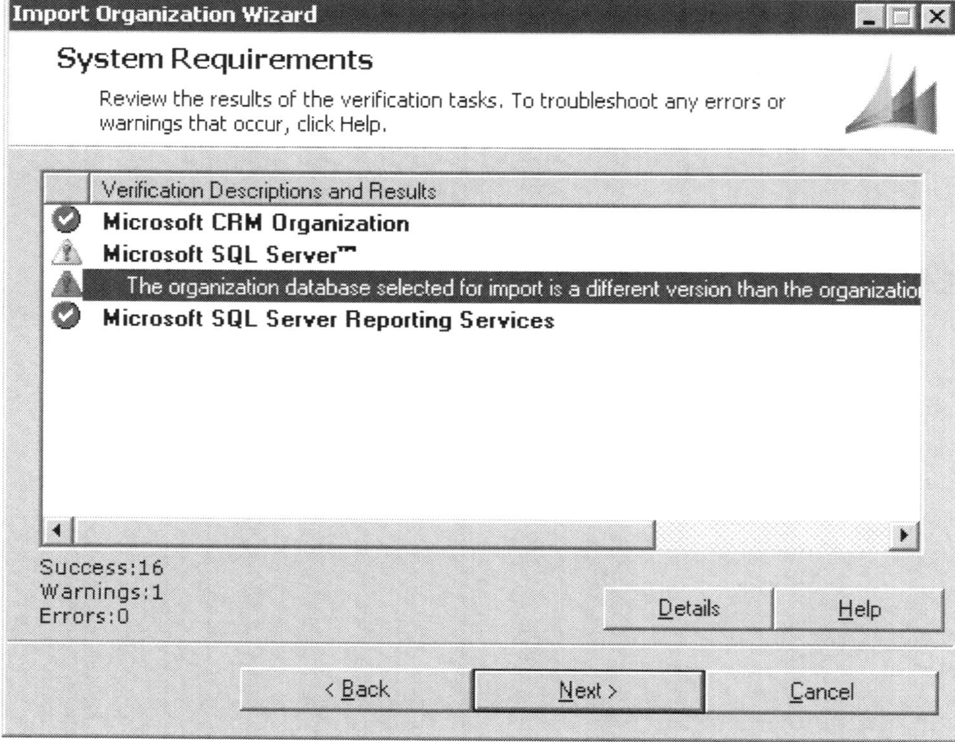


**Figure 24.9**

h. On the **System Requirements** screen, you will most likely receive a yellow exclamation warning stating that **The organization database selected for import is a different version than the organization database that is currently deployed**. You can safely ignore this warning as long as your new CRM cluster and your pre-cluster CRM organization that is being imported have the same version of CRM **Update Rollup** applied. Click on the **Next** button to continue.

i. On the **Ready to Install** screen, verify your selections, and then click on the **Import** button to complete the importation of your CRM organization.

j. If you have more than just one CRM organization to import then you'll want to repeat **Step 4** for each of them.

## Verifying the CRM Organization was Imported Successfully

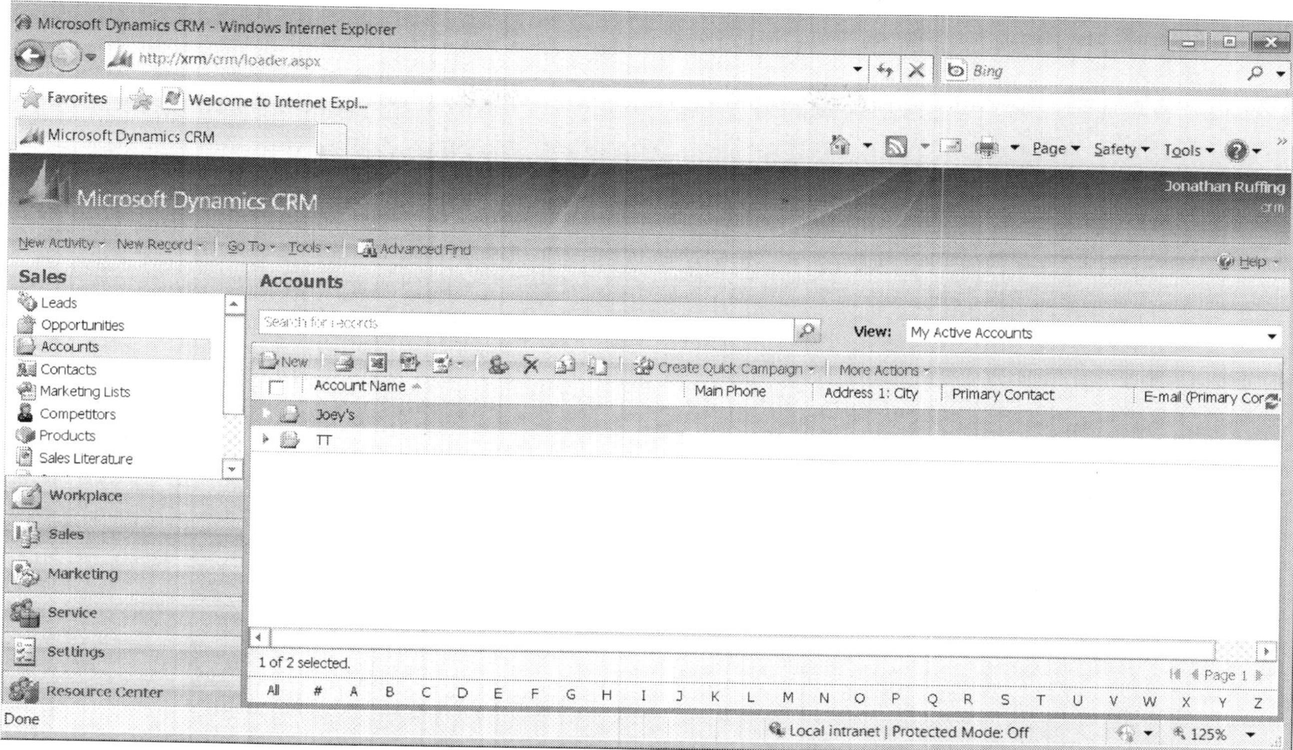


**Figure 24.10**

5. Now that we are finished importing our CRM organization(s) into our new cluster, we can test that each of our organizations are functioning correctly by logging into each organization via Internet Explorer. Enter your CRM NLB cluster's URL followed by your CRM organization's name in the following format to browse to your CRM website **http://<NLB_Cluster_Name>/<CRM_Organization_Name>** on the local subnet. Once logged in you can browse around within your CRM organization to verify all your data is there. For our project, we will enter in **http://xrm/crm** into Internet Explorer to login to our organization.

6. Once you have verified that your CRM organization(s) are operational, you want to apply Microsoft's latest **Update Rollup** for the **CRM Server** role on each of your CRM NLB cluster nodes. This will update your newly imported organization(s) to the latest update level and will also save you steps later by you only having to apply the most recent cumulative Update Rollups once for each of the remaining three CRM components to be installed.

# Chapter 25: Installation and Configuration of the CRM SRS Data Connector when Utilizing an NLB Cluster

The CRM SRS (SQL Reporting Services) Data Connector handles the reporting connections and security for our CRM between our front-end CRM servers and our back-end SQL cluster. Since we want our CRM application to be highly available and accessible from the internet we will need to utilize Microsoft's Network Load Balancer (NLB), Active Directory Service Principle Names (SPNs), Active Directory Trust Delegation, the CRM SRS Data Connector and the CRM Internet Facing Deployment (IFD) Tool. Unfortunately, Microsoft's CRM installation guide states that if you use the CRM 4.0 Internet Facing Deployment (IFD) Tool that you then should not install the CRM 4.0 SRS Data Connector for security, but instead only use Active Directory's Trust Delegation to facilitate your security. When utilizing Microsoft's NLB in conjunction with CRM it is required that you use both the CRM SRS Data Connector and Service Principle Names (SPN's) to maintain your reporting and authentication across the nodes of your NLB cluster. To overcome this slight shortcoming on CRM's part we will use a Microsoft supported workaround by making one small registry change before installing our CRM SRS Data Connector. Once complete with this chapter, we will have our CRM SRS Data Connector installed and be ready to move on to configuring our CRM deployment for internet access.

## Editing the Registry for CRM to Ignore Checks during the Installation of the CRM SRS Data Connector

During the CRM SRS Data Connector install we will receive an error concerning SQL Server Reporting Services and CRM application pool (CRMAppPool) using the same CRM service user account. The Microsoft Dynamics CRM 4.0 Installing Guide on page 2-21 outlines that it's not recommended to use the same active directory user account for CRM SRS Data Connector as you do for the CRM application pool due to a potential security risk. Unfortunately, when using the Microsoft software based Network Load Balancer (NLB) you have to use the same Active Directory user account due to only one user account being able to have the NLB's computer addresses set for its ServicePrincipalName (SPN) attribute. To be able to continue pass this security warning during the install, we will need to edit CRM's registry settings to Ignore Checks while the CRM SRS Data Connector is being installed.

**NOTE:** If you feel that the security risk as outlined on page 2-21 of the Microsoft Dynamics CRM 4.0 Installing Guide is too great for your environment, then your only other option would be to install a hardware load balancer in place of Microsoft's software based Network Load Balancer.

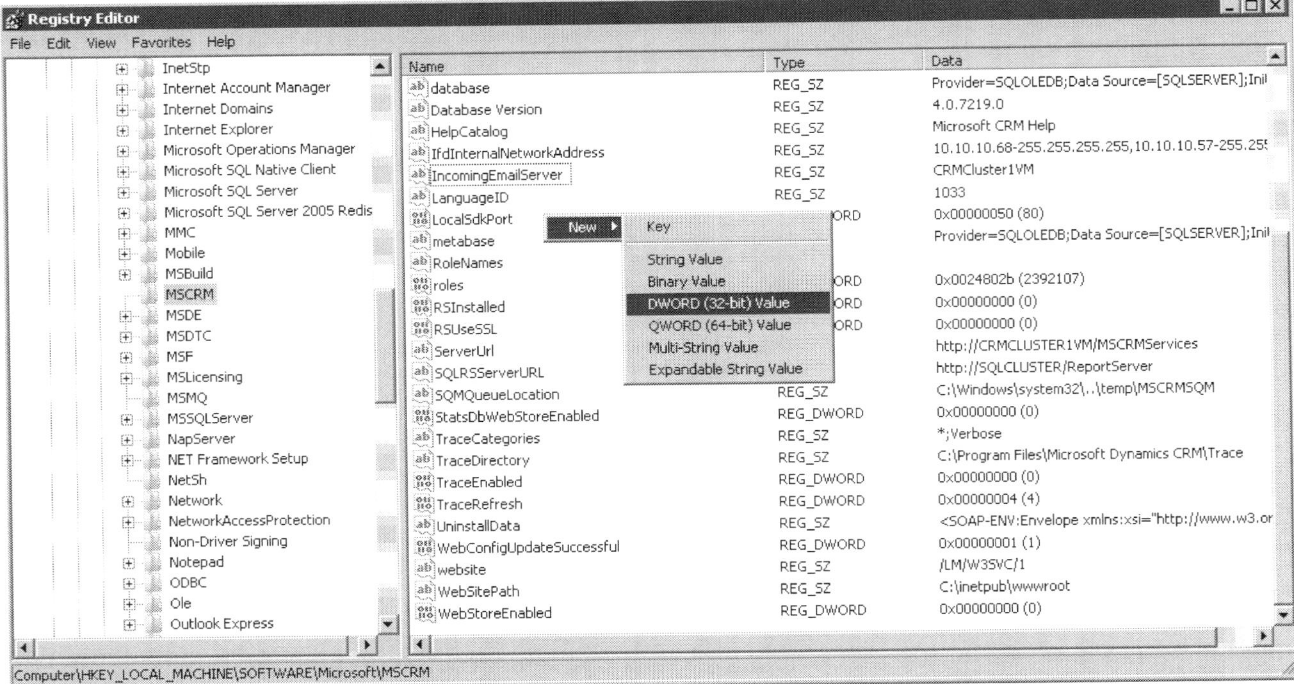


**Figure 25.1**

1. On each of your CRM NLB cluster nodes go to the **Start button\Run** field, type in the command **Regedit**, and then hit the **Enter** key.

    a. In the **Registry Editor's** left pane, browse to **HKEY_LOCAL_MACHINE\SOFTWARE\Microsoft\MSCRM** key.

    b. In the right pane, right click in the white area of the screen, and then select the **New\DWORD (32-bit) Value** option, as shown in **Figure 25.1**.

        i. Name the new value **IgnoreChecks**, and then hit the **Enter** key to save your changes.

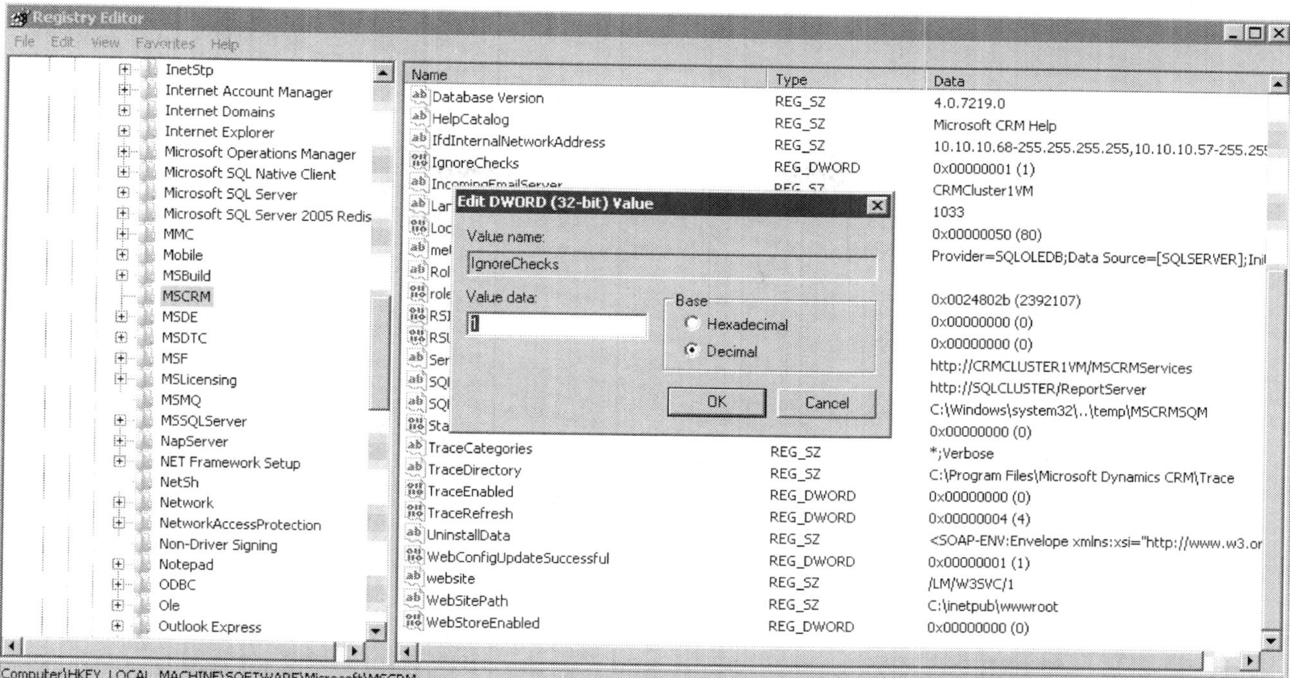


**Figure 25.2**

ii. Right click on the newly created **IgnoreChecks** value, and then select the **Modify** option.

iii. Set the **Value Data** field to **1** and the **Base** value field to **Decimal** as shown in **Figure 25.2**, and then click on the **OK** button.

iv. From the toolbar of the **Registry Editor** console select **File**, and then the **Exit** option to close the console.

v. You will need to reboot each of your CRM NLB clusters node for the registry changes to take effect. Remember, it is always a good practice to shutdown your CSV virtual machines from within the Failover Cluster Manager console.

vi. Repeat **Step 1** to modify the registry settings on each of your remaining CRM NLB cluster nodes.

## Installing the CRM SRS Data Connector on each of the CRM NLB Cluster Nodes

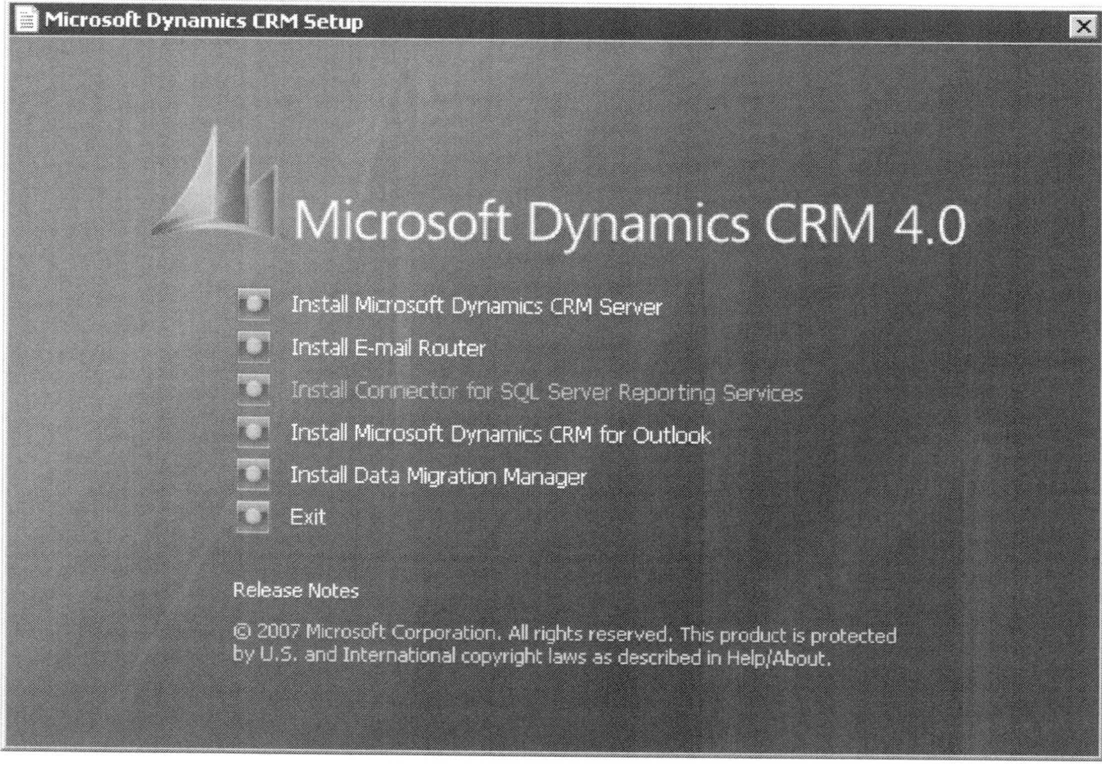


**Figure 25.3**

2. Launch the CRM 4.0 install by inserting the DVD or by double clicking on the **Splash.exe** in the root of the install files.

3. On the **Microsoft Dynamics CRM Setup** screen, select the **Install Connector for SQL Server Reporting Services** option, as shown in **Figure 25.3**.

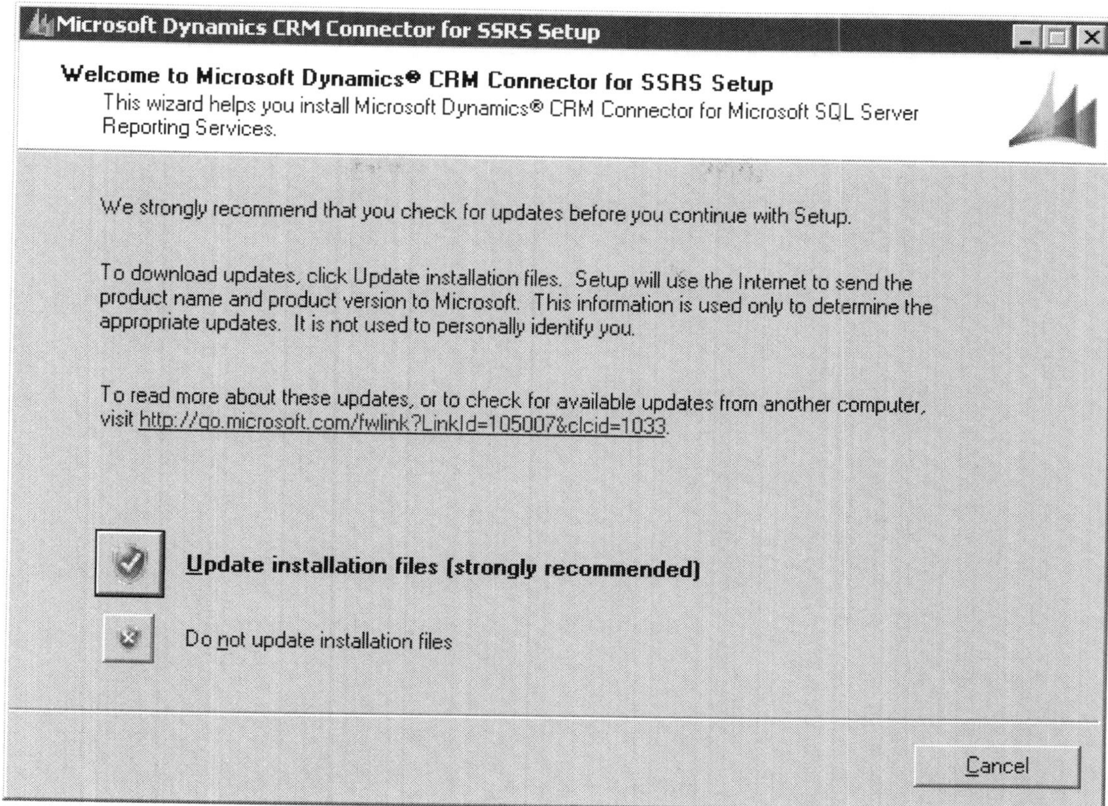


**Figure 25.4**

a. On the **Welcome to Microsoft Dynamics CRM Connector for SSRS Setup** screen, click on the **Update installation files (strongly recommended)** button.

b. On the **Checking for Update** screen, click on the **Next** button to continue.

c. On the **License Agreement** screen, select the **I accept this license agreement** bullet, and then click on the **I Accept** button to continue.

d. On the **Install Required Components** screen, click on the **Install** button, and then click on the **Next** button to continue.

## Installing the CRM SRS Data Connector- Specifying the SQL Cluster as the Database Server

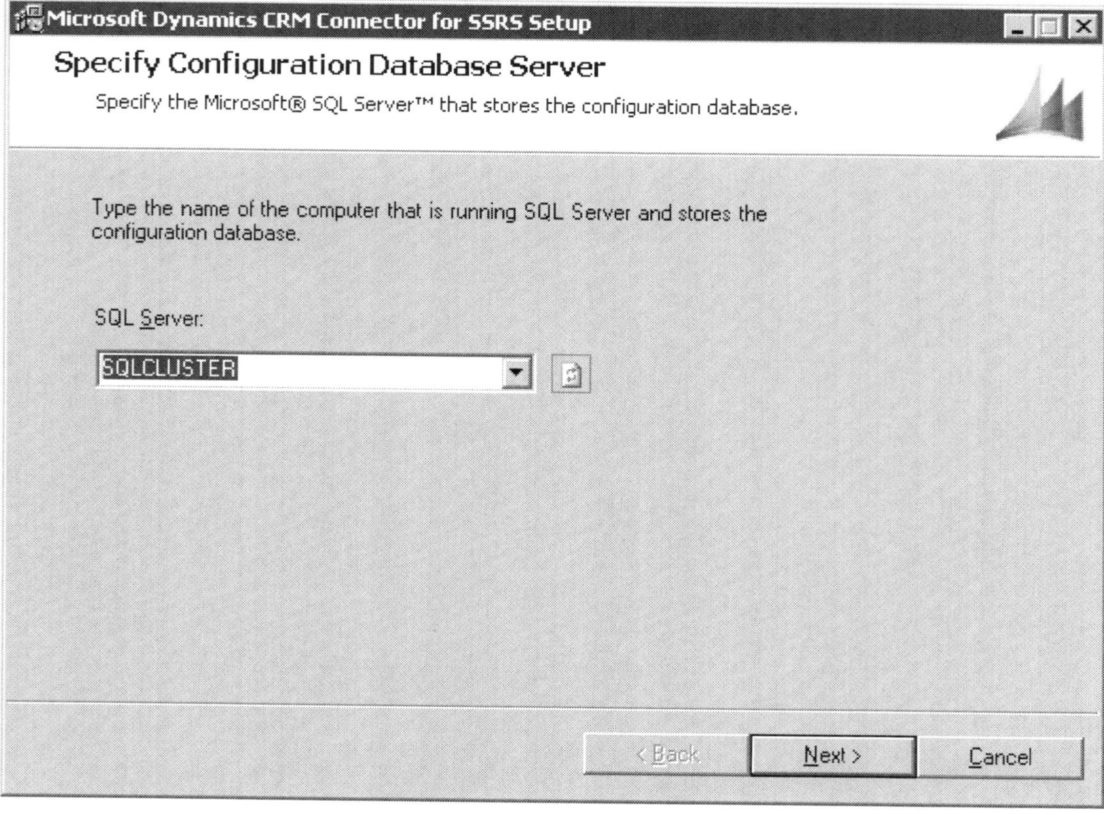


**Figure 25.5**

e. On the **Specify Configuration Database Server** screen, enter in your SQL cluster's name, and then click on the **Next** button to continue. For our project, we will enter our SQL cluster's name of **SQLCLUSTER**, as shown in **Figure 25.5**.

# Installing the CRM SRS Data Connector- System Requirements Error

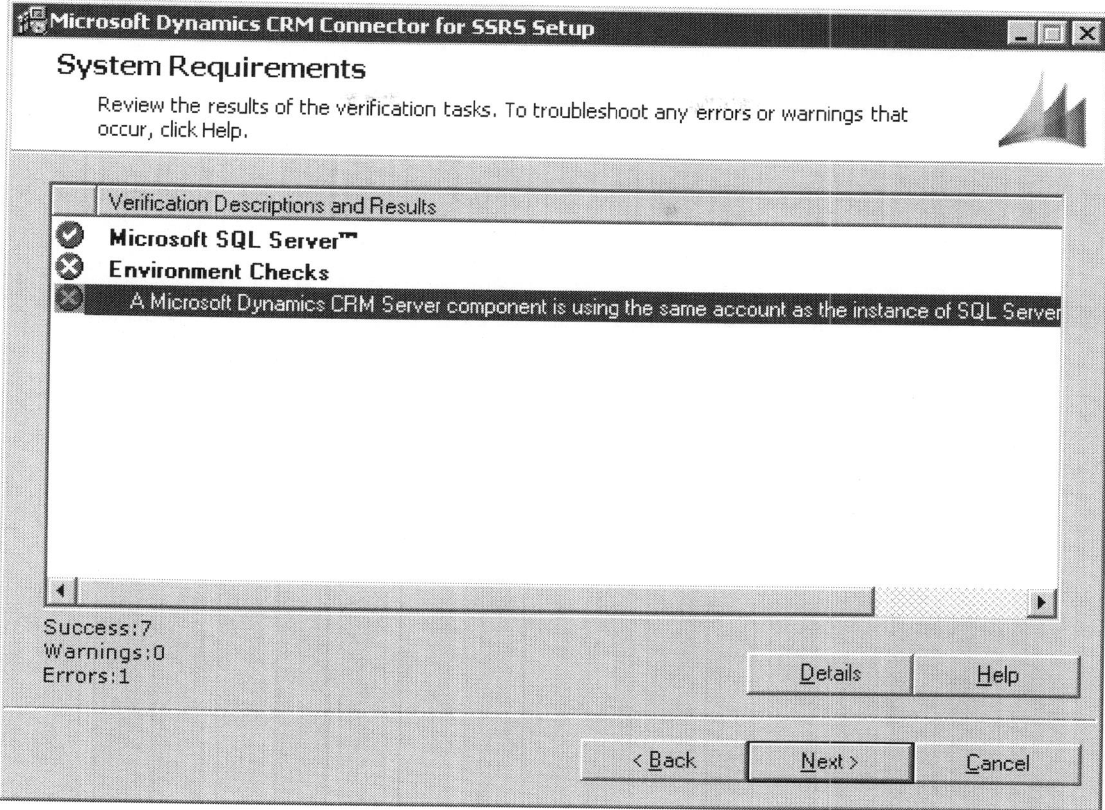


**Figure 25.6**

f. On the **System Requirements** screen, you will receive a red **X** error stating **A Microsoft dynamics CRM Server component is using the same account in the instance of SQL Server Reporting Services** which you can safely ignore, and then click on the **Next** button.

**NOTE:** If you didn't add the IgnoreChecks registry value, then you won't be able to continue as the Next button will be grayed out.

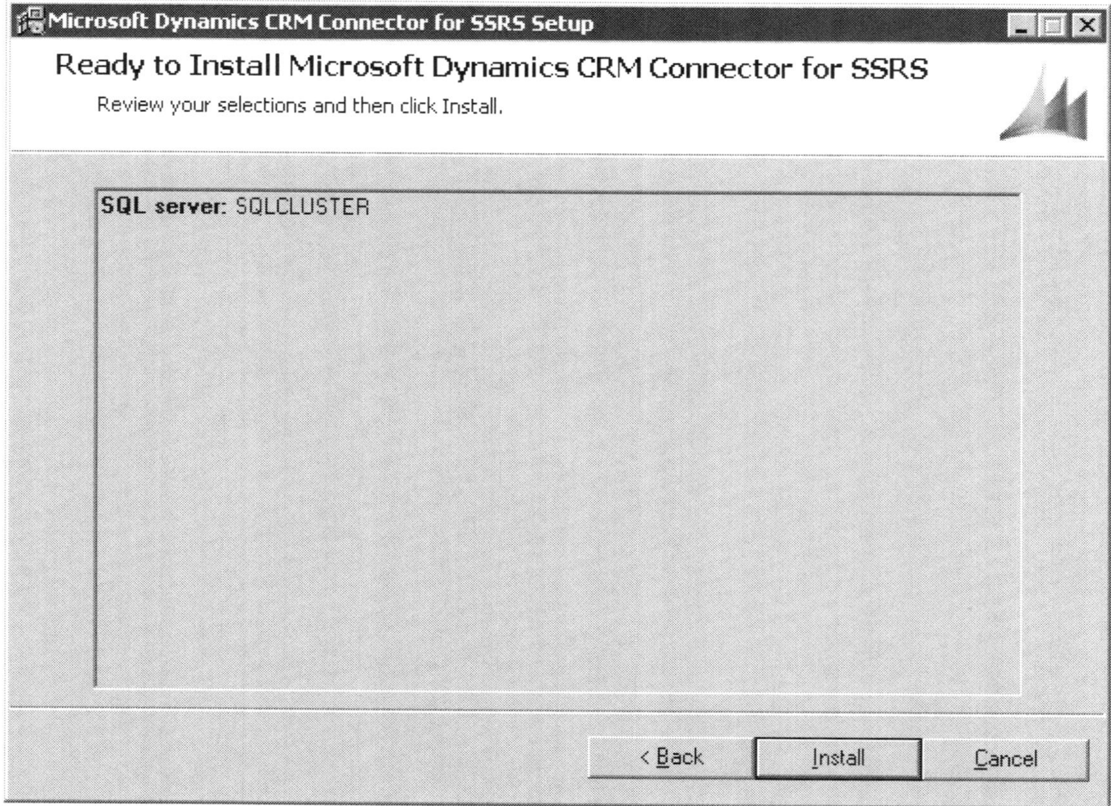


**Figure 25.7**

g. On the **Ready to Install Microsoft Dynamics CRM Connector for SSRS** screen, click on the **Install** button, and then click on the **Finish** button to complete the installation.

4. On each CRM NLB cluster node with the newly installed CRM SRS Data Connecter, apply the same level of **Update Rollup** for **CRM SRS Data Connecter** as you installed for your **CRM Server** component.

5. Repeat the steps in this chapter for each of your CRM NLB cluster nodes that have SQL Reporting Services installed.

   NOTE: We will test out our CRM reports in **Chapter 26, Step 9** after we have completed our CRM's internet facing configuration.

# Chapter 26: Installation and Configuration of the CRM Internet Facing Deployment (IFD) Tool when Utilizing an NLB Cluster

The Microsoft Dynamics CRM Internet Facing Deployment (IFD) Configuration Tool enables you to configure your CRM 4.0 deployment to be accessible from the internet. In this chapter, we will cover the intricacies of how to configure the CRM IFD tool for our particular network environment. Once we have our configuration complete, we will test access to our CRM organization through the internet, and also verify that our CRM SRS reporting is functioning correctly.

## Prerequisites- Setting Up Internet DNS Records

1. The first prerequisite is to create an internet DNS Host (A) record at our internet service provider for each of our CRM organizations that we want to be available from the internet. The internet DNS Host (A) record that you create has to include your CRM organization's name as a sub-domain/prefix. For example, in our project our CRM's organization name is **CRM** and our company's internet domain name is **www.ScreamPublications.com** which makes the internet DNS record that we need to add as **http://crm.screampublications.com** or **https://crm.screampublications.com** when using https. If you have any additional CRM organizations that you want to make available from the internet, then you'll need to also create an internet DNS record for each of those CRM organizations as well. As an example, if we had a second CRM organization named **Production**, then we would also need to create an internet DNS record of **http://production.screampublications.com**, and so on. You do not need to make all your CRM organizations accessible from the internet as you can choose to make just one or two accessible. The internet DNS record is what determines if a CRM organization is available from the internet or not. If the CRM organization doesn't have an internet DNS record created for it then that organization is not accessible from the internet as there is no URL to access it. Your internet DNS Host (A) records should point at your firewall's WAN IP address and then your firewall should have a policy pointing this incoming traffic to your CRM NLB cluster's IP address. For our project, we will create the internet DNS (A) record of **http://crm.screampublications.com** for our CRM organization named **CRM**.

## Prerequisites- Configuring the Internet Firewall

2. Now that we have our internet DNS record(s) pointing at our firewall, we will need to add a **Network Address Translation (NAT)** policy to our internet firewall that points our incoming CRM traffic on port **HTTP** or **HTTPS** to our CRM NLB cluster's IP address. For our project, we will create a **NAT** policy to point our incoming **HTTP** internet traffic to our CRM NLB cluster's IP of **10.10.10.59**.

## Downloading and Installing the Microsoft Dynamics CRM Internet Facing Deployment (IFD) Tool

3. Browse to Microsoft's software download website at **www.microsoft.com/downloads**, and then enter **Microsoft Dynamics CRM Internet Facing Deployment Configuration Tool** in the search field which will bring you to the tool's download screen. Download the **CRM40IFDTool.zip** file and then extract the .zip file on one of your CRM NLB cluster nodes.

4. Place a copy of the extracted **CRM4IFDTool.exe** program in the **C:\Program Files\Microsoft Dynamics CRM\Tools** directory on each of your CRM NLB cluster nodes.

5. Right click on the **CRM4IFDTool.exe** program, and then select the **Run As Administrator** option.

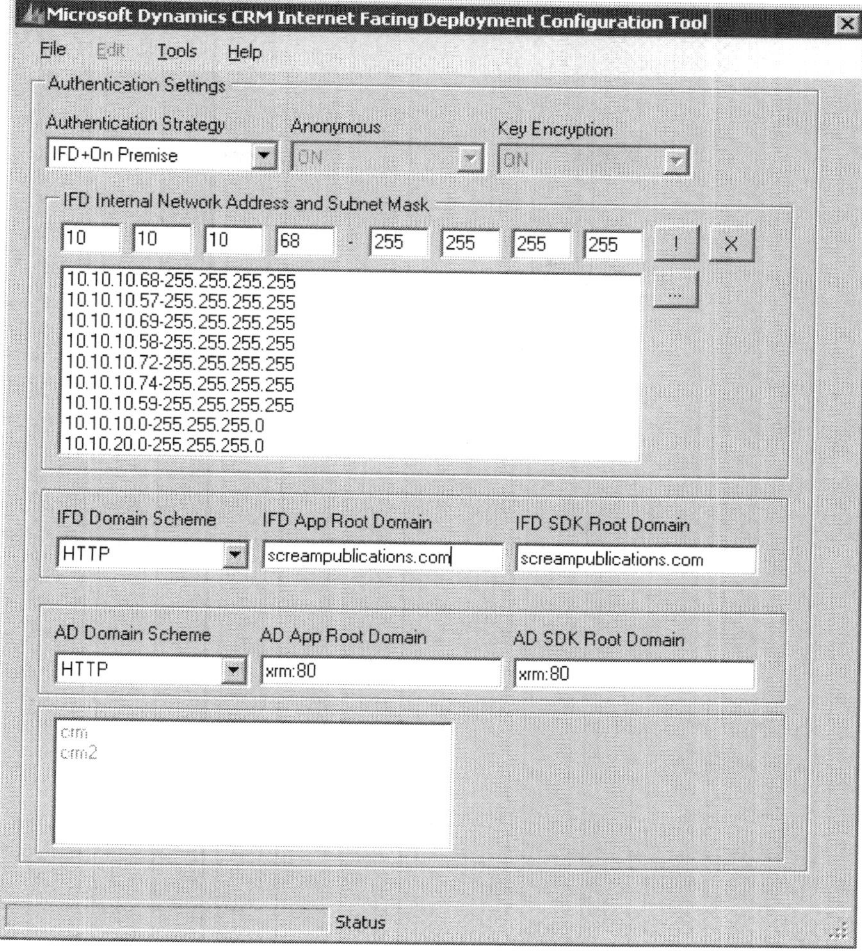


**Figure 26.1**

6. On the **Microsoft Dynamics CRM Internet Facing Deployment Configuration Tool** screen, select the **IFD+On Premise** option for the **Authentication Strategy** dropdown field.

   a. Fill in the following fields of the **Microsoft Dynamics CRM Internet Facing Deployment Configuration Tool** screen with your CRM cluster's configuration details, as explained in the steps below.

      i. For the **IFD Internal Network Address and Subnet Mask** field, add the **IP Addresses** and **Subnet Masks** of your **CRM NLB cluster nodes**, **CRM NLB cluster**, and any **internal subnets** that your clients will access the CRM NLB cluster from.

         1. Enter in your **IP Address** and **Subnet Mask** for both the **Client** and **Client NLB** network adapters of each of your **CRM NLB cluster nodes**, and then click on the **! exclamation** button to add the addresses. For our project, we will add our **CRMCluster1VM's Client10** network adapter's IP of **10.10.10.68** with the subnet mask **255.255.255.255**, and then we will also add its **Client10 NLB** network adapter's IP of **10.10.10.57** with the subnet mask **255.255.255.255**. We will repeat the process for our remaining **Client10** and **Client10 NLB** network adapters belonging to our remaining CRM NLB cluster nodes named **CRMCluster2VM** and **CRMCluster3VM**, as shown in **Figure 26.1**.

2. Enter in your **IP Address** and **Subnet Mask** for your **CRM NLB cluster**, and then click on the **! exclamation** button to add the addresses. For our project, we will enter our CRM NLB cluster's IP of **10.10.10.59** with the subnet mask **255.255.255.255**, as shown in **Figure 26.1**.

3. Enter in your **IP Addresses** and **Subnet Masks** for each of your **internal subnets** that your clients will be accessing your CRM NLB cluster from. As an example, in our project we have three internal subnets **10.10.10.0/24**, **10.10.20.0/24** and **10.10.30.0/24** that we want to allow clients access from, so we will add the IP address of **10.10.10.0** with the subnet mask of **255.255.255.0**, the IP address of **10.10.20.0** with the subnet mask of **255.255.255.0** and the IP address of **10.10.30.0** with the subnet mask of **255.255.255.0**, as shown in **Figure 26.1**.

b. For the **IFD Domain Scheme** and **AS Domain Scheme** fields, select either **HTTP** or **HTTPS** for which protocol your CRM internet traffic will use. For our project, we will select **HTTP** for both fields, as shown in **Figure 26.1**.

c. For the **IFD App Root Domain** and **IFD SDK Root Domain** fields, enter your **CRM's root internet domain name** that you created an internet DNS record for. The internet domain needs to be just the root internet domain name without any sub-domains or prefixes. For our project, we will enter **screampublications.com**, as shown in **Figure 26.1**.

d. For the **AD App Root Domain** and **AD SDK Root Domain** fields, enter your CRM NLB cluster's internal DNS name. For our project, we created an internal DNS Host (A) record for our CRM NLB cluster's IP of **10.10.10.59** called **xrm**, so we will enter **xrm** for both of these fields, as shown in **Figure 26.1**.

e. Click on the **File** option on the toolbar at the top of the screen, and then select the **Apply Changes** option to save your configuration.

f. Click on the **Tools** option on the toolbar at the top of the screen, and then select the **Check DNS** option to verify that the CRM Internet Facing Deployment Configuration Tool can resolve your internet DNS records for each of your CRM organizations.

g. To exit the CRM Internet Facing Deployment Configuration Tool, click on the **File** option on the toolbar at the top of the screen, and then select the **Exit** option.

7. Repeat **Steps 4-6** on each of your CRM NLB cluster nodes.

# Verifying that the CRM IFD Configuration was Successful

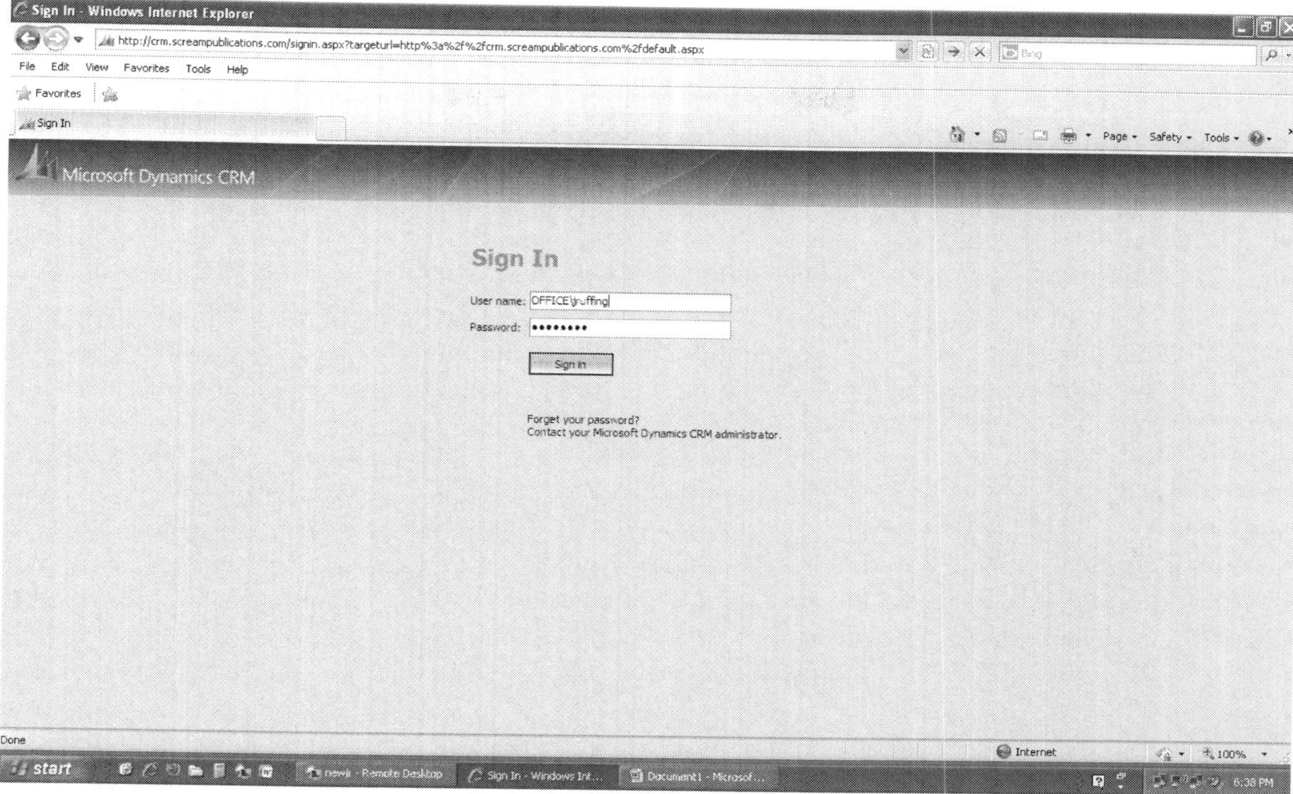


**Figure 26.2**

8. After using the CRM IFD Configuration Tool to configure each of our CRM NLB cluster nodes, we will want to test our configuration from the internet when outside the local network where our CRM NLB cluster is hosted. From externally on the internet, browse to each of CRM organization's URLs using Internet Explorer. When you receive a blue login screen as shown in **Figure 26.2**, then your IFD deployment has been successful and you should be able to login with a valid CRM user account. Your CRM URL's login screen should resolve to the following format **http://<Your Crm Org>.domain.com/signin.aspx** by automatically adding the **/signin.aspx** to the end of the URL. For our project, we will browse to **http://crm.screampublications.com** to login.

   **NOTE:** If instead you receive a Windows login pop-up screen, then this tells you that something is wrong with your IFD configuration due to CRM trying to authenticate via Windows Authentication vs. with CRM's IFD Authentication Mode. In which case, you'll need to review your IFD's configuration before continuing.

# Verifying that the CRM IFD and SRS Data Connector are Working Together

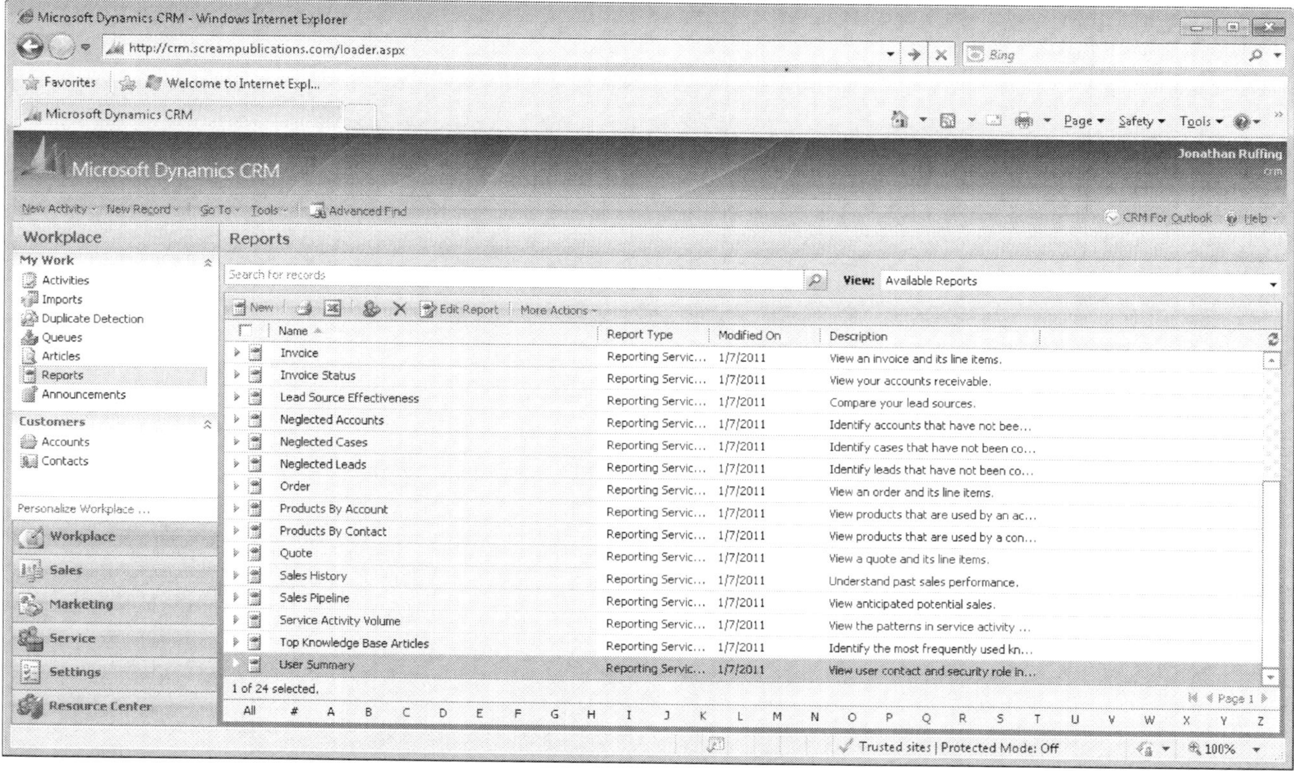


**Figure 26.3**

9. Once you're logged in, you'll want to test running some reports to verify that your **CRM SRS Data Connector** is functioning correctly as well. Click on the **Workplace** button in the left pane of the CRM screen, and then select the **Reports** option from the list under the **My Work** section of the left pane. Browse to the **User Summary** report in the right pane, and double click on it to launch the report screen.

## Verifying that the CRM SRS Data Connector- Running a Test Report

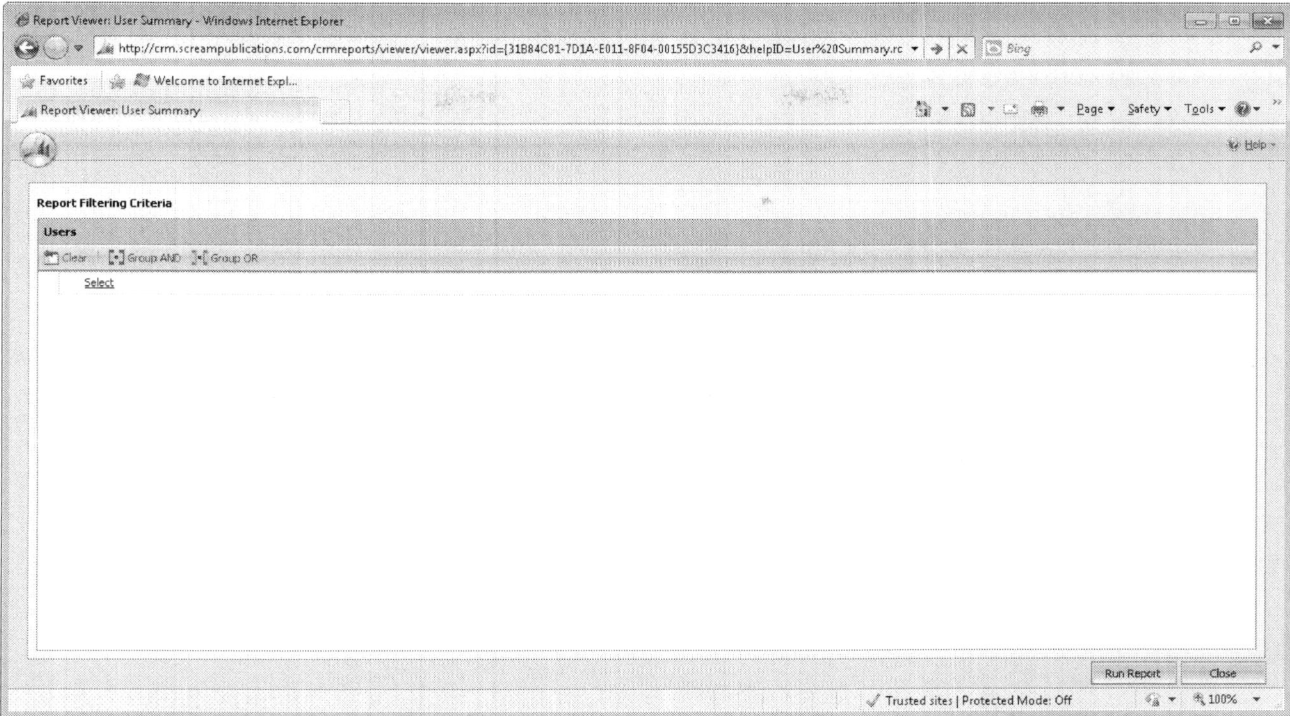


**Figure 26.4**

a. On the **Report Viewer: User Summary** screen, click on the **Run Report** button in the lower left hand corner of the screen.

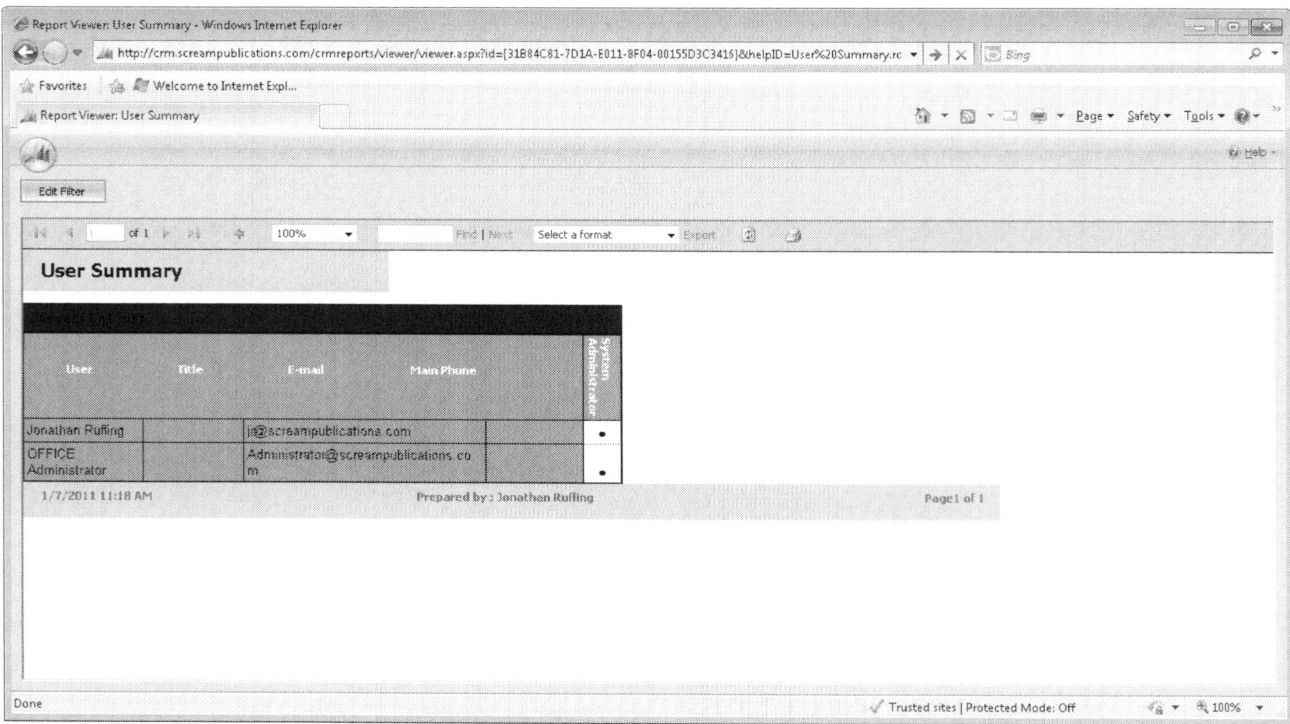


**Figure 26.5**

b. As long as you receive a screen with a layout similar to what is shown in **Figure 26.5**, then your **CRM IFD** and **CRM SRS Data Connector** for reports are functioning correctly. Your report can display with or without data as long as you didn't receive any SQL Reporting Services error.

# Chapter 27: Installing, Configuring, and Clustering the Microsoft Dynamics CRM E-mail Router

Once we have all our CRM organization(s) imported and/or created, then we can begin to install and configure the Microsoft Dynamics CRM Email Router role. The Email Router filters through CRM users Exchange mail to find and upload emails that apply to CRM. There are a few different ways that you can configure the CRM Email Router to filter and upload users' mail. You can choose to have the Email Router filter through your CRM user mailboxes at the Exchange server level or you can choose to utilize a forward mailbox where your CRM users' mail would be forwarded from their Outlook and/or from their Exchange web mail (OWA) to a specific mailbox that is then filtered by Email Router. Regardless of which method you choose, you will also need to determine what specific types of email are uploaded into your CRM database. You can specify which emails are uploaded based on different criteria such as if the email came from a lead, contact, or an account.

Microsoft recommends only having one instance of the CRM Email Router service running at a time. This is due to the fact that multiple instances of the CRM Email Router service have no way of communicating with each other to insure that they both don't upload the same emails into CRM twice. We will overcome this limitation and create a highly available solution for our CRM Email Router service by utilizing a Windows active/passive cluster. Within one of our existing Windows clusters we will create a new generic service to host our CRM Email Router. This generic service will need to have its own small shared disk on our SAN to host the CRM Email Router's application files. Once our CRM Email Router service has been clustered it will be able to failover between our cluster nodes independently from our other clustered resources within the same cluster. Since our front-end CRM servers are clustered applications themselves this makes them ineligible to host our clustered Email Router service.

You can choose to create a new active/passive Windows cluster that is dedicated only to hosting your CRM Email Router service or you can choose to use one of your already existing Windows clusters such as your SQL cluster. Choosing to place your clustered CRM Email Router service on your already existing SQL cluster is the easiest method as you do not need to create a new Windows cluster just to host your Email Router service. Further, your clustered Email Router service will be able to failover independently of your clustered SQL resources and thus allowing you to balance your workload across each of your SQL nodes. In this scenario, you would simply have your Email Router service active on your passive node of the SQL cluster. In addition, you'll also gain the benefit of better utilizing the processing power of both your SQL nodes vs. just having one active node for all your resources while the other node sits by in a purely passive/standby mode. For our project, we will create a generic service to host our CRM Email Router on our already existing Windows cluster that hosts our SQL resources.

## Installing the CRM E-mail Router Cluster- Initial Node

The installation steps are basically identical for each of our cluster nodes. The only difference is that all the configuration of the Email Router will take place on our initial node. Once we have our stand alone Email Router up and functioning on our initial node we will then copy its application files onto our shared disk to make it highly available. For our project, we will use our already existing Windows cluster named **WinSQLCluster** to host our clustered CRM Email Router service.

## Installing the CRM E-mail Router- Prerequisites

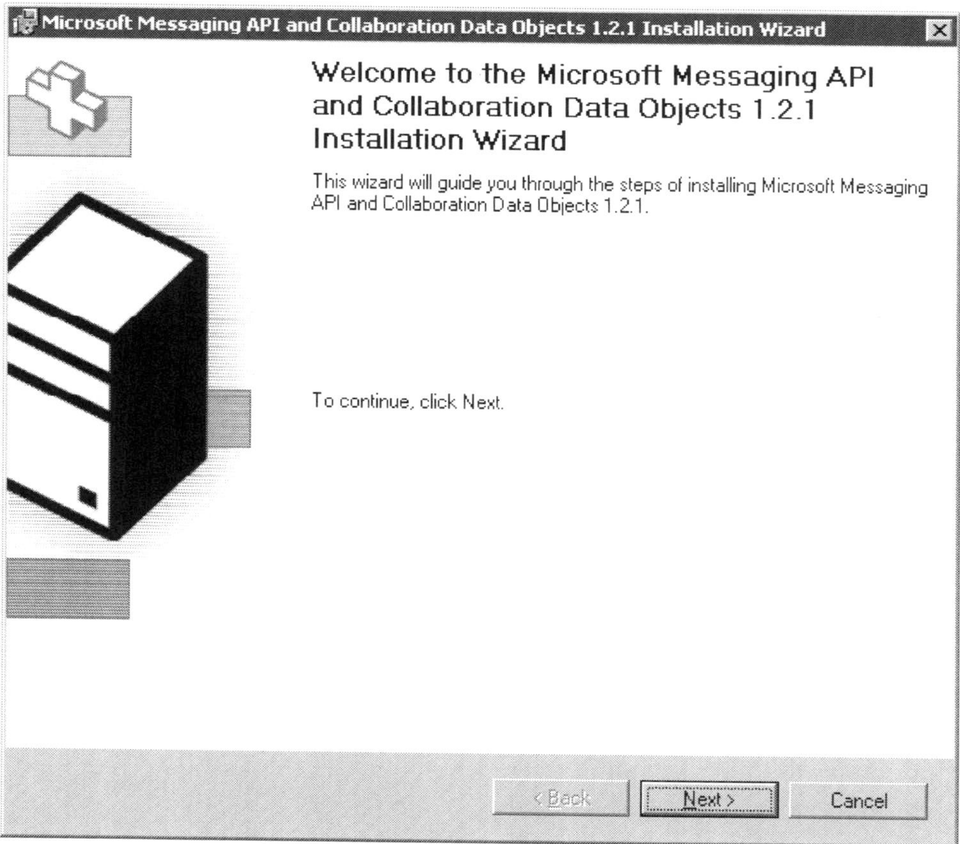


**Figure 27.1**

If you are using Exchange Server 2007 or later, then you'll need to install the Microsoft Messaging API (MAPI) and Collaboration Data Objects (CDO) 1.2.1 as a prerequisite to installing the CRM Email Router. These components are required for the CRM Email Router to be able to make connections to the Exchange server.

1. On the initial node, download and install the **Microsoft Exchange Server MAPI Client and Collaboration Data Objects 1.2.1** from Microsoft's download website at **www.microsoft.com/downloads**. For our project, we will install the **Microsoft Exchange Server MAPI Client and Collaboration Data Objects 1.2.1** prerequisite on our **WinSQLCluster** cluster's first node named **SQLCluster2VM**.

## Installing the CRM E-mail Router- Launching the Install

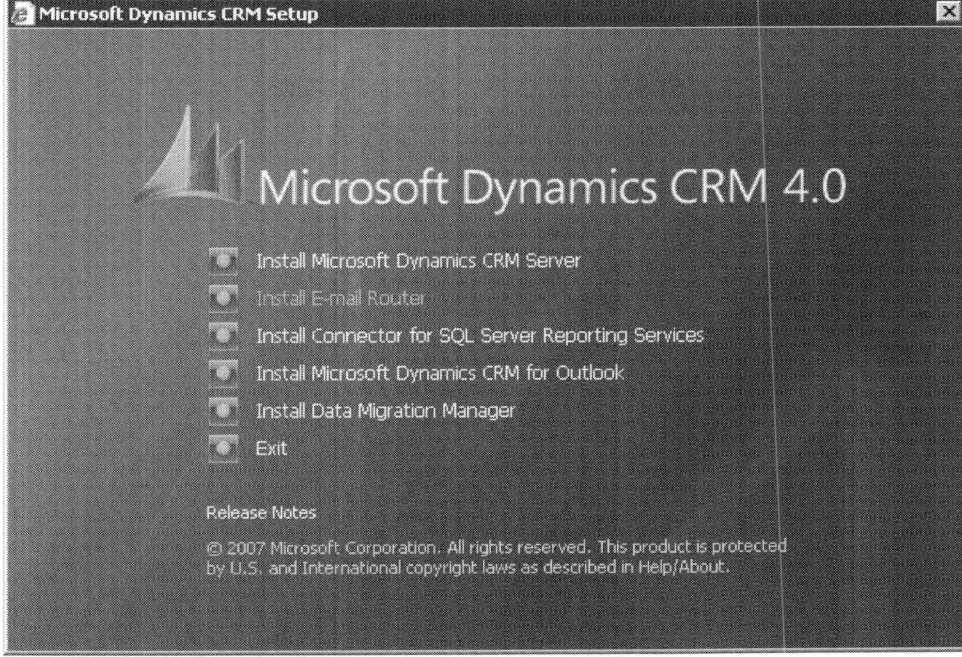


**Figure 27.2**

2. Launch the CRM 4.0 install by inserting the DVD or by double clicking on the **Splash.exe** in the root of the install files.

3. On the **Microsoft Dynamics CRM Setup** screen, select the **Install E-Mail Router** option, as shown in **Figure 27.2**.

    a. On the **Welcome to Microsoft Dynamics CRM Setup** screen, click on the **Update installation files (strongly recommended)** button.

    b. On the **Checking for Update** screen, click on the **Next** button to continue.

    c. On the **License Agreement** screen, select the **I accept this license agreement** option, and then click on the **I Accept** button to continue.

    d. On the **Install Required Components** screen, click on the **Install** button to continue.

    e. Verify that all the components installed successfully, and then click on the **Next** button to continue.

## Installing the CRM E-mail Router- Selecting Router Components

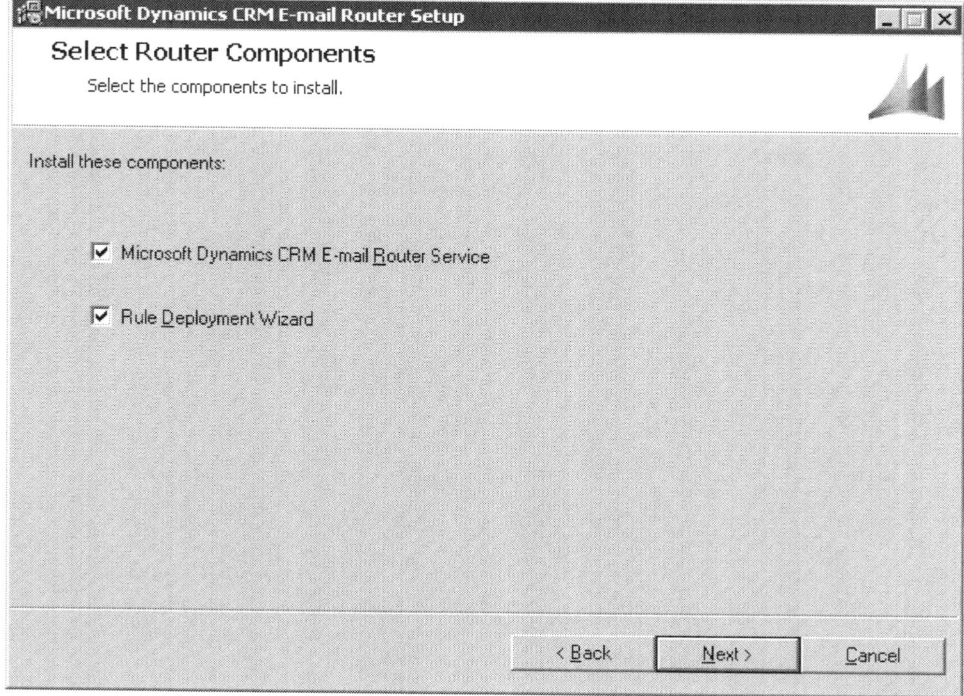


**Figure 27.3**

f. On the **Select Router Components** screen, select the router components you want installed, and then click on the **Next** button to continue. For our project, we will select both the **Microsoft Dynamics CRM E-mail Router Service** and the **Rule Deployment Wizard** components to be installed, as shown in **Figure 27.3**.

g. On the **Select Install Location** screen, choose your install location, and then click on the **Next** button to continue. For our project, we will leave the default install location.

h. On the **System Requirements** screen, verify the results are successful, and then click on the **Next** button to continue.

i. On the **Ready to Install the Application** screen, unselect the **Launch Configuration Manager after the installation completes** checkbox at the bottom of the screen, and then click on the **Install** button to continue.

j. On the **The Microsoft Dynamics CRM E-Mail Router has been successfully installed** screen, click on the **OK** to complete the install.

## Applying the Update Rollup to the CRM E-Mail Router

4. Install the **Update Rollup** for the **CRM E-Mail Router** component to the same level as your other CRM components are currently updated to.

## Configuring the CRM E-mail Router Security- Assigning the CRM Service User Account Permissions

Some of the permissions for your CRM service user account have already been outlined in Chapter 22. In this section, we will recap the permissions that apply to the CRM Email Router, and then expand further on the permissions that have to be set from within CRM itself for our CRM service user account. The following is an overview of the permissions required for the user account that is used in our Email Router's configuration.

- The user account that the Microsoft CRM Email Router service runs under must be a member of the Active Directory CRM security group PrivUserGroup. This group was created during the CRM installation and resides in the Active Directory Organizational Unit that you chose for CRM to use during the installation.

- When setting up access credentials for configuration profiles within the Email Router Configuration Manager the user account specified must be a CRM user within the CRM organization being configured to use the Email Router. In addition, this user account must have the CRM role of system administrator.

- If you choose to use the Local System Account for your access credentials, then the computer account of the server that the Email Router is installed on must be a member of the PrivUserGroup CRM security group.

- If you choose cluster your CRM Email Router service, then each of the cluster node's computer accounts must be a member of the PrivUserGroup CRM security group.

## Configuring the CRM E-mail Router Security- Adding PrivUserGroup Members

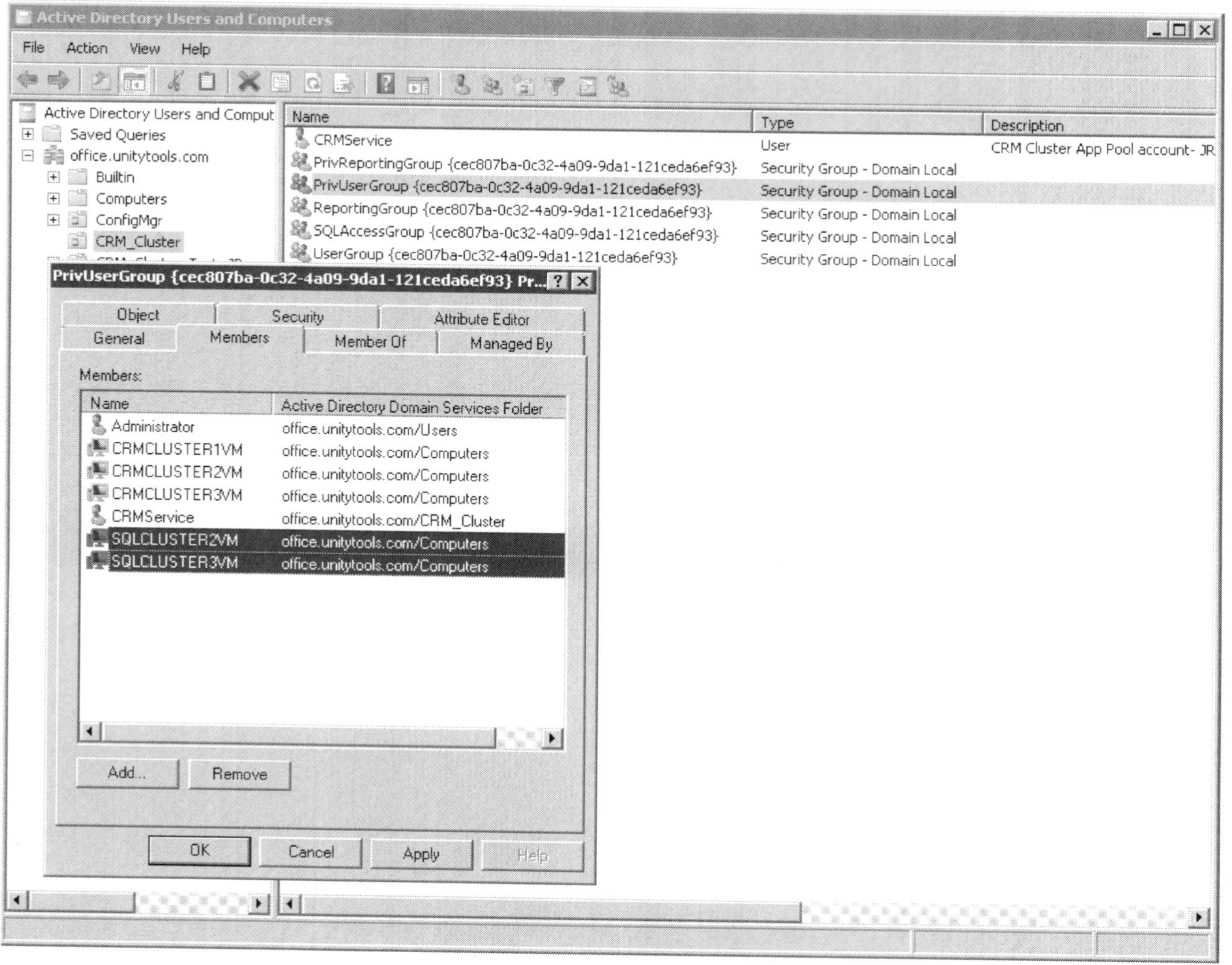

Figure 27.4

5. On the **Domain Controller**, open the **Active Directory Users and Computers** console, and then browse to your **CRM Organizational Unit**.

   a. Double click on the CRM **PrivUserGroup** security group to open its **Properties** screen, and then add the computer accounts for each of the cluster nodes that will host your clustered **CRM E-mail Router** service. Click on the **OK** button to exit and save your changes. For our project, we will add our SQL cluster nodes **SQLCluster2VM** and **SQLCluster3VM**, as shown in **Figure 27.4**.

# Configuring the CRM E-mail Router Security- User Account and Startup Type

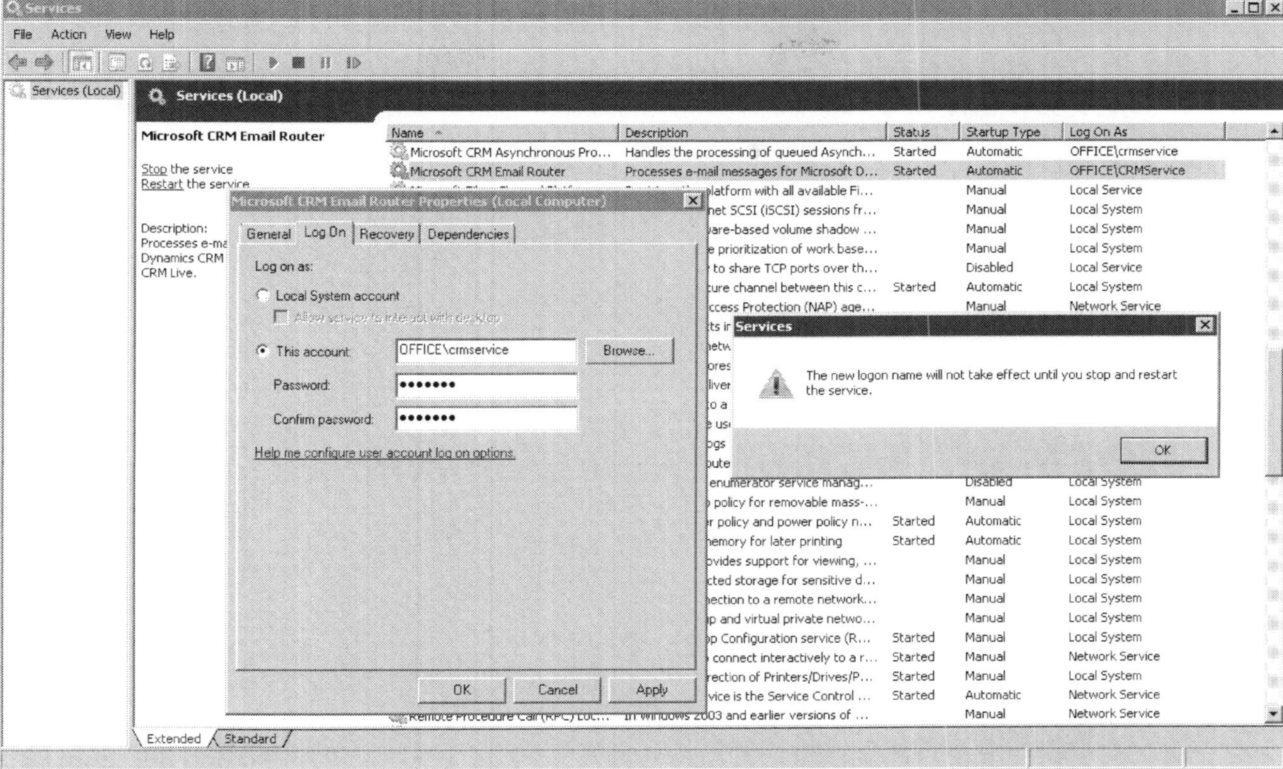


**Figure 27.5**

6. On each server where the CRM Email Router is installed, browse to **Administrative Tools\Services**, and then double click the **Microsoft CRM E-mail Router** service to open its **Properties** screen.

   a. On the **General** tab of the **Properties** screen, select the **Manual** option from the **Startup type** dropdown field. When a service is going to be clustered in an active/passive mode you need to set the startup type to manual so that the cluster can start and stop to service as needed during failovers.

   b. On the **Properties** screen, click on the **Log On** tab.

      i. On the **Log On** tab, select the **This account** option, and then enter your **CRM service** user account name and password. For our project, we will set the service to run under our **CRMService** user account, as shown in **Figure 27.5**. If you're not familiar with this custom CRMService user account that we created earlier, then please refer to **Chapter 22** on CRM security.

      ii. Click the **OK** button to save the changes to the **Properties** screen.

      iii. On the pop-up screen stating that the **The new logon name will not take effect until you stop and restart the service**, click on the **OK** button.

   c. Right click on the **Microsoft CRM E-mail Router** service, and select the **Restart** option so that your changes to take effect.

## Configuring the CRM E-mail Router Security- Adding the CRM Service Account to the CRM Organization(s)

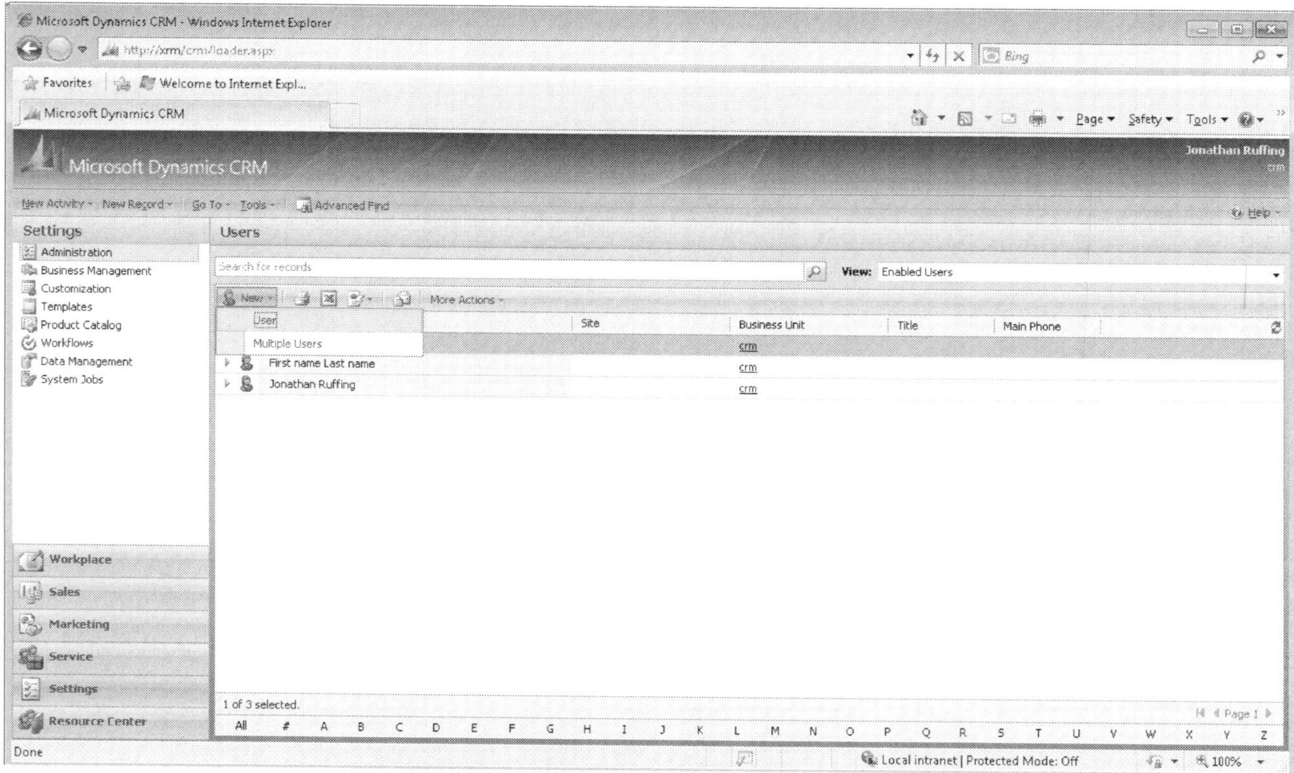

**Figure 27.6**

7. Connect to your CRM organization through **Internet Explorer**, click on the **Settings** button in the lower in left hand pane, and then select the **Administration** sub-category from the upper left hand pane.

   a. Click on the **Users** category in the right hand pane, and then on the **Users** list screen, click on the **New** button at the top of list screen and select the **User** option from the dropdown box, as shown in **Figure 27.6**.

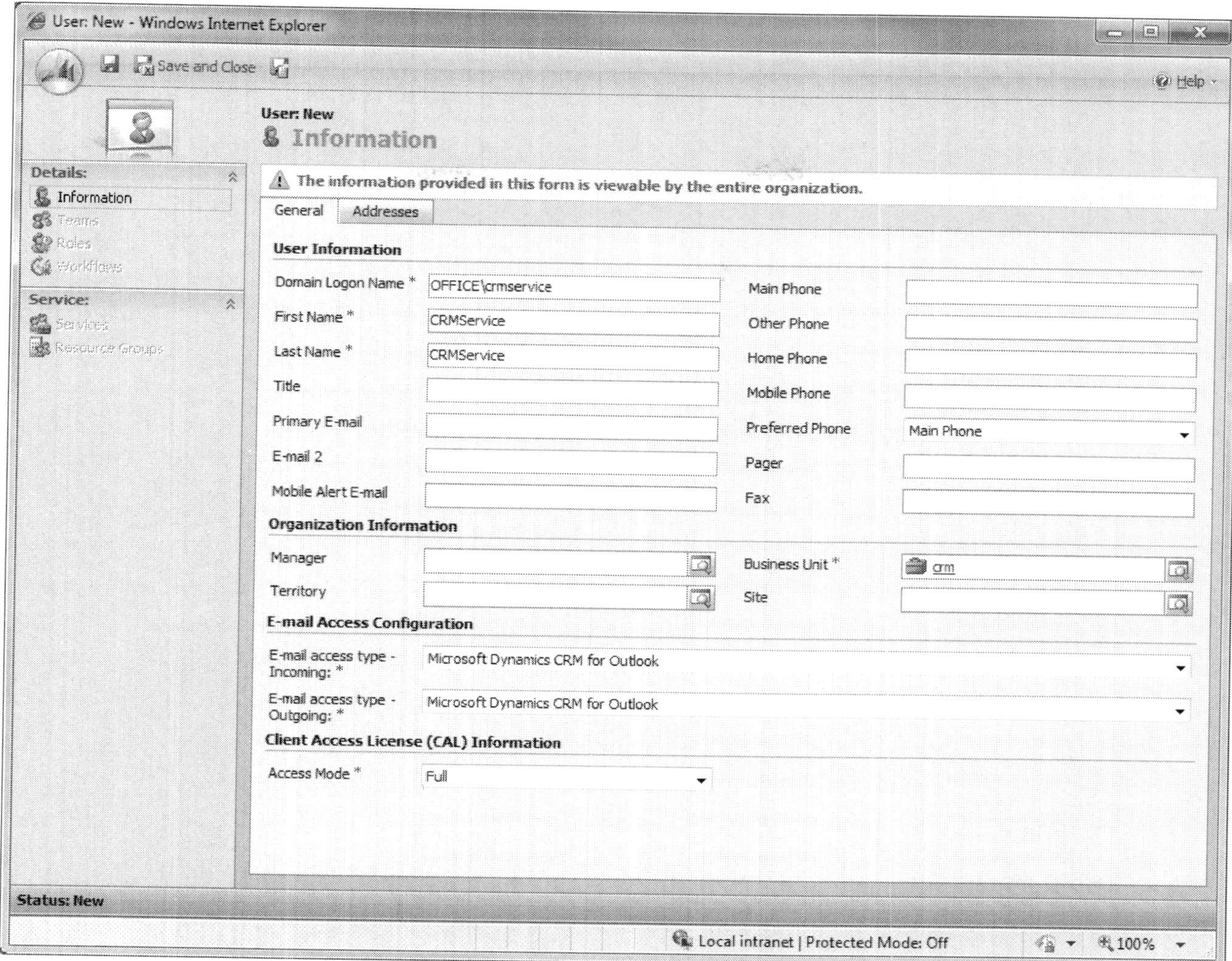


**Figure 27.7**

b. On the **User: New** screen, enter in your Active Directory **CRM service** user account's name in the **Domain Logon Name** field. For our project, we will enter **OFFICE\crmservice** for our **Domain** and **CRMService** user account names, as shown in **Figure 27.7**.

   i. Fill in the **First Name** and **Last Name** fields with your CRM service user account's names, and then click on the **Save and Close** button to add the user.

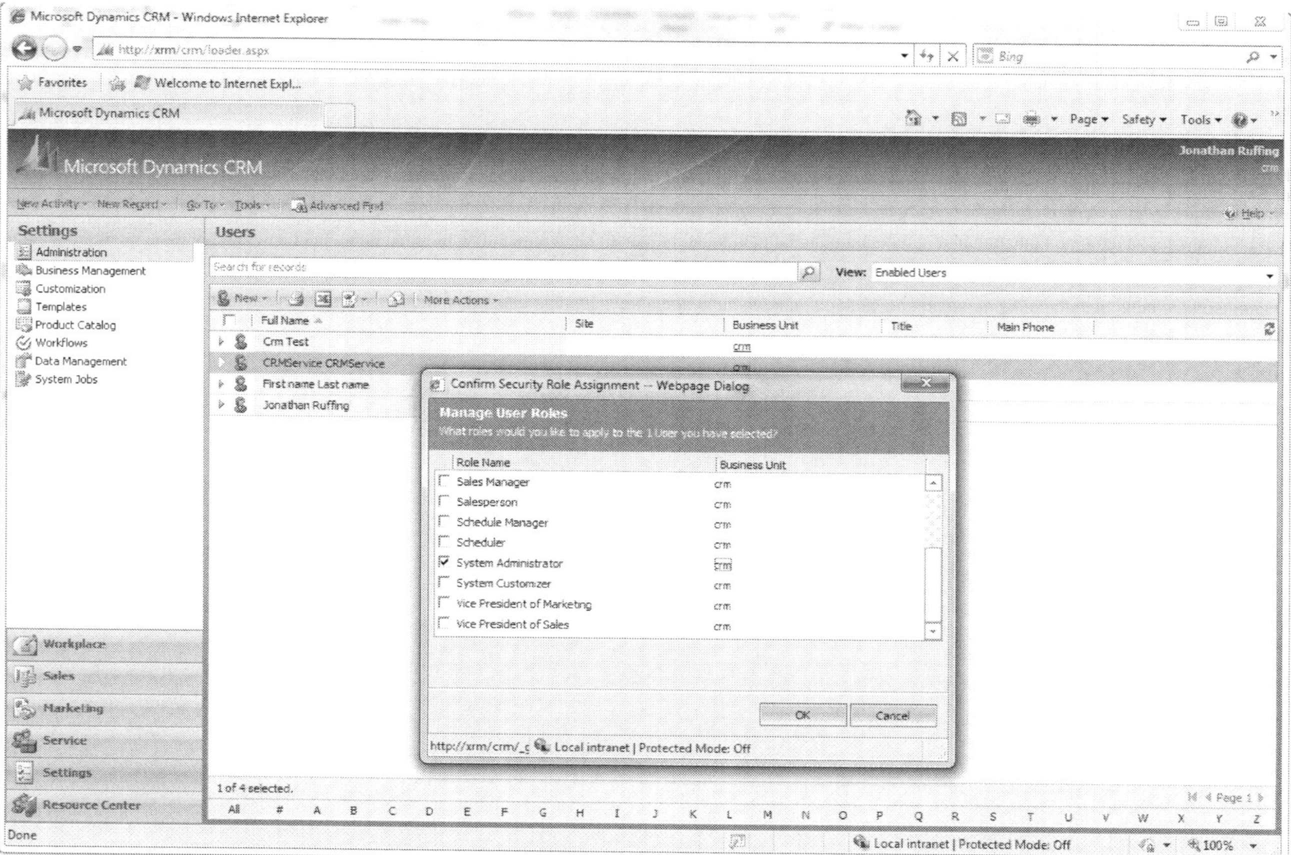


**Figure 27.8**

c. On the **Users** list screen, highlight your newly added **CRM service** user account, and then click on the **More Actions** button at the top of the list screen. Select the **Manage Roles** option from the dropdown.

   i. On the **Confirm Security Role Assignment** screen, select the **System Administrator** role, and then click on the **OK** button to save your changes.

8. Repeat **Step 7** for each **CRM Organization** that will use the **CRM E-mail Router**.

## Granting the CRM Service User Account Access to Exchange Mailboxes

For each CRM user or queue that will use the CRM Email Router you need configure your CRM service user account to have Send As and Full Access permissions to each of their Exchange mailboxes. We will cover how to add these permissions by both the using Exchange Management Shell (EMS) and from within the Exchange Management Console (EMC). The method when using the Exchange Management Console applies to Exchange Server 2007 SP1 or later, while the method when using the Exchange Management Shell applies to Exchange 2007 or later. If you are using Exchange Server 2003 you will need to use the Active Directory Users and Computers console to assign these permissions. Perform the following steps for each of your CRM users and queues by either using the **Exchange Management Console** in **Steps 9-11** or by using the **Exchange Management Shell** as outlined in **Steps 12-13**.

## Configuring the CRM E-Mail Router- Granting the Send As Permissions with the Exchange Management Console (EMC)

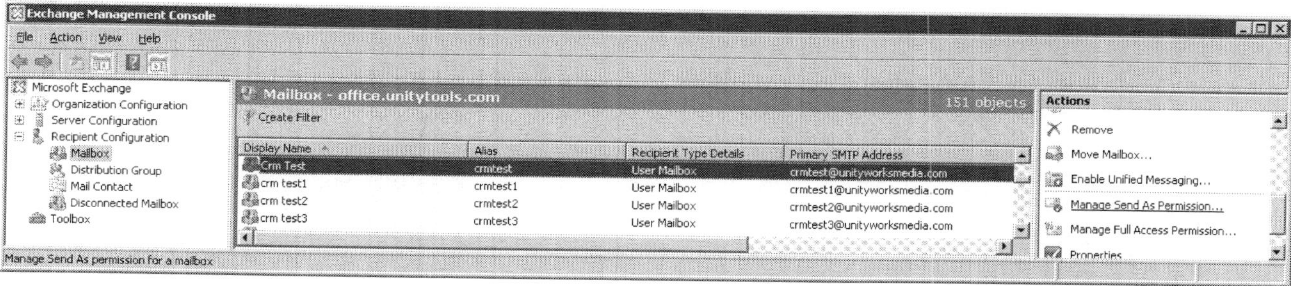


**Figure 27.9**

9. Go to your Exchange mail server and launch the **Exchange Management Console**. Browse to the **Recipient Configuration\Mailbox** node in the left pane, as shown in **Figure 27.9**.

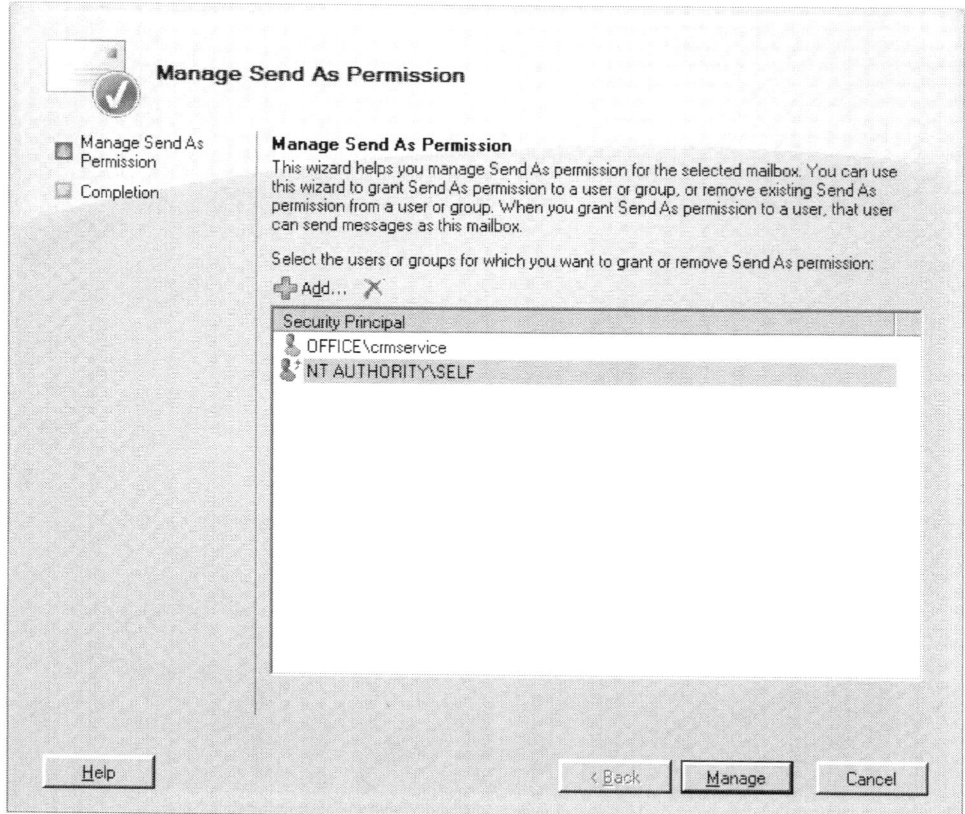


**Figure 27.10**

10. Highlight the CRM user or queue's mailbox in the center pane, and then click on the **Manage Send As Permission...** option in the right **Actions** pane of the Exchange Management Console.

    a. On the **Manage Send As Permission** screen, add the Active Directory user account that you created for your **CRM service** account, and then click on the **Manage** button to continue. For our project, we will add our CRM service user account named **CRMService**, as shown in **Figure 27.10**.

    b. On the **Completion** screen, click on the **Finish** button to complete setting up the permissions.

## Configuring the CRM E-Mail Router- Granting Full Access Permissions with the Exchange Management Console (EMC)

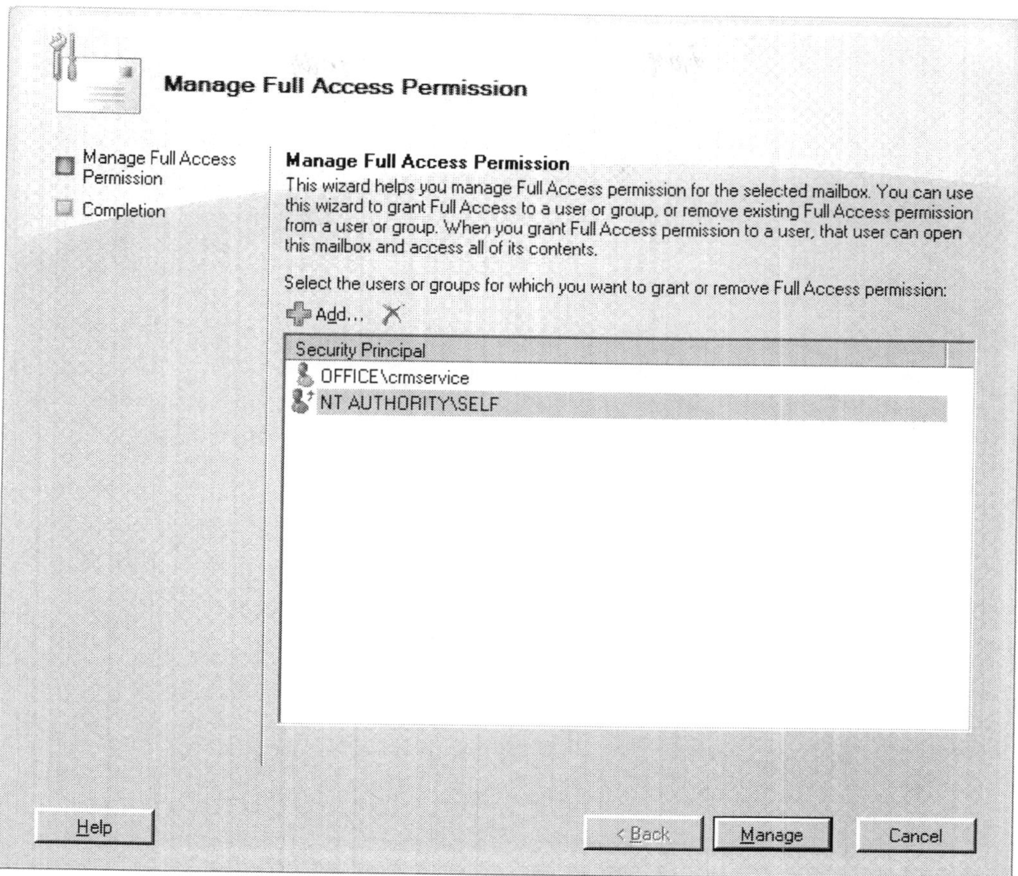


**Figure 27.11**

11. While the CRM user or queue's mailbox is still highlighted, click on the **Manage Full Access Permission...** option in the right **Actions** pane of the Exchange Management Console.

    a. On the **Manage Full Access Permission** screen, add the Active Directory user account that you created for your **CRM service** account, and then click on the **Manage** button to continue. For our project, we will add our CRM service user account named **CRMService**, as shown in **Figure 27.11**.

    b. On the **Completion** screen, click on the **Finish** button to complete setting up the permissions.

## Configuring the CRM E-Mail Router- Granting the Send As Permissions with the Exchange Management Shell (EMS)

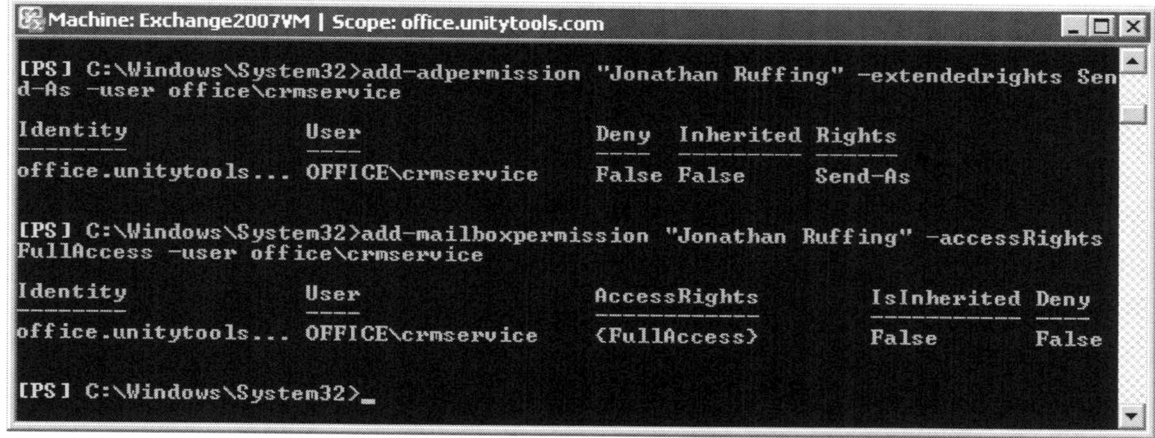


**Figure 27.12**

If you prefer using the Exchange Management Shell (EMS) to add the Send As and Full Access to your CRM user mailboxes then follow the below steps.

12. Go to one of your Exchange mail servers, and then launch the **Exchange Management Shell** with the **Run as administrator** permission. Run the following command to grant the **Send As** permission.

    a. Type in the following command into the **Exchange Management Shell** to add the **Send As** permission to a CRM user or queue's mailbox. You need to replace the **<CRM_User_Or_Queue's_Mailbox_Name>** with your CRM user or queue's mailbox's **Display Name**, and then also replace the **<AD_Domain\Your_CRM_Service_User_Account_Name>** with your **Active Directory Domain** and **CRM Service** user account names.

    **Syntax:**

    **add-adpermission <CRM_ User_Or_Queue's_Mailbox_Name> " -extendedrights Send-As -user <AD_Domain\Your_CRM_Service_User_Account_Name>**

    For our project, we will use the following command to grant our **CRMService** user account the **Send As** permission to the user account **Jonathan Ruffing**, as shown in **Figure 27.12's** first command.

    **Project example:**

    **add-adpermission "Jonathan Ruffing" -extendedrights Send-As -user office\crmservice**

## Configuring the CRM E-Mail Router- Granting Full Access Permissions with the Exchange Management Shell (EMS)

13. While still in the **Exchange Management Shell** run the following command to grant the **Full Access** permission.

    a. Type in the following command into the **Exchange Management Shell** to add the **Full Access** permission to a CRM user or queue's mailbox. You need to replace the **<CRM_User_Or_Queue's_Mailbox_Name>** with your CRM user or queue's mailbox's **Display Name**, and then also replace the **<AD_Domain\Your_CRM_Service_User_Account_Name>** with your **Active Directory Domain** and **CRM Service** user account names.

       **Syntax:**

       **add-mailboxpermission "<CRM_User_Or_Queue's_Mailbox_Name>" -accessRights FullAccess –user <AD_Domain\Your_CRM_Service_User_Account_Name>**

       For our project, we will use the following command to grant our **CRMService** user account the **Full Access** permission to the user account **Jonathan Ruffing**, as shown in **Figure 27.12's** second command.

       **Project example:**

       **add-mailboxpermission "Jonathan Ruffing" -accessRights FullAccess -user office\crmservice**

14. Grant your **CRM Service** user account the **Send As** and **Full Access** permissions for each of your CRM user and queue mailboxes that will be using your CRM Email Router by either repeating **Steps 9-11** using the **Exchange Management Console (EMC)** or by repeating **Steps 12-13** using the **Exchange Management Shell (EMS)**.

## Changing the CRM E-mail Access Configuration- Users

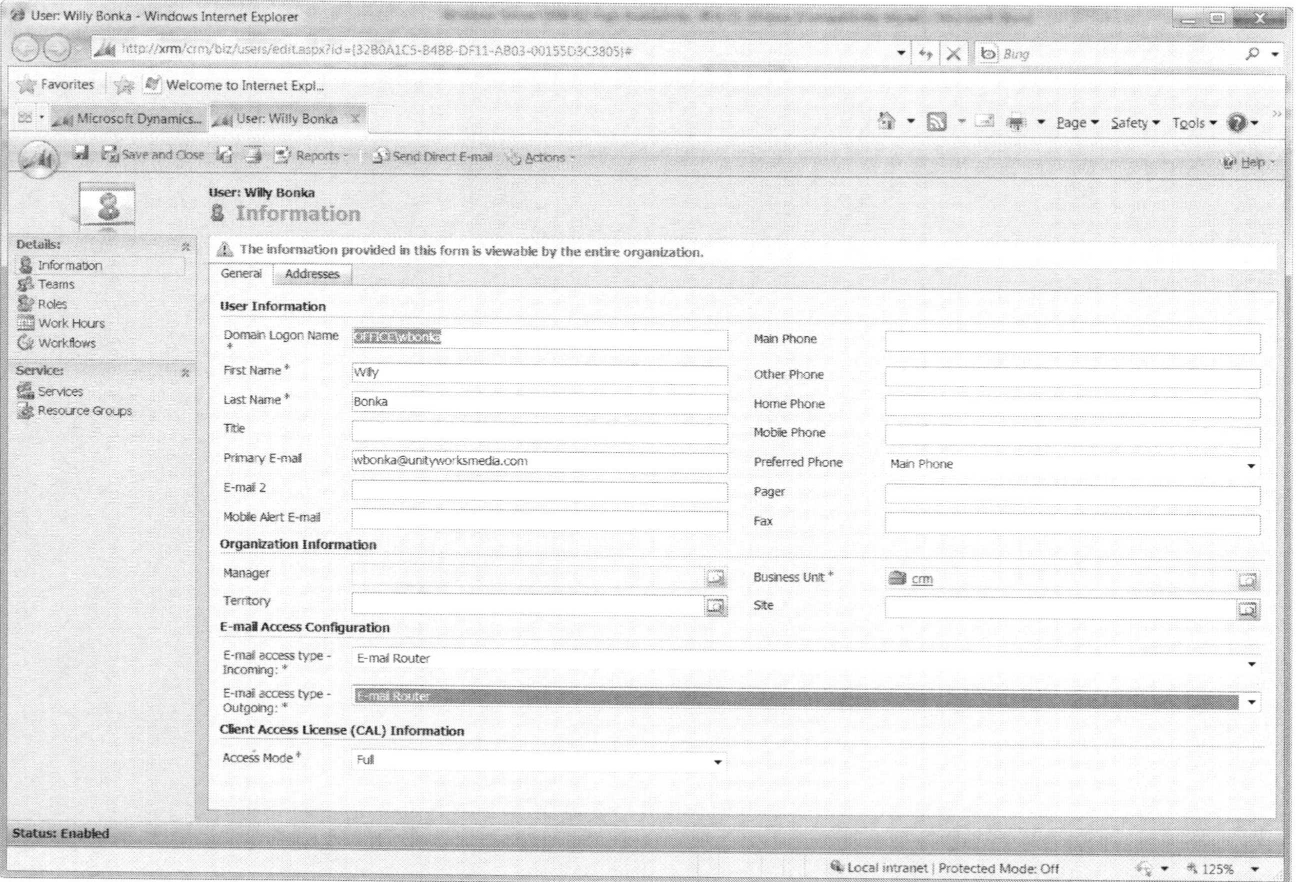


**Figure 27.13**

Unfortunately, this is where some real pain comes in concerning Microsoft Dynamics CRM 4.0. You have to manually set each individual CRM user and queue to use the Email Router for their incoming and outgoing email access configuration fields from within each CRM organization. This is one of the biggest let downs with CRM 4.0 as there is no way to centrally configure multiple users and queues to use the Email Router.

15. Login to each CRM organization that you want to configure to use the Email Router, click on **Settings** option in the bottom of the left pane, and then click on the **Administration** sub-category option in the top of the left pane.

    a. Click on the **Users** option in the right pane, which will bring you to the **Users** list screen. From here you'll need to open each user account, and then change both the **E-mail access type- Incoming** and the **E-mail access type- Outgoing** fields to use the **E-mail Router**, as shown **Figure 27.13**.

    b. Repeat **Step 15** for each **CRM Organization's Users** that will use the **CRM E-mail Router**.

## Changing the CRM E-mail Access Configuration- Queues

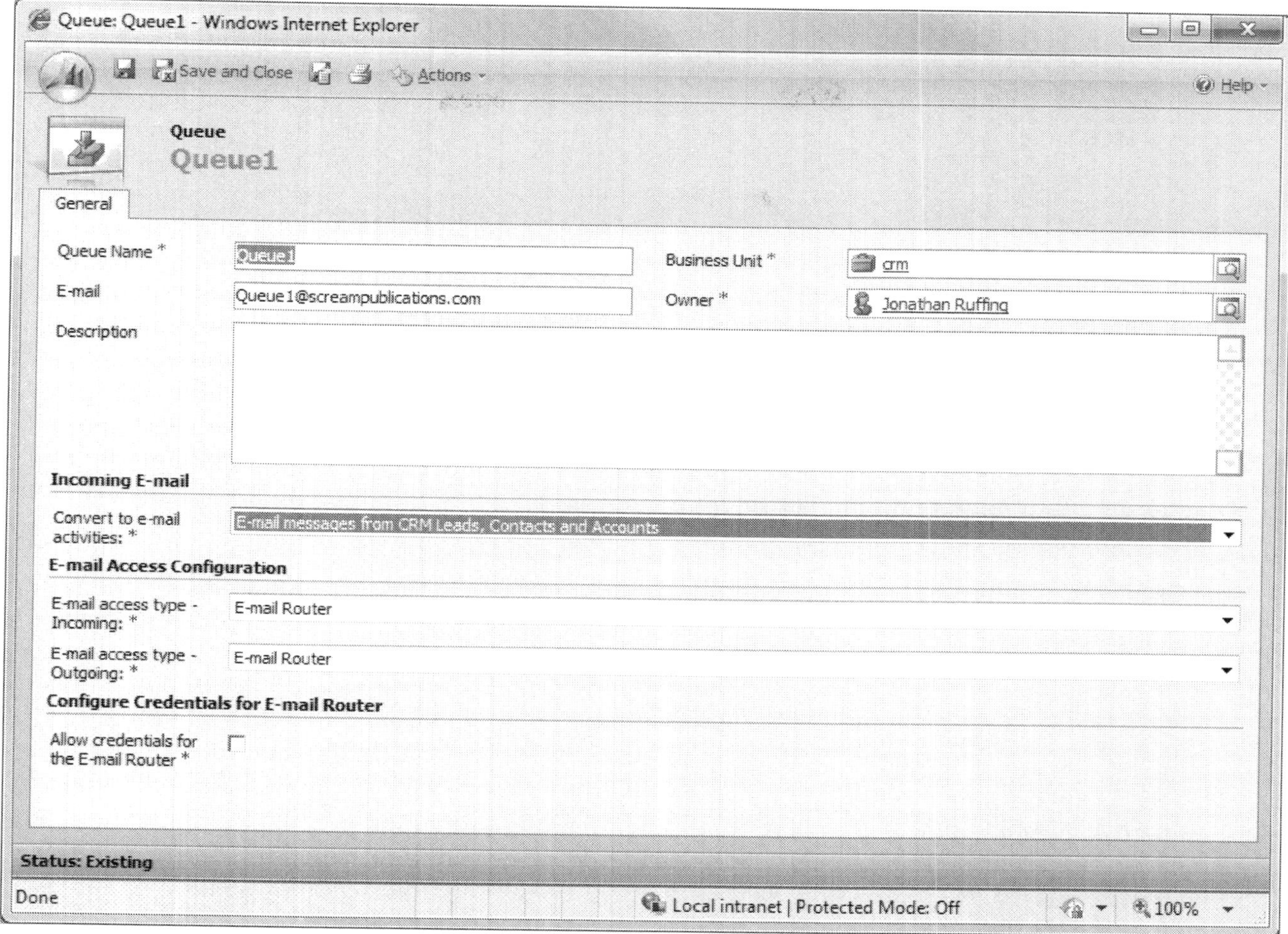


**Figure 27.14**

16. Return to the main CRM screen, click on the **Settings** option in the bottom of the left pane, and then click on the **Business Management** sub-category option in the top of the left pane.

    a. On the **Queues** list, open each queue's screen that will use the Email Router, and then set both the **E-mail access type- Incoming** and the **E-mail access type- Outgoing** fields to use the **E-mail Router**, as shown **Figure 27.14**.

    b. You can also at this time set the types of emails that will be converted to **Activities**, by changing the **Convert to e-mail activities** field to the option of your choice. For our project, we will set the **Covert to e-mail activities** field to only perform this action for **E-mail messages from CRM Leads, Contacts and Accounts**, as shown in **Figure 27.14**.

    c. Repeat **Step 16** for each **CRM Organization's Queues** that will use the **CRM E-mail Router**.

## Creating a Deployment within the E-mail Router Configuration Manager

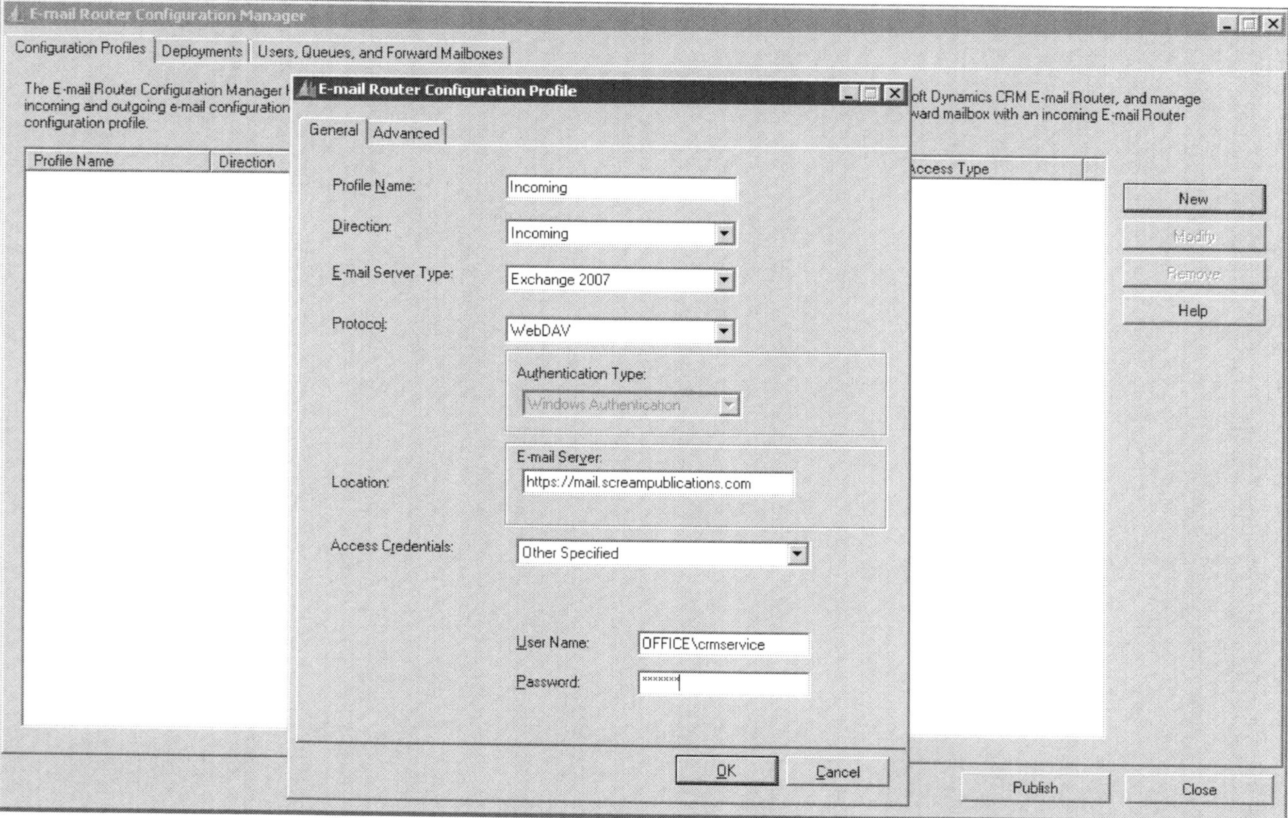


**Figure 27.15**

17. Go to the initial node that you installed the CRM E-mail Router on, and then browse to **Start\All Programs\ Microsoft Dynamics CRM E-mail Router** and select the **Microsoft Dynamics CRM E-mail Router Configuration Manager** option.

## E-mail Router Configuration Manager- Creating an Incoming Profile

18. Click on the **Configuration Profiles** tab, and then click on the **New** button.

    a. For the **Profile Name** field, enter the name for your incoming profile. For our project, we will simply name the profile **Incoming**.

    b. For the **Direction** field, select the **Incoming** option from the dropdown box.

    c. For the **E-mail Server Type** field, select your version of **Exchange Server** that you're using. Depending on the what version of **CRM E-mail Router Rollup Update** you have installed, you may or may not have the **Exchange Server 2010** option available from the dropdown box.

    d. For the **Protocol** field, select the **WebDAV** option from the dropdown box if you are using **Exchange 2007** as in our example. If the **WebDAV** option for **Exchange 2007** is unavailable, then select the **Exchange** option from the dropdown box instead. Again, depending on which version of the **CRM E-mail Router Rollup Update** you have installed, you may or may not have the **WebDAV** option available from the dropdown box. If you selected **Exchange 2010** for the previous **E-mail Server Type** field then this field will be grayed out with the **Exchange Web Services** option automatically selected.

e. For the **Location** field, enter the URL for your **Outlook Web Access (OWA)** site if you are using **Exchange 2007** as in our example. Most likely your web mail URL uses the **HTTPS** protocol, so make sure you include the **https://** prefix in your URL. The URL cannot include slash suffixes like **/owa**, so even if your web mail URL has a /owa on the end of it you do not want to include it in your URL. For example, in our project will use **https://mail.screampublications.com** for our URL. If you are using **Exchange 2010** then enter **https://<Your Exchange Server's NetBIOS name>/EWS/Exchange.asmx** for the **Location** field.

f. For the **Access Credentials** field, select the **Other Specified** option from the dropdown box, and then enter your **CRM Service** user account credentials. This is the user account that you granted the **Send As** and **Full Access** permissions to for your CRM user Exchange mailboxes. For our project, we will enter our domain name followed by our CRM Service user account named **CRMService**.

g. Once you're finished, click on the **OK** button to save your **Incoming Profile** configuration. If you're using **Exchange 2007**, then your **Incoming Profile** configuration should look similar to **Figure 27.15**.

# E-mail Router Configuration Manager- Creating an Outgoing Profile

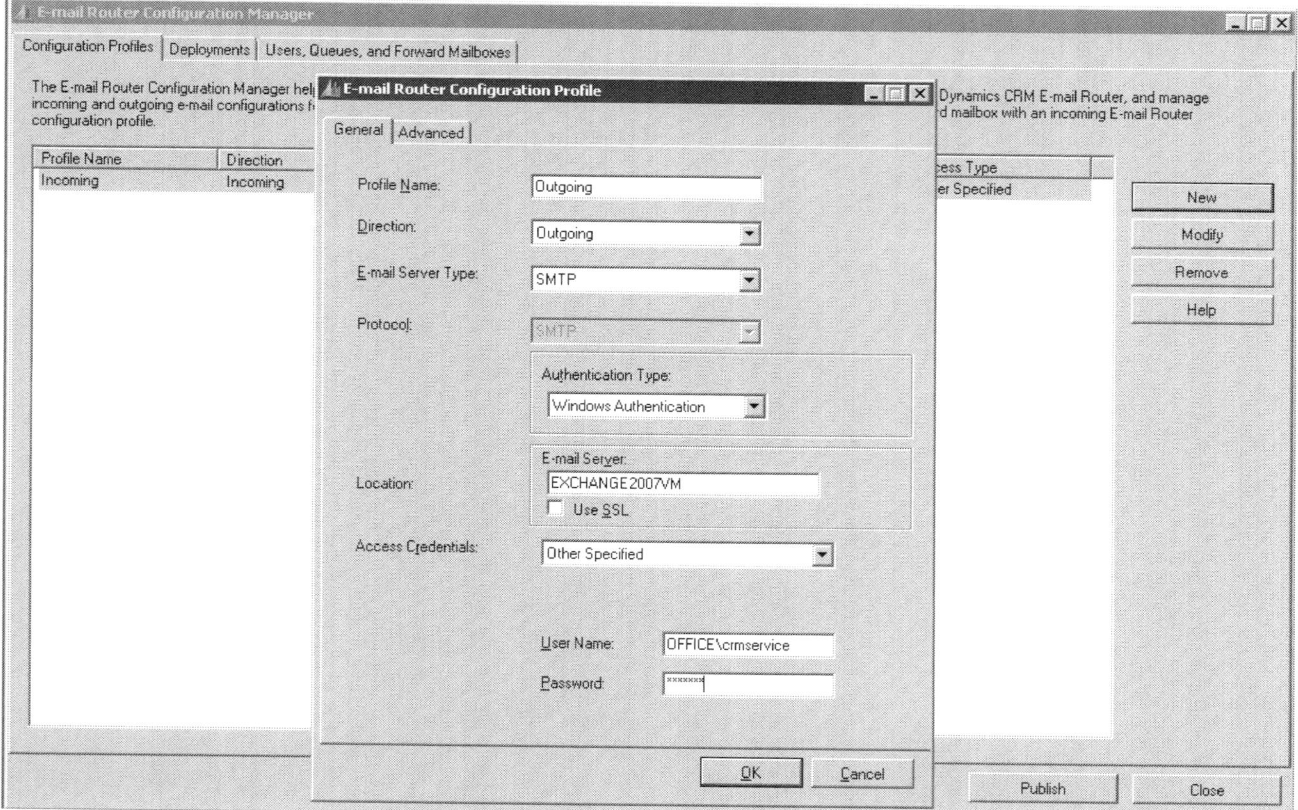

**Figure 27.16**

19. While still on the **Configuration Profiles** tab, click on the **New** button again.

    a. For the **Profile Name** field, enter the name for your outgoing profile. For our project, we will simply name our profile **Outgoing**.

    b. For the **Direction** field, select the **Outgoing** option from the dropdown box.

    c. For the **E-mail Server Type** field, select the **SMTP** option from the dropdown box.

    d. For the **Authentication Type** field, select **Windows Authentication** option from the dropdown box.

    e. For the **Location** field, enter your Exchange server's internal **NetBIOS** name. Make sure not to use the Fully Qualified Domain Name (FQDN) here, but instead just the Exchange server's name without specifying the domain name.

    f. For the **Access Credentials** field, select the **Other Specified** option from the dropdown box, and then enter your **CRM Service** user account. This is the user account that you granted the **Send As** and **Full Access** permissions to for your CRM user Exchange mailboxes. For our project, we will enter our **Domain** and **CRM Service** user account credentials of **OFFICE\crmservice**, as shown in **Figure 27.16**.

g. Once you're finished, click on the **OK** button to save your **Outgoing Profile** configuration. Whether you are using **Exchange 2007** or **2010** your **Outgoing Profile** configuration should look similar to **Figure 27.16**.

## E-mail Router Configuration Manager- Creating a Deployment

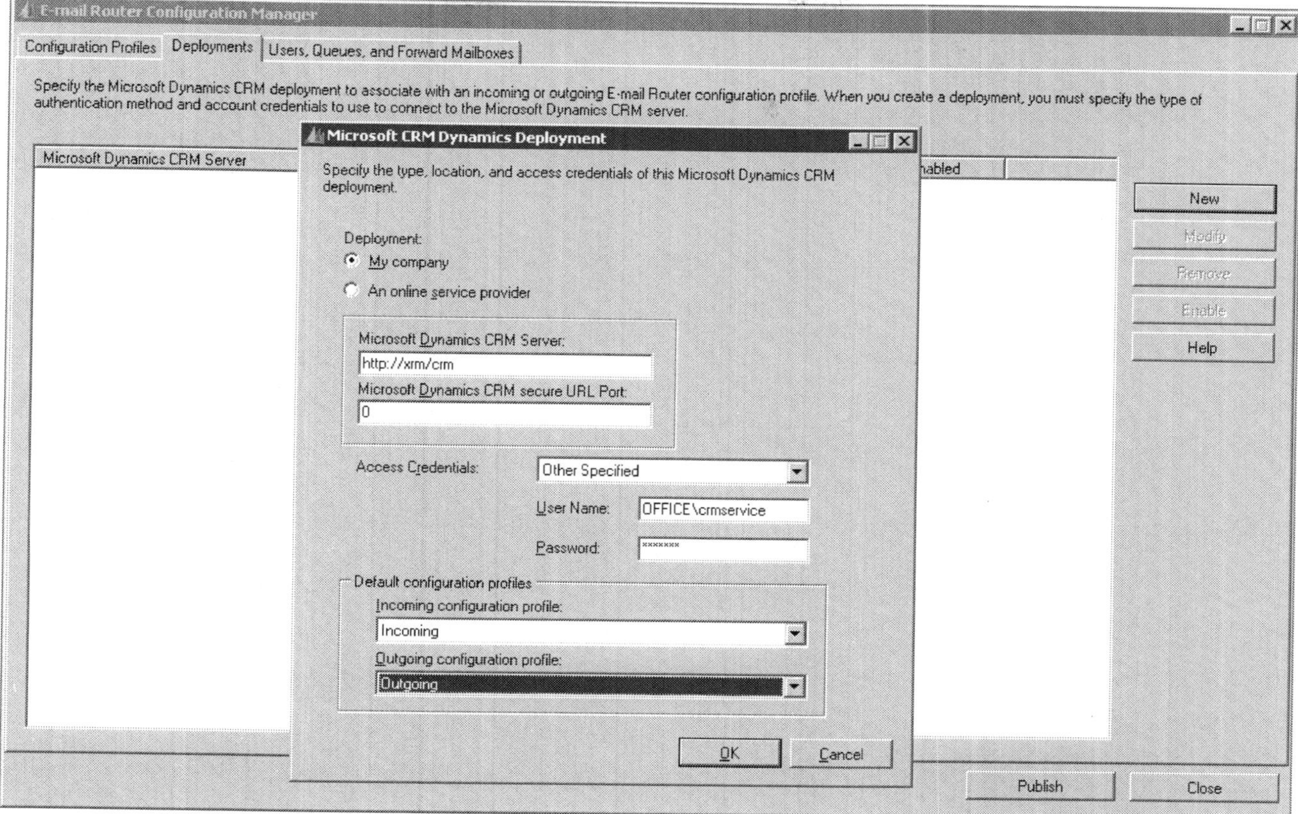


**Figure 27.17**

For each or your CRM organizations that will use the Email Router you have to create a deployment configuration. We will use our incoming and outgoing profiles that we just created for our deployment configuration. You can use the same set of profiles for multiple deployments if you so choose.

20. In the **E-mail Router Configuration Manager** console, click on the **Deployments** tab, and then click the **New** button.

    a. For the **Deployment** section, leave the default set to the **My company** option, as shown in **Figure 27.17**.

    b. For the **Microsoft Dynamics CRM Server** field, enter in your **CRM NLB cluster's URL** that you use to access this particular CRM organization. For our project, we will enter our URL of **http://xrm/crm** for our CRM NLB cluster's name of **xrm** along with our CRM organization's name of **crm** for our deployment.

    **NOTE:** The CRM organization name is case sensitive and needs to match what is listed in the **CRM Deployment Manger** under the **Organizations** node.

c. For the **Microsoft Dynamics CRM secure URL Port** field, you can leave the default port of **0** unless your CRM server has SSL enabled in which case you would input the port number here. For our project, we will leave the default port number set **0**.

d. For the **Access Credentials** field, select the **Other Specified** option from the dropdown box, and then enter your **CRM Service** user account. This is the user account that you granted the **Send As** and **Full Access** permissions to for your CRM user Exchange mailboxes. For our project, we will enter our CRM Service user account named **CRMService**.

e. Once you're finished, click on the **OK** button to save your **Deployment** configuration. Whether you are using **Exchange 2007** or **2010** your **Deployment** configuration should look similar to **Figure 27.17**.

f. If you have other CRM organizations that you'd like to use the Email Router, then you'll need to repeat **Step 20** to create a deployment configuration for each additional organization.

**NOTE:** You can choose to use the same incoming and outgoing configuration profiles for each of your additional CRM organizations.

## E-mail Router Configuration Manager- Loading Data

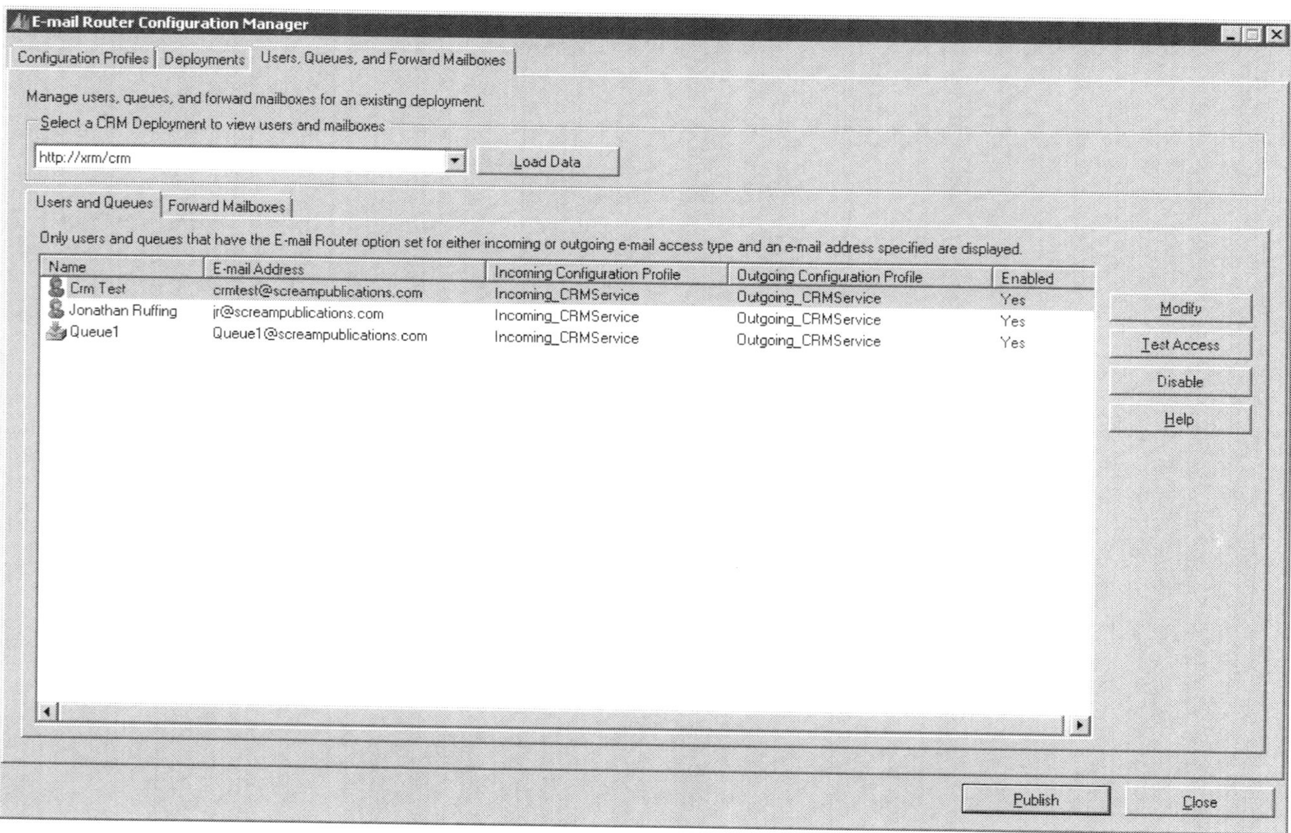


**Figure 27.18**

21. In the **E-mail Router Configuration Manager** console, click on the **Users, Queues, and Forward Mailboxes** tab.

a. For the **Select a CRM Deployment to view users and mailboxes** field, select your CRM Deployment URL from the dropdown box, and then click on the **Load Data** button. This will load your CRM users and queues that have been set to use the E-mail Router from within CRM.

b. Once your users and queues have loaded, then click on the **Publish** button in the lower right hand corner of the screen, as shown in **Figure 27.18**. This will save the E-mail Router's configuration to the server it's hosted on. When you receive the pop-up screen stating **Configuration Changes have been saved and the E-mail Router settings have been published**, click on the **OK** button to continue.

## E-mail Router Configuration Manager- Testing E-mail Router Access to Exchange Mailboxes

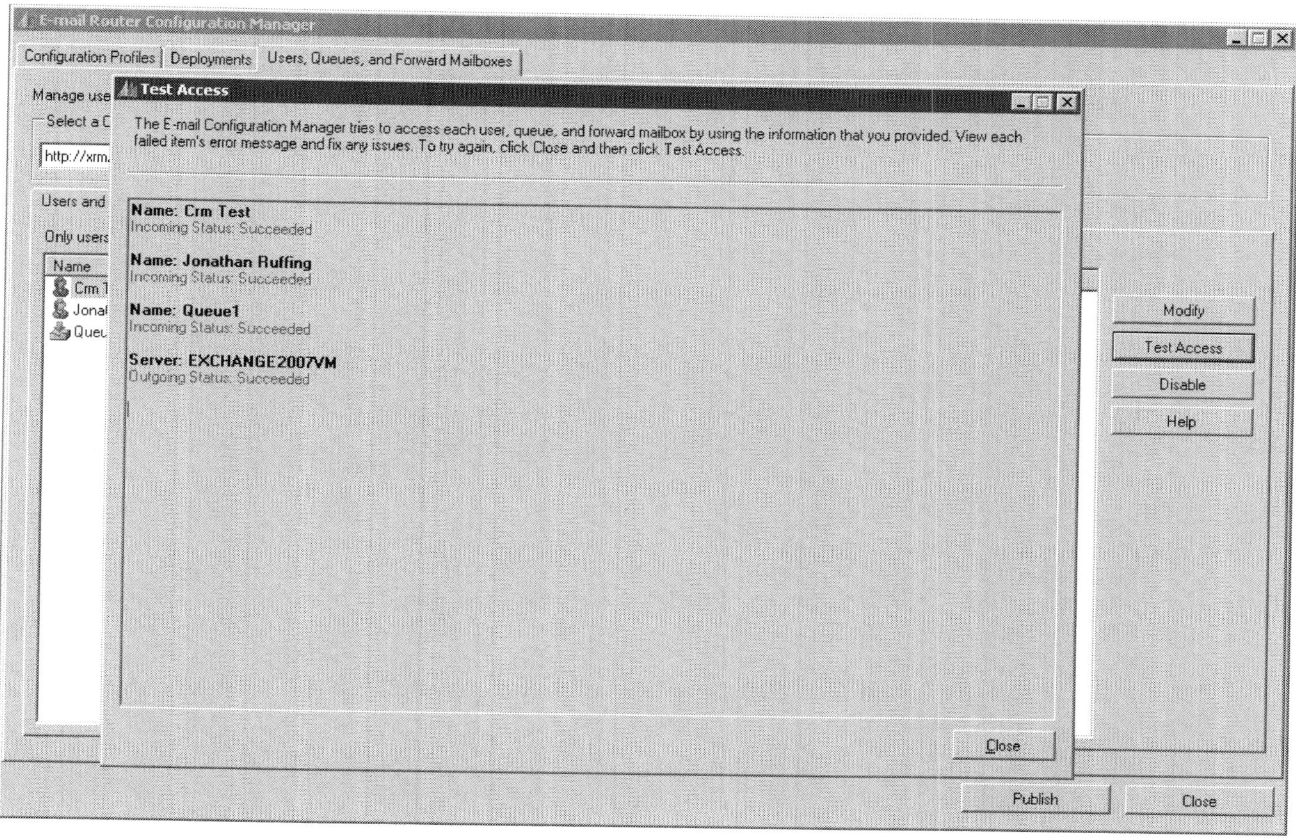


**Figure 27.19**

22. In addition to publishing the configuration, we want to click on the **Test Access** button on the right hand side of the screen. This will test the sending and receiving of emails for each CRM user and queue currently loaded. You should receive test results similar to **Figure 27.19** with green text stating that the test **Succeeded**. Once complete testing, click on the **Close** button to exit the **Test Access** screen.

    a. Login to each of your CRM organizations and then create some test email activities to verify that emails are successfully being sent to and from CRM.

    b. Repeat **Steps 21-22** for any additional CRM organizations that you have configured to use the E-mail Router.

## Creating the CRM E-mail Router Service's Shared Disk on the SAN

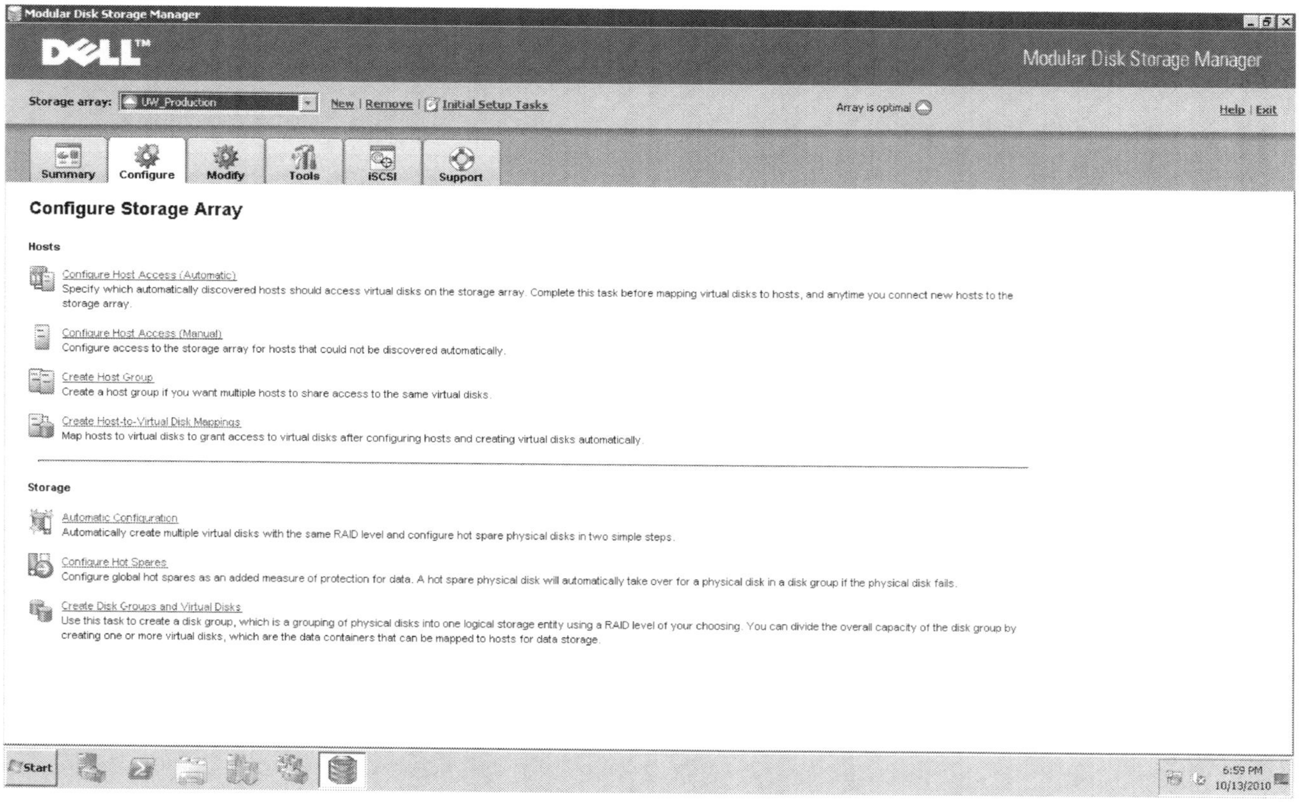

Figure 27.20

23. In these steps we will create a very small virtual disk on our SAN to host our CRM E-mail Router's application files. Go to the server that you use to manage your SAN, and then launch the **Dell Modular Disk Storage Manager (MDSM)** console by going to **Start button\Dell\MD Storage Manager**.

24. Click on the **Configure** tab, and then select the **Create Disk Groups and Virtual Disks** link, as shown in **Figure 27.20** at the bottom of the screen.

# Creating the Virtual Disk- Selecting the Disk Group

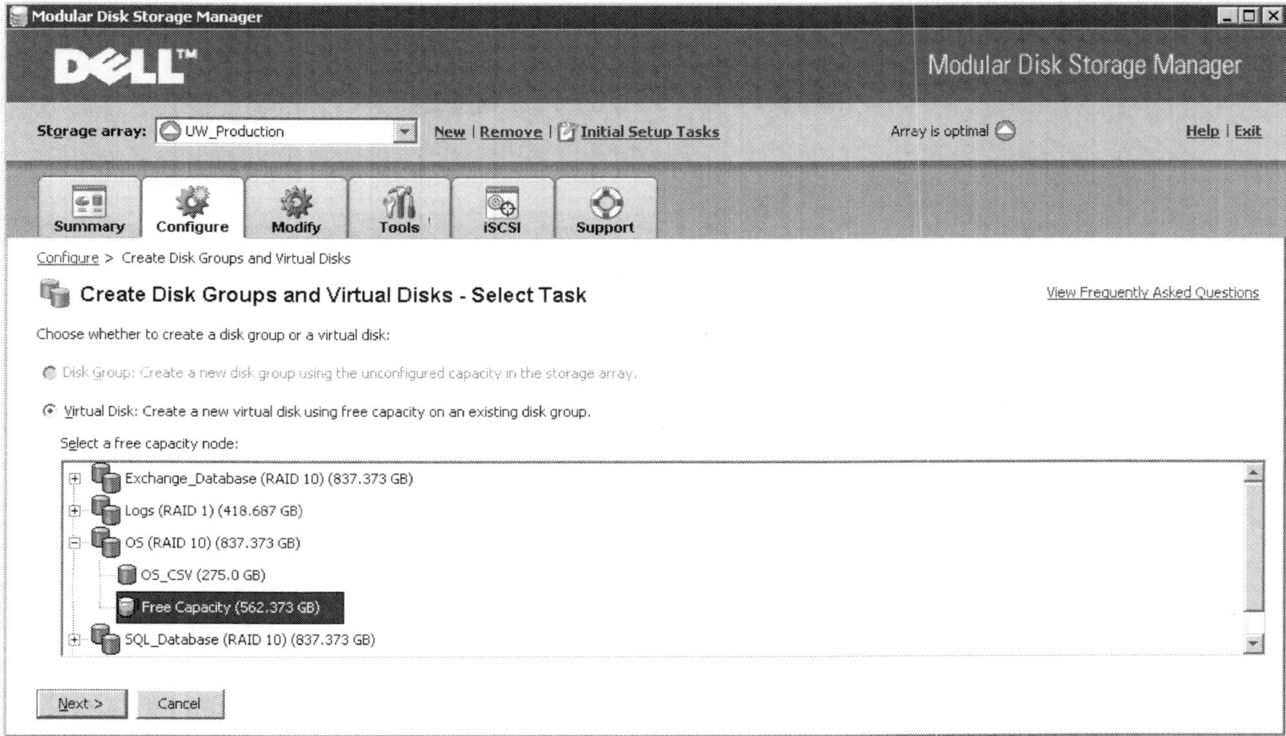


**Figure 27.21**

a. On the **Create Disk Groups and Virtual Disks – Select Task** screen, select the bullet next to the **Virtual Disk: Create a new virtual disk using free capacity on an existing disk group** option.

    i. For the **Select a free capacity node** field, highlight the free capacity of the disk you want to use, and then click on the **Next** button to continue. The CRM E-mail Router virtual disk can be very small such as one GB so shouldn't have to worry about capacity, but instead should focus on placing the virtual disk in the best location on your SAN. For our project, we will create the virtual disk on the same RAID array as our **OS_CSV** virtual disk, as shown in **Figure 27.21**.

## Creating the Virtual Disk- Specifying Capacity and Name

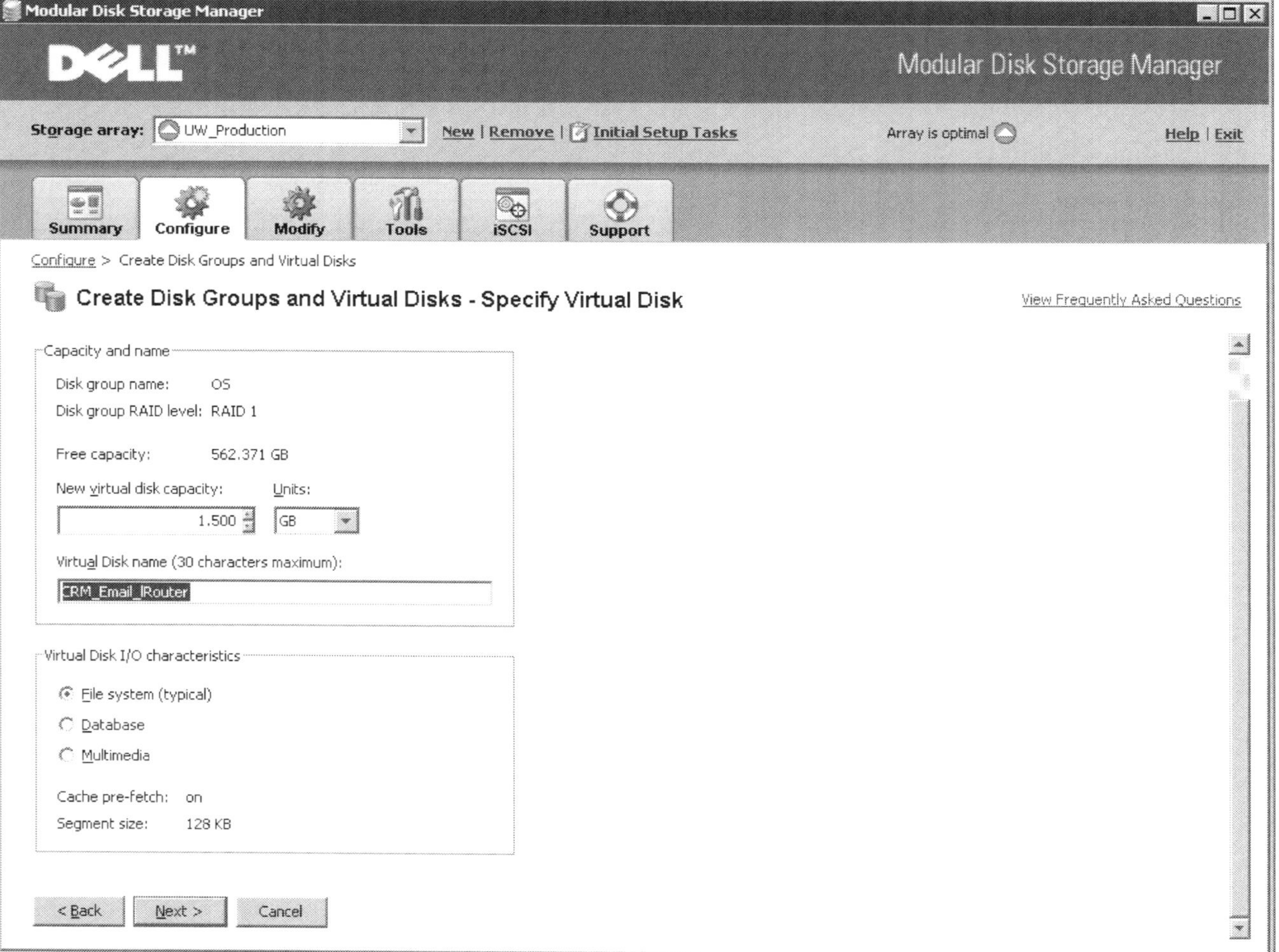


**Figure 27.22**

b. On the **Create Disk Groups and Virtual Disks – Specify Virtual Disk** screen, enter in the capacity you want for the **New virtual disk capacity** field, and then select the unit size for the **Units** dropdown field. For our project, we will enter **1.5** for our capacity with the **Units** field set to **GB**.

   i. For the **Virtual Disk name** field, enter the name you want for your virtual disk. For our project, we will name our virtual disk **CRM_Email_Router**, as shown in **Figure 27.22**.

   ii. For the **Virtual Disk I/O Characteristics** field, select the type of file system you want, and then click on the **Next** button to continue. For our project, we will select the **File system (typical)** option, as shown in **Figure 27.22**.

## Creating the Virtual Disk- Specifying the Host Group and LUN Id

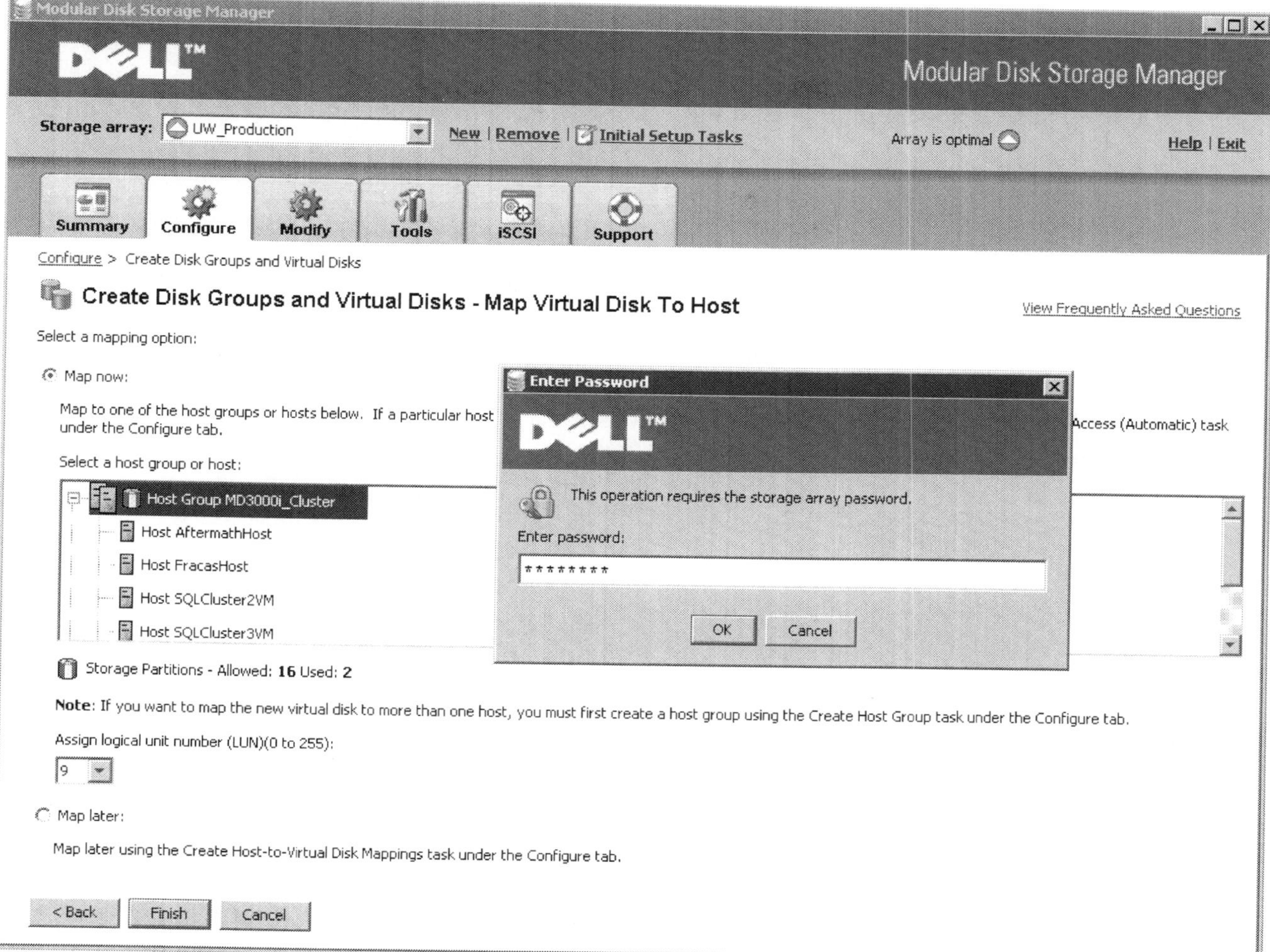


**Figure 27.23**

c. On the **Create Disk Groups and Virtual Disks – Map Virtual Disk To Host** screen, select the **Map now** option, and then highlight the host group that will have access to the virtual disk for the **Select a host group or host** field. For our project, we will select the host group named **MD3000i_Cluster**, as shown in **Figure 27.23**.

   i. For **Assign logical unit number** field, select the LUN Id you want from the dropdown field, and then click on the **Finish** button to create the virtual disk. For our project, we will assign the next lowest available **LUN** number of **9**, as shown in **Figure 27.23**.

   ii. On the **Enter Password** pop-up screen, enter your write permission password, and then click on the **OK** button to complete the changes.

iii. On the **Create Disk Groups and Virtual Disks – Complete** screen, click on the **No** button to return to the main menu.

## Configuring the Virtual Disk- Bringing the Shared Disk Online

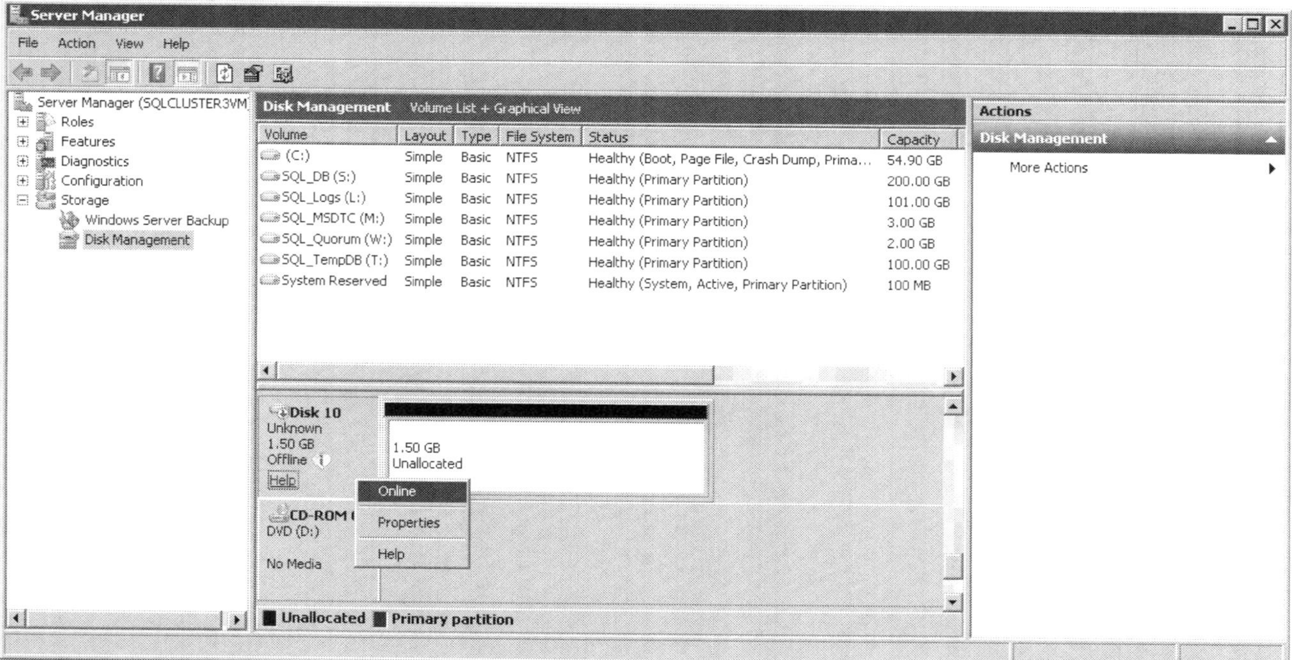


**Figure 27.24**

25. Open the Windows **Server Manager** on the cluster node that you want to have initial control of your shared disk by going to the **Start** button, and then right click on the **Computer**, and select the **Manage** option.

    a. Expand the **Storage** node in the left pane, and then highlight the **Disk Management** node to view the newly attached drive in the right pane. If your new drive doesn't appear right away, then right click on the **Disk Management** node, and select the **Rescan Disks** option a few times for the drive to show up.

    b. Right click on your **CRM E-mail Router** disk's gray area where it shows the **Disk** number, and then select the **Online** option. For our project, we want to bring online our **1.5GB** virtual disk that we created for our **CRM_Email_Router** disk, as shown in **Figure 27.24**.

    c. The disk should now have the **Status** of **Not Initialized**. Right click on the disk's gray area where it shows the **Disk** number, and then select the **Initialize Disk** option.

        i. On the **Initialize Disk** screen, unselect any other disk checkboxes except for your CRM E-mail Router disk, and then click on the **OK** button to continue.

d. Right click on the unformatted disk's white area where it says **Unallocated**, and then select the **New Simple Volume** option.

   i. On the **Welcome to the New Simple Volume Wizard** screen, click on the **Next** button to continue.

   ii. On the **Specify Volume Size** screen, leave the defaults with all available space selected, and then click on the **Next** button to continue.

   iii. On the **Assign Drive Letter or Path** screen, you want to assign a drive letter that corresponds to what the disk is. For our project, we will assign the drive letter as **R:** to help us associate the shared disk with our router.

   iv. On the **Format Partition** screen, enter the name for your CRM E-mail Router's disk in the **Volume label** field, and then click on the **Next** button to continue. For our project, we will simply name our disk as **CRM_Email_Router**.

   v. On the **Completing the New Simple Volume Wizard** screen, click on the **Finish** button to complete the wizard.

## Configuring the Shared Disk to Host the CRM E-mail Router

Now that we have our CRM E-mail Router service functioning on our initial cluster node we are ready to configure our service to run from our shared disk. We will first create a directory structure on our new disk, and then assign it the necessary permissions. After this, we will copy our CRM E-mail Router's service files into our new directory structure. Once we have our service files place, we will need to edit our service's registry settings on each server to point at our new shared disk's location.

## Configuring the Shared Disk- Creating the Directory Structure

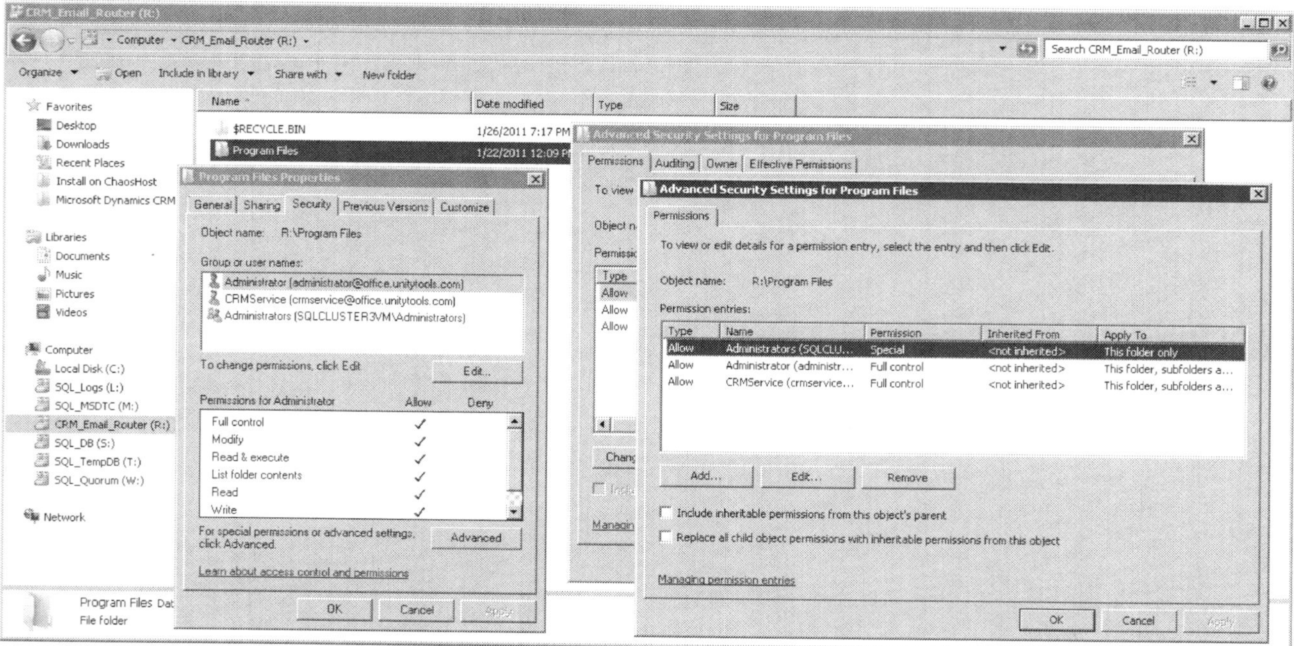


**Figure 27.25**

26. Open **Windows Explorer**, and then browse to your newly created shared disk.

    a. On your new shared disk, create a new folder named **Program Files**.

    b. Right click on the newly created **Program Files** folder, and then select the **Properties** option.

        i. On the **Properties** screen, click on the **Security** tab, and then click on the **Advanced** button.

            1. On the **Advanced Security Settings for Programs Files** screen, click on the **Change Permissions** button.

            2. On the second **Advanced Security Settings for Programs Files** screen, unselect the **Include inheritable permissions from the object's parent** checkbox, and then click on the **Remove** button of the **Windows Security** warning screen.

## Configuring the Shared Disk- Assigning Permissions

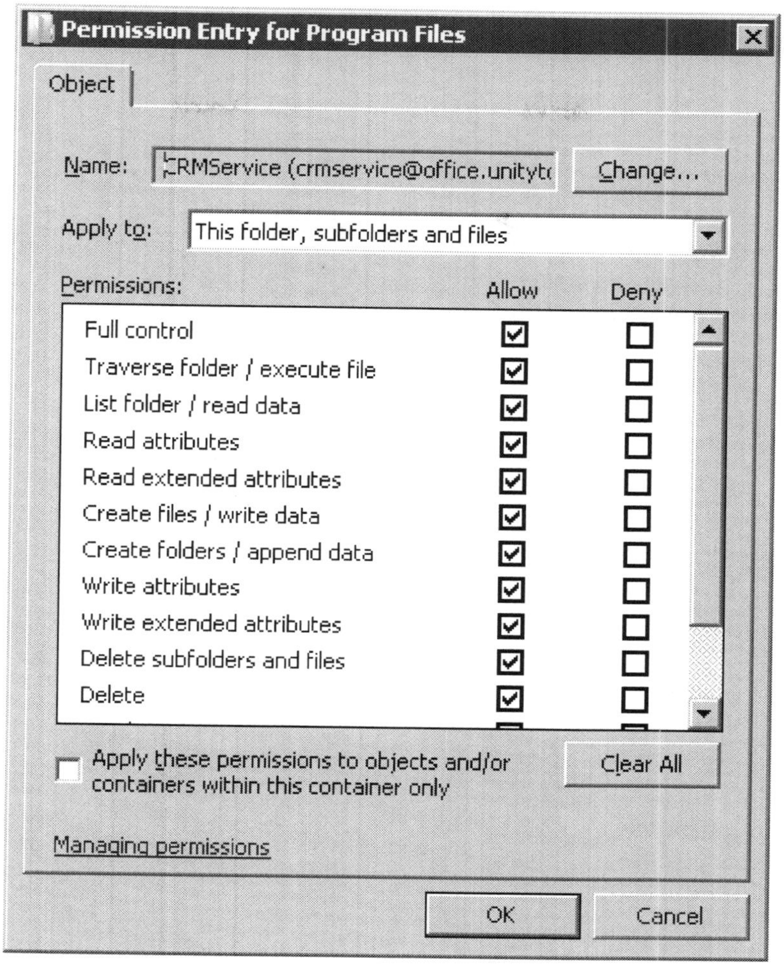

Permission Entry for Program Files

Object

Name: CRMService (crmservice@office.unityt
Change...

Apply to: This folder, subfolders and files

Permissions: Allow Deny

Full control
Traverse folder / execute file
List folder / read data
Read attributes
Read extended attributes
Create files / write data
Create folders / append data
Write attributes
Write extended attributes
Delete subfolders and files
Delete

Apply these permissions to objects and/or containers within this container only
Clear All

Managing permissions

OK Cancel

**Figure 27.26**

3. On the **Advanced Security Settings for Programs Files** screen, click on the **Add** button, and then add your **CRM service** user account.

4. On the **Permissions Entry for Program Files** pop-up screen, select the **Allow** checkbox for the **Full Control** row, and then click on the **OK** button to continue.

5. Repeat **Steps 3-4** to add your **Domain Administrator** with the **Full Control** permissions as well. For our project, we will add our **Domain Administrator** and our **CRMService** user account, as shown in **Figure 27.25**.

6. Once complete, click on the **OK** button of each of the security screens to save your changes and exit.

## Configuring the Service for Clustering

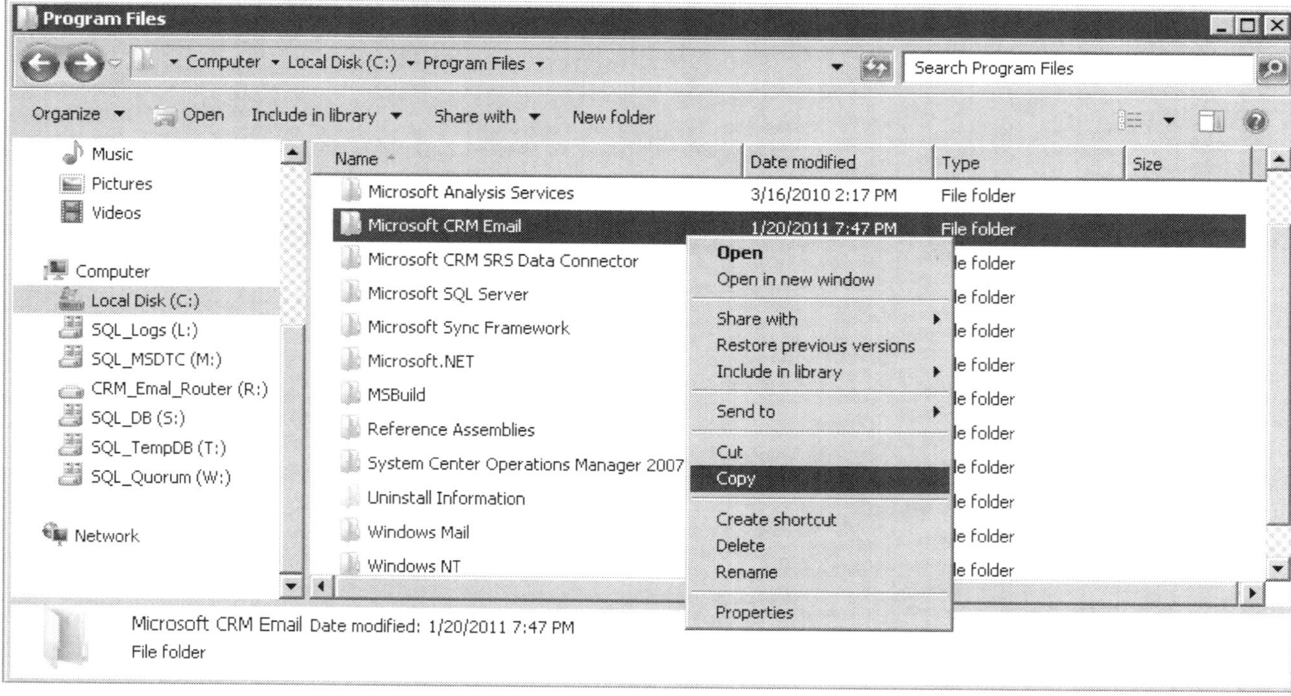


**Figure 27.26**

In this section, we will place our CRM E-mail Router's service files onto our newly created shared disk. Once we have our service files on the shared disk, we will then modify the registry path on our servers to point at our service's new location.

## Configuring the Service for Clustering- Placing the Application Files on the Shared Disk

27. While still in **Windows Explorer** on the initial node, browse to the **C:\Program Files** directory.

    a. Right click on the **Microsoft CRM Email** folder, and then select the **Copy** option. By default the E-mail Router files are located at **<Drive:>\Program Files\Microsoft CRM Email** directory.

    b. Browse to your shared disk's **<Drive:>\Program Files**, and then **Paste** the copied **Microsoft CRM Email** folder onto your shared disk. For our project, we will paste the **Microsoft CRM Email** folder into our **R:\Program Files** directory on our shared disk.

# Configuring the Service for Clustering- Modifying the Registry's Path

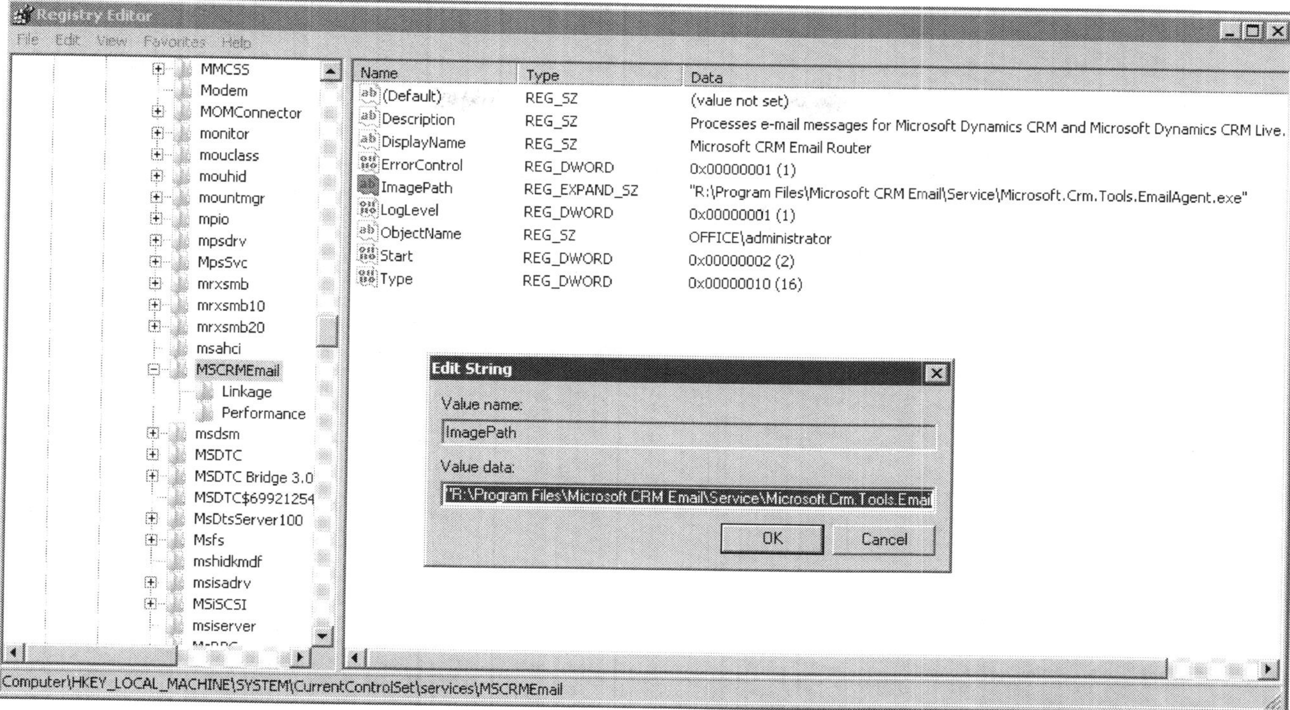


**Figure 27.27**

28. While still on the initial node, launch the **Registry Editor** console by going to **Start\Run**, and then entering the command **regedit**.

    a. Browse to the **HKEY_LOCAL_MACHINE\SYSTEM\CurrentControlSet\Services\MSCRMEmail** key, right click on the **ImagePath** value in the right pane, and then select the **Modify** option.

    b. Modify the **Value data** field's path to the location of your **CRM E-mail Router's** service files on your shared disk, and then click on the **OK** button. Since we already created the same Program Files directory structure our shared disk we should only need to modify the drive letter of the path. It is a good practice to create the Program Files folder on our shared disk, as this will alert other IT staff to not to manually delete or change these files. For our project, we will modify the **Value data** field's path to **"R:\Program Files\Microsoft CRM Email\Service\ Microsoft.Crm.Tools.EmailAgent.exe"**, as shown in **Figure 27.27**.

    c. Go to the **Start\Administrative Tools\Services** console, right click on the **Microsoft CRM Email Router** service, and then select the **Restart** option for your registry changes to take effect.

## Installing the CRM E-mail Router Cluster- On Secondary Nodes

In this section, we will perform the same basic CRM E-mail Router installation and registry modification steps as we did on the initial node, however for any additional cluster nodes we only have to perform a few of the previously outlined steps. Follow the steps referenced below for each of your additional nodes. Once we have the CRM E-mail Router installed and configured on our secondary node(s), then we will be ready to add the service to our Windows cluster.

29. On your passive node, install the prerequisite **Microsoft Exchange Server MAPI Client and Collaboration Data Objects 1.2.1 (MAPI)** software, as outlined this chapter's **Step 1**.

30. Install the **CRM E-mail Router** role, as outlined this chapter's **Steps 2-3**.

    a. During the installation process, make sure to unselect the **Launch Configuration Manager** checkbox in **Step 3-i**. We have already setup our E-mail Router's configuration using our initial node so there is no need to perform any configuration from our secondary node(s).

31. Install the same version of CRM **Update Rollup** for you E-mail Router as your other CRM roles have installed, as outlined in this chapter's **Step 4**.

32. Configure your **Microsoft CRM Email Router** service's **Startup type** and **Log On** user account, as outlined in this chapter's **Step 6**. For our project, we will use our **CRMService** user account.

33. Modify your secondary node's **ImagePath** registry key to point at the **CRM E-mail Router's** service files on your shared disk, as outlined in this chapter's **Step 28**.

    a. When you come to **Step 28-c**, **Reboot** the server instead of restarting the service for your changes to take effect. You will only be able to start the Microsoft CRM E-mail Router service on the server that it is the current owner of the shared disk, so the only way for your registry changes to take effect is by rebooting the passive node.

## Creating a Clustered Generic Service for the CRM E-mail Router

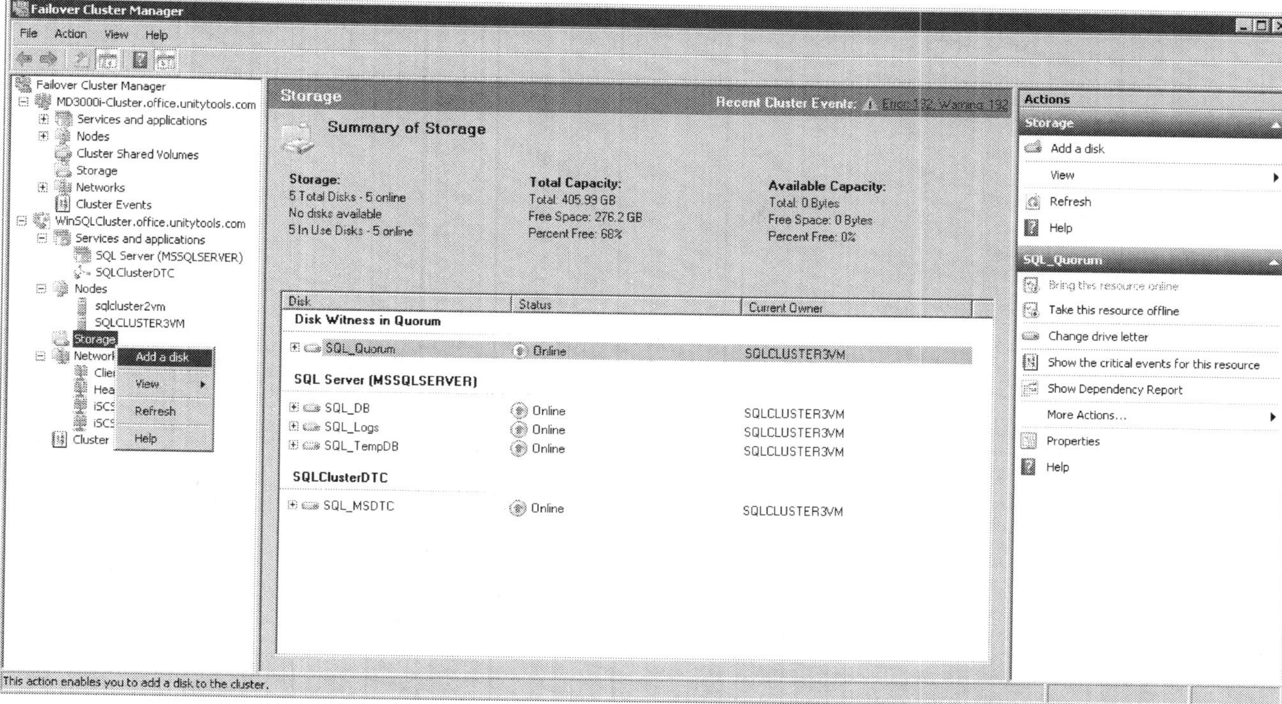

**Figure 27.28**

We are now ready to add a Generic Service to our Windows cluster to host our clustered CRM E-mail Router. The service will need its own disk, so we will begin by adding our E-mail Router's shared disk to the Windows cluster.

## Creating the Clustered Generic Service- Adding the Shared Disk

34. Open the Windows **Failover Cluster Manager** console on one of your cluster nodes, and then browse to the **Windows active/passive cluster** that will host your CRM E-mail Router service.

    a. Right click on the **Storage** node in the left pane, and then select the **Add a disk** option. For our project, we will add our shared disk for the CRM E-mail Router to our Windows cluster named **WinSQLCluster**, as shown in **Figure 27.28**.

    b. On the **Add Disks to a Cluster** screen, unselect all other disks except your newly created disk for the CRM E-mail Router service, and then click on the **OK** button to continue.

## Creating the Clustered Generic Service- Renaming the Shared Disk

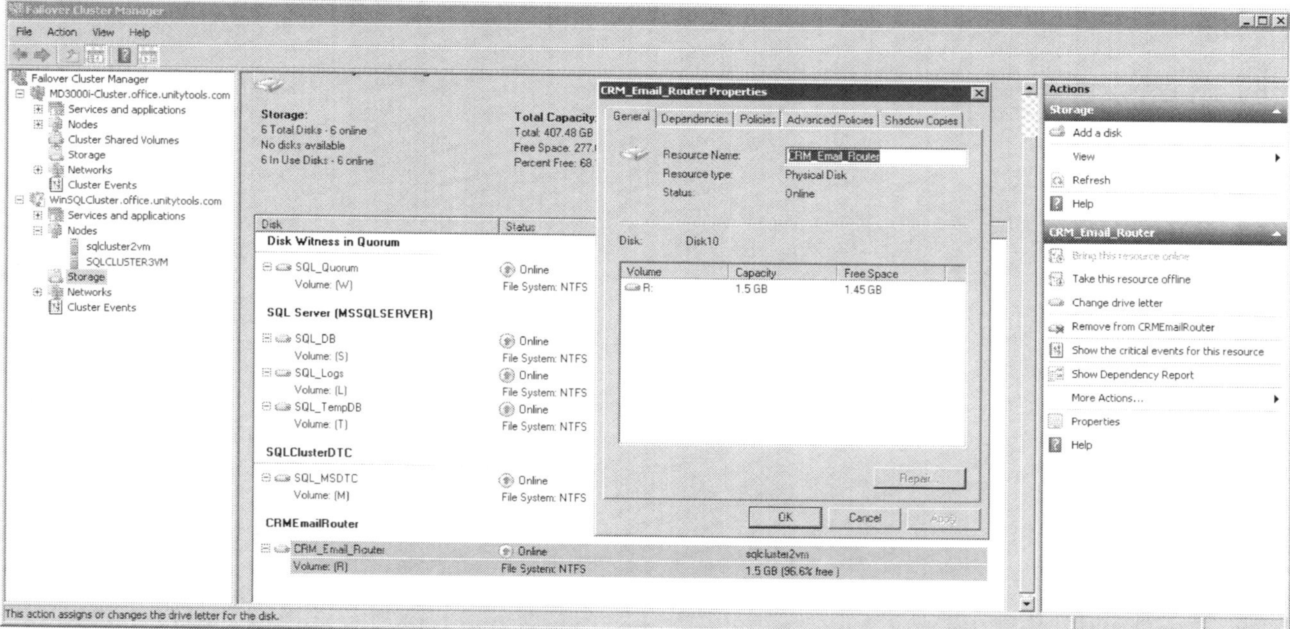

**Figure 27.29**

c. In the center **Storage** pane, right click on your newly added disk, and then select the **Properties** option.

   i. On the **General** tab of the **Properties** screen, change the **Resource Name** field to a descriptive name for your CRM E-mail Router, and then click on the **OK** button to save your change. For our project, we will rename our disk to **CRM_Email_Router**, as shown in **Figure 27.29**.

# Creating the Clustered Generic Service- Adding the Service

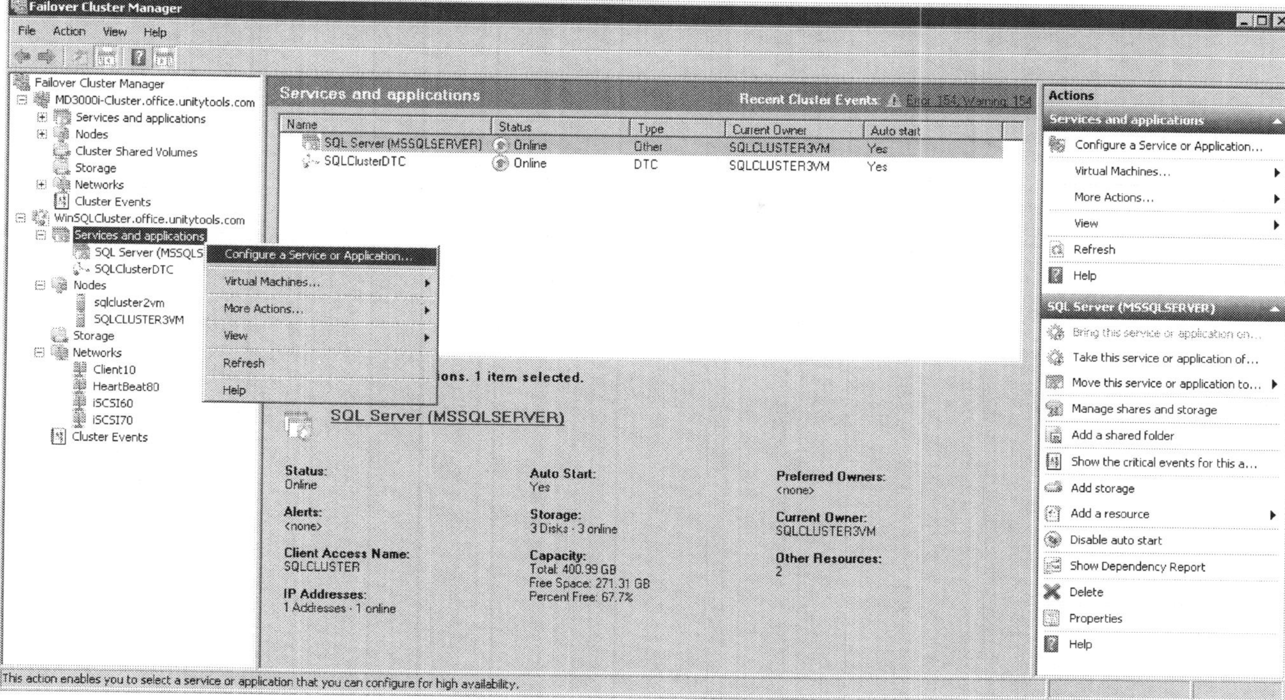


**Figure 27.30**

35. In the left pane of the **Failover Cluster Manager** console, right click on the **Services and applications** node of the Windows cluster that will host your CRM E-mail Router, and then select the **Configure a Service or Application** option.

    a. On the **Before You Begin** screen, click on the **Next** button to continue.

## Creating the Clustered Generic Service- Selecting the Type of Service

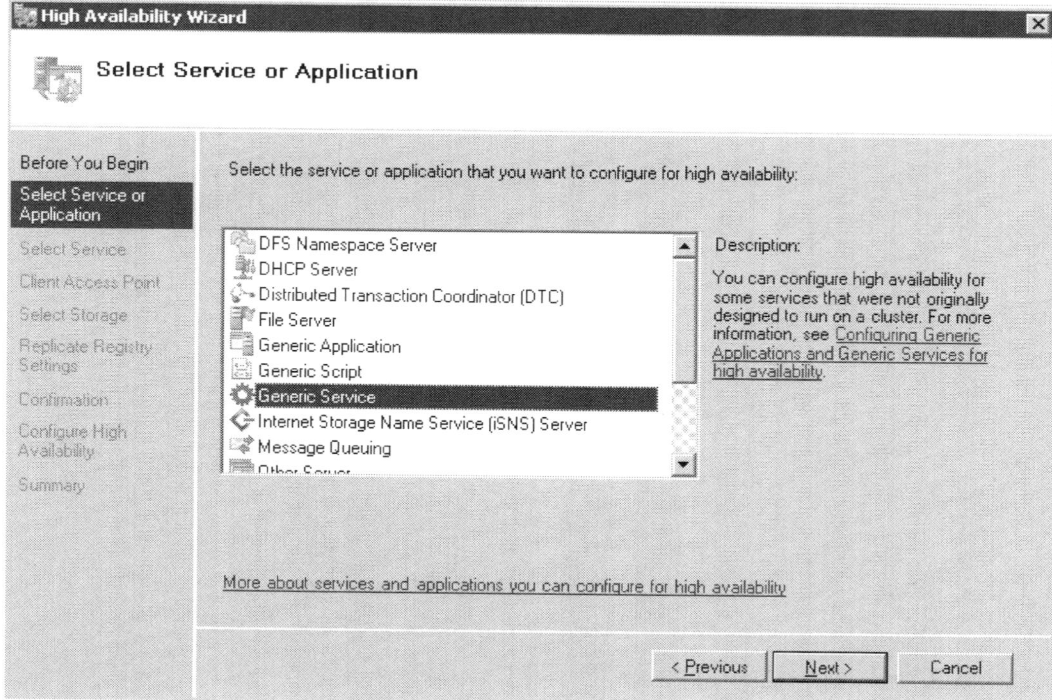


**Figure 27.31**

b. On the **Select Service or Application** screen, select the **Generic Service** option, and then click on the **Next** button to continue.

## Creating the Clustered Generic Service- Selecting the Microsoft CRM Email Router Service

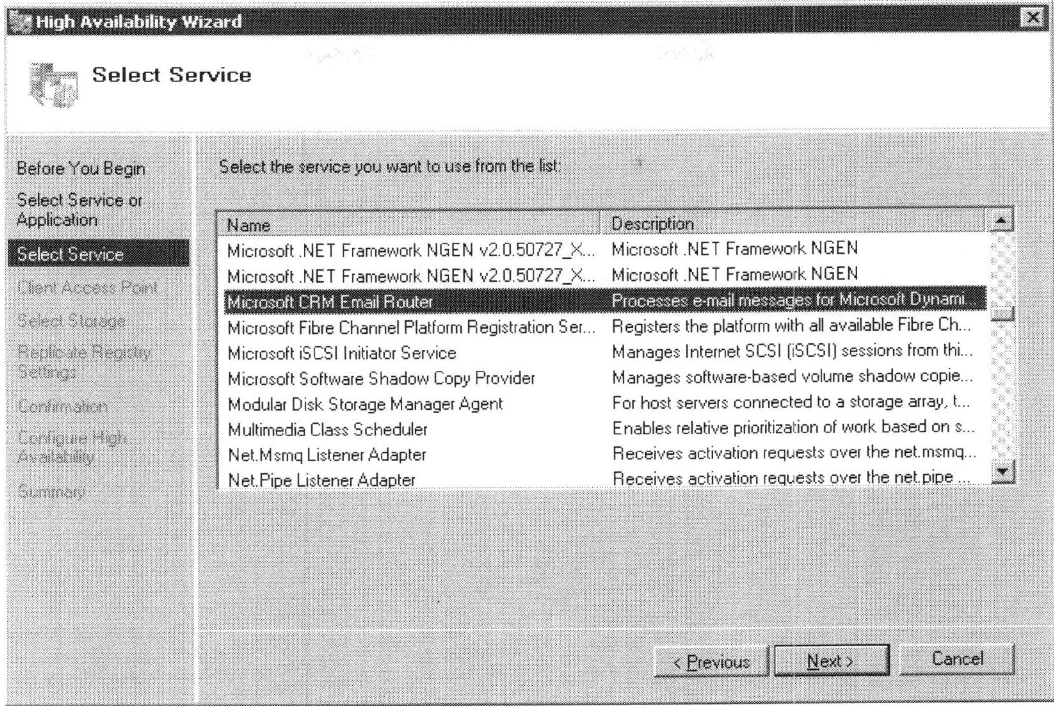


**Figure 27.32**

c. On the **Select Service** screen, select the **Microsoft CRM Email Router** option, and then click on the **Next** button to continue. If the Microsoft CRM Email Router service doesn't appear here, then most likely you don't have the service set to manual for its startup type or the service hasn't been installed on at least two nodes of your cluster.

## Creating the Clustered Generic Service- Creating the Client Access Point

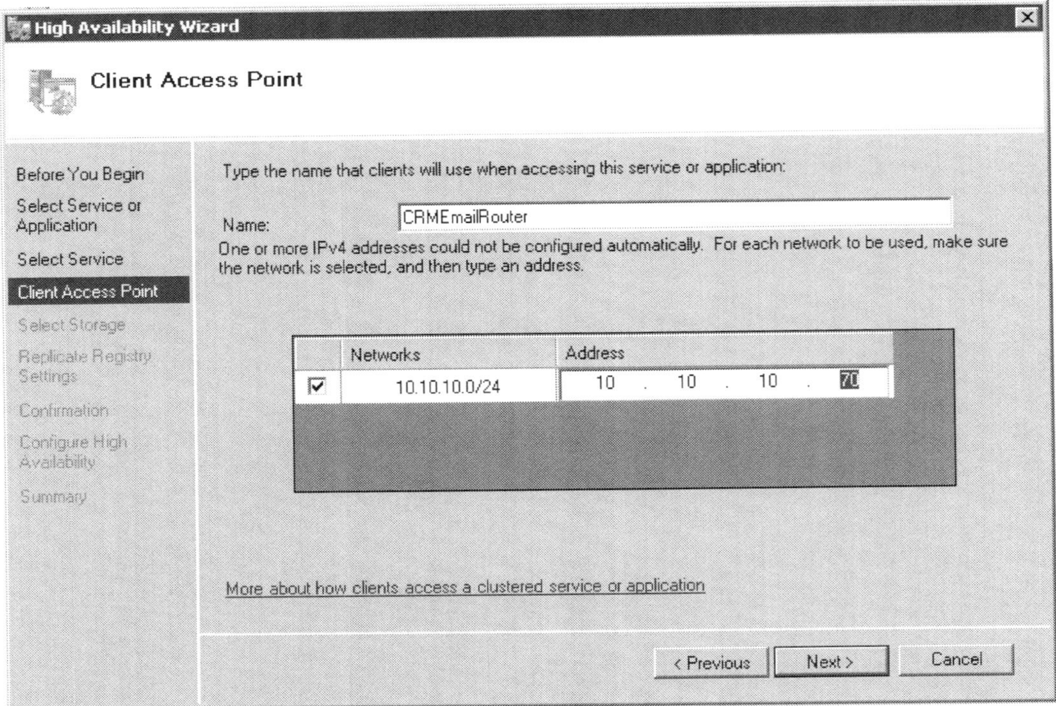


**Figure 27.33**

d. On the **Client Access Point** screen, enter the name for your CRM E-mail Router service in the **Name** field. For our project, we will name our service **CRMEmailRouter**, as shown in **Figure 27.33**.

   i. For the **Networks** field, enter the IP address that your CRM E-mail Router traffic will be sent to, and then click on the **Next** button to continue. This name and IP address will automatically be added to your Active Directory integrated DNS as a Host (A) record, the same as your other clustered resources were when you initially created your Windows cluster. For our project, we will assign the IP address of **10.10.10.70**, as shown in **Figure 27.33**.

## Creating the Clustered Generic Service- Selecting the Shared Disk

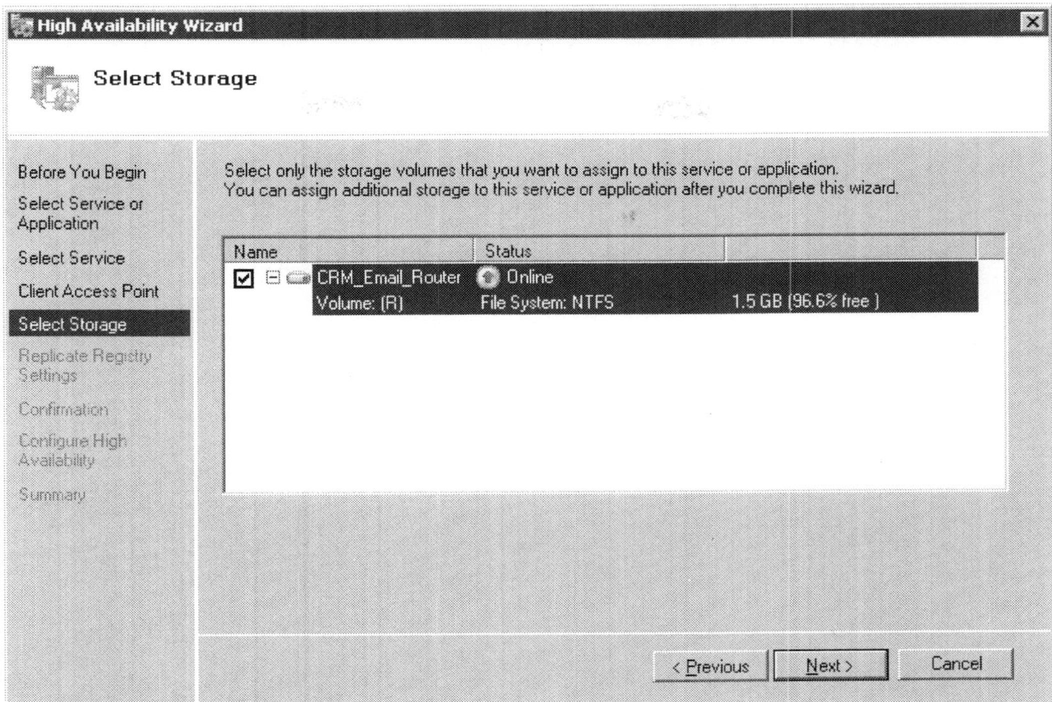


**Figure 27.34**

e. On the **Select Storage** screen, select your CRM E-mail Router shared disk, and then click on the **Next** button to continue. For our project, we will select our disk named **CRM_Email_Router**, as shown in **Figure 27.34**.

## Creating the Clustered Generic Service- Entering the Registry Settings

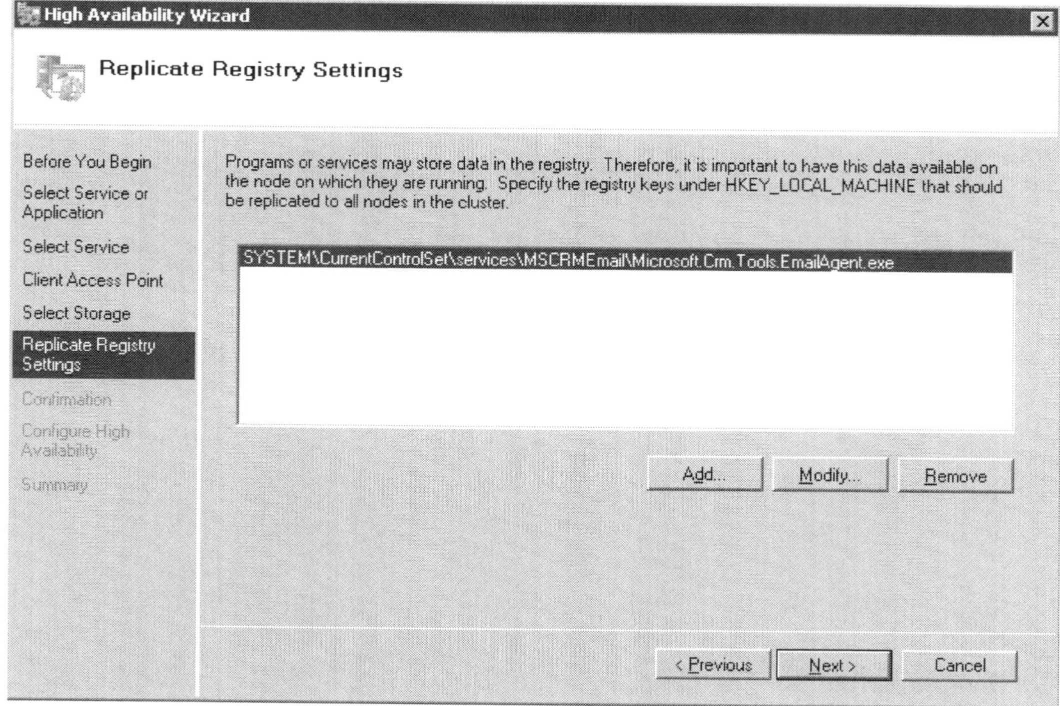


**Figure 27.35**

36. On the **Replicate Registry Settings** screen, click on the **Add** button.

    a. On the **Registry Key** screen, enter in the registry path of **HKEY_LOCAL_MACHINE\SYSTEM\CurrentControlSet\services\MSCRMEmail\Microsoft.Crm.Tools.EmailAgent.exe** with no spaces in the string, and then click on the **OK** button to save your changes. Your registry key should appear as in **Figure 27.35**.

37. On the **Confirmation** screen, verify your settings are correct, and then click on the **Next** button to continue.

# Creating the Clustered Generic Service- Verifying the Settings

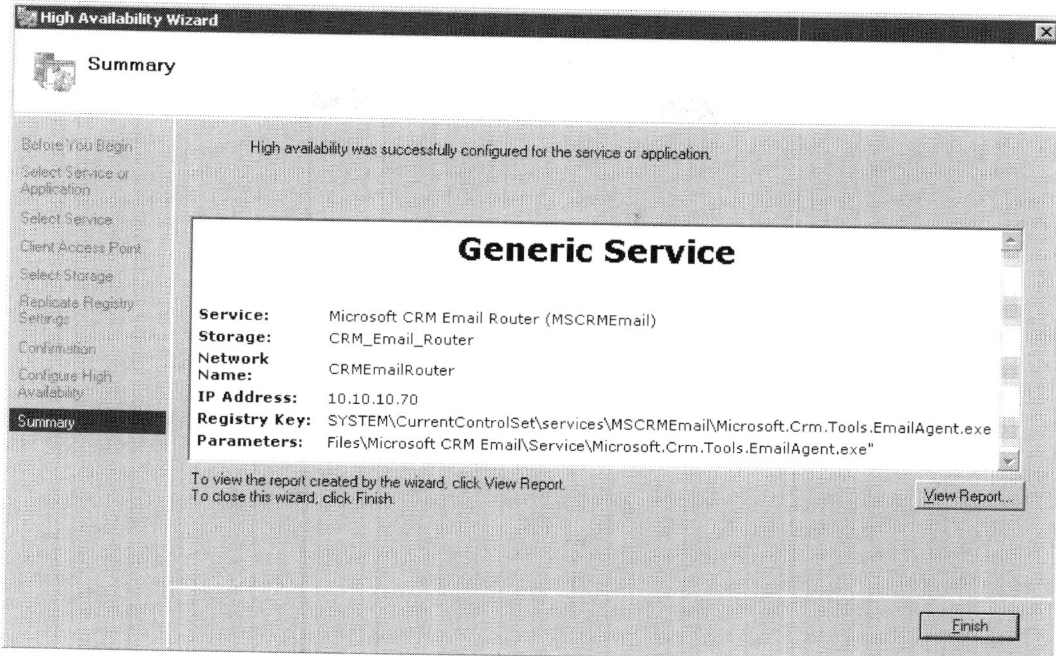


**Figure 27.36**

38. On the **Summary** screen, click on the **Finish** button to create the clustered Generic Service. You may have noticed on the Confirmation and Summary screens that the Parameters path was missing your shared drive letter and part of the Program Files folder's name. This is apparently a bug in the High Availability Wizard that we will need to manually correct in the next couple of steps.

# Creating the Clustered Generic Service- Correcting the Parameters Path

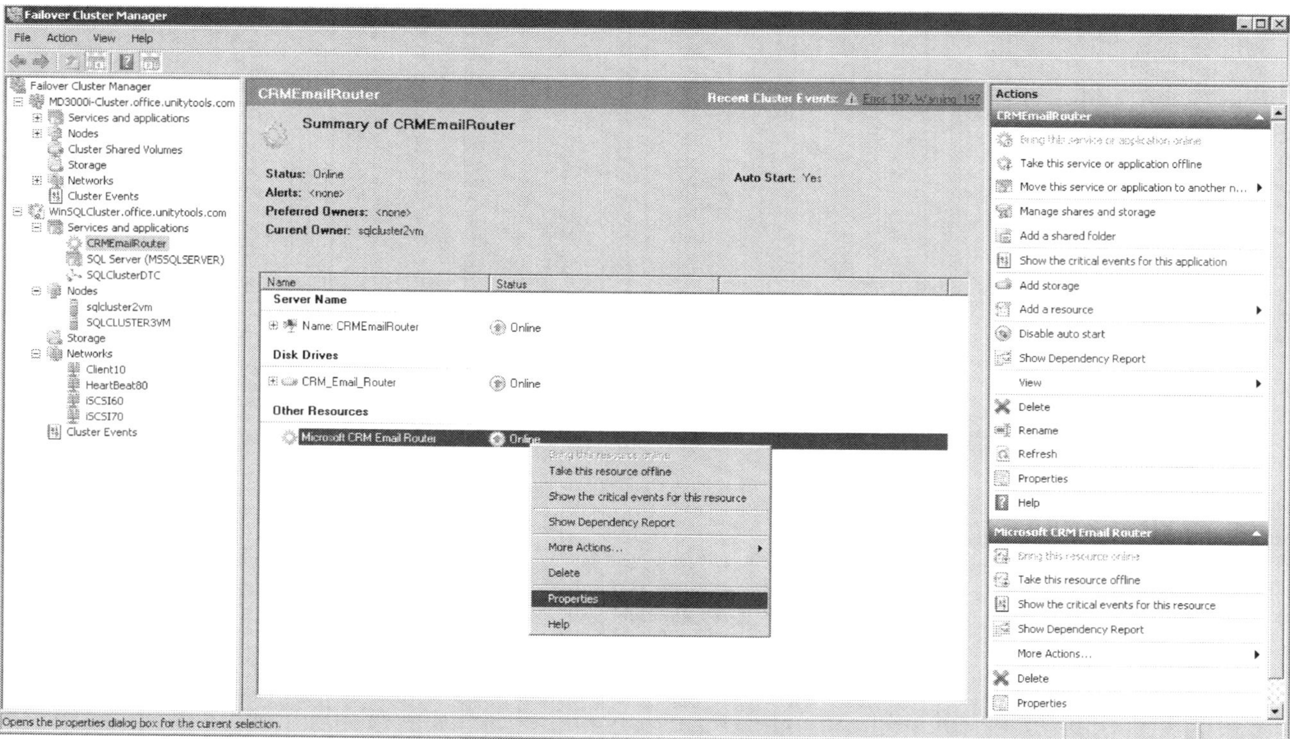

**Figure 27.37**

39. In the left pane of the **Failover Cluster Manager** console under the **Services and applications** node, highlight your newly created **CRM E-mail Router** service. For our project, we will highlight our CRM E-mail Router service with the name of **CRMEmailRouter** in the left pane.

    a. In the center pane, right click on the **Microsoft CRM Email Router** resource listed under the **Other Resources** section, and then select the **Properties** option.

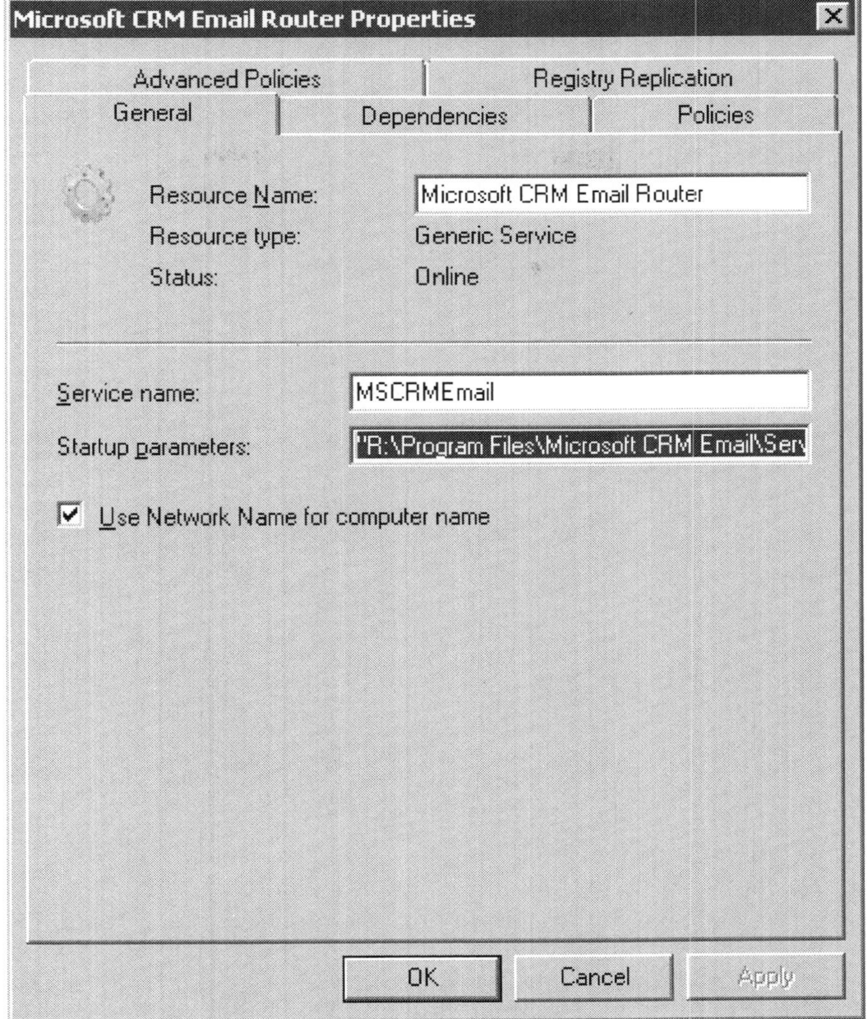


**Figure 27.37**

b. On the **General** tab of the **Properties** screen, modify the **Startup Parameters** field to have the full path to the **Microsoft.Crm.Tools.EmailAgent.exe** file on your shared disk, and then click on the **OK** button to save your changes. Most likely you are just missing the beginning of the path. Make sure to include double quotas at the beginning and end of the path to account for the space in between Program and Files. For our project, we will add the missing **"R:\Program** to our path to end up with the full path of **"R:\Program Files\Microsoft CRM Email\Service\Microsoft.Crm.Tools.EmailAgent.exe"**, as shown in **Figure 27.37**.

   i. On the **Please confirm action** pop-up screen that states **The properties were stored, but not all changes will take effect until the Microsoft CRM Email Router is taken offline and then online again**, select the **Yes** option.

   ii. On the **Information** pop-up screen that states **Microsoft CRM Email Router is back online**, click on the **OK** button.

# Testing Failover of the CRM E-mail Router Service

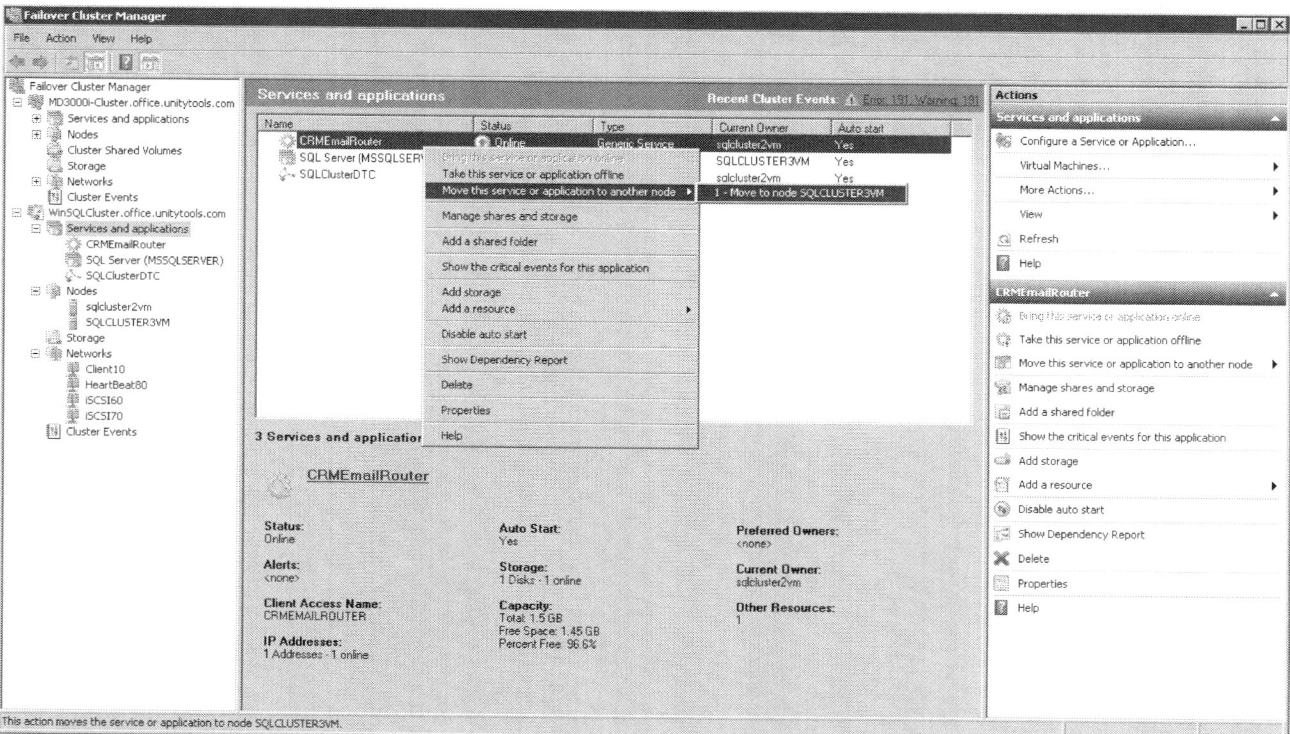


**Figure 27.38**

40. In the left pane of the **Failover Cluster Manager** console, highlight the **Services and applications** node.

    a. Right click on the **CRMEmailRouter** service in the center pane, select the **Move this service or application to another node** option, and then select your passive cluster node. This will failover your newly clustered CRM E-mail Router service to your passive node. Once the failover has completed successfully, you will want to confirm that your CRM E-mail Router is sending and receiving emails correctly. If you placed your clustered CRM E-mail Router service on your SQL cluster as in our project, then you may want to leave your E-mail Router service active on your passive SQL cluster node to balance some of the workload between your nodes.

# Chapter 28: Configuring Microsoft Dynamics CRM for Outlook Clients to Connect to the New NLB Cluster

The last step in setting up our CRM NLB cluster is to reconfigure our Microsoft Dynamics CRM for Outlook clients. In this chapter, we will cover how to connect our pre-existing and new clients to our cluster by running the Microsoft Dynamics CRM for Outlook Configuration Wizard. Once we are finished with this chapter we will have successfully built a completely redundant and highly available system to host our SQL and CRM applications.

## Configuring the CRM Client for Outlook- Launching the Configuration Wizard

1. On each of your CRM for Outlook user computers make sure that the **Microsoft Outlook** program is closed, and then install the CRM **Rollup Update** for Outlook to the same version level as the rest of your CRM components have installed.

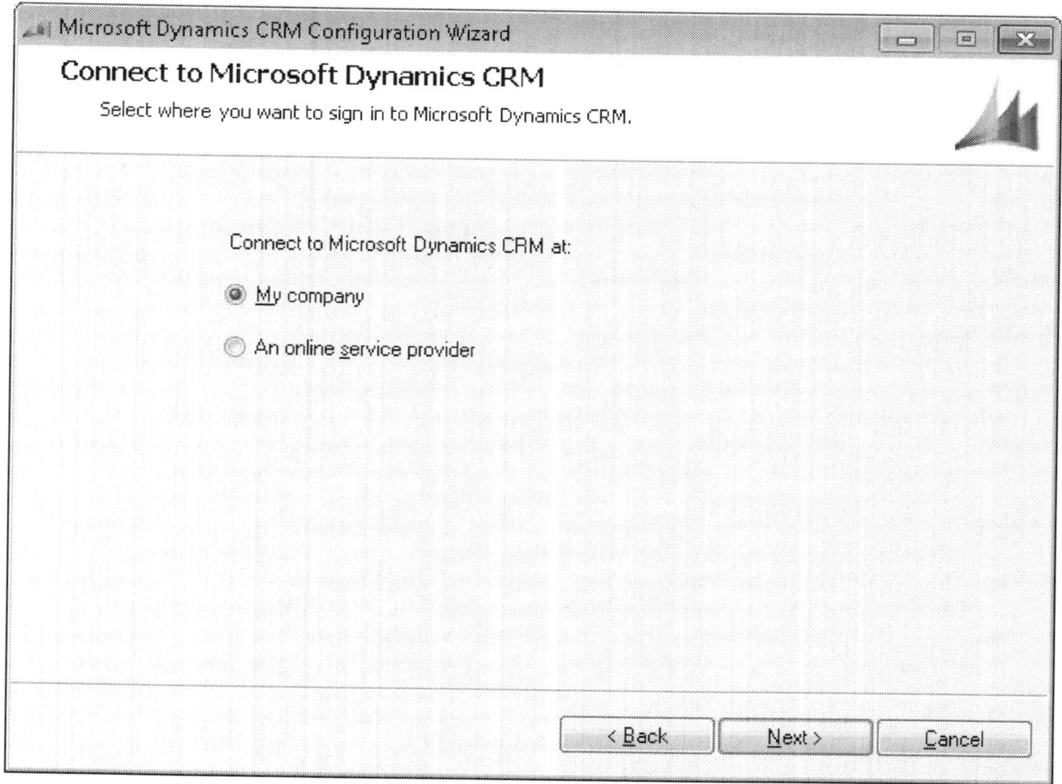


**Figure 28.1**

2. Launch the **Configuration Wizard** on the client machine by going to the **Start button\All Programs\Microsoft Dynamics CRM 4.0**, and then selecting the for the **Configuration Wizard** option. Select the defaults for the installation except where outlined in the following steps.

a. On the **Select where you want to sign in to Microsoft Dynamics CRM** screen, select the **My company** option, and then click on the **Next** button to continue.

## Configuring the CRM Client for Outlook- Specifying Web Addresses

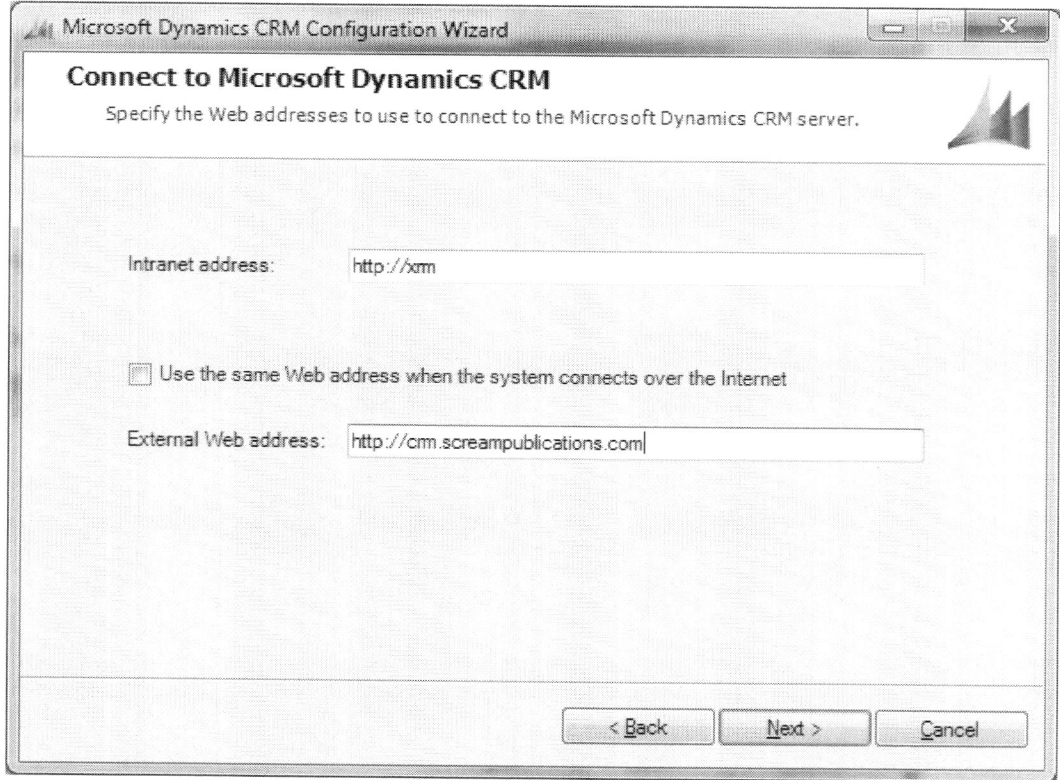


**Figure 28.2**

b. On the **Specify the Web addresses to use to connect to the Microsoft Dynamics CRM** screen, enter your **CRM NLB cluster's internal URL** for the **Intranet address** field. For our project, we will enter our **CRM NLB cluster's internal URL** of **http://xrm/**, as shown in **Figure 28.2**.

   i. If this computer remains on the internal LAN at all times, then you can leave the rest of the settings on this screen at their defaults and click on the **Next** button to continue. If the computer is mobile and used the internet as well as on the internal LAN, then unselect the **Use the same Web address when the system connects over the internet** checkbox, and enter in your CRM organization's internet URL in the **External Web address** field. For our project, we will enter the internet URL of **http://crm.screampublications.com** for access to our organization named **crm**, as shown in **Figure 28.2**.

## Configuring the CRM Client for Outlook- Selecting the Organization

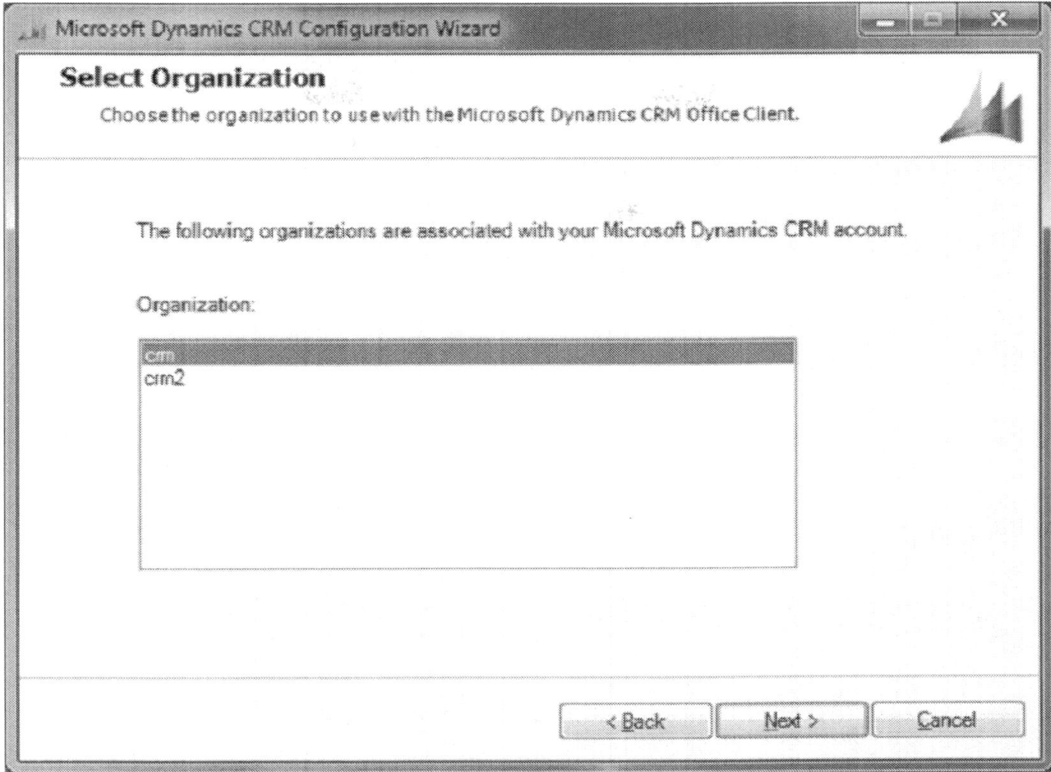


**Figure 28.3**

c. On the **Select Organization** screen, select the organization that the **CRM for Outlook** client will connect to, and then click on the **Next** button to continue. For our project, we will select our CRM organization named **crm**, as shown **Figure 28.3**.

d. On the **System Requirements** screen, click on the **Next** button to continue.

e. On the **Configuration Complete** screen, click on the **Finish** button to complete the configuration changes.

3. Repeat **Step 2** for each of your **CRM for Outlook** client computers that you want connected to your new CRM NLB cluster.

# Index:


.NET Framework, 210

## A

acronyms, xxii
Active Directory client subnet, 83, 119, 127, 134, 187-188, 190, 192, 194, 205
Active Directory domain, 9-10, 19-20, 26, 100, 188, 215, 287, 289, 334-335
Active Directory User and Computers, 278-279
active node, 124, 155, 158-159, 171, 206, 321-322
active/active, 2, 8, 187
active/passive, 2
ADSI Edit tool, 286-289
adsiedit.msc, 286
advanced IPv4 properties, 193
allocation unit size, 54, 75-79
Analysis Services, 124, 145-146
Analysis Services user accounts, 124
applying updates, 171, 190
authentication, 142, 149, 158, 162, 219, 221, 227, 229, 241, 285, 315, 340
authentication mode, 124, 142
auto-mapping, 301

## B

best practices, xxiii, 9, 38, 99, 161
binding orders, 90, 95-96, 107
BIOS, 80
Broadcom, iii, 30-33, 93
Broadcom Advanced Control Suite (BACS), 32-33

## C

client access point, 127, 360
client subnet, 4, 9-10, 20, 24, 26, 83, 119, 127, 134, 192
cluster disks, 7, 85, 118, 121
cluster IP, 198, 205, 239
cluster name, 5, 83, 119, 127, 177, 341
cluster service, 134, 159, 160
Cluster Shared Volumes (CSV), 2-3, 5, 7, 52, 55, 59, 61, 74-76, 79-81, 84-87, 90, 100, 115, 118, 125, 172-191, 196, 202, 307, 345, 379
- ClusterStorage Volume, 74, 173-175
- shared disk(s), 2, 74, 80, 84, 174-175
- virtual machine(s), 59, 75, 172-176, 182-191, 196, 202, 307

Clustered Generic Services and Applications, 355-364
- adding services and applications, 357
- client access point, 360
- Microsoft CRM Email Router Service, 359
- parameters path, 363, 364
- registry settings, 362
- selecting type of Services and Applications, 358
- shared disk, 355, 361
- startup parameters, 365

ClusterStorage Volume. *See* Cluster Shared Volumes (CSV)
CRM E-mail Router
- E-mail Router cluster, 322, 354
- E-mail Router Configuration Manager, 337, 338-339, 341-343
- Exchange mailboxes, 331, 334-335, 339, 343
- Full Access permissions, 331, 333-335, 339-340, 342
- incoming profile(s), 338-339
- loading data, 342
- outgoing profile(s), 339, 340
- queue(s), 331-332, 335-337, 343
- Send As permissions, 331-332, 334-335, 339-340, 342
- testing access, 343

CRM E-mail Router cluster
- additional node(s), 354
- Generic Service, 321, 322, 355, 363
- initial node, 322-322, 352-354
- parameters path, 363-364

router components, 324
secondary node(s), 354
security, 325-328
service startup type, 327, 354, 359
shared disk, 344
CRM for Outlook, 292, 367, 369
Configuration Wizard, 367
Web Addresses, 368
CRM Internet Facing Deployment (IFD) Tool, 257, 313
CRM Service user account, 278-281, 283-284, 287-291, 305, 325-326, 329-333, 351, 354
CRM Update Rollup(s), 292, 303, 324, 354
CRM user account(s), 251, 278, 301-302, 317


# D


database files, 163
Dell OpenManage Switch Administrator, 12, 16, 17
Dell PowerConnect 5424 switch(s), 12
Dell PowerEdge R710 server(s), 10, 19-20, 32, 80
Dell PowerVault MD3000i iSCSI SAN, 3, 9, 19-21, 40, 52, 55, 58
disk groups, 3, 51-52, 55, 58-59, 64
disk layout, 56
Distributed Transaction Coordinator (DTC), 6, 57, 125-127, 135, 157, 322
service, 126, 157, 322
DNS properties, 100, 106
DNS record, 313
drive(s), 52, 54, 59, 73, 75, 76-77, 114, 128, 136, 162, 237, 253, 267, 289, 348, 349, 350, 353, 363
dual RAID controllers, 3


# E


edit user mappings, 302
erasing switch configuration, 12-14
errors, 2, 91, 124, 132, 134, 180, 205, 248, 250, 264, 275
ethernet management ports, 26
Exchange Management Console (EMC), 331-333, 335
Exchange Management Shell (EMS), 331, 334-335


# F


failover cluster, 2, 5, 80-82, 84-85, 115, 118, 120, 125, 134, 148, 150, 156, 159-160, 177, 181, 183, 307, 357, 364, 365
flow control, 12, 18
format, 54, 73, 75-76, 78, 100, 114, 288, 295, 304, 317, 349
front-end application, 135-136, 141, 172-173, 187, 190, 200, 208, 251, 275
front-end application servers, 135-136, 141, 172-173, 190, 275


# G


Generic Service. *See* CRM E-mail Router Cluster
global hot spare, 55
ghost network adapters. *See* phantom network adapters


# H


heartbeat subnet, 4, 9, 11, 38
High Availability Wizard. *See* Windows Failover Cluster Manager
highly available, 2, 80, 124-125, 128, 135, 150, 159, 177, 187, 201, 265, 305, 321-322, 367, 379
host group, 62, 69, 71-72, 100, 113, 347
HOT TIP(s), xxiii, 52, 54, 75
HTTP/FQDN, 288
HTTP/NetBIOS, 288
Hyper-V, 80
Hyper-V Manager, 91, 100-101, 173, 175-177, 183, 188-189
role, 80
server(s), 91, 95
virtual networks, 29, 90, 93-96, 102
VLAN, 29


# I


initialize disk, 74, 348
instance name(s), 124, 137, 153, 217, 225, 233, 235, 237, 247

Internet Explorer security
disabling Protected Mode, 243, 245
local intranet zone, 243-245
disabling LoopbackCheck, 246
Internet Information Services (IIS) 6.0, 286
Internet Information Services (IIS) 7.5, 284-285
Internet Information Services (IIS) Manager, 284-285
IP Properties screen, 36-38
IPv4 settings, 27-28
iSCSI
connection(s), 4, 10-11, 69, 90, 112
host port(s), 27, 45
network, xx, xxi, 4, 9-10, 12, 15, 18-20, 27, 29, 30-33, 35-38, 41, 45-48, 109-111, 379
network adapter, 9, 30, 35, 111
network topology, 4
optimizing switches, 12
ports, 18
iSCSI Initiator, 21, 23, 29, 40-42, 44-50, 69-70, 100-101, 111-112
discovery portal(s), 42
target(s), 44-48

# J

jumbo frame(s), 12, 15-17, 31, 34, 109-110

# K

Kernel-mode authentication, 285

# L

live migration, xx, xxiii, 2, 80, 182, 379
logical unit number (LUN), xxiii, 51, 54, 59, 62-66, 347

# M

MAC address(s), 187, 190, 194, 199
mapping
virtual disk(s), 62, 347
user(s), 302
MD3000i, xxii, xxiii, 2-3, 5, 9, 19-21, 23, 25, 40, 42, 45-48, 50, 52, 55, 58, 60, 71-72, 83, 111, 113
MDSM, 19, 21-24, 26-27, 40-41, 58-59, 61-64, 111, 344
metric settings, 90, 95, 98, 108
Microsoft Cluster Service (MSCS), 134
Microsoft Distributed Transaction Coordinator (MSDTC), 6, 57, 63, 114, 117, 120, 124-128, 135, 148, 157, 171, 322
service, 125-126, 157, 322
cluster IP, 127
Microsoft Dynamics CRM 4.0
backing up database(s), 295
CRMAppPool, 277, 283-284, 305
CRMAppPool identity, 277
database(s), 256, 262, 277, 280, 295-298, 321
Deployment Manager, 276, 294, 297
DNS records, 257, 313-314, 316
E-mail Router. *See* CRM E-Mail Router
E-mail Router role, 262-263, 274, 282-283
Full Access permissions, 277
IgnoreChecks, 306-307, 311
IIS Application Pool, 283
importing organization(s), 292, 297
install type(s), 255, 269
Internet Facing Deployment (IFD), 313, 320
Internet Facing Deployment (IFD) Tool, 313
mapping users, 301-302
organization(s), xx, 251, 256-259, 292, 294, 296-297, 299, 303-304, 313, 321, 325, 328, 336, 341-344, 368-369
Organizational Unit (OU), 251, 253, 260, 277-280, 287, 325-326
PrivReportingGroup, 277, 279
PrivUserGroup, 277, 279-280, 283, 325-326
ReportingGroup, 277
restoring database(s), 296
security accounts, 253
security groups, 277-280, 283
Server role, 251, 253, 255, 262, 269, 282, 305
services, 282-283
SQLAccessGroup, 277, 279, 283
SRS Data Connector, 276-277, 290, 292, 305, 308, 310-311
System Requirements screen, 264, 275, 303, 311, 318-320, 324, 369

testing reports, 319
trust delegation, 290-291, 305
Update Rollup(s), 292, 293, 304, 312, 324
URL(s), 257
UserGroup, 277
website, 285, 304
mixed mode authentication, 142
Modular Disk Storage Manager (MSDM), xxiii, 19, 21-24, 26, 40, 58-59, 61, 70, 111, 113-114, 344
multi-homed server(s), 194-195
Multi-Path Input/Output (MPIO), xxiii, 9-10, 25, 30, 53
Multi-path Redundancy, 9, 19, 23, 44, 45, 46, 47, 48, 112

# N

naming convention(s), 29, 103
NetBIOS, 288, 340
netsh interface ipv4, 34-35, 110, 195
network adapter(s), xxiii, 9-10, 15, 20, 29, 30-32, 33-38, 50, 90, 92-95, 96, 98-100, 103-108, 110-111, 187-188, 190-196, 199, 202, 205, 315
security settings, 195
power management, 99
Network Load Balancer (NLB) , xx-xxii, 2, 8, 187-189, 195, 205, 208, 285-286, 290, 305, 379
additional node(s), 201, 202, 203, 204, 205, 275
cluster IP address, 198
cluster parameters, 198
default state, 207
host parameters, 197, 203, 207
initial node, 187, 196, 201
port rule(s), 197, 199-201, 204
seconday node(s), 187
stopping traffic, 206

# O

offline, 2, 19, 65, 73, 134, 150, 159, 187, 201, 262, 365
online, 2, 57, 65, 73-74, 80, 88, 100, 114, 124, 148, 150, 160, 171, 173, 181, 183, 188, 207, 262, 276, 348, 365

# P

partition alignment, iv, 54, 78, 79
partition(s), xxi, 73, 75, 76, 78, 79, 100, 114
passive node(s), 135, 159, 160, 171, 276, 321, 322, 354, 365
phantom network adapters
removing, 103-104
physical disk groups, 3, 52
physical hosts, 2, 90, 173, 182, 184-185, 187, 379
physical servers, xx, xxi, 2, 4, 20, 57, 69, 70-71, 80-81, 91, 96, 99, 100-101, 106-107, 113, 124, 187, 379
power management, 99
prerequisites, xx, 19, 20, 80, 124, 129, 150, 151, 187, 209, 210, 379
Windows clustering, 80
Project
Client10 network adapter, 103, 107, 188, 191, 194-196, 202, 315
CRMCluster1VM node, xxii, 2, 173-174, 176-177, 179, 196, 209, 216-217, 233-235, 248-249, 280, 291, 315
CRMCluster2VM node, 2, 173, 176-177, 179, 202, 225, 235, 237, 280, 291, 315
CRMCluster3VM node, 2, 173, 176-177, 179, 202, 232, 235, 238, 275, 280, 291, 315
CRMClusterVM, 2, 5
CRMService user account, 208, 215, 221, 229, 278-281, 283-284, 287, 291, 327, 329, 332-333, 339-340, 342, 351, 354
Heartbeat80 network adapter, 103, 107
iSCSI target(s)
first target, 44
fourth target, 48
second target, 45
third target, 47
iSCSI60 network adapter, 103, 107, 110-111
iSCSI70 network adapter, 103, 107, 110-111
MD3000i-Cluster, xxii, 2, 5, 71, 83
SQL_DB shared disk, 2, 62, 114, 120, 139, 143, 144, 146, 147
SQL_DTC shared disk, 2, 157
SQL_Logs shared disk, 2, 63, 114, 120, 139
SQL_Quorum shared disk, 2, 64, 114, 120, 123

SQL_TempDB shared disk, 2, 64, 114, 120, 139, 162, 165
SQLCluster2VM node, 2, 101, 105, 118, 129, 159, 322, 326
SQLCluster3VM node, 2, 101, 105, 150, 151, 156, 157, 326
SQLClusterDTC, 6, 127, 157
VLAN10 network, 30, 39, 92-94, 103, 188, 190
VLAN60 network, 14, 30, 35, 39, 94, 103
VLAN70 network, 14, 30, 39, 94, 103
VLAN80 network, 39, 94, 103
WinSQLCluster, 2, 6, 7, 119, 150, 322, 322, 355
XRM, 2, 8, 205, 239-240, 244, 257, 259, 272, 288, 300, 304, 316, 341, 368

# Q

quorum, 3, 56-57, 63-64, 74-76 79, 80, 84-85, 88, 118, 122, 123
disk, 57, 80, 122

# R

RAID array(s), 3, 52, 55, 143, 161
RAID controller(s), 3, 52, 55, 60
RAID level, 51, 52, 53, 58, 60
regedit, 206, 246, 353
registry, 104, 137, 246-247, 305, 307, 311, 350, 352-354, 362
Registry Editor, 246-247, 306-307, 353
Reporting Services. *See* SQL Reporting Services
Reporting Services Scale-Out Deployment. *See* SQL Reporting Services Scale-out Deployment
router(s), 15

# S

SAN. *See* Storage Area Network (SAN)
SAS drives, 3, 52
SATA drives, 52
sector alignment, 54, 78
Service Principle Names (SPN), 208, 264, 286-287, 305
shared disks, 73-74, 79-80, 84, 100, 113-114, 118, 121, 124, 139, 143, 146
behavior, 73
initialization, 74
spindles, 54
SQL Server 2008/R2
additional node(s), 124, 150
application, 133, 150, 156
authentication, 142
cluster node(s), 57, 101, 122, 124, 135, 159, 171, 325-326, 276, 365
clustering, 57, 100, 107, 124-125, 135, 171, 208
directories, 143
Distributed Transaction Coordinator (DTC). *See* Distributed Transaction Coordinator (DTC)
feature selection, 124, 136, 213
feature(s), 124, 135-136
initial cluster node, 114, 124, 128, 147, 150, 154, 208
instance configuration, 137, 214
instance name, 153
instance(s), 124, 135, 137, 150, 168, 169, 217, 225, 234, 235, 237, 248
Management Studio, 124, 137, 149, 158-159, 162, 164, 167, 169-170, 295-296
node(s), 101, 118, 124, 128, 150, 155, 167, 296
passive cluster Node, viii, 159
Reporting Services (SSRS). *See* SQL Server 2008/R2 Reporting Services (SSRS)
Reporting Services Scale-out Deployment. *See* SQL Server 2008/R2 Reporting Services (SSRS)
script, 164
secondary cluster node(s), 155
Service Pack(s), 129-130, 147, 151-152, 155, 209-210, 216
Service Pack 1 (SP1), xxi, 57, 124, 127, 129-130, 143, 146, 147, 151-152, 155, 208-210
service startup type, 141
service(s), 124, 141, 148, 154, 157
temporally database files (TempDB), 161, 164-166
virtual machines, 2, 4, 74, 90, 100-102, 105, 111, 113, 118, 134
SQL Server 2008 R2, xx-xxi, 1-2, 119, 124, 129-131, 143, 146-147, 151-152, 155, 168, 170, 208, 209, 212, 216, 239, 292, 379

SQL Server 2008/R2 Reporting Services (SSRS), xx-xxi, 135-136, 187, 208-210, 213-216-244, 246-250, 276, 278, 300, 305, 309, 312, 320, 379
.Config File, 239-242
database credentials, 221, 229
database name, 220
authentication method tag, 239
authentication type, 219, 227
hostname tag, 239
initial node, 208, 209, 234, 236
Report Manager URL, 224, 232, 249
ReportServer database, 217-218, 226, 228, 234
Reporting Services Configuration Manager, 216-217, 224-226, 232-238, 242, 247
Scale-out Deployment, xx-xxi, 135, 208-209, 216, 233, 235, 247, 379
synchronizing encryption key(s), 235-237
URL root tag, 239-240
Web Service URL, 223, 231, 248
static IP address(s), 36-38, 100, 106, 194
Storage Area Network (SAN), xx-xxi, xxiii, 2-4, 9, 11, 15, 19-21, 24-27, 29, 35, 40-52, 55, 57, 60, 62, 69, 71-73, 76-77, 79-80, 100-101, 110-114, 121, 124-125, 143-144, 147, 161-162, 321, 344-345, 379
subinterface. *See* netsh interface ipv4
switch, 4, 10-18, 20, 38
synonyms, xxiii

# T

TCP/IP Offload Engine (TOE), 50
TCP/IP overhead, xxiii
TCP/IPv4, 36-38, 98, 106, 108, 192-193
TCP/IPv6, 191
TempDB file(s). *See* SQL Server 2008/R2 temporally database file(s)
testing
communications, 170
failover(s), 156-159, 365
high availability, 156
TOE. *See* TCP/IP Offload Engine (TOE)

# U

user account(s), 141, 145, 154, 190, 208, 215, 219, 221, 227, 229, 251, 261, 265, 273, 277-278, 281-284, 287-289, 291, 302, 305, 325-326, 329-336, 339-340, 342-343, 354

# V

Validate a Cluster Wizard. *See* Windows Failover Cluster Manager
virtual disk(s), 2-3, 7, 40, 51-52, 54-55, 57-58, 59-60, 62-65, 69, 71-74, 76, 79, 101, 114-115
mappings, 62, 65-66, 72
ownership, 55
Virtual Hard Disk (VHD), xxiii, 3, 51, 52, 54, 55, 57, 58, 59, 61, 62, 65, 66, 74, 103, 144, 147, 162, 173, 344, 345, 346, 347, 348
fixed, xxiii
image, 103
virtual machine(s), xx-xxiii, 2, 4-5, 7, 40, 57, 69, 74, 80, 84, 90, 98, 100-107, 110-111, 113-115, 118, 122, 124-125, 128, 148-150, 162, 172-191, 196, 202, 206, 307, 379
advanced policies, 185
application, 178
configuration advanced policies, 186
virtual servers, 208
Virtualization Technology (VT), 80

# W

warning(s), 2, 14, 66, 82, 118, 124-125, 132-134, 209, 244-245, 264, 303, 305, 350
web user interface, 12
Windows
authentication, 149, 158, 162, 285, 317, 340
cluster(s), xxi, 2, 5, 74, 80, 82-83, 91, 95, 101, 115, 118-120, 122, 124-125, 129, 134, 148, 150-151, 156, 173-176, 321-322, 354-355, 357, 360, 379
clustering, 26, 82
CSV cluster, 172, 177, 187
failover cluster(s), xxii, 2, 3, 5, 6, 20, 81, 118, 355
Failover Cluster Manager. *See* Windows Failover Cluster Manager

feature(s), 80, 100, 115, 188
firewall, 133, 150, 167-168, 170, 190, 209
Installer, 210
Roles, 116, 251, 265
Server 2008. *See* Windows Server 2008
Server 2008 R2. *See* Windows Server 2008 R2
Server Manager. *See* Windows Server Manager
updates, 190
Windows Failover Cluster Manager, 5, 20, 118, 355
Add Node Wizard, 150
adding disk(s), 84, 120, 355
adding disk(s) to CSV, 87
adding DTC Service, 125-126
adding Generic Service. *See* Clustered Generic Service
adding Services and Applications, 125, 177, 357
adding virtual machine(s) to CSV, 177-181
advanced policies, 185
assigning cluster IP, 119, 127, 360
assigning cluster name, 119, 127, 360
Cluster Shared Volumes (CSV), 5, 7, 15, 84-87. *Also see* Cluster Shared Volumes (CSV)
ClusterStorage Volume(s). *See* Cluster Shared Volumes (CSV)
configuration advanced policies, 186
configuring Startup Parameters, 365
configuring Storage Witness, 123
configuring quorum disk(s), 84, 88, 122
creating client access point, 127, 360
creating cluster, 81, 118-119
creating Generic Service cluster. *See* Clustered Generic Service
enabling Cluster Shared Volumes (CSV), 86
failover, 156-159, 365
High Availability Wizard, 177-180, 358-363
managing CSV virtual machine(s), 182-186
Nodes node, 151, 159
renaming cluster disk(s), 85, 121, 356
Services and Applications node, 5-7, 148, 156-157, 182-185, 357
setting preferred owners, 184
Storage node, 7, 84-85, 115, 120, 348, 355
shutting down virtual machine(s), 183
Validate a Configuration Wizard, 82, 118
validation report, 82, 119
Windows Server 2008, xx-xxi, xxiii, 2, 30, 42, 74, 80, 93, 101, 124-125, 127, 129-130, 140, 147, 151-152, 155, 173, 182, 187, 194, 209-210, 243, 246, 285-286, 379
Windows Server 2008 R2, xx, xxiii, 2, 42, 74, 80, 101, 124-125, 129-130, 147, 151-152, 155, 173, 182, 187, 209-210, 243, 285, 379
Windows Server Manager, 54, 73-74, 80, 116, 188, 251, 265, 281, 348

Made in the USA
Lexington, KY
23 March 2013